I0825325

The Collected Works of J. Krishnamurti

Volume XIV

1963–1964

The New Mind

COLLECTED WORKS VOLUME 14

Photo: J. Krishnamurti, ca 1965 by Frances McCann

P.O Box 1560, Ojai, CA 93024

Website: www.kfa.org

Printed in the United States of America

ISBN 13: 9781934989470
ISBN: 1934989479

Contents

Preface vii

Talks in New Delhi, India 1

First Talk, October 23, 1963 1
Second Talk, October 27, 1963 7
Third Talk, October 30, 1963 13
Fourth Talk, November 3, 1963 20
Fifth Talk, November 6, 1963 27
Sixth Talk, November 10, 1963 33
Seventh Talk, November 13, 1963 39

Talks at Rajghat School, Banaras, India 47

First Talk, November 24, 1963 47
Second Talk, December 1, 1963 56
Third Talk, December 8, 1963 66

Talks in Madras, India 77

First Talk, January 12, 1964 77
Second Talk, January 15, 1964 82
Third Talk, January 19, 1964 88
Fourth Talk, January 22, 1964 94
Fifth Talk, January 26, 1964 100
Sixth Talk, January 29, 1964 106
Seventh Talk, February 2, 1964 112

Talks in Bombay, India 121

First Talk, February 9, 1964 121
Second Talk, February 12, 1964 127
Third Talk, February 16, 1964 134
Fourth Talk, February 19, 1964 141
Fifth Talk, February 23, 1964 147

Sixth Talk, February 26, 1964 154
Seventh Talk, March 1, 1964 161

Talks in Saanen, Switzerland 169

First Talk, July 12, 1964 169
Second Talk, July 14, 1964 174
Third Talk, July 16, 1964 180
Fourth Talk, July 19, 1964 187
Fifth Talk, July 21, 1964 192
Sixth Talk, July 23, 1964 197
Seventh Talk, July 26, 1964 203
Eighth Talk, July 28, 1964 208
Ninth Talk, July 30, 1964 214
Tenth Talk, August 2, 1964 219

Talks in New Delhi, India 225

First Talk, October 21, 1964 225
Second Talk, October 25, 1964 231
Third Talk, October 28, 1964 238
Fourth Talk, November 1, 1964 244
Fifth Talk, November 5, 1964 251
Sixth Talk, November 8, 1964 258
Seventh Talk, November 11, 1964 263

Talks at Rajghat School, Banaras, India 271

First Talk, November 20, 1964 271
Second Talk, November 22, 1964 280
Third Talk, November 24, 1964 288
Fourth Talk, November 26, 1964 296
Fifth Talk, November 28, 1964 302

Questions 311
Index 315

Preface

Jiddu Krishnamurti was born in 1895 of Brahmin parents in south India. At the age of fourteen he was proclaimed the coming World Teacher by Annie Besant, then president of the Theosophical Society, an international organization that emphasized the unity of world religions. Mrs. Besant adopted the boy and took him to England, where he was educated and prepared for his coming role. In 1911 a new worldwide organization was formed with Krishnamurti as its head, solely to prepare its members for his advent as World Teacher. In 1929, after many years of questioning himself and the destiny imposed upon him, Krishnamurti disbanded this organization, saying:

Truth is a pathless land, and you cannot approach it by any path whatsoever, by any religion, by any sect. Truth, being limitless, unconditioned, unapproachable by any path whatsoever, cannot be organized; nor should any organization be forced to lead or to coerce people along any particular path. My only concern is to set men absolutely, unconditionally free.

Until the end of his life at the age of ninety, Krishnamurti traveled the world speaking as a private person. The rejection of all spiritual and psychological authority, including his own, is a fundamental theme. A major concern is the social structure and how it conditions the individual. The emphasis in his talks and writings is on the psychological barriers that prevent clarity of perception. In the mirror of relationship, each of us can come to understand the content of his own consciousness, which is common to all humanity. We can do this, not analytically, but directly in a manner Krishnamurti describes at length. In observing this content we discover within ourselves the division of the observer and what is observed. He points out that this division, which prevents direct perception, is the root of human conflict.

His central vision did not waver after 1929, but Krishnamurti strove for the rest of his life to make his language even more simple and clear. There is a development in his exposition. From year to year he used new terms and new approaches to his subject, with different nuances.

Because his subject is all-embracing, the *Collected Works* are of compelling interest. Within his talks in any one year, Krishnamurti was not able to cover the whole range of his vision, but broad applications of particular themes are found throughout these volumes. In them he lays the foundations of many of the concepts he used in later years.

The *Collected Works* contain Krishnamurti's previously published talks, discussions, answers to specific questions, and writings for the years 1933 through 1967. They are an authentic record of his teachings, taken from transcripts of verbatim shorthand reports and tape recordings.

The Krishnamurti Foundation of America, a California charitable trust, has among its purposes the publication and distribution of Krishnamurti books, videocassettes, films and tape recordings. The production of the *Collected Works* is one of these activities.

New Delhi, India, 1963

First Talk in New Delhi

I think it would be wise from the very beginning to understand each other. For me there is only learning and no instruction. That is a very important thing to understand. The speaker is not teaching for you to learn. Together, we are going to investigate, to learn. And to investigate, to learn, one must know what it is to observe—because through observation alone we learn to observe, to be conscious of all the things, not only outwardly, but also inwardly, both outside the skin as well as inside the skin—the events, the reactions, the innumerable impressions and tensions. To observe these is to learn from them, and therefore immediately one becomes for oneself both the teacher as well as the disciple.

One learns, and to learn one has to observe. But most of us do not observe. We do not take *what is,* but we come to it with our opinions, with our judgments, with our condemnations and approvals. So we look at things through the screen of our own prejudices, of our own ideas and opinions. When we do observe, we investigate the truth of opinions rather than fact itself. So we never learn.

We know what the facts are in the world and though those facts are constantly impinging on the mind with great virility, with an immediate demand for action, we never learn from these facts because we approach them with our own conditioning, with our own peculiar, opinionated, dogmatic mind, with a mind which is afraid to investigate, to discover, to see what is new. So we approach the many facts with this peculiar half inattention, though all those facts demand action, demand a complete revolution in the state of the mind. Therefore we never learn.

During the talks here, together we are going to find out for ourselves. To find out you need a certain energy, an energy that is not the friction that comes through opinion, through conflict, through argument; but that energy comes only when you perceive what is true for yourself. And if I may point out, it seems to me that it is very important to understand the relationship between you and the speaker. Here, there is no authority of any kind whatsoever. We are both investigating, discovering. We are both searching out to discover what is true and immediately, totally, to deny what is false. Otherwise, we cannot go very far, and we have to go very far and very deeply to understand, to act, for action is demanded. And to act one must observe the facts as they are about one.

So, first, let us look at the things about us outwardly because you cannot go very far, deeply within, if we do not understand what is the outward movement of life. I mean by that word *understand* to be conscious of it—

not necessarily that one has to act definitely in a certain manner with regard to outward things, but to be conscious of them, to be aware of them, to know their content, their meaning, their significance. Because you will see that as we begin to understand the outward things of life, we begin to go inwardly naturally from the understanding of what is without. But without understanding the outer, the tide that is going out, you cannot flow with the tide that is coming in.

So, there is no division as the outer and the inner. It is a tide that has a movement that goes out infinitely far, and when you ride that tide, when the mind is of that tide, then that very tide carries you within very far, infinitely. But you cannot ride the inner tide, as most religious people try to do, without understanding the outer, the whole significance of existence, the outer existence, the daily acts, the daily faults, the reactions, the responses, the fears, the greeds, the ambitions, the corruption, the envy, the frustrations, and the agonies. Without understanding all these, there is no meaning in the search for truth, which demands an astonishingly sharp, healthy, sane, rational mind, not a crippled mind, not a mind that is frightened, not a mind that is greedy, seeking, wanting, groping after something—those are all indicative of an unhealthy mind.

So, what we are going to do is first to observe, perceive the facts as they are in the world—not your fact and my fact, not your opinion and my opinion, not observe dialectically because that is the art of investigating the truth of opinions. We are not concerned with opinions, nor with agreements. We are concerned with observing the actual facts, the *what is*. And to observe *what is* very clearly and to see the full significance of those facts, naturally we must look at it without all our conditioning. That is where the difficulty is going to lie because you have opinions, you have values, you approach them as a Hindu, Buddhist, Christian, or what you will, with your nationalities, with your peculiar idiosyncrasies—and these prevent you from observing, from looking. Observation is an art. It is not easily learned. One has observed neither the sunset nor the stars, neither the trees nor the facts, outwardly or inwardly.

So, if we are going to travel together—and I hope we will, during these talks—we have to observe scientifically, ruthlessly, and with great intelligence. I mean by that word *intelligence* not knowledge. Intelligence is not knowledge. A man who has read a great deal, who has accumulated knowledge, is not necessarily intelligent. I mean by that word intelligence the capacity for insight, to see immediately what is true, to see what is false immediately and deny the false totally. That requires intelligence—which is not a thing to be cultivated. You have to perceive that which is true immediately, and you can only perceive what is true immediately if you understand the whole process of your reasoning, your incapacities, your shelters, your fears, your greeds—all this human psychological structure.

So, we are going to observe the facts, the *what is*, because for me, the very act of observation is action. Action is not something apart from the act of observation. To see something totally—that very seeing is total action. I will go into that presently during these talks.

So, at the present moment in the world, as you and I and all know, there is great poverty—not only inwardly but outwardly—lack of food, the appalling poverty of the whole of Asia and Africa. And there are tremendous technological changes going on, changes that are not in the thing that is changed but in the process of change, in the very change itself, not in what is changed. Do you understand the change? What was invented yesterday becomes obsolete by tomorrow; the thoughts that you have had about this or that, about

God, about economy, about what you should do—they have already changed. There is a terrific movement of change going on in the world.

As the earth is broken up into fragments, so our thinking is broken up as the artist, as the politician, as the economist, as the businessman, as the yogi, as the sannyasi, as the man who is seeking truth, as the social reformer—they are all functioning in fragments, all saying, "We are going to solve this human problem." You can endlessly explore these fragments and their activities—which would be a waste of time. You can see the fragmentation going on—the classes, the nations, the religious divisions, the sectarian divisions, those who believe in this and those who do not believe in that, the one savior and the many saviors, one country against another and therefore cultivating nationalism. These are going on in the world, and they have been going on for some thousands of years, millennia, and none of us have solved this problem of living. And all religions have failed completely—whether you are a Hindu who reads the Gita and recites the innumerable phrases, or whether you are a Catholic, or whether you are a Muslim or a Buddhist. They have no meaning any more because they are not realities. You can escape through them. You can shut your eyes to all the process of living and escape through a narrow channel of what you call religious thinking; but that does not solve your agony, the agony of man, the despair, the sorrow, the appalling misery, confusion. You have to solve your problem, and therefore the urgency of solving the problem is immediate. It is something vital that demands your immediate action.

So you see all this in the world. There is the politician functioning in his own way—in the most confused, ruthless, corrupting way, fragmentarily—and there is the other, the religious man. By the politician, I mean also the businessman, the technician—the whole modern civilization which is fragmentary—with his education, escapes, drinks, amusements, and all that. And then there is the other, the man who escapes or avoids, who lives there and tries to find reality somewhere else, through his religion, through his tradition. There is no answer in either—neither in communism nor in yoga. There is no answer because you can see what is happening in the world. A wise man knows these, observes these, and totally denies them both. Do you understand? We are human beings, not Hindus, not Muslims, not patriotic Indians.

It is a human problem whether you live in Russia or in America or in India or in China. It is a human problem we are confronted with. We have suffered too long. We are confused. Our actions are very limited. We have always looked to another to save us. All those have failed, totally. I think that is the first thing one has to realize, not cynically, not with bitterness; that is a fact. They have no meaning any more; they have a meaning only for those who want to escape, like taking a drink. You can get drunk on whiskey or on the idea of God—both are the same. You are no more holy when you get drunk on an idea than when you get drunk through whiskey. So, we have to have a total perception of these fragmentations of existence, to observe them. And to observe, as I have pointed out, you need a very clear mind. You can have a clear mind if you want it. It is not very difficult to think clearly, sanely, rationally. And you can only do it when you have no fear.

So by observing, you learn. The very facts teach you, the very facts give you information that you can no longer be a Hindu or a Christian or a Buddhist. You have to become a human being and solve your problems immediately because there is no leader any more, politically or religiously. There are leaders technologically—that is all. The scientists, the professors, can give you information, but they cannot remove all your sorrows, the agony of existence, the despair that follows everyone. Nobody can solve this for you. And therefore, how you observe, what you do with what you have observed directly—that matters enormously.

The act of observation demands discipline. Please follow this closely. I am using the word *discipline* not in the orthodox sense of control, approximation, effort—that is what is generally implied in discipline. Approximation to an idea, to a symbol, to a pattern; control through fear, through subjugation, through reward and punishment; and conformity to a pattern—that is what is implied in the ordinary sense of the word discipline. The religious discipline, the military discipline, the discipline of education, the discipline of going to the office, however boring, tiresome, futile, empty it is—it brings about a certain discipline in which is involved conflict, approximation, control. And that discipline is considered highly necessary because it helps you to fit into a social pattern, or into a religious pattern, or into a political pattern, the party discipline, and so on and on.

I am not using that word discipline in that sense at all. To me such discipline is most destructive, whether it is religious discipline or the political or the military—one must be careful when one talks about discipline in this country; well, it is up to you. The discipline I am talking of is something entirely different; I am not using that word in the context of the old pattern at all. I am using that word discipline to mean the discipline that comes through observation, through observing clearly, factually. In the very process of observation, this discipline of which I am talking comes into being. To observe that flower, if you do at all observe a flower, demands a great deal of attention—to look at it without naming it, without saying, "It is a rose; I like that color; I do not like that color," or "I wish I had it"—without all that, merely to observe demands a great deal of attention. But to observe that way, you have to be aware of the chattering of the mind. We must be aware how we are distracted by our words, by our desires, by our urges, by our demands that prevent us from looking, seeing, observing, listening.

So the very act of observation is discipline. Do please understand this. This is really quite important. Once you grasp this, you will see the whole significance of all these talks. It is one simple fact: that is, you have to observe yourself, all your reactions, all the psychological conflicts, demands, urges, tensions, fears, greed—just to observe, not to deny them, not to accept them, not to evaluate, not to compare or judge or deny, but just to see. In that very act of seeing you become conscious of all your demands, urges, fears, complexes, greed, etc.; and to be aware of them demands discipline. So this whole process of looking, listening, is in itself a discipline in which there is no conflict, no contradiction, no conformity, no approximation to any pattern. Therefore you break down all your conditioning immediately. You try this; try it as I am talking, not when you go home. There is no time; there is only the present, the active present, now, not the present of the existentialist, but the actual moment you are listening, observing—not only listening to the speaker, but also observing yourself observing all your reactions, your fears, your anxieties, your despairs, the ambitions, the greeds, the fears; just to observe, not to do away with them.

You will see that very observation, to see very clearly, brings about an astonishing freedom in discipline. That is absolutely necessary if you and I are going to travel together—and we are going to travel together. Because when you observe the facts of the world, there must be a new man born out of this confusing conflict, misery, and despair; there must be a new mind, a new man, a new entity. And nobody is going to create that new entity except yourself. That is why through observing you will see that you will deny totally, not partially or fragmentarily, but completely, deny everything of authority—the gods, the religions, the rituals, the Gita, the Bible—everything you destroy to find out. For that there must be a new thinking, a new way of looking. There must be a revolution in the mind so that you can look at all these problems with a fresh mind, not with a mind that is dead, corrupt, decaying with age. You need a new, fresh mind to solve this immense problem of living.

There must be a mutation. You know that word ***mutation*** is now being used a great deal not only among the scientists but among others. May I go into it a little bit?—because it is quite interesting. To us, change is gradual; time is involved in change—"I will be this tomorrow; I won't be that tomorrow." Time is involved in change. In mutation time is not involved; the whole process of the mind, thought, has undergone a tremendous change, revolution—not in terms of time. I am going to go into that during these talks. That is what is demanded—a man totally born anew in a timeless state so that he can bring about a complete revolution in the world. And you need a revolution, not an economic or a social revolution. I am not talking of a superficial or fragmentary one, but of a revolution in the whole psyche, in the whole makeup of man so that he is no longer a businessman, no longer a religious man, separated, no longer an artist, a politician, but he is a total human being who is completely sensitive to the whole process of living.

You know what I mean by *sensitive:* to be sensitive to the stars, to be aware of them, to be aware of the beauty of a tree, to be aware of that noise, that hammering going on, to be aware of the world, to be aware of your own agonies, hopes, fears, to be aware of all the falsity of existence invented by the politicians, by the religious people. To be sensitive to all these means you begin to live. But you cannot be sensitive if you are so conditioned. If you are burdened with your fears, with your agonies, you are not aware, there is no attention.

So all these things are necessary, not only to understand this extraordinary world where there is immense material progress, but also what they are doing in Europe through the common market—the astonishing progress, the material well-being they are bringing about, the technological, lightning changes that are going to liberate man and give him freedom, where a whole factory can be run by a couple of men, and the electronic brains that think, that write music, that translate. And then there is the whole experiment that is going on among certain people: taking drugs to see if they can expand consciousness. But this expansion in consciousness, or in technology, or the pursuit of being completely physically well is not going to answer any of these problems.

We must go beyond all that. And that means a new mind; a new being must be born, not in your sons, not in the future, but it must be born now, in you. And that is the urgency. I mean exactly what I say; I am not a politician. I mean precisely, verbally, intellectually, and—if you like to use that word—spiritually, I mean exactly what I say, that there is no time. We have to make ourselves into a new human being immediately, and that is where the beauty of it lies. When you introduce time, you have sorrow and the ways of sorrow. So from the very beginning of this investigation and observation, this clear discipline in freedom comes into being, and that is absolutely necessary. Then the mind becomes sharp through observation;

then the mind becomes healthy, not afraid; then it has no authority.

And out of this observation comes energy. You must have energy, not the energy that is produced through conflict, through friction. With that we are all familiar. Through control, through suppression, through tension, through contradiction you have a certain energy. The more you are aware of your contradictions, the more tense you become, and out of that tenseness there is a certain form of energy. You may have a certain capacity; then, you write a book or become a politician or God knows what else. I am not talking of that kind of energy. I am talking of that energy that is born within in which there is no conflict, that energy that has never been contaminated by effort. Only these two are absolutely essential to go any further, to discover for oneself, not through any books, not through any religious leader—put them all away for God's sake; the world has gone beyond all that.

To find out for yourself as a total human being, you must have this extraordinarily subtle discipline and this energy. Otherwise you will never find what is true. You may talk about it, but the reality of it, the beauty of it, the very essence of it you will never come to know. Because to find what is true, that which is immeasurable, which is beyond all words or description, you need an amazing energy, not the energy they talk about of being a bachelor—that is all infantile, immature thinking. I am talking of an energy that has never known what it is to be in conflict, an energy that is uncontaminated by our petty desires; and that comes—and that you must have—only when you understand this observation which is itself discipline. Then you go very far. Then you enter into a world in which all knowledge has ceased, and then the mind is a fresh, young, innocent mind. And certainly it is only the innocent mind—however much it may be experienced, however much it may have learned—that can put all that aside and be innocent. It is only that innocent mind that can understand that which is without limit, which is immeasurable. And that is the only religion. There is no other religion. Every other religion that man has put together can be torn down because man has put it together through his fear, through his ambition. Through his despair and sorrow he has built this thing called religion, highly organized or individual; that is not religion. Religion is the discovery of what is true for oneself, which is not opinion, which is not based on authority. It is a living thing from moment to moment, to be discovered, to be lived, to be looked at, to be seen—the beauty of it. You cannot do it if your mind is destroyed by authority, by tradition, by nationalities, by fragmentation.

That is why by observing the world, the things that are going on outwardly, that tide of observation brings you within. And from that observation you begin to know yourself, not according to any psychology, not according to certain statements, however ancient. It is then you begin to know yourself as you are, never accepting a thing—that you are the atma, the soul, this and that; they have all lost their meaning. Please believe me; no, please do not believe me. (Laughter) They have lost their meaning because you are in sorrow. There is death; there is appalling misery, not only collective, but individual. There is mounting despair. It is there; you have not solved it. You have to solve it, completely resolve it—not in fragments, bit by bit, day after day—immediately cut at the root of the whole thing. Then you become a new man. Then, out of that comes a different life, a different way of living in this world, not away from this world.

That is why it is very important from the very beginning of these talks to understand that there is only learning, not the accumulation of learning. You cannot learn if you are accumulating—then you belong to the past, you are a dead human being. You only learn as you are living, moving, running, flowing; and that demands your complete attention.

And virtue comes with attention, not the stupid morality of a certain society—that is not virtue. Virtue comes out of this attention. It is a thing that is not to be cultivated. It is like a perfume, it is there and therefore can never be destroyed. All these things are necessary if you go very far, deeply, beyond the measure of time and beyond the measure of words. Then you do not invite that which is the immeasurable; it is there.

October 23, 1963

Second Talk in New Delhi

As we were saying the other day, it is obviously an absolute necessity to bring about within each one a radical revolution, a change in mutation at the very root of consciousness. I feel that unless this takes place totally, the many confusing and contradictory problems in all our relationships at all the levels of our consciousness can never be solved. The search for truth, for reality, is not possible in a world in which there is not only outward contradiction but inward self-contradiction. It is not possible for one to discover that extraordinary thing called reality if there is no corresponding total clarity, not according to any particular formula or a concept, but that clarity that comes about through understanding, through the awareness of the total boundary of one's consciousness.

You know it is very difficult to understand the meaning of words and also to be free of words. Most of us who understand English understand more or less the meaning of words. Words have their reference in the dictionary, or we give a particular significance to words. And I feel it is very important not to be caught in words. Most of us live with words; for us words have an extraordinary significance. All our thinking, our feeling, is limited by words. Words and symbols play an enormous part in our life; and to really comprehend those words and to be free of words and to go beyond the words is very important for the man who would really understand what is truth.

So, before we go this evening into this question of what is conflict, and if it is at all possible to be free of conflict, we must, it seems to me, understand the structure of words, the meaning which we give to a particular word, and discover through the awareness of the word how the mind is caught in a web of words. Because we live, most of us, by formulas, by concepts, either self-created or handed down to us by society, which we call ideals, which we call the necessity to have a certain pattern according to which we live. If you examine those formulas, those ideas, those concepts, and those patterns, you will see they are words, and those words control our activities, shape our thoughts, make us feel in a certain way. Words condition our thinking, our being.

Please do give a little attention to this. A mind caught in words is incapable of being free. A mind functioning within the pattern of a formula is obviously a conditioned, slavish mind. It is incapable of thinking anew, afresh. And most of our thinking, most of our activity, our thought, is within the boundaries of words and formulas. Take a word like *God, love.* What extraordinary images, formulas, come into your mind! A man who would find if there is God, who would find out what love implies or means, obviously must be free of all concepts, all formulas. And to be free of the formula, of the concept, the mind refuses to break through because there is fear. So, fear takes shelter in words, and we battle over words. So, the first thing for a man who would really go into this seriously—to the very end, to discover if there is or if there is not a reality, a thing that is beyond the measure of words—is that he must absolutely understand words and be free of formulas.

So, before we go very deeply into the question of conflict—which I will do presently this evening—I may use words which may have a particular meaning to you. And if I may earnestly request, don't translate what is said in terms of your own meaning. Just listen. Don't interpret, don't compare, but just listen. Because most of us do not listen. We do not know what it means to listen to somebody. It is as much an art to listen, as any other form of activity is. Every activity is an art; even your going to your office—it is an art, there is beauty in it. And one has to listen without comparison, without evaluating what is being said in terms of words—that is all that you are going to do; you will listen with words which you already know; but that is not listening. A mind that listens is completely attentive, not in the framework of words—it wants to find out. And to find out, the mind must be astonishingly alive; and a mind is not alive when it is caught in a formula, a religious or an economic or a social formula, either of Karl Marx or of this fantastic idea of nonviolence in this country, or according to the Gita or other books. To listen implies an astonishing awareness, not only of your own words, of your own formulas, but putting them aside, to listen, to find out what the speaker is saying—not to argue, not to agree; it is very cheap to argue and to agree or to contradict. But you have to understand, to find out whether what the speaker is saying is false or true—not according to a formula, not according to what you know. Because what you know is merely a series of words which have been handed to you or the things which you have experienced, which again establish a further strengthening of your conditioning, and with those words you listen; and therefore you never learn.

So, we have to be really earnest in this matter. There must be a few of us who are serious, who want to discover for themselves—not according to what some teacher, some book, or some political group has said, but to discover for oneself—what is the fact, the actual reality of things. For this, one must be free of these formulas and be capable of listening completely. We are not dealing with propaganda, we are not trying to convert you to anything, or to make you think differently, because thought is not going to bring about a revolution. On the contrary, the very cessation of thought is the beginning of a mutation. So, do please understand that we are not dealing with opinions or analyzing opinions or introducing new formulas, howsoever subtly—which is the way of propaganda. We are dealing, if we are at all serious in these matters, with facts. The man who is earnest begins to live, not the man who is not earnest—he does not live, he just dissipates not only his energy but his relationships—to such a man there is no reality, there is no way out of this enormous misery and confusion and sorrow. It is only to the serious man, to the earnest man, that life opens.

So the very art of listening is the beginning of understanding—the art of listening. When you do listen, it is not a matter of control, not forcing yourself to listen to something, because the moment you make an effort to listen, you cease to listen. Here, we are not making an effort to listen. We want to find out. And to discover something new, which we are going to discover as we go along together, your mind must be free—not always comparing, judging, evaluating, condemning, agreeing, not agreeing, chattering, but just listening not only to the play of words but to the play of thought, and also going beyond the word, the thought, the idea. Then, you will see, if you so listen, that without your wanting, without a deliberate, purposive, directive action taking place, there has already taken place a mutation. This is an important thing to understand. That is, any purposeful action based on a desire, on a motive, will not bring about a revolution, a mutation in consciousness, because such a motive, such a desire is still within the formula, within the conditioning by the old pattern. What we are concerned with—those who are serious—is the breaking down totally of our conditioning so as to see something totally new. And the world situation, not only now, but also in the future, at all times, demands a mind that can see the true and act, not as an idea but as an action that is ever present—which we will go into presently.

What I want to discuss this evening is the conflict within and without, and whether it is at all possible, living in this world, to be free of conflict totally, not partially. To be totally free of all conflict—is it at all possible? Don't say, "It is," or "It is not." A serious mind does not take such a position; it inquires. And the mind must be free of conflict, obviously—free of conflict which creates confusion, contradiction, various forms of neurosis. If it is not free of this confusion, how can such a mind see, understand, observe? It can only spin with a lot of words about truth, nonviolence, God, bliss, nirvana, and all the rest of the words—they have no meaning at all.

So, a mind that would seek or that would find reality must be free of conflict at all levels of consciousness—which does not mean pursuing peace, retiring from the world, going to a monastery, or meditating under a tree; that is merely an escape. It must be free totally, completely, at all levels of one's consciousness, of all conflict so that the mind is clear. It is only a mind that is clear that can be free, and it is only in complete freedom that you can discover what is true.

So we have to investigate the anatomy, the structure of conflict. You are not listening to me, you are listening to your own consciousness. You are listening, observing, seeing the conflict in your own life—whether it is in the office, whether it is with your wife or husband, or with your children, with your neighbor, with your ideals—observing your own conflict. Because what we are concerned with is the revolution in you, not in me, revolution within each one, radically, at the very root of one's being; otherwise, it is all a superficial change, an adjustment which has no value whatsoever. The world is undergoing tremendous changes not only technologically but morally, ethically; and merely to adapt oneself to a change does not bring about clarity of vision, clarity of mind. What brings about this extraordinary clarity is when the mind has understood, totally, the whole process of conflict within and without; and that very understanding brings freedom. And therefore such a mind is clear, and in that clarity there is beauty. Such a mind is the religious mind, not this phony mind that goes to a temple, repeats words endlessly, performs ceremonies ten thousand times—they have no meaning anymore.

So, what we are concerned with, this evening, is the understanding of conflict; understanding—not how to get rid of conflict, not how to substitute conflict by a series of formulas called peace, or to resist conflict, or to avoid conflict, but to understand it. I hope I am making myself clear when I use the word *understand.* You know, to understand something is to live with it, and you cannot live with something if you resist it, or if you substitute through your fear that which is a fact, or if you run away, or if, when you are in tremendous conflict within yourself, you seek peace—which is just another form of escape. I am using the word understand in a particular sense, that is, to face the fact that you are in conflict, and to live with it completely—

not to avoid it, not to escape. And then you will see if you can live with it, not translate it, not try to put all the collected opinions of every person upon it, but live with it—which you are going to do this evening even though it is for ten minutes.

First of all, there is conflict not only at the conscious level of the mind but also unconsciously, deep down. We are a mass of conflicts, contradictions, not only at the level of thought, but also at the level which conscious thought has not penetrated. Please, you must give your attention. Don't bother with who is coming or who is going. Sirs, we are dealing with very serious problems. We are not children. This requires all your attention, and you cannot give your attention if you are watching somebody, if you are listening to some other factor. This demands complete attention on your part. You are in conflict whether you like it or not; your life is a misery, confusion, a series of contradictions—violence and nonviolence. All the saints have destroyed you with their particular idiosyncrasies, with their particular patterns of violence and nonviolence. To break all that, to find out for yourself demands attention, an earnestness to go through right to the very end of this question of violence, of this question of effort, conflict.

So, please listen. We are in conflict. Everything we do brings conflict. We do not know a moment, from school days until now, when we are not in conflict. Going to the office, which is a terrible boredom, your prayers, your search for God, your disciplines, your relationships—everything has in it a seed of conflict. It is fairly obvious to any man who wants to know himself; when he observes himself as though in a mirror, he sees he is in conflict. And what does he do? Immediately he wants to run away from it, or to find a formula which will absorb that conflict. What we are trying to do this evening is to observe this conflict, not to run away from it.

Conflict arises when there is contradiction in our activity, in our thought, in our being, outwardly and inwardly. Conflict we accept as a way of progress. Conflict for us is a struggle. The adjustments, the suppressions, the innumerable contradictory desires, the various contradictory pulls, urges—all these create conflict within us. We are brought up to be ambitious, to make a success of life; and where there is ambition, there is conflict—this does not mean that you must go to sleep, that you must meditate. But when you understand the very nature of conflict, a new energy comes, an energy which is uncontaminated by any effort; and that is what we are going to find out.

So, first of all, to be aware that we are in conflict, not how to transcend it, not what to do about it, not how to suppress it, but to be aware and not do anything about it—that is necessary. We are going to do something about it later, but first not to do anything about what you have discovered, about the fact that you are in conflict, that you are trying to escape in different ways from that conflict. That is the fact, and when you remain with that fact for a few minutes, you will see how your mind resists remaining with the fact. It wants to run away, to act upon it, to do something about it. It can never live with that fact. And to understand something, you have got to live with it, and to live with it you have to be extremely sensitive. That is, to live with a beautiful tree or a picture or a person—to live with it is not to get used to it. The moment you get used to it, you have lost the sensitivity to it. That is a fact. If I get used to the mountain where I live all my life, I am no longer sensitive to the beauty of the line, to the light, to the shape, to the extraordinary brilliance of it in the morning or in the evening. I get used to it—which means I become insensitive to it. In the same way, to live with an ugly thing demands equal sensitivity. If I get used to the dirty roads, to the dirty thoughts, to the ugly situations, to put up with things, if I get used to them, I again become insensitive. So to live with something, whether it is beautiful or ugly, or a thing that brings sorrow—to live with it means to be sensitive to it and not get used to it. So that is the first thing.

Conflict exists because we have not only contradictory desires but all our education, all the psychological pressures of society bring about, in us, this division, this cleavage between *what is* and 'what should be', between the factual and the ideal. And we are ridden with ideals. A mind that is clear has no ideals. It functions from fact to fact and not from idea to idea. We know the nature of conflict not only at the conscious level but at an unconscious level. I do not want to discuss this evening what is conscious or what is unconscious; we will do that another day. We are now concerned with conflict, conflict throughout the total being of ourselves, not merely at the conscious levels, but at the unconscious level. There is conflict. Now, any effort to be free of it involves another conflict. Please see this. Any effort to be free of conflict involves another series of conflicts. It is fairly obvious, fairly logical. So the mind has to find a way of being free of conflict without effort. Do you understand the problem? If I resist conflict, or if I resist all the patterns, all the intimations which are involved in conflict, that very resistance is another contradiction and therefore a conflict. Am I making myself clear?

Look, sirs, let me put it very simply. I realize I am in conflict. I am violent, and all the saints and all the books have said I must not be violent. So there are two things in me contradictory: violence and also that I must be nonviolent; that is a contradiction, either self-imposed or imposed upon me by others. In that self-contradiction there is conflict. Now if I resist both, in order to understand or in order to avoid conflict, I am still in conflict. The very resistance creates conflict. That is fairly clear. So to understand and be free of conflict, there must be no resistance to conflict, there must be no escape from conflict; I must look at it, I must listen to the whole content of conflict—with my wife, with my children, with society, with all the ideas that I have. If you say it is not possible in this life to be free of conflict, then there is no further relationship between you and me. Or if you say it is possible, again there is no relationship between you and me. But if you say, "I want to find out, I want to go into it, I want to tear down the structure of conflict which is being built in me and of which I am a part," then you and I have a relationship; then we can proceed together.

So every form of resistance and escape and avoidance of conflict only increases conflict. And conflict implies confusion. Conflict implies brutality, a hardness. A mind in conflict cannot be compassionate, nor have that clarity of compassion. So the mind has to be aware of this conflict without resistance, without avoidance, without an opinion put upon it. Please follow this thing. In that very act there is a discipline born—a flexible discipline, a discipline which is not based on any formula, on any pattern, on any suppression. That is to observe the whole content of conflict within, and that very observation brings naturally, effortlessly, a discipline. And you must have this discipline. I am using the word *discipline* in the sense of clarity, in the sense of a mind that thinks precisely, healthily; and you cannot have a healthy, sane, clear mind if there is conflict.

Therefore the first essential thing is to understand conflict. Perhaps you will say, "I am not free of conflict. Tell me how to be free of conflict." Do you follow? That is the pattern you have learned. You want to be told how to be free, and you will pursue that pattern in order to be free from conflict and therefore still be in conflict. That is fairly simple. So there is no "how." Please understand this. There is no method in life. You have to live it. A man who has a method to achieve nonviolence or some extraordinary state is merely caught in a pattern; and the pattern does produce a result, but it will not lead to reality. So when you ask, "How am I to be free from conflict?" you are falling back into the old pattern—which indicates that you are still in conflict, that you have not understood, which means again that you have not lived clearly with the fact.

So, being in conflict implies a confused mind, and you can see this all over the world. Every politician in the world is confused and has brought misery to the world. Equally, the saints have brought misery to the world. And if you are earnest and would be free of conflict, you have to abolish totally all authority in yourself because for a man who wants to find truth, there is no authority—neither the Gita nor your saints nor your leaders—nobody. That means you stand completely alone. And to stand alone—that comes about when the mind is free from conflict.

You see, most of us want to avoid life, and we have found several ways and methods of avoiding this thing called life. Life is a total thing, not a partial thing. Life includes beauty, religion, politics, economics, relationships, quarrels, the misery, the torture, the agony of existence, the despair—all that is life, not just one part, one fragment of it; and you have to understand the totality of it. And that requires a mind healthy, sane, clear. That is why you have to have a mind without conflict, a mind that has no mark of conflict, that has not been scratched. That is why conflict in any form can only be understood by being aware.

I mean by "being aware," observing it. To observe demands that you should not look at it with an opinion. You should look at it, but not with your ideas, with your judgments, with your comparison, with your condemnation. If there is a condemnation, a resistance, you are not observing; therefore, your concern then is not conflict. You cannot look at anything without an idea, and that becomes your problem. You want to observe conflict, but you cannot observe conflict if you bring in an opinion or an idea or an evaluation about that conflict, or resist it. Your concern then is to find out why you resist, not how to understand conflict—why you resist. So you have moved away from conflict and become aware of your resistance. Why do you resist? You can find out why you resist. For most of us, conflict has become a habit. It has made us so dull that we are not even aware of it. We have accepted it as a part of existence. And when you come upon it, when you see it as a fact, then you resist it, or you are trying to avoid it, trying to find a way out of it. To observe the fact that you resist is far more important than to understand conflict—how you are avoiding it, how you are bringing a formula to it. So you begin to observe your formulas, your opinions, your resistances. By being aware of all these, you are breaking down your conditioning, and therefore you are able to face conflict. When you have broken down your conditioning, your resistance, your formulas, then you can face conflict.

So to understand conflict and therefore to be free of it, not eventually, not at the end of your life, not the day after tomorrow, but immediately, totally—and it can be done—demands an astonishing faculty of observation which is not to be cultivated, because the moment you cultivate it, you are back again in conflict. What is demanded is the immediate perception of that total process, of the total content of consciousness—immediate observation and therefore seeing the truth of it. The moment you see the truth of it, you are out of it. And you cannot see the truth of it if, in any form whatsoever, at whatever level, you try to resist, avoid, or impose upon it certain formulas which you have learned.

So, that brings up a very important question—which is that there is no time for change. Either you change now or never. I do not mean "never" in the orthodox sense or in the Christian sense of "eternally damned"—I do not mean that. I mean: you change now in the active present—that active present may be tomorrow but still the active present. And it is only in the active present that there is a mutation, not the day after tomorrow. This is very important to understand. We are so used to an idea, and then we try to put that idea into action. We first formulate logically or illogically—mostly illogically— an idea or an ideal, and try to put that into action. So there is a gap between action and the idea; so there is a contradiction between the idea, the ideal, and the action. The action is the living present, not the idea. The formula is merely a fixation; the active present is the action. So if you say, "I must be free of conflict," that becomes an idea. And there is a time interval between the idea and the action, and you hope that during that time interval some peculiar, mysterious action will take place that will make you bring about a change. You understand? I hope I am making myself clear.

If you allow time, then there is no mutation. To understand is immediate. And you can only understand if you observe completely, with all your being—to listen to that airplane, to the hum of that with all your being, not to translate it, not say, "That is an airplane," or "How disturbing it is," or "When I want to listen to him, that plane is going on"; then that becomes merely a distraction, a contradiction, and you are lost. But to listen to that airplane completely, with all your being, is to listen to the speaker also with all your being. There is no division between the two. There is a division only when you want to concentrate on what is being said, and that becomes a resistance. But if you are completely attentive, then you are listening to that airplane, and you are also listening to the speaker.

In the same way if you are completely aware of the whole structure, the anatomy of conflict, then you will see that there is an immediate change. Then you are out of conflict completely and totally. But if you say, "Well, will it always be so? Will I always be free of conflict?" then you are asking the most foolish question. Then it indicates that you are not free of conflict, that you have not understood the nature of conflict. You only want to conquer and be at peace.

A mind that has not understood conflict can never be at peace. It can escape to an idea, a word called peace; but it is not peace. To have peace demands clarity, and clarity can only come when there is no conflict of any kind, totally—which is not a process of self-hypnosis. When the mind has understood and therefore is free, such a mind alone can go very far. It is only the mind that has understood conflict with all its violence, with all its insanities—and nonviolence is a form of insanity because the mind has not understood violence—that can go very far. A mind that is forcing itself to be nonviolent is violent. Most of your saints and teachers are full of violence; they do not know the clarity of compassion. And it is only the compassionate mind that can understand that which is beyond words.

October 27, 1963

Third Talk in New Delhi

I wonder what the purpose of a gathering like this is. What do you, if I may ask—not that you are going to reply—expect from this? What do you want out of a gathering or meeting like this? I do not know what you want. Each person has his own particular problem which he wants resolved, and hopes he would find here, there, somewhere or other, an answer to an agony, to a despair, to an intense searching problem which he has. But I know what the speaker intends. He wants to convey something not only linguistically, verbally, but also to convey through the word something beyond the word. And to convey that thing beyond the word, the word must be understood, and also the mind must be able to communicate, to receive, to comprehend, to understand—and that is where our difficulty lies.

Most of us have innumerable problems—economic, social, family, personal, collective, national, international, every kind of problem, at every level of our existence—some very simple and others extraordinarily complex. We try to solve each problem in isolation as though it were something separate from the rest of our existence. But no problem is separate, whether it is an economic problem or your personal, individual problem. All problems are interrelated. And we have to know how to understand the extraordinary relationship of each problem, without trying to find an answer to the problem as a thing apart. For this we need a new mind, not a mind that is integrated, not a mind that is in fragmentation and is put together as an integration.

There is no such thing as integration; a thing that is broken up cannot be integrated. What is demanded is a new mind, not the approach of the old mind with all its superstitions, fears, dogmas, nationalities, authorities, traditions. There must be a new mind which sees the relationship of every problem with another problem, an interrelated comprehension of the whole. A problem cannot be answered. There is no answer to our human problems. Perhaps there may be an answer economically, technologically; but psychologically there is no answer.

The answer is in the problem itself—how we understand it, how we approach it, what we do and how we act with that problem. When a mind seeks an answer, a solution to this extraordinary, human, psychological, complex problem, there is no answer. What we have to do is to understand the problem, to investigate it, to go into it with all our being, and to go into it completely, totally. We cannot approach it with a fragmentary mind, a mind that has divided life into the economic world and the spiritual world, that avoids the one and goes off to the other, denies the one and accepts the other. It is the old mind that does it—the mind that is conditioned, that has not understood the problem. The problem, the crisis, the challenge is in you, and you have to reply adequately. You are the world, and you have to respond to this as a human being—not as an Indian, a Sikh, a Muslim, or a Christian—they are all outdated, they have no meaning any more. It is important how you, as a human being, respond to this.

The world is really you, whether you accept it or not, whether you like it or not. And if you merely try to answer all these extraordinary problems as though they are separate, independent, or if you approach them from a nationalistic or a class point of view, you will not reply adequately to these extraordinary challenges.

You need a new mind, a new way of thinking, and a new way of feeling, a new way of being. I would like, this evening, to go into that. But before I go into it, each one of us must see the necessity of denying the old mind, of putting away the old mind. You cannot put away something unless you completely, totally, understand it, see the implications involved. You cannot destroy the old mind and grope after the new mind. You have to understand the old mind, but to understand you must give your attention. And this attention will bring about a revolution, a mutation in the mind; you don't have to do a thing, only you must give your complete attention. So our question is not merely the freedom of the old, but in freeing the mind of the old, what is important is the manner, the way that it is done.

I hope this is very clear between you and me: We are trying to understand the problem of existence with all its ramifications, with all its fragments. There must be a total answer—not a political answer, not a sociological or scientific answer. If we try to answer the problem partially, our problems will increase a thousand times. So there must be a total approach so that this approach can bring about naturally, without effort, without conflict, a tremendous mutation in the whole of consciousness itself. That is our problem, that is the central issue with which we are confronted.

I hope it is clear between you and the speaker that we are not dealing with any particular, single, isolated problem of human existence, but we are concerned with putting away the old mind and thereby bringing about the new mind. The new mind is not a mind put together by us, by our travail, by our misery, by our anxiety, despair, and agony. We have to understand all these agonies, despairs, conflicts, miseries, confusions; and the way we understand, the way we approach that complex, psychological structure of a human being is important. And out of that understanding comes the new mind. There is no new mind if you are ambitious, greedy, envious, superstitious, ignorant. So, we have to understand the fact as it is—not have an idea about it, not inquire into what the new mind is and speculate endlessly about that.

We are concerned with a deep, psychological revolution, an explosion at the very root of our being, because everything around us has failed. All the religions, education, nationalities, economic societies—everything that man has put together brings more misery, more confusion. This is obvious. So, what we need—not eventually, but now, in the present, in the active daily living—is a tremendous revolution, a mutation. So, if that thing is clearly seen by each one of us, then the question arises: How is the mind that is crippled with the old to slough it off, how is it to put it away easily, without any effort, without any struggle? The problem then is: Is it possible for a mind that has been so conditioned—brought up in innumerable sects, religions, and all the superstitions, fears—to break away from itself and thereby bring about a new mind? I hope I am putting the question clearly.

The old mind is essentially the mind that is bound by authority. I am not using the word *authority* in the legalistic sense; but by that word I mean authority as tradition, authority as knowledge, authority as experience, authority as the means of finding security and remaining in that security, outwardly or inwardly, because, after all, that is what the mind is always seeking—a place where it can be secure, undisturbed. Such authority may be the self-imposed authority of an idea or the so-called religious idea of God which has no reality to a religious person. An idea is not a fact, it is a fiction. God is a fiction; you may believe in it, but still it is a fiction. But to find God you must completely destroy the fiction, because the old mind is the mind that is frightened, is ambitious, is fearful of death, of living, and of relationship; and it is always, consciously or unconsciously, seeking a permanency, security.

So, that is the old mind, and I am going to go into that. Now, I am going into it verbally; naturally, the only means of communication between the speaker and you is to use words. But if you twist the words, if you interpret the words to suit your own convenience, your own fiction, your own myth, then communication immediately ceases because you move away into the realm of your particular fancy, of your particular ideas. So, as the speaker is going into it, you have to listen not only to the word but also to the meaning of that word, see how you react to that word—please follow all this—and how you deal with the thing that the word awakens in you. You understand? I hope I am making myself clear. I am going to go into something rather complex, verbally complex. And most of us—being intellectually, verbally, very complicated, very clever—will translate it into intellectual terminology, into a concept, and leave it there. But what the speaker proposes is something entirely different. He proposes that when you leave this place, you have completely understood the whole significance of what he is saying; and in the very act of understanding you are free from the things that are destroying you, and free of the mind that is dead, crippled, corrupt, and that cannot possibly understand the new.

If you observe, there is ever-increasing knowledge, more and more information. We are the entities made up of knowledge which is memory; we are not so sharp, clear, quick as the electronic brain, but we function along that same process, in the same field. We are a bundle of memories and nothing else. Don't say, "Are we not the atma, the super-soul?" They are just words and they have no meaning. Somebody has told you about them and you repeat them—which is still a form of memory. We are a bundle of memories; that is the fact.

Now, what is the relationship of knowledge to freedom? How far is knowledge essential to freedom? Is knowledge opposed to ignorance, and what is ignorance? And this freedom, if there is such a thing—does it come from knowledge?

So, we are first going to understand what we mean by that word *ignorance.* For the speaker, ignorance essentially does not mean the lack of book knowledge—anybody can learn how to read and write and go to the office, go to the factory. I am using the word ignorance in the sense of having no knowledge of the whole psychological structure of oneself, not knowing yourself. Please listen carefully: not knowing yourself—not "not knowing the atma"; the man who repeats the word *atma* does not know what it means. What you know is yourself. You are a bundle of memories, and it is no good repeating what tens of thousands or millions of people have said. You have to find out. To find out you must inquire, and to inquire you must have freedom and not everlastingly repeat what the Gita, the Bible, the Koran, or your guru says—it has no meaning anymore; probably it never had except for those people who want to avoid, to escape, to bypass living with all its problems. The man who bypasses existence—living, the actual present—is not a religious man at all. He may go to all the gurus, all the ashrams, to every religion, but he is not a religious man. A religious man has the new mind—the mind that has no fear, that is not ambitious, that is without conflict.

So, ignorance is the lack of self-knowing. By self I mean the self that functions everyday—not the big self with a big, capital *S*—I mean the self that goes to the office, that quarrels, that is greedy, that is afraid of death and of living, that seeks, that gropes after, that suffers, that is in conflict, that agonizes over everything, that does not care. Without knowing that self, to try to find out what the supreme self is, is sheer nonsense—that is fiction for a man who does not know himself. So, the man that does not know that he is a bundle of memories—both the conscious as well as the unconscious, the totality of his being—that person is ignorant. Now, this person has to understand the whole structure of his memories and responses according to that memory, to observe, to be aware, to watch. You see, most of us do not want to do that; we would rather go to somebody and be told what to do. It requires attention to watch yourself. To watch yourself requires infinite love—not chastisement, not condemnation, not evaluation. It requires love so that you watch out of extraordinary clarity—just observe, just see.

As all of us are a bundle of memories and are adding every day to that bundle more and more, what is the relationship of that bundle—which is the creator of problems—to the thing that it seeks, which is freedom? Because you must be free. That is absolutely essential; otherwise, you can never discover anything. And this freedom is not a reaction to bondage, it is not freedom from something. If it is freedom from something, then it is a reaction and therefore not freedom. If I am free from pride, and I know that I am free from pride, then it is not freedom from pride. Freedom is something that cannot be cultivated, that cannot be sought. It comes with an extraordinary vitality, with a fury, with an intensity, only when you begin to understand the whole psychological structure of yourself. So that is the issue.

Because you are the world, you have to act, you have to think, you have to feel in the world that is undergoing tremendous changes, that is made corrupt by the politician, by the religious people—I am using the word ***religious*** in the wrong sense of the word, that is in the sense of "made ugly by the saints, by the organized religious dogmas, beliefs"; they are not religious people at all, and this world is made ugly by them. We live in that world and we have to understand that world. And to understand you must observe. And observation is not merely of the world outside you because the world outside you is the 'you' inside as well, the observer. There is no division between the world and you; you are the world. So how you observe yourself is of the highest importance. This observation of yourself is not the isolation of yourself from the world. Please do understand this. You are the world, the world in which you are born, in which you are educated—the family, the social, psychological structure of the society about you, the economic conditions in which you live—which shapes your mind, your thought, your feeling. So you, as a human being, have to understand this. And in the process of understanding, in the very act of understanding, the new is born.

How do you observe yourself? What is observation and what do you observe? Who is the observer? Do you follow? You have to observe. Obviously that is essential. You have to see because when you see, you begin to care. If you saw that dirty road, if you really saw the starvation, the poverty, the degradation, the corruption in this country—if you really saw it, you would care, you would do something, you would act. But you do not care because you do not see. And when you do see, you want some social action to take place, and therefore you wait.

To see is to care. To observe is to love. I am using the word *love* as a total thing—not the divine love, the sexual love, the personal love; those are all mere ideas; we are not dealing with ideas, we are dealing with facts. If you observe a dog, then you will begin to love that dog. If you observe your children, you will begin to love those children—not your particular children, but children. You will watch them intensely, completely, when they are sleeping, waking, crying, being naughty. In the same way, when you observe yourself, you will care. Sirs, I hope I am making myself clear. You will care for what you observe, and therefore you will not condemn what you see. You won't say, "I am ugly; I am beautiful; I am this; I am that." You won't say that because you will care when you are watching. Therefore when you watch, when you observe, you will see that you are observing without condemning, without bringing all the past experience into your mind, which either accepts or denies what you observe.

You see, sirs, we do not know what it means to love; we don't. We beget children, we are married, we have families, but we do not know what it means to love. If we loved, if there was love, if there was care, then we would find ways and means to fill the stomachs of the poor, build houses, do something drastically, independent of the ugly politicians with their words. We do not know what it means to love. And love cannot come to you if you do not understand yourself. That is the only solution in the world—to care profoundly.

So to understand yourself, there must be no authority—the authority of a memory, of a previous observation. You understand? Look! When you observe a child whom you love—if you love at all—that implies a tremendous thing. To love somebody—that means "to care." When you observe a child, what is happening? You watch. If you care, you do not condemn, you watch; you don't push him, you don't direct him, you don't say, "This is right; this is wrong." You want to find out about the child, what he thinks, what he feels. You want to establish a sensitive relationship with the child because you care, you love—that he must be brought up properly, that he must have the right education entirely different from this rotten education, that he must not merely live for a job and die in a job. In the same way, in that extraordinary sensitive observation which comes with care, you watch yourself without authority, you watch yourself without the previous knowledge of what you have observed and learned. Are you following this, or is it too difficult? If I observe myself from what I have learned from my previous observation, I am not observing—I am merely observing from the experience which I have had yesterday, and that experience is going to dictate how I shall observe; therefore, it prevents me from observing. If you observed your child who has been naughty yesterday, and with that knowledge you observe him today, you are not observing him. That knowledge is going to dictate how you should observe him today. That previous knowledge becomes your authority. That knowledge is the tradition, what the guru, what the saints, what society has said, and with that you observe, and therefore it is not observation at all.

If you are really interested to observe and therefore really care, then all the tradition, all the authority of yesterday or ten thousand yesterdays drop away from you. Then you are observant every minute, watching, looking, listening, because you have the feeling of care, affection, love. These are not ideas; don't nod your heads in agreement. This is your life we are talking about—not my life—your life which is so torn apart, which has no meaning any more, hedged about with so many anxieties, fears.

So a mind that is observing itself is watching the words, the gestures, the ideas, the feelings, the reactions, putting up with insults, inviting flattery. As you begin to observe yourself, you will see that all authority—as tradition, as what people will say and won't say, all the authority of the guru, of the book—comes to a complete end because then you become a light unto yourself. And that is absolutely essential because nobody can give you truth, nobody can point it out to you. Because truth is not something that is static. It is a living thing, a thing that is moving swiftly. It is not a word. And to find that, the mind must be equally swift and equally without a word. So if you really care and therefore observe, you will find that out of that observation comes freedom.

But, you see, most of us are so crippled by authority, both outwardly and inwardly. We respect authority, and authority is one of the most difficult things to be free from. Authority is different from law. Don't mix the two. The law of the road, the law of the country, the law that says that you must pay tax—that is entirely different from the authority of fear, the authority of a mind that is seeking security, the authority of a mind that has many experiences and uses those experiences to understand the living present. Because that authority is of time, of yesterday; it is not a living thing. And a dead thing shapes the living thing. A dead thing judges in its observation and says, "This is right, this is wrong; this is the right value, this is the wrong value." As you observe in the world now, all values are going, all values have gone. Psychologically, inwardly, we still have values, and with those values we observe. So to observe implies care, and when you care there is no condemnation, no comparison. You don't compare your child with his elder brother; you love that child. It is only when you do not care, when there is no love, you begin to compare and say, "You are not so good as your elder brother."

There is not only the authority of the conscious mind of which one is aware in daily process—the authority of your experiences of which you are conscious and which guides you, shapes you and controls you—but also there is the authority of the unconscious. I do not know if you yourself have gone into it directly—probably not. First of all you have neither the time nor the inclination. But probably all of you have read Freud and a few other psychologists or your own particular religious books which describe your consciousness, and you repeat it after them and think you have understood. What I am talking about is something direct, to be lived, discovered, understood immediately, as the speaker is talking.

There is the conscious as well as the unconscious—the thing that is hidden. The daily mind that operates, that goes to the office, that has technical knowledge of how to run a machine, what to do; the mind that is educated by the modern system to become a lawyer, a politician, a technician, a laborer—that is the conscious mind. There is the unconscious mind deep down, the racial instinct, the inherited racial knowledge, the things that are hidden which have never been uncovered, looked into—all that is part of you. I am not going to go into the details of the unconscious because that would demand quite a lot of inquiry, and that is not the purpose for the moment.

There is the unconscious. To inquire into that and to remove from it all authority—because otherwise there is no freedom, otherwise there is no discovery of the new—you must observe. You cannot possibly discover what is new with the eyes of the old. Life demands that every minute you look at it anew. And in looking at it anew, there is beauty. To look at the tree, the person, the mountains, the dirt, the squalor, to see all that anew demands that you shall be free. Our question is now not only how to free the conscious mind but also how to be aware of the authority that is in the conscious mind and also of the authority that is in the unconscious mind—which is much more difficult. To observe your secret thoughts, your secret motives, the fears that have not been discovered, the hopes, the sorrows, the longings, the deep motives—to discover those, to bring them out to the surface demands an extraordinarily sharp mind. And the mind is sharp only when it is quiet. The conscious mind which observes the unconscious can only observe when it is completely quiet. I hope I am making myself clear. The conscious mind (Do you understand what I mean by the conscious mind? I have explained it enough) has to be quiet, not forced to be quiet, not made quiet. If you would understand your child, you have to observe him quietly, haven't you?

So the conscious mind becomes quiet when you are inquiring into the unconscious. You will see also that the two are not separate—it is one movement, one process, which has been divided for convenience as the conscious and the unconscious. As you begin to understand the conscious mind, you will also begin to see that there is an understanding of the unconscious.

And the moment you see the necessity of being completely free from all authority—which you don't because your fear prevents you—when you go through like a flame through fear, when you see the poisonous nature of authority—whether it be of the guru, of the book, of a word, of a symbol, or the psychological authority of a nation, of a group—when you see that authority destroys, corrupts the mind, and therefore the mind cannot possibly think clearly, when you see the truth of all that, then you will begin to observe the conscious as well as the unconscious, and thereby free yourself from authority.

Authority is of the old. Authority is never the new, it is never the living. The thing that is beautiful has no authority. How can innocence have authority? How can love have authority? So a mind that is ridden by authority, whether it is the authority of the wife over the husband or of the husband over the wife, of the book, of the guru—all authority, the ugly nature of which we all know—a mind that is seeking security and therefore clinging to authority, when that mind sees, when it observes with care, you find that all authority ceases.

Then you are a light unto yourself. And there is great beauty and freedom in that light, and then you begin merely to observe. What is light in itself does not demand any experience, does not seek, because there is no 'more'. And that light has no shadow. To come to that light, you cannot invite it, you cannot sacrifice something for it. That light comes of its own accord, sweetly, uninvited, with a fury that will never leave you. But for it to come there must be no authority—which means the old is dead, the old mind is dead and gone. It is only such a mind which is really, truly, the religious mind.

October 30, 1963

Fourth Talk in New Delhi

I would like, this evening, to talk about thought, time, and sorrow. But before I go into that, I would like to point out how important it is to listen because most of us hardly ever listen to anything. To listen properly without projecting your own particular prejudices, idiosyncrasies, and all that you have learned is very difficult—to listen with intense curiosity as though you are for the first time learning, for the first time inquiring, and as though the whole field is open to you; and to go step by step into it without any conclusion, without any memory, inquiring, moving, running, seeing, finding out. Such an act of listening needs attention—not the attention of concentration, not the attention that you give when you are seeking profit or when you want something—and you listen without wanting, without seeking, but merely inquiring. And to inquire really deeply, you need freedom, and the act of listening is freedom. Once one understands this extraordinary act of listening or seeing immediately, comprehending something instantly, then you will see that action is totally different from the action that is derived with an idea or from an idea.

For most of us action is divided. There is a gap between idea and action. We have the formula, the pattern, the concept, the prototype; and according to that we act or approximate our action to that idea. That is our conditioning, that is the way we live—that is, the whole series of our actions is based on that. First we conceive, formulate, create a prototype—the ideal, the thing that should be—and then according to that we live, we act. And thereby our problem is how to bridge the gap between the action and the idea, how to bring the two together? And in that, there is conflict; in that, there is duration of time, because we need time to complete the action according to the idea.

So, what I want to say this evening is that the mind that gives root to a problem ceases to act because action is always in the living present, in the active present. When the problem becomes something to be solved eventually, then the idea becomes important, not the action.

Please, this is very important to understand because of what I am going to say presently. I have not prepared the talk. I am thinking aloud, and you have also to think within yourself aloud, think of your own processes, be aware of them so that we can go together.

For me there is no action if it is preceded by an idea. If action is conditioned by an idea, by a formula, by a concept, action then is not important, but the idea is important, and therefore, there is a conflict between action and idea. Is it possible to act immediately without idea?—which is, after all, what we call love. Is it possible to see the truth of something immediately, instantly, and act instantly on that which is seen—not consider the consequences, the effect, the causes, but act instantaneously on that which has been seen as true? Do think about this.

Therefore, what is important is to see immediately the truth of something or the falseness of something. And you cannot see the truth or the falseness of something if you have an idea about it. Love is not an idea, love is instant action. When you bring an idea, when you have ideas about love—what it should be, what it should not be—then it ceases to be love; it is merely a process of thought. So, this must be very clear before we proceed into what I am going to say—that it is possible to act without an idea, which does not mean that action will be irrational, or that action will be postponed, or that action will be conditioned. That is, as long as ideas have supreme importance—for most of us they have—then action becomes irrelevant. Then we find that how to put those ideas into action becomes extraordinarily difficult.

So, the question is how to see the truth immediately. By *truth* I mean the truth of everyday living, everyday talk, the truth or the falseness of what you think, what you feel, to discover the truth of your motives, your daily activities, revealing your feeling instantly—the truth that is behind them. I am talking of that truth, not of the ultimate, because you cannot go to that extraordinary cause, the really immeasurable, without understanding the everyday truth of life—which is everyday activity, everyday thought. So, you have to perceive the truth instantly and not have ideas about what is truth; and seeing the truth instantly is to act immediately. If you see a snake, you act immediately; there is not the idea first and then action; there is a danger, and your whole response to that danger is immediate; there is no interval of time which is idea. The response is instantaneous, and that instantaneous response is real action.

As I said, I am going to talk this evening about thought, time, and the ending of sorrow. Before we can go into the question of the ending of sorrow—which is what most of us want—we must understand sorrow. We are all steeped in sorrow of some kind or other—not only the personal sorrow, but also the sorrow of man, the wars that bring sorrow, the immense stupidity of man who postpones and does not face facts, the sorrow of frustration, the sorrow of ambition, the conflict between good and evil, the desire to fulfill, with which comes the extraordinary shadow of sorrow. There is sorrow of every kind—the little sorrow and the immense concealed sorrow of centuries. We want to end it. At least those of us who are serious want to find out whether it is possible to end sorrow instantly—not the method because that involves time.

Now, to answer that question really deeply and fundamentally, you have to inquire into what is thought, because if there were no time for thought, there would be no sorrow. If you didn't think about something, if you didn't think about the death of someone whom you love and therefore didn't give thought the quality of time—the continuation of thought—there would be no sorrow. I do not know if you have thought about this. For most of us, to think is to be in sorrow. Is it possible to end sorrow, to end thought? I am going to go into that.

So, first we have to inquire into what is thinking. Please, if I may suggest, watch yourselves how you respond to this question: What is thinking? Probably, most of us have not asked that question at all. If you do ask that question, what is your response? Please do ask that question and find out what your response is, not tomorrow, but actually as you are listening; please find out for yourself what is thinking. I ask you the question: What is thinking? Now, what is going on in your mind? Your memory is responding, trying to find an answer according to what you have learned or what you have experienced, what books you have read, what somebody has said about it. So your mind, in accepting that challenge, that question, is searching. And during the interval between the question and the answer is time, and in that time what you consider is thought is merely looking for a response through the memory of what you have learned, what you have seen, what you have heard.

So, thought is the response of memory and nothing else. If you had no memory, you could not think. So, the response is of memory which is experience, which is knowledge, which is the accumulated, inherited, endless experience of man. According to the condition of your memory—whether you are a Christian, whether you are a Sikh, a Buddhist, this, or that—you respond; and that response, you think, is extraordinarily important. You do not see how you are conditioned, how your brain has been washed according to a certain pattern—Catholic, communist, Hindu, and so on, whether it is modern or ancient, whether it is the everyday conditioning, or whether it is the extraordinary conditioning of centuries—and how, according to that, you reply. The search for the answer, in order to find the answer to a question which you have been asked, is what you call thinking. This is really looking into memory; and then, having found an answer, you reply. That is the first stage.

If the question is very familiar, you answer immediately; there is no time needed to think, or rather to look into memory. I ask your name, and your immediate response comes because you are very familiar with it. If you are asked a much more complicated question, the time interval is much greater. During that time interval you look, you listen, you wait, you ask. You may take a second or ten days or a year, but that is the process that goes on. Then the third stage is when you ask a question which has no answer—a real, fundamental, ultimate question. Then your mind says, "I do not know." There, your mind, your thought, is no longer seeking an answer from somebody because nobody has answered that question, nobody can answer that question—no saint, no teacher, no guru, no savior, nobody can answer that question. And you say, "I do not know." It is very important to understand the state of the mind that says, "I do not know"—which is not a denial. It does not know. If I ask you, "What is God? What is truth?" and if you are really, deeply honest, you would say, "I do not know." If you are dishonest, you will begin to describe.

So, it is very important to understand the mind that says, "I do not know." Such a mind is not waiting for an answer; it is not expecting, it is not seeking because it does not know where to seek. It has no memory. It does not look into all the records to find out the answer because there is no record. You can repeat what somebody else has said, but that is not answering the ultimate question which demands an answer.

So, this is what happens to most of us—the first two, not the third. The familiar question is answered immediately, but the more complex question takes time, the time interval being much longer or shorter. During that time you are looking, watching, hoping, waiting, expecting. With those two we are very familiar, but with the third we are not. And we cannot be familiar with the third because we have never inquired within ourselves to find out for ourselves, most seriously, what is truth, what is God, what is this whole process of monstrous living, injustice, brutality, inhumanity to man, because we just live on the surface and are easily satisfied with our pleasures and evade our pains. So for a man to find out, really and for himself, what is truth—not the truth according to some saint or to some leader of a sect—his mind must be completely unknowing, which means free from the known.

So, we see what thought is. Thought is the response of memory which, if you observe, is functioning on the same lines as the electronic brain. An electronic brain has information fed into it, and it functions through association, banks of memories, and responses which it has learned; if you put a question to it, it answers it instantly. Our brains function on the same lines. So, that is thinking. We can go much more deeply into it, but that is enough.

We think that time is necessary for action, to resolve a problem. By a problem I mean a human problem. I am not talking of a mathematical or technological problem, but I am talking of a human problem: sorrow, anger, brutality, violence, greed, envy, the appalling misery, the boredom in which we live, the repetition of something day after day—whether it is pleasurable, sexual, or going to the office—and the boredom of it. I am talking of the human, living problem. To resolve, to completely understand a human problem, the mind must not give root to that problem—which is time. Suppose you are jealous, envious, in a large way or in a petty way. You battle with jealousy, envy, day after day, or you accept it. You say that it is a part of existence, that it is a part of our daily civilized life to battle with each other for a position, for this and for that. You are used to it and you accept it. And in accepting it, in getting used to it, you have given soil to the problem because it goes on and on, day after day.

Now the question is, how to end a problem immediately so that the mind is fresh, alert, for the next problem. Because life is a problem. Life is constantly challenging you, never for a moment is it quiet. It is demanding, questioning, asking, pushing; and you must respond adequately, completely. And you cannot adequately respond, respond fully, if you have problems which are eating into your mind and your heart. So, not to give continuity to a problem, you must solve it immediately; that is, you must not think in terms of time, in terms of tomorrow, that you will eventually solve it.

So you have to ask yourself one fundamental question: Is it possible to end every problem as it arises, instantly? That is, is it possible to see the truth of every problem immediately? The very perception of what is true is action and therefore the resolution of that problem.

By *time* I mean psychological time—not the time by the watch: today, tomorrow, this hour, or the next hour. I am not talking of chronological time; I am talking of psychological time. The mind seeks an answer through time because we are used to the idea of gradualness—"I will achieve eventually; I will be made perfect eventually; I will reach God, if there is God, eventually." So we give psychologically a continuity to a problem, and gradualness creeps in when we have not really perceived what is true.

Now, what gives continuity to thought? I have put that question: What gives continuity to thought? You do not know the answer. So your memory is searching. You are searching in your memory for an answer. Now, if you do not do either, you will say, "I do not know." If you are really honest, you will say, "I do not know, I have not thought about this." If you really do not know, then you will see the truth of what I am going to say, immediately.

There is continuity to thought only when you think about something constantly. If you think about something which gives you pleasure from time to time, you have established a continuity. If you do not like something and you think about it, you have also given to it continuity. It is as simple as that. That is, if you have something that gives you great pleasure—sex or what you will—and when you think about it, when you think of your gods, your jobs, your pleasures, your pains, you have given a duration to all that. Not to think about pain is comparatively easy, but not to think about pleasure is much more difficult.

So you begin to see the nature of psychological time that the mind is caught in. It has established a duration, a continuity, by thinking about something—the something which gives pleasure or pain; a thing which it wants to avoid consciously, but which unconsciously, deep down, it is thinking about, looking at, watching. It is not only outwardly, consciously, that you give continuity to thought, but also unconsciously there is a duration to thought. If I were to die tomorrow and I had time to think about it, I would be tremendously upset about it. I would be frightened; I would want to believe in this and believe in that, and do all kinds of things through my fear because my mind is worried, anxious, and fearful. Therefore, it has given it a duration, and during that duration, there is born fear. If there were no duration but only action immediately—that is, if I am to die instantly, now, as I am speaking—then there is no fear; an act has taken place, a complete act in which there is no element of fear at all. That is what I mean when I talk of psychological time brought about when thought gives duration, a continuity, by thinking about it.

There is sorrow in the world. Man has been struggling with this question for centuries upon centuries, and he has never been able to find a way out. He has found many ways of escaping from it, avoiding it—taking drugs, drink, running away through various religious and social entertainments, but he has never solved it. He has never said, "This is the end of this extraordinary thing called sorrow."

And we are going to go into that now. Is it possible to end sorrow instantly? By *sorrow* I mean not fragmentary sorrow but the total sorrow of man, the total sorrow in which the human being is caught, both the conscious as well as the unconscious sorrow. You know what sorrow is? The fact, not the word, not the symbol that awakens the picture which gives you sorrow. You understand what I am saying? Not the word, not the picture that awakens sorrow, but the actual fact of sorrow. The symbol, the picture, the idea, the word, the experience, the memory—all that gives you sorrow, but that sorrow is not the living sorrow, the thing that is so tremendously vital. There is the sorrow that comes when someone whom you love dies. There is the sorrow of love not finding a response. There is the sorrow of frustration. There is this unresolved brutality and violence of war; the ugliness of man to man; the sorrow that is going on in this world, in this country, in this town; the sorrow of ambition wanting to climb the ladder of success, seeking power, oppressing others democratically or tyrannically; the sorrow of a husband who is dominated by his wife or of the wife dominated by the man; the sorrow of postponement, the ignorance; the collective sorrow of centuries, of all the sufferings that man has been through, of which one is rarely conscious because one is so occupied with one's own little sorrows; the sorrow of man—not the Indian or the European or the American or the Russian—but man, the man in conflict, conflict between good and evil, the conflict of violence.

There is immense sorrow. Personal sorrow, if you observe, has a good deal of self-pity in it, and therefore it is no longer sorrow because it is tinged, it is hedged about, by personal hope. In this personal sorrow there is self-pity—an ugly thing. Watch your own sorrow and you will see. If you have sorrow, you will see that most of it is self-pity—the sense of loneliness, of being left alone, having no companion, nobody to talk to who will really understand you. There are innumerable kinds of sorrow, and the greatest sorrow of all is the sorrow of not being able to see the truth immediately.

To see the truth immediately, there should be no self-pity, no fear, no knowledge of what other people have said, whoever they be. Then you are face to face with a fact, and you don't bring to that fact opinions, conclusions, concepts, your own personal or collective experience. You are faced with something real: a fact is always real. So there is this sorrow. The more you think about it, the more there is sorrow—not only personal sorrow but the collective sorrow of man. You cannot avoid thinking about it because you are caught in it. My wife leaves me, if I have a wife; someone whom I like is dead; I cannot succeed; I am not so clever as you are; the brutality of modern life; the total indifference; the lack of care; the utter lack of compassion, love—to be faced with all that, not theoretically, but actually, awakens sorrow. To face every day, as you walk down the streets, the ugliness, the total indifference of man to man—to face that fact is an extraordinary awakening of sorrow.

Now, is it possible to end sorrow without becoming indifferent, callous, not caring, and to find that extraordinary beauty of love? To find that out you have to begin by inquiring into thought and not giving continuity to that thought. You have to watch every pleasure and not give it continuity, to watch every pain, psychological hurt, flattery, to watch it and not to give it continuity; so that you will find that though you think instantly and respond instantly, there is no continuity, and therefore you are able to face the fact that you are full of self-pity, that you are lonely, and that you are faced with the fact of ambition and frustration.

So you deal with facts. My son is dead—I am not talking of death; we will talk about it at another time. I am talking about the fact: my son is dead. What takes place? Immediately I am in sorrow. There is a shock, a sudden realization that he is gone, in whom I had invested my immortality, my fulfillment, my hope, the name, and so on—the shock of being left alone. When I come out of that shock, I feel tremendously in sorrow; there is grief. Then I try to find an answer to it—a temple, a priest, a book, a drink, an avoidance or acceptance, rationalizing that sorrow or trying to find a lovely beautiful theory about it—I believe in reincarnation, karma, and all the rest of it—all words, words, words. So I never face the fact. The fact is that my son is dead. Why should there be self-pity? It is a fact I loved him; I loved him because he was my son. I had invested in him. I have no companion and so on. Thought is in operation. You follow? Thought is giving continuity to the picture of the son whom I had. And thought, by giving it a duration, is continuing in sorrow.

So can I face the fact? When I face the fact, there is no thinking, there is only observing—observing the whole content of my thinking, of my feeling, of my hope—being aware of that fact and my relation to that fact without any twist, without dodging, without escaping. You will see, if you have gone through this, that by facing the fact every day about every thing—all the time facing facts, not opinions, not ideas, not judgments—you will observe your own reactions, you will know what you are thinking, what you are feeling, consciously as well as unconsciously. You become totally aware of yourself, of all your foibles, of your secret hopes, fears, longings, motives—both conscious as well as unconscious. Then you will see that sorrow which has a motive is no longer sorrow, and that it is self-pity. When you realize the truth of that, the ending of your personal sorrow comes. In that ending there is also the ending of self-pity, loneliness, the hopes, the fears, and all the other things that are involved.

But there is a greater sorrow still, the sorrow of war. How man has suffered through war! There is the brutality of the ambitious people, the pseudo-religious politician everlastingly quoting the Gita or something or other, and dominating, crushing people democratically and tyrannically. There is the sorrow of man who has invented time and therefore postponement—eventually coming to the truth—that is the greater sorrow. It is necessary to understand it, to resolve it and yet not be indifferent, to have real love for people—which is to care; and you cannot care if you are nationalistic, if you belong to any religion or have any belief.

So the ending of sorrow is the beginning of self-knowledge, and without the ending of sorrow there is no ending of thought. The ending of thought is necessary because then real meditation begins. Thought cannot be ended by control, by suppression, by concentration, by any exclusive process. Thought must be understood, gone into, searched out, and not be given duration through pleasure or through pain. When thought ends—and thought can only end through self-knowledge—then real meditation begins. Real meditation is not the meditation that you all practice, if you do at all, because what you practice is too immature, too juvenile. We will go into that if there is time—"time" in the sense of chronological time.

What is important is to face the fact and not give time to the fact. You have to observe the fact of your anger, your brutality, your indifference, your ambition, your greed, to face that and resolve it immediately; and you can resolve it immediately only when you understand this whole problem of thinking. After all, thought is not very important. What is important is immediate action. Look at all the people in the world who are starving, who have no education, who live in misery, who are ill fed! The pseudo-religious politicians are not concerned with feeding the poor; they are concerned with who is going to feed the poor, which party, which group—the Americans or the Russians. They are not seriously concerned with the feeding of the people. So they take sides, and in the meantime the poor man dies.

We live like that; our lives are like that because we have divided ourselves into classes, into groups, into nationalities, into various compartments. In that there is tremendous sorrow for a man who observes all these. And you have to solve that sorrow also, to end it, so that the mind becomes innocent. It is only the innocent mind that has lived a thousand experiences and yet is free—it is only that innocent mind that can see the ultimate, the extraordinary thing called the nameless.

November 3, 1963

Fifth Talk in New Delhi

To commune with each other our minds must be at the same level with the same intensity, and we must have the same urgency. We must both have, if we are going to commune with each other, a sharpness, a clarity, an understanding of not only the words but also the significance that lies beyond the words. We must, each one of us, if we wish to commune with one another, obviously have the capacity to meet each other equally, at the same level, and continue to hold that level. Otherwise, our communion, our communication is cut short, especially when we are discussing matters that are very difficult, psychological, and need a great deal of thought and penetration inside.

This evening, I want to go, if I may, into something which requires a great deal of insight and understanding. I hope that we can maintain our communion with each other all the time. After all, love is that state of being or that state when two people or many people meet each other at the same level, at the same time, with the same intensity. Otherwise, love becomes merely a sentiment, a remembrance, and all communication then ceases. In the same way, to take a journey together into something that requires a very subtle, penetrating look, observation, one must have this intensity—not sporadically, not occasionally—and continue in that state of intensity because what we are trying to do at these gatherings is not to exchange ideas, not to discover for ourselves which is the best opinion and to discuss those opinions. What we are trying to do is to find out for ourselves, for each one of us, what is true and what is false. And to find it out, to observe it and to have a feeling for it, we must not only listen but also observe how we listen, with what quality of mind we observe.

I want to talk this evening about something which is called death. And to go into the whole problem of death, not theoretically but factually, you need humility. I am using that word *humility* not as a virtue that is cultivated by the vain, by the proud, but as that natural state of mind which comes about when you are really inquiring and really wanting to find out for yourself. Because virtue does not grow within the borders of time. It is a flower that comes into being involuntarily. One hasn't to search for virtue or to cultivate virtue. If you do, it ceases to be virtue. To see the truth that to cultivate virtue is no longer virtue demands a mind that is in a state of humility, because without humility you cannot learn. I am using the word *learn* not in the sense of accumulation which is knowledge. We are using that word learning in the sense of a mind that is not seeking for something, that is not searching for an end with a motive, that is pliable, quick, that is able to see what is true immediately. And to do that you need an extraordinary humility which has in it that peculiar quality of austerity of observation. Austerity, as we know it, is harsh, brutal; it becomes narrow, bigoted, opinionated, dogmatic—but that is not austerity. We are using the word *austerity* in the sense that a mind that has observed, that has seen what is true, is, out of that very observation, in a state of freedom out of which there comes the discipline which is austere.

There must be that austerity with humility. And at that level we are going to commune with each other this evening. You are not going to learn from the speaker anything. If you do, the speaker becomes the authority. Therefore, you cease to be really an observer—a man who is earnestly seeking what is true and putting away what is false; you will become merely a follower, and a follower can never find out what is true. Truth has to be discovered from moment to moment, and you have to discover it—not merely follow the description verbally. You have to find it with all your being, and to find it, you need humility.

One of the things that one observes in the world and within oneself is the peculiar state of mind that is constantly declining, deteriorating. I do not know if you have observed for yourself your own mind—not theoretically, not in terms of a formula or in terms of success and nonsuccess, but with the quality of the mind that can sustain efficiency, clarity, the capacity to observe what is true, without an opinion, without a thought. When one observes not only the minds of others but also one's own mind, one finds that there is a slow decline, not that one has ever reached a height from which one declines; one finds that one does not have the sharpness, the clarity, the energy, the precision required for observation, for a reasoned observation without any sentimentality. Most of us are dull, settled in comforting belief—have a job, a position, a family to maintain—and we live in the darkness of security. When one begins to observe for oneself one's own mind, one must have seen for oneself how the mind, as it grows, as the physical organism matures, gradually begins to decline. We accept this disintegration, this deterioration, and we are not aware. And when we do become aware of it, it becomes a tremendous conflict—how to maintain the mind that is getting worse, that is declining? Probably we have never put to ourselves the question whether the mind need ever decline. Probably we have never found for ourselves by putting that question whether it is possible to stop the deterioration, the decline.

After all, the decline of the mind, the worsening of sensitivity, the coarsening of all our observation—that is truly death, is it not? So, must we not find out for ourselves whether it is possible at all times to sustain a quality of mind that knows no decline? When I use the word *mind*, I include in that the brain—the totality—not just the capacity to acquire a particular technique and to function along that technique for the rest of your life and then die. I am using the word mind in the sense not only of the conscious mind but also of the unconscious mind in which the brain is included—the brain with all its reactions, the brain that thinks, that acts, that gets irritated, that responds to all the nervous strains. And as we observe, as we grow older, this thing begins to decline. Observe the old people, observe all the old politicians, observe how even the young people want to fall into the groove of a particular thought and run along that groove.

So, it seems to us that it is very important to find out for ourselves whether it is possible to sustain that clarity of observation actually, not theoretically—actually in the sense of the living present, in the active present. I use that word *present* not in the sense of time as tomorrow or yesterday, and now. The active present is always present; it has no tomorrow or yesterday. You should not have the idea that you will have this active, vital energy tomorrow; but you have to be aware of the active present with all your capacity, not technological capacity only, but with all your aesthetic powers, with your affections, with your sorrows, with your miseries, the frustrations, the ambitions, and the failures and the hopeless agony. Is it possible to be aware of all that and to sustain clarity of observation and innocency of inquiry? If this is not possible, whatever action we do has no vital meaning; it becomes mechanical.

Please observe your own minds. You are not listening to the speaker. Don't be caught in the words of the speaker. He is merely describing, and what is described is not the fact. The word is not the thing, the word *tree* is not the fact, which is the tree. And if you would observe the tree, the word has little importance.

So, we are asking a fundamental question, and you have to find out and discover the truth of it. The question is: Can the mind ever not lose its clarity, its capacity to reason—not according to some prejudice, not according to a particular fancy or opinion or knowledge—and to sustain itself in a healthy state without any dark, unexplored, rotting corners? Is it possible? To find that out, one has to be aware of the causes of this decline. Now, we are using the word *cause* merely to indicate the source from which the mind is made dull. By discovering the cause, you are not going to free the mind. You may discover the cause of your illness, but you have to do something about it, you have to go to a doctor, you may have to have an operation; you have to act. But most of us think that by merely discovering the cause, we have solved the whole thing. And so the repetition goes on. The repetition is one of the factors of deterioration—the repeating process, the formation of habits and living in those habits. So, the discovery of the cause is not going to free the mind from the factor of deterioration.

One of the major factors of deterioration is imitation, psychological imitation—not putting on a shirt or a coat, or going to the office, or learning a particular technique which you repeat; that is too superficial. It is the habit-forming mechanism of the mind which, in psychological states, functions in beliefs, in dogmas, in opinions. If you observe, you will see how your mind functions in habit. It functions in habit because it is essentially afraid not to be secure. So, one of the real factors of deterioration is fear, psychological fear, not the natural normal fear of being bitten by a snake and therefore protecting oneself—that is a different matter.

You know, one of our difficulties is that we are always satisfied with the obvious answers, and we always put the obvious questions. Take the problem of simplicity—"to be simple." Our immediate response, which is fairly obvious, platitudinous, and banal, is: You must have only two clothes and have only one meal, and then you are supposed to be very, very simple. That is not simplicity at all—it verges on exhibitionism and traditional acceptance of what it is to be simple. But simplicity is something entirely different. To be simple means a mind that is clear, without conflict, that has no ambition, that is really incorruptible by its own desires. But we are so easily satisfied by the obvious. We say that a man is a saint because he leads a very simple life, has one meal a day and two clothes; and we think we have solved the problem of simplicity. He may be having a hell of a time inside. And a man who is in conflict, however saintly he is, is not a simple man, nor is he a religious man.

So, in trying to find out what are the factors of degeneration, one must not be satisfied with the obvious questions and the obvious answers. One must push those aside and go behind, tear down to find the truth of the matter, and that requires energy. And that energy can only come when you are really not concerned with what is going to happen with your particular life when you are simple. To find out the factors of deterioration, you must inquire, you must ask the fundamental question whether a mind can live without habit, nonconforming. This means the whole inquiry into authority, not only the authority imposed, but also the authority of one's own experiences, knowledge, visions, and all the rest of it. So one begins to see that there is deterioration as long as there is conflict of any kind, at any level, consciously or unconsciously. And most of our lives are a hideous conflict, without any resolution, without any issue—endless conflict.

So the question is whether habit, conflict, and imitation can end, not eventually, not when you die, but now, in the active present. By imitation I mean not the superficial imitation but the psychological, deep-rooted imitation which is called a method, conforming to a discipline, to a pattern—the Hindu pattern, the American pattern, or the Russian pattern, or the Catholic pattern, and so on. That imitation comes only when there is the urge, the search for comfort in security—psychological security. We seek psychological security inwardly, and therefore there is no outward security for any of us. If you think that over, you will see the truth of the matter. We have no time to go into all the details now.

The desire to be secure breeds fear, fear to live and fear to die. Fear is not an abstract thing. It is there actually like your shadow. Every minute of the day it is there—fear of your boss, fear of your wife, fear of your husband, fear of losing. And with that fear we try to live. So we do not know what it is to live. How can a mind that is afraid, live? It can build a shelter; it can warm itself; it can isolate itself; it can follow a pattern, a religious illusion, a fiction—it can live in all that, but it is not living. And this fear makes death as something far away. We put fear many years ahead of us, a great distance between that fact and the illusion which fear has created and which we call living. So our life is neither rich nor full—I do not mean full by knowledge, book learning, or reading the latest book and talking about it endlessly. I mean "rich life" in the sense: it understands; it is clear, sharp, awake, alive, full of energy, and efficient in its own observation and discipline; and therefore it can see a tree and enjoy the tree, look at the stars, look at the people without envy. Therefore such a life is not a life of ambition, greed, and the worship of success.

Please, sirs, the speaker means exactly what he is talking about. These are not just words which you listen to, and then you go back to your old life again. We are talking about something very, very serious. There must be a new generation, new people, new minds, not the dead old minds with their fears, with their corruption, with their nationalities, with their petty little governments.

A new human being must be brought into being to solve this immense problem of living, and nobody is going to create that human being except you and me. And you have to do it—not in some future generation, but immediately, which means one has to see the urgency of the thing. You know, when you see the urgency of something that needs to be done immediately, urgently, all your capacities, all your energy, all your efficiency, come into being. You do not have to cultivate them; they are there when you feel the urgency of something—like the urgency of being hungry—and then you act.

We do not know what it is to live, nor do we know what it is to die. The thing that you call "living" is a torture with occasional pleasure which is a sensation—being well-fed, having a good meal, sex, driving in a good car or wanting to drive in a good car, or being envious of those who are driving in a good car, and so on. That is our life. Please observe yourself, and you will see what an ugly, brutal thing living has become—without any love, without any beauty, without any care. That is our life and we are satisfied with that. We put up with it. We do not say, "I am going to break through and find out." We invent all kinds of spurious and phony reasons.

And to live fully, completely, you cannot possibly have an ideal over there and you live over here. So the ideal has no meaning; it is a fiction. What is a fact is your daily travail, daily anxieties, hopes, fears; that is the actual, and to that we become accustomed. And with the memory of our tortures, hopes, fears, ambitions, we turn to look at death which is far away. So what happens? We are frightened of death and we are frightened of living.

Now, to find out what is death demands a mind that has no fear. I do not know if you have observed the pilots—the persons who fly those extraordinary airplanes that go two thousand miles and more an hour—how they are trained more than all the yogis put together. They have to face death, and therefore their response must be immediate, unconscious. They are trained for years to face death—to survive they must respond immediately to all the instruments, to all the orders. That is one way of not being afraid of death—that is, to train yourself so completely, so involuntarily that you die at the orders of another for your country and all the rest of that nonsense. Then there is death by suicide: that is, you face life and life has no meaning; you have come to the end of things, and you jump over the bridge or you take pills. Then there is the other way, the so-called religious way: you have extraordinary beliefs in reincarnation, in resurrection; and death you rationalize because you are going to live the same kind of hideous life in the next life with torture, agony, despair, with lies, with hypocrisy; and you are satisfied by these beliefs because temporarily they give you comfort, they hide your fear.

Now all those ways of dying are very ordinary, unreal, and undependable. We are talking of dying of a different kind, which is to live with death. You understand? To live with death, not to have this time interval between you and the eventual end. The eventual end may be fifty years or a hundred years hence; or the doctors or the scientists may add another fifty years to it; but the inevitable end is always there. We are talking of a voluntary living with death. I am going into that because that is the only way to resolve the whole question of death, not through beliefs, not through ideals, not through the structure of fear, and all the rest of the paraphernalia.

And to find out what is death, there must be no distance between death and you who are living with your troubles and all the rest of it; you must understand the significance of death and live with it while you are fairly alert, not completely dead, not quite dead yet. That thing called death is the end of everything that you know. Your body, your mind, your work, your ambitions, the things that you have built up, the things that you want to do, the things that you have not finished, the things that you have been trying to finish—there is an end of all these when death comes. That is the fact—the end. What happens afterwards is quite another matter; that is not important because you will not inquire what happens afterwards if there is no fear. Then death becomes something extraordinary—not sadistically, not abnormally, unhealthily—because death then is something unknown, and there is immense beauty in that which is unknown. These aren't just words.

So to find out the whole significance of death, what it means, to see the immensity of it—not just the stupid, symbolic image of death—this fear of living and the fear of dying must completely cease, not only consciously, but also deep down. Most of us want to die, wish to die, because our lives are so shallow, so empty. And our life being empty, we try to give significance to life, meaning to life; we ask, "What is the purpose of living?" Because our own lives are so empty, shallow, worthless, we think we must have an ideal to live by. It is all nonsense. So fear is the origin of the separation between that fact which you call death and that fact which you call living. What does it mean actually, not theoretically? We are not discussing theoretically; we are not discussing merely to formulate an idea, a concept; we are not. We are talking of facts, and if you reduce a fact merely into a theory, it is your own misfortune. You will live with your own shadow of fear, and your life will end miserably as it has begun miserably.

So you have to find out how to live with death—not a method. You cannot have a method to live with something you don't know. You cannot have that idea and say, "You tell me the method, and I will practice it, and I will live with death"—that has no meaning. You have to find out what it means to live with something that must be an astonishing thing, actually to see it, actually to feel it—to be aware of this thing called death and of which you are so terribly frightened. What does it mean to live with something which you don't know? I don't know if you have ever thought about it at all in that way; probably you have not. All that you have done is, being frightened of it, you try to avoid it, you do not look at it; or you jump to some hopeful ideal, belief, and thereby avoid it. But you have really to ask the fundamental question, which is to find out what death means, and if you can live with it as you would live with your wife, with your children, with your job, with your anxiety. You live with all these, don't you? You live with your boredom, your fears. Can you live in the same way with something that you don't know?

To find out what it means to live, not only with the thing called life, but also with death, which is the unknown, to go into it very deeply, we must die to the things that we know. I am talking about psychological knowledge, not of things like your home, your office: if you don't have them, you won't get your money tomorrow, or you lose your job, or you have no food. We are talking about dying to the things that your mind clings to. You know, we want to die to the things which give us pain; we want to die to the insults, but we cling to the flattery. We want to die to the pain, but we hold on like grim death to the pleasure. Please observe your own mind. Can you die to that pleasure, not eventually, but now? Because you do not reason with death, you cannot have a prolonged argument with death. You have to die voluntarily to your pleasure which does not mean that you become harsh, brutal, ugly, like one of these saints; on the contrary, you become highly sensitive—sensitive to beauty, to dirt, to squalor—and being sensitive, you care infinitely.

Now, is it possible to die to things, to that which you know about yourself? To die—I am taking a very, very superficial example—to a habit, to put away a particular habit either of drinking or smoking, having a particular kind of food, or the habit of sex, completely to withdraw from it without an effort, without a struggle, without a conflict, without saying, "I must give it up." Then you will see that you have left behind the knowledge, the experience, the memories of all the things that you have known and learned and lived by. And therefore you are no longer afraid, and your mind is astonishingly clear to observe what this extraordinary phenomenon is of which man has been frightened through millennia, to observe something which you are confronted with, which is of no time, and which in its entirety is the unknown. Only that mind can so observe which is not afraid and which is therefore free from the known—the known of your anger, of your ambitions, your greeds, your petty little pursuits. All these are the known. You have to die to them, to let them go voluntarily, to drop them easily, without any conflict. And it is possible—this is not a theory. Then the mind is rejuvenated, young, innocent, fresh; and therefore it can live with that thing called death.

Then you will see that life has an entirely different substance. Then life and death are not divided; they are one because you are dying every minute of the day in order to live. And you must die every day to live; otherwise, you merely carry along the repetition like a gramophone record, repeating, repeating, repeating.

So when you really have the perfume of this thing—not in somebody else's nostrils, but in your nostrils, in your breath, in your being; not on some rare occasions, but every day, waking and sleeping—then you will see for yourself, without somebody telling you, what an extraordinary thing it is to live, to live with actuality, not with words and symbols, to live with death and therefore to live every minute in a world in which there is not the known, but there is always the freedom from the known. It is only such a mind that can see what is truth, what is beauty, and that which is from the everlasting to the everlasting.

November 6, 1963

Sixth Talk in New Delhi

I would like this evening to talk about something with which you may be familiar. Probably you are familiar with the word and not with the fact. And to go into it, as we shall during this evening, we must have a critical capacity. Most of us accept very easily—we accept authority, tradition, and the easy way of life—and thereby lose the critical observation. And when we do observe, our criticism is very superficial, casual, or it is made from a particular point of view, and therefore becomes narrow, cynical, or merely destructive. Destruction is good—one must destroy to create. But casual criticism or a gesture or a word does not lead anywhere. And this evening, at least for this hour, one should have the capacity critically to observe not what the speaker is saying but the natural, spontaneous responses that arise within each one; and one should observe those reactions and not accept them or casually put them aside. One should observe so that one may be able to go into that process which is called meditation.

Without right meditation—not the traditionally accepted, monotonous, repetitive, so-called meditation which is utterly futile and juvenile—if there is no right meditation, life becomes very superficial. I mean by "life" the whole content of it, the extraordinary beauty, the sorrow, the anxiety, the utter shallowness, the lack of sensitivity, the despair, the hopes, the fears, the agonies, the total process of living. And we are going to go into that this evening. But if you would take the journey together, there must be really critical observation, never accepting a thing, either what the speaker says or what you observe of your own reactions. Because it is only a very sharp, clear, healthy, sane mind that is capable of meditation. If we merely accept, we destroy all feeling. Acceptance is a form of imitation, and meditation is not imitation, it is not repetitive. You have to accept certain obvious things, like keeping to the left side of the road, paying taxes, and so on; it is the obvious, superficial authority. But we are talking of authority at quite a different level—the psychological acceptance of authority which comes into being when there is the search and the demand for security, and therefore we accept.

Please observe your own minds in operation rather than merely casually listen to the speaker. Because if one is not aware of one's own process of thought, one will not be able to follow or be able to criticize with an extraordinary passion. Because passion is necessary, and there is no authority when there is passion.

As most of us are merely yes-sayers, we do accept; and when we do accept, all feeling is made dull. We are not affected deeply, we have no feeling when we observe the things about us—the tree, the squalor, the poverty, the ignorance, those in power who destroy. For most of us feeling is subtle; when we feel very strongly about something, that very feeling breeds sorrow. When you see the poverty, the utter callousness of people—whether they be the high politicians or the low cunning operators in a particular party, they have no feelings—when you do feel and when you observe yourself, you will find there is a great deal of sorrow involved in it. There is grief not only when there is the feeling about your own particular little sorrow of not having a good position, of being insulted by your boss every day, or by the loss of a particular person, but also when there is the feeling, as a human being, for the whole world, for another human being. To see how power destroys and corrupts, and to feel very strongly, passionately, about these things, every form of acceptance must be put aside.

And it is only when you begin to feel very strongly, out of that feeling there is love. It is only in that state that you can cooperate, because we live by cooperating and we destroy each other when there is no cooperation—and that is what is happening throughout the world. We have intellectually, verbally, cultivated our brains, our thoughts; but we do not feel strongly. And when we do feel very strongly, we do the most stupid, silly things: trying to convert people to a particular form of belief, or joining a peace march, or this, or that.

I am talking of something entirely different. We are talking about feeling, for itself, without sorrow. Because the moment there is sorrow, there is a feeling that you must do something immediately; then that feeling loses itself in organization. You observe all this in yourself. And then the feeling gets dissipated, lost. Love cannot be organized, and it is only a man who loves that can cooperate. The world needs cooperation, the feeling of cooperation; there is the necessity, the urgency, to cooperate—not according to a particular pattern, not with the government or against the government, not with a particular authority or with a particular system. We cooperate when we agree, but our agreement is merely, generally intellectual, verbal. Love does not agree; love is not an idea with which you agree or disagree. You do not agree with the heat of the sun; it is there burning, destroying, creating, making things new.

So there is cooperation right through life, not at one level of life only, but right through—this feeling of working together efficiently, living together, not dividing the earth into yours and mine, into America, Russia, India, and all the stupid, political, national, linguistic divisions—feeling together. Unfortunately, only hate brings us together. When we are attacked, we all come together, but hate is not love. It is only when a man really feels when he sees the squalor, the dirt on the road, feels the inward poverty of the politician, sees the utter cupidity of the saints and their followers—to feel for all these is part of meditation. Meditation is not just a word. I am sure that word has awakened in you the traditional form, the traditional way of meditation.

You see, we need a fresh mind, a new mind, because it is only a new mind that can create, bring about, a new world—not the traditional mind, not the mind that accepts and performs a routine day after day. We need a mind that is in revolution, not a mind that is merely in revolt. There is a difference between revolt and revolution. One can revolt against something: that revolt is merely a reaction; it is life revolting against a particular form of society, a particular order, a psychological insistence of a particular society. But revolution is something entirely different. To deny completely the whole psychological structure of society, not just parts of it, but the totality of it, needs an extraordinary capacity to be critical. And you can only criticize sanely when there is real feeling. As we were saying, what is necessary is a mind that is incorruptible, a mind that is made new.

Now, we are going, this evening, to go into this question and to bring about that mind instantly. Because it must be brought about instantly; it cannot take place in time—then corruption sets in. That instant mutation is revolution, not revolt. And the inquiry sanely, logically, through the observation of every process of your own thinking and feeling—to observe—is the beginning of meditation. A mind that is not made new, that has the whole weight of the past, merely reacts; it can never be still, quiet. So we are going into a problem which is extremely subtle, which needs all your attention, and therefore not accepting or denying what the speaker is saying. You need merely to observe at the highest capacity of critical awareness in which there is no choice, no comparative condemnation.

For most of us, to meditate is a problem of conflict because thought wanders all over the place, and to make that thought quiet is a battle, is a conflict. And when there is conflict, there is no understanding. It is merely a battle between 'what should be' and *what is*, and a mind caught in this battle cannot possibly ever know what is the right way, the right process of meditation. So we must understand this whole process of thinking—not how to still thought, not how to control thought. Every schoolboy knows how to control thought. When he wants to look out of the window and the teacher says, "Look at your book," he is frightened and looks at the book. We have known that art of concentration. But to inquire into this whole process of thinking—to find out whether thought can ever be still—demands attention, and we are going to go into it.

As I have pointed out, meditation is an extraordinary thing. There is an extraordinary beauty in it. It gives the mind a sensitivity and heightens its sharpness so that your whole life is lived completely, fully, in the active present. For most of us do not live totally, with all our conscious and unconscious states and beyond. We only touch at the periphery, and this peripheral touch we call living—with all its agonies, contradictions, bestialities, cruelties, flatteries, insults, and all the rest of human existence. That is where we touch. We are talking of a meditative mind that is totally aware, not only of the peripheral movement, but of the whole content of consciousness, and thereby goes beyond it. Otherwise that is not meditation; otherwise, it is mere self-hypnotism, caught in a series of ideas, in images, in a conditioned projection of Christ or Buddha or Sri Krishna or your particular guru, seeing visions and getting terribly excited about those normal conditional responses which have no meaning at all.

So we are talking about something entirely different. We are talking about a meditative mind that is in the full flow of life without fear and therefore without hope, without despair, and therefore seeing beauty, living in a state of complete cooperation and therefore in a state of love. That is what we are going into.

As we said just now, we have to understand or to find out the beginning of meditation. If you do not understand the beginning, you will not understand the end because the end is in the beginning, not away, not at a distance. Therefore you have to understand completely what the beginning is—completely, with all your being. So, if I may suggest or request, please don't say at the end, "You have not taught me how to meditate. I haven't a silent mind. So what am I to do?"—those are questions that are utterly immature. Those questions indicate a mind that has not gone into itself and discovered the whole process of its own thought, the flowering of its whole being.

All we know is the observer and the observed—which is the experiencer and the thing experienced, or the thinker and the thought. That is all we know. That is a fact which you will find out for yourself when you observe yourself: the thinker trying to control thought, the thinker trying to shape thought, the thinker trying to impose discipline, trying to understand this thing, this thought, that wanders away from moment to moment. And so we know only the contradiction and the conflict between the thinker and the thought. Please, you are not listening to me, to the speaker; you are observing yourself. What the speaker says is of very little importance. What is important is to observe how your own mind is operating and merely to listen to the speaker so that he acts as a mirror for your observation and nothing else. And you will see how this process, this conflict, is our life.

From the moment we are born until we die, this battle goes on, day after day, endlessly: the thinker accumulating, chastening his thought, refining or controlling; and what he wants is completely to control all thought. So the thinker lives in a state of sterile decay because he has controlled all thoughts. That is all that your meditation means—just to control your feelings, your thoughts, the duties, the responsibilities, the ugliness of your life. And in that framework you try to meditate. Therefore you may alter your character a little bit, here and there; you may become a little more quiet, more considerate. But character—which is really the reaction to a particular society—however necessary, will not bring in the freedom of a mind that can meditate, of a mind that is in a state of an extraordinary ecstasy; and there is that ecstasy.

So the question then is: Is it possible to remove totally this conflict between the thinker and the thought? Please see the problem, understand the problem, first. If you exercise will to bring about a complete harmony between the thinker and the thought, between the innumerable experiences of the past and the present movement of experiencing which is the response of the past in the present, if you merely exercise a decision, exercise will to control, who is the entity that exercises that will? It is still the thinker. You may call it the higher self, the atma, or give it all kinds of superficial or traditional names, but it is still within the field of thought. Therefore what is within the field of thought is not the real. Thought is merely the response of memory. You have been brought up to believe in the atma, and another man might not be brought up to believe in anything. You are just conditioned. Because you use the word *atma* or the word *God*, you are not godly. To find God, to realize that extraordinary thing, you need a mind that is astonishingly new, innocent, a mind that has that energy which is not contaminated by conflict.

So what is necessary is not will but being aware of this duality, of this contradiction between the thinker and the thought—just to be aware, just to see, just to observe. You will find that really to observe is one of the most difficult things, and that very observation itself is discipline—not the discipline enforced.

So meditation then is the observation of yourself—just to observe the movement of your own being, to observe your thought—not to correct thought, not to put them in certain categories of good or bad, but just to observe. When you so observe, you will see that there is no thinker and the thought, that there is only a state of observation—not that you observe. This is very important to understand because most of us—not most of us, all of us—are secondhand human beings. Sirs, please do not take notes; just listen, listen with your hearts, not with your minds only. We are secondhand human beings. There is nothing new, original, pristine, uncorrupt. We are all put together by society—which again is a fact. How can a second-hand mind, though it has had a thousand experiences, discover something that has never been touched by thought? How can a second-hand mind discover the energy that has never known what it is to be in conflict, that is something beyond time, beyond all forms of the known? Do what you will, meditate for the rest of your life traditionally, you will never free that mind. You will never bring about a new mind unless you have totally, completely understood the whole process of experiencing and thinking. It is only when you have really understood the problem of experiencing and thinking that the mind can be still.

For most of us experience is very necessary. We are fed up with our daily experiences, daily going to the office, with the usual sexual enjoyments. We are fed up with the traditional acceptances, and we want something more. We want to experience something much more. So what do we do? We take drugs—that is the latest craze. We take drugs which will give us heightened sensitivity, which will expand slightly our consciousness; and in that state we have extraordinary feelings—there is no distance between the flower and you, between the sky and you, between the tree and you; there is no distance between you and your feeling, between you and the state of being; you are completely unidentified and are one with all that. Not that I have taken that drug, but I have talked to people who have. But that experience is still within the field of time, within the field of consciousness. That does not bring about that extraordinary freedom from the known.

So you have to understand experience. Please, from the moment I began the talk this evening until now, it has been a process of meditation. If you have not understood this, you won't go any further.

A mind that is made up of experience is a secondhand mind because there is nothing new in experience—however deep, however wide the challenge may be. Because when there is a challenge, you respond according to your conditioning. If you are a politician, you will obviously respond as a politician to a demand, to a challenge that asks you to respond totally. You as a politician will respond according to your party politics, to your country, to your fears, to your desire for power or to remain in your position, and all the rest of the stupid nonsense that goes on in this world. If you want a wider, deeper, more extensive experience, you will experience according to your conditioning, whatever that be.

A mind that has understood experience, and therefore is free from the demand for experiencing, is in a state where there is no experience. It is only the mind that has no experience that is an innocent mind. And it is only the innocent mind that can observe that which is beyond the measure of time. Therefore meditation is the understanding of experience. Do follow all this. A mind that is freeing itself from experience is a light, a fire, without a shadow; it is completely a light to itself. How can such a mind demand experience? It is only the mind that is seeking, wanting, desiring, hoping, escaping—it is only such a mind that wants more and more experience. So meditation takes place when the mind understands and is freeing itself from all experience.

But to free oneself from all experience, to understand experience rightly, one has to understand the conscious and the unconscious mind. The conscious mind—we know what it is: the educated, the technological, the present mind that has learned how to read and write, to go to the office, to follow the leaders, to accept the traditional forms of belief in gods and goddesses, and all the rest of it. That is the superficial mind. Then there is the whole unconscious mind—the unconscious mind with its motives, with its collected and collecting, accumulated and accumulating impressions, the residue of a particular race, all man's endeavor. It is there, hidden, deep down in you. You may be a Hindu; outwardly, you may smoke, you may drink, and you may carry on, highly civilized; but deep down, you have still whole centuries of propaganda, centuries of assertions, centuries of beliefs. You are conditioned deep down as a Hindu. That demands exploration. That demands understanding. That demands that you must be totally free, that all conditioning must be broken down.

Now the question is: Is it possible to inquire into the unconscious? I have not the time to go into it too deeply, but I hope you will follow this. Unless you understand the unconscious completely—do what you will consciously—your meditation or your inquiry or your seeking God or trying to become nonviolent and all the rest of it has no meaning because the unconscious shapes our thought and our feeling. So you have to inquire into it. You understand? You have to find out about the unconscious, about something of which you don't know. You don't know your unconscious; you may have some hints, some intimations of it, through dreams and so on. You don't know the depth of it, the contours of it, the frame, the boundaries of it. You have to know this. And to find out about the unconscious, your conscious mind must be completely quiet.

The conscious mind is in constant battle; the conscious mind is ambitious, greedy, envious, frightened, licking the boots of those in power, showing respect to those people in power and not showing respect to anybody else; the conscious mind is only put together by the psychological structure of society. That conscious mind must be completely quiet—that means you must be free from ambition, not verbally; you must be free from the desire for power, position, prestige; you must be free from fear and therefore in a state of complete humility; it is only then the superficial mind is quiet. Then you will find, when the superficial mind is quiet, the whole content of consciousness comes into view. You understand?

By analyzing the unconscious—you know the analytical process—you will never solve this problem. In the analytical process there will always be the analyzer who is conditioned, and therefore whatever he analyzes is still conditioned. Therefore the analytical process has no value, nor has the self-introspective process any value. But what has value is for the conscious mind to be aware of the psychological structure of the particular society in which it is caught, and to be free of that psychological structure. Only then will the conscious mind be quiet, completely quiet; but the unconscious mind is not yet quiet. Then you will see, the conscious mind is very quiet, not at any given moment, but all the time—as you are going to the office, as you walk home, as you bicycle, as you go in a bus. This quietness is not enforced. Because you understand how important it is for the superficial mind to be quiet, the necessity of it, the urgency of it, the superficial mind is quiet. You cannot make it quiet—because then it becomes stupidly dull, inactive, and is not aware; and all the beauty of life slips by.

So the conscious mind, by observing the necessity of quietness, is quiet. Then the unconscious projects all the things, all its contents—as you observe a tree, as you observe a woman, as you observe a man, as you observe a child, all the responses, the motives, the hidden dark corners of the mind spill out—and they are understood immediately because the conscious mind is not judging, is not evaluating, is not comparing. It is there, watching, completely still, because it is no longer seeking, no longer wanting experience. Then you will see, if you have gone as far as that, that the whole content of consciousness is empty.

These are not words. Don't repeat it afterwards and ask, "How is the conscious to be emptied?" Either you are doing it or you will never do it. If you are doing it, you will go on for the rest of your life. If you are not doing it now, you will never do it because this is not an act of memory, this is an act in the living present. Because you understand, that very understanding is an action which goes on and on in spite of you, whether you like it or not.

Such a mind is not a mind which is concentrating because what is there to concentrate upon? It is aware, it is attentive. A mind that is concentrated on something narrow, exclusive, itself becomes exclusive and therefore inattentive; it is merely focused on a particular thing. What we are talking about is a mind that has understood this whole problem of experience—the contradictions, the conflicts, the miseries—and therefore has become completely attentive and is in a state of complete attention. Such a mind can then concentrate; then it won't be exclusive. As I said in the beginning, all this is part of meditation—all this from the beginning until now. Then you will see, from this—naturally, as a flower opens—there comes a stillness, a quietness of the mind. And such stillness of the mind is absolutely necessary for a man who would discover what is true.

Such a mind has no belief, is not seeking, is not wanting more experience. Then out of that complete quietness—in which thought is not, but the mind is completely aware—out of that stillness there comes quite a different movement. Please, you will naturally translate what I am saying, what we are talking about, into your own terminology—*samadhi* and all the rest of the words which you use. The moment you translate what is being said into your own terminology, you have stopped meditating. You have to break down all the words, all the terminologies, all the traditions, all the things that man has put together in his fear, in his hope, in his despair.

Then you will see that the mind is completely alone; there is a quality of incorruptibility. And a mind that has completely understood and is free of the whole psychological structure of society—only such a mind is innocent and can see that which is eternal, which has no name, which cannot be put into words, which cannot be experienced.

November 10, 1963

Seventh Talk in New Delhi

This is the last talk. This evening I would like to range over a large field and to go into things that may perhaps be rather abstruse and perhaps, verbally, not communicable.

For most of us word and action are so wide apart. We are satisfied with words. The more significant the word is, the more we are satisfied; it is unrelated to our daily living, to our daily activity. Most of us are incapable of action except within the narrow groove of everyday habit, everyday idea, a custom, a formulated opinion. And to go beyond the everyday activity and the everyday thought seems so utterly barren and difficult. But it is necessary to go beyond all that to really find an answer to the absurdity of our daily existence. As our existence is hopeless, miserable, and so utterly superficial, we try to find a satisfactory answer. And that answer we are satisfied with when it is comforting, when it gives us an opportunity to escape from our daily boredom, sorrows, and the utter despair of a life that has very little meaning. And we are satisfied with words; we live with words and we live upon words. I am afraid words have never solved any problem—economic, social, or so-called religious.

It is very difficult for most people to put away the word, the idea, the formula, and think of the whole issue anew. We have to think of the whole issue anew as though each one of us has no one to lean on, no one to look to, no leader, no spiritual precepts, because they have had no effect at all on our daily life. So we have to think of the problem entirely, wholly, as though you and I are facing the issue anew, afresh—and not to bring in all our old ideas, concepts, not to quote everlastingly from the sacred books. You have an old pattern, or you have a new theory if you are a communist, and you function on those lines. But it seems to me the problem is so vast, so complex, so interrelated, that we must approach it as though we are approaching it for the first time, if it is possible at all, and look at "living," actual living, not the abstract idea of living, not the abstract idea of what living should be—the ideal which is utterly valueless and nonsensical, which is a fiction that has no validity at all. We must be able to look at *what is* actually, with clarity, with an energy, with a drive, so that we really understand the full, deep significance of our life, of our living. And it seems to me that it is the most important thing to do when we are confronted with an extraordinary problem.

The problem is not only here in this country but everywhere else—the utter meaninglessness of life, the absurdity of this life. Saying, inventing, or thinking about phrases and terms like *God* and all the rest of it has no meaning any more. Life, as it is, means going to the office, earning a livelihood, going to the temple occasionally and calling the priest to perform your marriages, death ceremonies, and so on. All these have become utterly meaningless, and so we begin to invent or give significance to life. If you have a very clever, philosophical mind, you give a new meaning and you persuade thousands of people to think along that line. If you are in despair, you invent a philosophy of despair, or you try to recall the past, to revive the old, ancient ways of life. Because the present has no meaning at all—the way we live, the way we think, the way we go about with all our ambitions, corruption, anxieties, and despair—we are in constant battle with ourselves, with our neighbors, with society, with the world. And for what? When we put that question, we try to find an answer. We try to find an answer according to our conditioning and be satisfied with that explanation—which is again living on words, living on ashes, that have no meaning at all.

So if we look around, we will see actually that religions have no meaning any more. You verbally repeat certain phrases because that is the habit, that is the custom, that is the usual polite thing to do—but it has no meaning at all any more—probably never had. And as religion has lost its significance, we turn to science as if that is going to solve everything—going to the moon, inventing new ways of production, automation, electronic brains, etc. We always look outwardly to find an answer to a deep psychological problem. And as that has not succeeded, we turn to the expert, the specialist in economy or in politics. This is what we are actually doing, this is what is actually taking place in the world.

I think it is important for each one of us to realize, to see actually the fact, the *what is*—not to have an opinion about it, not to come to a conclusion. And you can't come to a conclusion because whatever conclusions you come to are insufficient to resolve the problem, which is too vast. Or we may get lost in nationalism, the poison of modern existence; and also there is always the threat of war. And when none of these finds an answer, then we take to drugs, various forms of drugs, which psychologically stir you up to a heightened perception. So one observes this right through the world—not only in this unfortunate country, but right through. We have not solved the problem of starvation, and probably we will never solve it the way we are going because the problem of starvation is not of a particular country or of a particular party. It is the problem of the world. We are human beings interrelated with each other, and we all of us have to solve this problem together, but the politicians and their helpers prevent this. So when you see actually what is happening, is there an answer? Is there a way out of all this, out of this deep, fundamental anxiety, fear, frustration, and hopeless despair? You may not know it, you may not be even conscious of it, but it is deep down; if you can explore into your unconscious, it is there.

Is there an answer to this, and how do we find it? When you put a question like this, it is so easy to say, "Yes, there is an answer: seek God, or join this religion or that sect, or do some social reform, and so on." But every action, every attempt to solve this problem does not solve the essential problem of human existence—man's misery, his despair, his exhausting frustration. Please, I am not exaggerating. You may be satisfied with the little that you have, with your little philosophy, with your little gods, with having a good job, and all the rest of it. And you may say, "Why bother about all this? Life is short, and we will eventually die. Perhaps we may live or we may not. Don't bother about all this; just live, have a good time." But only those who are really serious can live, and do live, completely, totally. I mean by "the serious" those who go to the very end, who try to find out for themselves the answer, who are not thwarted by any personal ambition and personal pleasures, but who really want to find out.

So what is the answer? Does it lie in collective activity or in individual activity? Is there such a thing as the individual apart from the collective, psychologically? You may be physically apart, but psychologically is there an entity who is totally separate, alone, in the sense of being unique, individual, undivided? There is no such human being. You are the collective. I know that is heresy for the religious man. But if you examine yourself, you will see that what you think, all your habits, your ways of thought, your feelings, are controlled, shaped by the society in which you live. You are a Hindu because you have been told you are a Hindu, or you are a Muslim or whatever you are, and you think in that pattern. And there is the whole block, which is the collective, against the individual. Neither has found the answer, neither will find the answer. So how do we find the answer?

Having stated the problem, and seeing the problem very clearly—not only verbally but deeply and psychologically—how are we to be aware of the problem? You understand what I mean? Is it a problem that is put to you by somebody, and therefore you make it your problem? Or are you aware of the problem yourself without being told of the problem? Surely, the two things are entirely different. If you accept the problem from another, it has no validity, it has become very superficial. But if it is an intrinsic problem, it is a problem with which you are confronted every day, battling with it, seeking, finding out, inquiring, because it is your despair, your agony, your frustration. It is like the problem of a man who is hungry—either he is told that he is hungry, and therefore he becomes hungry, or he is actually hungry; these two states of being are entirely different.

If you and I are actually aware of this extraordinary problem of living, not escaping, then when the speaker is beginning to go into it, you and I, being aware, have a relationship; then you and I can meet at a certain point. But if it is not an actual, abiding, exhausting problem to you, then you and I will have no communication. You live at one level, and the speaker lives at another level. How are we aware of this problem? Please, this is very important. I am going to go into it, because it is very important to find out how we are aware. Are we aware of it merely as it affects us personally, or are we aware of it as a human, extensive, living problem of man—not of a particular man? I mean by that word *aware* not merely verbally but seeing the significance—comprehending nonverbally the state of your observation, how you observe this deep, anxious frustration, misery, and sorrow which each one of us has.

How is one aware of it? Are you aware of it as a fact, or are you aware of it as it is verbally described? Am I making myself clear? Do I perceive, see, or observe merely verbally, or do I observe completely, without words? Because what we want to convey is that as long as there is conflict in observation, we shall not find the answer. As long as you put it outside of yourself, outside the skin as it were, and then observe it, then there is no answer to that, then it becomes superficial. Then it is a surface reaction to which you will find an answer which will be satisfactory to you, and you will stop with that. But if in the process of observation there is no conflict, then you are only observing, and therefore there is no sense of distance between you and the thing which you observe—which means no conflict, which means there is no observer observing something outside himself. I hope you are following all this. What I want to get at is that the religious spirit is the only answer. There is no other answer.

But to understand this religious spirit which I am going to go into, we have to understand this kind of observation in which all conflict has completely come to an end; otherwise, you cease to observe because then you come to what you observe with your opinions, with your conditioning, with your ideas, with your hopes, fears, despairs, and all the paraphernalia of modern existence. Unless we completely remove this conflict in observation, we shall not find the real answer—which means that when you are able to look completely, objectively, you are able to observe, see, listen without any directive, without any motive, without any purpose; you merely observe.

Surely that is the only scientific observation; that is the only way to look, to listen to somebody—not to agree or disagree; that is so futile and empty. But to listen without conflict so that you find out whether the speaker is telling the truth or the falsehood is difficult. We have to find this out for ourselves; nobody on earth, whoever he may be, can give it. You have to find it out yourself because it is your life, your misery, your despair, your hopeless frustration. And when you find it, it is not an individual finding. It is the discovery of something which is true, and what is true is not personal or collective. When you find this out, then you can cooperate; then cooperation has got a different meaning when truth is functioning—not your particular form of truth, not your limited, inner voice which has no meaning at all. The man who talks about his inner voice is obviously giving out his personal conclusion—psychologically, all these are very explainable.

So before we go into this whole religious spirit, we have to inquire really deeply into it, not verbally but actually, not in any sense of seeking some kind of comfort or an opiate. This observation is absolutely necessary so that the mind can look, can listen, can observe without any sense of conflict at itself, at its own misery, at its own anxiety, at its own frustration, and at the frustration of man throughout the world. Because if you are not capable of looking at this vast complex problem of human existence, if you will not be able to observe it without conflict, without judging, then whatever answer you will find out will be superfluous. But if you can observe it without conflict, then you will find out; you will begin to inquire into and discover for yourself the religious spirit.

For me, revolution is absolutely necessary—not at the economic or social level; that is no revolution at all. I am talking of a religious revolution. Please, we have to understand these two words *religious* and *revolution.* And this revolution is instantaneous—it must be instantaneous; if it has duration, if you say it will happen in a few years, then it is not revolution. It must be instantaneous and immediate. And I am going to go into it and also into what we mean by the word religious.

First of all, to inquire and to find out what is true, you must negate. You must see what is false and put it away immediately—not according to your convenience, not when you want to put it away or when it suits you. Religion is not belief; religion is not a hypothesis, a convenience, a reasoned end of a mind which is conditioned with fear, hope, and despair. The religious mind has absolutely nothing whatsoever to do with any dogma, with any belief, with any idea or command or sanction of another. Please see the importance of this. The religious mind has no authority and therefore does not belong to any organized religion—Christian, Muslim, Hindu, or any other organized religion. After all, all the organized religions, are merely propaganda. You have been told over and over again from childhood that you are a Hindu, you are a Muslim, you are this or you are that, you must believe and you must not believe—and you repeat it. And in your fear, in your misery, in your anguish, you hope there is God or you believe in God. To find out if there is God, you must destroy completely all belief—which means all fear must cease. So religion is not belief; religion cannot be organized; religion is not the everlasting repetition of either the Mass or the puja, or the everyday whispering of words.

When you listen, how do you listen? Are you listening objectively, observing the fact without conflict? A religious mind stands completely alone and therefore is not dependent on society or on dogmas or on rituals or on the paraphernalia of so-called religion—how do you listen to that? Most of you, being a Hindu or a Sikh or whatever you are, will listen, will naturally react and say, "How can you say such a thing." Therefore you have established a conflict between what is a fact and what you want that fact to be. To find out—not to be told, not to repeat everlastingly—if there is something which is beyond words, beyond the measure of time, beyond all thought, you must obviously negate completely everything you have been told. They may all be wrong, including your gurus, your saints, your ancestors, the sacred books. Why should you accept them? You only accept when you have not understood, when you are frightened, when you want some comfort in this dark, mad, confused world.

So religion is not the repetition of words, nor is it belief in God or no-God. The communists are trained, are educated not to believe, as you are educated to believe. There is not much difference between the two. You are no more religious because you believe. Probably you are worse because you don't care, you don't see the ugly brutality of this monstrous world that is going on round you—the utter indifference, the callousness, the insensitivity.

Now, how do you deny matters normally? If you deny all the so-called religions without deeply understanding the whole significance of this psychological structure, if you merely deny them, then you are back again in the same problem; you have not answered it. But if you understand it—that is, if you understand the whole structure of fear, the whole anatomy of authority, whether it is the authority of the past or of the present, the authority of a particular guru or of the books, or the authority involving this extraordinary sense of obedience—then you can look, then your denial will have meaning, and therefore you are out of it, not eventually but immediately; on the instant you are out. The moment you see something false, the moment you see a dangerous snake or a dangerous animal, you are gone, you are finished with it, and you never touch it again. This means the mind is no longer confused about things, is no longer in conflict between the false and the true. The false has gone completely, so the mind has purged itself, emptied itself, of the false. So religion is something that can only come about through the negative approach—not through the positive, dogmatic, assertive, propagandistic approach. You can only come to religion negatively. But the negative approach is the most positive; the other approach is not at all positive; it is nothing. And in the very act of denying, you are discovering what is false, and out of that you begin to see what is true.

Now we mean by revolution something that is not an idea separated from action. It is not a planned revolution. The very term *planned revolution* is contradictory in itself. It has no meaning. A planned revolution is merely conforming to a pattern established by another, whoever it is. That is not a revolution; it is only an action based on an idea formulated according to a certain pattern—which is a reaction according to which you must act. You approximate your action according to that reaction, and therefore it ceases to be action; there, the idea is more important than action—than to do, to act, to function. The revolution of which we are talking is not an idea carried out in action; therefore, in the action brought about by this revolution, there is no conflict, no approximation, no imitation of an idea. Please do see this. Perhaps it is something new which you have not read or heard, and therefore you are a little bit bewildered, and you say, "How can you act without an idea?"

You know what love is? Love is not an idea. Love is not a formula according to which you live. Love is not a concept according to which you approximate your action. Love is something in action, immediately. And when you bring an idea, it is no longer love. We have an idea of what love should be. Therefore we have stopped, we have ceased to love. We know the idea of what love should be—it must be chaste, it must be nonphysical, it must be divine, it must be this, it must be that. All such ideas are established in words, in patterns, in formulas; and we do not know what it means to love, to care, to have real feeling for people, for things, for trees, for animals. We have divorced love because we are so crowded with ideas of what love should be—that is the very depth of our existence.

The saints have told you that to find God, you must renounce, you must have no sexual relationship, you must not look, you must not have feelings, you must suppress, you must subjugate, you must destroy. What happens when you sit on a feeling? It pops up in another direction. You are boiling inside and you suppress; you say, "In order to find God, I must live a bachelor's life"; and so you go round and round in a circle, never finding God and never understanding the whole problem. So idea and action create real hell in our lives, real misery in our lives, when we separate the two.

Is it possible to act without idea? It is possible. And it is only possible when you observe without conflict, and therefore there is action instantly. And that action is not conformity. That action is an extraordinary releasing process, and therefore that action is revolutionary.

Now we begin to see what is the religious spirit. The man who has ideals is not religious. Take the question of nonviolence. You love that word in this country; you don't know a thing about it. It is just a word to cover up your violence, because you are violent. If you are not violent, do you think you would allow even for a minute all the things that are going on round us—the brutality, the callousness, the indifference, the complete lack of respect? By "respect" I do not mean the respect that you have for your bosses—that is not respect. I mean when you have respect, you have respect for everybody, not for the ugly people in power. So the religious mind is really the revolutionary mind because it is acting without idea and therefore instantly. It is only such a mind that is new, fresh, innocent, decisive, young. It is only the young mind that can decide, that can say, "That is so," not out of impetuosity, not out of some personal opinion, but because it sees actually without contradiction, and observes what is true; it is only the innocent mind, the young mind, that can do this.

And the religious mind, the religious spirit, is not divorced from beauty. We will have to examine semantically the meaning of this word *beauty*. Look at your religion! There is not even one atom of beauty in it. Is there? Look at it. Beauty implies the highest form of sensitivity—not for pictures, but the sensitivity of a mind that is alive, fresh. And therefore for that mind everything, even the most ugly thing, has its own beauty—this is not an idea. We have in this country divorced beauty from religion, and therefore we have ceased to be religious. Because, your saints have said, "Beauty implies the woman or the man; therefore, do not be sensitive, but suppress, hide, run away; don't look; suppress your passions; you may be boiling inside, but suppress it."

To find God, you must have an extraordinary energy. You do need an energy of which I am going to talk presently. Having divorced beauty from religion, you have ceased to be religious. For you, things like the tree, the color of the sky, the light on the water, or a bird on its wings do not matter. But you repeat the word *God*, quote the Gita, this and that, endlessly. So your lives have become harsh, brutal. And the saints have insisted on austerity. So you say, "I must suppress." But you know, austerity is the most lovely thing, not the austerity practiced by your saints and the rest of the gang—I am using that word "gang" purposely without any disrespect. To feel the sense of austerity is a lovely thing. It is not harsh. And you can be austere only when there is sensitivity. To be sensitive—to have all your nerves, your eyes, your ears, function at the highest level—requires an astonishing awareness of every movement of your thought: whether you are suppressing, why you are suppressing. Then you are alive, you are watching every word, every gesture, every movement of your body and eyes. And out of this astonishing awareness, sensitivity, there comes an austerity without harshness, without bigotry, without cruelty. Therefore out of this comes the religious revolution, which in essence is the highest form of intelligence—which is to be highly sensitive, not to have your particular likes and dislikes which everybody has, but to be sensitive to the whole human existence with all the complexities, with all the problems, with all the despairs, anxieties, sorrows; to be aware of them, to watch them. And in the very process of such observation there is discipline, and that discipline is austere, without any sense of suppression. Then the religious spirit, the religious mind, is in a constant state of revolution—I have explained that; I won't go back. It is only that mind that can find this energy.

There is an energy, a source of energy, which can never be touched by a mind in conflict, by the so-called religious mind—do what it will. Man is seeking this energy because that is the source, the origin. Don't give it a name; it has no name. It is an energy. And it is only that energy that is creative—not the painter, not the writer, not the people who are trying to be creative, to think creatively; they are not creative. It is only the religious mind that is in a state of revolution; that is clear. It is only such a mind that can find the source of this energy in action because that energy comprehends the whole. That energy does not comprehend nor try to answer in particular fragments, but it deals entirely with the whole problem of man—not at one particular level of his particular problem. You have lost that energy—not lost; probably you never had it. You have really to discover it—not to be told like a lot of infants—really to find it out through the religious revolution, through the sense of the highest beauty.

This demands all your attention, and that attention is virtue. The cultivated virtue is no longer a virtue; it is just a habit formed to function in a particular pattern. Virtue is something out of time. It cannot be cultivated—you are virtuous, or you are not. Think of cultivating humility! Just think of that absurdity: a vain man trying to cultivate humility! He will remain at the end still vain. He has learned the word humility and has covered it up. To have this humility you have to destroy completely, consciously as well as unconsciously, all vanity or pride, and on the instant, not gradually.

So the religious mind has no time. Therefore it has no idea as a psychological idea according to which it is functioning. The religious mind is acting—not socially, economically, politically. It is acting because it has found, it has discovered, that source which is uncontaminated by thought, uncontaminated by conflict. It is only the mind that understands the true religious spirit that can find that thing which is beyond all words.

November 13, 1963

Banaras, India, 1963

First Talk at Rajghat

I will talk to you for about half an hour or so, and then perhaps you will be good enough to ask questions, and we can discuss them. Perhaps this might be worthwhile.

It seems to me, not only now but always, that a new mind, a mind that can consider all the many problems from a totally different dimension is necessary because the problems are increasing in every field; man's anxiety, his despair, the agony of his violence and hatred all over the world is increasing—one kills for an idea. And technologically, you may go to the moon; but the human problems of violence, of real sympathy, love, affection, are not solved at all. And wars are on the increase—there is the threat of war, there is more division between man and man. And one sees, all over the world, the fantastic illusion, the fiction of ideals which have no meaning at all; and ideals have become astonishingly important.

We—especially the so-called religious people, the so-called idealists, the nonviolent people—live in a world of fiction. We are not facing facts, the actualities, the *what is* of everyday human existence. And if one observes, one finds there is more conflict, without as well as within—not only physical conflict, an act which kills, but also the conflict within—inside the skin, inside the heart, inside the brain; and there is the conflict between nations, between classes. And unfortunately in this country, there is conflict between people who speak different languages, between the rich and the poor.

If one observes a little more deeply, there is conflict within at all levels of our existence—not only at the conscious level of our daily hopes, daily activities, and daily feelings, but unconsciously, deep down. There is always a battle going on—an endless battle which perhaps ends with death. There is unceasing violence outside and within. And we try to escape from this violence through ideals, through every form of religious fantasy. But the fact remains that there is this extraordinary violence and conflict within each one. Apparently, we do not give our whole heart and mind to understand this conflict, this violence. When you give your mind, your body, your heart, your nerves, everything that you have, you understand and resolve this conflict. But apparently we do not do that. We rather put up with the conflict and escape through some ideation. All ideation is fiction; it has no reality at all. What has reality is the actual—the actual thing that you can observe, put your hands upon. But apparently ideals give us a fantastic escape from the actual thing.

Not only have we conflict within ourselves, but we add to it another conflict, the conflict of ideals—how to approximate our activities, our doing, our thought, to a certain pattern which we call the ideal. You know what happens in this country, the country which has everlastingly preached nonviolence. Nonviolence is obviously a fiction, it has no validity at all; and yet we are carried away by this word. What has reality is violence, this conflict, this agony, this terribly complex existence of life. Instead of giving our hearts to understand it, to resolve it, and to go completely beyond it, we pursue this fiction, this myth. We see not only that we have this incessant conflict, but we also add another. This becomes hypocritical as is shown in this country which has talked about ahimsa and nonviolence—which is all sheer, brutal, ugly nonsense.

Our problem is surely not only to find the cause, not only to be aware of the conflict, of the violence within, but having discovered it, having seen it as a fact, as an actuality, to give our hearts to it—and apparently we cannot do that. You know, to understand something, to understand even the most scientific question, the scientist must give his mind, his labor, his thought, his heart to it. And the really first-class scientist does this at least in his laboratory; he is completely there. He is a completely different human being once he leaves his laboratory. But when he is in his laboratory, he has only one complete intensity to discover, to understand what is under the microscope and go on with it until he discovers everything that has to be understood about that particular thing. But apparently we cannot do that. Though we are broken, we are in chaos, though our life is shattered, made ugly, though our life is petty, narrow, small, and stupid, we won't give our minds, our hearts, to understand this thing. I wonder why we are so fragmented, broken up.

It is important, I think, to find out what it is to listen, to find out how we listen. There is a statement being made by the speaker. How do you listen to it? Do you listen to it as something foreign, as a series of words put together which you casually hear, which has a vague peripheral meaning, as something that you have heard or that has very little meaning? Or, do you listen to find out if what the speaker is saying is true or false?—not agreeing with him, not rejecting what he says. And to find out, you have to listen. And to listen is one of the most difficult things. We can't listen completely, continuously. We listen intermittently, sporadically, now and then.

To listen implies that you have to have a certain quality of attention. To listen means that you have not to bring your own opinions, not to bring your own ideas, the commitments that you have, the knowledge, the inferences, the comparison that you make—all those have to be put aside so as to listen really, completely, to what another person is saying.

You happen to be here to listen to the speaker; if you cannot listen that way, then what is being said is merely a series of words casually formed together, and all communication between you and the speaker ceases.

We are talking about something very, very serious—not something which you do occasionally when you have time, when you have nothing else to do. We are dealing with life. And you have to listen to find out how to resolve this extraordinary conflict in which one is. Because this conflict is not merely of the particular, but it is also the conflict of the world, the collective—the two things are not separate; it is one continuous movement, like a tide that goes out and comes in. And you have to resolve this conflict as an individual, not as a group, not as the collective that wants to work for peace—that will follow much later. We will always begin at the wrong end.

It is important to understand this and give our hearts and minds to find out if this conflict, misery, sorrow, despair, and anxiety can be resolved. What we propose to do during the three Sundays we are meeting here is to go into the question of whether a new mind can come into being. And a new mind is only possible when all the conflicts at every level of our being—the conflict of the unconscious, the conflict of the verbal, the conflict of the intellectual, and the conflict at the level of our daily existence—are wiped away. We have to see whether that conflict can be completely, totally, wiped away. Because it is only then that we can have the new mind—a mind that can proceed, a mind that is young, fresh, innocent, a mind that can ask.

You see another peculiar thing in our life. We think that every action needs conflict. To overcome that conflict, we have a pattern called an idea, and according to that idea, action is made to conform; and so conflict increases in action. So, is it possible—not theoretically, not ideationally, not in some far-off places, not in an ecstatic heaven—is it possible actually to eliminate conflict altogether if I am going to see? Naturally that is a vital question. Because if the mind were not in conflict, then there would be affection, love; there would be clarity; then you and I would not be against each other; you wouldn't have your own opinions, ideas, your beliefs which are so extraordinarily important that you fight with another for your beliefs and dogmas. Then we would look at things, then we would consider what is important and would inquire into those things with which we are concerned.

So, is it possible to end conflict? If you say it is not possible to end conflict in life, in living, then you stop inquiring. Please understand this. You may say it is not possible, as most people say. The whole of the communist world, ideologically and actually, says, "Conflict cannot be wiped away from the human mind. It is part and parcel of human existence"; then you must have conflict. You don't do it either. You say, "Let us refine conflict, let us make it better, let us fasten it, let us put it in a gold frame, and all the rest of it."

Just as there are those who say it is not possible, there are those who say, ideologically, verbally, it is possible if you follow a certain discipline and a certain rule of life. They say that if you believe in God, if you sacrifice yourself for certain ideas and so on, eventually you will have peace. Eventually means at a distance, at the end of some years, but we want peace now, like a hungry man wanting food. So if you belong to either of these categories—one who says that it is not possible and the other who says that it is possible only through time—then you and I can have no relationship because it is absolutely essential to end this conflict immediately, not in time.

If you say it is possible, then you do not do anything about it because possibility is merely an idea. And if you say it is not possible, again you belong to the category of the man that says, "Conflict is there, put up with it, make the best of it." You do not belong to either of the two: that is the only intelligent approach. Then, when you approach a problem, you start with the fact that there is conflict, and you will begin to inquire whether it is possible to end it, neither accepting that it can be ended nor asserting that it cannot be ended; your mind is then in a position to look at the fact; and that is what we must establish between us.

We are not concerned with the state of the mind which says, "It cannot be," or "It is possible." When a man is hungry, he wants food and not the possibility of having food. That is the first thing to establish: that you are concerned with the understanding of conflict and whether it is possible to end that conflict, not in the world outside—that is one of our fantastic escapes—but in yourself, because you are the world, you are all the environmental influences, conditions, forces of the world, you are the center of all that. Without understanding this, merely to go out to reform this world has no meaning at all; that way you create more mischief—which the idealists, the reformers do now; they are really the most dangerous people. So is it possible to end conflict?

What do we mean by conflict? To be insulted, to be battling, to have the constant struggle to maintain and sustain certain ideas, language, ideals. The conflict that goes on within one: "I am loved," or "I am not loved," or "I want more love," or "I want to fulfill"—and in the very act of fulfillment there is frustration. "I am a little man and I want to become the big man, the big noise"—there is the conflict because it is not possible for everyone to become the big man. "I am greedy, I want to be good, and I want to flower to goodness"; there is the other side of me which is ugly, which is dull, which is stupid, so there is the battle between stupidity and intelligence. The conflict of a mind that must be always wanting more experiences, more intelligence, more things as well as intellectual capacities—that is what we call conflict. And we are saying, "Is it possible to end conflict?"

First of all, to find out for oneself whether it is possible or not, one has to look at the actuality, one has to observe the actuality, the real thing. It is very important to understand what we mean by "observation," by "looking," by "seeing the fact." How does one observe? You understand? I am in conflict with myself. I want to understand it. In order to understand something, I must look, I must observe. What do we mean by observation? How do we look? Because if I do not know how to look, I shall not be able to understand it. If I am not observing, I shall not be able to unravel, to learn about it. Therefore the first thing you have to understand is how to look, how to observe.

How do you observe a tree, if you ever do? How do you look at a tree? Do you ever look at a tree? You are so highly, intellectually, spiritually evolved! If you ever look at a tree, how do you look at it? You say that it is a mango, a tamarind, a peepul, or whatever the tree is. And by the very act of giving it a name, you have already distracted your observation; the word prevents you from looking at that tree. I do not know if you have noticed all this. You want to look at the tree, and in the very act of looking, you have named the tree; and in the very naming of that tree, your mind has gone away from observation; so the word prevents you from looking. Most of us do not even care to look, but if we do look, the word distracts. That is the first thing to find out: to observe a thing, the word must not interfere—not that you are going to suppress it, not that you are going to discipline yourself not to use the word. It is as simple as that; if you want to see something clearly, no verbal distraction must take place.

Then the word is associated with opinion. The word by itself is nothing, but behind the word there are innumerable associations: pleasure, pain, opinion, judgment, evaluation, comparison, condemnation. Behind the symbol, all these associated, related thoughts lie; and all these prevent you from looking, especially at something which requires complete attention. It is very simple to look at a tree—the tree is static. But to look without the interference of association, without all the implications which a symbol evokes, requires astonishing attention and real interest in the thing which we are observing. Therefore, when you observe there is no contradiction, or you observe the contradiction when you begin to observe. When you begin to observe violence, the violence in yourself, the opposite of that violence, which is nonviolence, may occur because you are trained by the saints, by literature, by the past, by society, by all the things that you have been brought up in, to introduce the opposite. If you are not aware of it while you observe, if you do not see it the moment you introduce the opposite, you are not observing. So the art of observation is as difficult as, or perhaps more difficult than, getting a PhD or any other technological degree because it requires a tremendous interest in the very act of living.

So the first thing to understand is this complex violence of human thought and human being—not only the human being outside, but also the human being inside. To observe that, you need interest in the thing which you are observing—interest, nothing else. And that interest cannot be stimulated; you cannot by drink or by a pill or by going to a temple understand violence—all that is an escape. And when you are interested, you begin to observe; then you begin to learn "how to observe." That very observation, you will find, brings its own discipline—not the stupid discipline imposed by society, or the discipline you impose upon yourself endlessly, because that discipline breeds conflict. In the discipline of observation, there is no conflict. A man who would really resolve this problem, this complex, perplexing, destructive thing called violence, which is outside the skin as well as inside the skin—what that man has to learn is how to observe.

You cannot learn from another. There is no teacher. You cannot practice learning. You learn by the very act of doing. If I am interested to find out how a motorcar runs, I open the hood and look, observe, watch, see how everything is put together—the piston, the sparking plug, and all the rest of it. In the very act of observation, I am learning. Not that we learn first and then apply; that is what most of us do, and therefore we are not learning at all, we are merely applying something that we already know, or that we have learned, or that we are being told. We never have this extraordinary capacity and beauty of observation. That is the first thing to understand.

But to go beyond all this—to go beyond all violence, all man's stupidity which has been imposed upon us and which we have cultivated ourselves—requires earnestness. One must be earnest—not in pursuing an ideal which is childish and immature—one must have the serious intent that comes when one wants to find out and to go to the very end of that thing so as totally to be free from it. It is only the serious mind that can live richly, fully, in this world.

Perhaps you will ask some questions about the things we have been talking about.

•

Question: Does the recognition of a thing prevent one from observing it? You may not name it.

KRISHNAMURTI: What do we mean by the words *to recognize?* We are not splitting hairs to be dialectically argumentative. You know what dialecticism is? It means to discuss and see the truth of an opinion. We are not discussing opinions, we are discussing facts. Therefore we are not dialectically arguing about anything, we are not concerned with opinions. So we are considering what we mean by the words to recognize. It is very important to understand this thing. I recognize you because I met you yesterday or last year; I say you are that person. That is one thing: outwardly I recognize you. But during the interval of a year, a day, or an hour, you may have undergone a tremendous transformation. There might have been sorrows, despairs, hopeless misery. I do not recognize you there. Only outwardly I recognize you, and that recognition comes through memory—I have a memory of having met you the day before yesterday, and I recognize you today; I recognize you physically and nothing more. When I say I know you, I only know the physical contour of your face. I cannot know you because in the interval you might have changed tremendously or might not have changed; so only experience gives recognition; otherwise, I cannot recognize. Please go with me a little, and you will see what it is leading to.

I have an experience of sorrow, which I have named as sorrow, and when it recurs, I say that is sorrow. The first experience of sorrow has left a memory, and that memory reacts when a similar, or somewhat similar, sorrow arises; there is again recognition. Memory reacts through recognition. I meet that tree and say, "It is a tree and it is not a car." Please watch this. The moment I say that is a tree, I have recognized it as a tree; that very recognition as a tree is a distraction which prevents me from observing. I do not say it is a car; I know it is a tree. I won't mistake it as a human being—I wish I could; the tree is more beautiful than a human being, generally. I am not distracted, I say it is a tree, I do not confuse. But I see that the very process of recognition becomes a distraction from observation.

Can a mind look at something, though it recognizes it, without bringing in all the associated memories of that recognition? Please be quiet. Do think about it; do not reject it. Because you will see that unless you understand this very deeply, your mind is merely in a mechanical state, your mind follows merely a repetitive process—adding and subtracting—and you will keep this mechanism going on all the time.

I have learned something. I have had an experience of something, and with that experience I look. And I do not really look because the experiences, the memories, the associations prevent me from looking. Therefore, there is a continual mechanism of recognition, acceptance, denial, or gathering to yourself. This is the mechanical process that is going on all the time, consciously or unconsciously. If you want to look at something anew, as though you are meeting it for the first time, you have to have a mind that is not cluttered up with all the past, and you have to look at it without bringing up all the associations.

Question: What is the root, what is the source of imitation and fear? How is one to be free of them?

KRISHNAMURTI: I have to repeat your question. Please correct me if I do not repeat it properly. The question is, "What is the root of imitation and fear? Is it at the conscious level or at the unconscious level? And is it possible to be free of imitation and fear?"

Do you want to discuss this now, or should we discuss it next Sunday when we talk about fear and its consequences? We are now talking about something which is not completely related to this question. This morning we are trying to talk about the art of observing, the art of seeing.

Question: What is the significance of words? Have words any significance? If we cannot use words, how do we communicate?

KRISHNAMURTI: First of all, the word is not the thing. The word *tree* is not the tree. But the word tree for most of us, is the tree. You understand? When we use the word tree, immediately the image of a particular tree arises in our mind—the tree that has given us pleasure, the tree with which we are familiar. But the word is not the tree. So one has to be aware of this fact that the word, the symbol, becomes much more important than the fact. To a Christian, the symbol—the image, the cross—is much more important than all the facts associated with that symbol. To you the symbol of some goddess or some god or image is much more important than the fact. So if you want to think clearly, simply, directly, you have to realize the importance and the unimportance of the word and not get caught up between the two.

When we use the word *understanding,* does the word create or bring understanding, or is understanding independent of the word? I say, "I understand what you say. I understand very clearly that the ideal of nonviolence is sheer rubbish." I say, "I understand." What do you mean by the word understanding? What is the state of the mind that says, "I understand"? I say something, and you say, "How true that is! I understand it." What is the state of the mind that says, "I understand it"? In that state the mind has grasped something. When does understanding take place? I have stated verbally a certain thing. You have heard it, and you say, "I understand it." You can only understand something directly, as a fact, when the mind is not projecting its own opinion, conclusion, concept, but is listening so as to have an immediate communication with the speaker. The person who says, "I understand," has gone beyond the word; the word has become irrelevant—that is, he has grasped the significance of the word and gone beyond it. The mind can only go beyond the word when it is attentively observing so that it is not caught in the word, and therefore it becomes quiet, somewhat quiet, and in the space of that second of quietness, it can see something true and therefore say, "I understand." The word has significance only as long as it is not caught between the word and the fact.

Question: You have said that ideas prevent action. Is not that statement itself an idea?

KRISHNAMURTI: The gentleman says that I have said that ideas prevent immediate action, and he asks if that statement is not itself an idea. I have already said that the word is not the thing. I have said: Ideas prevent immediate action—which is a fact. If I have an idea and I see you starving, I begin to say that India must be saved and all the rest of it; I become a politician or a social worker, and I do not see you are starving.

Question: Is it not helpful to have a teacher, a guru, to instruct and guide me?

KRISHNAMURTI: The word is not the thing. To you who are so trained and conditioned, a guru is astonishingly important. Then you begin to defend, to hide behind words. What I said was something entirely different. I said learning is far more important than the teacher. The teacher is not at all important. Please follow. Learning is far more important than any guru, any book, any scripture in the world—those are irrelevant; so they have to be put away in a cupboard and locked up, or thrown down the river, including the saints. What is important is to learn. Now, how do you learn? What do you mean by learning? This is really very important.

What do you mean by learning? We generally mean that one learns from something, from some experience, from some example, from some observation. I learn from an experience that has left a mark, left some knowledge. When I have the next experience, I look at that experience through this knowledge and add to that knowledge. This process is what is called learning. Please follow this. I have an experience, I have learned from that experience, and with that knowledge I approach the next experience; and what I have learned from that new experience is added on to the old. I keep this going. So what we generally mean by learning is an additive process, adding, adding. We are just adding. We are not learning. I will explain what I mean by learning.

We know now what we do—this mechanical process of adding to something which we already know. And that process we have called learning. I do not call that learning at all; that is only a mechanical process that is going on—a self-possessive, defensive, reactionary process that goes on. To learn something new is something entirely different. To learn implies something new. For example, I learn how this machine is working. The implication behind that word is: It is something new, learning is something new, not adding something to what is already known. Therefore learning means a constant newness; otherwise, the mind cannot learn.

Listen, sir. I have said something new just now. I am telling you that to learn implies no additive process. Adding to something which you already know or discarding something which you already know—that is not learning. I say that to you, and you say, "What do you mean? How do you know? What are you talking about?" So you don't listen; you have already discarded what is being said, you have already stated, "I don't understand what you are saying." You do not say, "Perhaps there may be something in what you say; I will listen to what you say." All that you say is, "Can I add that which you say to something which I already know?" I say: Don't do that, but listen to find out what is being said, don't add. Because if you add, you are not listening; then your mind is a mere machine which is running automatically, reactionally, mechanically—adding, subtracting, dividing. But to learn, your mind must be fresh; otherwise, you cannot learn. Learning is a process of being constantly inquisitive, constantly aware, not constantly adding and making yourself dull.

So learning is an astonishing thing. You cannot learn from a teacher. You can only learn from observing—observing what another says, observing to see whether there is truth or whether there is falsehood in what he says, or observing to see the truth in the false. Your mind must be constantly alert, watchful; then only can it keep its freshness all the time and not become dull by adding, adding.

Question: Scientific or technological progress is made by the new knowledge that has been learned being added to the old knowledge. How can you say that this is not learning?

KRISHNAMURTI: Have you all heard the question? The questioner says that technological knowledge is an additive process wherein you keep on adding, adding. You cannot discard all that and restart to know what the atom is all over again. You already know a great deal about it, and you can start from there. Is not human understanding also the same? That is, people have already inquired, found out what you are; all that you have to do is to accept what they have said as knowledge and go on from there; otherwise, you will have to start right from the bottom again. That is the question.

Look at the implications in that question. Technological knowledge and adding more and more to it is what the scientists, the physicians, the businessmen know. The whole world of technological progress and of electronic brains is based on that. Then there is the other: the psychologists, the saints, and others have laid down, have said, what you are; will you accept them and start? Or, do you say, "I am not going to accept anybody, not even the greatest of people, but I am going to find out"?

Not that I start at the bottom. Here I am—this complex human being which is the residue of all human beings. What is the good of what Buddha, Shankara, or your own pet guru has said about this? I have to find out, to watch, to observe. It looks like starting from the bottom, but I observe what I am. I know what I am, and I also know the conflict between 'what I am' and 'what I should be'. I observe all the fantastic ideas about the supreme self, the big self with a capital *S*, the higher self, and all the rest of it. In the very process of observation, I also learn about myself, not adding more and more to myself; I am learning. Therefore, living, being, is a constant change. And to understand this constant change, the mind must be fluid, sensitive, unaccumulating, every moment of the day. This does not mean starting from the bottom of the thing. On the contrary, the very observation gives me the intensity to start anew, watching everything in me.

Question: It requires a good deal of energy to observe oneself. How is one to get that energy?

KRISHNAMURTI: The question is: "Every man needs a great deal of energy to observe himself. From where is he to get this energy? How will energy come for every man to observe himself?"

The energy of a scientist is understandable because he is objectively working at something, putting his heart in it. He is ambitious, he is greedy, he is conscious of everything that is going on. He divides himself—that is, he escapes from his daily life into his laboratory, and there he is energetic. But we are talking of a different kind of energy, aren't we?

It is obvious that we need a tremendous lot of energy to observe the whole of the psychological structure of a human being. Now, how do we get this energy? Obviously, the first obvious thing is not to escape. The moment you escape from the fact of what you are, to move away from it is the lessening of this energy. The moment you cease completely to escape from the actual of what you are, there is greater energy. When you say, "I must be that," you escape. The fact is: You are violent. When you say, "I must not be violent, I must be nonviolent," you escape from the fact; and as you have escaped from the fact, you are lessening your energy. When you are confronted with the fact, any attempt on your part to translate what you see of that fact according to what you already know, or to suppress it, or to change it, is an escape; it is a deterioration of that energy.

Any approach to the fact of what you are actually, through any opinion, judgment, evaluation, condemnation, and so on, takes away your energy. A mind has energy only when it is completely with the fact and does not try to do something about that fact.

Question: Is it possible to be free from conflict without ending it?

KRISHNAMURTI: Of course it is not possible. How can I be free from conflict if I do not end conflict? I must end conflict—that is what we are talking about. When I have a pain, I can only be free when that pain goes.

Question: When you decide to do something, why is there conflict in that decision?

KRISHNAMURTI: That is very simple, isn't it? First, don't decide. (Laughter) You laugh because you do not understand.

What is involved in a decision? I decide to do this and not that; that has already created a conflict. But when you see the truth of this and the truth of that—either the truth of this and the falseness of that, or the falseness of this and the truth of that—when you see the truth, that seeing will act; it is not a decision.

Therefore do not decide, don't choose; then there is no conflict. See what is true—that requires astonishing intelligence. You cannot see what is true when you take what Shankara or any other person has said as true and follow him.

So a mind that chooses is always in conflict. But a mind that sees what is true acts instantly on that perception; it is not in conflict. Such action is the only action.

Question: Not to choose is also a choice—is it not?

KRISHNAMURTI: It is up to you, sir.

November 24, 1963

Second Talk at Rajghat

If I may, I shall talk for about half-an-hour or so, and then perhaps you will be good enough to ask some questions.

I think it would be deeply interesting, not as a curiosity, to find out what one is vitally interested in. Perhaps that interest varies according to circumstances, pressures, and strains. Either we deal with the immediacy of the strains and the problems, and therefore are merely satisfied with superficial answers, or through these superficial, intermittent, passing problems, crises, and strains, there might arise, if one is persistently inquiring and is vitally interested, a deeper awakening of interest. Perhaps each one of us, not only individually but collectively, might have this interest and might be seeking an answer.

Before we go into that, I think we ought to be clear that there is no collective action or individual action. We are the collective. If we understand what is action, then it won't be collective or individual. This unfortunate division as the collective and as the individual seems to me so utterly fallacious. I know it is a common way of dividing life as personal and collective, individual and universal, and all the rest of it. But if one examines a little more closely and deeply, one finds that there is no such thing as the individual—this comes at a much later stage of our inquiry. But for most of us there is only a collective attitude and activity, collective conditioning. If you look at yourself, you will find you are the collective, you are the result of all the various pressures, strains, and cultures. So, really to inquire into what the vital interest is, perhaps one will come to it not as an individual or as the collective, and will therefore answer the problems not individually or collectively. We have to find out what is the vital interest that must exist in a world where there is chaos, brutality, violence, upheavals, miseries, despair—what is the real demand. Perhaps if we can really ask that, then we might be able to attack the problem. And in the very understanding of the problem, it will be neither the collective nor the individual. Because, after all, your problem is my problem, it is everyone's problem. You are unhappy, so is another. It isn't your particular individual problem which you have so carefully nurtured or cultivated, or hope to resolve. It is the problem of man.

So, what is man's fundamental interest? You can only put that question when you put it yourself, not as an individual. Because you are not an "individual"—you may have a separate body, a certain series of nervous, neurological, psychological reactions, but as an individual you are not. You are a mere human being conditioned, shaped, by society, whether that society is a thousand years old or a month old. So, if we could find out what is the deep, vital, continuous interest, perhaps, in understanding that, the minor problems of everyday existence will be solved. I am afraid it is not worthwhile merely trying to resolve the immediate peripheral problems because there will be no end to them. But if you could get at the root problem, if you can so put it, then from there you can explore. Then the so-called daily problems of existence may be resolved.

So, what is it we are really seeking? Perhaps, we will say we are seeking God, we are seeking truth, we are seeking happiness; or if we are trained in a particular culture, in a particular society, we say we want nirvana and this or that—not ideationally, but actually. I do not know if you see the difference. The idea is entirely different from the actuality. The idea is nonexistent. When a man talks about liberation, to him liberation is an idea; it is what he has learned, what he hopes for, what he wishes. But the idea is entirely different from the actual. The actual is: We are mistaken, confused; we are in misery; we are in insecurity, and we are everlastingly seeking security; we want to be loved; we want to love; we have fear, despair—not only are these the actual things of our daily life, but also these are deep down in our consciousness. Surely, it is only when the mind is very clear, healthy—which means, free from all this confusion, completely free from the conflicts, the miseries, the despairs, the anxieties—only when the mind is quiet, that it can seek; perhaps then, it won't seek at all; it is something entirely different.

So, either we deal in abstraction—which has no value at all—or we deal with the fact, the *what is*, and from there proceed. To put it differently, without understanding the whole psychological structure of one's being, without inquiring, understanding, resolving the structure of the way one thinks—consciously or unconsciously—the motives, the purposes, the fears—it seems to me utterly vain, meaningless, to deal in abstractions: what is God, what is this, and what is that. All this has no meaning unless you are very clear, unconfused. A mind that has totally put away all conflict, that conflict has never touched—it is only such a mind that can discover what is truth, what is real, if there is God, and so on.

So it seems to me, the primary interest for any healthy mind has to be with facts as they are. A human being living is this world has not only to acquire food, clothes, and shelter but also to resolve the psychological conflicts, stresses, strains, fears. For this, the first thing that one has to do is to know oneself—not as an idea, but actually to understand the movement of thought which is not logical, which is capricious, vagrant, without purpose, and occasionally with purpose. One has to understand this whole mechanism of thought, not logically but actually, what it is. If we are really examining it logically, then all that logic—which is never spontaneous but a reasoned, calculated process—can produce is only a computer. That is what we are becoming, if we are at all aware; we are becoming rather poor imitations of the extraordinary machines called computers. If we merely look at ourselves logically, cultivate memory which will direct what we should do and what we should not do, then such logical, consecutive action will inevitably lead to mechanistic activity—which is that of the computer.

I do not know if you have followed all the things that are going on in the world. We, human beings, whether we are religious, whether we are scientific, or whether we are extraordinarily clever, are all becoming imitations of computers. Our chief concern is the cultivation of memory, logical memory: "I have done this, and I must do that; I should be that; I am not that, but I am going to make an effort to be that." All this is based on memory, and logical memory leads to a life of the computer. I am not saying that you should be illogical; on the contrary, we should be aware of the process of a mind that merely functions on memory. I hope we can go into this because this is very important. There has to be a quality of spontaneity—that is, you have to discover yourself anew each time, to see yourself actually as something that is changing all the time. You have spontaneously to see this change that is going on all the time. And if you can observe it, see it, spontaneously, then the mechanistic process of memory will have very little significance.

I do not know if you have observed yourself. If one observes oneself, one finds that one obviously desires certain changes, certain conformities, certain modifications and that those desires for modification, for change, are really based on memory, on association, on the pattern established by society of which one is a part. So, to understand oneself, there must be spontaneity. But to observe freely is one of the most difficult things to do. Because, after all, the mind, the being, is in constant movement, is in constant change under various conscious or unconscious strains, pressures; when we look at that mind, that being which is undergoing change all the time, with a memory which is stabilized, then we shall not be able to understand it. I do not know if I am making myself clear. If I want to understand you, I must look at you afresh; I cannot look at you with all my memories—whether you have slandered me, whether you have flattered me, whether you have been kind or unkind to me, and so on. These memories, obviously, prevent me from understanding.

So, is it possible to look at oneself? It is imperative to look at oneself. If you do not understand yourself, there is no basis for any thought, for any clarity; then you will just live in a world of words, of ideas, which have no relation to daily existence, to what is happening in the religious world. There is a wide gulf between idea and action, between your daily existence and all your demands about God, about truth. When a man is in confusion, he has to understand confusion and be clarified; and out of that clarity he can look. But being confused, to seek God, to seek truth, is absurd and has no meaning. The whole structure of the mind is confused, and one has to look at it not in the mirror of memory but anew each time; one has to look at each thought, each feeling, each reaction, as though one is looking at it for the first time. Is that possible? If it is not possible, we will merely cultivate more and more memory, make it more and more refined and ultimately become extraordinarily mechanistic—and a computer can do it much better than our little mind.

So, if it is clear, the question is: Is it possible to look at yourself, to look at every thought as it arises, as though you are meeting it for the first time? Otherwise, you merely translate or interpret what you see according to your memory, and therefore, you won't understand the actual movement of thought which may have its source in the past but which may appear as new. You have to look at it anew. If this is clear, then we have to find out, if it is at all possible, the relationship between memory and perception, seeing.

How do you observe, see? Do you observe, see, through thought? Or do you actually see? Do you see me, the speaker, through all the knowledge, information, reputation, ideas, that you have? Do you merely have the opinion which you have cultivated about the speaker? Or do you actually see? Do you follow what I mean? I think this is very important, if you could really understand this very simple fact: Do you actually see, or do you see through your memories? Seeing through your memories is not seeing. Is it possible to look, to see, to observe, without the whole response of the mechanism of memory in operation? Otherwise, it will be merely carrying on something of the past, a modified continuity of what has been; and therefore, the mind is never fresh, never young, never innocent to look, to observe.

To observe, we need a fresh mind, we need a deep mutation. Mutation, the word itself, implies a complete change without cause, a complete revolution. And we need such a mind because the problems are so immense, not only in India, but all over the world—the problems of starvation, overpopulation; the problems of progress; the mind becoming more and more superficial, more and more mechanical; and deep down, the agony, the despair, the frustration; wars; the longing for peace; the conflict between two powerful blocks, each demanding a certain type of action, a certain way of living. When you look at all these enormous, complex problems, you need to have a fresh mind, not an old, traditional, decrepit mind; you need to have a mind that is no longer caught in any pattern of thought—it is the patterns of thought that have brought about the present state of affairs.

So, you need a fresh mind. That means a complete mutation, not in time, but out of time. And that can only take place if you can observe without the whole mechanism of memory coming into operation. As a problem itself, it is very interesting. Whether you can do it or not—that depends on you. As an issue, as a question, as an inquiry, it is extremely interesting. We need a fresh mind, obviously; we need a mind that can look at things anew, without awakening the whole power of memory. And it is only possible if you can look at yourself—the self being not the higher self or the lower self but the ordinary self; this division as the high with a capital H, is an idea, not a fact. If you can see the motives, all the movements, conscious as well as unconscious, of every desire, of every thought, of every feeling; if you are totally aware of all that without any choice; if you can just observe, neither condemning nor comparing; if you can see this in operation—then out of that comes a fresh mind, a mind that is spontaneous. And it is only such a mind which has emptied itself of all memory that can function, if necessary, with freedom; it is only such a mind that can meditate. And that is real mutation and nothing else.

Let us discuss. You may ask questions.

Question: My memory is inherent in me, it is part of me. How can I get rid of it?

KRISHNAMURTI: The gentleman says that memory is inherent, is a part of us, and it is very difficult to get rid of it.

I do not say that we should get rid of it. You cannot get rid of memory. Please look at it! You are logically functioning now. You say, "I must get rid of my memory in order to have a fresh mind," and you will find methods of getting rid of certain memories logically; and you will end up mechanistically. What I said was that one must understand this whole mechanism of memory—not get rid of it; you cannot. The idea of getting rid of memory is nothing; you must understand it.

Now, what do you mean by understanding? It means to observe it in action, not to do anything about it, just to observe it. Now, you react to everything; there is no space between that reaction and the fact. You have to have this empty space in which memory does not continuously jump in.

Question: It is only with my memory that I can recognize something. Can I recognize you if I have no memory of you?

KRISHNAMURTI: The question is, "How can I recognize you if I have no memory?"

You cannot. You met me yesterday or a week before, and you say you recognize me because you have memory. But what has happened during that week, during those twenty-four hours? I have changed a great deal; there has been a change, a variation, due to various considerations, pressures, challenges to which I have answered inadequately, and therefore conflict and so on.

You only recognize me, the form, and nothing else; and that form too is changing. So, obviously, you must, unless you have amnesia, have memory; that capacity must exist.

But if I insulted you, if I robbed you, if I cheated you, if things have happened to you—all that comes into operation when you meet me the next time; and so you push me aside, you cut me. You know that I have insulted you, that I have done you harm consciously or unconsciously; yet, you have to be aware of all that without letting your present relationship with me be interfered with by the memories of the past.

Question: Does this not imply that if I have been robbed once by somebody, I should not allow that memory to operate when I meet him again, and thus I allow myself to be robbed again by that person?

KRISHNAMURTI: The gentleman says that I should allow myself to be robbed again.

Is that a serious question? Or, are you merely trying to defend a particular pattern of thinking? If it is really a serious question, naturally you will protect yourself from being robbed. You do not want to be robbed twice by the same person. You may be robbed by another person, by a politician, but you do not want to be robbed by the same person twice. So you keep at a safe distance from him, but you look at him with a different spirit.

Question: Does mutation come about naturally, spontaneously? Or is it caused by an outside agency?

KRISHNAMURTI: Why do we divide the outside agency and the inward spontaneity?

The speaker tells you something. The speaker is the outside agency, and he says that you must have mutation, deep down. And obviously what he says is reasonable, and you see the necessity of it; then you begin to inquire, "Is it possible or not possible?" If it is possible, how is that spontaneity to come about? Does it come through an outside agency—that is, through outside pressures, challenges, demands, culture, and all the rest of it? Or does it come about when one understands these outward pressures with all their limited restrictions and so on?

By understanding these outside influences, you are free from them, and therefore you are then faced with the simple fact that mutation must take place without any pressure, without any cause. Otherwise, you are merely yielding to circumstances, pushed by a motive.

Comment: Sir, you have not explained why we divide.

KRISHNAMURTI: Why do we divide?

You ask a question and then wander off. I said very clearly why we divide the outer and the inner. It is a total process; by understanding the outer, you will come to the inner; and by going, penetrating, deeper and deeper into the inner, you will find out whether that mutation is possible at all. But merely asking a question and leaving it has no meaning. You have to grapple with this question and find out for yourself. And to find out for yourself, you must either reject the challenge or observe how you respond to that challenge. If you respond verbally—that is, intellectually—then it is not a challenge at all. But if you respond with your whole being—that is, physiologically, nervously, with your eyes, with your ears, with your heart, with your mind—then that challenge will, by the very response, open the door to further inquiry. But unfortunately, we do not want to listen to anything intensely, we do not want to feel intensely about anything. Probably, most of us have little passion—perhaps it is reserved for physiological, sexual passion and for nothing else. You need to have tremendous passion to find out what truth is. You cannot have passion if your heart is barren, controlled, beaten—that is what most of you are.

Question: If the mutation you talk of takes place, how can I do my present job, how can I maintain my present relationship with persons and things?

KRISHNAMURTI: The gentleman says that if mutation takes place, we will lose our job, our relationship.

Is that so? Find out. You are speculating, aren't you? A hungry man does not speculate; he wants food and he is not satisfied by words. I am afraid most of us are satisfied by words; we have been fed by words for so many centuries. We are talking of something quite different—of experiencing directly, inquiring directly, not speculating.

Question: What is the use of your talking? Why do you talk?

KRISHNAMURTI: Sir, why do you learn? Why do you learn to read, why do you learn anything—about history, geography, mathematics? Why do you study at all? Either you study to make the mind intelligent, sharp, clear, precise, or you study merely to pass an examination and to get a job—which becomes a burden and in which you die. In the same way, we are talking because one sees we must learn about life and look at it differently.

That is as simple as that.

Question: What is the aim of human life? What is the purpose of human life?

KRISHNAMURTI: It is very simple, is it not? To live, to live vigorously without conflict, without misery, without despair; to love people. You cannot love if you have sorrow. Sorrow and love do not go together. So, if you want to find out what is love, sorrow must end. And can sorrow end—not only the little sorrow, but the sorrow that destroys human beings? Or, is that a part of the inevitable process of existence?

To end sorrow, one has to go into the whole problem of what is suffering—the physical pain as well as the psychological pain—and whether it can end. Without ending sorrow, you cannot possibly have or know or understand what love is. You may talk about love like a man who is ambitious. How can the ambitious man have sympathy, affection for somebody? You listen and you say, "It is right, logical," but in your heart you are ambitious; there is no relationship between what you listen to and what you actually are. But if you take what you actually are and go into it with passion—not with calculated fears and hopes—then out of that—you will find out for yourself whether sorrow can end.

Question: Is it possible to be free of fear?

KRISHNAMURTI: Fear exists not only at the conscious level but deep down at the unconscious level. There is the fear with which we are familiar and to which we have become accustomed. There is also the fear deep down, hidden, concealed. Is it possible to be free of all fear?

To understand that, one must understand the whole content of consciousness. Now, you have to understand the fact, not what consciousness is according to somebody—whether that somebody is a great saint or great teacher or whatever he is. You have to understand the consciousness which is you—not in terms of what you have learned from some book or from what you have been told—you have to observe. And that is what we are going to do, if you will follow what I am going to say.

This whole consciousness is of time—time being thought, thought being the response of memory, memory being the past, the past moving through the present to the future in a limited way or in an expansive way. The whole structure of the conscious as well as the unconscious is in the framework of time—time being not only chronological time but also psychological time. That is a fact, whether you agree or disagree; it is not a matter of agreement or disagreement; it is so.

We have divided this consciousness as the superficial and the hidden. The superficial is the educated mind, the modern mind—it goes to the office, however bored it is; it passes examinations; it has certain technological knowledge; it reads newspapers and reacts. That is the superficial mind. And then there is the hidden mind. The hidden mind is all the latent factors of the past; certain parts of it are awake, other parts of it are asleep.

I wish you would listen to this, actually observing your own state of consciousness. I am only using the words to describe; do not depend on the description, but watch it. Then you will go much further, deeply.

Now, how do we deal with the superficial fears? We either escape or take a drink or go to church or repeat some mantra or read a book. And reading a book, going to the temple, seeking God, or taking a drink are all the same because they are all escapes from the fact of the fears of which you are conscious. Secondly, in regard to the unconscious with which we are not familiar, we have to get acquainted with it—and it is difficult. There is the hidden part of me, the hidden part of you with which you are not familiar, as familiar as you are with your conscious mind. To become familiar with it, to know all the contents of it, requires an attention, an observation which is attentive—not in terms of condemnation or justification, but merely attentive.

Attention is necessary in order to find out the whole content of the unconscious. I mean by *attention* a mind that is attentive without any subjective or objective condemnation, a mind which is merely attentive. I must go into the meaning of the word attentive. Because most of us do not know what it means; we know only what it is to be concentrated, to focus the attention, to focus the thought on a particular thing. And in that focusing of the thought on a particular thing, which is called concentration, there is an exclusive process—you are putting everything aside. Therefore, concentration is a form of resistance. Concentration is not attention because in attention there is no resistance. Attention can concentrate; even then, it is not exclusive.

One must be very clear between these two facts: the implication of concentration, and the implication of attention. In attention, there is complete emptiness; otherwise, you can't attend. Now, if you are attentive, you listen to that noise of the train on the bridge, you listen to the hoot of the train, you listen to the speaker, you watch the colors of the various people, you see the sparrows flying across the room, you see the people there—their smiles, their yawning, their scratching. But if you are concentrated, you cannot be aware of all this extraordinary movement.

So, you need attention to observe the unconscious; otherwise, you cannot observe it. This means that the conscious mind must not seek any result, it must not wish to transform what it sees, it must not try to interpret what it sees according to its likes and dislikes. So the conscious mind must be attentively aware, which means "aware without any preoccupation." The conscious mind must be in a noninterpretative, noncondemnative state; this means it must be quiet—quiet, not forced, not compelled. And that is only possible when there is no ambition, when the conscious mind is psychologically free from society—then the conscious mind is completely quiet; even the brain cells which are being highly sensitive, highly aware, are quiet; the conscious mind can be quiet because there is no resistance. When the conscious mind is quiet—which means when the conscious mind is attentive—it has no thought, it is empty but aware; then it can observe. This observation is not analytical or interpretative. I won't go into the question of analysis: who is the analyzer or who is the analyzed. This attention has no introspective or analytical quality; the conscious mind merely observes.

Then what is the unconscious? I am merely describing verbally. You can add more words, more description, but that will not help you to understand the unconscious. And you have to understand the whole content of the unconscious, not only the superficial, but also the hidden; otherwise, you cannot possibly go beyond. You may talk everlastingly about God, truth—that is all too childish, immature. Unless the mind can comprehend the depth, the superficiality, the movement of every conscious and unconscious thing within the field of time, unless the mind understands all that, it cannot possibly under any circumstances go beyond itself. And it must go beyond itself to understand what is truth—even the truth of everyday, the daily truth, not the ultimate. So, you have to observe the unconscious or the subconscious, whatever name you give it. The word, the name, is not the thing. We are talking about the thing and not about the word, not about the symbol. When you are observing the thing, the word becomes unimportant.

As we said, the whole of consciousness is of time. The unconscious is the past with all its traditions and authorities and experience—not only the experiences of the present, but the experiences, the knowledge, the authorities of centuries and centuries of man—because you are the result of all men, not just one man. It is too narrow, limited, if we say that the unconscious is merely the result of one individual life, striving, striving, striving—it is not a fact. The unconscious is the whole endeavor of man's existence, his conflicts, his hopes, his fears, his despairs. The whole of that is the unconscious, the collective, as well as the collective operating through the so-called individual, the motives, the urges, the hidden recesses of the mind, of which the conscious mind is not aware at all, and which occasionally, through dreams, come into being. I am not going into dreams now; that will take too long. So, all that is time, obviously—time as the past operating in the present, which becomes the future; the yesterday, moving into today, becomes the tomorrow. That is how we live.

Being attentive, one can observe this process of time. Time becomes mechanical—"I have done this yesterday, and the result of that is today, which will operate on the events, the challenges of tomorrow." The mind which is consciousness, the mind which is asleep or awake, hidden or open—that mind is the result put together by time. Your mind is the result of time. Now, please listen to this carefully. Is it possible for that mind to be free of time? Do not say yes or no. Do not put a superficial question: "Is it possible? Must I catch my train? What about my lunch?" I am talking about the working of the mind at a deeper level. The mind has to be free of time.

Without being free of time, you cannot be free of fear. Because, fear is the result of thought; if you did not think, if you had no thought about tomorrow, you would not be afraid of tomorrow. If there is no process of thinking with regard to something, of which you think you are afraid, there will be no fear. If death comes to one instantaneously, one has no fear of death. So thought which is the instrument of time, which is the response of memory, which is the past—that creates time; and out of that there is fear. Thought is the origin of fear; time gives soil to fear. So one has to understand fear and be free of fear—not the fear of the snake, but this deep-down fear which gives sorrow, the fear which prevents affection, the fear which clouds the mind, the fear which creates conflict, the fear which brings about darkness. Most of us live in darkness and die in darkness. If one would really understand that fear, one must understand this whole process of consciousness which is of time.

Question: Are we not the creatures of destiny?

KRISHNAMURTI: Is that of very great importance? Are you not the creatures of environment? When you are a Hindu, a Muslim and when you are so conditioned, obviously, you can foresee that you are the creatures of your condition and therefore of time, the creatures of a particular culture.

What is important to you to ask that question? Is it to find an answer to it? Or, have you put the right question? That is not the right question because it has no meaning.

We live in this world, you and I. We are confused, we are unhappy; there is immense struggle, conflict. Is it possible to be free of all this? Or, are we everlastingly destined to live like this? If you say that we are destined to live in this chaos, in this confusion, in this conflict, and it is inevitable, then there is no problem; once you accept that as inevitable, you have no problem. Then you have the problem: how to decorate your conflict, how to make it a little more refined—but, deep down, you have no problem. But if you say, "Is it possible to step out of it completely?" then it becomes an astonishing, vital, question. And to answer it, not verbally, not theoretically, to answer that actually, in daily living, you need tremendous vitality. And to have that vitality, you have to observe, you have to be alive, you have to be intensely sensitive.

Question: Is everything preordained? What is the truth of it?

KRISHNAMURTI: Obviously, if you are lazy, if you accept, if you function mechanically, you become a poor imitation of the computer. That is your destiny obviously; that is the truth.

To be free of destiny, you have to reject it. And to reject psychologically, you need vitality. I am not talking about putting on clothes or doing silly absurd things that people do. You have psychologically to reject the whole structure of society of which you are a part—not reject it, but deny it. If you reject it, deny it, in life and not in idea, then you are free of all destiny, nothing is ordained.

I said that a man who functions within the psychological field of a social structure is destined; almost certainly he will function like a cog in a machine. But when a man rejects that psychologically—not being ambitious, not being greedy, not following, not accepting authority, and so on—when he rejects all the psychological structure of the society of which he is, he rejects because he has understood all that. When a man has understood and therefore denies all that, for him there is no destiny; he is not a slave to circumstances.

Question: Is there not a middle course?

KRISHNAMURTI: There is no middle course. Either you are that or this. There is no halfway—that is what we all want; we want the darkness of insecurity and the freedom of life; but we cannot have both. We want to be hot and cold. Do you know what happens when you mix very hot water and very cold water? It becomes lukewarm. And that is what you are: you have become lukewarm. We need to have the fire.

Comment: But lukewarm may be the truth. It is life.

KRISHNAMURTI: Yes, lukewarm, if you like—lukewarm water, lukewarm emotions, lukewarm living. Is that the middle path? No, sir. Don't say yes.

The middle path means to see the false, and to see the truth in the false, and to walk in the middle. That is, when you know what is truth, when you see what is false, then, out of this perception, you walk. It is neither the middle nor the center.

Question: What is really the difference between the brain and the mind?

KRISHNAMURTI: The brain—we know what it is. The brain—the cells, the nerves, the responses, and all that—is the inherited, animal instinct. Do not deny it. Biologically it is so. The brain is a part of the mind. The mind is the whole, and the brain is the fragment. Between the fragment and the whole, the relationship is tenuous. When you understand the whole structure of man—the brain, the mind, the feeling, the struggle, the conflict—the mind then has no limits, no frontiers. What is the relationship of darkness and light?

Comment: But in the physical body, the brain is the medium.

KRISHNAMURTI: It is obvious.

Question: You have said that one must look at the unconscious without interpretation; but the interpretation arises from the unconscious. What is one to do?

KRISHNAMURTI: I said that the conscious mind has to be quiet, uninfluenced, not drilled into quietness; and that it is only possible for the conscious mind to be still when it has understood the psychological structure of the society in which it is living, and nothing more. The interpretation comes much later.

What is the act of interpretation? When do we interpret? When we do not see things directly, then interpretation takes place. When I see that, I do not need to interpret. That is obvious. But, later on, I begin to interpret, and interpretation comes and interferes.

But I say: Look at it without interpretation; that can be done at any level, at any time. Try to look at a flower, do it some time; try to look at it without interpretation. Interpretation is a distraction. When you see the flower and you say it is a rose, the word that arises when you see the flower is a distraction from your observation of that flower. When you are interpreting, saying, "That is beautiful, I wish I had that," that interpretation becomes a distraction from seeing per se. The moment you have understood this process, that interpretation can stop. With regard to the deeper interpretation, I said that first you must make the superficial mind quiet—not make it, but it must become quiet. Then, whatever interpretation or intimation that comes from the unconscious—you will be able to deal with it and break it down. If you do not understand how the conscious mind interprets everything, even the minutest thing, then you will never be able to understand the unconscious.

Question: How can you understand a human being without interpreting?

KRISHNAMURTI: Have you ever noticed when the state of understanding comes? Have you ever noticed how, when you say, "I understand something," that comes?

Comment: It comes instinctively, by intuition.

KRISHNAMURTI: I do not understand what that word *intuition* means.

Comment: I do not understand what you say, sir.

KRISHNAMURTI: What is the state of mind that says, "I understand"? You say, "I understand what you are talking about; I see what you say very clearly; I understand it immediately." What do you mean by saying, "I understand," and what is the state of mind which says, "I have understood"? You mean you have learned from what has been said. I will go into it, you will see.

What we are asking is: What is the state of mind that understands, that says, "I understand, I see"? First of all, such a state of mind has no distraction; it is not distracted by the noise, by the color, by any movement; there is no sense of distraction, and therefore there is no distraction. Because it has seen each distraction, the word *distraction* does not exist in such a mind. Then, what takes place?

When there is no distraction, there is attention; and that attention is silence—there is no operation of thought at all. The mind is completely empty and therefore silent. And when you say something true, I say, "I understand, it is true"; when you say something false, I say, "It is false." So understanding is only possible when there is empty, silent attention in which there is no sense of distraction at all.

Before you understand what the state of mind is that understands, you have to go into the question of distraction. When you want to be concentrated on something, and your thought goes off, the going off is equally a distraction. I want to know why it goes off. That indicates that that particular thought has some interest. So, the mind examines every thought, every wandering off, never saying it is a distraction. Therefore, such a mind is astonishingly awake, very intelligent, sharp, clear, because it is not in a battle with concentration and distraction. Therefore, it is watching everything.

Question: Is there anything to do after watching?

KRISHNAMURTI: All that you have to do is merely to watch. That is the greatest action. Out of that is action—and that is the only action.

December 1, 1963

Third Talk in Rajghat

After talking for about an hour or so, perhaps we can discuss the problems with which, I am sure, most of us consciously or unconsciously are concerned.

There is the question of deterioration—the decline not only physiologically but also psychologically; the decline of the body, the organs; the decline of the mind; the decline, the disintegration of strong, passionate feelings; the decline of clarity, of the capacity to observe. If one has enough vitality when one is young, one has the capacity to observe the things about one, the everyday events of life, the dirt, the squalor, the misery; one has the capacity to question, the capacity of the inquiring mind. If one observes, one will naturally be aware not only of the decline of this capacity but also of the disintegration about one in every field of life.

One must have asked or inquired or tried to find out what is the cause of all this—what is the cause of the decline of the mind. Obviously, it is very clear why the body disintegrates—through old age, lack of right food, and the purely physical strain of disease, all the various physical pressures, adjustments. That, one can expect; that, one sees, is inevitable. The scientists and the doctors may discover some kind of medicine or some kind of food that will prolong physical existence, but there will still be decline—the physical organ wearing itself out through constant use. One has naturally, sanely, to accept this. But is it also necessary for the mind to disintegrate, to decline?

I am going to go into that, if I can, this morning—not as a mere descriptive analysis with which you either agree or disagree. We are not here, I hope, in a state of mind which agrees or disagrees. We are investigating, we are inquiring—not merely verbally, not merely intellectually as a passing amusement for an hour, but actually investigating—into this very process of decline. This investigation has to be in ourselves, rather than the investigation of words and opinions, because mere analysis and examination of opinions has very little value. You have your opinion and I may have mine, but opinions do not bring about the understanding of what is true; they have never brought it about, nor will they ever bring it about.

So, we are going actually to investigate, to inquire into this process of decline. To inquire, you have to watch yourself, you have to observe your own decline, if you are in a state of decline—obviously, not accepting or rejecting, but inquiring. And that is one of the most difficult things to do because we are not used to inquiring into ourselves. We never question the activities, the responses, the thoughts of ourselves. We accept them, or our prejudices dictate, so there is no inquiry at all. This morning, if we can, we are going together to inquire into this whole process of decline, the psychological decline, the disintegration of a mind which should be healthy, which should have the capacity to function at all levels of its being—not to have any dark, concealed, hidden corner, but to be totally aware—and to discover the root of this decline.

So, that is what we are going to do this morning. Naturally I have to talk, but the words do not act as an inquiry. Words have little meaning unless you use the words and go beyond the words—then the inquiry becomes extraordinarily interesting and alive. One sees within oneself various strains at various levels, tensions, pressures—the family pressures, the strain of being with people, the strain of going to the office, the strain of relationships of various kinds at various levels. In modern civilization, these pressures are increasing more and more. Unless we understand and resolve these pressures, the strains, there must be disintegration. That is an obvious fact, that is clear. A machine which is not well oiled does not function perfectly, and it wears itself out very rapidly—that is an obvious mechanical fact. In the same way, a mind, a consciousness, declines, which is constantly under strain, constantly in friction at all levels, not just at one level.

And all the levels at which the mind functions are covered by the word *relationship.* As long as there is friction of any kind in relationship—relationship with ourselves or relationship with the world at any level, at any time—there must be disintegration. Is it ever possible to be free, totally, not partially, of the strains, to be completely conscious of the strains, of the conflicts, of the innumerable pressures, conscious as well as unconscious? Is it possible to be completely aware of them and to be free of them?

To find out, one has to go into this question of action; because life is action, life is relationship which is action, everyday action—from the action of cleaning your teeth to the most absurd or complicated action. Life is a series of either related or unrelated activities; the more sane it is, the more related it is, the more unbalanced the life is, the more disjointed it is. Please follow all this, not verbally but inwardly. We are dealing with life, not with words; we are dealing with activities, facts, everyday incidents; we are dealing with everyday life. And without understanding that life completely, totally, you cannot go very far. You may spin a lot of words about God, religion, silence, and so on—it has no validity at all, it has no substance, it has no foundation, it is just an escape from the actuality.

You are dealing with everyday activity—the activity of any movement of your hands, of your gesture, of an opinion; the activity of what to do and what not to do; the activity of various desires, compulsions, urges—not a sublime, grand, superact; not a heroic act. If you do not understand that, if you are not fully aware of the whole significance of a particular act, either an act related with all the other series of acts or merely a disjointed act, if you do not understand action, obviously, there must be not only friction, strain, but also distortion, an illusion. When a man believes in God, it is an absolute illusion. Whether there is God or not, he has to find out; to have a belief is obviously immature, obviously without any substance.

We are dealing with action at all the levels of our being—not only the physical, but the emotional, the psychological, the mental, the unconscious, the conscious act—because that is life. Life is all relationship or action. You cannot escape from these two facts, though action and relationship are synonymous. By *action* we mean that which was done, and that which has to be done, and that which is going to be done. It is a movement, either a continuous movement or a disjointed movement. With most of us, it is disjointed. We live at different levels; there is the office; there is the family; there is public opinion; there are my fears and my gods, my opinions, my judgments, my conditioning; and there are the various pressures, influences of society and so on. We live at different levels, disjointed, unrelated with each other. The man who talks everlastingly about God—his life, his way of thinking, is complex.

We are inquiring into action—that is, that which is to be done, that which has happened and which has acted, and the future act to do which is not only physical but also psychological. If you observe, you will see that act is based upon an idea, the idea being a reasoned-out thought or merely an impulse or an idea formulated or concealed through fear, through ambition, through anxiety. We get the pattern of an idea, the idea being not only words put together but a thought according to certain prejudices, desires, pressures, demands. We create the pattern of an idea—an ideological, sublime pattern or a stupid, illusory pattern—and according to that idea we act or we try to act. That is our whole life.

Please, this is very important to understand: that, for us, the idea, the formula, the pattern, the concept, is far more important than action; and for us, what is important is to act according to the pattern, the ideal. If you observe, you will find that is what is taking place all the time; there is no instant when this is not taking place unless there is a crisis. If the crisis is tremendously great, there is an immediate response—not of an idea according to which you are acting, but immediate action. If you see something cruel, or if a house is on fire, or if a child is in danger, there is then an immediate challenge and an immediate response. Otherwise, we are always functioning according to a pattern, or we are attempting to act according to a formula, to an idea. Please do relate what we are saying actually to yourself, and see if it is so.

So, there is the idea and there is the action, two different things. Then, we ask ourselves how to carry that idea out in action, how to approximate that action to the idea; and so there is always a strain, a conflict between the action and the idea. That is, to put it differently, there is always an observer and the thing observed; there is always the experiencer and the thing experienced—the thinker and the thought. So long as there is this division between the idea or the pattern and action, there must be conflict. Please do follow this. A mind functions perfectly, as is the case with a machine, only when there is no friction; then it cannot possibly wear itself out, it cannot possibly disintegrate or degenerate. It is only when there is a strain of any kind, when there is friction, that it begins to wear itself out.

So, is it possible to live without any friction, without any strain? If it is not possible, then you cannot possibly go any further, you cannot possibly inquire, except verbally. But actually to inquire and go into what is reality, if there is something beyond the measure of thought, it is necessary to realize this absolute fact—that as long as the mind is in conflict of any kind, conscious or unconscious, it cannot possibly go beyond its own limits. It is very important to find out and to be aware of this fact of the idea or the concept, and action.

I mean by that word *aware* something very simple—to be aware of this room, of this hall; to be aware of the people with their coats and various colors; to be aware of the light on the leaf outside the window; just to be aware, not to say, "I like this, I do not like this; this is nice, this is not nice; this is right, this is wrong"; just to be aware of the outline of the leaf, the outline of these pillars. All that is factual; you cannot alter it. "To be aware" means to observe and then to be aware of one's reactions to all the things one observes. You have to be aware of your reaction to that noise of the train going across the bridge, to be aware of the people coughing, yawning; you have to watch, to be aware of all that, seeing what is outside and also the responses which you give to it. And if you begin very simply, you can go very far in this awareness.

So, when you are aware of this division between idea and action, what it involves—which is, to suppress, to approximate, constantly to try and adjust action with a pattern—you see that there is never a moment when action is for itself. For me, that is one of the fundamental reasons for this disintegration, the degeneration of the mind that is in conflict, that is constantly in friction with itself.

Now, when you observe why the idea becomes important, when you are aware why the pattern has assumed such an extraordinary significance, you can see why it does. Because, first of all, it tends to postpone action: I am violent, and I have this marvelous idea of nonviolence which is an ideal, and I can pursue that ideal and not act because I am still trying to be nonviolent. Therefore, it is an escape from the fact of violence. If I have no ideal of nonviolence, I can deal with the fact.

So, the ideal becomes a distraction; the ideal is a fiction, a myth; it is not a reality. The reality is *what is,* which is violence. And we think that by having an ideal like nonviolence, we can push violence out of ourselves—which never takes place, which can never take place. Because when we deal with facts alone, there is an operation, not when we deal with ideas. So that is one of the reasons: An idea or a pattern offers a means of postponing, of escaping from the fact; and the idea becomes important to give continuity to a particular act. I did this yesterday, I will do this today and tomorrow—it gives a continuity or becomes a habit which prevents action. This is merely carrying out a certain formula, and therefore it becomes mechanical. Life is not mechanical; it has to be lived, it is action changing every minute.

So, ideas offer a means of postponing action. Therefore the more the ideas, the more ideals you have, the more inactive you are. Please do see this: When you act from an idea, you are not active because you are living your life in a world of fiction without any reality. So, escape, postponement, offering a continuity which gives you a habit, and functioning from a habit—that is memory and therefore mechanical. So, you can see ideas do not bring passion. I think it is very important to understand this: To act, you must have passion; to do, you must have strong feelings; otherwise, it becomes mechanical. You cannot have strong, intense, immediate feeling and passion if you have ideas. And you can only act when you are passionate, when you feel very strongly; otherwise, it becomes merely an idea which creates friction.

So, one has to see the whole significance of this psychological process of bringing about a formula according to which one wants to live and function. In being aware of all this, we see that our whole life, from the moment we are born to the moment we die, is a constant battle; and to escape from this pattern, we create an idea; we never face the battle, we never understand it, and we are never free of it. And we cannot be free of it as long as we have an idea and function within the pattern of that idea. A man who would have a very clear, perceptive mind, a mind that is without friction, without fear, without any form of suppression and therefore without any friction, must totally comprehend that this process of fabricating patterns, however pure, however lovely, however noble, is the central fact of disintegration and degeneration.

It is only when the mind is not functioning in the pattern of ideas but is only concerned with action—which is to be completely cognizant of the fact and therefore to be passionate—that it can go beyond; it is only such a mind that can find out if there is or if there is not something everlasting.

Question: Is it true that literature is the criticism of life?

KRISHNAMURTI: We are talking of something else, not of literature. Perhaps you would keep that question for the day when we all meet the students. We are discussing something which is not literature, and perhaps we should confine ourselves to the things that we have talked about this morning.

Question: We are infants in observation. Should we not have some help from people who know how to observe?

KRISHNAMURTI: Why don't we talk simply? Now, who is going to help you? Your guru, your teacher—what you call the double lines, like the railway? Listen very carefully. We want double lines so that we will always function mechanically on those two lines. An engine is never free; it functions only on those two lines. That is what you want.

"To observe"—what does it mean? To observe, to see, to listen—it is very simple, is it not? You observe the trees, the flowers, the birds, the squalor, the dirt on the road, the poor people, the rich people. You just observe. Nobody can teach you how to see; you just see. And you have to find out for yourself whether you see what is there, or whether you see or you think you see what is not there. We think we see with our eyes, but we see much more with our mind actually. The eyes see a certain amount, but the mind actually sees much more than the eyes.

If you are not alert, watchful, looking, you never see. Most of us do not see at all even the obvious things: the size of this hall, the people who sit next to us, the color, the shape of the window. And we say, "Teach me how to look at that window"—which means, "Teach me how to love." Can any one teach you how to love? The books, the saints, the so-called teachers say what love is—love is this, love is that, love is not that. And you have therefore an idea of what love is, and you try to conform to that pattern; and then you are dead—that is not love. Nobody can teach you—it is a hideous idea that somebody can teach you what love is; it is a monstrous, ugly, brutal thing.

You have to feel. And you can only feel when you observe. You see everyday the squalor of the filthy streets, and you get used to it because you have never watched, because you have never looked. When you look, you can never possibly get used to anything. The guru, the teacher, cannot teach you what love is. If they teach you what love is, do not follow them.

When you begin to observe, you will become sensitive, you will become alive. And from that sensitivity, you will have feeling. When that feeling becomes strong, you will be a flame. And from that flame there is action. And that is real compassion. And only that can alter this world, not all the infinite planning by the clever politicians, by the engineers building new dams—they are necessary, but they are not going to create a new world. And we need a new world, a new mind.

Question: When you wrote At the Feet of the Master, *did you not follow the double lines?*

KRISHNAMURTI: The gentleman asks, "When you wrote *At the Feet of the Master* did you not follow the double lines?" Look, sirs, those double lines have been forgotten, and they have gone down the river long ago. We are no longer children, but we want to be perpetual children to be told what to do. Whether it is by the Master or by the saint or by God, we want to be told because we do not want to go wrong, because we are frightened. A mind that is frightened, a mind that complies, obeys, and follows—such a mind is a dead mind.

Question: What is the right understanding for the attainment of bliss?

KRISHNAMURTI: All that we have been saying this morning has to be understood. If we understand this whole structure of conflict within and without and therefore we are free of that conflict, then there is bliss. But a mind which is in conflict and speculates about bliss will never know what bliss is. So, we must first find out what we mean by that word *understand*. When do you say, "I understand"?

If you have said, "I really understand something," do you know what it means to understand something? What do we mean by that word understand? I understand the verbal meaning; because I know English, I understand the words that you have used. Is that what we mean by understand? you have only understood the meaning connoted by those words—we do not mean that. If you and I know English, and if I say that this is a microphone, you understand. This is verbal. Surely, we do not mean merely that. When we use the word understand, it has much more significance. A man who superficially just runs about with a lot of words, may be satisfied with hearing some statements verbally.

But to a man who says, "I really understand what you are talking about," the word understand has a very deep significance. He has not only heard the words but also related those words to action. The mind has understood the relationship of the words and action upon itself—which means it is being aware of the whole content, the significance of all the implications; and the understanding of those implications, conscious or unconscious, is a total thing, not just a verbal understanding. We are talking of a total understanding. When you understand something totally, there is immediate freedom. It is only a partial understanding that is so destructive.

One has to understand the whole psychological structure of one's own being—"being" not with a capital B—that is, the being of everyday life, everyday aspirations, fears, anxieties, worries, jealousies, pains, pleasures. When one understands that completely, totally, then one can proceed to find out what bliss is. A petty mind, a small mind, asking what bliss is, can only find what is its own pettiness—which it calls bliss. The pettiness of the dull, weary mind has to be broken down; then only can it proceed. Then perhaps, there is nowhere to go. Then, the thing is there when all search, all demand, all seeking comes to an end.

Question: At certain periods, the mind is very alert, sees everything, sees every detail—the ants, the flowers, the birds, and so on—with clarity, with simplicity, with care; it sees everything. At other moments it is dull, weary. Why?

KRISHNAMURTI: The state of mind may depend on what you have eaten, on your not having enough sleep and therefore being wearied, on your being self-concerned, perpetually in conflict with yourself. For a single minute, when all that has come to an end, you are watching; and out of that simplicity, out of that freedom from self-concern, you see everything in detail. And you cannot see if there is no affection, if there is no feeling. For most of us, life is such a drab, dull, weary process within the petty limits of our own thoughts and feelings; naturally that predominates, and there are very rare moments when the other takes place.

Question: Is the conflict within oneself not better than the conflict outside? Is it not more significant, better manageable, more worthwhile, more significant than the conflict in society outside?

KRISHNAMURTI: So, you say that there is society outside, and there is the 'you' with its own conflict separated from society. Now, are you not society, are you not the environment? You are a part of the whole social structure; you are a Hindu, a Muslim, or a Buddhist, or a Christian. You have been educated within the pattern. You have withdrawn from this total consciousness, and then you say that this battle within that limited consciousness is better than the battle outside. How can one separate oneself? Is that not an illusion? One has to understand the total consciousness which is the human consciousness—not yours which you have separated through segregation, and which you say is yours. The mind is the total. You cannot possibly exist away from society. You are the result of all the conflicts, the wars, the historical events, the pressures, the religious propaganda; all that you are.

One has really to understand the nature of conflict—not your conflict or the world conflict, but the conflict of a human being, the conflict of the human being next to you and of the human being which you are. To separate the inside and the outside seems to me to be an illusion leading nowhere. As you are a part of society educationally and religiously, and as you are also psychologically that structure, you have to understand that structure. And to understand it, you have to understand the outside as well as the inside; you cannot separate the two; they are one movement, and in understanding the one, you are understanding also the other.

Question: If life is continuous action, how can there be inaction?

KRISHNAMURTI: This is a verbal limitation. I said life is action. But one can make that life inactive, as most of us have done. One can live in a world of friction or fiction and say, "I am active." But I say that living in the world of idea, pattern, formula, is inaction. There is action only when the mind is free from the formulation of ideas, patterns, or systems. That is all.

Question: We understand you intellectually, but we do not really understand you. What can we do about it?

KRISHNAMURTI: Nothing. Is this not an extraordinary idea that you understand me intellectually, but not really? What you mean is: You have heard the words and you understand the meaning of those words. This you call intellectual understanding. I wonder whether you have got intellectual understanding! At least that means you have thought over it. But you haven't thought. You use a very important word *intellectual* for that something which every schoolboy understands—which is to understand the meaning of the word. Either you understand intellectually and emotionally with all your being, or you do not understand at all.

Question: How does one get that alert mind which you talk about?

KRISHNAMURTI: You cannot get it by a method. I have explained it very clearly. You cannot get it through any system. Because if you have a system, you are caught again in the pattern, and therefore you are not free. You can have that alert mind only when you observe yourself, when you observe the trees, the birds, the people, the ways of your thought, your feelings, how you sit, how you yawn, how you eat. Then out of that observation, your mind becomes sensitive. Then when you are sensitive, there is feeling. You cannot stimulate feeling by a system, by saying, "Do this, and you will get it."

Question: What is the function of a teacher in a school or in a college?

KRISHNAMURTI: Apparently in a school, in a college, as it is, it is merely to give information. You know some books, and the poor chap does not know; you tell him about the books. As he has to pass an examination in order to get a job, he repeats what you have told him. He is asked some questions and he becomes a BA or MA or PhD. That is what the parents are concerned with and what the professors and teachers are mostly concerned with. But a real teacher is something entirely different, surely, not your guru. A teacher implies the one who teaches, who helps another to learn.

There is only learning, there is no teaching; you can give information, but you cannot help another to learn. There is information and there is learning. So, do not let us confuse them. To learn implies a mind which is not accumulating. You cannot learn if there is accumulation. If there is accumulation, then it becomes merely memory which is mechanical; then that mechanical memory makes you rather an imperfect computer. Do you know what a computer is? It is an electronic machine built on the same principles as the human brain, and it functions according to what it has been told—the information, the memory, the reaction through association. When you give those electronic machines a lot of information, they store it up; and when you ask a question, they reply according to what they have been told. This is what all of you, ladies and gentlemen, do. That is all. But really to find out, really to learn, you must go beyond the mechanical method of adding, cultivating memory.

Question: How can we avoid the decline, the disintegration of the mind, due to old age and disease?

KRISHNAMURTI: The brain is a part of the mind, and when the brain is diseased, you cannot function. So, how can you prevent the disintegration of the physical organism?

There is such a thing as psychosomatic disease. Physically, what kind of mental life you lead, what kind of mental efforts, strains, you have—that affects the system, the organism, the brain. So, when there is a cessation of conflicts, struggles, fears, then the body becomes more healthy. The physical body may not last for three hundred years but only for twenty years; but it will live those twenty years a strong, healthy life. That is all.

Question: The individual is related to society. And when there is so much conflict within society, how can an individual be completely free from it?

KRISHNAMURTI: We are talking about the psychological relationship of the one with the many, which is society—not about the relationship of everyday activity. The question is, "When the many are in conflict, will not the one be affected and therefore disintegrate?"

Is it possible psychologically to free oneself from society? That is the real question. Society being the structure of authority, of power, with all the implications such as greed, envy, ambition, corruption, is it possible for one to free oneself from that? Is it possible for you living in a society which is greedy, which is acquisitive, which is insisting on power, position, to be free for yourself from greed, not to seek power? I know that power gives you position, money, cars, corruption, and all the other evil things of all power. Power, whether it is the minister's power or spiritual power, is essentially evil. Surely, one can free oneself from that, can't one, and not seek power—not seek power over anybody: one's wife, one's husband, one's children, one's servants; not seek any form of power, which means not only physical power but power through ideas; not try to dominate anyone through any form of compulsion, ideationally or subtly; not want to be in a position of leadership. Can't every person work with that, and free himself from that? Surely that is possible; then you are free from the psychological structure of society.

Question: You see some persons very rich and others very poor. Don't you want to do something about it?

KRISHNAMURTI: The gentleman says that when you see luxury, poverty, you want to do something about it; but you cannot deal with this enormous poverty, the poverty not only outside but within. When you see the poverty, the starvation outside the skin, and all this enormous poverty within, and when you cannot do anything with it, the questioner says you are in conflict.

Please look at all the implications!

You want to do something to prevent, to bring about the cessation of, the starvation in this country. Then what happens? You join the socialist, the communist, or the capitalist movement; you are caught in that; you will become a member of the party, and you will always postpone doing something about starvation. Then, what are you to do? If you join a party, socialist or communist, what happens? Each party wants to solve poverty, starvation, according to its ideas, according to its patterns; and so each party wants to start from its pattern. So, the two parties are at war with each other, and the poor chap in the meantime is hungry everlastingly. So, what is one to do?

Is that a problem of yours, an actual problem like being hungry? Do not bring in your personal issues. You realize that no one in the world is interested vitally, strongly, in completely eradicating poverty. They all say they are interested, but their interest is ideational, not actual. So, what do you do when you feel actually, vitally, that starvation should be stopped? You give what you have, what little you have. What else can you do? You talk, you find out what are the reasons, the causes, that prevent human beings all over the world from acting together to stop this starvation right through the world. Of the several causes that are preventing this, the first is nationality—to belong to a nation, as an Indian, as a Buddhist, as a Christian, as a communist, as a capitalist. Then there is the desire on the part of each one to be psychologically secure—not physically secure because physically one must be secure. The more you demand psychological security, the more darkness you create the more uncertainty you create, in the world. So, you have to tackle your thinking; you have to do all the things you can to prevent the separative sovereign states, nationalities, linguistic states, and all such things that are going on in the world.

Question: Is what you have said any different from what the Gita says?

KRISHNAMURTI: I am afraid I do not know what the Gita says, I have not read it; you apparently have read it, and you say, "Is what is said in the Gita any different from what you are saying?" Look at what has taken place within your own mind! You have read it, you have certain interpretations about it, or you have read the interpreter's interpretation of it and that is fixed in your mind. Then you come here and you listen. But you do not really listen. You hear a series of words; you know the meaning of those words, and then you compare and say, "Are they any different?" What value has that statement "Are they different?" What has value is whether you have understood, whether you love—not what the Gita says.

One of the best things that can happen to this country is to burn all the books and start again. Then you are forced to think for yourself; you have to work for yourself, to find out—not quote everlastingly some book. I do not know why one particular book should have much more significance than any other book.

Do you see, sir, what you have done in this process? You have lost all sense of inquiry. What the Gita says is quite enough for you, and you repeat it and become sterile. You are destroyed by authority; you have not inquired, you have not gone into yourself; you do not question, you do not ask. You never question if there is God—that would be terrible. But the Gita says, "There is," or some other book says, "There is," and this is quite enough for you. So, you lose all sense of inquiry.

There is great beauty in inquiry. And to inquire, you must be astonishingly alive, watchful.

Question: If I watch violence passionately with care, will that free me from violence?

KRISHNAMURTI: The question of violence—has the questioner tried it, or is it merely an idea to him: If I do this, will I get that?

What does "watching passionately" mean? To watch with care, as when you watch a child with care. What happens when you watch a child with care? You do not condemn it, do you? You do not say that child is not so clever as the other child. Probably you do—which means you really do not care. You do not watch that child when you are comparing, when you are condemning, when you are judging. When you condemn violence through nonviolence as an idea and when you want to get rid of it, you do not observe all the psychological implications and the structure of violence. It is only when you observe completely, there is an end to violence. You can do this; if you do, then you will find out for yourself. Do not ask anybody, but do it and find out.

Question: Can the mind be in such a state that is free from ideas?

KRISHNAMURTI: I have just explained the whole thing.

Question: What is philosophy, and is it useful for us?

KRISHNAMURTI: For most of us, philosophy is learning all that the other philosophers including yourself have said. It certainly is not philosophy—dealing with ideas and systems of ideas. Philosophy means obviously, as we were talking the other day, love of wisdom. Neither have we love nor do we listen. We talk, we discuss in philosophic terms, but we do not know what wisdom is, and we do not know what love is. You cannot buy wisdom, and no teacher, no guru, no book, will give you wisdom.

Wisdom begins when sorrow ends. Wisdom is a thing that comes through self-knowing—knowing yourself, knowing every movement of your thought, every feeling, every reaction. And as you understand all about yourself, there is that emptiness; and in that emptiness there is wisdom.

Love cannot be taught, nor is it to be found in any book. It comes stealthily, unknowingly, when you begin to observe, to see, to feel, to hear the things and the mutterings of the world. And out of that there comes sensitivity, and then there is the beginning of that which is called love.

December 8, 1963

Madras, India, 1964

First Talk in Madras

I should think it must be a great concern for most of us to observe the deterioration in the character, in the stability, in the nature of man. One observes it at all the levels of activity. Especially in this country one notices it much more—this country which was supposed to be very religious by tradition, by its inheritance, and the constant repetition of certain religious phrases and ideas. One observes that the deterioration is much deeper, much wider, and apparently very few people are concerned about it. If they are concerned, they try to revive what has been; they go back to the old, ancient traditions, customs, habits, and attitudes of thoughts and values. Or if they are concerned, they turn to an economic or social solution. But apparently, those who take life seriously either escape into what has been, or escape into their old fanciful ideas, or pursue a new conception, a new formula, sociologically or religiously.

Being aware of the world and also of this country, especially of this country, it seems to me that what is needed is a total revolution in consciousness. And that revolution cannot take place if you are fooling around with beliefs and ideas and concepts. We cannot find a way out of our confusion and misery and conflict by constant repetition of the Gita, the Upanishads, and all the sacred books—that may lead to hypocrisy and double life and to everlasting moralizing, but not to facing realities at all. What we have to do, it seems to me, is to be aware of the conditions of our daily existence, of our sorrows, of our miseries, of our confusion and conflict, and try to understand them so deeply that we lay a right foundation and, from there, start. There is no other way out. We have to face ourselves as we are, not according to any pattern, not according to any idealization. We have to face actually what we are, and from there begin to bring about a radical transformation.

You might say, "What is the effect or value of an individual changing? How will that transform the whole current of human existence? What can an individual do?" I think that is a wrong question because there is no such thing as an individual consciousness; there is only consciousness of which we are a part. You might segregate yourself and build a wall of a particular space called the 'me'. But that 'me' is related to the whole, that 'me' is not separate. And in transforming that particular section, that particular part, we will affect the whole of consciousness. And I think this is very important to realize—that we are not talking about individual salvation, or individual reformation, but about being aware of the particular in relation to the total. Then out of that realization comes action which will affect the whole.

When one considers what is taking place in the world—how the minds of human beings have become mechanical, repetitive, how the minds of human beings are separated into nationalities, into groups divided by technological knowledge, and with religious divisions as Hindu, Muslim, and Christian and so on—it seems to me that a wholly different action is necessary. We must find, obviously, a different source, a different way of life which will not be contradictory to our daily living and yet bring about a deep religious comprehension of life.

For me what is important is not only the immediate response to the various challenges—a response which will be adequate—but also a response that is the outcome of a deep religious life. I mean by a religious life not a ritualistic, a conformative life to a particular pattern, but a religious life that comes with the understanding of oneself. Because without knowing oneself, actually what one is—however crooked one is, however deceptive, cunning, hypocritical, petty minded one is—one has no basis for any real religious action or religious thought.

So, it seems to me, anyone who is really, deeply concerned not only with the world situation but to find the truth, to find out if there is something beyond the measure of the mind—he must totally comprehend himself. And during these talks here, that will be our only concern. Because that is the spring, that is the source of our thought, of our being, and of our action. Without self-knowledge, without understanding the self—not the higher self and the self with the big *S*, but the ordinary self, the self that daily goes to the office, that is passionate, that is angry, vicious, cruel, hypocritical, conforming—without understanding that totally, completely, with all one's being, every action, every thought, every idea will only lead to further confusion and further misery.

And it seems to me we have got an immense task, and that task demands seriousness. I mean by that word the capacity to pursue a truth, an observation, to the very end. Because we are not serious people at all, we are very superficial, we are easily distracted, we are easily satisfied. But to inquire into oneself deeply, one must be extraordinarily serious and continue in that seriousness. And that requires energy; you cannot be serious if you have not got energy. That energy has to be not a sporadic, casual energy but a constant energy that can observe a fact as it is, and can pursue that fact to the very end—an astonishing energy, both of the mind and of the body.

And to have energy, there must be no conflict because conflict is the major factor of deterioration. We are people educated to live with conflict. All our life is a conflict—within oneself and without; with the neighbor, with ourselves, and in our relationships. Everything that we touch, both psychologically and ideationally, does breed conflict. And conflict is the major factor of deterioration.

And it seems to me, to understand this conflict, not partially but totally, is the major task of a human mind. Because only when there is complete cessation of conflict, then only is there the ending of all illusion, then only can the mind go very deeply into the question of what is true, if there is something beyond time. And it is only such a mind that can discover what is love and discover that state of mind which is creative, because every other form is speculation. And a religious mind does not speculate; it only moves from fact to fact. And that fact is not observable if there is conflict of any kind, strain of any kind.

So, our chief problem is, it seems to me, that we have completely lost religion, the religious spirit. You may have temples, go to the temple, put on the sacred thread, and all the rest of that immature nonsense, but we are not religious people at all. And the problem of the world cannot be solved at any level except at the religious level. And the really religious life is a life that is lived with the comprehension of conflict and freedom from conflict.

So, our first concern then is the understanding of conflict, within and without. Actually the two are not separate. The world is not separate from you and me; you are the world and the world is you. This is not a theory; but, if you observe, this is an actual fact. You are conditioned by the society in which you live—a communist, a socialistic, a capitalistic, or some other society. You are a so-called individual born in this country and brought up according to a certain tradition, believing in God or not believing in God. You are shaped by society, by circumstances. Your beliefs, your conduct, your way of thinking are all the result of your conditioning by the particular society in which you live. That is an obvious, irrefutable fact. And we have separated the world as something different from ourselves because the world is too much, with all the pressures, the strains, the conflicts, the innumerable demands, and the way of life. And we retreat from that into ourselves, into our beliefs, into our hopes and fears and speculative concepts. So there is a division between ourselves and the world. But if you observe, you will see that the world is not different from ourselves—it is like the tide that goes out and comes in. Without understanding the world outside, you cannot possibly understand the within. And to understand it, you must observe it—not from any particular point of view, but as a scientist observes. The scientist observes only in his laboratory. We, as living human beings, have to observe the world daily, in our relationships, in our activities. And as I said, to understand this whole complex, harrowing, despairing life—a life in which there is no love, no beauty—we must understand conflict.

Conflict arises, surely, when there is contradiction—contradiction of various desires, various demands, both conscious as well as unconscious. But most of us are aware of these conflicts. And if we are aware, we have no answer for them; so we retreat from them, we escape from them, into religion, social work, or various forms of amusement, entertainment, such as going to a temple, going to a cinema, or taking a drink. And it is only possible to resolve these conflicts when the mind is capable of understanding itself.

Now I am going to go into this question of conflict. To understand conflict you have to observe yourself. And observation demands care. Care means sympathy, affection, like caring for a child—not denial, not condemnation. When you care for a child, you observe the child, you do not condemn him, you do not compare him. You watch him endlessly with affection, with immense understanding; you study him, all his moves, his phases, his mischievousness, his tears, his laughter. And to watch demands care. So, in observing oneself completely, the first thing one has to have is care and, therefore, never a moment of condemning, justifying, or comparing, but mere observation of what is taking place, every moment of the day, whether you are in an office, or going in a bus, or talking to somebody, and so on. You have to observe yourself so completely with such infinite care that out of that care comes precision, a unique precision—not vague ideas, ineffectual action.

So, to observe yourself there must be complete care. A caring mind, a mind that is aware of itself, in the very process of its observation of itself, is beginning to learn about itself. Learning is something entirely different from accumulating knowledge. I think this has to be understood very carefully.

Most of us accumulate knowledge. From childhood until we die, we record; our mind becomes a tape on which everything is recorded. And from that record we act, we think, we respond; and to that record we are adding everyday, consciously or unconsciously. We store up every experience, every information, every incident, every memory. And this we call experiencing. This we call learning. But that is not learning at all; learning is something entirely different. The moment you accumulate, you cease to learn. Because it is only the fresh mind, the young mind, the mind that observes with care, that learns.

I think we must see the difference between the two. Technological knowledge is accumulative. You add more and more, and from that knowledge you act. If you are an engineer, if you are a physicist, you gather all the information, as much of it as possible, and from that you act. So there is never freedom. It is always acting from what it has learned, from what it has acquired. At the level of technological knowledge, such action, such memory, such accumulative process, is absolutely necessary. But we are talking of something entirely different—that to observe with care implies no additive process. Because if you are merely adding, acquiring, then, the next minute you observe, you are observing from that which you have accumulated, and therefore you cease to observe. Please understand this.

It is very important to understand that when a mind, merely acquiring, adding to itself, observes from knowledge, what it observes is tainted by its previous comprehension, by previous knowledge; and therefore such a mind is incapable of learning a fresh fact. And life is fresh; living is something totally new, every minute of the day. And we lose that freshness, that extraordinary sense of vitality, beauty, and enormousness by always approaching it through our accumulated knowledge and, therefore, never learning but merely adding to what has been and from that addition looking and hoping to learn.

So, a mind that is serious, that is aware of the world situation, sees that the whole world is in turmoil—there is a steady decline in every country; only a few people can function mentally, perhaps freely, but the rest merely imitate; they are poor imitators of computers; they are ineffective. The sorrow, the misery, the anxiety, the despair, which are facts; not your beliefs, not your hopes, not your gods; the fact of despair, of anxiety, of the extraordinary continuity of sorrow, endless sorrow; the increasing hatred and brutality—that is the world of which you are. And it is the function of a very serious mind to understand this and to go beyond it. A serious mind has to observe it. That is, you have to observe yourself because you are the world, because you are in misery, in sorrow, in loneliness, in despair, anxiety, fear, driven by ambition, greed, and envy—you are that. You are not what you think you are—namely you are God and all the rest of it; that is just speculative nonsense. You have to start from facts, and you have to learn about yourself.

So, there is a difference between learning and accumulating knowledge. Learning is infinite; there is no end to learning about yourself. And therefore that mind which is not accumulative but is constantly learning can then observe its conflicts, its stresses, and all the pains and the secret desires and fears. If you can do that, not casually, not once in a while, but every day, every minute—it can be done—if you watch it constantly, then you will see you have an extraordinary energy. Because then self-contradiction is being understood.

I mean by that word *understand* not something intellectual. A mind that is in fragmentation can never understand. When we say, "I understand something intellectually," what we really mean is we hear the word and understand the word—this is totally unrelated to understanding. Understanding implies not only the semantic nature and the meaning of the word but also the understanding of the whole content of that word and being totally aware of its significance as it applies to ourselves, completely. So understanding is not merely a matter of mentation, an intellectual process. You can understand something only when you give your mind, your body, your senses, your eyes, your ears, everything. And out of that understanding is total action, not a fragmentary, contradictory action.

So our concern then is to understand—especially for those who are really serious; and life demands that you be serious because you cannot live in this world casually. You cannot be concerned merely with your own worries, with your own amusements, with your own fears. You are a part of the world, and you have to understand yourself and the world. And this understanding demands extraordinary seriousness, and the task is immense. And when you are serious, you have to go to the very end of that understanding, you have to see the whole implication of existence.

Then conflict is something that we have to understand—understand, not overcome, not try to deny it, not try to escape from it, but understand it, see the whole meaning, be aware of the various contradictions in word, in thought, in action. Most of us lead double lives, or triple lives, or many lives! We function in fragments, our being is fragmentary; we want to be worldly; we want all the comforts—which we should have. Comfort is obviously necessary, but with that comfort goes the demand for security. And we want not only to be secure in our jobs—which is a natural, healthy response—but also to be secure psychologically, inwardly.

Is it possible to be psychologically secure at any time—which is to be psychologically secure in our relationships and to be psychologically secure with that with which we are identified? It is necessary obviously to be secure outwardly. Outwardly, it is absolutely necessary to have a house, a home, a job; but we are not content with that. We want to be psychologically, inwardly, secure; and then the trouble begins. We never inquire if there is such a thing as inward security, but we say we must be secure inwardly, and thereby begins the illusion. And from that moment begins a whole series of conflicts, endless conflicts.

So we have to find out for ourselves the truth of this enormous question of psychological security—not what somebody else says. Psychologically we are insecure, and therefore we create gods, and these gods become our permanent security! This breeds conflicts. Do you understand what we mean by conflict? We mean the contradiction, the fragmentary action, the disjointed thoughts, one desire opposing another desire, one demand contradictory to another demand, the pressures of the world and the inward demand to live peacefully with the world, the demand to find something beyond the everyday monotonous, stupid existence, being caught in the everyday existence and despairing, never having an answer to this despair, and immense sorrow—not only personal sorrow but the sorrow of the world—and never finding a way out of this sorrow. All these breed contradiction, of which you may be aware consciously or unconsciously. Where the mind is in contradiction, there must be conflict.

And obviously, a mind that is in conflict cannot proceed further; it can proceed in illusion, but it cannot proceed to find out if there is something beyond time, beyond the measure of man. Surely, that is the function of religion. It is the function of a religious mind to find out what is true. And the truth does not possibly lie in a temple, in a book, however old. You have to discover it for yourself. You cannot buy it through tears, through prayers, through repetition, through rituals—in that way lies absurdity, illusion, insanity.

So a serious mind has to be aware of this conflict. I mean by "being aware" to observe, to listen. Listening is an art. Really, it is quite an extraordinary art to listen to a sound. I do not know if you have ever listened to a sound—the sound of a bird on a tree, or the distant hoot of the horn of a car. By listening, not by judging, not by identifying that particular noise with a particular bird or a particular car or a particular radio in the next house, but merely by listening, you will see, if you so listen, how astonishingly sensitive you become. Your mind becomes astonishingly alert if you merely listen—not interpret what you hear, not try to translate what you hear, not identify what you hear with what you already know; all these prevent you from listening. But if you merely listen—listen to your thoughts, listen to your demands, to the despair of your being, not try to interpret it, not translate it, not try to do something about it—then you will see your mind becomes astonishingly clear.

And only a very clear mind, a healthy mind that is sane, rational, logical, that has no conflict, conscious or unconscious—it is only such a mind that can proceed to discover for itself if there is a reality. It is only such a mind that is a religious mind. And it is only such a mind that can solve the problems of this world. The problems of the world are innumerable, and they are multiplying. And if you cannot answer them logically, sanely, healthily, from a mind that is completely free from all conflict, you are merely creating more confusion, more misery for the world and for yourself.

So, the first thing that one has to find out for oneself is to observe with care and to listen to all the mutterings, the fears, the delusions, the despairs of one's being. And then you will see for yourself—and that needs no proof, no guru, no sacred book—if there is a reality. And you will find in that an extraordinary sense of release from all sorrow. And in that, there is clarity, beauty, and the thing that human minds now lack, which is affection, love.

January 12, 1964

Second Talk in Madras

To understand something completely, however trivial or great, one must give complete attention, untrammeled and free. Otherwise, one cannot understand—especially those things that demand careful study and intimate knowledge. To give attention there must be freedom; otherwise, one cannot attend. You cannot give yourself completely over to something if you are not free. And to understand the extraordinary thing called truth, which is yet simple and at the same time quite complex, one must give this untrammeled attention. And, as I said, freedom is essential. For truth does not belong to any religion, to any system, nor is it to be found in any book. You cannot learn it from another, nor can another lead you to it. One must completely understand it and give oneself to it. So, you must come to it free, untrammeled, and with a state of mind that has understood itself and, therefore, is free from all illusion.

Freedom—to be free—is becoming more and more difficult. As society becomes more complex and as industrialization becomes wider and deeper and more organized, there is less and less freedom for man. As one observes, when the state becomes all-powerful, when there is social welfare, the care of the welfare state over the citizens is so complete that there is less and less freedom, outwardly. And outwardly one becomes a slave to society, to the pressure of society; in this pressure of organized existence there is no longer the tribal existence but the industrialized, organized, centralized control. Outwardly, there is less and less freedom. Where there is more progress, there is less freedom. This is obvious, as you see in every society becoming more complex, more organized.

So, outwardly there is the pressure of the control, the shaping of the mind of the individual—technologically, industrially. Being so outwardly held, there is naturally the tendency to become inwardly, psychologically, more and more entrenched in a particular pattern of existence. Again this is an obvious fact. So, for one who is serious enough to find out whether there is such a thing as reality, to find out what is truth—the truth not put together by man in his fear, in his despair; the truth that is not a tradition, a repetition, a thing that is an instrument of propaganda—to find that out, there must be complete freedom. Outwardly perhaps, there may not be freedom, but inwardly there must be absolute freedom.

And to understand this question of freedom is one of the most difficult things. I do not know if you have gone into it at all. Even if you have thought about it, do you know what it means to be free? By freedom I do not mean the abstract, ideational freedom, liberation—that is too abstract, too far away; it may have no reality at all; it may be the invention of a mind that is in despair, in fear, in agony, and that has constructed verbally a pattern, hoping to achieve a verbal state, but not an actuality. We are talking of freedom, not in abstraction but actually; we are talking of the everyday freedom, inwardly, in which, psychologically, there is no bondage to anything. Is that possible? Theoretically and ideationally it may be possible. But we are not concerned with ideas, with theories, with speculative religious hopes; but we are concerned with facts.

Is it possible for a mind, psychologically, inwardly, to be totally free? Outwardly you may go to the office every day, belong to a certain class of people, to a particular society, and so on—which you must, which is absolutely necessary to gain a livelihood. But will the stresses and strains of outward conditioning, outward conformity to a pattern of a particular society—will that control the psyche, the whole process of our thinking? And is there such a thing as complete psychological freedom? Because without freedom, absolute psychological freedom, there is no possibility whatsoever of finding reality, finding out what God is—if there is such a thing. Freedom is an absolute necessity, and most of us do not want to be free—that is the first thing to realize.

So, is it possible to be psychologically free so as to discover for oneself what is truth? Because in the very process of understanding or in the very act of understanding what is truth, you are able to help your fellow man; otherwise, you cannot help; otherwise, you bring more confusion, more misery to man—which again is obvious, which is shown by all these things.

Truth which is made manifest by another or described by another or told by another—however wise, however intelligent—is not truth. You have to find it, you have to understand it. I withdraw that word *find*—you cannot find truth; you cannot set about deliberately, consciously, to find it. You must come upon truth darkly, unknowingly. But you cannot come upon it if your mind, if your psyche, inwardly is not completely, totally free.

To discover anything, even in the scientific field, the mind must be free. The mind must be untrammeled to see something new. But most of our minds, unfortunately, are not fresh, young, innocent—to see, to observe, to understand. We are full of experiences, not only the experiences that one has gathered recently—I mean by "recently" within the last fifty, sixty, or a hundred years—but also the experience of man, ageless. We are cluttered with all that, which is our knowledge, conscious or unconscious; the conscious knowledge is what we have acquired through education in the modern world, at the present time.

Now, it is important, when you are hearing these words, that you are actually listening. I think there is a difference between listening and hearing. You can hear words and interpret those words, giving your own particular meaning or the meaning according to a particular dictionary, and remain at the level of purely verbal communication. And when you are so hearing words intellectually, there is either agreement or disagreement. Please do follow this a little bit. We are not exchanging opinions. We are not dialectically investigating the truth of opinions. We are investigating, trying to understand truth—not the truth of opinions, not the truth of what other people have said. If you listen—which is entirely different from hearing—then there is neither agreement nor disagreement. You are actually listening to find out what is true and what is false—which is not dependent on your judgment, or on your opinion, or on your knowledge, or on your conditioning.

So, you have to listen, if you want to be serious. If you merely want to be flippant and have intellectual amusement, that is all right too. But if you are really serious and want to have urgency to find out what is truth, you have to listen. The act of listening is not agreement or disagreement. And that is the beauty of listening. Then you comprehend totally. If you listen to that crow, then you will see that you are listening so completely that you are not comparing, that you are not interpreting the sound as the sound of a crow. You are listening purely to the sound, without interpretation, without identification, therefore not comparing. And that is the act of listening.

Now, if we are communicating with each other verbally—and that is all we can do—then you must not only hear the word—that is, the nature and the meaning of that word—but also listen without agreement or disagreement, without comparing, without interpreting; you must actually give complete attention. Then you will see for yourself, immediately, the whole significance of what is implied in that word *freedom.* One can understand it immediately. And all understanding, the act of understanding, is immediate, whether it is tomorrow or today. And the state of understanding is then timeless; it is not a gradual, accumulative process.

So, we are not merely communicating verbally with each other, but also we are actually listening to each other. You are listening to yourself as well as hearing the speaker. What the speaker is saying is irrelevant, but what you listen to is relevant—please, this is not being clever. Because it is the listener, you, that has to find out what is truth; and it is the listener that has to understand this whole structure, the anatomy, the depth, and the fullness of freedom. The speaker is merely verbally communicating. And if you merely hear the words and say, "This is your opinion, this is my opinion; I agree, I disagree; this is what Shankara or Buddha has said," then you and I are not communicating. Then we are merely indulging—at least you are—in opinions. So we must be very clear, from the very beginning, that we are not only hearing the verbal communication—the word, the meaning of the word, and the nature of the word—but are also listening.

So you have a double job—hearing the words and listening. Naturally, when you hear the word, the word has a meaning, and that meaning evokes certain responses, certain memories, certain reactions. And at the same time you have to listen without reaction, without opinion, without judgment, without comparison. So, your task is much greater than the speaker's; it is not the other way round, which most of us are used to; the speaker does all the work and you just listen, agree or disagree, and go away elated, amused, intellectually alerted; and such a state has no validity at all—you can just as well go to a cinema.

But the man who is serious has the seriousness that demands complete attention, an attention that will go right through. Such a man must know this art of listening. If you know the art of listening, there is nothing more to be said. Then you will listen to the crow, to the bird, to the whisper of the breeze among the leaves; and you will also listen to yourself, to the mutterings of your own mind, to your own heart, and to the intimation of your own unconsciousness. Then you are in a state of acute, intense listening, and therefore you are no longer indulging in opinions.

So, if you are at all serious, you would listen that way; and you must listen that way. Because, as I said, freedom is absolutely necessary for the understanding of what is truth. And without understanding it, life becomes very shallow, empty; you become merely mechanical. And in the act of understanding what is true—which is to listen—life begins anew.

Our minds are not fresh. Our minds have lived a thousand years—please do not bring in reincarnation; if you bring in reincarnation, you are not listening. When I used the words *thousand years,* I mean not only "you" but "man." You are the result of a thousand years of man. You are a vast consciousness; only you have appropriated a part of it, built a wall round it, enclosed it, and you say, "That is my individuality." And when I say "thousand years," I am not talking of that enclosure—a barbed wire enclosure which most people are. I am talking of that state of consciousness which is immense, wide, which has had a thousand experiences, and which has been encrusted, burdened, weighted down by tradition, by knowledge, by every form of hope, fear, despair, anxiety, agony, greed, ambition—not only the ambition of the enclosed, but also the ambition of "man." So our minds are made dull by the past—again, that is a psychological fact; it is not your opinion against mine.

So, with that mind, with that psyche which has experienced, which has retained every scar, every memory, every movement of thought as memory—with that you approach life. Or, with that you approach that thing which you want to discover—what is truth? And obviously, you cannot. Like for anything else, you must have a fresh mind. To look at a flower, though you may have seen it for the last ten years, to look at that flower anew, as though you were seeing it for the first time in your life, you must have a fresh mind—a fresh, innocent, tremendously alert mind. Otherwise, you cannot see—you see only the memories which you have projected into that flower, but you do not see the flower. Please do understand this.

Once you understand the act of seeing as the act of listening, you will have grasped something extraordinary in your life; it will never leave you again. As our minds are so jaded, made dull by society, by circumstances, by our own fears, despairs, by all the brutalities, the insults, the pressures, the mind has become mechanical, dull, stupid, heavy. And with that mind we want to understand; obviously we cannot.

So the question is: Is it possible to be free of that? Otherwise, you cannot see even the flower. I do not know if, when you get up early in the morning, you see the Southern Cross—the stars in the heavens. If you have at all looked at the sky—which I doubt—perhaps you have seen the stars, you know their names, you have placed them. And after seeing them for a few years, a few days, or a few weeks, you have forgotten, and you say, "This is Jupiter, Mars, this and that." But to wake up in the morning, look out of the window or step into the street and see it afresh with unclouded eyes, with an untrammeled mind—then only can you understand the beauty and the depth and the silence that is between you and that. Then only can you see. And for that, you must be free; you cannot bring all your experience, and look.

So, our question then is: Is it possible to be free of knowledge? Knowledge is the immediate past which accumulates. Every experience that you have is translated and stored and recorded; and with that record you approach the next experience. And, therefore, you never understand experience; you are merely translating each challenge according to the response of the past and, therefore, strengthening the record. This is what is taking place in the electronic brain, in the computer. Only we are a poor imitation of the mechanical, wonderful instrument called the computer. Is it possible to be free? Otherwise, you cannot possibly find out what is truth—you might talk about it everlastingly as the politicians quote the Gita. So, you have to inquire. And the inquiry is not verbal, intellectual; but it is the state of mind that is listening.

Knowledge becomes our authority—as tradition, as experience, as what you have read, as what you have learned, and as the authority asserted by those who say they know. The moment you say you know, you do not know! Truth is not something you can know about. It has to be perceived from moment to moment—as the beauty of the tree, the sky, the sunset. So, knowledge becomes the authority which guides, which shapes, which gives us courage, which gives us the strength to go on. Please follow all this because we have to understand the anatomy of authority—the authority of the government, the authority of the law, the authority of the policeman, the psychological authority which is your own experiences and the traditions that have been handed down, consciously or unconsciously; they become the guide, they become a warning signal as to what to do and what not to do. It is all in the realm of memory. And that is what we are actually. Our mind is the result of a thousand experiences with their memories and with their scratches, of the traditions handed down by society, by religion, and of the traditions of education. With that mind so burdened with memory, we try to understand something which cannot be understood through memory. So one has to be free from authority.

I do not know if you understand the meaning of that word *authority.* The meaning of that word in itself, is "the origin; one who originates something new." Look at your own religion! I don't know if you are at all a religious person—probably you are not. You mutter a lot of words, go to the temple, repeat some words—which you call religious. Now what an extraordinary weight of tradition the so-called spiritual leaders and saints have established in your minds—the Gita, the Upanishads, Shankara, and other interpreters of the Gita! These interpreters take their stand on the Gita and interpret, and you go on interpreting. And that interpretation you consider to be most extraordinary, and the one who interprets you call a religious man. But that person is conditioned by his own fears; he worships a particular stone, either made by the hand or by the mind! That tradition is driven into you through the propaganda of a thousand years—not through recent propaganda—and you accept it; and that shapes your thinking.

So, if you would be free, you have to wipe away all that—wipe away Shankaras, Buddhas, all the religious books and teachers—and be yourself, to find out. Otherwise, you cannot know the extraordinary beauty and the significance of what is truth, and you will never know what love is.

So, can you, who have been shaped by Shankaras, by the many saints, by the temples, wipe them all out? You have to wipe them out. You have to stand completely alone, unaided, without despair, without fear; only then can you find out. But to wipe away, to deny totally—not negatively to say, "Let it go," but to deny completely—you have to understand this whole anatomy and structure, the being of authority; you have to understand the man that seeks authority. You cannot remove authority from the man who wants it because that is his only solace, that is his bread and butter—as it is of the politician, of the priest, or of the philosopher. But if you want to understand the extraordinary thing called truth, you must have no authority. Because it is only the fresh mind, the innocent mind, the young, vibrant mind, that can understand these things, not the mind driven, shaped, weakened, burdened by the past. Either it is so, or it is not so. Either you say, "It is not possible to be free of the past, this knowledge, this authority which the mind seeks because of its own poverty, because of its own despair, as something to lean on; the mind can never be free from authority, the past, the things that it has learned, acquired, amassed." Or you say that the mind can be free of the past. But you have to find out; you cannot say that it can be free, or that it cannot be free—that is merely indulging in an opinion, and that is absolutely worthless; that has to be left to the philosophers. If you want to find out, you have to inquire into whether it is possible or not; you cannot accept or deny.

So you have to learn about knowledge and authority. When you are learning, there is no contradiction because you are learning. But if you are merely acquiring knowledge, then there is contradiction. Please do see this thing. If you are merely accumulating knowledge, then you will be in conflict because the thing which you are acquiring knowledge about is a thing living, moving, changing; and, therefore, between what you have accumulated and the reality, there is a contradiction. But if you are learning about it, then there is no contradiction; therefore, there is no conflict. Therefore the mind that is learning is gathering energy because it is not in a state of conflict. But when a mind is accumulating and from there adding, looking, observing from knowledge, then there is contradiction; then there is conflict and, therefore, dissipation of energy.

So the man who learns has no conflict, but the man who is merely gathering information in order to live according to a particular pattern established by himself or by his society or by some religious person whoever he is—that man is in contradiction and, therefore, in conflict.

And, as we said the other day, conflict is the very essence of disintegration. Conflict arises not only from the past but also in relation to the present. The conflict also arises when you have ideals—that you must be this or that you must be in such and such a state—marvelous, ennobling ideas. It is very important to understand the nature of an ideal. The ideal is not the reality. An idea, projected by a mind which is in conflict, becomes an ideal according to which it must live; and therefore the mind is in conflict, in contradiction. But a mind that is listening to a fact, not to an ideal—such a mind is not in conflict; and, therefore, it is moving from fact to fact. And therefore, such a mind is in a state of energy. And without this energy you cannot go very far. You are merely dissipating it in contradictions, in trying to become this and not that.

So you have to observe, you have to listen, you have to see the fact—the *what is*—and remain with that fact. And this is an extraordinarily difficult thing to do.

Obviously you have not thought about all this, or it does not come to you naturally, as the rains come out of the sky. You are hearing this, probably for the first time, or you have read about it. As the speaker has talked about it many times, you say, "Well, he is back to his old words." But if you are listening, if you are aware of what the speaker intends, then you will see as a fact that what you have is knowledge, and you will remain with that. The fact is that you are completely the past in relation to the present; the past may be modified, changed, but still you are always moving, being, in the past.

Now, what do we mean by "to live with that fact"? That is, not to accept it, not to deny it, but to listen to it—to listen to all the subtle movements, intimations, the questions, the answers it prompts; not to deny it because you cannot, because then you may end up in an asylum. That is what it means actually to observe the fact and to live with it.

Now, when you live with something—with your wife, with your children, with a tree, with your idea—either you get accustomed to it so that it no longer exists, or you live with it, observing everything. The moment you get accustomed to something, you become insensitive. If I get used to this tree, then I am insensitive to this tree. If I am insensitive to the tree, I am also insensitive to the dirt as well as to the people; I am insensitive to everything. But to be attentive to something is not to get used to it, not to get used to the dirt, the squalor, the family, the wife, the children. Not to get used to something requires a great deal of attention and, therefore, energy. I hope you are following this.

So, a mind that would understand what is true has to comprehend, not ideationally, the whole significance of what is freedom. Freedom is not liberation in some heavenly world, but it is the freedom of every day, the freedom from jealousy, the freedom from attachment, the freedom from ambition, the freedom from competition—which is the 'more', "I must be better; I am this and I must become that." But, when you observe what you are, there is no becoming something else than what you are; then there is an immediate transformation of that *which is.*

So, a mind that will go very far must begin very near. But you cannot go very far if you merely verbalize on something that man has created as truth, as God. You must begin very near and lay the foundation. And even to lay that foundation, there must be freedom. And, therefore, you lay your foundation on freedom, in freedom—thus, it is no longer a foundation; it is a movement, it is not something static.

It is only when the mind has understood the extraordinary nature of knowledge, freedom, and learning that conflict ceases; only then does the mind become very clear, precise. It is not caught in opinions, in judgments; it is in a state of attention, and therefore it is in a state of complete energy and learning. It is only when the mind is still that it can learn—not "learn about what?" It is only the still mind that can learn, and what is important is not what it learns about but the state of learning, the state of silence in which it is learning.

January 15, 1964

Third Talk in Madras

I would like this evening to talk about fear. One has to go into it deeply and not merely find some superficial remedy or a concept or an ideal to be applied as a means of getting rid of fear—which is never possible. I would like not only to go into it verbally but also to go beyond the word and inquire nonverbally if it is at all possible to be utterly free from fear, both the biological, physiological fear as well as the psychological fear.

For most of us, the word plays an important part. We are slaves to words. Our thinking is verbal, and without words, it is hardly possible to think. Perhaps there is a thinking which is nonverbal, but to understand the nonverbal thinking, we must be free of the word, the symbol, the verbal thinking. But for most of us, the word, the symbol, plays an extraordinarily important part in our life. And the mind is a slave to words—words like *an Indian, a Hindu, a Brahmin,* this or that. And to go into this question of fear very deeply, one must not only understand the meaning of the word but also free the mind of the word—if it is possible—and thereby understand profoundly the significance of fear.

To inquire very deeply, there must be a sense of humility—not as a virtue. Humility is not a virtue, it is a state of being—you are or you are not. You cannot come by it, you cannot cultivate it; you cannot be vain and put a layer of humility on that vanity—as most of us try to do. We are going to learn about fear. And to learn about fear and its extraordinary importance in life, its darkness and its dangers, one must learn about it. And, therefore, there must be that state of unapprehensive, unrewarded, not-sought-after humility.

For most of us virtue is merely a thing that we cultivate as a means of resistance to all the demands of our own desires as well as the demands of a particular society in which one happens to be. But virtue is something not within the field of time. It cannot be accumulated, it cannot be cultivated. It is, for example, "being good," not "becoming good." The two things are entirely different. To flower in goodness is entirely different from becoming good. Becoming good is a means of a reward or punishment or resistance; in that, there is no flowering.

In the same way, there must be humility as an immediate state, but not as a state that you acquire. It is only that state that can comprehend, understand and learn. Because there is only learning, and not being taught and acquiring information—especially with regard to nontechnological matters. You can acquire information, knowledge, about mathematics. But you have to learn about fear, not from books, not from psychological study, but through observation of oneself. And you cannot learn if there is no humility. So, one has to be both the teacher and the disciple for oneself, the disciple being the mind that learns. The person with the mind that learns is not a disciple that submits, accepts, follows. The person who submits, follows, is not seeking truth; he is merely conforming to a pattern of good behavior which, he hopes, will ultimately reward him by giving him what he calls truth.

So, humility is something that is a state of mind in which there is no fear. Humility is different from respect. You can respect another, and because you respect, there is no disrespect. You respect the governor, the prime minister, and kick your servant; in that, there is disrespect. So, humility has nothing whatsoever to do with respect; it is a quality of the mind. And it is only a mind that has humility that can learn. Therefore, it is only humility that can follow precisely every movement of thought. Because the mind is in a state of learning, it is in a state of attention, not concentration. We will discuss attention and concentration at another time when we talk about meditation.

We are talking this evening about fear. We are inquiring whether it is at all possible—not verbally, not ideationally, not theoretically, but actually—to be deeply, fundamentally, radically free of fear. I do not know if you have ever put that question to yourself—probably you have not. We accept fear, psychological fear, as inevitable, and therefore try to suppress it, or try to run away from it. But when you do put that question whether it is at all possible to be completely, totally free of fear, you discover something extraordinary for yourself, which is a state of mind that has not only humility but a quality of being completely in a state of innocency. We are going to talk about it this evening.

We are talking of fear, not about any fear. There is fear of various kinds, outwardly and inwardly, inside the skin and outside the skin. Outside the skin there is danger. Fear means danger—danger of losing a job, danger of death, an accident; fear of not having a particular position, not fulfilling, not having enough money; fear of poverty, discomfort, disease, pain. Physical pain one can fairly deal with; there is a remedy—the doctor or the acceptance of a particular pain. One accepts a physical pain when one is conscious or aware that the physical pain does not distort the mind, does not make thought bitter, anxious, and when the mind is watching itself so that it does not create, or is not afraid of, a future pain. One can deal with all that fairly intelligently, with fair balance and understanding. But we are talking about psychological fear which is much more complex, which needs astonishing inquiry and attention to go into. Because one can see very well that if there is any kind of fear in any form, psychologically, it distorts all perception.

As I said the other day, you are not merely listening, you are not merely hearing words, but you are listening and hearing at the same time. The speaker is merely using words to communicate. The nature of the word and the understanding of the word depend on both of us. But the art of listening is entirely yours. If you merely listen to the words and do not go directly where those words indicate, then you are stopping at hearing the words and proceeding no further. And as I said, we are learning. To learn there must be humility, and to learn one must listen, one must hear. To hear, to listen, to penetrate requires attention in which there is no resistance. That is, you hear the sound of that horn of the motorcar, of the crow, of the coughing; and at the same time you are so attentive that you hear the word and you comprehend the meaning of that word intellectually, through your ears and all the nervous system and all the rest of it; and also there is the state of learning. And it is only such a mind that can go profoundly into this question of love.

We all have fear of various kinds, psychologically. Most of us have uneasily accepted them because we have found no way. We know various forms of fear: fear of death; fear of public opinion; fear of not being able inwardly to achieve, to gain, to arrive, to fulfill in something; the fear of not conforming; the fear established by an ideal. Please follow this a little bit. Most of us are rather simple idealists—simple in the sense "without much thought behind it." We are conformists, the yes-sayers, but never the no-sayers. We are conforming and we are driven by society to conform, to imitate, to comply.

This is what is happening in this country at the present time. You have all been ideationally nonviolent. You have accepted it verbally—perhaps not actually. But you have preached it, moralized about it endlessly. The saints, the politicians, and all the people who want to do good politically, have preached this thing all over the world, beginning as a means of a political instrument and action. You have accepted and followed it for years as an ideal. And suddenly you have an incident, and you all become military-minded with equal eagerness. And nobody objects to this extraordinary contradiction. A whole generation that had accepted nonviolence is now being trained to accept violence!

Do you see the importance of this state of a mind that accepts the contradictions with equal ease? Surely such a mind, because it has accepted ideals, can be driven, like so many animals are driven. But a mind that is understanding fear has no ideals; therefore, it cannot be driven by any propaganda, by any politician, by any book, by any teacher, or by society. Such a mind, which is not driven or which is not conforming to a pattern of ideals, is facing each minute of every action and every thought, understanding every movement of thought and feeling, the actual, the factual, the *what is* which is much more significant than 'what should be'.

'What should be' is the ideal; therefore, it is nonexistent, illusory, it has no meaning whatsoever. But *what is,* the actual, is of immense significance; it is that alone that can be transformed, not 'what should be'. So, with complete understanding you will wipe away all ideals. Therefore there is one burden the less—not that you become something different. When you wipe away the ideal, you are actually confronted with the fact of *what is*—the fact that you are violent. And you can deal with that fact. But if you are all the time becoming nonviolent, pretending, hypnotizing yourself, you are in a state of delusion. And generally such people are neurotic. But a man who is completely aware of himself has no ideals; he moves from fact to fact—which is the psychological fact of himself, the *what is.*

So, one of the factors of fear has been removed. Please do understand the enormous significance of this. The moment you are free of ideals—which are nonexistent, which have no reality—you are confronted with *what is.* That is, you are violent; and when you are aware of yourself as being violent, you can deal with it; and there is no hypocrisy, there is no pretention, there is no putting on of a mask of nonviolence, with burning hatred inside! So if you understand that, not verbally but actually, then you are free of this extraordinary contradiction of 'what should be' and *what is.* And you have removed with one stroke this contradiction; and, therefore, you are able to face this whole problem of conformity. Then there is no conformity but only the understanding of the fact of violence.

Our society is based on violence—violence which is competition, ambition, each one out for himself, isolating himself. You may say, "You must love your neighbor"—it is excellent! But at the same time you cannot be ambitious. The two, love and ambition, do not go together because you are competing in your office for a better position, a better job, more money—you know the whole business of it!

So, you have to understand this process of ideals: how we project these ideals in order to escape from the fact, and the ideals encourage, bring about, conformity and contradiction and conflict and therefore bring about fear. You have to understand this whole structure of ideals. You cannot understand merely intellectually. There is no such thing as intellectual understanding; when you say, "I understand intellectually," you mean that you understand the meaning of the word. Understanding implies understanding totally with your mind, verbally, emotionally, intellectually, with all your being; and that understanding is complete, instantaneous. And if you understand this—about ideals, conformity, contradiction—then you have removed one major factor of fear.

Please, as the speaker talks, go into it yourself; do not merely hear the words and, just to agree, say, "What are you going to say next?" The next, what will come, I do not know yet; what will come will be equally difficult if you do not go into it yourself. We are moving, journeying together, lightening the mind from one of the major facts of fear.

Then, there is this whole question of discipline—which is, psychologically training ourselves to conform to a particular pattern, the so-called religious pattern or the moral pattern of a particular society. Discipline actually, verbally, means "to learn." I do not know if you have ever thought about discipline, if you have ever attempted disciplining yourself actually—not theoretically, but actually—to find out if you can discipline yourself, and what is entailed in it. If you have gone into it, you will see that there is resistance—resistance to a particular desire or to a particular want or to a particular impetus, urge; resistance or suppression which is control. All suppression, resistance, control, is contrary to learning. If I learn about something, anger for example, not only am I aware I am angry, but also I observe the cause, the causation of that anger—anger being the reaction and so on—I go into it, I understand it. In that process of understanding there is no resistance, there is no need to control, because out of that understanding comes a different kind of discipline which is the act of learning.

I do not know if you follow all this. What we need is a free mind, not a disciplined mind—disciplined in the ordinary sense of that word—not a mind trained to conform to a particular pattern. The disciplined mind is a dead mind; it is a bureaucratic, narrow, petty, little mind; it is never free. And it is only the free mind that can understand, go beyond, take an infinite journey within itself.

So, a mind that is merely disciplining itself—which is to resist, to control—is a mind that cannot possibly understand the nature of fear. We try to find the cause of fear. We say, "I am afraid because of that," and we think it is very important to find the cause of fear; but it is not at all important. We think that, by understanding the cause, we shall be rid of fear. If you observe, you will find that you may know the cause, but fear still goes on. So, the mere psychological search for the cause of fear is not the freeing of fear. That is one of the factors.

Then, there is the real factor that demands a great deal of understanding; and I am going to go into it now. There is, in all of us, the observer, the thinker, and the thought—two separate states; one is the thinker, the observer, the experiencer, and the other is the thing experienced, the thing observed, the thought. The two, as far as most of us are concerned, are separate; there is a tremendous division between the two. Please observe; do not accept or deny what is being said. Please observe yourself; allow the speaker to be merely a mirror in which you are observing so that you see the actual, not what you would like to see.

There is a division between the thinker and the thought. And then there arises the question: How to bridge between the thinker and the thought? The thought creates the idea, the idea being rationalized thought; or many rationalized thoughts are put together as an idea, as a conclusion, as a concept. There is the thinker, and there is the concept which he has formulated through thought and which becomes the pattern. Therefore the thinker separates the concept away from him. So there is the conflict between the thinker and the thought because he is always trying to correct the thought, to change it, to modify it, or to give it continuity.

Now, is this division actual? This division does exist. But is there such a thing as a thinker apart from thought? If you do not think at all, where is the thinker? Please, listen. I am not putting a rhetorical question for you to answer, to agree or disagree with. If you put it to yourself as you are doing now, you will have to find out if, when there is no thinking of any kind, there is any center from which to think. There is only thought, and thought creates the thinker for various psychological reasons, for security, as a means of further experience, as a center from which to act, and so on and so on.

So, there is this division between the thinker and the thought; and, therefore, there is conflict. As long as this division exists, there must be fear. The thinker is then trying to control fear, he is trying to dominate fear; he tries to resist fear, to get rid of it. Therefore he is always looking at it as though it is something apart from himself, and therefore he is never free of fear. So, again, that is a major cause of continuity of fear. As long as there is a division between the observer and the thing observed, there is contradiction, there is division. The fear is there, and he is here; and observing fear, he wants to get rid of it; therefore, he seeks all the methods of getting rid of fear.

If there is no thinker, but only the state of fear—the state of fear, not the entity that experiences fear—then you can understand it, go into it. I will go into it a little bit.

What is fear actually—the psychological fear? It is a state when you are aware of danger psychologically—of losing your wife, of losing a job, and so on. Psychologically, what is that fear? Surely, it is time. If there were no time, then there would be no fear. Because I can think about something—think about the danger, think about losing a job, think about death, think about the interval between the actuality and what might be—the lag of time is the cause of fear. If there were no time at all, if there were no tomorrow as when there is the thought "What will happen tomorrow?" if the mind were only concerned with the actual state of fear, then what would take place? There is chronological time by the watch. But if there is no psychological time, not only the time of tomorrow, but the time of yesterday—that is, if thought does not think about what might happen tomorrow, or if thought does not go back into what has happened and relate it to the present—then you are confronted not with fear but only with a state.

If you have observed in yourself, do you know what actually takes place when you are afraid, when there is psychological danger? Suppose I am afraid, for example, of being found out what I am. If you found out about me, I might lose my reputation, my position, and all the rest of it. So, I put on a mask. And behind that mask, there is always anxiety, a sense of guilt, a sense of watching, so as never to remove that mask so that you will see something behind. That is my actual state. What you see is the mask, not my state; but what is behind the mask is my actual state, and I am afraid of this. Now, what is going on? You are not sufficiently interested in me to remove the mask and look. Because you have your own masks, many of them, you are not concerned. But I am thinking that you might look. The "might," the future, and the past, that I have done something which you might discover—I am caught in time. The process of thinking has made this time, and in that time—which may be a split second or a day or ten years—thought is caught. Thought has created that time by thinking that you might look behind my mask. So, thought creates fear—fear comes because there is time. You cannot abolish it, you cannot say, "I shall not be afraid of time." You have to understand this extraordinarily subtle process.

Then, if you have gone sufficiently into the matter, you will also find that you really, actually, never experience that state of fear. It is not like standing at the edge of a precipice physically, or being confronted by a poisonous snake. There you are; it is there immediately, it demands an immediate response. But probably most of us have never confronted actually the state of fear because we come to it through words, and words create the fear. Please go with me. Take, for example, the word *death.* I am not talking of death; we will discuss it at another meeting. We are talking of the word, like *God,* like *death,* like *communism,* and so on. The word plays an extraordinarily important part. The word death evokes all kinds of images, all kinds of fears—the word or the symbol or the thing that you have seen in the street, the dead body which is a symbol. So, the word creates that fear.

So you understand what is involved in this extraordinary process of fear—word, time, ideal, discipline, conformity, and this division between the experiencer and the thing being experienced. All that is involved when you begin to inquire into fear, and you have to understand it totally, not in fragments. And if you have gone that far, you have to go much deeper still into this whole question of the conscious and the unconscious.

Most of us live on the surface. All our jobs, all our routine, all our sensations are on the surface. We never delve, go, to the very depth of our consciousness and find out. And to find out, the superficial mind which is always active must be quiet.

The mind has to be totally free of fear because if there is any shadow of fear at any level of your consciousness, unexplored, hidden, concealed, that will project an illusion that will darken. The mind that would really understand what is true, the real—the extraordinary state of mind that comprehends that thing called truth—must have, psychologically, no fear of any kind. There is the natural fear when you meet a snake, you jump away from it—that is quite natural; there must be that fear; otherwise, you will become neurotic; that is a normal reaction of a good, healthy mind. But we are talking of psychological fear, which is a neurotic state. A mind which would really understand, take a journey into the most extraordinary thing called reality and go deeply into it—where there is no measure, no time, no illusion, no imagination—must be completely free from fear. And, therefore, such a mind is always living, neither in the past nor in the future. Do not translate it immediately as a thing in the present, as some of the bigger philosophers, disappointed philosophers, talk about the present; that is to live completely in the present, to accept everything—good, bad, indifferent—in the present, to live there and make the best of it. I do not want to name the particular philosophy—what I have said is good enough; we know what it is.

So, a mind that is aware of all the things that are connected with fear is not concerned with the past, but as the past arises, it deals with it, not as a steppingstone to the future. Therefore such a mind is living in the active present, and therefore comprehends every movement of thought, feeling, fear, as it arises. There is a great deal to learn. There is no end to learning. Therefore, there is no despair, no anxiety. This you must have completely in your blood so that you are never caught in the things that have been done or that will be done in the future, so that you are never held in time as thought. It is only the mind that has emptied itself of all this fear that is empty. Then in that emptiness it can understand that which is supreme and nameless.

January 19, 1964

Fourth Talk in Madras

It seems to me that one of the major problems that confronts each one of us is an utter lack of intense feeling. We have a certain emotional, sustained excitement about activities—what should be done or what should not be done. But we are rather warm about things that really do not matter at all. And it seems to me that there is lack of passion—not for a particular end to be achieved, not for some objective to be gained. I am talking of the sense of an intense, strong feeling.

Most of us have petty minds—small, narrow minds fixed in a petty groove—that run along very smoothly unless there is some kind of an accident; and then there is trouble, and afterwards they get back under another routine. The petty mind cannot face problems. It has innumerable problems, the whole problem of living. And it invariably translates these extraordinarily significant problems of life into its own petty, narrow, limited understanding and tries to twist this enormous stream of existence, the stream of life, into its own petty, little channels. And that is what we are confronted with now—probably always. But it is much more so now, as the challenge is much greater and demands a response equally intense, equally strong, equally living.

This sense of passion is not a thing that you cultivate easily by taking some kind of a drug, getting into a hypnotic state about some ideals, and so on. This passion comes naturally—it must. I am using the word *passion* purposely. For most of us, passion is employed only with regard to one thing, sex; or you suffer passionately and try to resolve that suffering. But I am using the word passion in the sense of a state of mind, a state of being, a state of your inward core—if there is such a thing—that feels very strongly, that is highly sensitive—sensitive alike to dirt, to squalor, to poverty, and to enormous riches and corruption, to the beauty of a tree, of a bird, to the flow of water, and to a pond that has the evening sky reflected upon it. To feel all this intensely, strongly, is necessary. Because without passion life becomes empty, shallow, and without much meaning. If you cannot see the beauty of a tree and love that tree, if you cannot care for it intensely, you are not living. I am using the words "you are not living" deliberately because, in this country probably, religion is utterly divorced from beauty.

Without being sensitive to this extraordinary beauty of life, the beauty of a face, the line of a building, the shape of a tree, a bird on the wing, and the morning song—if one is not aware of all that, if one does not feel all that very strongly, obviously, life, which is cooperation and relationship, has no meaning at all; then one merely functions mechanically. So, I would like to talk about that, this evening.

That passion is not devotion, is not sentimentality; it has nothing to do with sensation. The moment passion has a motive, or is aroused by a motive, or is for something, it becomes pleasure and pain. Please see this; I do not have to go into details because I want to go further into this thing. If passion is aroused sexually or for some purpose, if passion has a cause, if it has an end in view, then in that so-called passion there is frustration, there is pain, there is the demand for the continuity of pleasure and therefore the fear of not having it, and the avoidance of pain. So, a passion with a motive, or a passion which is aroused, invariably ends in despair, pain, frustration, anxiety.

We are talking about passion without a motive—which is quite a different thing. Whether it exists or not is for you to find out, but we know that passion aroused ends in despair, in anxiety, in pain, or in the demand for a particular form of pleasure. And in that there is conflict, there is contradiction, there is a constant demand. We are talking of a passion that is without motive. There is such a passion. It has nothing to do with personal gain or loss, or all the petty little demands of a particular pleasure and the avoidance of pain. Without that passion you cannot possibly cooperate, and cooperation is life, which is relationship. Such cooperation is not for an idea; you cooperate not because the state drives you, not for a reward, not for the avoidance of a punishment, not for working for some economic ideal, a utopia; you cooperate not for working together because of some ideal—all those, for us, are not conducive to cooperation.

I am talking of the spirit of cooperation. If we do not cooperate, there cannot be relationship. Life demands that you and I cooperate, do things together, work together, feel together, live together, see things together. And this "togetherness" must be at the same time, of the same intensity, at the same level; otherwise, there is no togetherness. And if one observes more and more this rather sad and destructive world, the mind is becoming mechanical, routine-bound, technologically held in a narrow groove. And therefore, gradually, the sense of intensity, the sense of feeling strongly about anything fades away. And if you cannot feel strongly, obviously the mind is insensitive, dull, fearful, and all the rest of it.

So, the passion we are talking about is a state of being. It is really quite extraordinary, if you go into it; it is not tinged with suffering, it has no self-pity, it has no sense of fear. And to understand it, we must understand desire. Especially all those people who have been brought up on religious ideas, religious sanctions in a particular society where apparently the so-called religion plays an important part, think that to realize what they call God, the mind must be without desire; they consider that desirelessness, to be without desire, is one of the primary, important things. Probably you know all the books talking about this, all the *slokas,* and all the rest of the business. We have killed all passion successfully, except in one direction—sexually. And, we have tamed desire. Society, religion, living together—we have made of all that a thing that has no vitality because we have the idea that a man, a being, a human entity that has got strong feelings verging on an intense desire, cannot possibly understand that which is so-called God.

What is wrong with desire? You all have it, either very strongly or in a weak, dull manner; everybody has desire of some kind or another. What is wrong with it? Why do we so easily agree to subjugate, to destroy, to pervert, to suppress desire? Because apparently desire brings conflict—the desire to have wealth, to have a position, to have fame, all the rest of it. And to achieve fame, to have possessions, to feel very strongly, implies conflict, disturbance; and we do not want to be disturbed. That is all what we are seeking essentially, deeply—not to be disturbed. But when we are disturbed, we try to find a way out of it, and settle back in a comforting state where nothing will disturb us.

So, for us, desire is a disturbance. Please follow this. These are all psychological facts—it is not a matter of whether you accept it or do not accept it, whether you agree or disagree. These are facts, not my facts. Desire then becomes a thing that must be controlled, that must be suppressed; and so all our effort goes into this—that, at any price, we are not to be disturbed, and that anything that disturbs must be suppressed, sublimated, or put aside.

Please, as we said the other day, as we keep repeating at every talk, what is important is not to hear the words but actually to listen. There is a great beauty in listening. This evening, there was a bird outside the window, a kingfisher. It had a large beak, brilliant feathers, intensely blue in color. It was calling; another bird of a similar kind, a kingfisher, far away, was answering. Just to listen to it—not to say, "That is a kingfisher. How beautiful!" or "How ugly!" "I wish that crow would stop cawing!"—I do not know if you have listened with that state of mind. Just listening, where there is no profit, where there is no utilitarian purpose, when you are not getting something, when you are not avoiding something. Or seeing the sunset, that brilliant glow of an evening, that Venus clear and the slip of a young moon—just to look at it and to feel it very strongly.

And if you do listen in that happy manner, with an ease, without any strain, then that very act of listening is a miracle. It is a miracle, because in that action, in that moment, you comprehend all of the act of listening, understanding, seeing; and you have broken down the walls, and there is space between you and the world and the thing you are listening to. And you must have this space to observe, to see, to listen; the wider, the deeper that space, the more beauty, the more depth there is. A different quality comes into being when there is this space between you and the thing that you are listening to.

I am not being poetical, sentimental, or romantic. But we do not know how to listen, just to listen—to the wife, or to the husband, who is nagging or quarreling or angry, who is bullying. If you just listen, you understand a great deal; then the heavens are wide open. Do it sometimes; do not try it, but do it, and you will find out for yourself.

In the same way, I hope you are listening. Because what we are talking about is something beyond the mere word. The word is not the thing. The word *passion* is not passion. To feel that and to be caught in it without any volition or directive or purpose, to listen to this thing called desire, to listen to your own desires which you have, plenty of them, weak or strong—when you do that, you will see what a tremendous damage you do when you suppress desire, when you distort it, when you want to fulfill it, when you want to do something about it, when you have an opinion about it.

Most people have lost this passion. Probably one has had it once in one's youth—to become a rich man, to have fame and to live a bourgeois or a respectable life; perhaps a vague muttering of that. And society—which is what you are—suppresses that. And so one has to adjust oneself to you who are dead, who are respectable, who have not even a spark of passion; and then one becomes a part of you, and thereby loses this passion.

To understand this whole problem of desire, we must understand effort. Because from the moment we go to school until we die, we are making effort; our mind, our psyche, is a battleground. There is never a moment of quietness, ease, freedom; we are always battling, striving, pushing, gathering, avoiding, accumulating—this is our life! I am not describing something which is not. Our life is a constant effort. I do not know if you have not noticed that when you do not make an effort—which does not mean you stagnate, which does not mean you go to sleep—when your whole being is without effort, then you see things very clearly, very sharply, with a vitality, with an energy, with a passion.

And we make effort because we are driven by two or more contrary desires. We are always opposing one desire by another desire, the desire to have and the desire not to have—if you are at all caught! But if you have one desire, then there is no problem. You pursue that one desire ruthlessly, logically or illogically, and with all the things entailed—pain, pleasure. But most of us, being a little civilized—not too much civilized—have these contrary desires, and so there is a battle.

There is this religious sanction that you must be without desire—the pattern, the ideal laid down by this teacher or that teacher, by this guru or that guru, repeating, repeating. There is that pattern established in the consciousness through centuries of propaganda which you call religion. And also there is the desire, your own instinctual desire of everyday demands, pressures, strains. So there is a contradiction between the two. And you have to suppress the one and accept the other, or deny the other and pursue the one that you have—all that implies effort.

For me, every act of volition, that is, every act of desire—and desire is a reaction—must entail effort and contradiction, and therefore implies a mind broken, torn between innumerable desires. For example, you see something, a car, a beautiful car; you touch it sensationally; then you have the desire to possess it. Or you may have any other form of desire—you can observe for yourself how desire comes into being. When any desire arises in you, you are also aware of the traditional desire to suppress it—which is deeply rooted in all people. But as the desire arises, you have to be aware of it, to understand it, to listen to all the promptings—to listen, not to deny it, not to suppress it, not to put it aside, not to run away from it. You cannot run away from desires.

All the saints and all the yogis are driven, torn by desire. When they put on their loincloth and ashes, they think they lead a very simple life. Not a bit of it—inside they are boiling, of which they are conscious or unconscious; and they do not know what to do. And so they make their life and their society with their saints an ugly, brutal, venomous thing full of hatred. Because, if you do not understand desire, you create enmity, you have antagonisms. And no amount of preaching brotherhood has any meaning at all if you do not understand this extraordinarily simple thing called desire. If you deny desire, if you say, "I have had an experience with that desire, and I must no longer have it," then you are merely comparing it, the living desire, with something which you already had—which has become a memory which is going to control—and you are caught again in the battle.

But as each desire arises—it does not matter if it is for a most simple thing—you have to watch it coming, living, flowering, getting new vitality. And if you do not suppress it, if you do not compare it, if your past memory of that particular experience does not dominate it, and if you can look at it with that space, then you will see that particular desire is being transformed into an intensity of feeling without an object, into a feeling. But for most of us will is necessary, or at least we think will is necessary. Will is the cord twisted of many desires. And the moment you have the will to do or the will to deny, you are in a state of resistance. And, therefore, you are back again in a state of conflict.

What we are talking about is a mind that is mature, that has understood conflict. A mind that has understood conflict, that has understood this whole question of desire with all its problems, that has matured—only such a mind can understand what is real, what is true. No other mind, not the mind that has suppressed desire, can understand what is real. Because to understand what is true, you must have passion. Passion is this extraordinary thing that drives you, not aroused, not pushed by some desire. That is a flame, and without that you cannot bring about a change in the world because the world is full of problems.

And, as you are a part of the world, you are full of problems—the little quarrels with your wives, with your husbands; the brutality, the problem of starvation in this country, in the East, in Asia; the problems of war; the thing called peace; the problem of cooperation. There are problems; you cannot avoid them. They are there every minute; consciously or unconsciously, they are impinging on your mind. Either you understand them as they arise, as you are conscious of them—that is, you resolve them immediately—or you carry them over for the next day. The carrying over for the next day is the real problem—not whether you solve the problem or not. Because when you carry them over for the next day, that is what makes the mind dull, stupid; you give time for the problem to take root in your mind. Therefore, you give strain, stress to the brain cells, and the brain cells get tired. A brain that is tired cannot possibly understand. You need a fresh mind each day. So you have to understand problems—not carry them over.

And to understand a problem, the first thing is not to say, "I must resolve it, I must find an answer, I must find a way out of it; how am I to find the right answer to it?"—

not to worry like a dog with a bone. That is all that you do, and the more you worry, the more you think you are serious! Please observe your own minds, your own life, not what the speaker is saying. And to resolve problems—to resolve them, not to carry them over—you have to look at them; you have to be sensitive enough to observe the implications, the meaning, the inwardness of a problem. That means you have to listen to it—to listen to all the whispers, to all the significance of a problem, not merely verbally, but to see, to feel, to touch the problem with your eyes, with your nose, with your ears, with your whole being. That means not to be caught in the word which points to the problem. I do not know if you understand that the word is not the problem. The word *tree* is not the tree. But, for most of us, the word is important, not the thing behind the word; the symbol has much more significance than the fact.

So a mind has to be alert, alive, watching, listening to every problem. The problem is there, and you cannot deny a problem. A problem means a response to a challenge, and you respond either totally, completely, or inadequately. The inadequate response to the challenge creates the problem. You are not all the time awake, you cannot be aware, you cannot be sensitive all the twenty-four hours of the day; so, your responses are inadequate, and this creates the problem; and then you do not meet the problem immediately. To meet completely the immediate problem—the thought, the feeling—is not to try to solve it, not to run away from it, not to compare it, not to say, "This is the way to solve it"—all the murmurings, the stupid things the mind and the brain go through hoping to understand the problem. To meet it completely is to listen to it, to be sensitive. And you cannot be sensitive if you are running away, if you are suppressing, if you have an answer to the problem.

So we begin to see that the mind has to be alert and sensitive. I am using the word ***mind*** as the interplay between the brain and the thing that controls the brain; the mind is not only the nerves, the brain cells, but that which is both beyond and made up of the cells—the total thing. The mind which most of us have is so burdened, heavy with innumerable problems, and every day we add more to them. And so our whole being becomes dull, and we lose all sensitivity. And when we are not sensitive, we make effort. Please see the vicious circle that we are caught in.

So, the understanding of desire is necessary. You have "to understand desire," not "to be without desire." If you kill desire, you are paralyzed. When you look at that sunset in front of you, the very looking is a delight, if you are at all sensitive. That is also desire—the delight. And if you cannot see that sunset and delight in it, you are not sensitive. If you cannot see a rich man in a big car and delight in that—not because you want it but you are just delighted to see a man in a big car—or if you cannot see a poor, unwashed, dirty, uneducated human being in despair and feel enormous pity, affection, love, you are not sensitive. How can you then find reality if you have not this sensitivity and feeling?

So you have to understand desire. And to understand every prompting of desire, you must have space, and not try to fill the space by your own thoughts or memories, or how to achieve, or how to destroy that desire. Then out of that understanding comes love. Most of us do not have love, we do not know what it means. We know pleasure, we know pain. We know the inconsistency of pleasure and, probably, the continuous pain. And we know the pleasure of sex and the pleasure of achieving fame, position, prestige, and the pleasure of having tremendous control over one's own body as the ascetics do, keeping a record—we know all these. We are everlastingly talking about love, but we do not know what it means because we have not understood desire, which is the beginning of love.

Without love there is no morality—there is conformity to a pattern, a social or a so-called religious pattern. Without love there is no virtue. Love is something spontaneous, real, alive. And virtue is not a thing that you beget by constant practice; it is something spontaneous, akin to love. Virtue is not a memory according to which you function as a virtuous human being. If you have no love, you are not virtuous. You may go to the temple, you may lead a most respectable family life, you may have the social moralities—but you are not virtuous. Because your heart is barren, empty, dull, stupid, because you have not understood desire. Therefore life becomes an endless battleground, and effort ends always in death. Effort always ends in death because that is all you know.

So, a man who would understand desire has to understand, has to listen to every prompting of the mind and the heart, to every mood, to every change of thought and feeling, has to watch it; he has to become sensitive, become alive to it. You cannot become alive to desire if you condemn it or compare it. You must care for desire because it will give you an enormous understanding. And out of that understanding, there is sensitivity. You are then sensitive not only physically to beauty, to the dirt, to the stars, to a smiling face, or to tears, but also to all the mutterings, the whispers that are in your minds, the secret hopes and fears.

And out of this listening, watching, comes passion, this passion which is akin to love. And it is only this state that can cooperate. And also it is only this state that can, because it can cooperate, know also when not to cooperate. Therefore, out of this depth of understanding, watching, the mind becomes efficient, clear, full of vitality, vigor; and it is only such a mind that can journey very far.

January 22, 1964

Fifth Talk in Madras

This evening, I would like—if I may—to talk about time, sorrow, and death. It is a wide field to cover in an hour. And at all times, communication is difficult. To commune with one another requires a certain intensity, a meeting of two minds at the same level, at the same time, and with the same intensity; otherwise, communion is not possible. We may intellectually or verbally agree or disagree, but that is not communion. Communion is a relationship which is extraordinarily intense. And that intensity must exist between two minds, at the same time and at the same level; otherwise, communion becomes merely verbal or interpretative or superficial.

To talk about death, sorrow, and time requires an infinite patience. Patience is not the thing that you cultivate in order to acquire a certain technique or to form a certain habit. To go very deeply into anything, especially psychologically, you require a certain quality of the mind that is willing to go step by step and not come to any conclusion at any time, not conceive or formulate at any time, but merely proceed from observation to observation, from clarity of understanding to further clarity of understanding. I am using the word *patience* in that sense. That requires an extraordinary state of mind—not a superficial mind that agrees or disagrees or, while hearing, compares with what it has read or heard; such a mind is not in a state of communion.

We have to talk about something, this evening, which requires an astonishing amount of attention—not concentration—an attention in which there is no exclusion, even of that noise, and in which that hideous noise is not allowed to interfere. Then only, in that state of attention, we can commune and go into something which is extraordinarily difficult.

But, to understand anything one must directly experience it, not verbally. Actually to experience something demands that you and I be together and have the same look, the same ear, the same eye, the same voice to understand; otherwise, you and I are not at the same point, at the same level, with the same intensity. We have to understand this problem of "time." Because, without understanding it, we shall not understand the extraordinary thing called death.

I mean by the word *understand* not a verbal, intellectual, fragmentary comprehension, or an informed mind which has gathered a lot of information and compares, judges, evaluates from what it has gathered—such a mind is not in a state of understanding; it is not capable of understanding. Again understanding is another strange phenomenon of the mind. You understand only when you totally listen, completely, with all your being, with your mind, with your heart, with your body, with your eyes, with your nerves, completely—then only you understand something totally. And unfortunately, we never give ourselves to understanding. We have never given ourselves to anything.

You have to give yourself completely to this comprehension of time, sorrow, and death. And you cannot give yourself if there is no understanding of fear, of time. Death must be a very strange phenomenon as life is. And to understand it, to go into it, with your heart and not with your words, you require a mind that is sharp, clear, that can reason logically, sanely, with complete confidence—not the speaker's confidence but your confidence. Otherwise, you cannot take a journey into this strange land, and if you cannot take the journey, you have not lived.

So, we are going to talk about time. Probably, most of you have not thought about it at all, or if you have thought about it, you have thought what will happen to you tomorrow or ten years later. You have not thought about it, probably, as a factor in life. By the word *time* I mean psychological time, but not chronological time which is by the watch—as yesterday, today, and tomorrow, the next hour, and what you are going to do after this meeting. Probably you have thought about that because you were forced to, but you have not gone beyond to inquire into, to find out for yourself, the tremendous significance of time. We have never brought time to a crisis. We have always avoided it. We have never felt our way into this thing called the past, the present, and the future, this continued existence as the past, the present, and the future, with all the turmoil, anxieties, guilt, pain, joy, and all the other things which the human mind goes through, through this period of time as yesterday, today, and tomorrow.

And without fully comprehending the significance of time, you will not be able to understand what is sorrow. And where there is sorrow, there is no love; and without love you will never understand what is death. So you have to take the journey with the speaker—not verbally, because that is very superficial and has no meaning whatsoever. You have to take the journey with all your being, without any resistance or agreement, completely giving yourself over to that understanding.

Time, for most of us, is a movement as the past expressing itself in the present, conditioning the future. And also time is a gradual process of achievement. We use time to postpone; we use time as a means of change from this to that. And can there be no time at all? Time exists only for a man who thinks in terms of the past through the present into the future—his achievements, his cultivation of virtue, capacity, learning techniques, and so on; all those remain at the level of achievement, development, and gathering. So, we use time, and a mind that is caught in such usage of time cannot understand this—that there is probably no time at all.

Consider a man who has been to his office for thirty or forty years of his life as a scientist, as an engineer, as a physicist, as a bureaucrat. How can such a man who has given himself to the office for this period of forty years, understand something which is not the office, the routine? His brain cells are used up, warped, twisted, worn out; and they are not fresh, young, eager, alert, alive. His reactions are slow. He has been ambitious, he has been driven by ambition, greed, position, power; and he has used time. Time has withered him, time has made his mind go into decay. Such a mind—most of our minds are like that—when it approaches this problem of time, is incapable of understanding the full meaning of it. But such a mind has to understand time, and it can only understand when it is aware of the problem and aware that it has been destroyed by forty years of office routine. When such a mind realizes that, it can bring the whole of time into one minute and comprehend it completely—that is to bring time to a crisis.

Time is continued existence—what has been, what will be, and what is. That is all we know. Our memories, our experiences, the things that we have heard and stored up, the experiences that we met with in the past, which give more strength to the past—all that gives us continuity of existence. The memory, the pleasure, the pains, the insults, the angers, the brutalities, the venomous states of hatred, envy, jealousy, the competition, the ambitious drive, and ruthless desire—this continuity of existence is what we call life. We never bring this whole existence into one minute and clear it, but we keep on repeating, repeating, repeating. And what we call life is caught up in the net of time, and so there is always tomorrow full of pain, anxiety, and sorrow.

And time is what gives pain and pleasure. For thought has continuity. You think about something that gives you pleasure, and you keep on thinking about it—either it is sexual, or it is your position, or it is the thing that you are going to achieve. The thinking about it gives it continuity—as when you think about pain, how to avoid it, and so on—that thinking gives continuity to pain. Please observe yourself—observe how you give continuity to the existence which you call life, which is full of anxiety, despair, agony, with passing pleasures, because you think constantly about it; therefore, you live in time, in psychological time. Therefore, the past—with all its memories, with all the scars of pleasure, pain, with all the things that it has acquired, heard, the tradition—shapes the present, and the present shapes the future. So we become slaves to time.

You have to find out for yourself—you are not to be told—if there is time at all. If actually you had no tomorrow, your whole life would be transformed immediately; then you would throw away all the rubbish from your minds, all the things that you have acquired, learned, heard; and you will be so tremendously active—then you have no time; and therefore, there is no time.

A mind that has no time can then look at death with quite different eyes. Then death is not something in the distance, an interval of years, with old age, with all the agonies and pains; it is not over there and you over here—it is this space which is time. It is this "time" that you dread, that you are afraid of, not of death. And time brings decay; it does not enrich, it does not mature. Do not compare it to the fruit of a tree—for that, you need time; there you need sunshine, rain, darkness, nourishment; and then when the fruit is ripe, it drops. But we have no time. If you look to time, you are caught in sorrow.

Then you are thinking in terms of what has been, what will be, what must be. And to understand sorrow, with its pain—physical pain, emotional anxiety, the sorrow of someone whom you have lost, and the pain of it—you must not look to time, you must have no time.

I do not know if you have gone through sorrow. But most of us avoid sorrow, or worship sorrow, or accept it. You go into any church in Europe or in this country, and you see how sorrow is worshiped! And here, in this country, you have explanations for sorrow, karma and so on; you have never objected, totally, with all your being, to be in sorrow. You have accepted sorrow—and that is the sad part of sorrow.

What is sorrow? Have any of you really known any sorrow? The word *sorrow* has its memories—the memory of self-pity, the memory of the things that have been, the things that you did or did not do with your friend, with your wife, or with your child, whoever it is. The memory, the picture, the word, the symbol, creates that feeling of sorrow; and then we say, "We must avoid it, we must find out a reason for it"; then we are going to invent, then we look to the future as a means of conquering something. If there were no time at all, no tomorrow, then you would not accept sorrow, then you have no time to think at all—for thought breeds sorrow. I do not know if you have noticed that either sorrow is personal or it is the sorrow of man—man who has suffered, who has been driven, who has been bullied, who has been made to do things and believe and accept through propaganda of a thousand years or ten thousand years. There is sorrow of man as a whole, and there is the sorrow of a particular human being. My son dies; I have a picture of him in my mind. I have invested in him all my hope, my pleasures; it is 'me' continuing in that person, and he dies. And I am being bereft of everything that I had; I find myself suddenly alone, suddenly lonely.

Do you know what it means to be lonely? Have you ever experienced actually that state of complete isolation in which there is no relationship to anything, no identification with another—your wife, your children, your country—in which you are completely cut off from everything? When you feel lonely, your past has no meaning, your experiences have lost their significance; your job, your family means nothing; though you are surrounded by a crowd, you have no relationship with anything. I do not know if you have ever been through that state of loneliness. If you have not, you will never know the end of sorrow. Because that is the path that is part of you—this intense, complete isolation, this loneliness. And from this loneliness we are always, consciously or unconsciously, escaping—through drink, through sex, through gods, through prayers, through every form of deceit.

And this loneliness has to be understood. Every one of us, in his secret mind, knows loneliness—not in the sense of experiencing but in the sense of knowing it verbally through intimations, through occasional glimpses of it. He knows it but cannot understand it, cannot live with it, cannot cope with it; he runs away and tries to fulfill in so many ways. But this thing goes on relentlessly; it is there. So, when my son dies, I am confronted with that; I translate my sorrow into every form of escape from that. You know all the dozen escapes—I think about meeting my son in heaven, I have conclusions, explanations such as reincarnation! Again time comes in—that is, I will meet him, I will do this with him, it is my karma, it is that, it is this. By escaping, you have admitted time. And the moment you admit time, you admit sorrow, and therefore sorrow and time bring about decay, deterioration of the mind.

So, when there is sorrow, one must not escape from loneliness but understand it completely. Do you know what it means to live with something, unpleasant or pleasant? It requires a great deal of energy to live with something. To live with a tree, with a family, with squalor, with dirt, with anything, you need tremendous energy; otherwise, you get used to it. Probably you have got used to the sunset, to the water of the river when it is calm, when the sky is upon it. When you have got used to something, you no longer notice it. The moment you have got used to it, you are not living. And that is what we do.

We put up with governments, with our families, with our quarrels, with our sorrows, with dirt, with squalor, with misery, with everything, because we have got used to them. First there is a shock, pain; and then gradually we find ways and means of getting used to it which is time. I get used to my son's death; therefore, I have accepted sorrow; and, therefore, out of that comes self-pity. If there is no self-pity at all, then you will be understanding sorrow, you will grapple with it immediately because sorrow must end.

And the ending of sorrow is the beginning of wisdom. You cannot gather wisdom from books, from attending schools. Wisdom comes to a man only with the ending of sorrow. That means you have to understand this problem of thought and time. We like sorrow! If you took down the picture of that one whom you loved from the wall of your room or from the wall of your mind, you would think it would be a terrible thing. You really do not love that person; you love the memory of him who, at one time, was pleasant. You do not think about him, of all his stages, your quarrels with him, your anxieties, your competition. All that, you do not have. You would just have the one picture that you like, and you do not want to let that go. Because if you let it go, you are by yourself, lonely, lost; and so sorrow begins again.

But a man who rejects sorrow, who would not accept it, who has no philosophy, no church, no formulas, no beliefs—it is only such a man that can look at this extraordinary thing called sorrow. And to end sorrow, one must go into this whole question of memory and understand where memory is necessary and where memory is detrimental. If one has traveled so far, not verbally but actually, then one can face death.

There is the old age and the pain of old age—the physical faculties deteriorating. But we have spent forty years in an office, grinding away, and our mind has lost its quickness, freshness. Even in youth, we have lost it. Please observe yourself. Don't listen to the speaker; what the speaker is saying has very little value if you are not actually observing yourself. So you have to observe your own process of thinking, not rejecting it, not condemning it, but watching the flow, the actual process of your own thinking.

We have never gone into the question of death. We have always found beliefs, consolations, ideas, and formulas which will protect us against death. But death is there for everybody—from the greatest philosophers to the poor woman on the street. For most people, death is something away from life, because they have not understood life. Life is an extraordinary field in which we live. Sorrow, pain, anxiety, affection, sympathy, hatred, everlasting fear, the false gods, the temples, the corruption, the competition—all that is life. We do not understand that. Yet, we cling to it desperately because that is all we know. We do not know anything else, and we do not want to know anything else!

And so, not having understood living, naturally we avoid death and put it at a distance, away from you and me. And to understand life, you must give yourself to life. To understand pain, anxiety, despair, affection, you have to give yourself, to give your whole being to it. Then you will see that living and death are not separate. To live, you must die every day; otherwise, you cannot live. Merely living in memory, in your pictures, in your formulas, in your beliefs—that is not living. The moment you have understood, the moment you have given your being to life, then you will see that you are dying—not withering, not decaying, not degenerating. I am talking about dying psychologically.

When you are dying psychologically, you are always living with death. Then death is not something far away, something to be afraid of, something which you dread. Because to live completely, every minute, every day, you have to die to the past every minute, every day—and that is what is actually going to take place when you die. There, you cannot argue with death, you cannot postpone it, asking of it a favor for another year. It is there, whether you like it or not. And a man who is afraid of death is not living, because he is afraid of life.

Do please understand this very simple fact in life: You do not know how to live when you are living always in pain and anxiety, fear, hope, and despair; that is a battlefield. I mean by "living," living when none of these exist, when you are no longer competing with anybody, when there is a total, complete cessation of sorrow—not a fragmentary cessation. And there is such a thing as a complete ending of sorrow. And when you so live, you will see that to live, you have to die to everything that you know. Then life and death are not separate.

I hope you are listening not merely to the words, not with the intention of gathering a few ideas to refute them or to collaborate with them or to say that the speaker is right or wrong. We are taking a journey together. And to take a journey, you cannot journey on words; it must be actual treading, not only hearing the noise of your footsteps, but also listening to your words, to your thoughts, to your feelings.

Then you will see that where there is freedom from the known, there is death; then you are not bothered at all whether there is reincarnation or not. And besides, what continues? Only your thought, your memory, continues—not the so-called spiritual essence. If it is the spiritual essence, you cannot think about it. The moment you think about it, you have reduced it into the field of time, the field of sorrow; therefore, it is not the spiritual essence at all but merely a product of thought. When we talk of the soul as something that will continue, we are still within the realm of thought. Where thought merely dominates, that thought creates fear. Then you are caught in the whole vicious circle of time, sorrow, and the fear of death.

So, to understand death and sorrow and time, one must give oneself to living. And to live you must be highly sensitive—not with your traditions. You must be sensitive with your nerves, with your eyes, with your body, with your mind, with your heart. And you cannot be sensitive if you have got used to anything—used to sex, used to anger, used to having a family around you, used to the squalor of a road, used to the lovely sunset in the clear sky, or used to your own vulgarities, your own cruelties and unobserved gestures and words.

So, one has to be astonishingly awake and sensitive. Then you will know what it means to die and what it means to live totally—in the sense that a mind has no future, no tomorrow, because it has no past; it is no longer becoming, it simply is flowing, living, moving. And a thing that moves, flows, has no death. But death only exists for him who desires continuity. But if a man dies every minute to everything—to every pleasure, to every pain, to every habit, good or bad—then he will know for himself what is beyond death, what is beyond this agony of life. There is something beyond—not because the speaker says so. You have to find it out. But to find out there must be no sorrow, because where sorrow abides, there is no love. And without love you will never understand what death is.

January 26, 1964

Sixth Talk in Madras

I would like this evening, if I may, to talk about meditation. I would like to talk about it because I feel it is the most important thing in life.

To understand meditation, to go into it very deeply, one must, first of all, understand the word and the fact. For most of us are slaves to words. The word *meditation* itself arouses in most people a certain state, a certain sensitivity, a certain quietness, a desire to achieve something or the other. But the word is not the thing. Because the word, the symbol, the name—if it is not totally understood—is a terrible thing. It acts as a barrier, it makes the mind slavish. And the reaction to the word, to the symbol, makes most of us act because we are unaware or unconscious of the fact itself. We come to the fact, to *what is* with our opinions, judgments, evaluations, our memories. And we never see the fact—the *what is.* I think that must be clearly understood.

To comprehend every experience, every state of mind, the *what is,* the actual fact, the actuality, one must not be a slave to words—and that is one of the most difficult things. The naming of it, the word, arouses various memories; and these memories impinge on the fact, control, shape, offer guidance to the fact, to the *what is.* So, one must be extraordinarily aware of this confusion and not bring about a conflict between the word and the actuality, the *what is.* And that is a very arduous task for a mind; that demands precision, clarity.

Without clarity, one cannot see things as they are. There is an extraordinary beauty in seeing things as they are—not in your opinions, your judgments, your memories. One has to see the tree as it is, without any confusion; similarly one has to see the sky on the water, of an evening—just to see, without verbalization, without that arousing symbols, ideas, and memories. In that there is extraordinary beauty. And beauty is essential. Beauty is the appreciation, the sensitivity to things about one—to nature, to people, to ideas. And if there is no sensitivity, there will be no clarity; the two are together, synonymous. This clarity is essential if we would understand what meditation is.

A mind that is confused, a mind caught up in ideas, in experiences, in all the urges of desire, only breeds conflict. And a mind that would really be in a state of meditation has to be aware not only of the word but also of the instinctive response of naming the experience or the state. And the very naming of that state or experience—whatever the experience be, however cruel, however real, however false—only strengthens memory with which we proceed to further experience.

Please, if I may point out, it is very important to understand what we are talking about because if you do not understand this, you will not be able to take a journey with the speaker into this whole problem of meditation.

As I said, meditation is one of the most important things in life—or, perhaps, the most important thing in life. If there is no meditation, there is no possibility of going beyond the limits of thought and mind and brain. And to go into this problem of meditation, from the very beginning one must lay the foundation of virtue. I do not mean the virtue imposed by society, a morality through fear, through greed, through envy, through certain punishment and reward.

I am talking of virtue which comes about naturally, spontaneously, easily, without any conflict or resistance, when there is self-knowing. Without knowing yourself, do what you will, there cannot possibly be the state of meditation. I mean by "self-knowing," knowing every thought, every mood, every word, every feeling; knowing the activity of your mind—not knowing the supreme self, the big self; there is no such thing; the higher self, the atma, is still within the field of thought. Thought is the result of your conditioning, thought is the response of your memory—ancestral or immediate. And merely to try to meditate without first establishing deeply, irrevocably, that virtue which comes about through self-knowing is utterly deceptive and absolutely useless.

Please, it is very important for those who are serious to understand this. Because if you cannot do that, your meditation and actual living are divorced, are apart—so wide apart that though you may meditate, taking postures indefinitely, for the rest of your life, you will not see beyond your nose; any posture you take, anything that you do, will have no meaning whatsoever.

So, the mind that would inquire—I am using the word *inquire* purposely—into what meditation is, must lay this foundation, which comes about naturally, spontaneously, with an ease of effortlessness, when there is self-knowing. And also, it is important to understand what this self-knowing is, just to be aware, without any choice, of the 'me' which has its source in a bundle of memories—I will go presently into what we mean by awareness—just to be conscious of it without interpretation, merely to observe the movement of the mind. But that observation is prevented when you are merely accumulating through observation—what to do, what not to do, what to achieve, what not to achieve; if you do that, you put an end to the living process of the movement of the mind as the self. That is, I have to observe and see the fact, the actual, the *what is*. If I approach it with an idea, with an opinion—such as "I must not," or "I must," which are the responses of memory—then the movement of *what is* is hindered, is blocked; and, therefore, there is no learning.

To observe the movement of the breeze in the tree, you cannot do anything about it. It moves either with violence or with grace, with beauty. You, the observer, cannot control it. You cannot shape it, you cannot say, "I will keep it in my mind." It is there. You may remember it. But if you remember it and recollect that breeze in the tree the next time you look at it, you are not looking at the natural movement of the breeze in the tree but only remembering the movement of the past. Therefore you are not learning, but you are merely adding to what you already know. So, knowledge becomes, at a certain level, an impediment to a further level.

I hope this is very clear. Because what we are going into presently demands a mind that is completely clear, capable of looking, seeing, listening, without any movement of recognition.

So, one must first be very clear, not confused. Clarity is essential. I mean by "clarity," seeing things as they are; seeing the *what is*, without any opinion; seeing the movement of your mind; observing it very closely, minutely, diligently, without any purpose, without any directive. Just to observe demands astonishing clarity; otherwise, you cannot observe. If you would observe an ant moving about, doing all the activities it does—if you come to it with various biological facts about the ant, that knowledge prevents you from looking. So you begin to see immediately where knowledge is necessary and where knowledge becomes an impediment. So there is no confusion.

Where the mind is clear, precise, capable of deep, fundamental reasoning, it is in a state of negation. Most of us accept things so easily; we are so gullible because we want comfort, we want security, we want a sense of hope, we want somebody to save us—Masters, saviors, gurus, rishis; you know the whole mess of it! We accept readily, easily; and equally easily we deny, according to the climate of our mind.

So, "clarity" is in the sense of seeing things as they are within oneself. Because oneself is a part of the world. Oneself is the movement of the world. Oneself is the outer expression which is the movement that goes inwardly—it is like the tide that goes out and comes in. Merely to concentrate on, or observe, yourself apart from the world leads you to isolation and to all forms of idiosyncrasy, neurosis, isolating fears, and so on. But if you observe the world and follow the movement of the world, and ride that movement as it comes within, then there is no division between you and the world; then you are not an individual opposed to the collective.

And there must be this sense of observation, which is both explorative—which is exploring—and observing, listening, and being aware. I am using the word *observing* in that sense. The very act of observation is the act of exploration. You cannot explore if you are not free. Therefore, to explore, to observe, there must be clarity; to explore within yourself deeply, you must come to it each time afresh. That is, in that exploration you have never achieved a result, you have never climbed a ladder, and you never say, "Now I know." There is no ladder. If you do climb, you must come down immediately so that your mind is tremendously sensitive to observe, to watch, to listen.

And out of this observing, listening, seeing, watching, comes that extraordinary beauty of virtue. There is no other virtue except that which comes from self-knowing. Then that virtue is vital, vigorous, active—not a dead thing that you cultivate. And that must be the foundation. That is, the foundation for meditation is observation, clarity, and virtue, in the sense we mean—not in the sense you have made virtue a thing to be cultivated day after day, which is mere resistance.

Then, we can see from there the implications of the so-called prayers, the so-called repetition of words, mantras, sitting in a corner and trying to fix your mind on a particular object or a word or a symbol—which is to meditate deliberately. Please listen carefully. Taking a deliberate posture or doing certain things to meditate deliberately, consciously, only implies that you are playing in the field of your own desires and your own conditioning; and, therefore, it is not meditation. One can see very well, if one observes, that those people who meditate have all kinds of images; they see Krishna, Christ, Buddha, and they think they have got something—like a Christian seeing the Christ; that phenomenon is very simple, very clear; it is a projection of his own conditioning, his own fears, his own hopes, his desire for security. The Christian sees the Christ as you would see Rama or whatever your particular pet god is.

And there is nothing remarkable about these visions. They are the product of your unconscious, which has been so conditioned, so trained in fear. When you become slightly quiet, up it pops with its images, symbols, ideas. So, visions, trances, pictures, and ideas have no value whatsoever. It is like a man repeating some mantra or some phrase or a name over and over and over again. When you repeat a name over and over and over again, what happens, obviously, is you make the mind dull, stupid; and in that stupidity it becomes quiet. You can just as well take a drug to make the mind quiet—and there are such drugs—and in that state of quietness, in that drugged state you have visions. Those are obviously the product of your own society, of your own culture, of your own hopes and fears; they have nothing whatsoever to do with reality.

Prayers are equally so. The man who prays is like a man who has his hand in another man's pocket. The businessman, the politician, and the whole competitive society are praying for peace; but they are doing everything to bring about war, hatred, and antagonism—it has no meaning, it has no rationality. Your prayer is a supplication, asking for something which you have no right to ask—because you are not living, you are not virtuous. And you want something peaceful, great, to enrich your lives; but you are doing everything opposite to destroy—becoming mean, petty, stupid.

So, prayers, visions, sitting in a corner upright, breathing rightly, doing things with your mind are so immature, juvenile; they have no meaning for a man who really wants to understand the full significance of what meditation is. So a man who would understand what meditation is puts all this aside completely, even though he may lose his job; he does not immediately turn to a petty god in order to get a job—that is the game you all play. When there is some kind of sorrow, disturbance, you turn to a temple, and you call yourself religious! All these must be completely, totally set aside so that they do not touch you. If you have done this, then we can proceed into this whole question of what is meditation.

You must have observation, clarity, self-knowing and, because of that, virtue. Virtue is a thing that is flowering in goodness all the time; you might make a mistake, do things ugly, but they are finished; you are moving, are flowering in goodness, because you are knowing yourself. Having laid that foundation, then you can put aside the prayers, the muttering of words and taking postures. Then you can begin to inquire into what is experience.

It is very important to understand what is experience because we all want experience. We have everyday experiences—going to the office, quarreling, being jealous, envious, brutal, competitive, sexual. In life, we go through every kind of experience, day after day, consciously or unconsciously. And we are living on the surface of our life, without beauty, without any depth, with nothing of our own which is original, pristine, clear; we are all secondhand human beings, quoting others, following others, empty as a shell. And naturally we want more experience other than everyday experience. So, we search for this experience either through meditation or through taking some of the latest drugs. LSD 25 is one of these latest drugs; the moment you have taken it, you feel you have "instant mysticism"—not that I have taken it. (Laughter)

We are talking seriously. You merely laugh at the least provocation; therefore, you are not serious; you are not going step by step into it, watching into yourself; you are just listening to words, going along riding on words—which I warned you against at the beginning of the talk.

So, there are these drugs which give you an expansion of consciousness, make you highly sensitive for the time being. And in that state of heightened sensitivity you see things—the tree becomes most astonishingly alive, bright, and clear and with an immensity. Or, if you are religiously-minded, you, in that heightened state of sensitivity, have an extraordinary sense of peace and light; there is no difference between you and the thing observed, you are it, and the whole universe is part of you. And you crave for these drugs because you want more experience, a wider and deeper experience, hoping that experience will give you significance to life; so you begin to depend.

Yet, when you have these experiences, you are still within the field of thought, within the field of the known.

So you have to understand experience—that is, the response to a challenge, which becomes a reaction; and that reaction shapes your thought, your feeling, your being. And you add more and more experiences, you think of having more and more experiences. The more clear the memories of those experiences are, the more you think you know. But, if you observe, you will find that the more you know, the more shallow you become, the more empty. Becoming more empty, you want more experience, and wider. So you have to understand not only all that I have said previously but also this extraordinary demand for experience. Now we can proceed.

A mind that is seeking experience of any kind is still within the field of time, within the field of the known, within the field of self-projected desires. As I said at the beginning of the talk, deliberate meditation only leads to illusion. But yet, there must be meditation. To meditate deliberately only leads you to various forms of self-hypnosis, to various forms of experience projected by your own desires, by your own conditioning; and those conditionings, those desires, shape your mind, control your thought. So a man who would really understand the deep significance of meditation must understand the significance of experience; and also his mind must be free from seeking. That is very difficult. I am going to go into that presently.

Having laid all this as a basic thing, naturally, spontaneously, easily, then we must find out what it means to control thought. Because that is what you are after; the more you can control thought, the more you think you have advanced in meditation. For me, every form of control—physically, psychologically, intellectually, emotionally—is detrimental. Please listen carefully. Do not say, "Then, I will do what I like." I am not saying that. Control implies subjugation, suppression, adaptation, shaping the thought to a particular pattern—which implies that the pattern is more important than the discovery of what is true. So control, in any form—which is resistance, suppression, or sublimation, in any form—shapes the mind more and more according to the past, according to the conditioning in which you have been brought up, according to the conditioning of a particular community, and so on and on.

It is necessary to understand what is meditation. Now please listen carefully. I do not know if you have ever done this kind of meditation; probably you have not. But you are going to do it now with me. We are going to take the journey together, not verbally, but actually, to go through it right up to the end where verbal communication exists. That is, it is like going together up to the door; then either you go through the door, or you stop on this side of the door. You will stop on this side of the door if you have not actually, factually, done everything that is being pointed out—not because the speaker says so, but because that is sane, healthy, reasonable, and it will stand every test, every examination.

So now, together, we are going to meditate—not deliberately meditate because that does not exist. It is like leaving the window open and the air comes when it will—whatever the air brings, whatever the breeze is. But if you expect, wait for, the breezes to come because you have opened the window, they will never come. So, it must be opened out of love, out of affection, out of freedom—not because you want something. And that is the state of beauty, that is the state of mind that sees and does not demand.

To be aware is an extraordinary state of mind—to be aware of your surroundings, of the trees, the bird that is singing, the sunset behind you; to be aware of the faces, of the smiles; to be aware of the dirt on the road; to be aware of the beauty of the land, of a palm tree against the red sunset, the ripple of the water—just to be aware, choicelessly. Please do this as you are going along. Listen to these birds; do not name them, do not recognize the species, but just listen, to the sound. Listen to the movement of your own thoughts; do not control them, do not shape them, do not say, "This is right, that is wrong"; just move with them. That is awareness in which there is no choice, no condemnation, no judgment, no comparison or interpretation, but mere observation. That makes your mind highly sensitive. The moment you name, you have gone back; your mind becomes dull because that is what you are used to.

In that state of awareness there is attention—not control, not concentration. There is attention—that is, you are listening to the birds, you are seeing the sunset, you are seeing the stillness of the trees, you are hearing the cars go by, you are hearing the speaker, and you are attentive to the meaning of the words, you are attentive to your own thoughts and feelings, and to the movement in that attention. You are attentive comprehensively, without a border, not only consciously but also unconsciously. The unconscious is more important; therefore, you have to inquire into the unconscious.

I am not using the word *unconscious* as a technological term or a technique. I am not using it in the sense in which the psychologists use it but as that of which you are not conscious. Because most of us are living on the surface of the mind: going to the office, acquiring knowledge or a technique, quarreling, and so on. We never pay attention to the depth of our being, which is the result of our community, of the racial residue, of all the past—not only of you as a human being but also of man, the anxieties of man. When you sleep, all these project themselves as dreams, and then there is the interpretation of those dreams. Dreams become totally unnecessary for a man who is awake, alert, watching, listening, aware, attentive.

Now, this attention demands tremendous energy: not the energy which you have gathered through practice, being a bachelor and all the rest of that stuff—that is all the energy of greed. I am talking of the energy of self-knowing. Because you have laid the right foundation, out of that comes the energy to be attentive, in which there is no sense of concentration. Concentration is exclusion—you want to listen to that music and you want also to hear what the speaker is saying, so you resist that music and try to listen to the speaker; so you are really not paying complete attention. A part of your energy has gone to resist that music and a part of it is trying to listen; therefore, you are not listening totally; therefore, you are not being attentive. So if you concentrate, you merely resist, exclude. But a mind that is attentive can concentrate and not be exclusive.

So out of this attention comes a brain that is quiet, the brain cells themselves are quiet—not made quiet, not disciplined, not enforced, not brutally conditioned. But because this whole attention has come into being, naturally, spontaneously, without effort, easily, the brain cells are not perverted, not hardened, not coarsened, not brutalized. I hope you are following all this. Unless the brain cells themselves are astonishingly sensitive, alert, vital, not hardened, not beaten, not overworked, not specialized in a particular department of knowledge, unless they are extraordinarily sensitive, they cannot be quiet. So the brain must be quiet but yet be sensitive to every reaction, be aware of all the music, the noises, the birds, hearing these words, watching the sunset without any pressure, without any strain, without any influence. The brain must be very quiet because without quietness—uninduced, not brought about artificially—there can be no clarity.

And clarity can only come when there is space. And you have space the moment the brain is absolutely quiet but yet highly sensitive, not deadened. And that is why it is very important what you do all day. The brain is brutalized by circumstances, by society, by your jobs, and by specialization, by your thirty or forty years in an office, grinding away brutally—all that destroys the extraordinary sensitivity of the brain. And the brain must be quiet. Then from there, the whole mind, in which is included the brain, is capable of being completely still. That still mind is no longer seeking, it is not waiting for experience; it is not experiencing anything at all.

I hope you are understanding all this. Perhaps you aren't—it doesn't matter! Just listen. Do not be mesmerized by me but listen to the truth of this. And perhaps then, when you are walking in the street, sitting in a bus, watching a stream or a rice field, rich and green, this will come unknowingly, like a breath from a distant land.

So the mind then becomes completely still, without any form of pressure, compulsion. This stillness is not a thing produced by thought because thought has ended, the whole machinery of thought has come to an end. Thought must end; otherwise, thought will produce more images, more ideas, more illusions—more and more and more. Therefore, you have to understand this whole machinery of thought—not how to stop thinking. If you understand the whole machinery of thought, which is the response of memory, association, and recognition, naming, comparing, judging—if you understand it, naturally it comes to an end. When the mind is completely still, then out of that stillness, in that stillness, there is quite a different movement.

That movement is not a movement created by thought, by society, by what you have read or not read. That movement is not of time, of experience, because that movement has no experience. To a still mind there is no experience. A light which is burning brightly, which is strong, does not demand anything more; it is a light to itself. That movement is not a movement in any direction because direction implies time. That movement has no cause because anything that has a cause produces an effect, and that effect becomes the cause and so on—an endless chain of causation and effect, the effect becoming the cause. So there is no effect, no cause, no motive, no sense of experiencing at all. So, because the mind is completely still, naturally still, because you have laid the foundation, it is directly related to life, it is not divorced from everyday living.

Then, if the mind has gone that far, that movement is creation. Then there is no anxiety to express because a mind that is in a state of creation may express or may not express. That state of mind which is in that complete silence—it will move, it has its own movement into the unknown, into that which is unnameable.

So the meditation which you do is not the meditation of which we are talking. This meditation is from the everlasting to the everlasting because you have laid the foundation, not on time but on reality.

January 29, 1964

Seventh Talk in Madras

This is the last talk in Madras. I would, if I may, like to talk about what is the religious mind—not theoretically, not as a speculation, not because we have nothing else or better to do, nor merely out of curiosity. To inquire into anything, especially into matters that require a great deal of penetration, an enormous amount of intelligence, you need energy. If you do anything efficiently, clearly, to the very end and carry it out fully, you need to have an abundant and inexhaustible energy. That is taken for granted by most of us. To go to the office every day of your life for thirty years and more of boredom, you need energy if you would not be destroyed by the boredom, by the routine, by all the insults, and so on.

And especially when we are inquiring into psychological matters, we need energy that is not motivated by any desire, by any purpose. We need simple energy. And for most of us that energy is lacking. We pursue something that we like, which is gratifying, to the very end of it. And for that we have plenty of energy—whether it is good, bad, or indifferent; whether it is worthwhile or not; whether there is any significance or not in action. If we want to do a certain thing, we will go at it with a great deal of zeal and energy.

And to inquire into what is the religious mind—which we are going to do this evening—we need energy, the energy that comes from facing facts, from facing *what is.* Any avoidance of facing *what is* is a waste of energy. Whether they are agreeable, dissatisfactory, or repellant, we have to face things. And to understand *what is* nonspeculatively, to realize it actually as you would realize, as you would see, the sunset or the tree or the blue sky, we must face facts. If we would realize what actually is a religious mind, we have to face certain things and not escape from them. If you notice, all our life is a series of escapes—escape from boredom, escape from routine, escape from fear. We have various kinds of escape; whether we are conscious of them or not, there they are as actual as the tree behind you or in front of you. And not to escape but to face things as they are actually, to see *what is,* requires an unvaried attention, requires a passion; that passion comes from the energy which is the natural outcome of facing *what is.*

And if you would, kindly follow the speaker to the very end, not agreeing or disagreeing, not verbally or intellectually. Because we are not going to discuss opinions—then you can agree or disagree, then you can say "I like" or "I do not like." And we are not exploring the truth of opinions, there is no truth in opinions—it is your opinion against another; and in that you can either agree or disagree or turn your back on it altogether; but we are not doing that. We are facing facts, facing actually *what is.* Otherwise, we will not have the energy to pursue logically, reasonably, sanely, totally, to the very end of what is a religious mind, and realize it by discovering it.

For facing *what is,* we need energy—that is an obvious fact. And we need to have that energy in abundance because most of us are terribly lazy, not only physically, but also mentally. We would rather accept than inquire; we would rather put up with things, however uncomfortable, however ugly, than break through. We would rather bow to obey an authority, than totally deny an authority and find out.

So with most of us there is this enervating laziness. What is important is to realize this laziness, not what to do about it. Because if you do something about it, you are wasting your energy. But if you face the actual fact that you are lazy, that very confrontation begins to set about a psychological activity naturally, spontaneously, from which you derive energy which banishes away your laziness. Do this sometime, and you will see this for yourselves. And as for most of us our culture, our civilization, is a series of escapes, the objects of our escapes have become much more important than those from which we are running away.

Please, as the speaker has often pointed out in these talks and previously, do not merely hear the words. Words are like the breeze. You cannot live on words, you cannot catch words and live, you cannot exert all your mind and energy on words. You have to go beyond the words. Words are merely symbols, means of communication. And to commune with each other, we must not only hear the word but also comprehend the meaning and the significance of the word. And to understand the meaning of the word is not to be caught in the word because the word is not the thing. The word is never the thing. The word *sky* is not the sky. The word is only a symbol and not the actuality.

And to find out the actual, not merely the meaning of the word, you and I—because we are together going to inquire into this thing called the religious mind—must be in communion, with a sustained—not only intellectual or verbal, but a sustained—intensity, clarity, and go to the very end of it, without slackening, without letting go. Therefore if one would understand this extraordinary thing called religion and the whole significance of it—which man has been trying to find for centuries upon centuries—you must give your whole heart and mind. Therefore merely to stop at a word when you are really hungry has no meaning. So we must sustain an intensity at a level where both of us meet at the same time, constantly and to the very end. Because only then is any communion possible.

So, as we were saying, our life is a vast series of escapes—escapes from our boredom, our loneliness, our fears, our pettiness, all the things that man has cultivated as a means of avoidance of facing things as they are. We have many escapes, of which one may be actually conscious or unconscious. To discover the unconscious escapes, one needs a very alert, watchful mind—that is, one needs constantly to watch every movement of thought and feeling. Because in that area of watching—that watching being negation, not a positive search, but a state of mind which is observing—every movement of the unconscious, with all its intimations, is received and understood.

There are many escapes, conscious as well as unconscious—as I have said—from boredom, from routine, from the extraordinary pettiness of our lives. You may be very intellectual and may have a good, high position in a government; but your heart and your mind, everything, may be small, petty, shallow; you are bored and you are escaping from that, either through drink, sex, or through God—they are all on the same level when you are escaping. So, to be aware of this, to be conscious of this, brings about energy.

I am going to go into this because, without this energy, if you do not have it from the very beginning of this talk, you will not be able to proceed further; then halfway you will give it up, and it will become a theory, a verbal explanation, which has very little significance.

For most of us, life—the very act of living—has become a problem. I mean by that word *living* going to the office, seeing the squalor in the street, the utter misery of man, poverty, negligence, squalor, the innumerable insults we receive, the joys, the pleasures, the anxieties, the despairs, the affections, the sympathies, and ultimately that thing called death. That is the whole of our life, that is part of our existence. We do not understand it, and everything that we touch becomes a problem. I mean by "problem" something that is not resolved immediately and is carried over for the next day.

Our whole life is a problem. And not being able to solve it, we try to run away; and sex is one of the things to which we run away and escape because intellectually, emotionally, in every way, we are uncreative, we are secondhand, and there is nothing original, there is nothing pristine, clear, beautiful, unspoiled, untrammeled. We are secondhand. All our education is a repetition of something that we have merely acquired as information to get a job, to earn a livelihood. And, therefore, life becomes a terrible boredom.

Or, we try to give significance to life; we say "What is the purpose of living?" as though living has a purpose. You live richly, completely, fully—there is no purpose. Beauty has no purpose. But our life being what it is, tawdry, empty, without much meaning, we are bored in the very act of everything that we do. I do not think we realize how bored we are. That is why religious organizations exist—to escape from this boredom, from this loneliness, from this shallow existence. There are these innumerable swamis, yogis, and all the rest of that business; naturally we are blocked everywhere, and sex is the only escape for most of us. Having that escape, that becomes an astonishing problem, a moral problem, whether it is right or wrong and so on; and then we get caught up in it. We have to understand the bondage that the mind is laden with, bound to; we have to understand the whole field of desire, the innumerable appetites, and to break through them—that is to be free, both intellectually and emotionally. Without understanding them and breaking through them, there is only one release, sex. And we wish sex in different forms: as beauty, as taste, as morality, as the things that should be and should not be.

Please, we are talking not about something outrageous, not about something theoretical; but it is your life. And when you escape, the thing to which you escape becomes more important than the thing from which you are escaping—your sex becomes important; God or non-God becomes important. We want to find a significance in life—the ultimate peace, the permanency, the everlasting something in which time is not, and all the innumerable theories. Because one is escaping, the more one can escape, the more one thinks one is religious. When you so completely identify yourself with an idea called God, that is not a reality because you cannot possibly, under any circumstances, identify yourself with reality. If you do, it is not reality. To perceive reality, your mind must be completely free from all these things which make you identify, your mind must be free from fear.

We want to identify ourselves with a nation, with the family, with the community, with a particular form of commitment of social activity, and ultimately with the state; or, if the state is not fashionable, then we identify ourselves with God. This identification through an organized religion, or through your own particular fancy of what God is, your particular mythology and your particular vision of that mythology, is another escape. And, therefore, the people who so completely identify themselves with the state, with the nation, with God, with some activity—they have a certain form of neurotic energy. But that energy is destructive, deteriorating, contradictory.

So one has to be aware of this fact that there is always this desire to identify with a group, with an idea, with a particular person, and so on. When you identify yourself with something, when you escape, when there are problems, you are losing energy. And a mind that would go into this question of what is reality, what is the religious mind, must be free from every form of boredom, from escape in all its multitudinous forms—not just one form—including your churches, gods, religions, gurus. When you cease to escape, then alone can you understand.

I hope you are listening and, therefore, realizing your escapes, and putting an end to these escapes immediately, not tomorrow. If you postpone, that is also an escape from facing the fact of your commitment, whether your commitment is to art, or whether your commitment is to beauty, to music, to literature, to social work. Because this commitment, this escape, this boredom prevents you from seeing yourself actually as you are. If you understand as you are actually, then you come to an ultimate thing which is your sense of complete loneliness.

But most of us, by our activities, by our thoughts, by the culture in which we are born, by our ideas—we isolate ourselves. We live in a family, with a wife and children, in a society, in a community and talk about brotherhood, tolerance, friendship, love, and all the rest of the words that we use endlessly. If you go beyond those words, inwardly, there is this loneliness; and from there begin all the escapes. And when you face that loneliness, understand it, not run away from it, understand it and live with it—as you would live with a tree, with a cloud, with squalor—then out of that living comes beauty.

So, the religious mind then is the mind that has no fear. And that is one of the most difficult things to understand—to be completely, totally free of fear, not fear in a certain form, but totally. You may be afraid of death or you may be afraid of your wife or husband; you may have fear, from the meanest to the highest form of fear—if there is a highest form of fear. And to understand that fear and to be free, you must investigate it, you must look.

Now freedom is not from something. If you are free from something, you have only learned how to resist it, how to avoid it, how to circumvent it, how to go beyond it. But if you understand it, then you are free. Therefore freedom is something per se, not from something. And that freedom you must have completely because otherwise you create illusions.

The so-called religious mind is a superstitious, dull, accepting mind, with innumerable beliefs, because basically there is fear. You know, people run to the temple because there is some misfortune, because they are not making enough money—money is their God. Or because they are frightened that someone will not get well, they run to the temple to do some repetitive puja, which has no meaning at all. And such a mind is considered to be astonishingly religious—which is sheer nonsense!

A man who is free from fear is not seeking God. Please understand this; a man who is really free from fear is not seeking favors from anything, from anybody—least of all from the gods that man has created. And to understand this recurring, constant fear, you must understand yourself, go into yourself and face *what is*—that is, your loneliness, your boredom, your escapes, the virtues and the moralities that you have cultivated as a means of resistance, which are not virtue or morality at all. Virtue is something entirely different; virtue is a perfume, it is a beauty that comes with wisdom. And wisdom comes with self-knowing—knowing not the big self, but the ordinary self, the everyday self, knowing all the movements, the beauty, and the ugliness of that self. Out of that comes wisdom. And then only there is freedom—that means freedom not only from fear but also from authority.

We are going to find out for ourselves by inquiring into what is the religious mind, the origin, the source of reality—the thing that is beyond words, beyond measure, beyond thought; a movement without a core. And to inquire into that, every form of authority must come to an end. Especially the mind that seeks authority in books must know itself. Books have no authority. The Upanishads, the Gita, the Koran—they have no authority, they are just printed words like any other book. But it is your mind that seeks authority, confirmation, comfort, in those books; and that gives them sacredness. So, you have to understand this whole anatomy of authority and be free from it.

Then from this observation, from this awareness in which there is no choice, an awareness which is negative, watching, you have passion. You know, for most of us, that word is identified with lust, with appetite. And you have been told that a religious man is not lustful; he must be without desire, he must twist himself, torture himself to the pattern established by somebody or other. You want to achieve that thing which he has achieved because you are frightened of life. And therefore you destroy yourself, torture yourself, twist yourself to fit into the pattern established by society, by organized religion; so you remain secondhand.

Please follow all this. We are secondhand people; there is nothing original. And the religious man is in search of the original, not the secondhand. And no god is the original because the original is beyond man's thought, man's structure, beyond the things man has put together as religion, in which are included all the rituals and the repetitions and all the absurdities.

So, a mind that is free from fear has also understood completely, and is free from, authority—the authority that the mind seeks to bolster itself up with, to find out whether it is doing right or wrong, with the desire to be guided, to be helped; such a mind can never be a religious mind. Obviously, a religious mind will never touch politics because politics is concerned with the immediate—"the immediate" in the sense of time interval in which something has to be done, in which there is corruption, chicanery, double talk, nationality, and all the other things that go in the name of politics.

So, a religious mind is a mind that is alone. There is a difference between loneliness and aloneness. You cannot come to this aloneness if you have not understood completely the extraordinary nature of loneliness and gone through it—if you have not understood it completely, tasted it, smelled it, been familiar with it, been in complete contact with it, having never a moment to avoid it either through sex or though various forms of escape, been completely related to it, not verbally but actually. This word *loneliness* is not the fact. And what most of us are frightened of is the word, not the fact, because the word separates the thought from the fact. So you have to understand the whole structure of the word and how we are slaves to words. All this demands tremendous energy.

A religious mind is not the mind that escapes, that avoids the world, puts on a loincloth and becomes simple, outwardly. The outward simplicity is mere exhibitionism! The inward simplicity is much more demanding, much more austere; it has no outward show. And the religious mind has this inward understanding—not control, not shaping the thought after a pattern which has been laid out by another, whoever he may be, and which demands suppression, obedience.

I am talking of the austerity that comes with self-knowing. And that is much more austere because that demands precision, that demands reasoning, not fragmentary thinking. And that demands constant watchfulness of every thought, of every feeling, to be totally aware, so that there is a total action, not fragmentary action—bureaucratic at one level, but superstitious, ugly, brutal, silly, stupid, at another level; running to the temple because someone is dying or crying, or because one wants more money. So a religious mind is a mind that is completely alone. Aloneness is not isolation; it is the actual state of cooperation. You cannot cooperate if you are not alone. Generally you cooperate only when there is a reward or punishment, when you are getting something, when you want to do something together under an authority, under the umbrella of ideas. When you are working for a utopia or an ideal, you are really not cooperating; the idea attracts you, you are absorbed by the idea; and when you disagree with the idea, you break away. That is what is happening with all the communities. In this utopia, ideal society, state, everybody is against another! The communist world is like that too; though they started out to have an idealistic, utopian world, the competition there is more brutal, more ruthless; and they are all trying to cooperate with the state—communes, collective farms; forcing people to cooperate; therefore, inwardly battling, destroying, watching for ways and means where you can go against all this. That is not cooperation.

Cooperation comes only when you are alone, where there is this sense of complete aloneness, which is the outcome, a natural outcome, of a mind that has no escapes, no fear, no authority, and has understood this whole problem of energy. Then it is in a state of cooperation. And, therefore, being in a state of cooperation, it also knows when not to cooperate.

So, there is this sense of aloneness. Perhaps some of you have gone thus far, not verbally, but actually; not as an experience once in a while, but clearly, right through. It is not a state to be achieved or a thing to be experienced; it is there. This aloneness is a state of mind when the mind has emptied itself of all its contents. Just as a room or a cup is useful when it is empty, when it is not cluttered up with furniture and so on, so also it is only when the mind is completely empty of ideas, beliefs, and dogmas that it can proceed. Only then, out of this emptiness, is there action. Action then is not an idea; action then is not an approximation of an idea; it is not an idea; action then is not an idea. Action then is not an approximation to a pattern, an idea, a thought, a symbol.

Such a mind is like a drum. The other evening, there was a *mridangam* being played. It was empty, and every finger that touched it gave the right note, gave the pure sound. But if that drum were full, there would be no sound; it would be discordance.

That emptiness of the mind cannot be produced; the mind cannot be made empty, cannot be put together to be empty. That emptiness comes as a sunset comes of an evening, full of beauty, enchantment, and richness; that comes as naturally as the blossoming of a flower when there is no fear, when there are no escapes, when there is no boredom, and when there is no seeking. And that is the most important of all—there must be no seeking because you cannot find. You cannot find the everlasting. That which is beyond time you cannot search out. It may come to you, but you cannot go to it because your minds are too shallow, petty, empty, full of ambition, fears, ugliness, and distortion. Therefore the mind must empty itself, not because it wants that. Because, when you want that, you have a motive; and the moment you have a motive, you have lost your energy.

Therefore, it is only the mind that is completely empty that is in a state of inaction; that inaction is action. And it is only such a mind that is being passionate; it is only such a mind that can live with beauty and not get used to beauty—the beauty of a tree; the beauty of a face; the beauty of an eye, of a smile, of the ugly, dirty road, the squalor, the dirt, the poverty. It is only the passionate mind that can live with it and not get distorted.

And it is only such a mind that is so completely empty that is in a state of meditation. Do not translate it as *samadhi* and all the rest of the absurdities that you have learned. It is not that at all, it is something entirely different. The word is not the thing. If you have not found it for yourself, everything that somebody says is a lie to you—it does not matter who it is, Shankara downwards or upwards.

Truth you have to find out for yourself. You have to walk the path alone, and there is no path to truth. Truth is the vast ocean which has not been charted; it is fathomless; you have to find it, walking endlessly. And the endlessness becomes a torture, a thing that you are frightened of, if you have not understood the beginning of what we have been talking about. Then there is no time. Then you are living so completely in that emptiness that time has gone, and there is only the present, this active present.

I do not know if you have ever noticed a bird on the wing, a leaf falling, or the sun on the water, or the reflection of the moon on the water. If you have noticed, if you have seen the beauty of it, in that moment there is no time. It is there endlessly, unspoiled, incorruptible, timeless. Similarly, a religious mind is that. And it is only such a religious mind that can receive the immeasurable, the nameless.

February 2, 1964

Bombay, India, 1964

First Talk in Bombay

Those of you who are going to come to all these talks—you have an arduous, persistent, and strenuous inquiry to make. We have to take a very long journey together. And that requires a mind that is capable of instant perception, a mind that is not fixed to any particular point of view, or to any conclusion, or to any formula. We are going to inquire together into this vast problem of living, as a total problem—not as any particular problem, but life as a whole. And to inquire very deeply into that, one requires a mind that is subtle, that is free, that is capable of reasoning and sanity; and the mind must be very healthy.

Most of us who are desirous of inquiring within ourselves are merely satisfied with words and are not capable or are not willing to go beyond the words. So, what we are going to do in all these talks is that we, the speaker as well as you, are both, together, going to cooperate freely in a spirit of inquiry. In this country especially, one finds this spirit of inquiry has completely come to an end; we have lost the urge of inquiry, of searching out, penetrating, having a deep insight. And to comprehend the things that we are going to talk about during these seven discourses demands a mind that does not agree or disagree, that does not easily accept or easily deny; it requires a mind that is capable of looking, observing, seeing, listening.

The thing that we are going to inquire into demands a total freedom—freedom from everything, not from a particular quality or a particular condition. Because truth is something that cannot be found unless you discover it for yourself. It is utterly useless to repeat what somebody else has said. What somebody else has said with regard to truth becomes a lie if you do not discover it for yourself. And to discover it for yourself you need a very quick, a very free mind. And we are going persistently, ardently, to inquire into the source, into the very foundation of what is truth. And we are going to go into it right from the beginning to the very end, touching the whole of life. And this demands seriousness.

Most of us are not serious. You may listen to many talks, you may read a few books and be capable of discussion, and you may intellectually accept a certain norm of thought, but that does not indicate seriousness. I mean by seriousness that intention to go through to the very end and not get distracted or sidetracked, to go to the very root of things, and to find out for yourself what this extraordinary thing called truth is. Because unless you find it, each one of you, life becomes very empty. You may play with a lot of things, you may go to many shrines, many teachers, but unless you, as a human being living in this world—and this world is so tortuous, miserable, anxious—find it for yourself, life becomes utterly stupid, shallow, empty. And most of our lives are empty. You may be very clever in acquiring knowledge, you may be a great student of the past, you may repeat endlessly the sacred books—all of which indicate a mind that is not very serious.

And what we are going to discuss and talk about during these seven talks demands an extraordinary amount of seriousness, deadly seriousness. Most of us want to be distracted; most of us escape from the central issue; we do this and ten different things. And this also is surely the central issue. And what we are going to do during these talks is to uncover this root from which we can flower in goodness, in beauty. Only then can we understand this extraordinary thing called life, with its vastness and its great simplicity and its variety of complexities, and meet the various challenges of daily existence.

So your task is strenuous: You have not only to hear the words, and comprehend the meaning of those words, but you have also to listen—that is, to go beyond the words because words are merely symbols. The word is not the real; it indicates, it signifies, it gives you direction; but most of us stop there, and with these words we either disagree or agree. But I feel if we could listen, then perhaps inadvertently, without our knowing consciously, we would catch a glimpse of the beauty of something that is beyond the measure of words and the measure of thought. But one has to have this state of mind that is capable of listening.

Listening is an art. You are not going to develop it in the sense of true time. There is only the instant that is the true time; there is no other time, except chronological time. And you listen so that in that instant, you catch the whole significance immediately. That listening to that instant brings about an extraordinary revelation which actually transforms one's whole existence. I feel that this listening is extraordinarily important.

Please do differentiate between hearing and listening. You are naturally now hearing the words, and you will translate those words according to your comprehension of English and according to your likes and dislikes, whether you agree or disagree. And you will see that we are not discussing opinions. There is no truth in opinions; one opinion is as good as another. We are not dialectically exploring—dialectically in the sense of finding the truth of opinions and discussing those opinions—we are not doing it. We are not agreeing or disagreeing.

We are exploring. And to explore really, ardently, with a passion, we need to have this attention, which is the act of listening—the act of listening to everything: to the crows, to that kite, and listening to the speaker, not trying to find out if he is telling truth or falsehood, but merely listening, suspending your capacity to judge, to evaluate, to condemn. If you listen in that sense—listen in a state of emptiness, if it could be so put, or listen out of emptiness—then the very act of listening begins that instant in which there is comprehension, which alone brings about transformation. Because we need a tremendous revolution, not only outwardly, but inwardly—especially inwardly.

I do not think we realize how important it is that there should be this spontaneous, not calculated, not brought about according to your formula, but an instant perception of what is true—and that very perception should act in life. And that action in life can only come about when there is this act of listening. A mind has to be very aware of its surroundings, not only outwardly to all the squalor, the dirt, the beauty of a tree, of a sunlit cloud, but also inwardly so as to listen to all the whispers, mutterings, secret desires, all the urges and compulsions—to listen to them without any judgment, just to listen and to perceive *what is*. And that alone brings about an extraordinary revolution, psychologically, and therefore outwardly.

As one observes throughout the world, wherever one is, there is a general decline, a general disintegration. And especially in a country which is supposed to be very old and ancient like this, there is disintegration at all levels. Politically there is corruption, tyranny, personal worship, the desire for power and position on the part of the politicians; there is corruption at that level from the top to the bottom. In the world of business there is also corruption, decline; you are only concerned with making money, and not making, helping, the other also to live happily, richly, in a happy environment. So there is corruption there too, a decline, a disintegration, degeneration. Then there is also decline in the family. When the family becomes all-important, as one observes, the family then is merely the continuity of oneself, enlarged; and when one is concerned with oneself, everlastingly calculating, then one is the root of corruption. And then there is corruption in relationship with one another.

Life is relationship. To live in this world you must be related, because you can't exist in isolation. To be related means also to cooperate: cooperation is "working together." You cannot work together if one dominates the other, if one has a particular idea and forces the other to accept it. Cooperation can only exist when there is real affection, sympathy, pity, a sense of togetherness. This does not exist at all in this country. Ideologically, yes! That is, in the sense of words—that we must all work together, that we are brothers, that there is one life—you know all that nonsense that we repeat endlessly. But actually, factually, in every moment of our life, it does not exist.

So we do not know what it means to cooperate. We know to cooperate with the state from which we are going to gain our livelihood, or with an idea for a utopia, because that is going to profit us; or we know cooperation under authority, which is compulsion, conformity. But the cooperation we are talking about is entirely different. That cooperation comes only when you care. *Care* is a very simple word, but it has a deep meaning—to care for somebody, to care for a tree, to care for a bird. We do not care—please, I am not moralizing; you must leave it to the politicians. I am merely pointing out to you how important it is to live in this world with care—to care for the room in which you are living, to care how you eat, what your behavior is, what your manners are.

Please, I am going to go into it because you have to understand the meaning of this word care. To care how you dress, how you talk, what your gestures are, how you treat your neighbor, how you look at life, how you educate your children; to care—from that sense of caring, there comes sympathy, there comes affection, and you can go, you can ride on that affection and you know what love is. And you have to have that sense of caring from the very beginning—how you use words, how you speak to another. Don't brush all this aside and say that you know all this, you have heard this, you have read about this, you have listened to this thing, that we must love, a hundred thousand times. We are stating something which is true.

You have to understand truth in that little word care and listen to that word, and understand it. That word means being sensitive—to be sensitive to another; sensitive to the sky, to the bird, to the tree, to the beauty of the sunset, to the sun on a lovely cloud. If you are not sensitive completely, vulnerably, you will never know what love is. You may have married, you may have children, you may have relations, but you will have no love. The very beginning of reality is at the first step—that is to care.

And there is not only corruption at every level of our life, but there is also death in religion. We are not religious people at all. Please listen carefully, don't agree or disagree. I say we are not religious people. You may go to temples, you may read the Gita, quote endlessly Shankara or some other teacher—you may just as well quote a detective story—and you may perform innumerable rituals. But you are not religious people.

Religion is something entirely different; that is, to find the root of things, to find out for yourself what is truth and live in that, live with it endlessly so that every act and every word and every gesture has a meaning, beauty. And you cannot live that way unless you have passion. And to discover truth you must have passion, an ardent, burning inquiry; and for that you need great energy. Please see, observe all the misery, despair, inward stagnation, inward emptiness, inward rot that is going on, and also technologically what is happening in the world. There is the electronic brain, there is automation. There are extraordinarily rapid changes in technology—what was yesterday is no longer today, it has already moved; the change is much more rapid than the thing that is changing. And unless inwardly, inside this skin, we are very alive, we also will become mechanical. Monkeys have painted pictures. Electronic brains have written poems; they calculate much more quickly than the human mind, though the human mind has put them together. They translate books and solve mechanical problems immediately. These electronic brains are doing most extraordinary things. Man is going to the moon. Outwardly there is extraordinary knowledge, information almost about everything. And inwardly, if you observe yourself, you will see how dead you are. It is only a dead thing that adapts itself to the mechanical things of life, that shapes itself to the form demanded by society.

Do listen to all this. We are not talking vainly because we have nothing else or better to do, nor are you listening for an hour because you happen to have an hour. We are talking of deadly serious things, things that are terribly serious. You have no time to waste. You have only one life—whether you live a future life is irrelevant. You have only this period and you have to completely transform yourself inwardly—that is your task; that is the only thing you have to do. If you don't transform yourself, there is not only this contradiction between the dead or decaying thing of which you are inwardly and this rapid change that is going on technologically, outwardly, but also you have to adjust yourself to that. And a mind that merely adjusts itself to a pattern becomes a dead thing itself.

Anybody can adjust himself to an environment—which we all do because it is the easiest thing to do. But we have to be so alive inwardly that the environment plays very little part. And what we are discussing, what we are going into, is to bring about this state of aliveness, an alertness, a quickness; and that demands an astonishing seriousness on your part.

So, we have to consider what the world outwardly is, and also to be aware inwardly how things are, inwardly in ourselves. Constant conflict—that is all we know; endless conflict in ourselves, projected in the world as war, hatred, ambition, greed, thirst for power, for position. Inwardly we are in a state of constant battle. A mind that is in conflict is a dull mind; conflict makes it dull, stupid. It is not "how to be free of conflict"—I am going to go into that. But first listen to what conflict does, not how to get out of it. If you understand, if you see the poisonous nature of conflict, if you see the deadliness of conflict, the brutality, the insensitivity that conflict brings about, if you really understand conflict, then you are out of it, instantly.

But, you see, we have got so used to conflict. Conflict with the world, with your neighbor, with your children, with your wife; conflict in the office; conflict between groups, between families, between societies, communities, nations; and conflict between divergent, contradictory desires, the compulsions, the urges—you know all this, especially the inward conflicts if at all you are aware, if at all you are watching. When you are aware of this conflict, you want to be out of that conflict; you do not want to understand it, you do not sit with it, you do not care for it—that is, you do not care to understand what that conflict is; that is, you do not look at conflict with affection but with an urge to be rid of it.

Conflict comes when there is contradiction, when there are two desires, pulling in different directions. And so we say we should be without desires, or have only one desire for truth or whatever it is. So you have conflict, not only the conscious conflict, but also the unconscious conflict in which you have been brought up—the society in which you live, the jobs you do that are utterly boring, endless routine, going to the office from morning till night for thirty or forty years of your life. And during those thirty or forty years, you are muttering about religion, God, spirituality, truth; but your main interest is the office, money, family, position; so you are in conflict. That is a fact. Now, being in conflict, you try to escape. The first escape is to get rid of it; that is our instant reaction to every form of conflict. The ultimate escape is war, outwardly—to kill and to be killed.

So, conflict exists when there is self-contradiction, when inside you there is this sense of wanting to do that and also at the same time wanting to do something else—like wanting to smoke, and because you have heard the doctors make the recent announcement that smoking produces cancer, you are frightened. You want to give up smoking, and at the same time you have the habit—it is conflict on a very, very simple, stupid level. But you can go further and further, deeper, into this thing of conflict, of contradiction.

Now, if we understand one thing about conflict, it is this: The whole conflict of life must be understood instantly, not one by one. Because you have no time to examine every conflict as it arises, to analyze, to go into it, to become aware of the cause of it. You follow? To do all the various conflicts one by one is merely a fragmentation, and you cannot put various fragments of contradiction together and make it a whole. But if you take one contradiction, one conflict, the simplest possible, like smoking, and merely listen to it, not saying, "I must give it up or not give it up," then you listen to the whole problem of conflict. This demands patience, and to listen, to observe, you need care.

You are understanding now what an important place "care" has got—care to understand what that conflict is. And when you care, you have patience. When you care, you don't condemn, you don't judge; you look, you observe, you see. If you care for a tree, you water it, you prune it, you give manure to it, and all the rest of it; you look after it; you don't condemn it; you don't say it is going to be a bigger tree or a smaller tree. You care for it, and therefore all comparison ceases. Because you love that tree, you have planted it, watered it every day, protected it; you are looking at it, and in that state there is no condemnation, no judgment; it is just observation.

In that sense, we have to observe with care this vast thing called "conflict," in which we have been brought up. And to look at it, there must be no condemnation, obviously, no comparison, no desire to be out of this conflict. Because the moment you desire to be out of one conflict, you are going to create another conflict as a means of escape; and so you are seeing that through the first conflict you have many other conflicts. So our life becomes a vast field of conflicts.

That is the first thing to realize: that a mind in conflict day after day, a mind that is worn out with problems—problems of society, problems of family, problems of its own, any problem—becomes dull. Problems do not sharpen the mind. What sharpens the mind is freedom to look at the problem. And you need to have a very sharp mind, a sensitive mind, not a clever mind, not a mind that is full of erudition; you need to have a mind that is clear, that is free to observe, to listen, to see.

And what is utterly important is that each one of us does bring about a deep, fundamental revolution in himself. Because, you see, if you have observed the world, the world is yourself—the thing outside you is yourself, you are part of the world. You are not different from the world. You might like to think you are, but you are not; when you say you are a Hindu, a Parsi, this or that, something or the other, you are being conditioned by society to think that way.

You are part of the environment, part of this outward flow which comes inwardly. The two things are not separate. Unless you understand the outer, you do not understand the inner; from the outer you must come to the inner—not start from the inner. You must understand the world, the things that are going on: the vast changes, the corruption, the ugly brutality of existence, the insensitivity, the pettiness, the shallowness of the human mind, and all the false gods. And all gods are false, they are man-made—made by man because he is frightened. A man who is not frightened, a man who sees clearly, who reasons with care—he does not invent gods. That is something entirely different.

So we need a complete revolution, not in any time, but now, actually on the instant. Please see—even intellectually, verbally—the importance of this state: that you have no time, that there is no time. For when you admit time and say, "I will change gradually; change is an evolutionary process; time will bring about a change," when you rely on time, then you are merely continuing what has been, as a "modified continuity." And that is not a revolution, that is not a change, that is not a complete transformation.

You need transformation, you need a very deep revolution. Because without religion—not this phony thing called "religion"—without uncovering for yourself what is real, what is true, the beauty of truth, and the extraordinary meaning of that word, unless you find it out for yourself, any outward transformation, any outward adjustment to conditions, to the environment, to new inventions, will make you all the more dull, more mechanical, more stupid, more clever, but not a human being, totally alive.

So, whether you want it or not, as a human being living in this despairing world, in this world where there is so much corruption, degeneration, you need this immense change taking place in you. And it cannot be brought about through the "will." I am going to go into all this during the talks that are following, but I am just pointing out to you that it cannot be brought about through will, through a deliberate act. Because, then, it is merely conforming to a pattern; and a mind that conforms to a pattern has not the least idea of what this tremendous revolution means.

So this revolution can only come about when you listen with that care to the world outside you, to all the ugliness, the corruption, the desire for power, the politicians and their words and their chicanery, the businessman with his gods and temples, who is out to make money. You know all this is going on in this mad, stupid world. Unless you understand all that, you cannot come within. When you understand the world, you will inevitably come within on the tide of this understanding of the world. When you come inwardly, then you will have to listen much more; and that is our difficulty because we do not know how to listen to ourselves.

We have never listened to ourselves. We know we have only said to ourselves, "I must, I must not; this is right, this is wrong; this is bad, this is good; I must conform to this; I must do this," or "I must not do this." That is only what we have said. We have never listened to ourselves—listened with care so that everything, every detail is revealed. And that is the beginning of self-knowing. Without self-knowing, you have no basis for any action because then all action leads to misery, to despair.

Therefore, a man who would understand what truth is must begin with himself, must begin to know himself. All the intricacies, all the hints and intimations, the ugliness, and the beauty, the murmur of every thought and everything—all that he must know. There must not be one corner untrodden. It must all come out, and it does, if you listen with care. That is why you must begin to care for the things that you do, how you dress, what you say, how you behave, how you are polite, how you conform, how you talk to your servants, if you have servants, how you talk to the boss.

You have to listen with care. And out of that listening comes sensitivity, a sharpened mind. It comes naturally; you don't have to sharpen your mind through conflict. But that sharpening, that natural sharpening without bitterness, without harshness, comes only when you begin to care; and that care brings about a state of attention in which there is listening. Then on that wave you can proceed deeply.

All religions have failed. Religion has nothing to do with beliefs and dogmas—organized belief is merely propaganda. What we need now is not to go to the past, to revive the past. You cannot revive the dead; it is gone, it is finished. Now you have to come alive, totally alive, to find out for yourself what truth is. You have no leader, you have no guru, you have no teacher. You have to find out the flower of goodness, the expanding beauty, and that reality that is beyond the words, beyond the measure of thought—you have to find it out for yourself.

February 9, 1964

Second Talk in Bombay

The problem of communication is always a difficult matter. To commune with one another about serious subjects requires, I should think, a certain quality of attention. Because most of us, when we are trying to communicate something to another, are not clear ourselves; and the other is not actually paying attention or listening—he is burdened with his own problems, with his own anxieties, with his own fears. And so communication becomes extremely strenuous, extremely difficult.

To partake in a talk like this we must both be—the speaker as well as you who are listening—in a state of communion. We must be able to commune with each other. That is, we must both be in a state of intense attention, at the same time and at the same level. If the speaker wishes to say something, as he is going to do, which demands an insight—not a mere verbal acceptance or denial, but an insight—a deep, intimate insight into the whole problem, you and the speaker must meet, commune with each other at the same level, with the same intensity, at the same time. Otherwise there is no communion, there is no communication. You may hear the words and interpret the words according to your fancy, according to your comprehension of a particular language; but really to be in a state of communion requires that you and the speaker both feel intensely at the same time, be in communion with an intensity, at a level that demands your complete attention; otherwise, there is no communication.

I do not know if you have ever communed with yourself—not meditate, but just be in communion, in communication, in contact, in touch, with yourself. If you have ever been in touch, in contact, in communion, with your own mind, with your own heart, you will know that to be in communion requires a certain quality of attention. You must be able to follow swiftly, you must be able to see rapidly the meaning of the word, as well as the significance that lies beyond the word. Communion or communication is only possible when we both understand the nature and the meaning of the word and the significance of the word.

It seems to me, especially when we are dealing with matters that require a great deal of insight, a subtlety of thought, a rapidity of pursuit, you require not only to be in communion with yourself but also to be in communion with the speaker. So your task as a person who is hearing is doubly difficult because you have not only to understand and be in communion with yourself but also at the same time hear the words, and not give a particular importance to, and halt at, the words. You also have to listen with care, with an intensity which does not pervert, which does not translate, which does not compare; you actually have to be in a state of acute communication with yourself as well as with the speaker. That demands a great task, that is a tremendous task. Because we are not just speaking casually about something that does not matter—political or some social reform. But we are talking about something that touches the human being right to the very core of his existence.

We said, in the last talk that we had here, that we are going to the very root of things, to question, to inquire into the very substance of our being. And that requires not only that you be aware of your own states of mind and heart but also at the same time and at the same level, with the same intensity, listen to what is being said. So, if I may point out, your task is much more strenuous. You are not just casually listening, agreeing or disagreeing. We are really exploring into the whole structure of our mind and of our being. And you are doing it in cooperation with the speaker, and therefore you must be in communion with the speaker as well as with yourself. Otherwise all communication between the speaker and yourself ceases immediately; you are off at a certain point, and the speaker is off at another point or pursuing his line.

So I hope you see the task set before you for yourself. I am not setting it for you; you are setting it for yourself. And that is the only way to be in communion with another—whether it be with nature, with a cloud, with the beauty of a sunset, or with your wife and children, with your neighbor, with your boss. You must be in that state of attention where we both have a direct relationship about which we are thinking, talking, or listening. Please see the importance of this; otherwise, you and the speaker have no relationship.

When that is clear, not only inwardly but also outwardly, when your mind is not wandering or tired or thinking about something, when you are listening—not interpreting, not comparing, not evaluating, but actually listening—then you will find that we are both taking a journey together into the very depth of our being and, there, are discovering all the tortures, all the difficulties, all the problems that live in our minds and hearts.

I want to talk this evening about the nature of conflict, and whether it is at all possible to be free totally of all conflict. By conflict I mean the struggle, the perpetual worry, anxiety, despair, the misery, the fears, the conflicts, the struggle that exists within and without, the sense of insecurity, being insecure and seeking an undisturbed state, a permanent state. There is also the conflict that exists between the conscious and the unconscious, the conflict of various desires, the conflict of ambition, the conflict of fulfillment, the conflict of frustration, the conflict of wanting to find out what is truth, and thereby increasing the conflict more. Because we are living in this world and trying to adjust ourselves to this world and to the idea which we have established as a pattern, as an ideal, we are thereby increasing our conflict.

The speaker is going to go into all that, and you are going to listen. But you are not merely listening, accepting or denying, to a talk by somebody outside of you, sitting on the platform. You are listening to yourself with a mental ear, an ear that is completely capable of listening to every movement of your own thought and feeling with clarity, with precision, with reason and sanity.

Most of us seek security of some kind because our life is an endless conflict, from the moment we are born to the moment we die. The boredom of life and the anxiety of life; the despair of existence; the feeling that you want to be loved, and you are not loved; the shallowness, the pettiness, the travail of everyday existence—that is our life. In that life there is danger, there is apprehension; nothing is certain; there is always the uncertainty of tomorrow. So you are all the time pursuing security, consciously or unconsciously; you want to find a permanent state, psychologically first and outwardly afterwards—it is always psychological first, not outward. You want a permanent state where you will not be disturbed by anything, by any fear, by any anxiety, by any sense of uncertainty, by any sense of guilt. That is what most of us want. That is what most of us seek outwardly as well as inwardly.

Outwardly we want very good jobs; we are educated, technologically, to function mechanically in a certain bureaucratic way, or whatever it is. And inwardly we want peace, a sense of certainty, a sense of permanency. In all our relationships, in all our actions, whether we are doing right or wrong, we want to be secure. We want to be told: This is right, this is wrong; don't do this, do that. We want to follow a pattern because that is the safest way to live—either the pattern set by you or by another, by society, by the guru, or by your own ideals and impressions. So there is this constant demand for outward security as well as for inward security. The inward security is made much more complicated when there is the authority of an idea.

We mean by an idea the ideal, the pattern, the example, the formula, the hero. That is permanent, and towards that we are striving. And therefore there is always a distance between *what is* and 'what should be', and therefore there is a conflict. When the mind is seeking security, you must have authority—whether it is the authority of society, of law, or whether it is the authority set by society as an ideal, as a person who will tell you what to do and what not to do. And ultimately the perfect security that we seek is in God. That is the pattern according to which we have lived for centuries upon centuries.

Man has existed as man, as has been discovered, for nearly two million years. And there are paintings and all kinds of things to indicate that man has always been in this constant anxiety, constant fear, constant state of apprehension—it is a stream on which man has floated, all the time seeking, seeking, and in the very search, establishing the authority of a book, of a person, of an idea. And consciously he is doing this.

Observe, please, as I said, your own mind, your own life. That is what you are really interested in mostly—outwardly, security: money, position, power, comfort; and inwardly, an undisturbed state free from all anxiety, free from all problems, free from all sense of danger, imminent or in the distance. That is our life. And we have accepted this pattern of existence, we have never questioned it. When we are very disturbed, we try to run away from it through temples, through various other forms of escape. We have never questioned and never inquired into ourselves whether there is such a thing as security, consciously or unconsciously. And we are going to question now. You may not like it, you may resist it, because we are not used to facing things at all, we are not used to looking at ourselves as we are. We would rather see things that are not there, or imagine things that should be there. Now we are going to look into *what is* actually.

First of all, is there such a thing as inward security in relationship, in our affections, in the ways of our thinking? Is there the ultimate reality which every man wants, hopes, pins his faith to? Because the moment you want security, you will invent a god, an idea, an ideal, which will give you the feeling of security; but it may not be real at all—it may be merely an idea, a reaction, a resistance to the obvious fact of uncertainty. So one has to inquire into this question of whether there is security at all at any level of our lives. First, inwardly, because if there is no security inwardly, then our relationship with the world will be entirely different; then we shall not identify ourselves with any group, with any nation, or even with any family.

Therefore, we must first inquire into the question whether there is a permanency, whether there is such a thing as "being secure." This means that you and I are willing happily, easily, without hesitancy, to look into ourselves. Because we are bound by authority—again outer and inner: the authority of society, or the authority which we have established for ourselves through experience, or the authority given to us by tradition. We are trained to obey because in obedience there is security. And to find out if there is such a thing as security, one must be completely free from all authority. This is very important to understand because all religions have maintained that there is a spiritual, permanent entity—call it by different names, the soul, the atma, or whatever you like to call it. And we have accepted it because of propaganda, conditioning, our own fears, our own demands for security. We have accepted that as a comforting, actual thing, as reality. And there is the whole world which says: There is no such thing, it is just a matter of belief, it has no validity. That is the communist world whom you call the atheist, the ungodly—as though you are very godly because you have a belief.

So, a man who would inquire into this question of security must be completely, totally free of every form of authority—not the authority of the law, not the authority of the state, but the authority that the mind seeks or establishes in a book, in an idea, in an experience, in life. Please follow all this, consciously or unconsciously. Only such a mind that is free from authority can begin to inquire into this immense problem of security. Otherwise, you and I would have no communion because I say there is no such thing as security, psychologically.

If you try to find security in God, it is your invention. You are projecting your desire in a symbol which you call God, but that has no validity at all. So you have to be free of authority in that sense. The mind seeks authority, establishes authority, in an ideal, in a formula, in a person, in a church, in a particular belief, and conforms, obeys. It has to be free of that, not only consciously but unconsciously—which is much more difficult. Most of us, the so-called educated people, do not believe in God because it is not very important, because we either have a very good job or we have a fair bit of money, and belief in God is just an old-fashioned idea; and so we throw it out of the window and carry on. But to inquire into the unconscious and be free of the unconscious urge to find authority is much more strenuous.

I am not going into the unconscious very deeply, I am touching it briefly. The unconscious is the past of many thousands of years. The unconscious is the residue of the race, of the family, the collected knowledge. The unconscious is the whole tradition which you may deny consciously, but it is there. And that becomes our authority in moments when there is trouble. Then the unconscious says: Go to church, do this and do that, do puja—whatever you do. The prompting, the hinting of the unconscious with all the past becomes the authority—which becomes our conscience, the inner voice, and all the rest of it. So one has to be aware of all that, understand it and be free of it, in order to find out if there is security, and to live in the truth which you discover for yourself whether there is security or not.

Also we find a great deal of security, psychologically, emotionally, in identifying ourselves with an idea, with a race, with a community, with a particular action. That is, we commit ourselves to a certain cause, to a certain political party, to a certain way of thinking, to certain customs, habits, rituals, as the Hindu, the Parsi, the Christian, the Muslim, and all the rest of it. We commit ourselves to a particular form of existence, a particular way of thinking; we identify ourselves with a group, with a community, with a particular class, or with a particular idea. This identification with the nation, with the family, with a group, with a community gives you also a certain sense of security. You feel much more safe when you say I am an Indian, or I am an Englishman, or I am a German, whatever it is. This identification gives you security. One must be aware of that, too.

So, when you put to yourself the question whether there is security or not, the problem becomes extremely complex if you don't understand directly the question, not all the side issues. Because it is the desire to be secure, when there is probably no security at all, that breeds conflict. If psychologically you see the truth that there is no security of any kind, of any type, at any level, there is no conflict. Then, you are creative, volcanic in your action, explosive in your ideas; you are not tethered to anything. Then you are living. And a mind that is in conflict, obviously cannot live clearly with clarity, with an immense sense of affection and sympathy. To love you must have a mind that is extraordinarily sensitive. But you cannot be sensitive if you are perpetually afraid, perpetually anxious, perpetually worried, insecure, and therefore seeking security. And a mind in conflict, obviously, like any machine that is in friction, is wearing itself out; it becomes dull, stupid, bored.

So, first then, is there such a thing as security? You have to find it out, not me. I say there is no security of any kind, psychologically, at any level, at any depth. It is not a reality to you. If you repeat it, you will be telling a lie because it is not true to you. So you have to find it out because it is an urgent problem, because the world is in a chaos, the world is in a dreadful condition of despair, violence, brutality. By "the world" I mean the world you live in—not Russia, China, or England, but the world round you—the family, the people you come in contact with. That is your world. In that world, if you look deeply and not just casually pass by, you will find this immense sense of despair, anxiety, degeneration, a constant imitation. And to understand this life with all its vastness and the extraordinary beauty and the depth of life—not imaginary depth, not imaginary beauty, but the actual, palpitating, vital, strong beauty of life, of existence, of living—your mind must be completely in a state where not a scratch of conflict has remained.

So you have to find out for yourself, and you are finding out for yourself. If you feel that there is security inwardly, then you will be living in a perpetual state of conflict. You will be living in a perpetual state of imitation, obedience, conformity, and therefore you will never be free. And your mind must be free completely; otherwise, it cannot see; otherwise, it cannot understand. If it is not free, it cannot see the beauty of a tree, or the loveliness of the cloud, or the exquisite smile on a face.

Is there security? Is there permanency which man is seeking all the time? As you notice for yourself, your body changes, the cells of the body change so often. As you see for yourself in your relationship with your wife, with your children, with your neighbor, with your state, with your community, is there anything permanent? You would like to make it permanent. The relationship with your wife—you call it marriage, and legally hold it tightly. But is there permanency in that relationship? Because if you have invested permanency in your wife or husband, when she turns away, or looks at another, or dies, or some illness takes place, you are completely lost, you become jealous, you are afraid, you run to the temple, you do puja, you invite all kinds of nonsense.

Please observe your own mind, observe your own life. Because if you do not understand your life—the misery, the unhappiness, the constant battle of your life, of your everyday existence—you cannot go very far. You may talk about God, you may talk about love, you may talk about beauty—they have no validity at all. To go very far you must begin very close. And the closest thing to you is yourself; there you must begin.

So you have to inquire and find out for yourself if there is such a thing as security, permanency, an undisturbed state. Not what other people have said, Shankara or somebody else—wipe them out for the moment; they have no truth in your life; they have as much truth as a good detective story. What is truth is your life—the battle, the misery, the conflict, the problems. Unless you understand that field completely, you cannot possibly go any further; if you do, you will be going into an illusion, a fancy, a myth that has no validity at all.

Now, when you begin to inquire, you inquire to find out what is true, what is factual—factual in the sense of psychologically what is actual—not what you would like it to be, not what you think it ought to be. The actual state of every human being is uncertainty. Those who realize the actual state of uncertainty either see the fact and live with it there or they go off, become neurotic, because they cannot face that uncertainty. They cannot live with something that demands an astonishing swiftness of mind and heart, and so they become neurotic, they become monks, they adopt every kind of fanciful escape. So you have to see the actual, and not escape in good works, good action, going to the temple, talking. The fact is something that demands your complete attention. The fact is that all of us are insecure; there is nothing secure.

The fact is that there is nothing certain, nothing. My son may die, my wife may run away, I may fall ill—nothing is certain. Now why don't we accept it and live with that? Do you know what it means to live with it?

Have you ever tried to live with something and not get used to it? You know, one can get very easily used to a tree, to the beauty of a sunset—that is very easy. But to live with a tree, to see the sunset every day anew, to see the leaf as though you are seeing it for the first time, with clarity, with an intensity, with a sense of the extraordinary beauty of that leaf—that requires not memory; that requires that you should look at it anew, each day, afresh, with an intensity.

So one has to live with uncertainty. Because it is only the mind that is uncertain that is creative—not the mind that has continuity; not the mind that is completely secure and then creates, writes a poem; that is too immature, too juvenile. When you live in that state of complete, inward uncertainty, then you will see that you meet every problem of life at any level, any crisis, any challenge, with clarity, with swiftness. Because, for most of us, the inadequacy of response to a challenge is the beginning of conflict. Life is constantly giving us—each one, in different ways according to one's temperament and taste—challenges, conscious or unconscious, all the time, twenty-four hours of the day. How do you respond completely, each time, so that there is no conflict at all? Your response has to be completely adequate, and you cannot keep this up all the time. When there is inadequacy of response, it creates a problem; then one has to meet that problem immediately and resolve it immediately. And that can only happen when your mind is completely in a state of movement, untethered, living, vital. And you can only be vital, moving, tremendously active, in inaction, only when the mind is completely free from all the fears of security.

But you see, for most of us, our everyday life—going to the office, the family, the sex, the money, pleasures—brutalizes us. I do not know if you have considered a man who has spent thirty or forty years of his life going every day to the office! Look at his mind! He cannot function in any other way except in that. Like a doctor who specializes in a particular disease—his heaven will be that disease. And after spending thirty or forty years, your mind is worn out; it is not fresh, it is not young, it is not innocent; it is being brutalized, specialized, beaten, shaped; and so it keeps to itself tight in a corner, and life goes by. That is what you all want your children to be—to have a good job for the next thirty or forty years so that they will be dull, stupid, not capable of facing life. That is all you are concerned with.

There are wars; man is destroying man; there is terrible cruelty; everyone is out for himself, in the name of God, in the name of society, doing good, going and helping people and all the rest of it, using everybody to profit oneself or for the idea with which one has identified oneself. That is the state of man. I am not using the word *individual* because individual is something entirely different. There is real individuality only when you are alone, when you are completely free from all social, environmental control and shaping. You are a man, a human being tortured, caught in this terrible world of misery; and you cannot escape from it. It is a fact. You have got to grapple with it; you have to put your teeth into it. And that requires energy, and that requires passion. And that passion and that energy you cannot possibly have if you waste your life in conflict.

So from the beginning to the end, a mind has to understand this immense problem of struggle, trying to become something endlessly, everlastingly—and that we consider evolution. When one struggles everlastingly to become, fight, fight, there is never a moment of actual peace—not imagined peace, not the peace of the stagnation of the mind that says, "I have found God, I have found some reality and I am happy with it." If a man has not understood conflict, if he has not understood his being, if he has not gone into himself deeply, widely, with clarity, then he has no peace, do what he will. He may pretend to others; then he is a hypocrite. But to find that reality, one must completely understand this question of security, be free and live in that state of uncertainty.

For most of us life is empty. Being empty, we try to fill it with all kinds of things. But if you understand this question of security and insecurity, you will find, as you go into it deeper and deeper—I am using the word *deeper* in the sense of noncomparatively—that it is not a question of time. Then you understand completely this problem of security and conflict. Then you will find—find, not believe—for yourself a state where there is complete existence, complete being, in which there is no sense of fear, no anxiety, no sense of obedience, compulsion; a complete state of being; a light that does not seek, that has no movement beyond itself.

February 12, 1964

Third Talk in Bombay

This evening we are going to paint a verbal picture. The words are not important. You have to hear the words and not be caught by the superficial meaning of those words; it is like looking at a painting. Generally we want to know who the painter is and begin to compare him with other painters, or we bring in our own knowledge about painting and begin to interpret, tear to pieces, the construction, the depth, the light, the color; and we think we understand the painting. So, this evening, we must be rather cautious not to be caught in words or by words. Because most of our minds are slaves to words; we are slaves also in practically every way. Especially words play an extraordinarily important part in our life; words are loaded with significance, with meaning. And we do not listen, we are incapable of listening because the words awaken various symbols, various ideas, fears, hopes, anguishes.

What is important is really to listen with a free mind, a mind that is not merely rejecting or accepting words but has a depth of feeling, a quality that sees what is true and what is false immediately, not based upon knowledge. Because knowledge never gives you the perception of what is true. What gives free insight is total freedom. And we are going to talk about that this evening.

The word *freedom* is heavily loaded, politically, religiously, socially, and in every way. That word is really an extraordinary word with a tremendous significance and depth; we have loaded it, like *love,* with all kinds of meaning. There is political freedom, social freedom, freedom of opportunity to work; there is freedom from religious dogmas, beliefs; freedom from immediate responsibilities, problems, anxiety, fears. Freedom from so many things, the mind wants. And we have built a verbal structure which gives us the appearance of freedom, but we do not know what it means to be really free, to feel it, not to argue about it, not to define it, not to say, "What do you mean by freedom?" We do not know the quality of it, the feel of it, the demand for it—not at any particular level but totally.

Without total freedom, every perception, every objective regard, is twisted. It is only the man who is totally free that can look and understand immediately. Freedom implies really, doesn't it, the total emptying of the mind. To completely empty the whole content of the mind—that is real freedom. Freedom is not mere revolt from circumstances, which again breeds other circumstances, other environmental influences, which enslave the mind. We are talking about a freedom that comes naturally, easily, unasked for, when the mind is capable of functioning at its highest level.

Most of our brains are lazy. Our brains have thickened, have been made dull through education, through specialization, through conflict, through every form of psychological, inward struggle as well as outward compulsions. Our brains function only when there is an immediate demand, when there is an immediate crisis. But otherwise we live in a state of hypnotic, monotonous life, functioning lazily with our jobs and tasks; so our brains are not sharp, alert, awake, sensitive, functioning at their highest capacity.

If the brain does not function at its highest capacity, it is not capable of being free. Because a dull, shallow, limited, narrow, petty mind merely reacts to its environment, and through that reaction it becomes a slave to that environment. And from this arises the whole problem of extricating oneself from the environment, and not being a slave to every form of influence, direction, urge. So what is important is the quality of feeling to be utterly free.

There are two kinds of freedom: one is the freedom *from* something, which is a reaction; and the other is not a reaction, it is *being free.* The freedom from something is a response, depending on our choice, on our character, on our temperament, on various forms of conditioning. Like a boy who is in revolt against society—he wants to be free. Or like a husband who wants to be free from his wife, or a wife from the husband; or free from anger, jealousy, envy, despair. Those are all reactions, responses to given circumstances, which prevent you from functioning freely, easily.

We want personal liberty. And that liberty is denied in a society where the mores, the customs, the habits, the traditions are tremendously important; then there is a revolt. Or there is a revolt against tyranny. So there are various forms of revolt, responses to immediate demands. Really that is not freedom at all because every reaction breeds further reactions, which create further environments through which the mind becomes a slave again; so there is a constant repetition of revolt, being caught by circumstances, revolt against those circumstances, and so on, endlessly.

We are talking of a freedom which is not a reaction. The mind that is free is not a slave to anything, to any circumstances, to any particular routine; though it is specialized to do a certain functional job, it is not a slave to that, it is not held in that groove; though it lives in society, it is not of society. And a mind that is emptying itself of all the accumulations of everyday reactions, all the time—it is only such a mind that is free.

We live by action. Action is imperative, it is necessary. There is the action born of idea and there is the action born of freedom. We are going to go into something that needs the quickness of your brain, not your agreement or your disagreement. The house is on fire, the world is on fire, burning, destroying itself; and there must be action. And that action does not depend on your ideas about the fire, on the size of the bucket, or what you will do. You act to put out that fire. To put out that fire, you cannot have ideas about that fire: who set the house on fire, what is the nature of the fire, so on and on, speculating about the fire. There must be immediate action. This means the mind must undergo a complete mutation.

Man has lived for a million and seven hundred and fifty thousand years, nearly two million years, biologically has accumulated so many experiences, so much knowledge, and has lived through so many civilizations, so many pressures and strains. You are that man, whether you know it or not. Whether you acknowledge it or not, you are the man, you are the result of two million years. Either you continue evolving slowly through pain, suffering, anxiety, all kinds of conflicts, endlessly, or you step out of that current altogether, at any time, like stepping off a boat on to the bank of the river—you can do that at any time. And it is only the free mind that can do it.

Action—that is, to do, to be—if it is born of an idea, is not liberating, is not freeing the mind. And most of our actions are born from a formula, from a concept; and so they are not liberating, they are not freeing the mind. Please, if I may suggest, don't merely listen to the words; observe your own minds in operation. Watch yourself and see what your actions are, and what they are based on. You are not agreeing or disagreeing with the speaker. The speaker is merely indicating what is actually taking place, actually *what is.* If you do not observe *what is* in yourself but merely are listening to the speech, then you will go away with ashes, with emptiness; you will have nothing; you will have wasted an hour, a precious hour of an evening.

You have to watch yourself, watch the operation of your own mind. And that is extremely strenuous because you are not used to watching the activity of a thought. You have to watch the operation of your mind—not guide it, not shape it, not tell it what it should think or what it should not think, but merely observe the reactions of the brain as it listens to the words, as it listens to the crows, as it sees the trees, the evening light, the breeze among the leaves, the shape of a branch, the darkness of a trunk against the evening sky—you have just to watch it. When you so observe it, there is a quickening of the brain. But when you direct that observation—what it should do and what it should not do—then you are reacting and making the brain dull and heavy.

To understand what is freedom and action, you must understand the whole process of your own thinking; that is, you must know yourself. And that is one of the most difficult tasks that you can possibly undertake. Because to know oneself implies a mind that is capable of looking at itself without the previous knowledge which it has acquired. If you look at yourself with the knowledge that you have got, then you are merely projecting or translating what you see according to the past, and therefore not looking at yourself. So to look at yourself demands a freshness of mind, each minute. That is where the arduousness comes in. Please understand this. Because if you do not understand what is being said now, then when I go into the problem of freedom, you will not be able to take it up and go into it.

We are talking about the whole human being, the psyche, the inward activity, the quality of the brain as well as the mind. The brain is part of the mind and the mind is part of the psyche; the entirety is the mind. So one has to understand the whole functioning of oneself.

There is self-knowledge and there is self-knowing. Knowledge is merely an additive process. That is, you can add to it through experience, through further examination, through further exploration; and what you discover, you add to whatever you already know. Every experience is translated according to what you already know, experience being the challenge and the response to that challenge. Because we are having, every minute of our waking or sleeping consciousness, this challenge. When we respond to it adequately, totally, completely, the response does not create conflict and therefore keeps the brain astonishingly active at its highest pitch. But when we respond to the challenge according to our conditioning, to our knowledge, to our previous experiences, that response creates conflict between the challenge and the response.

If we observe ourselves, we shall find that most of us respond according to our knowledge, according to our experience, according to our conditioning either as a Hindu or a Buddhist or a Christian or a communist or a technician or a family man. Such a man has acquired lots of experience, and having accumulated, he reacts. And with that knowledge he looks at himself. Then he says, "This is good, this is bad; this I must keep, this I must reject." When he does that, he is not looking at himself; he is merely projecting his knowledge upon what he sees, and translating what he sees, or interpreting what he sees, in terms of his experience, of his knowledge, of his conditioning.

Please observe this in yourself. The mind that responds to a challenge with previous knowledge is not a mind that is learning; it is merely adding to what it already knows. A mind that learns, or is in a state of learning, is always in a state of knowing, observing. I think these two things must be very clear to each one. Because learning is something entirely different from acquiring knowledge. Learning—to learn—demands that your brain functions at its highest level. But you cannot learn if you merely come to it with an additive mind, with a mind which says, "I am going to add to what already I know."

A mind that is demanding experience and has accumulated experience is never in a state of learning. It is very important to understand this. Because this thing called the 'me', the self, is always in a state of mutation, always changing, moving; it is never static. Every thought, every feeling, which you already know, when you observe it with knowledge, you have reduced to a static state. I will explain it a little more.

You know we have so many feelings. You look at the beauty of a sunset and you may have immediately a certain response. I do not know if you have ever looked at a sunset. I doubt it. I doubt if you have ever watched a tree. The limb of a tree, the beauty of the light, the freshness of the leaves, the movement of a leaf in the breeze—have you ever watched it? In this country beauty has gone. You have destroyed the feeling for beauty because your saints have said you must not look at beauty. Because, for you beauty is identified with desire, with lust for a woman or for a man; you are being told for thousands of years that you must be desireless. And with the attempt to be desireless, you have destroyed the feeling for beauty, the sense of loveliness, seeing something that is perfectly lovely.

Please watch yourself. See how insensitive your mind has become. When you have a feeling of pleasure, pain, of a spontaneous joy of something, the moment you feel it, there is an immediate response to it by naming it, you name it instantly. Please follow this, observe it in yourself. Because all this if you don't follow, when I talk about freedom—it will mean nothing to you. I am talking about a mind that does not name. When you have a feeling, you name it instantly, you give it a name. The very process of naming it is the state of nonobservation. And you name it in order to fix it as an experience in your memory, and then, the next day that memory which has become mechanical wants it repeated. Therefore when you look at the sunset the next day, it is no longer the thing that you looked at spontaneously the first day. So the naming process of any feeling, any observation, prevents you from looking.

Have you ever looked at a flower? There are two ways of looking at a flower: either botanically or nonbotanically. When you look at a flower botanically, you know the species, the color, the kind, what it is; when that interpretation comes in between, you are observing it botanically; when that comes in, you can't see the flower. Please observe this. When you say, "That is a rose. How lovely!" you have already ceased to look at it. Because you have identified that rose with what you have already called a rose, that identification with the past prevents you from looking at the actual rose in front of you.

Similarly, when you look at yourself, when you identify a particular feeling, a particular state, a particular experience, by naming it, you have identified yourself with that feeling through a name which is out of memory, from the past, and therefore you are incapable of looking, observing, listening, seeing that feeling. So this identification, this naming, this symbol which has become so astonishingly important in your life prevents you from looking, feeling deeper, completely.

Take a man whom you call a sannyasi. He is a symbol of the renunciation of the world. The symbol, the outward garb, you respect. For you the outward garb is of extraordinary significance; it does not matter what he is inside. He is being tortured by his hopes, by his sexual demands, by his complex memories, his desire to be like somebody else; this constant imitating process is going on in him, and therefore struggle, conflict, subjugation, control, suppression. You are not interested in that; what you are interested in is the symbol. In the same way, the name, the word, has become a symbol, which prevents us from looking deeper.

So one has to be extremely alert when one watches oneself. Because without knowing yourself, you can't live; you are a dead entity. You are talking, you are reading a book and repeating the book endlessly—the Gita, the Upanishads, or any other silly book. You follow? I said any other silly book because the moment you repeat, you have ceased to understand, you have dissociated it from your actual daily living. What matters is not the book but your daily living, daily feelings, daily anxieties, miseries, the way you think. So you have to know that. Because, without knowing that, you have no foundation, you have no basis for any thought, for any reason; then you are merely functioning mechanically or neurotically.

And to know yourself is the most arduous task that you can set to yourself. You can go to the moon, you can do everything in life; but if you don't know yourself, you will be empty, dull, stupid; though you may function as a prime minister or a first-class engineer or a marvelous technician, you are merely functioning mechanically. So feel the importance, the seriousness of knowing yourself. Not what people have said about yourself, whether you are the supreme self or the little self—wipe away all the things that people have said, and observe your own minds and your own hearts, and from there function.

To know oneself, knowing, is the active present; and what you have learned, knowledge, is the past. The past cannot dictate to the active present. When it does, you create more conflict. But you cannot reject the past either; it is there, in the conscious as well as in the unconscious. And you have to have knowledge. It would be absurd for a scientist to wipe away all the things that he has learned, accumulated, through centuries; it would be absurd for an artist to wipe away his knowledge of how to mix colors and all that. But not to let the past interfere with the active present—that is what we have to understand.

One has to look with eyes, with a feeling, with a mind, with a brain that is intensely active. And the brain ceases to be intensely active the moment you name something, give it a symbol. A man who is studying himself, who is observing himself, is not interpreting, is not comparing; he is merely observing. That is why I said, when you observe a flower, just observe it. Listen to those crows cawing away before they go to sleep; just listen to it without resistance, without any urge to listen to the speaker and to resist the noise of those crows; just listen to everything. Then out of that listening you can pay attention to what you want to listen to. But if you resist the noise of the crows, then you are in conflict. Therefore you have no energy to listen.

So, please observe yourself. That observation is absolutely necessary because if you don't know yourself, you become a hypocrite. All the politicians, all the gurus, all the interpreters, have made you a hypocrite because you don't know what you think, what you are, actually. It is only when you know yourself that you can, from there, function as a total human being, not in fragments. So to know yourself is to observe yourself. And to observe yourself there must be freedom, and that freedom is not a reaction. You have to observe, to listen to those crows freely. If you listen to those crows freely, you are also listening freely to the speaker; but if you resist the crows, you won't listen to the speaker. Do please see the importance of this: In observation, in looking at yourself, every form of resistance such as naming, which is the operation of the past upon the present, destroys, prevents your observation.

So through observation you are learning, constantly learning. And to learn you need a heightened sensitivity, a brain that functions completely at its highest level. When the brain functions at its highest level, there is no time to name the thing that you are observing; then there is immediate action—that is what we are coming to.

For most of us action is derived from an idea, a formula, a concept, an ideal. There is the ideal, and according to that you approximate the action and try to conform to that idea. Look at what has happened in this country with which you are probably very familiar. You have preached and practiced and shouted abroad, nonviolence. That has been your slogan for twenty or thirty years, or whatever it is. And suddenly there is an incident and you have all become violent. Now violence is the fashion. You have forgotten all that has been said about nonviolence. Now you have the army, conscription, every student going into the army—you know the whole business. And you accept it equally as easily as you accepted nonviolence. You don't say, "Stop, let us look at it and let us find out." You have accepted nonviolence easily because it suited you; now you are accepting violence as easily because it suits you. So your ideal of nonviolence has no meaning at all.

And all our ideals, however sublime, however lovely, however beautiful, have no meaning. Because they create conflict between *what is* and 'what should be'. What is important is *what is,* and not 'what should be'. Please do understand this very simple fact, psychological fact: What is important is *what is.* You are angry, you are violent, you are cruel, you are hateful, you dislike, and you protect your security at any cost—that is the fact; not your nonviolence, ahimsa, which is sheer nonsense. When you observe *what is,* without the ideal—which is a distraction from *what is,* an avoidance of *what is*—then you either say, "Well, I accept *what is* and live with it, be miserable with it," or you have a direct action upon it, or it has a direct action upon you. So, what is important is to be capable of observing actually *what is*—whether you are angry, lustful, wanting this and that. You know what human beings are inwardly. To observe it without naming it, without saying, "I am angry, I must not be angry," but just to observe it; to know what it means, the depth, the extraordinary feeling that lies behind all the subtleties, the secrets—if you so observe, then you will see that out of that observation there is freedom, and out of that freedom there is action immediately.

Because action means action in the present, not tomorrow. Action means the active present. And the active present can only act in the present, when there is not all this immense burden of fear, of guilt, of anxiety.

Therefore it is very important to understand the whole psyche, the whole consciousness of yourself. As I was pointing out earlier this evening, if one observes, one will find that the mind, not only the brain, but the totality of the mind, is emptying itself.

You know what is space? You know what space is? There is space between you and me—the distance. There is space between you and the tree, there is space between you and the crow and that noise. There is the space between you and the stars—the space, the distance, in which time is involved. Now, when you observe yourself, there must be space between yourself and that which you observe. And generally we do not have that space; we have crowded it with our ideas, with our opinions, with our judgments. So there must be space. And the mind must have space within itself. It is only in the space within the mind that there can be a mutation, that a new thing can be born. Surely, that space in the mind is when the mind is innocent.

The innocent mind has space like a child within the mother's womb. But a mind that is crowded, that is heavy with its own despairs, fears, joys, pleasures—such a mind is never empty; and therefore there is nothing new for it, nothing new can come. It is only in that emptiness that a new thing, a new mutation can take place. This emptiness, this space, is freedom. And for the space to come about, you have to understand this whole structure of yourself, the conscious as well as the unconscious.

Most of us live at the conscious level, very superficially, because most of us are occupied with our jobs, with our family, with our immediate necessities. We live on the surface. Society, education, the world—they all demand that you live on top. Below that top there is the great depth of your traditions, of your hopes, of your fears, of your gods; all the murky existence of your being is there—and you have to understand that too. So, for a mind that wishes to understand the unconscious, the conscious part has to be quiet for some time, or all the time; and then only all the unconscious begins to tell its story. To understand the unconscious, either you go through the process of analyzing and so on, indefinitely, or you cut through it. And you cut through it when you see the whole activity of yourself, without naming it, immediately.

And therefore freedom is not a reaction. Freedom is a state of being. Freedom is a feeling. You have to liberate yourself, free yourself, even in little things—you dominating your wife, or your wife dominating you, or your ambitions, your greeds, your envy. When you cut through all that, not taking time and discussing about it, then you will see that, without analysis, without introspective moods and demands, to observe—to see things as they are without self-pity, without the desire to change; just to observe—is to have that space.

And the moment there is that space untouched by society, then in that state there is a mutation, a mutation takes place. And you need a mutation in this world because that mutation is the birth of the individual. And it is only the individual that can do something in this world to bring about a complete revolution, a complete change, a complete transformation. What we need in this world at the present time is an individual who is born out of this emptiness.

Have you listened to a drum played often? The man who plays on it can produce any sound, and that sound is clear, sharp, bright, penetrating, only when that drum is empty. If that drum were full, there would be no clear, precise, lovely tone.

In the same way when the mind has space, there is this extraordinary quality of emptiness; then in that state it acts; and that action is the outcome of total mutation. It is only that mind that can understand that which is beyond itself.

February 16, 1964

Fourth Talk in Bombay

I want to go into something very widely and rather deeply this evening. I am going to describe a scene that took place. It actually happened. It is not an invention, it is not a story made up for the sake of making a story, but it actually took place.

We were sitting on the bank of a river, very wide, of an evening. The crows were coming back from across the river, and the moon was just coming over the trees. There was a cloud floating by, and all the evening sun was on it, full of brilliance and delight. The river was flowing richly, very quietly; but the current was strong, deep. Then across the river there was a man singing; I could hardly hear him, but occasionally a note floated across the water. It was really a very beautiful evening, full of charm. There was the strange silence that comes when the sun is about to set, and there was beauty that cannot be expressed in words—you felt it; you felt it through the very bones of your being. You saw that river every day and you saw the sun and the moon every day. But that evening there was a charm, full, quiet, and extraordinarily mysterious.

And the beauty that was there was so palpable, so extraordinarily real, as the tree across the river, as the boatman, as the fish that jumped out of that river. You felt it with a deep passion, with an intensity; nothing existed; there was neither form nor that peculiar emotion that comes when you see something very beautiful. Your mind, your body, your being was utterly still; and that beauty continued; you felt it throbbing in a deep silence. It was a beauty that had no emotional quality; there was no sentiment. It was naked, strong, vital, passionate; there was no sense of any sentimentality. It was like meeting something face to face that is real, naked, complete in itself. It did not want any imagination, any expression, any translation. It was there like a fullness, with a richness, with an extraordinary sense of magnitude and depth; one felt it. And the feeling, not the emotion, that is aroused when you see something extraordinarily beautiful has nothing to do with sentimentality, with emotion, with any memory—all that is banished, and you are there watching an extraordinary thing, a part of your whole being, alive, vibrant, clear, rich.

And there was a man sitting beside us. He was a sannyasi. He did not notice the water and the moon on the water. He did not notice the song of that village man from that village, he did not notice the crows coming back; he was so absorbed in his own problem. And he began to talk quietly with a tremendous sense of sorrow. He was a lustful man, he said, brutal in his demands, never satisfied, always demanding, asking, pushing, driving; his lust had no quietness; and he was striving and he was driven for many years to conquer it. And at last he did the most brutal thing to himself; and from that day he was no longer a man.

And as you listened, you felt an extraordinary sorrow, a tremendous shock, that a man in search of God could mutilate himself forever. He had lost all feeling, all sense of beauty. All that he was concerned with was to reach God. He tortured himself, butchered himself, destroyed himself, in order to find that thing which he called God. He had formed an idea, and according to that formula, he was living. The formula was real, not what he was seeking, not what he was trying to find out. What was real to him was the formula, the form the mind had created, which the saints, the religions, and society had said that he must do in order to find.

And there he was, lost, destroyed, without sensitivity to feel the extraordinary beauty of that evening. And as it got dark, the stars came out full, wide, with immense space; and he was totally unaware.

And most of us live that way. We have brutalized ourselves through different ways, so completely. We have formed ideas; we live with formulas. All our actions, all our feelings, all our activities are shaped, controlled, subjugated, dominated by the formulas which society, the saints, the religions, the experiences that one has had, have established. These formulas shape our life, our activity, our being. We are always approximating ourselves to these formulas, to these ideas, adjusting, conforming when these formulas become very strong. This is the case with most people; they have the formula—that is, what one must do and what one must not do, what is right and what is wrong. The pattern having been set, we torture ourselves to that formula in order to find God, in order to be happy, in order to achieve a certain state of tranquillity.

So our minds are always forming ideas, patterns, formulas, and we shape ourselves according to those formulas voluntarily, consciously or unconsciously, choosing some and rejecting others—rejecting those which are not pleasurable or which are not according to our tendencies, our idiosyncrasies, and our character. Formulas, patterns, are imposed by others, by society, by religion, by saints, by teachers. And if you observe your own life, you will see that you live, have your being, and act according to a formula. We are never free of a formula. There, in the instance mentioned already of the sannyasi, he went through extreme torture because he believed in a formula, because he believed in an idea, which is an extreme form of neurosis. But those of us who have not such compulsive demands—we have our formulas according to which we are torturing ourselves, night and day, consciously or unconsciously, all the time.

As long as the formula, the pattern, the idea exists, there must be conflict between that idea, that formula, and *what is.* And one must realize that conflict in any form, under any guise, for any purpose, noble, ultimate, under any circumstances, is a torture; it is a thing to be completely, totally avoided—not that one must yield to what one wants; that is rather juvenile and it is not worthwhile even to go into it. We torture ourselves with what we should do, with what might be, what has been; and we never face *what is.* This torture man has considered necessary, through centuries upon centuries, to find God. In India they do it in one way, and in Christendom they do it in another way. And those people who do not believe in God, or something beyond, torture themselves with their ambitions, with their brutalities, with their compulsive demands, with their authoritarian rule, and in all other ways.

Reality, that thing which man has sought for a million years, that thing which is translated by different minds, by different people with different tendencies, under different cultures and civilizations—that cannot be understood, that cannot be reached by a mind which is merely tortured. That thing, it seems to me, can only be realized when the mind is completely normal, completely healthy, not tortured by any discipline, by any enforcement, by any manner or any kind of compulsion, imitation. Such a mind must come to it with youth, with freshness, untrammeled, unscratched, innocent, vital, healthy, completely original; otherwise, it will never find.

Because truth, the real God—the real God, not the god that man has made—does not want a mind that has been destroyed, petty, shallow, narrow, limited. It needs a healthy mind to appreciate it; it needs a rich mind—rich, not with knowledge but with innocence—a mind upon which there has never been a scratch of experience, a mind that is free from time. The gods that you have invented for your own comforts accept torture; they accept a mind that is being made dull. But the real thing does not want it; it wants a total, complete human being whose heart is full, rich, clear, capable of intense feeling, capable of seeing the beauty of a tree, the smile of a child, and the agony of a woman who has never had a full meal.

You have to have this extraordinary feeling, this sensitivity to everything—to the animal, to the cat that walks across the wall, to the squalor, the dirt, the filth of human beings in poverty, in despair. You have to be sensitive—which is to feel intensely, not in any particular direction, which is not an emotion which comes and goes, but which is to be sensitive with your nerves, with your eyes, with your body, with your ears, with your voice. You have to be sensitive completely all the time. Unless you are so completely sensitive, there is no intelligence. Intelligence comes with sensitivity and observation.

Sensitivity does not come with infinite knowledge and information. You may know all the books in the world; you may have read them, devoured them; you may be familiar with every author; you may know all the things that have been said; but that does not bring intelligence. What brings intelligence is this sensitivity, a total sensitivity of your mind, conscious as well as unconscious, and of your heart with its extraordinary capacities of affection, sympathy, generosity. And with that comes this intense feeling, feeling for the leaf that falls from a tree with all its dying colors and the squalor of a filthy street—you have to be sensitive to both; you cannot be sensitive to the one and insensitive to the other. You are sensitive—not merely to the one or the other.

And when there is that sensitivity with observation, there is intelligence to observe—to see things as they are without a formula, without an opinion; to see the cloud as the cloud; to see your own deep thoughts, secret demands, as they actually are without interpretation, without wanting them or not wanting them; just to observe, just to listen to the secret wishes; and to observe, as you sit in a bus with the other passengers; to see the passenger near you, the way he behaves, the way he talks; just to observe. Then out of that observation there comes clarity. Such observation expels every form of confusion. So with sensitivity and observation comes this extraordinary quality of intelligence.

Now, if I may point out, please listen to what is being said. Don't take notes. Just listen, as you would listen to a distant song, relaxed, easy, without any compulsive urge to find. Because if you have so listened, we will go very far together. Then you are in a state of neither accepting nor denying; then you are not using the petty little mind that says, "Prove it to me," that wants to argue, dissect, analyze. This does not mean that you swallow what is being said, or become sentimental and accept.

To listen demands tremendous energy. It is neither a sentimental state nor an emotional quality. To listen, you need a very clear, precise, reasoned mind, a mind that is capable of reasoning completely to the very end—that is a very healthy mind. And with that mind, just listen—not to what is being said, but listen to yourself. Listen to the whispers of your own mind, the promptings of your own heart; just listen to yourself. We are going to go into something that demands the fine art of listening; we are going to find out what is true.

When you discover for yourself what is true, then that truth acts. You do not have to act at all. Even in your office, in your home, when you are walking by yourself in solitude among woods and streams, that truth acts which has been discovered by you—not repeated by you because you have heard it said by somebody else. When you discover for yourself what is true and what is false, when you discover for yourself the truth in the false and the truth as truth, then that extraordinary thing has a quality of explosion; and that explosive quality heals and brings about action out of that pure health and clarity. That is what we are going to do this evening. By listening to the words of the speaker, you are going to discover for yourself the truth, and then let the truth operate, where it will, when it will. And when it operates, let it operate without your interference.

As we were saying, observation with this highest sensitivity brings about intelligence. Because without intelligence life is drab, shallow, repetitive, and has no depth and quality. And it is this intelligence that is going to bring about discipline.

When the origin of that word *discipline* is taken into consideration, to discipline means to learn—not to conform, not to follow a pattern set by yesterday or by a thousand yesterdays, or by the formula of tomorrow or ten thousand tomorrows. To discipline is to learn—not to conform, not to obey, not to accept, not to torture yourself by a pattern, by an idea, by a formula. What society, the religions, the technological jobs, and other things have made us do is to discipline ourselves—which is to conform, to imitate, to suppress, or to sublimate. That has not brought us clarity, freedom from confusion, freedom from sorrow; it has not freed the mind so that it can be quiet, feel intensely without any motive, without any future, without any past, just feel tremendously. We know the tortures of discipline.

Take the most insignificant thing like smoking and the conflict to give up smoking. What an extraordinary conflict you go through about a little thing—just to give up smoking! The doctors, the government have said it is bad for you, it may bring cancer; there is the fear, the punishment; yet, you go on. And in the very act of going on, there is conflict because you know that for your health, for various reasons, you should not smoke, but you go on as it has become a habit; and to break that habit you form another formula, another habit.

That is the way we live—always in a state of conflict, always breaking down one habit and falling into another habit of thought, of feeling, of sensation, of pleasure. The sexual habit, the drinking habit, the habit of seeking God because you are miserable—they are all the same, they are an escape from reality. And depending upon our tendencies, our erudition, our knowledge, our education, either we intensify that struggle, that conflict, through so-called discipline or depending upon our tremendous urge or our laziness, we play with discipline. So our minds are always shaped by society, by the church, by circumstances.

Please follow all this, I am talking about your mind. Don't be caught in the words which I am using. The words have no value at all. A word is a symbol, a word is a means of communication; it is like the telephone. If you use the telephone, you don't worship the telephone; what the telephone conveys to you is important.

We have lived with the disciplines, with the mores, with the customs that we call morality—the 'what should be' and 'what should not be'. This is the pattern of our existence—a torture, an ugly, ever-endless strife and misery.

Now, can one live without discipline? Because that way of disciplining, in which one has lived for centuries, is a terrible thing, is a most ugly form of existence; it only breeds a mechanical mind. You know what happens to a soldier who is trained day after day, for months, for years, to obey orders? Have you ever watched him? He functions mechanically, obeying; all spontaneity, all freedom has gone. You go to the office day after day for forty years; with that terrible boredom, what has happened to your mind? Watch it. You have trained yourself, you have conformed because you have a family, you have to earn a livelihood, you have to support the family—we know all the innumerable reasons.

So we have to find out how to live in this world which demands a livelihood, which asks that you do things, day after day, regularly, efficiently, constantly, that you have your own lustful desires, sex, and do not make it into a habit. You have also other urges that create habits. Please listen to this. We have to find out how to live in this world surrounded by all this with complete freedom, without a formula, without twisting the mind, without shaping it to conform, or without it being shaped by society.

Because a disciplined mind—in the sense a mind that conforms, a mind that accepts, a mind that follows, imitates, suppresses—is a stupid, dull, crippled mind; it is a dead mind—whether it is the mind of the holiest of the sannyasis or of the poor, wretched woman or of the man who steals. One has to live in this world without that kind of discipline because one understands it, one sees the truth of it.

You see what a discipline implies—conforming, imitating, suppressing, controlling, living within a certain framework, within a formula, within a pattern, whether it is established by society, by religion, or by your intellectual capacity or experience. Every form of discipline, according to that kind, is deadly, destructive; it makes the mind useless. You may function as a machine, but you cannot possibly, under any circumstances, find out what is truth. Because truth demands freedom; that is, it demands intelligence that is the highest sensitivity; and with this, it demands awareness, which is to observe.

Can you live in this world without this traditional, destructive discipline? Please follow it, please ask yourself. This world is becoming more and more mechanistic; every boy and girl is trained technologically, is shaped. To live in this world is to conform; otherwise, you are destroyed by society, you are pushed out if you are not a Catholic, if you are not a Muslim, a Hindu, or a Buddhist. Can you live in this world without this destructive, traditional weight of a discipline that corrupts, that destroys, that makes the mind ugly? Do you see the truth of that—not because I tell you, not because the speaker has pointed it out? If you will see the actual beauty of that, then you have to ask yourself if you can live in this world without discipline of that kind. Can you live without discipline, doing what you like, free? Can you? You cannot; if you do, you will be in a constant state of endless conflict.

So you have to find out for yourself if you can live with intelligence. We have explained what we mean by intelligence. It is not a definition of intelligence. It is not that you are going to repeat or dialectically say, "That is one opinion and there are other opinions." Discussing opinions and finding truth in opinions is the dialectical way of approach. We are not talking dialectically. We are stating a fact—whether you accept it or don't accept it is totally irrelevant. If you say, "That is your opinion, there are other opinions," we are not discussing opinions. There is no truth in opinions; there are a thousand opinions because there are a thousand men, and each has his own opinion. So we are not talking dialectically; trying to find out the truth of opinions by analysis leads nowhere. What we are pointing out is something entirely different.

We are saying that a mind that is extraordinarily alive and sensitive and awake, can, through the observation of *what is,* through the observation of facts, live in this world without this destructive discipline. A tree is a tree; it is not what you think about that tree. You have to observe *what is,* to observe what you are actually—not what you should be, not what other people have told you that you should be—to observe the color, the richness, the beauty of the sunset, the calm sea, and the extraordinary quality of a still night. Then out of that sensitivity and observation comes this living quality of intelligence.

Now, we need a certain kind of discipline—which is to learn. We are learning. There is no end to learning. Therefore, there is no end to the form of discipline that comes through intelligence. The other discipline—the traditional discipline, which is conforming, adjusting, forcing, suppressing—does not create intelligence, does not bring about this clarity, the beauty and the vitality of intelligence. But where there is intelligence fully operating actually, then out of that intelligence comes the discipline which is constantly learning. Do you know what it is to learn anything? To learn about a motorcar, about your job, how to cook, how to wash dishes, anything—to do it properly, efficiently, you have to be learning all the time. Now, when you are learning all the time, you do not say, "I have learned, and what I have learned is good enough; and therefore whatever happens is going to be something more learned and added to what I have learned." If you say that, you cease to learn.

When the mind is learning all the time, it brings about its own extraordinarily sweet discipline. In that there is no conformity; in that there is no pattern; in that there is no formula, suppression, obedience; it is living. And every living thing creates its own easy, swift, free efficiency of learning. From that comes the beauty of a mind that is so clear, and therefore it needs no discipline.

If you see this—see in the full sense, not merely hear what has been said—if you see with the inner eye, hear with the ear of the mind, then you will see for yourself the true nature of the old traditional, rotten thing called *discipline.* I am using the word *rotten* expressly, because when you look at your own mind, you will see how shallow, dull, insensitive it has become. If you understand this thing called discipline which has made man into an ugly thing, if you see the truth of that, it will drop away from you; you don't have to do anything. You see the truth of that or the falseness of that only when you are highly sensitive and, with that sensitivity and clarity, observe this whole formulation of discipline. Then you are out of it.

But you can't live, doing what you want, because your desires vary from day to day. When one desire is fulfilling itself, it is not satisfied with it; it becomes dissatisfied and seeks another. There is ever a constant change in the objects of desire. Desire remains the same, but the objects change. From childhood to manhood, the objects of desire change constantly, not the desire. And we think that if we replace all the objects with God, we have understood the whole phenomenon. Only we have moved away from the petty to the large, but it is still petty because it is still the object of desire.

So if you understand this whole process, then you will see that you can live in this world with all its challenges, with all its brutalities, because you have the extraordinary insight brought about by intelligence; then you will see that you can live, functioning as a human being who is intelligent, efficient, clear, unconfused. And you can only live that way if you understand how the mind forms, shapes, an idea, and how that becomes the formula according to which you are going to live.

We create formulas because they give us self-identified continuity. We create formulas because they give us a sense of worthwhileness. We breed formulas because they give us a sense of action, a sense of doing something. It is like a man who wants to help—he has a formula that he must help and that he knows what it is to help. It gives self-importance, and in that help, he is exploiting others for his own comfort, for his own well-being, for his own satisfaction.

The flower by the wayside, rich in color and beauty, does not talk about helping others. It is there, full of perfume, loveliness, and an extraordinary tenderness; it is for you to go to it, smell it, and enjoy it. It does not talk about help. But we, who want to be active with our petty, little minds, identify ourselves with ten different activities; we want formulas; we live by formulas and we die by formulas. We have formulas about love, we have formulas about death, and we have formulas about God. So words have become very important—not life, not living. Ideals, all the phony inventions of man in order to enclose himself into an escape from himself, have become important.

So, a mind that is capable of living in this world has to understand this formulation, this framing of ideas and living according to them. When once you see the truth of it, then you can ask a really fundamental question: Is it possible to live without any formula at all—a formula of the past, or a formula of the future? To find that state and to be in that state demands astonishing clarity in which there is no conflict, no torture of any kind, at any moment. Because a mind that is a light to itself, a mind that is completely awake—it is not tortured, it has no formula, it has no time.

February 19, 1964

Fifth Talk in Bombay

I would like, if I may, to talk over this evening something rather complex, but yet very simple. We need a great simplicity—not the loincloth simplicity, but of the mind that thinks clearly, simply, without any philosophy, without any system. Such a mind is a rare mind, and such a mind is necessary to understand something very complex, something that demands an approach that is not cluttered up, suffocated, by ideas, by words, by symbols, by all the various accumulations that man has gathered together through so many centuries. To go into the problem of sorrow, of time, and that strange phenomenon called 'death', one must have, it seems to me, an extraordinarily simple but a very penetrating mind.

When you are faced with something of a tremendous nature, words, dialectical and philosophical theories, opinions, have very little value. We are not dealing with theories, with a system of philosophy; but we are dealing directly, in immediate contact with sorrow. And to understand that ever-existing grief, one must put away any escape from that fact, any idea or any system of thought; one must come to it, if one can, with a sharpened mind and with an insight that one can have when one is confronted with something that one has to solve. Man has lived for so long, for so many centuries, with sorrow. We have become accustomed to it, we accept it, we philosophize over it, we try to find out explanations, the cause of it, and so on and so on. But we have not resolved it, we have not come to the end of it. Man, who has lived for such a long period of time, has not—except perhaps one or two—really stepped out completely, totally free from this thing called sorrow.

And I would like, if I may this evening, to explore together if it is at all possible to end sorrow. Not that there is an ending and therefore you believe in an ending of sorrow, but actually to take the journey of exploration together, if you are willing with the speaker to go into it—not intellectually or verbally, which has no meaning at all. To say, "I understand intellectually," or "Verbally, I comprehend what you are trying to say"—such statements have no value at all to a man who is really taking the journey into this question of sorrow. It is not that there is an ending or that it must continue, but we see that unless we solve it, unless we are entirely, deeply, everlastingly free from it, every movement, every thought, every action is within its shadow, within its darkness; and so, there is never a moment of freedom, of complete well-being, sane and rational, a cup that is full, overflowing, without a breath of sorrow.

To inquire into this thing, we must also keep in mind the question of time because they are tied together, they are not separate. It is not that I will understand sorrow and then I will be free of time, or in understanding time I shall overcome sorrow or completely comprehend this extraordinary mystery called 'death'—they are interrelated. If you do not end sorrow, you will not end or put a stop to time; and without putting a stop to time, you will not understand the extraordinary quality of death. So they are intimately related, one to the other.

All these talks here are related to one another. You cannot take one part of them and say that you will live with that part. Either you take the whole of it, the totality of all that is being said, or you reject it totally. You cannot take one fragment and live with it, try to comprehend it. You must take the whole. Similarly, if you would go into the whole question of sorrow, you have to take time, sorrow, and this thing called 'death'. Man has tried to solve, to overcome through every form of worship, theory, to free the mind from this dread of death, from this extraordinary fear of the unknown. So if you would comprehend the beauty of death, you must also go into the question of time and sorrow because death is something that is intimately connected with life—not at the end of life; it is not something you put away in the distance and look at it with a dread, with an apprehension, with an agony. Living is dying and dying is living, and one has to understand it—not theoretically, not quote the speaker as though one has understood him. We must together go into it. And I hope we shall have time, this evening, to go into this question of time, sorrow, and death.

We all know sorrow. There is the sorrow of a mind that has never fulfilled; that is poor, empty, dull; that has become mechanical, weary; that sees a cloud and does not know the beauty of that cloud; that has never been able to be sensitive, to feel, to comprehend and live. There is the sorrow of not achieving, not becoming, not being. There is the sorrow of disappointment in life. There is the sorrow of incapacity in the awareness of a very small, incapable mind, inefficient, limited, shallow. The sorrow of a mind that knows that it is stupid, dull, heavy; and, do what it will, it is never sharp, clear, tremendously alive—that also breeds sorrow.

There is every kind of sorrow that man can possibly invent or has been through. It is there persistently, continuously, willingly, or hidden deep down in the recesses of one's own heart which has never been explored, which has never been opened and looked at. There is the unconscious sorrow of man who has lived centuries upon centuries, has never solved this thing, the agony, the despair, the ambition. It is there. And we have never really come into contact with it; we have avoided it; we have run away through various forms, through hopes, through all kinds of intellectual, verbal theories and ideas. We have never directly come into a crisis with it and faced it, as we have never come into a crisis with time. One has to bring time into a crisis, and one has never confronted the whole problem of time.

So one has never gone into this extraordinary thing, this aching business called sorrow; and one cannot go into it if one avoids it. That is the first thing to realize—not to avoid it. We avoid it, either through explanation, through words, through conclusions, through formulas, or through drink, through amusement, through gods, through worship. The mind which wishes really to comprehend and put an end to sorrow has to stop completely every form of escape. And that is one of our most difficult things because we have a net of escapes, a complicated net of escapes. The word *sorrow* is an escape from the actual fact.

Please do listen with your heart and mind—not just verbally because that will lead you nowhere; you will leave this gathering empty-handed, with ashes. If you don't listen with that quality of attention, that is your affair, because we are talking about something that is yours, not mine. This is your problem; you have to deal with it, you have to live with it, you have to go beyond it. So you have to listen with intensity, with passion, with alertness. Don't say, "How am I to be alert, how am I to be passionate?" There is no "how," there is no system; it is like going to a doctor, when you have to be operated on. Then you are directly in contact with the fact that you have to be operated on. So you have to give your whole being to that decision whether you shall or you shall not be operated on. In the same way to really comprehend this thing called sorrow, every form of escape, the gods, the drinks, the amusements, the radio, everything must come to an end.

Because sorrow is thought and thought is time, you have to understand *time*. There is the time by the watch, as yesterday, today, and tomorrow. The sun sets and the sun rises—the physical phenomenon. The bus leaves at a certain time, and the train starts at a certain time—that is the time by the watch, chronological time. Now, is there any other time? Please put to yourself this question: Is there any other time, except chronological time? There is time as duration, apart from chronological time, the time by the watch. There is duration, continued existence: I was, I am, and I will be. The memories, the experiences, the various anxieties, fears, hopes—all that is there in the field of time as the past. And that past which is psychological, which is memory, that burden of yesterday with all its experiences—I carry it today; memory carries it today, and that memory is identified through thought as the 'me'. If there were no memory, if there were no identification with that memory from which arises thought, there would be no center as the 'me' that carries this burden from day to day.

So there is time by the watch. And there is psychological time—is that time valid? Is that true time? Is not time that interval between actions? When there is action which is spontaneous, real, actually there is no time. You have forgotten the past, the present, and the future while living in that state of action. But when action is derived from the past, you have introduced time into action. This requires your attention because we are dealing with an extraordinarily complex problem of action within the field of time and action outside the field of time—not theories, not what the Gita, the Upanishads have said.

When the speaker is talking about action, do not compare, do not say that is what the books have said; then you are not living with the question; you are living with what you have already heard or what somebody else has told you. What somebody has told you may not be true at all; it is not. You have to find it out, and there lies the extraordinary strength, the vitality, the beauty, and the originality. You have to be original—not quote what Shankara, Buddha, or anybody else has said.

You have to be original to find this out—not through the speaker. The speaker can only point out and use words. But you, through the act of listening, have to tear the words away and explore; you have to see if it is false or real. And you cannot see if it is false or real if you have brought along opinions, ideas, suspicions, fears—then you are not moving. What the speaker is doing is bringing time into a crisis. Because we use time as a means of escape. Or we have used time as the only present, the now, and so we make the best of life now, with all the despairs, agonies, anxieties, fears, hopes, joys. We say, "We only live a few years, and let us live with all that making the best of it." That is what we do, and that is what all the philosophers have done. And the people who have invented theories are deadly frightened of death too.

So we are concerned with time. And we say time is the interval between actions. A mind that is in action can be without time. Please follow this. A mind that is in action with an idea, with a motive, with a purpose, with a formula, is caught in time; and therefore that action, being incomplete, gives continuity to time. You know, for us time is not only psychological duration but also continued existence: that is, I will be that tomorrow or next year. The "will be" is not only conditioned by the environment, by society, but also by the reaction to that conditioning, to that society—that reaction saying to itself that it will be that, that it will reach it ultimately. When one says, "If I am not happy today, if I am not inwardly, deeply, widely, inexhaustibly rich, I will be," there is the deception of time. The man who thinks that he will be and is striving after the 'what will be'—for him, the greatest sorrow is time.

Is it possible for the mind to be always in instant action, spontaneously, freely, so that it has never a moment of time? Because time is peripheral thinking. All thinking is on the periphery, on the border—all thinking. Because thought is the response of accumulated memory, experience, knowledge; from that, there is thought which is reaction to the past. Thought can never be original. You may use words, which are of the past, to express the original; but the original is not of time. So, to find the original, the mind must be entirely free of time—psychological time, duration, the idea that "I will be, I will achieve, I will become."

The clerk, the poor man who goes every day by tube, by bus, to the office, for forty years in a crowded bus, smelly, dirty—his one hope is that one day he will become the manager. His wife goads him, society pushes him, drives him, to be somebody in this world, with a bigger house, more comfort, more joy. One must have physical joy, comfort. It is absolutely, scientifically possible for all human beings to have it now. But it is not happening because we are so stupid; we have divided ourselves into nationalities, into sovereign governments; we have provincialism, linguistic separateness, so on and so on. This is what is preventing us.

As the clerk wants to become the bank manager, and the bank manager wants to be a director, as the priest wants to become the archbishop, as the sannyasi wants to become, to reach ultimately something or other, so we approach our life with the same attitude. We have approached everyday living in terms of achievement; so, psychologically, we come to it, saying, "I must be good; I must do this; I must become." It is the same mentality, the same ambition; so we introduce time. We never question time. We never say, "Is it so? Shall I in ten years be happy, intelligent, aware, tremendously, inwardly rich, so that there is only one thing?" We have never questioned; we have accepted it as we have accepted everything—blindly, stupidly, without any thought, without reason.

So I say time is poison, time is danger, of which you are to be tremendously aware—as living with a tiger. You have to be aware every minute that time is a deadly, poisonous thing, unreal. You are living today, and you cannot live today completely, richly, widely, with an extraordinary sense of beauty and loveliness if you bring with it all of yesterday. So you have to go into this question of memory.

Memory, knowledge, experience, and all the scientific, technological accumulation as information—all this has vital importance when you are doing something material. In things with which you have to live, there memory must function most efficiently, like an electronic brain. I do not know if you know anything about the electronic brain that man has built. It can do most extraordinary things—it can paint, write poems, translate, even conduct an orchestra. But that electronic brain works on the information that man has fed into it, through association and all the rest of it. And to put a question to that electronic brain, you must use precise words; otherwise, it won't answer you. So there is a whole school now going into, investigating into, the question of action in language—but that is irrelevant for the moment.

So, most of us bring the past into the present, and the present becomes mechanical. You observe your own life and you will see how extraordinarily mechanical it is! You function like a machine, like a rather poor imitation of an electronic brain. Because you have accepted, you have got used to time. Now there is a life out of time when you understand the past, the past being memory and nothing else.

The memory as knowledge, accumulation of experiences, the things that man has gathered for millions of years—that is the past, conscious or unconscious; all the traditions are there. And you come to the present with that, the 'now', and therefore you are not living at all. You are living with memories, with the dead ashes of yesterday. Do watch yourself. Then, out of the dead ashes of memory, you invent the tomorrow: I will be nonviolent one day; I am violent today, and I will keep on polishing my lovely violence until, one day, I will be free and be nonviolent—which is so infantile, juvenile! You have accepted it; you do not spit on that idea. And there are people who talk such nonsense. You treat them as great people because you are caught in time, as they are caught in time. They are not liberating you, they are not making you face the fact of time—which is to bring the whole past into the present, as a crisis.

You know what happens when you are in a crisis—an actual crisis, not an invented crisis, not a crisis with words, ideas, and theories? When you are actually confronted with a crisis that demands your complete attention—complete attention being attention with your mind, your eyes, your ears, your heart, your nerves, the whole of your being—do you know what happens? Then, there is no past; then, there is nobody to tell you what to do; then, out of that tremendous attention comes spontaneity; then, in that state, there is no time. But the moment you begin to think about the crisis, the moment you begin to "think," all the past comes into action. Thought is the reaction of the past—association, and all the rest of it. And then you have the beginning of time and sorrow.

Therefore when a mind is not really in a state of action but in a state of inaction, from that comes further inaction, which is of time. There are two kinds of inaction. The inaction that time breeds, and the inaction which is the total state of the mind when it is confronted with a tremendous crisis. Out of facing a tremendous crisis, the mind itself is completely inactive—which is, free from all thought—and out of that inaction, there is action; and that is the only action that counts, not the other.

So, one has to understand the nature of time and the meaning of time. By the word *understand* I mean really one has lived with it, gone into it—not accepted any theory, any verbal explanation; and not escaped through the past, but has actually gone into this phenomenon of psychological time. When you go into it, you bring time into a crisis; then that crisis makes you completely attentive, and therefore the mind is in a state of action. The mind is always acting because, then, it is free from that state of the past and the future, which is time. And in that state, when the mind is not concerned with the past or the future, the present has a different meaning. It is not a theory, it is not a state of despair. So the ending of sorrow is the ending of thought, and the ending of thought is the beginning of wisdom. The ending of sorrow is wisdom.

You really have to understand death. By understand I mean to live with it—not at the end of your life when you are crippled, diseased, old, when your brain cells cannot function rationally, clearly, sharply, but while you are young, fresh, alive, active. To live with death, you have to understand life, not the life of somebody else, but your life—the daily life, your office, your tortures, your miseries, your hopes, the despairs, the wide field of living. If you don't know life, you don't know what death is. Do please listen to what is being said. These are not cryptic sayings which you have to think over tomorrow. You are living now, at this moment, not tomorrow. Therefore you have to listen—not put into memory and think over.

The speaker said just now that if you do not know what life is, you will never know what death is. And if you do not know what death is, you do not know what living is. So living is intimately connected with death. That which we call living, the everyday existence, is a torture, is a boredom, is a state of anxiety, despair, covered over with bright thought, innumerable masks of civilization. Your life is a petty life of quarrels, of jealousy, of envy. If you don't understand that, if you do not put an end to quarrels, to greed, to sorrow, to all the petty tyrannies of society—all societies are petty—if you do not understand life, then you are merely a tortured human being, and inevitably death is there waiting at a distance, perhaps ten years or forty years or one hundred years.

So there is the fear of the unknown—fear of the unknown as death, and fear of the unknown as life. Do you know what we mean by life? The waking and sleeping, and that interval between that waking and sleeping, which is darkness, misery, conflict, and endless effort—that is what we call living. We have never said, "Is that living?" We have accepted it, as we have accepted the squalor, the poverty around us, the starvation around us. You have accepted this as life, and this thing you want to continue; and that is why you are frightened of death—the known is better than the unknown. And the known is so petty, so utterly meaningless—the toil, endless until you die. Then you invent a significance to life, a purpose of life, and then discuss that.

So we never die to the life of misery, psychologically—that is, to be aware of it, to face it without any choice, without any condemnation, just to observe it completely, look at it without any verbal, intellectual formulation or any form of escape. When you are so confronted with the life that you live every day, when you are faced with it without any escape, you are in a state of crisis; that state is a state of tremendous passion—I am using the word *passion* not as lust.

Do you know how to die to a little thing effortlessly—to smoking, to any habit, to ideas, to fears? To die effortlessly to fear is to face fear and follow the whole thread of fear—not halfway. For fear is, like sorrow, an unending state for man—fear of loneliness, fear of public opinion, fear of the future, fear of the past, fear of not being, fear of not becoming. When you face fear, you have to go to the very end of it; and you can go to the very end of it only when there is no choice, when there is no verbal interference. And then you will find that there is an extraordinary sense of isolation, a thing like loneliness; you have to go through that.

So you have to die, die to everyday incidents and experiences and memory, whether they are pleasurable or painful. Because when death comes, you are not going to argue with it, you don't say, "I am going to keep that which is pleasurable; please take away that which is painful." It is going to take away everything. A man who says, "What happens after death? Do you believe in reincarnation? Is there a continuity of the 'I'?"—such a man will never know the nature of death. And if he does not know the meaning and nature of dying while living, he will never know what it is to live.

We do not know what love is. We know pleasure; we know the lust, the pleasure that is derived from that and the fleeting happiness which is shrouded off with thought, with sorrow. We do not know what "to love" means. Love is not a memory. Love is not a word, love is not the continuity of a thing that has given you pleasure. You may have relationship, you may say, "I love my wife"; but you don't love. If you love your wife, there is no jealousy, there is no dominance, there is no attachment.

We do not know what love is because we do not know what beauty is—the beauty of a sunset, the cry of a child, the swift movement of the bird across the sky, all the exquisite colors of a sunset. You are totally unaware, insensitive to all that; therefore, you are also insensitive to life.

So to find out what death is, one has to die every day to everything that one has gathered, remembered, and passed over. If you have ever died to a pleasure, you will know what it is to die actually—not theoretically, verbally, but actually to come to an end of pleasure, voluntarily, easily, without any sense of effort, reward, punishment, motive. If you know how to die to a little thing called pleasure, then you will also know how to die totally to the whole question of the past, to time and to sorrow. When you die every day to everything unhesitatingly, freely, with a full smile and delight in your heart, then you will know what death is.

Death is not something in the distance to be avoided, to be frightened of. It is there, whether you like it or not. It is there like beauty, like love. But we have put it at a distance, and the distance is time. And so we make time into poison. Therefore we neither live completely, totally, with a fullness, with complete intensity and passion, nor do we know what it is to live or to die.

To die is to end continuity: the continuity of a thought, of a pleasure, of an idea, of a problem. In that ending there is the beginning of innocence and therefore the beginning of the new. That which has continuity can never be the new, and therefore that which has continuity can never be love. Please, do understand this.

You need a different world, a different culture, a different society. Therefore you have to die to everything that you have known so that your mind is made fresh, innocent, and young. And in that innocency, in that freshness and youth, there is love. And when there is that love, there is that intensity of life, living. Living then is action: action which is all the time, not a moment of recess, of interval; it is there all the time completely. And to understand that, you have to die, so that the mind is always in a state of the unknown, free from the known. And then you will see that fear, sorrow, and the things that have shadowed man thousands upon thousands of years come to an end when your mind is made fresh by death.

February 23, 1964

Sixth Talk in Bombay

If you permit me, I would like to talk, this evening, about the meaning and the nature of meditation. To go into it rather deeply, one must not only use reason and see the limits of reason, but also one must have passion. For most of us passion is a thing that is derived or aroused, and we do not know passion without a motive, which is not aroused. For most of us, with our daily activities, with our innumerable responsibilities and commitments, much of our energy is absorbed, taken away, by the daily events, by the daily experiences, wrangles, miseries, conflicts, and sorrows. We have very little energy to take us very deeply into anything; we are satisfied merely to skip on the surface of things and be satisfied with a few phrases, limited experiences, and certain beliefs.

But really to go into something that demands our complete attention and our total energy requires reason, as a beginning. We would rather avoid not only that word but the implication of that word. We think it is not quite spiritual—if I may use that word *spiritual*—when we bring reason into it; we would rather be vague, sentimental, emotional, devotional, believing, living in a hypnotic state, and from there imagine, or have, some formula about God and all the rest of it. So we try to avoid reason.

We are using the word *reason* not in a philosophical sense with all its implications; we are giving to that word the simple meaning of great honesty in thought, sanity, a sense of clear insight, perception, where there is no deception or self-delusion. Without reason as a beginning, you cannot go very far. Because, without reason, you are inevitably led to all forms of delusions, misconceptions, fears, and all the rest of it. To understand the nature and the meaning of meditation, it is absolutely necessary to reason step by step so that your mind is sharpened, your brains are clear, without any distortion, without any pressure. It does not demand any belief, any system; but it requires a brain that is sensitive, sharpened, clear, that can go step by step, not illogically, not jumping, but with rationality, with sanity.

Without reason, passion becomes merely lustful, pleasurable. Passion which is aroused, which has a motive, becomes pleasure; and pleasure breeds pain, anxiety, fear. We are talking of a passion that is not aroused, that has no cause. Because such passion implies the fire of complete attention, complete giving oneself over to something, logically, sanely, reasonably, in which there is no commitment, no belief, no dogma. Without that passion one cannot go very far.

If you see a beautiful sunset on a lovely evening, if there is not that complete attention, that passion, when you look at it, it becomes merely another evening without much significance. If you look at the branch of a tree in sunlight just as the sun is setting, and if you are not capable of feeling tremendously the beauty, the extraordinary quality—not aroused by the branch, by the sunlight, but because you are in that state of passion—then every event, every incident, every scene, every experience becomes merely another routine, without much meaning, without much significance. And if we do not understand the meaning and the nature of meditation which is astonishingly important in life, we shall miss not only the depth but the beauty and the truth of life.

We are going to talk this evening about meditation and the meditative mind. To go into it very deeply, one must first lay the foundation, the foundation being self-knowing. Without knowing yourself completely, totally, without knowing yourself with all the intricacies of the mind, all the secret recesses of your heart and your desires, secret hopes and longings, you have no basis from which to start clearly, sanely, and widely. That foundation is absolutely necessary because otherwise you will deceive yourself; otherwise, meditation becomes merely a hypnosis, a hypnotic, self-suggestive state where you have visions, excitement, and every kind of delusion.

As we are going to take together a journey into this extraordinary thing called meditation, you and I have to lay that foundation. To lay that foundation there is no method. You have to understand yourself: your thoughts, your feelings, your activities, the way you speak, the way you talk, your gestures, your relationship, your jealousy, your anxieties, your fears, your guilts, and the innumerable escapes that you have established for yourself. You have to understand the totality of all this. Either you understand it in a flash completely—which can be done, and which does not demand time; and that is the only way—or you understand by a slow process of analysis, self-critical awareness, a process of elimination, a gradual exploration. This process, if you do that, will not, under any circumstances, establish righteousness; what it establishes is a peripheral action. Such action, however wide, however deep, is an action merely at the border, merely at the periphery of one's own being; and you can spend years, months, days, polishing it—that has very little value, except socially. Such action has no value whatsoever when you want to go into this question of finding out for yourself what is truth, if you are really inquiring into the source, the origin, the beginning of all things.

That foundation is not laid through the cultivation of the periphery. As it is necessary to take a bath every day, the peripheral cleanliness is necessary—a certain morality, a certain cleanliness of thought, action. But merely by everlastingly cleaning the periphery, the outward circle, the border, one will never find, or come to the center of things. So virtue is not of time, but yet the mind must be extraordinarily virtuous. Virtue is not a thing to be cultivated. Because the moment you cultivate a thing, it ceases to be virtue; it becomes a vice.

You cannot cultivate humility. It is only the vain man, the man who is proud, vain, arrogant—he cultivates virtue as a cloak to hide behind, as a mask behind which he can have full play for his vanity. But yet, there must be humility in the sense—a mind that does not obey, that does not follow, that has no pattern, no formula, no system, but is willing to learn; a mind that never climbs the ladder, but even if it has taken two steps, it comes down and begins again. There must be that sense of humility, not humbleness, not groveling, not the worshiping of a guru, but that quality of mind that has understood the nature of fear, the anatomy of authority that seeks someone to give it comfort, position, security. In the understanding of these things comes that sense of humility which is absolutely necessary if one would learn the nature of meditation, the nature of truth, the meaning of reality.

First of all, for most of us, life, the everyday living is a drab, shallow, ugly, petty, little thing. The quarrels, the office with its boredom, sex and its repetitive pleasures, the daily efforts, struggles—we want to escape from all that. And meditation, for most people, becomes an easy escape; they practice, they sit down and follow a system of thought, ideas, and a formula which again becomes very repetitive. And they do not mind such repetitive activity of the mind because they ultimately hope to achieve or gain or understand something which that system promises. That is not meditation at all, it is merely an escape from actuality, from *what is,* into self-hypnotic states.

And most people are satisfied with this formula of meditation, the repetition of words. If you go into it, you will observe that if you repeat over and over and over again a name or a sentence or a mantra or whatever you do, obviously such repetition dulls the mind, it puts the mind to tranquillity, to sleep; and that state of self-hypnotic, suggestive sleep is considered an extraordinary state that you have achieved. It is a form of hypnosis, and it is a very well-known phenomenon. In that state of hypnosis you may have visions which are the projections of your own background, of your own fears, of your own conditioning; and you get terribly excited about those. But that is not meditation.

And if one would go very deeply into this whole question of meditation, one has to drop that formula of meditation completely and totally. You cannot play with it. Because there must be no breath of any suggestion, any self-hypnosis, any directive; the mind must be completely clear, without any pressure, without any conditioning.

You know, as a Hindu, as a Muslim, as a Christian, or what you will, you may see your gods; those are the projections of your own background, your own desires; you will see your Masters, your saints, your saviors, your Krishnas, and your Ramas and all the rest of it; those are all juvenile, immature. To inquire into meditation, they must be entirely put aside, not forcefully, not surgically, but because you understand yourself.

And that is why self-knowing is extraordinarily important for a man who would go very deeply into meditation. And what is important is also to break down immediately the whole psychological condition of man, the psychological structure imposed by society, and by you through society—the psychological structure of greed, envy, ambition, the desire to be secure in a belief, in an idea, in a formula. And that breaking down of your conditioning as a Hindu, as a Christian, or what you will, can only be done instantly, when you bring the conditioning into a crisis, and that crisis demands your attention. Every crisis demands your attention—attention being that you give your complete energy, your complete thought, all your feelings, everything that the crisis demands.

You know, when you lose your job, when you are suddenly thrown out, or when there is sudden death, or you are faced with a real problem—not an imaginary, speculative problem, but an actual problem—that demands your attention. It is a big crisis and you have to answer it; you cannot avoid it, you cannot run away from it; it demands attention.

So one can bring the whole conditioning—I mean by the conditioning, the past of the race, of the family, of the name, of the culture, the superficial moralities—all that into a crisis in the present. And that is the only way to break down the conditioning of the mind; then the brain is sharpened and clear and free. So really for a mind that would go very deeply into meditation, these are absolutely, inevitably necessary; otherwise, you are fooling yourself with a lot of things that have no meaning whatsoever.

Then there comes the question of prayer. That is supplication; somebody is going to do something. A higher entity, a superior wisdom, a Master, a guru, a savior, somebody outside of your own clarity, understanding, is going to do something for you, for your people, for your race. That again leads to delusion. You may, through prayer, receive something—it is a well-known psychological phenomenon; it is not the moment now to go into that. You can pray for a refrigerator and you will probably get it—that is a very well-known phenomenon. So, that has to be abandoned too, that has to be completely put aside.

If you are following what we are talking about—and I hope you are doing it, not merely listening verbally, hearing the words, but actually following it step by step as the speaker is unfolding it—you will find that your mind now, your brain, is no longer functioning at the periphery, at the edge, at the boundary, but it is beginning to sharpen itself; it is beginning to clear itself of all the debris, of all the accumulation of the past; and therefore it is capable of looking, observing, listening.

Then there is the question of control of thought. Every form of control—every form, physically, psychologically, and mentally—is detrimental, is destructive. Please listen to all this. Don't say, "Must I not control?" but listen to the very end of this explanation. Every form of control implies subjugation, imitation, forcing, compelling. And in that is involved a great deal of effort: I must become that, I must discipline myself to that. When you do that, the mind and the brain are perverted; they are not clear. Only the mind that is not perverted, the brain that is not twisted, that has no pressure of any kind in any direction—it is only such a mind, such a brain, that can understand what is truth; not a brain, not a mind that is shaped through compulsion, through force, through imitation, through fear.

So one has to understand this whole problem of controlling thought. Everybody controls thought; every schoolboy is taught how to control, how to concentrate. One has accepted it as an axiom, as you all accept so many things in life. You never question, you never say no to anything that is serious. You may say no to some little things, but you never deny; and it is only through denial that you find out.

We are going now into this question of control and what is involved in it. Where there is control, there is waste of energy. You need tremendous energy to go to the very end of meditation, and therefore there must be no wastage of energy. This energy is not brought about through so-called sexual abstinence—that is only a peripheral cleanliness. This energy which you have to have can only come through clarity, when the mind is absolutely free, without any distortion, when the brain is highly sensitive—sensitive to everything, to every reaction, to the beauty of a sunset, to the cawing of a crow, to the squalor and the dirt on the road, to the intimations of your own unconscious, to your relationships, to the quiet night when you are by yourself either in a pleasant room or an ugly room; to be totally sensitive. And that can only be brought about naturally, spontaneously, easily, when we understand this question of control.

There is, for most people, "the thinker and the thought"; so there is a division between thought and that entity who is separate from thought. Observe yourself, please. You are not listening to my description and applying that description to yourself, you are actually watching yourself. If you observe yourself, you will see that there is the thinker apart from your thought, there is the observer of the tree and the tree—not the word but the actual fact; the word *tree* is not the tree. So there is "the observer and the observed, the thinker and the thought." And the thinker is always trying to shape thought, always trying to control, to guide thought—this is the origin of all effort, of all control—"I must be this, I must not be that, I must not smoke though I have the habit, and so on and on."

The 'I' and the thing observed, the thinker and the thought—unless you understand this thing, you are wasting your energy in control. You need every breath of energy, every unit of energy, and therefore there must be no effort. A machine, if there is any friction, wears itself out; it is not performing, functioning beautifully; it is not picking up. In the same way, if there is any kind of effort, at any level, it is a wastage of energy. And to understand the wastage of energy and to free the mind and the brain from this effort, one has to understand this division: the thinker and the thought.

You accept this division because you think the thinker is a permanent entity, a spiritual entity, the atma, the higher self—the names that one gives to this. If you observe that very carefully, the so-called higher self or the so-called atma, and all the rest of the things that you use and imply, is still within the field of time. Because man has thought of it—man, whether it be Shankara or your pet guru or somebody else, has thought of it—he has brought it into the realm of thought. And thought has created this superself, the super-atma, the higher self, which is guiding, which is shaping, which is controlling, which is creating this division.

Now, is there such an entity? The speaker says there is no such entity. It does not matter who says it—what there is, is thinking, thought and nothing else. Thought creates the entity as the thinker. Because if you have no thought, if you are in a state of amnesia, without memory, completely blank, then there is no thinker who has identified himself with innumerable experiences, ideas, beliefs, dogmas. So a man who would go very far into the understanding of the nature of meditation must understand this whole problem of thought, not controlling, not shaping, not guiding thought.

So one has to inquire into this whole question of memory, memory accumulated as knowledge, as experience, and stored up through association and all the rest of it, as in the mechanical computer—in the mechanical computer, in the electronic brain, man has built a series of memories, layers, banks of memories; and when those are called upon, the computer begins to think. The memory becomes the 'I', from which there is thought, from which there is reaction as thought. If you understand that, then there is only thinking. Therefore, there is no control of thought. Then you see the whole mechanism of thinking. Then you can proceed from there and inquire into this whole question of experience.

This is all part of meditation, from the very beginning of this talk until now. We are understanding the nature and the meaning of meditation, we are in a state of meditation. Don't say at the end, "What do you mean by meditation?" You are actually going through, with the speaker, taking the journey actually, into this extraordinary thing called meditation. Don't stop halfway. If you are tired, then that is all right. But you must go into it very, very deeply because life is very deep, not the shady thing that you call life—that is not life at all; that is just mechanical existence, a brutal, ugly, superficial thing that we call life. If you want to go into this extraordinary phenomenon of life and the depth and beauty of meditation, you have to take a tremendous journey. And we are taking it together.

So you have to inquire into this question of experience, which is still, like thought, a part of consciousness. Experience means going through something, however small, however immediate, however deep. That is, to every challenge there is a response. The challenge may be a tremendous crisis, and you respond adequately or inadequately or totally to that challenge or to that crisis. For most of us, the challenges are merely superficial, and we hardly know that there are challenges at all because our whole life is so mechanical, so superficial, so casual. And a man who has been through a hundred experiences, a thousand experiences, wants a new experience. Don't you know? Don't you all pray for something new to happen in your life, a new experience or a new vision—a new way of looking at a tree, a new way of looking at your wife, at your husband, to see in a new way the beauty of the sunset, the blue of the sky? Because we are so exhausted, we are so bored with our everyday experience. And every experience is within this consciousness of the 'me', of the thinker.

Thought, when pushed to the very extreme, steps beyond the borders of consciousness because there are no words, there is no memory—but that is a different matter. Most of us pray for new experiences. Please bear in mind that this is a part of your meditation, and we are taking the journey together.

The mind, the brain, your being, wants something new to happen; and you want a new experience. You want to expand your consciousness, and so you take a drug—there are many new drugs that give you the sense of expansion of consciousness. When in that state, you see things immaculately, you see everything afresh—the tree, the branch, the leaf—as you have never seen it before; for the first time, you see the splendor of light, the beauty of a leaf as it falls to the ground, because that drug has made your brain highly sensitive. There are drugs like LSD 25 and so on. And in that state, according to your conditioning, you respond. In that state, if you are a Christian, you see God; whatever it is, it is still within the field of the known, highly sensitized and therefore highly perceptive of a particular conditioning. Therefore mere experience has no value in meditation. Please, I am going to go a little bit into this.

There is always challenge and response, challenge from the outside and response from you. If you are aware of this challenge outwardly, then perhaps you will also be aware of rejecting the outer and becoming a challenge to yourself, all the time questioning—a challenge to yourself; nobody puts a challenge, not society, not incident, not environment; but you yourself are challenging everything you are doing and responding. You follow? There is the outward challenge to which you respond. And then there is the challenge which you yourself offer to yourself, questioning, asking, demanding, forcing, inquiring, pushing, driving. Then if you go still further into this question of experience, is it possible to live without experience at all, in which there is no challenge and no response, in which there is no crisis, big or small? Is it possible? It is possible only when the mind is so terribly awakened. How can there be a challenge to life?

So in meditation, there is no search for experience at all. Please follow all this. There is no search at all, not only for experience, but for every form of seeking, asking, questioning. Because only when there is no seeking and no asking, when there is no directive conditioning, when the brain has been sharpened to its highest sensitivity, when there is no sense of control but complete awareness, out of this comes the stillness of the mind—not the stillness that you are seeking, that you are cultivating; that is death, that is stagnation.

Out of this awareness of all that has been said until now, during this evening—awareness of those crows, awareness of the speaker, awareness of your reactions to the speaker and the words he is using, choicelessly, negatively observing, being so totally aware—out of this awareness there is attention. You cannot attend if you are not silent. You listen to those crows, actually listen, give your attention—not resistance. Listen to those crows and listen to the speaker simultaneously—not two different things. And to pay complete attention to the crows and to the speaker, and to watch your own mind, how it is working, you need that attention which comes out of complete silence. Otherwise, you are merely resisting the crows and trying to listen to the speaker; so there is a division, there is a conflict; so there is a pushing away, an exclusion—which is what most people do, which is concentration.

In concentration, if you observe, there are several things involved, as in the case of a child. Give the child a toy; the toy is so interesting that he is completely absorbed by the toy; he is not mischievous, he spends hours, days, in that toy; he loves it; the toy is so exciting, the toy has taken him over. That is part of concentration; nothing exists except the toy.

Part of concentration is this self-absorption, identified with the Masters, with the guru, with somebody, with your gods. You want to concentrate on your ideas, on your Masters, on your gurus, on your pictures—you know all that business man has invented. In that concentration there is exclusion; you are not aware, you are not attentive; you do not look at the tree, the bird, the passerby, the color of the sari; you are totally unaware.

And it is only the mind that is completely aware that is completely attentive. And this attention and this awareness can only come when there is total stillness. That stillness is absolutely necessary.

Perhaps some of you have really taken the journey with the speaker so far; you have actually, factually, walked step by step on this journey, until now. If you have done it, you will see that your mind is extraordinarily quiet. Please, I am not hypnotizing you—it is so immature, a trick of a clever charlatan. We are actually going through, actually living it; there is no pretension. Either you are there or you are not there. If you are not there, you have to begin right from the beginning and go through it.

So there is no sense of being hypnotized by somebody else, by his ideas or by his words or by your own longing to find the silence. It comes inevitably, as the sun rises in the east of a morning, when the mind has completely gone through all this and understood. Because it is the mature mind—the mind that is capable of looking at itself pitilessly, without any self-pity, without tears, without hope, without fear, the mind that is stark naked—that is capable of standing completely alone, not only in this world, but in the psychological world which is inside the skin, without looking for anybody, for any support, for any way of conduct, to be encouraged.

If you have gone that far, then you will see the mind is completely silent. In that silence there is no reflection. When you look into a well which is rich with water and quietness, you see your own face; the reflection of your own face is there in the water; and you can go on improving that reflection ad nauseam, changing it, modifying it. In that silence there is no reflection; as there is no thinker, there is no thought; it is devoid of all experience, but it is tremendously alive; it is energy, not death, not decay.

Now, so far, we can use words up to there. But to go further into this extraordinary silence, you not only have to proceed nonverbally, nonabstractly, but actually. And you cannot proceed actually unless you have come, step by step, where we are now. Perhaps some of you have gone through it, and you now begin to understand the nature and the meaning of meditation, and so are able to be actually in that silence, unimagined, not provoked, not premeditated—it is there.

In that silence, there is no onlooker, there is no entity that says, "I am silent." There is only silence, an immense space in which there is emptiness. Because unless the mind is empty, it cannot possibly see the new. When the mind is empty—not induced emptiness—when there is the sense of complete void, which is alive, vibrating, strong, potent, not dormant, not a state of blankness, then you will see that there is quite a different movement of creation.

You may say, "Are you not, when you are talking about that silence, observing that silence?" What we are saying is merely the word, but not the thing. The word *tree* is not the tree. The speaker is only describing; the word, the description, is not the effect. Therefore you can forget the word, forget the description, and be actually there.

If you are there, if the mind is totally aware in that quality of pure clarity, then out of that there is creation—creation not in the mundane sense of the word: painting a picture, writing a poem, creating the baby. Because the world is in a state of creation, the universe is, it is exploding. And only in that extraordinary silence which has no border, which has no depth, no height, no measures, out of this immense silence, one knows the origin, the beginning of all things.

February 26, 1964

Seventh Talk in Bombay

This is the last talk in Bombay this year. I think very few of us realize what tremendous problems we are confronted with; very few of us are aware of their total implication, and very few desire to do anything about them actually. We realize, intellectually or verbally, when we read in a newspaper an article or two, or when we read a book, the immense revolution that is taking place outwardly. I mean by *realize* actually be confronted with them, not intellectually or verbally—but come directly into contact with them. And when one does, one realizes with a tremendous shock that man has lived for a million years and more with very little comprehension, with very little change, and without transmutation or mutation—total mutation of the mind and the heart.

We have many problems: the utter lack of affection in the world, the sense of love which is completely absent; there is the problem of sex; then there is the question of guilt; and we have not comprehended fully what it means to be creative. We are confronted with these problems, and we have to answer them, each one of us. And it seems to me, one of our greatest difficulties is that we look to thought as a means of solution to all the innumerable problems.

Thought is of time, and thought cannot possibly solve the problems of our life. I think that is the first thing we have to realize. Thought has time and authority, and thought cannot, under any circumstances, solve or confront the many, many intricate problems of life. There must be a totally new approach, an operational approach that can be tested out, worked out by each one. And to understand the limitations and the importance of thought, one has to see the mechanical process of thinking, and the futility, the utter superficiality, of all the philosophies that we have, because they are the product of thought.

And we have to go beyond the limitations of thought, and that is one of our major problems. And also we have to understand that the way of so-called traditional religion does not lead anywhere, and that the so-called religions have to be totally abandoned. And we have to find out for ourselves what is an individual. And finally, one has to find out the importance of religion and, in the discovery of what is truth, see the emergence of a state of mind that is in mutation. This is what we are going to talk about this evening: religion, the individual, and mutation.

But before we go into that, one has to be very clear what the problems are that are facing each one of us. Because without understanding these problems, not merely verbally or intellectually, but actually, without realizing the implications of all these problems and thereby sharpening our brains, we shall not be able to meet these problems and to go beyond them. That is the first important thing.

One sees what is going on in this world. First, there is the mechanical, technological progress, so vast, so dynamic, so all-consuming, that, unless one understands it, one is caught up in the mechanical process of it, and there will never be freedom for man because man is going to have, through automation, through electronic brains, leisure. In fifty or more years, the economic problems of food, clothing, and shelter will be solved, and man will be left with leisure. Factories can be run by a dozen people or so, not by three thousand or thirty thousand people. The electronic brains, the computers, the machines that are going to correct machines—all these are actually produced now. And man—you—is going to have leisure.

And what is man going to do with that leisure? The organized religions are going to take over that leisure; amusement and entertainment are going to take over that leisure. This is going on. The church, the religious organizations, being aware of the implications of all this, are organizing themselves to control, to shape man's thought. And because they want it, there is entertainment—organized or individual amusements. So either we understand the whole significance of leisure, or we are going to be absorbed in these two channels and, as society, we will go on in a state of corruption.

Society is always in a state of corruption, and it behooves us to find out for ourselves how to come out of this corruption. You know what is happening in this country, as in the world? From the highest political office to the lowest, there is corruption. Everywhere in the world of art, music, there is tradition; there is no creation. Religion, as it is practiced now, is absolutely meaningless and utterly disastrous for man; it has no meaning; it is an escape from the actual life of boredom, of fear; and all the rituals, with their priests, have no meaning whatsoever, though momentarily they give a kind of sensation. And the worship of authority as the guru, as the leader, will lead man nowhere; for they totally deny freedom.

So these are some of the problems. First, there is no freedom. You have to work to have that freedom, and it is only in freedom you can discover what is truth. You will not have freedom through any form of government—communist, socialist, or otherwise. Governments are not going to solve your problems, nor science. You may go to the moon or go into the bowels of the earth, but the human mind will be the same, adjusting itself, modifying itself, carrying on at a superficial level of corruption, modifying, adjusting, reforming. Nor is any social reform, whatever its reputation, whatever its activity, going to give freedom to man. Every social reformation is the denial of the freedom of man because he sustains the corruption of society. Probably you know all this, probably you have vaguely thought about all this; and probably you find there is no way out of it.

So we are going to find out for ourselves if there is a way out of this chaos, this corruption, this utter decay. We have looked to an outside agency as God, to some spiritual authority, to help us out. And this has been going on for centuries upon centuries—seeking aid from outside, through prayers, through worship, through obedience, through the worship of a guru, of a saint, and blindly or intelligently following them. We have tried so many ways to escape from the chaos which man has created, which you and I have created, which is the result of our activity.

Society which is relationship is the result of your relationship with another. Environment has made you, and you have made the environment. Seeing all this, what is man to do? There is no escape. No outside agency, no gods, nobody is going to come from Mars or Venus, in flying saucers, to save us. No religion, no belief, no dogma is going to purify the mind and the heart so completely that you come out of this with beauty, with an extraordinary sense of compassion and love.

So what is it that we can do? First, we must actually deny—actually deny the religion that we know, actually deny society as it is. I mean by society the psychological structure of society of which we are a part. We must deny that totally. You must deny completely, with all your mind and heart, authority. And you must deny entirely, ruthlessly, every demand of help through an outside agency beyond yourself.

Please listen to this. We seek help because we are in a state of misery, confusion, conflict, and we want to be helped. We want somebody to tell us what to do. We want some guidance, we want to take somebody's hand in this darkness, who will take us to the light. We are so confused, we do not know where to turn. Education, religion, leaders, saints—all these have utterly failed; and yet, because we are in sorrow, because there is conflict and confusion, we look to somebody to help us. And probably that is why most of you are here, hoping in some way to catch a glimpse of reality, hoping in some way to be led to that beauty of life.

Now, if you will kindly listen with your inner ear, with clarity, you will see that there is no help. The speaker cannot help you; he refuses to help you. Please understand this. Go with it slowly. He refuses totally, completely, to help you.

What you want is to sustain the corruption, live in corruption, and to help in that corruption. You want to be helped a little bit to live comfortably, to carry on with your ambitions, with your ways, with your envies, with your brutalities; to continue in the everyday existence, and yet modify it a little—become a little more rich, a little more comfortable, a little more happy. That is all you want—a better job, a better car, a better position. You really do not want to be completely, entirely, free of sorrow. You don't want to find out what is love and the beauty of it, the immensity of it. You don't want to find out what is creation.

So what you really want is to be helped to continue in a modified form, in this wretched world, with the ugliness of your lives, with the brutality of your existence, with your everyday conflict. That is all you know; you cling to that and you want that modified. And anybody that helps you to live in that field—you think he is a great man, he is a saint, he is a marvelous savior.

Therefore, the speaker says he is not giving you help. If you seek help from the speaker, you are lost. There is no help from anybody, of any type—that is a dreadful thing to realize for oneself. You have to realize the appalling, frightening fact that you, as a human being, have to stand completely on your own feet; there are no Upanishads, no Gita, no leaders, nothing that can save you; you have to save yourself. You know what that does when you realize that fact? It is a fact. When you actually realize that fact, either you sink further in your corruption or that very fact gives you tremendous energy to break through the network of the psychological structure of society—break through, shattering everything. And then you will never seek help because you are free.

A free man, a man who is not frightened, who has a clear mind, whose heart is vital, strong, energetic—he does not want help. And we, you and I, have to stand alone completely, totally, with no help from anybody. You have sought help politically, religiously from the gurus, socially in every way; they have all betrayed you. There have been revolutions—political and economic revolutions, communism, social revolutions. They are not the answers; they cannot help you because they will bring more tyranny, more slavery.

It is only when you demand complete freedom and sustain that freedom that you will find, through the operational approach, reality; and it is that reality that will set man free—nothing else. And it is one of the most difficult things to realize that you have to stand completely alone, by yourself entirely.

It is only the man who is free that can cooperate. And it is the man who is free who says, "I will not cooperate." Cooperation, as it is generally understood, implies cooperating around a person, around an idea, or for a utopia, around the authority of a person, or the authority of an idea as the state. If you observe that kind of cooperation, it is not cooperation at all, it is mutual benefit; and when the authority changes, you change in order to derive your benefit from that; so it is a compulsive form of adjustment.

We are talking of cooperation which is entirely different because man must cooperate. We cannot live without cooperation. Life is relationship, life is cooperation. You and I cannot possibly exist without cooperation. But to cooperate there must be freedom. You must be free and I must be free to cooperate. Freedom does not mean doing what we like—being ruthless and all the rest of the stupid reaction connected with that word. It is only the man who is free to love, who has no jealousy, no hate, that wants nothing for himself, for his family, for his race, for his group—it is only the man who is free and knows the full significance of love and beauty that can cooperate.

So what is necessary is to understand this freedom. Thought does not bring about this freedom. Thought is never free. Thought is merely a reaction to accumulated knowledge as memory, as experience; therefore, it can never free man. And yet, everything that we do—every action, every motive, every urge—is based on thought. So one has to see for oneself the significance of thought, where it is necessary and where it is poison.

Mutation can only come about when the mind is totally empty of all thought. It is like the womb—a child is conceived in the womb because the womb is empty, and out of that a new birth is given. In the same way, the mind must be empty; it is only in emptiness that a new thing can take place—a totally new thing, not a thing that has continued through millennia.

So the question is then how to empty the mind—not the system. When I use the word *how*, it is not "Do these things and you will empty the mind." There is no system, there is no formula. You have to see the truth of that: that mutation is absolutely necessary for the salvation of man—for you and me, for our salvation, for our freedom, to be completely free from sorrow, from the agony of life.

You must have a mutation, a mind that is completely different, that is not the product of environment, of society, of reaction, of knowledge, of experience—all those do not bring about innocence, do not bring about freedom; they do not give this vast sense of space in the mind. It is only in that space that the movement of mutation takes place. And it is only that mutation that can save man because it is that mutation which brings about the individual.

We are not individuals. We have names, separate names. You have a separate body; perhaps, if you are lucky enough, you have a bank account; otherwise, you are not an individual inwardly, psychologically. You belong to the race, to the community, to tradition, to the past, and therefore you have ceased to be creative. You have ceased to be aware of the immensity of the width and the depth and the beauty of life.

Because we are not individuals, we do not know what it means to love. We know only what it means to love in which is contained jealousy, hate, envy, and all the mischief that thought can bring about. Do observe, if you will, your own so-called affection; observe yourself, your own affection for your wife and your family. There is not a spark of love; it is a unit of corruption, of attachment, pain, jealousy, ambition, and domination. You may beget children, but in that there is no love; it is pleasure. And where there is pleasure, there is pain. And a man who would understand this thing called "love" must first understand what it is to be free.

Then, there is the question of sex, which is a great problem in the world. You may be out of it because of your age or because you have forced yourself. You have no sexual life because you want to find God. I am afraid you won't find God. God wants a free man, a man who has lived, who has suffered, who is free. So you have to understand this question of sex.

Please listen to what the speaker says. You may not go completely to the very end of the journey, but listen. Listen without condemning, without justifying, without comparing, without bringing all the memories into operation. Just listen freely, happily. Because, if you know how to listen, then you will know when the mind is empty. There is nothing that you can do to bring about that emptiness. Every action on your part is the action of the past, of thought, of time; and time is not going to bring you that freedom. But listen, actually enjoy listening to the sound of a bird, the single sound, each sound separate, distinct, vital, clear; listen to that crow; listen to the speaker completely—to each word, each statement, without interpreting, without translating. Just listen. And out of that listening you will have the energy; out of that listening you will act completely, totally.

We do not listen. There are too many noises about us; inside us, there is too much talk, too much questioning, too much demanding, too many urges, compulsions. We have so many things, and we never listen to any one of them completely, totally, to the very end. And if you would kindly so listen, you will see that, in spite of yourself, the mutation, that emptiness, that transformation, the perception of what is true, comes into being. You don't have to do a thing because what you do will interfere, because you are greedy, you are envious, you are full of hate, ambition, and all the mischief that thought can make.

So if you can listen happily, effortlessly, then perhaps in the quiet, deep silence you will know what is truth. And it is only that truth that liberates, and nothing else. That is why you must stand completely alone. You cannot listen through another; you cannot see with the eyes of another; you cannot think with the thoughts of others. But yet, you listen through others, see through the activities, through the saints, through the dictum of others. So if you can put away all these secondary things, the activities of others, and be simple, quiet, and listen, then you will find out.

You know, when you look at a sunset or a lovely face or a beautiful leaf or a flower, when you actually see it, then there is space between you and that flower and that beauty and that loveliness, or between you and the misery and the squalor you see. There is space; you have not created it—it is there. You cannot do anything to make that space wide or narrow, it is there. But we refuse to look through that space simply, quietly, persistently. Through that space we project our opinions, our ideas, our conclusions, our formulas; and therefore there is no space. That space is covered over with yesterdays, with the memories, with the experiences of yesterday; therefore, we never see, we never listen, we are never quiet. So, if you will, do listen this evening, not being hypnotized—that would be absurd, that would be too immature—not accepting it, not denying it, because we are dealing with your life and not with my life; we are dealing with your sorrows, your miseries, your authorities, your despairs, and the agony and the boredom of life.

As we were saying, there is this question of sex, which has become tremendously important. Why? Look at your own lives. Why? First you have no other free pleasure. You are blocked intellectually; you repeat what others have said everlastingly, from childhood until you die. Your examinations, your education, your technological information—all this is repetition, repetition. You are blocked intellectually. You dare not think independently. You don't deny. You are yes-sayers. You are followers, you are worshipers of authority. Therefore you are blocked intellectually, and therefore you have only one thing where you are free, original—your sex.

Then emotionally, you are not free to express. There too, you are blocked, hindered, contained. You never enjoy the sunset; you never see the tree nor are you with the tree in full enjoyment, in the full beauty of that tree. So, emotionally, intellectually, you are starved, cut off; and beauty means nothing to you—nothing. Otherwise, this country would be different. You have divorced religion from beauty. You will never sit up of an evening, quietly looking at the stars, the moon, and the light on the water; you have the radio, the TV, the books, the cinema—anything but be alone with yourself to enjoy that which is about you. So emotionally, aesthetically, deep down you are completely blocked. So you have only one thing left—your own, original—and that is sex.

And when sex becomes the only thing, it creates havoc in one's life. And that too becomes repetitive, and that too leads to various forms of domination, compulsion, the agony of relationship. That too leads to brutality, to dulling the mind—this repetitive pleasure. So there is no love; there is no beauty in our life, no emotional freedom. And so the thing is left which is called sex.

Then there is no discovery, for yourself, of reality. Because religions have made you followers, not investigators, not explorers, not the people who will discover. You are merely people who repeat endlessly, go to the church or to the temple, or deny and merely live superficially. So religion actually has no meaning, except when you are in a state of fear, disease, or when you want some kind of comfort.

Please listen, don't get bored. This is your life. You have to face these things. And ultimately there is that creation—not of children—that creation which is beyond time and measure, which makes all things new all the time because it is out of time. But, yet, we are seeking always new expressions in the world of art, in the world of aesthetics. New expressions—that is all we are concerned with. We are not concerned with creation.

So those are the many problems that confront you, and you have to find out the right answer for yourself. And there is the right answer, which is that there must be complete freedom for you, complete freedom from this sociological structure, the psychological structure of society which is fear, greed, envy, ambition, the seeking of power, the seeking of position, depending on money. The corruption of society—one has to be free of that. And yet, one has to live in this world vitally, strongly, energetically. And to do that, you have to work; you have to work inwardly, ruthlessly, to strip yourself of all the debris of society, of all the corruption of society. When you realize that you have to do it for yourself, completely, and nobody is going to help you, you have a tremendous energy. Then, all your attention is given to that; then you have a mind, a heart that is tremendously alive, active.

So, self-knowing is operational; it is not a question of belief; it functions, it operates if you go after it steadily, day after day. Out of self-knowing comes awareness—that is to be aware of the birds, of the trees, of the squalor, of the dirt, of the beauty, of the color, of everything about you outwardly. Because the outward movement brings you the inward movement. You cannot ride on the inward without understanding the outward movement. They are one; they are a unitary process just like a tide on the sea that goes out and comes in. And you must ride on that tide without effort. You can ride on that tide without effort when you observe and when you listen to all the intimations of thought and the implications of your being, when you just listen. It does not demand analysis, introspection—that is deadly. All that it demands is that you look, that you listen, and that you keep that space between the observer and the thing observed. If you keep that space completely empty, there is neither the observer nor the observed; there is only a movement.

And out of this self-knowing, there comes freedom which nobody, no God, no saint, no society, can give you. You must have this freedom. Because, otherwise, the churches with their organized belief and entertainment are going to take over, and you will live mechanically, stupidly, worthlessly. And from this freedom comes that state of mind when the brain is highly sensitive because it has understood every movement of thought, every wave of feeling—because thought and feeling are not separate things; it is a whole process. And out of that understanding, out of that freedom, the mind is made young, fresh, and innocent. It is only out of this emptiness comes mutation, and from that alone there can be salvation for man. It is only when the mind has completely undergone this tremendous mutation out of time—not within the limits of society, but completely outside society; not becoming a sannyasi, that is too immature—when the mind has understood the whole fabric of society, which is yourself, and out of that understanding comes this extraordinary sense of aloneness.

Then you are completely, indissolubly alone. And only then, in that state of complete aloneness, does that movement which is the beginning and end of all things come into being. That is religion and nothing else. In that state, there is love, there is compassion and infinite pity. And in that state, there is neither sorrow nor pleasure, but a life that is vitally living, strong, vital, clear.

March 1, 1964

Saanen, Switzerland, 1964

First Talk in Saanen

As you know, there are going to be ten talks here and some discussions after all these talks are concluded, so we shall have plenty of leisure to talk things over together.

I would like to begin this morning by pointing out the extraordinary importance of freedom. Most of us do not want to be free. We have our families, our responsibilities, our duties—and in those we abide. We are hedged about by social laws, by a certain code of morality, and we are burdened with daily troubles and problems; and if we can find some kind of consolation, some means of escape from all this conflict and misery, we are very easily satisfied. Most of us do not really want to be free at all, in any direction, at any depth; yet it seems to me that one of the most essential things in life is to find out for oneself how to be completely and totally free. And is it at all possible for the human mind, being so heavily conditioned, so narrowly caught up in its everyday labors, so full of fears and anxieties, so uncertain of the future and constant in its demand for security—is it at all possible for such a mind to bring about in itself a radical mutation, which can take place only in complete freedom?

I think each one of us should be really concerned with this problem, at least for the three weeks that we are here. We should be concerned—not just verbally, but through the verbal or linguistic analysis we should go much more deeply into ourselves—to find out whether it is at all possible to be free. Without freedom one cannot discover what is true and what is false; without freedom there is no depth to life; without freedom we are slaves to every form of influence, to all the social pressures, to the innumerable demands that we are constantly faced with.

So, can you, as an individual, really go into yourself very searchingly, ruthlessly, and find out if it is at all possible for each one of us to be completely free? Surely, it is only in freedom that there can be change. And we do have to change, not superficially, not in the sense of merely pruning a little bit here and there, but we have to bring about a radical mutation in the very structure of the mind itself. That is why I feel it is so important to talk about change, to discuss it, and to see how far each one of us can go into this problem.

Do you know what I mean by change? To change is to think in a totally different manner; it is to bring about a state of mind in which there is no anxiety at any time, no sense of conflict, no struggle to achieve, to be or to become something. It is to be completely free of fear. To find out what it means to be free of fear, I think one has to understand this question of the teacher and the taught, and thereby discover what learning is. There is no teacher here, and there is no person who is being taught. We are all learning. So you have to be completely rid of the idea that someone is going to instruct you or tell you what to do—which means that the relationship between you and the speaker is entirely different. We are learning; you are not being taught. If you really understand that you are not here to be taught by anyone, that there is no teacher to teach you, no savior to save you, no guru to tell you what to do—if you really understand this fact, then you have to do everything for yourself; and that demands tremendous energy.

Energy is dissipated, degraded, totally lost when there is the relationship of the teacher and the taught; so during these talks here, and in the discussions that are to follow, I hope there will be no sense of any such relationship. It would really be marvelous if we could wipe that out completely so that there is only the movement of learning.

We generally learn through study, through books, through experience, or through being instructed. Those are the usual ways of learning. We commit to memory what to do and what not to do, what to think and what not to think, how to feel, how to react. Through experience, through study, through analysis, through probing, through introspective examination, we store up knowledge as memory, and memory then responds to further challenges and demands from which there is more and more learning. With this process we are quite familiar; it is the only way we learn. I do not know how to fly an airplane, so I learn. I am instructed, I gain experience, the memory of which is retained, and then I fly. That is the only process of learning with which most of us are acquainted. We learn through study, through experience, through instruction. What is learned is committed to memory as knowledge, and that knowledge functions whenever there is a challenge, or whenever we have to do something.

Now, I think there is a totally different way of learning, and I am going to talk a little bit about it; but to understand it, and to learn in this different way, you must be completely rid of authority; otherwise, you will merely be instructed, and you will repeat what you have heard. That is why it is very important to understand the nature of authority. Authority prevents learning—learning which is not the accumulation of knowledge as memory. Memory always responds in patterns; there is no freedom. A man who is burdened with knowledge, with instructions, who is weighed down by the things he has learned, is never free. He may be most extraordinarily erudite, but his accumulation of knowledge prevents him from being free, and therefore he is incapable of learning.

We accumulate various forms of knowledge—scientific, physiological, technological, and so on—and this knowledge is necessary for the physical well-being of man. But we also accumulate knowledge in order to be safe, in order to function without disturbance, in order to act always within the borders of our own information and thereby feel secure. We want never to be uncertain—we are afraid of uncertainty—and therefore we accumulate knowledge. This psychological accumulation is what I am talking about, and it is this that completely blocks freedom.

So, the moment one begins to inquire into what is freedom, one has to question not only authority but knowledge. If you are merely being instructed, if you are merely accumulating what you hear, what you read, what you experience, then you will find that you can never be free because you are always functioning within the pattern of the known. This is what actually happens to most of us, so what is one to do?

One sees how the mind and the brain function. The brain is an animalistic, progressive, evolutionary thing which lives and functions within the walls of its own experience, its own knowledge, its own hopes and fears. It is everlastingly active in safeguarding and protecting itself—and in some measure it has to be; otherwise, it would soon be destroyed. It must have some degree of security, so it habitually benefits itself by gathering every kind of information, obeying every kind of instruction, creating a pattern by which to live, and so never being free. If one has observed one's own brain, the whole functioning of oneself, one is aware of this patterned mode of existence in which there is no spontaneity at all.

Then what is learning? Is there a different kind of learning, a learning which is not cumulative, which doesn't become merely a background of memory or knowledge that creates patterns and blocks freedom? Is there a kind of learning which doesn't become a burden, which doesn't cripple the mind but, on the contrary, gives it freedom? If you have ever put this question to yourself, not superficially but deeply, you will know that one has to find out why the mind clings to authority. Whether it be the authority of the instructor, of the savior, of the book, or the authority of one's own knowledge and experience, why does the mind cling to that authority?

You know, authority takes many forms. There is the authority of books, the authority of the church, the authority of the ideal, the authority of your own experience, and the authority of the knowledge which you have gathered. Why do you cling to those authorities? Technologically there is need of authorities—that is simple and obvious. But we are talking about the psychological state of the mind; and quite apart from technological authority, why does the mind cling to authority in the psychological sense?

Obviously, the mind clings to authority because it is afraid of uncertainty, insecurity; it is afraid of the unknown, of what may happen tomorrow. And can you and I live without any authority at all—authority in the sense of domination, assertion, dogmatism, aggressiveness, wanting to succeed, wanting to be famous, wanting to become somebody? Can we live in this world—going to the office, and all the rest of it—in a state of complete humility? That is a very difficult thing to find out, is it not? But I think it is only in that state of complete humility—which is the state of a mind that is always willing not to know—that one can learn. Otherwise one is always accumulating and therefore ceasing to learn.

So, can one live from day to day in that state? Do you understand my question? Surely, a mind that is really learning has no authority, nor does it seek authority. Because it is in a state of constant learning—not only from outward things, but also from inward things—it does not belong to any group, to any society, to any race or culture. If you are constantly learning from everything without accumulation, how can there be any authority, any teacher? How can you possibly follow anyone? And that is the only way to live—not learning from books, I don't mean that, but learning from your own demands, from the movements of your own thought, your own being. Then your mind is always fresh; it looks at everything anew and not with the jaded look of knowledge, of experience, of that which it has learned. If one understands this—really, profoundly—then all authority ceases. Then the speaker is of no importance at all.

The extraordinary state that truth reveals, the immensity of reality, cannot be given to you by another. There is no authority, there is no guide. You have to discover it for yourself, and thereby bring some sense into this chaos which we call life. It is a journey which must be taken completely alone, without companions, with neither wife nor husband nor books. You can set out on this journey only when you really see the truth that you have to walk completely alone—and then you are alone; not out of bitterness, not out of cynicism, not out of despair, but because you see the fact that aloneness is absolutely necessary. It is this fact, and the perceiving of this fact, that sets one free to walk alone. The book, the savior, the teacher—they are yourself. So you have to investigate yourself, you have to learn about yourself—which does not mean accumulating knowledge about yourself, and with that knowledge looking at the movements of your own thought. Do you understand?

To learn about yourself, to know yourself, you must observe yourself with a freshness, with a freedom. You can't learn about yourself if you are merely applying knowledge, that is, looking at yourself in terms of what you have learned from some instructor, from some book, or from your own experience. The 'you' is an extraordinary entity; it is a complex, vital thing, tremendously alive, constantly changing, undergoing all kinds of experiences. It is a vortex of enormous energy, and there is no one who can teach you about it—no one! That is the first thing to realize. When one realizes that, really sees the truth of it, you are already liberated from a heavy burden; you have ceased looking to someone else to tell you what to do. There is already the beginning of this extraordinary perfume of freedom.

So I have to know myself because without knowing myself there can be no end to conflict, there can be no end to fear and despair, there can be no understanding of death. When I understand myself, I understand all human beings, the whole of human relationship. To understand oneself is to learn about the physical body and the various responses of the nerves; it is to be aware of every movement of thought; it is to comprehend the thing called jealousy, brutality, and to discover what is affection, what is love. It is to understand the whole of that which is the 'me', the 'you'.

Learning is not a process of laying the foundation of knowledge. Learning is from moment to moment; it is a movement in which you are watching yourself infinitely, never condemning, never judging, never evaluating, but merely observing. The moment you condemn, interpret, or evaluate, you have a pattern of knowledge, of experience, and that pattern prevents you from learning.

A mutation at the very root of the mind is possible only when you understand yourself; and there must be such a mutation, there must be change. I am not using the word *change* in the sense of being influenced by society, by climate, by experience, or by pressure in some other form. Pressures and influences will merely push you in a certain direction. I mean the change that comes about effortlessly because you understand yourself. Surely there is a vast difference between the change brought about through compulsion and the change that comes spontaneously, naturally, freely.

Now, if you are at all serious—and I think it would be rather absurd to come all the way to attend these talks in this heat, and put up with a lot of discomfort, if you were not serious—then these three weeks here will offer a very good opportunity for learning, for real observation, for deep inquiry. Because, you see, I feel that our life is so superficial. We know and have experienced a great deal, we can talk very cleverly—and we really have no depth. We live on the surface, and living on the surface, we try to make that surface living very serious. But I am talking about a seriousness that is not merely at the superficial level, a seriousness that penetrates into the very depths of one's own being. Most of us are not really free, and I feel that unless we are free—free from worry, free from habits, free from psychosomatic disabilities, free from fear—our life remains terribly shallow and empty, and in that condition we grow old and die.

So, during these three weeks, let us find out if we can break through this superficial existence that we have so carefully nurtured, and delve into something much deeper. And the delving process is not through authority, it is not a matter of being told by another how to do it—for there is nobody who can tell you. What we are here to do is to learn together what is true in all this, and once you really understand what is true, then all looking to authority is over. Then you do not need any book, you do not go to any church or temple—you have ceased to be a follower. There is a great beauty, a great depth, a great love in freedom, of which now we know nothing at all because we are not free. So our first concern, it seems to me, is to inquire into this freedom, not only through verbal or linguistic analysis, but also through being free of the word.

It is very hot, but I am afraid we have done everything we can to make the inside of this tent fairly cool. We can't have these meetings any earlier because many people come from a distance, so we shall have to put up with this heat as part of the discomfort.

You know, one has to discipline oneself—not through imposition or rigid control, but through understanding the whole question of discipline, learning about it. Just take this immediate thing: the heat. One can be aware of this heat and not be bothered by it because one's interest, one's inquiry, which is the very movement of learning, is much more important than the heat and the discomfort of the body. So learning demands discipline, and the very act of learning is discipline; and therefore there need be no imposed discipline, no artificial control. That is, I want to listen, not only to what is being said, but also to all the reactions which those words awaken in me. I want to be aware of every movement of thought, of every feeling, of every gesture. That in itself is discipline, and such discipline is extraordinarily flexible.

So, I think the first thing you have to discover is whether you—as a human being living in a particular culture or community—really demand freedom as you demand food, sex, comfort; and how far and how deep you are willing to go in order to be free. I think that is the only thing we can do at the first talk—or rather, that is the only thing we can do during these three weeks because it is the only thing we can share—that, and nothing else. Do you understand? Because everything else becomes mere sentimentality, devotion, emotionalism, which is too immature. But if you and I together are really seeking, inquiring, learning what it means to be free, then in that abundance we can all share.

As I said at the beginning, here there is no teacher, no taught. Each one of us is learning—but not about somebody else. You are not learning about the speaker nor about your neighbor. You are learning about yourself. And if you are learning about yourself, then you are the speaker, you are your neighbor. If you are learning about yourself, you can love your neighbor—otherwise, you cannot, and all this will remain mere words. You cannot love your neighbor if you are competitive. Our whole social structure—economic, political, moral, religious—is based on competition, and at the same time we say we must love our neighbor. Such a thing is impossible because where there is competition there can be no love.

So, to understand what love is, what truth is, there must be freedom—and nobody can give that to you. You have to find it for yourself through hard work.

July 12, 1964

Second Talk in Saanen

The other day when we met here, I was talking about the necessity of freedom; and by that word *freedom* I do not mean a peripheral or fragmentary freedom at certain levels of one's consciousness. I was talking about being totally free—free at the very root of one's mind, in all one's activities, physical, psychological, and parapsychological. Freedom implies a total absence of problems, does it not? Because when the mind is free, it can observe and act with complete clarity; it can be what it is without any sense of contradiction. To me, a life of problems—whether economic or social, private or public—destroys and perverts clarity. And one needs clarity. One needs a mind that sees very clearly every problem as it arises, a mind that can think without confusion, without conditioning, a mind that has a quality of affection, love—which has nothing whatever to do with emotionalism or sentimentality.

To be in this state of freedom—which is extremely difficult to understand, and requires a great deal of probing into—one must have an undisturbed, quiet mind; a mind that is functioning totally, not only at the periphery, but also at the center. This freedom is not an abstraction, it is not an ideal. The movement of the mind in freedom is a reality, and ideals and abstractions have nothing whatsoever to do with it. Such freedom takes place naturally, spontaneously—without any sort of coercion, discipline, control, or persuasion—when we understand the whole process of the arising and the ending of problems. A mind that has a problem, which is really a disturbance, and has escaped from that problem, is still crippled, bound; it is not free. For the mind that does not resolve every problem as it arises, at whatever level—physical, psychological, emotional—there can be no freedom and therefore no clarity of thought, of outlook, of perception.

Most human beings have problems. I mean by a problem the lingering disturbance created by one's inadequate response to a challenge—that is, by the incapacity to meet an issue totally, with one's whole being—or by the indifference which results in the habitual acceptance of problems and just putting up with them. There is a problem when one fails to confront each issue and go to the very end of it, not tomorrow or at some future date, but as it arises, every minute, every hour, every day.

Any problem at any level, conscious or unconscious, is a factor that destroys freedom. A problem is something which we don't understand completely. One's problem may be pain, physical discomfort, the death of someone, or the lack of money; it may be the incapacity to discover for oneself whether God is a reality or merely a word without substance. And there are the problems of relationship, both private and public, individual as well as collective. Not to understand the whole of human relationship does breed problems; and most of us have these problems—from which psychosomatic diseases arise—crippling our minds and hearts. Being burdened with these problems, we turn to various forms of escape: We worship the state, accept authority, look to someone else to resolve our problems, plunge into a useless repetition of prayers and rituals, take to drink, indulge in sex, in hate, in self-pity, and so on.

So we have carefully cultivated a network of escapes—rational or irrational, neurotic or intellectual—which enable us to accept and therefore put up with all the human problems that arise. But these problems inevitably breed confusion, and the mind is never free.

Now, I don't know if you feel the way I do about the necessity—not a fragmentary necessity, not the necessity of one day because you are suddenly forced to face an issue, but the absolute necessity, from the very beginning of one's thought about these things right through to the end of one's life—of having no problem. Probably you do not feel the urgency of it. But if one sees very clearly and factually, not abstractly, that to be free of problems is as much a necessity as food and fresh air, then from that perception one acts, both psychologically and in the business of everyday life; it is present in everything that one does and thinks and feels.

So, freedom from problems is the main issue, at least for this morning. Tomorrow we may approach it differently, but it doesn't matter. What matters is to see that a mind in conflict is a destructive mind because it is constantly deteriorating. Deterioration is not a question of old age or of youth, but it arises when the mind is caught in conflict and has many unresolved problems. Conflict is the core of deterioration and decay. I do not know if you see the truth of that. If you do, then the issue is how to resolve conflict. But first one must perceive for oneself the truth that a mind that has a problem of any kind, at any level, for any duration, is incapable of clear thinking, of seeing things as they are—brutally, ruthlessly—without any sentiment or self-pity.

Now, most of us are used to escaping immediately when a problem arises, and we find it very difficult to stay with the problem—just to observe it without interpreting, condemning, or comparing, without trying to alter it or do something about it. That demands one's complete attention, but to most of us no problem is ever so serious that we want to give it our complete attention because we lead a very superficial life, and we are easily satisfied by glib answers, quick responses. We want to forget the problem, put it away and get on with something else. It is only when the problem touches us intimately, as in the case of death, or a complete lack of money, or when the husband or the wife has left us—it is only then that the problem may become a crisis. But we never allow any problem to bring about a crisis in our life; we always push it away by explanations, by words, by the various things we use as a defense.

So, we know what we mean by a problem. It is an issue that we have not gone to the very end of and completely understood; therefore, it is not finished, it repeats again and again. To understand a problem one has to understand the contradictions—the extreme contradictions as well as the everyday contradictions—of one's own being. We think one thing and do another; we say one thing and feel quite differently. There is the conflict of respect and disrespect, rudeness and politeness. On the one hand there is a sense of arrogance, pride, and on the other we play with humility. You know the many contradictions we all have, both conscious and hidden. Now, how do these contradictions arise?

Please, as I have repeatedly said, don't just listen to the speaker, but listen also to your own thought; observe the operation of your own reactions, be aware of your own response when the question is put so that you become familiar with yourself.

Most of us, when we have a problem, want to know how to resolve it, what to do about it, how to go beyond it, how to get rid of it, or what the answer is. I am not interested in all this. I want to know why the problem arises; because if I can find the root of one problem, understand it, go to the very end of it, then I shall have found the answer to all problems. If I know how to look at one problem completely, then I can understand any problem that may arise in the future.

So, how does a problem arise—a psychological problem? Let us deal with that first because psychological problems distort every activity in life. It is only when the mind understands and resolves a psychological problem as it arises, and does not carry the record of that problem over to the following hour, or the following day, that it is capable of meeting the next issue with freshness, with clarity. Our life is a series of challenges and responses, and we must be capable of meeting each challenge completely; otherwise, every moment brings us further problems. Do you understand? My whole concern is to be free, not to have problems—about God, about sex, about anything. If God becomes my problem, then God is not worth seeking; because to find out if there is such a thing as God, a supreme something beyond the measure of the mind, my own mind must be very clear, innocent, free, not crippled with a problem.

That is why I have said from the very beginning that freedom is a necessity. I am told that even Karl Marx—the god of the communists—wrote that human beings must have freedom. To me, freedom is absolutely necessary—freedom at the beginning, in the middle, and at the end—and that freedom is denied when I carry a problem over to the next day. This means that I have not only to discover how the problem arises but also how to end it completely, surgically, so that there is no repetition, no carrying over of the problem, no feeling that I will think about it and find the answer tomorrow. If I carry the problem over to the next day, I have provided the soil in which the problem takes root, and then the pruning of that problem becomes still another problem. Therefore I have to operate so drastically and immediately that the problem comes completely to an end.

So you see the two issues. Whether it is a problem of one's wife and children, or the lack of money, or the problem of God—whatever it is, one has to find out how the problem arises, and also how to end it instantly.

What I am saying is not illogical. I have shown you logically, reasonably, the necessity of ending the problem and not carrying it over to the next day. Would you like to ask any questions about that?

Comment: I can't understand why you say that money is not a problem.

KRISHNAMURTI: It is a problem for many people. I never said it was not. Please, I said that a problem is something which you do not understand completely, whether it is with regard to money, sex, God, your relationship with your wife, with somebody who hates you—it doesn't matter what it is. If I have a disease or very little money, it becomes a psychological problem. Or it may be sex that becomes a problem. We are investigating how psychological problems arise, not how to deal with a particular problem. Do you understand? Good Lord, that is very simple.

You know, there are people in the East who give up the world and wander from village to village with a begging bowl. The Brahmins in India have established through centuries the custom that a man who gives up the world is to be respected, and the people must feed and clothe him. To such a man, money is obviously not a problem—but I am not advocating that custom here! I am just pointing out that most of us have so many psychological problems. Haven't you got problems, not only with regard to money, but also with regard to sex, God, relationship? Aren't you concerned about whether you are loved or not loved? If I have very little money and I want more, then that becomes my problem. I worry about it; there is a feeling of anxiety; or I become envious because you have more money than I have. All this distorts perception, and these are the problems we are talking about. We are trying to find out how a problem of this kind arises. I think I made that fairly clear—or do you want me to go into it further?

Surely, a problem arises when there is in me a contradiction. If there is no contradiction, at any level, there is no problem. If I have no money, I will work, beg, borrow—I will do something, and it won't be a problem.

Question: But what happens when you can't do anything?

KRISHNAMURTI: What do you mean, you can't do anything? If you have a technique or some specialized knowledge, you become this or that. If you are incapable of anything else, you go and dig.

Comment: After a certain age a man can't work at all.

KRISHNAMURTI: But he has the welfare state.

Comment: No, he hasn't.

KRISHNAMURTI: Then he dies, and there is no problem. But this isn't your problem, is it, madame?

Comment: It is not my own personal problem.

KRISHNAMURTI: Then you are talking about somebody else, and we are out of it. Here we are talking about you as a human being with problems, not about some relative or friend.

Question: He has no one to look after him but me. How am I to come and listen to you, and leave him helpless?

KRISHNAMURTI: Don't come.

Comment: But I want to.

KRISHNAMURTI: Then don't make it a problem.

Question: Are you saying that when an embarrassing or inconvenient situation exists, like the lack of money, the mind can rise above it?

KRISHNAMURTI: No. You see, you have already gone ahead of me, trying to resolve the problem. You want to know how to deal with the problem, and I haven't come to that yet. I have merely stated the problem, not what to do about it. When you say the mind must rise above the problem, or ask what a relative or friend is to do who is old and has no money, do you see what you are doing? You are escaping from the fact. Wait a minute, listen to what I am saying. Don't accept or reject what I am saying, but just listen to it. You are unwilling to face the fact that it is you who have a problem, not somebody else. If you can resolve your own problem as a human being, you will help another—or not, as the case may be—in resolving his. But the moment you go off to the problems of other people and ask, "What am I to do?" you have put yourself in a position in which you can have no answer, and therefore that becomes a contradiction.

I don't know if you are following all this.

Question: I am illiterate through a disability in childhood, and this has been a great problem to me throughout my life. How can I solve it?

KRISHNAMURTI: You are all terribly concerned about solving a problem, aren't you? I am not. Sorry. I told you right at the beginning of these talks that I am not interested in solving problems, yours or mine. I am not your helper or your guide. You are your own teacher, your own disciple. You are here to learn, and not to ask somebody else what to do and what not to do. It is not a question of what you should do about the crippled person, or about a person who hasn't got enough money, or about illiteracy, and so on and so on. You are here to learn for yourself about the problems you have, and not to be instructed by me. So please don't put me in that false position because I will not instruct you. If I did, I would become a leader, a guru, thereby adding to all the exploiting rubbish that already exists in the world. So we are here—you and I—to learn, and not to be instructed. We are learning, not through study, not through experience, but by being alert, awake, totally aware of ourselves; so our relationship is entirely different from that of the teacher and the taught. The speaker is not instructing you or telling you what to do—that would be utterly immature.

Question: When we are incapable of seeing all that is involved in a problem, how can we go to the root of it and resolve it?

KRISHNAMURTI: You are all so eager to find out what to do that you haven't given me a chance to go into it. Please do listen for two minutes, if you will. I am not telling you what to do about your problems. I am pointing out how to learn and what learning is, and you will find that as you learn about your problem, the problem comes to an end. But if you look to someone to tell you what to do about a problem, then you will become like an irresponsible child who is being directed by another, and you will have still more problems. That is straightforward and simple, so please, once and for all, get it clearly into your heart and mind. We are here to learn, not to be instructed. To be instructed is to commit what is heard to memory, but mere repetition from memory does not bring about the resolution of problems. There is maturity only in the movement of learning. The use of knowledge, of that which has merely been memorized, as a means of resolving human problems, is born of immaturity, and it only creates further patterns, further problems.

The mere desire to resolve a problem is an escape from the problem, is it not? I haven't gone into the problem, I haven't studied it, explored it, understood it. I don't know the beauty or the ugliness or the depth of the problem; my only concern is to resolve it, put it away. This urge to resolve a problem without having understood it is an escape from the problem—and therefore it becomes another problem. Every escape breeds further problems.

Now, I have a problem, and I want to understand it completely. I don't want to escape from it, I don't want to verbalize about it, I don't want to tell someone about it—I just want to understand it. I am not looking to anyone to tell me what to do. I see that no one can tell me what to do, and that if someone did, and I accepted his instruction, it would be a most foolish and absurd act. So I have to learn without being instructed, and not bring in the memory of what I have learned about previous problems in dealing with the present problem. Oh, you don't see the beauty of it!

Do you know what it means to live in the present? No, I am afraid you don't. To live in the present is to have no continuity at all. But that is a thing we will discuss some other time.

I have a problem and I want to understand, I want to learn about it. To learn about it, I cannot bring in the memories of the past in order to deal with it because the new problem demands a fresh approach, and I cannot come to it with my dead, stupid memories. The problem is active, so I must deal with it in the active present, and therefore the time element must be altogether put aside.

I want to find out how problems—psychological problems—arise. As I said, if I can understand the whole structure of the causation of problems, and am therefore free from making problems for myself, then I will know how to act with regard to money, with regard to sex, with regard to hate, with regard to everything in life; and I will not, in the very process of dealing with these things, create another problem. So I have to find out how a psychological problem arises, not how to resolve it. Do you follow? Nobody can tell me how it arises; I have to understand it for myself.

Please, as I explore into myself, you must explore into yourself also, and not just listen to my words. Unless you go beyond the words and look at yourself, the words won't help you at all; they will become a mere abstraction, not a reality. The reality is the actual movement of your own inquiry which discovers, not the verbal indication of that movement.

Is all this clear so far?

To me, as I said, freedom is of the highest importance. But freedom cannot possibly be understood without intelligence, and intelligence can come about only when one has completely understood for oneself the causation of problems. The mind must be alert, attentive; it must be in a state of supersensitivity so that every problem is resolved as it comes along. Otherwise there is no real freedom; there is only a fragmentary, peripheral freedom which has no value at all. It is like a rich man saying he is free. Good God! He is a slave to drink, to sex, to comfort, to a dozen things. And the poor man who says, "I am free because I have no money"—he has other problems. So freedom, and the maintenance of that freedom, cannot be a mere abstraction; it must be the absolute demand on your part as a human being because it is only when there is freedom that you can love. How can you love if you are ambitious, greedy, competitive?

Don't agree, sirs—you are letting me do all the work.

I am not interested at all in resolving the problem, or in seeking somebody who will tell me how to resolve it. No book, no leader, no church, no priest, no savior can tell me. We have played with all that for millennia, and we are still burdened with problems. Going to church, confession, prayer—none of those things will solve our problems, which only continue to multiply, as is the case now. So, how does a problem arise?

As I said, when there is no contradiction within oneself, there is no problem. Self-contradiction implies a conflict of desire, does it not? But desire itself is never contradictory. Surely, what create contradiction are the objects of desire. Because I paint pictures, or write books, or because of some stupid thing I do, I want to be famous, recognized. When nobody recognizes me, there is a contradiction, and I am miserable. I am afraid of death, which I haven't understood; and in what I call love, there is a contradiction. So I see that desire is the beginning of contradiction—not desire itself, but the objects of desire are contradictory. If I try to change or deny the objects of desire, saying that I am going to stick to just one thing and nothing else, then that again becomes a problem because I have to resist, I have to build up barriers against everything else. So what I have to do is not merely to change or reduce the objects of desire, but to understand desire itself.

You may say, "What has all this to do with the problem?" We think it is desire that creates conflict, contradiction; and I am pointing out that it is not desire but the conflicting objects or aims of desire that create contradiction. And it is no good trying to have only one desire. That is like the priest who says, "I have only one desire, the desire to reach God"—and who has innumerable desires of which he is not even aware. So one has to understand the nature of desire, and not merely control or deny it. All religious literature says that you must destroy desire, be without desire—which is rubbish. One has to understand how desire arises and what gives continuity to desire—not how to end it. Do you follow the problem? You can see how desire arises—it is fairly simple.

There is perception, contact, sensation—sensation even without contact; and out of sensation there is the beginning of desire. I see a car; its lines, its shape, its beauty attract me, and I want it. But to destroy desire is not to be sensitive to anything. The moment I am sensitive, I am already in the process of desire. I see a beautiful object or a beautiful woman—whatever it is—and there is the arising of desire; or I see a man with tremendous intelligence, integrity, and I want to be like that. From perception there is sensation, and from sensation the beginning of desire. This is what actually happens; there is nothing complicated about it. The complexity begins when thought comes in and gives desire a continuity. I think about the car or the woman or the man of intelligence, and through that thought desire is given a continuity. Otherwise it has no continuity—I can look at the car, and that is the end of it. Do you follow? But the moment I give an inch of thought to the car, then desire has continuity and contradiction begins.

Question: Can there be desire without an object?

KRISHNAMURTI: There is no such thing. There is no abstract desire.

Comment: Then desire is always connected with an object. But you said before that we have to understand the mechanism of desire itself, and not be concerned with its object.

KRISHNAMURTI: Sir, I have pointed out how desire arises, and how through thought we give continuity to desire. I am sorry, but we must stop now and continue next Thursday.

July 14, 1964

Third Talk in Saanen

There is, I think, a great deal of difference between communication and communion. In communication there is a sharing of ideas through words, pleasant or unpleasant, through symbols, through gestures; and ideas can be translated ideologically or interpreted according to one's own peculiarities, idiosyncracies, and background. But in communion I think there is something quite different taking place. In communion there is no sharing or interpretation of ideas. You may or may not be communicating through words, but you are directly in relationship with that which you are observing; and you are communing with your own mind, with your own heart. One may commune with a tree, for example, or with a mountain, or a river. I do not know if you have ever sat beneath a tree and really tried to commune with it. It is not sentimentality, it is not emotionalism—you are directly in contact with the tree. There is an extraordinary intimacy of relationship. In such communion there must be silence, there must be a deep sense of quietness; your heart itself almost comes to a stop. There is no interpretation, there is no communication, no sharing. The tree is not you, nor are you identified with the tree; there is only this sense of intimacy in a great depth of silence.

I do not know if you have ever tried it. Try it sometime—when your mind is not chattering, not wandering all over the place, when you are not soliloquizing, when you are not remembering the things that have been done or that must be done. Forgetting all that, just try communing with a mountain, with a stream, with a person, with a tree, with the very movement of life. That demands an astonishing sense of stillness, and a peculiar attention—not concentration, but an attention which comes with ease, with pleasure.

Now, I would like to commune with you this morning about what we were discussing the other day. We were talking about freedom, and the quality of it. Freedom is not an ideal, something far away; it is not the ideation of a mind held in a prison, which is only a theory. Freedom can exist only when the mind is no longer crippled by any problem whatsoever. A mind that has problems can never commune with freedom, or be aware of the extraordinary quality of freedom.

Most people have problems and just put up with them; they get used to their problems and accept them as part of their life. But those problems are not resolved by accepting or getting used to them, and if you scratch the surface, there they are, still festering away. And most people live in that state—perpetually accepting one problem after another, one pain after another; there is a sense of disillusionment, of anxiety, despair, and they accept it.

Now, if we merely accept problems and live with them, we have obviously not resolved those problems at all. We may say they are forgotten or that they do not matter any more, but they do matter, infinitely, because they pervert the mind, distort perception, and destroy clarity. If we have a problem, with most of us that problem takes up the whole field of our life. It may be a problem of money, of sex, of illiteracy, or of the desire to fulfill oneself, to become famous; whatever it is, we are so concerned with that one problem that it consumes our being, and we think that by resolving it we shall be free of all our misery. But as long as a narrow, little mind is trying to resolve its own particular problem, unrelated to the whole movement of life, it can never be free of problems. Every problem is related to another problem, and if you merely take one problem and try to resolve it fragmentarily, what you are doing is utterly useless. It is like cultivating one corner of a field and thinking that you have cultivated the whole field. You have to cultivate the whole field, you have to look at every problem.

As I was saying the other day, what is important is not the resolution of a problem but the understanding of it—however painful, however demanding, however imminent and pressing that problem may be. I am not being dogmatic or assertive, but it seems to me that to be concerned with only one particular problem indicates a very petty, little mind; and a petty, little mind which is everlastingly trying to solve its own particular problem can never find the way out of problems. It can escape in various ways, it can become bitter, cynical, or give itself up to despair; but it can never understand the whole problem of existence.

So, if we are to deal with problems, we must deal with the whole field from which problems arise, and not just with one particular problem. Any one problem, however intricate, however demanding or pressing it may be, is related to all other problems; therefore, it is important not to think of that problem fragmentarily—which is one of the most difficult things to do. When we have a problem which is urgent, painful, insistent, most of us think that we must solve it isolatedly, without taking into consideration the whole network of problems. We think of that problem fragmentarily, and a fragmentary mind is really a petty mind; it is—if I may use the word—a bourgeois mind. Please, I am not being insulting, I am not using that word derogatively, but simply as an indication of what the mind actually is. It is a mediocre mind that wants a particular problem solved isolatedly. A person who is consumed by jealousy wants to act on the spot, to do something about it, either to suppress his jealousy or to take revenge. But that particular problem is related very deeply to other problems, so we have to consider the whole issue and not just one part of it.

When we are discussing problems, it must be understood that we are not trying to find an answer to any problem. As I have pointed out, inquiry merely in order to find an answer to a problem is an escape from the problem. That escape may be comfortable or painful, it may demand a certain intellectual capacity, and so on; but whatever it is, it is still an escape. If we are to resolve our problems, if we are to be free of them, released from all the pressures which they entail so that the mind is completely quiet and can perceive—because it can perceive only in freedom—then our first concern must not be how to resolve any problem but to understand it. To understand is far more important than to resolve a problem. Understanding is not the capacity or the cleverness of a mind that has acquired various forms of analytical knowledge and is capable of analyzing a particular problem; but a mind that understands is in communion with the problem. To be in communion is not to be identified with the problem. As I said, to be in communion with a tree, with a human being, with a river, with the extraordinary beauty of nature, there must be a certain quietness, a certain sense of aloofness, of being far away from things.

So, what we are trying to do here is to learn how to be in communion with the problem. But do you understand the difficulty in this statement? When there is communion with another, the thought of the 'me' is absent. When you are in communion with your loved one, with your wife, with your child, when you hold the hand of a friend, in that moment—if it is not merely the phony sentimentality, sensation, and all the rest of it, which is called love, but something quite different, something vital, dynamic, real—there is a total absence of the whole mechanism of the 'me' with its thought process. Similarly, to be in communion with a problem implies complete, nonidentifying observation, does it not? Your nerves, your brain, your body—the whole entity is quiet. In that state you can observe the problem without identification, and that is the only state in which there can be an understanding of the problem.

You know, the so-called artist may paint a tree or write a poem about it, but I wonder if he is really in communion with the tree? In the state of communion there is no interpretation, there is no sense of communication, there is no searching for a way of expression. Whether or not you express that communion in words, on a canvas, or in stone is of very little importance; but the moment you want to express it, to show it, to sell it, to become famous, and so on, self-importance comes in.

To understand a problem completely is to be in communion with it. Then you will find that the problem is not at all important, and that what is important is the state of the mind which is in communion with the problem. Such a mind does not create problems. But a mind that is not capable of communion with the problem, that is self-centered, egotistic, that wants to express itself, and all the rest of those immature things—it is that petty mind which creates the problems.

So, as I was saying the other day, to understand the problem—any problem—you have to understand the whole process of desire. We are self-contradictory psychologically, and therefore in our action. We think one thing, and do another. We live in a state of self-contradiction; otherwise, there would be no problems; and self-contradiction arises when there is no understanding of desire. To live without conflict of any kind whatsoever, one has to understand the structure and the nature of desire—not suppress it, control it, try to destroy it, or merely indulge in it, as most people do. This does not mean going to sleep, vegetating, and just accepting life with all its degeneracy. What it means is seeing for oneself that conflict in any form—whether it is quarreling with one's wife or husband, with the community, with society, whatever it is—deteriorates the mind, makes the mind dull, insensitive.

As I said the other day, desire by itself is not in a state of contradiction—it is the objects of desire, and the reaction of desire to those objects, that create the contradiction. Desire has continuity only when there is the identification of thought with that desire. To observe there must be sensitivity; one's nerves, one's eyes and ears, one's whole being must be alive, yet the mind must be quiet. Then one can look at a fine car, a beautiful woman, a splendid house, or a face which is extraordinarily alive, intelligent—one can observe these things, see them as they are, and there the matter ends. But what generally happens? There is desire; and thought, identifying itself with that desire, gives it continuity.

I do not know if I am making myself clear. We will discuss this point a little later.

What is important is to observe without bringing in thought. Now, do not make a problem out of that statement. Do not say, "How am I to observe, how am I to see and feel without allowing thought to interfere?" If you perceive for yourself the whole process of desire, and the contradiction brought about by its objects, and the continuity which thought gives to desire—if you see this whole machinery in operation, then you will not ask that question.

You know, to learn how to drive a car, it is not enough just to be told about it. You have to sit at the wheel, start the car, put on the brakes, learn the whole movement of driving. In the same way, you have to know the extraordinarily delicate mechanism of thought and desire, and not just be instructed about it. You have to look at it, learn about it for yourself—and that requires a sensitivity of approach.

So, what is important is not the resolution of a problem but the understanding of the problem. A problem arises only when there is a contradiction, conflict; and conflict implies effort, does it not?—the effort to achieve, the effort to become, the effort to change this into that, the effort to bring one thing nearer and push something else away. This effort has its origin in desire—the desire to which thought has given continuity. So you have to learn about this whole process—learn, and not just be instructed by the speaker, which has no value at all. What you hear through the telephone may be nice, or it may be unpleasant; it may be real, or it may be stupid, completely false; but it is what you hear that is important, and not the instrument itself. Most of us attach importance to the instrument. We think the instrument is going to teach us something, and I have constantly warned against that particular form of stupidity.

You are here to learn, and you are listening, not just to the speaker, but to yourselves. You are in communion with your own mind; you are observing the operation of desire, and how problems arise. You are becoming intimate with yourself, and that intimacy can be deeply felt only when you approach the problem very quietly, without saying, "I must solve the beastly thing" and getting agitated or excited about it. You are finding out how a problem arises, and how thought perpetuates it by giving continuity to a particular desire. So we are going to learn about the arising of a problem and the ending of the problem—not through taking time to think it over, but the ending of it immediately.

Whatever the problem, thought gives it continuity. If you say something pleasing to me, thought identifies itself with that pleasure and wants to continue living in it; therefore, I regard you as my friend, and I see you often. But if you say something which insults me, what happens? Again I give continuity to that particular feeling by thinking about it. What you have said may be true, but I don't like it; therefore, I avoid you, or I want to hit you back. This is the mechanism that creates problems and keeps them going.

I think this is now fairly clear. By constantly thinking about something, one gives it continuity. You know the messy stuff you think about yourself and your family, all the pleasurable memories, and the illusions you have about yourself—you constantly think about all that, and therefore it has a continuity. Now, if you begin to understand that whole process and learn for yourself the ways of continuity, then when a problem arises, you can be in complete communion with it because thought doesn't interfere; and therefore there is the immediate ending of that problem. Do you follow?

Look, sirs, let us take a very common problem: the desire for security. Most of us want to be secure—that is one of the animalistic demands of human beings. Obviously you must have a certain security in the physical sense. You must have a place to live, and you must know where you are going to get your next meal—unless you live in the East, where you can play around with physical insecurity, wandering from village to village and all that kind of thing. Fortunately or unfortunately, you can't do that here; if you did, you would be put in prison for vagrancy, and all the rest of it.

In the animal, in the baby, in the child, the urge to be physically secure is very strong. And most of us demand to be secure psychologically; in everything we do, think and feel, we want to be secure, certain. That is why we are so competitive; that is why we are jealous, greedy, envious, brutal; that is why we are so terribly concerned about things that don't matter at all. This insistent demand for psychological security has existed for millions of years, and we have never inquired into the truth of it. We have taken it for granted that we must have psychological security in our relationship with our family, with our wife or husband, with our children, with our property, with what we call God. At all costs we must feel secure.

Now, I want to be in communion with this demand for psychological security because it is a real problem. Do you understand? Not to feel psychologically secure, for most of us, means going off the deep end, or becoming neurotic, peculiar. You can see this peculiar look in the faces of many people. I want to find out the truth of the matter, I want to understand this whole demand for security because it is the desire to be secure in relationship that breeds jealousy, anxiety, that gives rise to the hate and misery in which most of us live. And having demanded to be secure for so many millions of years, how is the mind, being so conditioned, to find out the truth of security? To find the truth of it, surely, I have to be in complete communion with it. I cannot be told about it by another—that would be too silly. I have to learn about it for myself. I have to investigate it, find out; I have to be in complete intimacy with this demand for security; otherwise, I will never know whether there is such a thing as security or not. This is probably the major problem with most of us. If I discover that there is no security at all, then there is no problem, is there? Then I am out of this battle for security, and therefore my action in relationship is entirely different. If my wife wants to run away, she runs away, and I don't make an issue of it, I don't hate anyone, I don't become jealous, envious, furious, and all the rest of it.

I see you are now paying close attention, all right! You are much more familiar with this sort of thing than I am. Personally, I don't want to make a problem of security; I don't want to create a problem in my life of any kind—economic, social, psychological, or so-called religious. I see very clearly that a mind that has problems is made dull, insensitive, and that only a highly sensitive mind is intelligent. And because this cry to be secure goes on so deeply and everlastingly in each one of us, I want to find out the truth of security. But this is a very difficult matter to inquire into because, not only from childhood, but from the very beginning of time, we have always wanted to be secure—secure in our work, in our thoughts and feelings, in our beliefs and our gods, in our nation, in our family and our property. That is why memory, tradition, the whole background of the past, plays such an extraordinarily important role in our life.

Now, every experience adds to my sense of security. Do you understand? Every experience is being recorded in memory, added to the storehouse of things that have happened. This accumulated experience becomes my permanent background as long as I live, and with that background I experience further; therefore, every further experience is added to and strengthens that background of memory in which I feel safe, secure. Do you follow? So I have to be aware of this whole extraordinary process of my conditioning. It is not a question of how to be free of my conditioning but of being in communion with it from moment to moment. Then I can look at the desire for security and not make it into a problem.

Is this clear so far? Would you like to ask questions at this point?

Comment: There is no communion because the mind is burdened with the 'I'.

KRISHNAMURTI: Sir, I am asking you something. I am asking you: What is communion? Now, what happens when you hear that question? The whole mechanism of your conditioned mind comes into operation, and you answer it; but you haven't really listened to the question. You may or may not have thought about it before. You may have thought about it casually, or perhaps you have read about it in some book or other, and you repeat what you have read. But you are not listening. When the speaker says to you, "Try being in communion with a tree," surely—if you are at all interested—you first have to find out what it means. Go and sit beneath a tree, or by the river, or in the shadow of a mountain, or just look at your wife, at your child. What does it mean to be in communion? It means that there is no barrier of thought between the observer and that which is observed. The observer is not identifying himself with the tree, with the person, with the river, with the mountain, with the sky. There is simply no barrier. If there is a 'you', with its complex thoughts and anxieties, that is observing the tree, then there is no communion with the tree. To be in communion with someone or something, demands space, silence; your body, your nerves, your mind, your heart, your whole being must be quiet, completely still. Don't say, "How am I to be still?" Don't make stillness another problem. Just see that there is no communion if the mechanism of thought is in operation—which doesn't mean you go to sleep!

Probably you have never done this; you have never been in communion with your wife or husband, with whom you sleep, breathe, eat, have children, and all the rest of it. Probably you have never been in communion even with yourself. If you are a Catholic, you go to church and receive what is called communion; but that is not it. All such things are immature.

When we talk like this about communion with nature, with the mountains, with each other, most of us don't know what it means, so we try to imagine it. Do you follow? We speculate about it, and we say it is the 'I' that is preventing this communion. For God's sake, don't make another problem of communion! You have enough problems already, so just listen. You are in communion with me, and I am in communion with you. I am telling you something, and to understand it you have to listen. But listening means effortless attention, giving your nerves a rest; it does not mean saying, "I must listen," and therefore screwing yourself up, tightening your nerves. It means that you listen pleasantly, easily, in silence, so that you find out what it is the speaker wants to convey. What he is talking about may be utter nonsense, or it may be something real, and you have to listen to find out—but that seems to be one of your greatest difficulties. You are not really listening; in your mind you are arguing with me, putting up a barrier of words.

I am saying that what is important in all this is to learn to be in communion with yourself in a pleasant, happy way, so that you follow all the little movements of your own thought and feeling as you would follow that stream. See every movement of thought, every movement of feeling, without trying to correct it, without saying it is good or bad, without all those silly, bourgeois judgments of petty, little minds. Just observe, and in observing, without identifying yourself with any thought or feeling, pleasant or unpleasant, you will find that you can have communion with yourself.

Most of us want to be psychologically secure; we insist on it, and that is why the family becomes a nightmare; it becomes a dreadful thing because we use it as a means of our own security. Then it is the nation that becomes our security, and we go through all this stupid nationalistic stuff. The family is all right, but when it is used as a means of security, it becomes a deadly poison.

To find out the truth of security, you have to be in communion with the deep-rooted desire to be secure, which is constantly repeating itself in different forms. You seek security, not only in the family, but also in memories, and in the domination or the influence of another. You return to the memory of some experience or relationship which gratified you, which gave you hope, assurance, and in that memory you take shelter. There is the security of cleverness, of knowledge; there is the security of name and position. And there is the security of capacity—you can paint, or play the fiddle, or do something else that gives you a sense of security.

Now, when once you are in communion with the desire that drives you to seek security, and you perceive that it is this desire that creates contradiction because nothing on earth is ever secure, including yourself—when you have found that out and have not merely been told about it, and have resolved the problem completely, then you are out of this whole field of contradiction and are therefore free of fear.

Is that enough for this morning?

I do not know if you are ever silent within yourself. When you are walking down the street, the mind is completely still, observing and listening without thought. When you are driving, you look at the road, at the trees, at the cars passing by—you just observe without recognition, without all the mechanism of thought coming into operation. The more that mechanism of thought operates, the more it wears out the mind; it leaves no space for innocency, and it is only the innocent mind that can see reality.

July 16, 1964

Fourth Talk in Saanen

There is, I consider, a vast difference between change and mutation. Mere change will not lead anywhere. One can become superficially adaptable, very clever at adjusting oneself to the different environments and circumstances of society, and to various forms of inward and outward pressure; but mutation demands a quite different state of mind, and this morning I would like to point out the difference between these two.

Change is alteration, reform, the substitution of one thing for another. Change implies an act of will, conscious or unconscious. And considering the confusion, the starvation, the oppression, the utter misery that exists throughout undeveloped Asia, there must obviously be a radical, revolutionary change. There must be not only a physical or economic change but also a psychological change—a change at all levels of our being, outward as well as inward, in order to bring about a better existence for man. I think this is fairly obvious and even the most conservative accept it. But even though we accept this obvious fact, I am afraid that most of us have not gone very far into the question of what is implied in change. Does adjustment, substitution, reform, go to any great depth, or is it merely a superficial polishing, a cleansing of morality in human relationship? I think we ought to understand pretty deeply and thoroughly what is involved in this process of change before we go into the question of mutation.

Though change is necessary, to me it is always superficial. I mean by change a movement brought about by desire or will, an initiative focused in a particular direction, towards a well-defined attitude or action. All change obviously has behind it a motive. The motive may be personal or collective; it may be manifest or ulterior; it may be a kindly, generous motive, or a motive of fear, despair; but whatever the nature of the motive, at whatever level, the initiative or movement springing from that motive does produce a certain change. I think this is fairly clear. Most of us are very susceptible, individually and collectively, to modifying our attitudes under influence, under pressure, and again when there is a new invention of some kind which directly or indirectly affects our life. We can be made to change our thoughts, orient them in a different direction, by a newspaper article, or by the propagation of an idea. Organized religion insists on educating us from childhood in a certain form of belief, thereby conditioning the mind, and for the rest of our life any change that we make is generally within the modified limits of that belief.

So, very few of us change, except with a motive. The motive may be altruistic or personal, limited or wide; it may be the fear of losing a reward or of not attaining some promised future state. One sacrifices oneself for the collective, for the state, for an ideology, or for a particular form of belief in God. All this involves a certain change, brought about consciously or unconsciously.

Now, what we call change is a modified continuity of what has been, and in this so-called change we have become very clever. We are constantly making new discoveries in physics, science, mathematics, inventing new things, preparing to go to the moon, and so on and so on. In certain areas we are becoming extraordinarily knowledgeable, very well informed; and this kind of change implies having the capacity to adjust oneself to the new environment, to the new pressures which it creates. But is that all? One perceives the implications of this superficial form of change. Yet one knows inwardly, deeply, that there must be a radical change—a change not brought about through any motive or as the result of any pressure. One realizes that there must be a mutation at the very root of the mind itself; otherwise, we are just a lot of clever monkeys with extraordinary capacities—we are not really human beings at all.

So, realizing all this deeply within oneself, what is one to do? One sees that there must be a revolutionary change, a complete mutation at the very root of our being; otherwise, our problems, both economic and social, will inevitably increase and become more and more critical. One needs a new, fresh mind—and for this there must be, right through one's consciousness, a mutation which is not brought about by an act of will, and which therefore has no motive.

I do not know if I am making myself clear.

Seeing the necessity of a change, one can exercise will to bring it about—will being desire strengthened in a particular direction by determination and initiated by thought, by fear, by revolt. But all such change—the change brought about by the action of desire, of will—is still limited. It is a modified continuity of what has been, as one can see from what is going on in the communist world, and also in the capitalist countries. So there must be an extraordinary revolution, a psychological revolution in the human being, in man himself; but if he has an aim, if his revolution is planned, then it is still within the limits of the known, and therefore it is not a change at all.

Look. I can change myself; I can force myself to think differently, to adopt a different set of beliefs; I can stop a particular habit, get rid of nationalism, reform my thinking, brainwash myself instead of being brainwashed by a party or a church. Such changes in myself are fairly easy to make, but I see the utter futility of all that because it is superficial and does not lead to a great depth of understanding from which one can live, be, and function. So what is one to do?

Do you understand my question? I hope I have made it clear.

If I make an effort to change, that effort has a motive, which means that desire initiates a movement in a particular direction. There is the action of will, and therefore any change which is brought about is merely a modification—it is really not a change at all.

I see very clearly that I must change, and that the change must come about without effort. Any effort to change defeats itself because it implies the action of desire, of will, according to a preestablished pattern, formula, or concept. So what is one to do?

I do not know if you feel the same way I do about all this—how extraordinarily interesting it is, not only intellectually, but as a vital factor in one's own life. For millions of years man has been making a ceaseless effort to change, yet he is still caught in misery, in despair, in fear, with only an occasional flash of joy and delight. And how is this entity, who has been so heavily conditioned for so long, to throw off his burden without effort? That is the question we are asking ourselves. But the throwing off of the burden must not become another problem because, as I pointed out the other day, a problem is something we do not understand, something we have not the capacity to go to the very end of and finish with.

To bring about this mutation—not "bring about," those are the wrong words. There must be a mutation, and this mutation must take place now. If you introduce time as a factor in mutation, then time creates the problem. There is no tomorrow, there is no time at all for me to change in—time being thought. It is now or never. Do you understand?

I see the necessity of this radical change in me as a human being, as part of the whole human race; and I also see that time, which is thought, must not be a factor in it at all. Thought cannot resolve this problem. I have exercised thought for thousands upon thousands of years, yet I have not changed. I carry on with my habits, with my greed, with my envy, with my fears, and I am still caught up in the whole competitive pattern of existence. It is thought that has created the pattern, and thought cannot under any circumstances alter this pattern without creating another—thought being time. So I cannot look to thought, to time, to bring about a mutation, a radical change. There can be no exercising of will, no allowing of thought to guide the change.

Then what have I left? I see that desire, which is will, cannot bring about a real mutation of myself. Man has played with that for centuries, and it has produced no fundamental change in him. He has also used thought as an instrument to bring about a change within himself—thought as time, thought as tomorrow, with all its demands, inventions, pressures, influences—and again there has been no radical transformation. So what is one to do?

Now, if one has understood the whole structure and movement of the will, then the will does not operate at all; and if one sees that the use of thought, or time, as an instrument of change, is merely a postponement, then the thought process comes to an end. But what do we mean when we say that we see or understand something? Is understanding merely intellectual, verbal, or does it mean seeing something as a fact? I may say that I understand—but the word is not the thing. The intellectual understanding of a problem is not the resolution of that problem. When we comprehend something only verbally, which is what we call intellectual understanding, the word becomes enormously important; but when there is real understanding, the word is not important at all; it is merely a means of communication. There is a direct contact with the reality, with the fact. If we see as a fact the futility of will, and also the futility of thought, or time, in bringing about this radical transformation, then the mind—having rejected the whole structure of will, of thought—has no instrument with which to initiate action.

Now, so far you and I have been in communication with each other verbally, and perhaps we have also established between us a certain communion. But before we proceed any further, I think it is important to understand what we mean by communion. If you have ever walked by yourself among the trees or a forest, or along the banks of a stream, and felt the quietness, the sense of living completely with everything—with the rocks, with the flowers, with the stream, with the trees, with the sky—then you will know what communion is. The 'you'—with its thoughts, its anxieties, its pleasures, memories, recollections, despairs—has completely ceased. There is no 'you' as an observer apart from the thing observed; there is only that state of complete communion. And that, I hope, is what we have established here. It is not a hypnotic state—the speaker is not hypnotizing you into it. He has very carefully, verbally, explained certain things. But there is something more which cannot be explained verbally. Up to a point you can be informed by the words which the speaker uses, but at the same time you have to remember that the word is not the thing, and that the word must not be allowed to interfere with your own direct perception of the fact. When you commune with a tree—if you ever do—your mind is not occupied with the particular species of that tree or with whether it is useful or not. You are directly in communion with the tree. Similarly, we must establish this state of communion between you and the speaker because what comes next is one of the most difficult things to talk about.

As I said, the action of will, the action of thought as time, and the movement that is initiated by any influence or pressure whatsoever, has come to an end. Therefore the mind—which has nonverbally observed and understood all this—is completely quiet. It is not the initiator of any movement, conscious or unconscious. Again, this is something that must be gone into before we can go a little further.

Consciously you may not want to act in any particular direction because you have observed the futility of every kind of calculated change, from that of the communist to that of the most reactionary conservative. You see how silly it all is. But inwardly, unconsciously, there is the tremendous weight of the past pushing you in a certain direction. You are conditioned as a European, as a Christian, as a scientist, as a mathematician, as an artist, as a technician; and there is the tradition of a thousand years, very carefully exploited by the church, which has instilled in the unconscious certain beliefs and dogmas. You may consciously reject all that, but unconsciously the weight of it is still there. You are still a Christian, an Englishman, a German, an Italian, a Frenchman; you are still swayed by national, economic, and family interests, and by the traditions of the race to which you belong; and when it is a race that is very, very old, its influence is much deeper.

Now, how is one to wipe all that away? How is the unconscious to be cleansed immediately of the past? The analysts think that the unconscious can be partially or even completely cleansed through analysis—through investigation, exploration, confession, the interpretation of dreams, and so on—so that at least you become a "normal" human being, able to adjust yourself to the present environment. But in analysis there is always the analyzer and the analyzed, an observer who is interpreting the thing observed, which is a duality, a source of conflict.

So I see that mere analysis of the unconscious will not lead anywhere. It may help me to be a little less neurotic, a little kinder to my wife, to my neighbor, or some superficial thing like that; but that is not what we are talking about. I see that the analytical process—which involves time, interpretation, the movement of thought as the observer analyzing the thing observed—cannot free the unconscious; therefore, I reject the analytical process completely. The moment I perceive the fact that analysis cannot under any circumstances clear away the burden of the unconscious, I am out of analysis. I no longer analyze. So what has taken place? Because there is no longer an analyzer separated from the thing that he analyzes, he *is* that thing. He is not an entity apart from it. Then one finds that the unconscious is of very little importance. Do you follow?

I have pointed out how trivial the conscious is, with its superficial activities, its ceaseless chatter, and so on; and the unconscious is also very trivial. The unconscious, like the conscious, becomes important only when thought gives it continuity. Thought has its place; it is useful in technological matters, and all that; but thought is utterly futile in bringing about this radical transformation. When I see how thought gives continuity, there is an end to continuity as the thinker.

I hope you are following all this—it requires very close attention.

The conscious, or the unconscious, has very little importance. It has importance only when thought gives it continuity. When you perceive the truth that the whole process of thinking is a response of the past, and that it cannot possibly meet the tremendous demand of mutation, then both the conscious and the unconscious become unimportant, and the mind is no longer influenced or driven by either of them. Therefore it is no longer initiating any movement; it is completely quiet, still, silent. Though the mind is aware that there must be a change, a revolution, a complete transformation at the root of one's being, yet it does not initiate any movement in any direction; and in that total awareness, in that complete silence, mutation has already taken place. So mutation can take place only in a nondirective way, when the mind is not initiating any movement and is therefore completely still. In that stillness there is mutation because the root of one's being is exposed and it withers away. That is the only real revolution, not the economic or social kind, and it cannot be brought about by will or by thought. It is only in that state of mutation that you can perceive something beyond the measure of words, something that is supreme, beyond all theology and all recognition.

I hope you have not been put to sleep! Perhaps you will be good enough to ask some questions.

Question: As far as I have experienced, thinking condemns me to isolation because it prevents me from communing with the things around me, and it also prevents me from going to the roots of myself. Therefore I should like to ask: Why do human beings think? What is the function of human thinking? And why do we so greatly exaggerate the importance of thinking?

KRISHNAMURTI: I thought we had gone beyond all that. All right, sir, let me explain.

Merely listening to an explanation is not seeing the fact, and we cannot commune with each other through the explanation unless you and I both see the fact and leave the fact alone, which is not to interfere with it. Then we are also in communion with the fact. But if you interpret the fact in one way, and I in another, then we are not in communion, either with the fact or with each other.

Now, how does thought arise—the thought that isolates, that does not give love, which is the only means of communion? And how can this thought come to an end? Thought—the whole mechanism of thought—has to be understood, and the very understanding of it is the ending of it. I will go into it, if I may.

Thought arises as a reaction when there is a challenge. If there were no challenge, you would not think. The challenge may take the form of a question, however trivial or however great, and according to that question you respond. In the time interval between the question and the response, the thought process begins, does it not? If you ask me about something with which I am very familiar, my response is immediate. If you ask me where I live, for example, there is no time interval because I do not have to think about it, and to your question I respond immediately. But if your question is a little more complex, there is a time interval—during which I am looking into memory—between your question and my reply. You may ask me what is the distance between the earth and the moon, and I say, "By Jove, do I know anything about that? Yes, I do"—and then I reply. Between your question and my reply there is an interval of time in which memory has come into operation and provided the answer. So when I am challenged, my response may be immediate, or it may take a certain length of time. If you ask me a question about which I know nothing at all, the interval is much longer. I say, "I don't know, but I will find out"; and not having found the answer among all the things that I remember, I turn to someone else to tell me, or I look it up in a book. Again, during this much longer interval, the thought process is going on. With these three phases we are quite familiar.

Now, there is a fourth phase, which perhaps you don't know or have never articulated, and it is this. You ask me a question, and I actually don't know the answer. My memory doesn't recollect it, and I am not waiting for anybody to tell me. I have no answer, and no expectation. I really don't know. There is no time interval and therefore no thought because the mind is not looking, not searching, not expecting. That state is actually a complete negation; it is freedom from everything the mind has known. And it is only in that state that the new can be understood—the new being the supreme, or whatever other word you care to give to it. In that state the whole process of thinking has come to an end; there is neither the observer nor the observed, neither the experiencer nor the thing that is experienced. All experience has ceased, and in that total silence there is a complete mutation.

July 19, 1964

Fifth Talk in Saanen

This morning I would like, if I may, to talk about something which seems to me very important. It is not an idea or a concept or a formula to be carried out. Concepts, formulas, ideas, really prevent deep understanding of facts as they are. By understanding a fact, I mean observing an activity, a movement of thought or feeling, and perceiving its significance in the very moment of action. The perception of a fact as it is must take place in the moment of action itself; and unless one comprehends facts to a great depth, one will always be hounded by fear.

Most of us, I think, have this enormous burden of conscious or unconscious fear. And this morning I would like to go into this problem with you and see if we cannot bring about a total understanding and therefore a complete resolution of fear, so that when one leaves this hot tent, one will literally and factually be free of fear. So may I suggest that you listen quietly rather than inwardly argue with me. We will argue, exchange words, verbalize our thoughts and feelings, a little later. But for the moment let us listen, in a sense, negatively—that is, without any positive assertion of the act of listening. Just listen. I am communicating with you—you are not communicating with me. I am telling you something. To understand what it is I want to convey, you have to listen—and in the very act of listening, you will be able to commune with the speaker.

Unfortunately, most of us are incapable of this negative, silent listening, not only here, but also in our everyday existence. When we go out for a walk, we do not listen to the birds, to the whisper of the trees, to the murmur of the river; we do not listen to the mountains and to the skies beyond. To be directly in communion with nature, and with other people, you have to listen; and you can listen only when you are negatively silent—that is, when you listen without effort, without mentation taking place, without verbalizing, quarreling, discussing.

I do not know if you have ever tried listening completely to your wife or husband, to your children, to the car that goes by, to the movements of your own thought and feeling. In such listening there is no action at all, no intention, no interpretation; and that very act of listening brings about a tremendous revolution at the very root of the mind.

But most of us are so unaccustomed to listening. If we hear anything contrary to our habitual thought, or if one of our pet ideals gets kicked around, we become terribly agitated. We have a vested interest in certain ideas and ideals, just as we have in properties, and in our own experience and knowledge; and when any of that is questioned, we lose our balance, we resist anything that is being said.

Now, if you will really listen this morning to what is being said, listen with alert, choiceless awareness, then you will find that you are following the speaker nonverbally—that is, without linguistic analysis—and are therefore moving with the meaning, the significance that lies beyond the word. It doesn't mean that you go to sleep, or that you are in some beatific state of self-satisfying sentimentality. On the contrary, listening requires a great deal of attention—not concentration, but attention. The two things are entirely different. If you listen with attention, perhaps you and I can go to those great depths at which creation can take place. And surely this is essential because a mind that is superficial, anxious, endlessly worried over many problems, cannot possibly understand fear, which is one of the most fundamental things in life. If we do not understand fear, there can be no love, nor can there be creation—not the act of creating, but that state of timeless creation which cannot be put into words, into pictures, into books.

So, one has to be free of fear. Fear is not an abstraction. Fear is not just a word—though for most of us the word has become much more important than the fact. I do not know if you have ever thought of getting rid of fear totally and absolutely. It can be done so completely that there is never a shadow of fear because the mind is always ahead of the event. That is, instead of pursuing fear and trying to overcome it after it has arisen, the mind is ahead of fear and is therefore free of fear.

Now, to understand fear, one has to go into the question of comparison. Why do we compare at all? In technical matters comparison reveals progress, which is relative. Fifty years ago there was no atomic bomb, there were no supersonic airplanes, but now we have these things; and in another fifty years we shall have something else which we don't have now. This is called progress, which is always comparative, relative, and our mind is caught in that way of thinking. Not only outside the skin, as it were, but also inside the skin, in the psychological structure of our own being, we think comparatively. We say, "I am this, I have been that, and I shall be something more in the future." This comparative thinking we call progress, evolution, and our whole behavior—morally, ethically, religiously, in our business and social relationships—is based on it. We observe ourselves comparatively in relation to a society which itself is the outcome of this same comparative struggle.

Comparison breeds fear. Do observe this fact in yourself. I want to be a better writer or a more beautiful and intelligent person. I want to have more knowledge than others; I want to be successful, to become somebody, to have more fame in the world. Success and fame are psychologically the very essence of comparison, through which we constantly breed fear. And comparison also gives rise to conflict, struggle—which is considered highly respectable. You say that you must be competitive in order to survive in this world, so you compare and compete in business, in the family, and in so-called religious matters. You must reach heaven and sit next to Jesus, or whoever your particular savior may be. The comparative spirit is reflected in the priest becoming an archbishop, a cardinal, and finally the pope. We cultivate this same spirit very assiduously throughout our life, struggling to become better or to achieve a higher status than somebody else. Our social and moral structure is based on it.

So there is in our life this constant state of comparison, competition, and the everlasting struggle to be somebody—or to be nobody, which is the same thing. This, I feel, is the root of all fear because it breeds envy, jealousy, hatred. Where there is hatred, there is obviously no love, and fear is generated more and more.

As I said, please just listen. Don't ask, "How am I not to be comparative? What am I to do to stop comparing?" You can't do anything to stop it. If you did, your motive would also be born of comparison. All that you can do is just to see the fact that this complex thing we call our existence is a comparative struggle, and that if you act upon it, try to alter it, you are again caught in the comparative, competitive spirit. What is important is to listen without any distortion, and you will distort what you are listening to the minute you want to do something about it.

So one sees the implications and the significance of this comparative evaluation of life, and the illusion of thinking that comparison brings understanding—comparing the works of two painters, or two writers; comparing oneself with another who is not so clever, less efficient, more beautiful, and all the rest of it. And can one live in the world, both outwardly and inwardly, without ever comparing? You know, to be aware of the state of a mind that is always comparing—just to recognize it as a fact and abide with that fact—requires a great deal of attention. That attention brings about its own discipline, which is extraordinarily pliable; it has no pattern, it is not compulsive, it is not the act of controlling, subjugating, denying, in the hope of understanding further the whole question of fear.

This attitude towards life which is based on comparison is a major factor in the deterioration of the mind, is it not? Deterioration of the mind implies dullness, insensitivity, decay, and therefore an utter lack of intelligence. The body is slowly deteriorating because we are getting old, but the mind is also deteriorating, and the cause of this deterioration is comparison, conflict, competitive effort. It is like an engine that is running with a great deal of friction—it cannot function properly, and it deteriorates rapidly all the time it is running.

As we have seen, comparison, conflict, competition not only breed deterioration but also fear; and where there is fear, there is darkness; there is no affection, no understanding, no love.

Now, what is fear? Have you ever really come face to face with fear, or only with the idea of fear? There is a difference between the two, is there not? The actual fact of fear and the idea of fear are two entirely different things. Most of us are caught in the idea of fear in an opinion, a judgment, an evaluation of fear, and we are never in contact with the actual fact of fear itself. I think this is something we have to understand rather widely and deeply.

I am afraid, let us say, of snakes. I saw a snake one day, and it caused me a great deal of fear, and that experience has remained in my mind as memory. When I go out walking of an evening, this memory comes into operation, and I am already afraid of meeting a snake; so the idea of fear is much more vital, more potent than the fact itself. Which means what? That we are never in contact with fear, but only with the idea of fear. Just observe this fact in yourself. And you can't artificially remove the idea. You may say, "Well, I will try to meet fear without the idea"; but you can't. Whereas, if you really see that memory and ideation are preventing you from being directly in communion with the fact—with the fact of fear, with the fact of jealousy, with the fact of death—then you will find quite a different relationship taking place between the fact and yourself.

To most of us, idea is far more important than action. We never act completely. We are always limiting action with an idea, adjusting or interpreting action according to a formula, a concept, and therefore there is no action at all—or rather, action is so incomplete that it breeds problems. But once you realize this extraordinary fact, then action becomes an astonishingly vital thing because it is no longer approximating itself to an idea.

Fear is not an abstraction, it is always in relation to something. I am afraid of death, afraid of public opinion, afraid of not being popular, of not being known, afraid of not achieving anything, and so on. The word *fear* is not the fact; it is only a symbol representing the fact; and for most of us the symbol is far more important than the fact—religiously, and in every other way. Now, can the mind free itself from the word, the symbol, the idea, and observe the fact without interpretation, without saying, "I must look at the fact," without any idea about the fact at all? If the mind looks at a fact with an opinion about that fact, then it is merely dealing with ideas, is it not? So this is something very important to understand—that when I look at a fact through an idea, there is no communion with the fact at all. If I want to be in communion with the fact, then the idea must completely disappear. Now, let us proceed from there and see where it leads.

There is the fact that you are afraid of death, afraid of what somebody will say, afraid of a dozen things. Now, when you are no longer looking at that fact through an idea, through a conclusion, through a concept, through memory, what actually takes place? First of all, there is no division between the observer and the thing observed, no 'I' separate from that thing. The cause of separation has been removed, and therefore you are directly in relation with the sensation which you call fear. The 'you' with its opinions, ideas, judgments, evaluation, concepts, memories—all that is absent, and there is only that thing.

What we are doing is arduous; it is not just a morning's entertainment. I feel that when one leaves this tent this morning, one can be deeply and completely free of fear—and then one is a human being.

So, you are now facing the fact: the sensation or apprehension which you call fear, and which an idea has brought about. You are afraid of death—I am taking that as an example. Ordinarily death is merely an idea to you; it is not a fact. The fact comes into being only when you yourself are dying. You know about other people dying, and the realization that you also are going to die becomes an idea which breeds fear. You look through the idea at the fact, and this prevents you from being directly in contact with the fact. There is an interval between the observer and the thing observed. It is in this interval that thought arises—thought being the ideation, the verbalization, the memory which offers resistance to the fact. But when there is not this gap, that is, when there is the absence of thought, which is time, then you are completely confronted with the fact; and then the fact operates on you—you do not operate on the fact.

I hope you are getting all this. Is it too much on a hot morning?

You see, I feel that to live with fear of any kind is—if I may use the word—evil. Living with fear is evil because it breeds hatred, distorts your thinking and perverts your whole life. So it is absolutely necessary for the religious man to be completely free of fear, outwardly and inwardly. I do not mean the spontaneous response of the physical body in safeguarding itself, which is natural. It is normal, when you suddenly see a snake, to jump out of the way—that is merely a self-protective physical instinct, and it would be abnormal not to have such a reaction. But the desire to be secure inwardly, psychologically, at any level of one's being, breeds fear. One sees all around one the effects of fear, and one realizes how essential it is for the mind not to be a breeding ground of fear at any time.

If you have listened attentively to what has been said this morning, you will have seen that fear is never in the present, but always in the future; it is evoked by thought, by thinking of what may happen tomorrow, or the next minute. So fear, thought, and time go together; and if one is to understand and to go beyond fear, there must be the understanding of thought as well as of time. All comparative thinking must stop; all sense of effort—in which is involved competition, ambition, the worship of success, the striving to be somebody—must come to an end. And when that whole process is understood, there is no conflict at all, is there? Hence the mind is no longer in a state of deterioration because it is capable of meeting fear and is not the breeding ground of fear. Now, this state of freedom from fear is absolutely necessary if one is to understand what is creation.

For most of us, life is a boring routine, and there is nothing new in it. Whatever new thing takes place, we make into a routine immediately. Someone paints a picture, and for a second it is a new thing—and then it is all over. Pleasure, pain, endeavor—it all becomes a routine, a bore, an everlasting struggle with very little meaning. We are always seeking for something new—the new in pictures, the new in painting. We want to feel something new, to express something new—something that will not immediately be translated in terms of the old. We hope to find some trick or clever technique through which we can express ourselves and feel satisfied—but that again becomes a terrible nuisance, an ugly thing, something to kick against. So we are always in a state of recognition. Anything new is immediately recognized and thereby absorbed into the old. The process of recognition is, for most of us, astonishingly important because thought is always functioning from within that field of the known.

The moment you recognize something, it ceases to be new. Do you understand? Our education, our experience, our daily living—all this is a process of recognition, of constant repetition, and it gives a continuity to our existence. With our minds caught in this process, we ask if there is anything new; we want to find out whether or not there is God. From the known we seek to find the unknown. It is the known that causes fear of the unknown, so we say, "I must find the unknown, I must recognize it and bring it back into the known." This is our search in painting, in music, in everything—the search for the new, which is always interpreted in terms of the old.

Now, this process of recognition and interpretation, of action and fulfillment, is not creation. You cannot possibly express the unknown. What you can express is an interpretation or a recognition of what you call the unknown. So you must find out for yourself what is creation; otherwise, your life becomes a mere routine in which there is no change, no mutation, and with which you get bored very quickly. Creation is the very movement of creation itself—it is not the interpretation of that movement on canvas, in music, in books, or in relationship.

After all, the mind has within it millions of years of memories, of instincts, and the urge to go beyond all that is still part of the mind. From this background of the old springs the desire to recognize the new, but the new is something totally different—it is love—and it cannot be understood by a mind which is caught in the process of the old trying to recognize the new.

This is one of the most difficult things to communicate, but I would like to communicate it, if I can, because if the mind is not in that state of creation, it is always in the process of deterioration. That state is timeless, eternal. It is not comparative, it is not utilitarian, it has no value at all in terms of action; you can't use it to paint your beastly little pictures or to write your marvelous

Shakespearean poetry. But without it, there is really no love at all. The love that we know is jealousy; it is hedged about with hate, anxiety, despair, misery, conflict—and none of that is love. Love is something everlastingly new, unrecognizable; it is never the same, and therefore it is the highest state of uncertainty. And it is only in the state of love that the mind can understand that extraordinary thing called creation—which is God, or any other name you like to give it. The mind that has understood the limitations of the known and is therefore free of the known—only such a mind can be in that state of creation in which there is no factor of deterioration.

Do you want to ask any questions on what we have talked about this morning?

Question: Is the feeling of having an individual will the cause of fear?

KRISHNAMURTI: Probably it is. But what do you mean by that word *individual?* Are you an individual? You have a body, a name, a bank account; but if you are inwardly bound, crippled, limited, are you an individual? Like everybody else, you are conditioned, are you not? And within that limited area of your conditioning, which you call the individual, everything arises—your miseries, your despairs, your jealousies, your fears. That narrow, fragmentary thing, with its individual soul, its individual will, and all that messy little stuff—of that you are very proud. And with that you want to uncover God, truth, love. You cannot. All that you can do is to be aware of your fragment and its struggles, and see that the fragment can never become the whole. Do what it will, the spoke can never become the wheel. So one has to inquire into and understand this separate, narrow, limited existence, the so-called individual.

What is important in all this is not your opinion or my opinion but to find out what is true. And to find out what is true, the mind must be without fear—so completely denuded of fear that it is totally innocent. It is only out of that innocence that there is creation.

July 21, 1964

Sixth Talk in Saanen

It seems to me rather important to find out for oneself what one is seeking. The word *seeking* has extraordinary significance, has it not? Apart from the dictionary meaning, the act of seeking implies that one is moving from the periphery to the center. And this seeking, this searching, depends upon one's temperament, upon environmental pressures and strains, upon the calamities of experience, the distresses of life, the innumerable travails of one's existence. All these factors force one to seek. If there were no pressure, no challenge, no calamity, no misery, I wonder how many of us would seek anything at all?

Searching implies going around looking in the hope of finding something, does it not? I looked up that word *searching* this morning in the dictionary. It comes from a Latin word, the implication of which is to go seeking, asking, demanding, inquiring, probing. And I wonder what we are probing for, what it is we are seeking! Can we ever find out? Or is it something vague, fleeting, constantly changing according to circumstances, according to one's temperament, one's peculiar pleasures and pains?

We are everlastingly talking about seeking, searching. What does that word imply? It implies that from the outside you gradually move to the center according to your own particular idiosyncrasies, tastes, and environmental pressures. It is like going from shop to shop trying on various suits until something fits you which you like, and you accept it. When you say you are seeking, what you really mean is that you are experimenting with different ideas, concepts, formulas, going from one religion to another, from one teacher to another, until eventually you find something you like, something that suits your own particular temperament and idiosyncracies. If you don't like what you find in the Occident, you turn to the Orient, with its ancient and complex philosophy, where there are innumerable teachers and gurus to choose from; and there you get caught up in a little pool of thought, imagining it to be the everlasting reality. Or, if you don't do that, you become a yet more ardent Catholic, or join the Existentialists—oh, goodness, there are so many of these things in the world! To me there is neither the East nor the West; the human mind is neither Oriental nor Occidental. Whatever their origin, all theologies are immature, as all philosophies are. They are the inventions of man, who, being caught in a prison of his own making, believes in something and around that belief creates a theology, or projects some extraordinary philosophy; and the more clever the philosopher or the theologian, the more acceptable he becomes to the public, to the reader, to the follower.

Now, is that what we are all doing here? You come and spend two or three weeks here, listening to what is being said. If you feel that it isn't quite satisfactory, that it doesn't give you everything you want, you turn to some other teacher, or take up some other philosophy, from which you get a little more satisfaction. So, unless you are permanently caught up in a little backwater of thought, you keep going until one year, perhaps, you come back here; and then you start all over again.

So I think we ought to understand this extraordinary phenomenon, whether in the West or in the East, of going from one thing to another, endlessly seeking, asking, demanding, probing. That is, I think we ought to be very clear in ourselves what it is we are seeking, and why—and whether there is any necessity to seek at all. Surely, all search implies a movement from the periphery to the center, from the circumstances to the cause, from the boundaries to the very origin of existence. That is, we move from the outer to the inner, hoping to find something real, deep, vital, something extraordinarily significant. In the course of this movement we struggle to practice different methods, systems, we torture ourselves with various forms of discipline so that at the end of one's life one is bruised, one's mind is almost crippled.

I am afraid this is the case with most of us. We move in from the periphery to the center because we want to find out how to be happy, what is truth, whether there is God, something everlasting; and therefore we are always struggling, conforming, imitating, following, brutalizing our minds and hearts with discipline, until we have nothing left of ourselves that is original, true, real. That is our life, and the greater the pressure, the pain, the fury of life on the periphery, the more we want to move towards the center.

Now, is there a coming to the center immediately—without this endless struggle to reach the center—and from the center, flowering? Do you understand my question? For millions of years we have struggled to go from the outer to the inner in order to find out what is real—and we have just seen what is involved in that process. So I say to myself, how absurd all that is. Why should I torture myself? Why should I copy, imitate, follow? Is there not a possibility of discovering or being at the very center, and flowering from there, instead of going the other way around? Because, to me at least, the other way around has no meaning; it has no significance whatsoever; therefore, I reject it completely. I don't want to torture myself, or follow anyone. I don't want to read a single book about philosophy or sharpen my mind with subtle argument—my mind has been made sufficiently sharp as it is through ambition, through anxiety and despair, through all the brutalities of life. And I don't want to practice another method, another system, or follow another guru, teacher, or savior—I don't want to do anything of that kind.

Please, I am thinking aloud, not just for myself, but to clarify certain things so that you and I can commune with each other about what is real, and not everlastingly struggle through reaction to move from the outer to the inner. I am putting into words what perhaps you may feel at rare moments, when you are fed up with everything—with your churches, with your politicians, with your banks, with the pettiness of your relationships at home, with the boredom of the office, with all the stupidities of life which are an insult to human dignity. Having spent twenty years or more going to the office day after day, or cooking food and bearing children one after another—having experienced the pleasure as well as the boredom, the pettiness, the despair of all that, you must sometimes have asked yourself if there is not a possibility of coming suddenly, unexpectedly, to the original source, to the very essence of things, and from there living, functioning, flowering, so that you never need read a single book, study any philosophy, worship any image or savior, because wherever you look, there is that center from which all action, all love, everything takes place.

The obvious fact is that—with our greed, jealousy, possessiveness, fear, with our sentimentality, our fleeting pleasures, our purr of self-satisfaction—we are animals, highly evolved animals. If you watch an animal, you will see it has the same conflicts that we have. The anthropoid apes are jealous and have their matrimonial difficulties. They unite in groups—first the family, then the tribe, and all that business—just as we do; and someone was saying the other day that these apes could sit in the United Nations quite as well as any human being! It is an obvious fact that our character, our devotion, our courage, our fear, our wars, our so-called peace, our struggles, all spring from this animal background. You don't have to dispute this with me. The biologists, the anthropologists are saying it is so—if you want authorities.

Now, is it possible to be free of all that, not eventually, by slow degrees, but can one cut it away at one blow so that it is over, and one has a morality, an ethic, a sense of beauty totally apart, something completely different from the animal background? Obviously, to live together in the world, we need a morality of social behavior; but at present our morality, our concepts of behavior—which are the formulas of our daily existence—are still of the animal, and we don't want to acknowledge that. We like to think, because we are a little more capable, more efficient, more inventive than the apes, that we are also more human; but even the apes use instruments to catch things; they invent as they go along, so there is very little difference between them and us.

So, there is this extraordinary activity of the animals, and the equally extraordinary activity of the human mind that wants to be secure, not only in the physical world, but also inwardly—which is still a result of the animal instinct. And there is at the same time the desire to find something real, original, a state that is uncontaminated, innocent. Now, is it possible to come upon that state suddenly so that it is not cultivated, not sought after? Because beauty cannot be cultivated, any more than love can. You must come upon it suddenly, as you would come upon a view which you had never seen before. All at once it is there in front of you, rich, full, vital, and you are part of it; and from there you live, you act, you are. Without making an effort, without disciplining, controlling, compelling the outer, without imitating, and all that, you suddenly come upon the well of life, the original spring of all existence; and when once the mind has drunk at that fountain, it has lived and it lives from there forever. Is such a thing possible?

Do you understand my question? This is not something sentimental or mystical; it is not something to get excited or inspired over, nor is it something that you intuitively feel. It is none of those things. As long as we are animalistic, with our envies, jealousies, despairs, this thing is not possible—the two can't go together. To cut away totally, at one stroke, the animal background, and then begin anew—is that possible?

I will show you how important, how necessary it is that it be made possible. If you admit time—yesterday, today, and tomorrow—then you are inevitably caught in the process of degeneration because you will always be looking to tomorrow, and there will always be a yesterday which conditions the present. So the mind, which is the result of centuries of time, has to forget time. Do you follow? It has to put away time altogether. Otherwise it is caught in the net of time, in the struggle to achieve, to become, to arrive—it goes through all that, which only leads to sorrow, misery, decay. So what is one to do?

I want to find out immediately what is true, and not wait a few seconds, or until the day after tomorrow; I want to be there. I am too impatient to wait. I have no use for time, for the idea of achieving something at the end of my life, or after ten thousand lives. That to me is utterly juvenile, immature. It is all an invention of the mind in its laziness, in its confusion, in its despair. I want to be so awake that when I open my eyes, my heart, my mind, the truth is there—and from there to function, to act, to live, to enjoy the beauties of the earth.

Now, we are going to talk about something which cannot possibly be copied, imitated. I am going to explore, and I hope you are going to explore with me. But if you merely follow me, then you are lost.

However different the varieties of temperament, all movement from the border to the center is a positive movement. It is a deliberate search, a reaction away from the border towards the center, a movement arising from the desire to find, and therefore involving discipline, imitation, following, obeying, the practice of a system. All this is a positive process—at least it is what you call positive.

Just follow this; don't inwardly argue with me. You will see how true it is as we go along. I am not mesmerizing or trying to put something over on you, nor am I doing any kind of propaganda—that is all too silly.

So one is aware of this positive movement, and one sees the whole significance of it. One sees it immediately, and not in a leisurely, inattentive manner, with the idea, "I will think about it tomorrow." There is no thought of tomorrow, there is no idea of "in the meantime." One sees it immediately, and therefore the positive movement ceases completely. One hasn't done anything; there has been no volitional act, no cause, no deliberate searching and coming to a result. One sees the immaturity of this positive movement, with its priests—one sees the utter futility of the whole of it. The priests, the churches, the theologies, the inventors of ideas—they all drop away because one perceives the truth that this positive movement from the periphery to the center can never reach the center. It is the movement of the outer trying to come within—and therefore always remaining the outer. One sees that fact with sharpness, with an extraordinary clarity; and then one begins to understand the beauty of negative movement—the negative movement of the mind which is not the opposite of the positive but which comes into being when the mind has understood the significance of all positive movement. So one's mind is no longer caught in the positive movement, and therefore it is in a state of negation. That is, having seen—not fragmentarily, but completely—the significance of this positive movement, the mind is no longer moving, no longer acting, doing; therefore, it is in a state which may be called negative. Do you understand? Let me put it differently.

Personally, I never read a book about all this. I don't want to; it doesn't interest me because I see in myself the whole of mankind—not mystically, metaphorically, or symbolically, but actually. I am you and the world. In me is the whole treasure of the world, and to discover it I have only to understand and go beyond myself. If I don't understand myself, I have no raison d'être, no substance; I am just a confused entity, and the more I seek, study, follow, the more confused I become. I depend on teachers, on my temperament, on my desires, and therefore my confusion grows.

So I see how important it is to understand myself totally, without effort—that is, without making the understanding of myself into a problem. To understand myself, I must have a mind that is not making any positive movement to correct, or not to correct, what it sees. As I said the other day, both the conscious and the unconscious mind are trivial, and I have to understand that triviality; I have to understand it immediately so that the unconscious doesn't play tricks, doesn't project some vision, some image, some secret desire, when I am not giving it complete attention—and which again becomes a problem.

Are you following all this?

I see that to understand myself completely requires a mind that is totally uninfluenced, without a motive, without a movement, a mind that is completely empty of positive action. And when with that clarity of mind I can look at myself, that very looking dissolves the triviality, which is the 'me'.

Please, I am not inventing a philosophy. And for God's sake, don't translate this as something peculiar to the Orient and all that nonsense. It isn't an idiosyncrasy of the speaker, who happens to have been born in a country where the sun is hot and makes the skin brown. Because of that heat and the sluggishness it induces, and out of poverty, there are those who go within, and from that going within they write philosophies, invent religions, gods, and all the rest of it. Leave that to them. I am not talking about that. I am talking about something which is neither of the East nor of the West, which is neither personal nor impersonal—it is what is true. One has suddenly come upon a state in which the mind is no longer driven by the desire to be gratified, no longer demanding or seeking experience. One has to come upon it, for there is nobody to teach it, and this requires energy. By energy I mean the focusing of all one's attention without any sense of distraction. Actually there is no such thing as distraction; there is only inattention. No? I am glad somebody doesn't agree.

Is there such a thing as distraction? As I am walking, moving, I look. My mind goes here and there, to different points, and if they move me, if they take me away from the main road, from the self-center, I call them distractions. But when there is no self-center, no straight path along which I am walking, there is no distraction.

This is very important to understand. If you understand this one thing very clearly, you will find that all effort to concentrate, with the conflict it creates, completely disappears; and then there is no distraction. Looking at the sky, seeing the face of a lovely child, hearing the stream rushing by and the terrific noise of a jet passing overhead, observing people, the politicians, the priests, listening to your own mind and heart, being aware of your own demands, your own despairs—in none of these, from the looking at the sky to the looking at yourself, is there distraction. It is all part of one whole, and that one whole can be seen only when there is complete attention; and complete attention is denied when you admit distraction. Oh, do see this!

When there is complete attention, you never regard anything as a distraction. Your sex, your jealousy, your anxiety, your fear, your love, your passion—nothing you look at is any distraction at all. Everything is within the flame of attention, and therefore there is nothing fragmentary. The politician, the priest, the ritual—they are all part of the whole. In the positive movement of the mind there is distraction, there is fragmentation; but when the mind has no movement and is therefore—if I may use the word—negative, there is no fragmentation of life. Then the cloud in the sky, the dust on the road, the flower by the wayside, and the whisper of your own thought are all part of the whole. But that wholeness can be understood only when the positive movement of the mind has completely ceased.

So you see for yourself that to come upon that center, that original source of things, which is the supreme, all movement of the mind must come to an end—but not through torturing the mind with discipline, or through posing so extraordinarily difficult or fantastic a question, as they do in certain sects, that the mind is shocked into silence. That is all utterly immature. From the beginning you must see the truth of every movement of your own thought and feeling; and you can do that only when the mind is completely 'negative', silent, quiet. And it can be done immediately. It is like stepping off the road—the road of positive action which man has habitually followed for thousands upon thousands of years. You can just step off that road without any expectation, without any demanding or seeking. But you can do it only when you see the whole movement of man, and not just the movement of a particular man; that is, when you see in yourself the movement of the whole. When you perceive all this at one glance—and that is all you have to do, nothing else—then you are already walking in freedom; and out of that freedom there is action which does not cripple the mind.

Will you please ask some questions about all this? Or is there nothing to ask?

Question: What is maturity?

KRISHNAMURTI: Are we talking about maturity? All right, sir, what is maturity? Has maturity got anything to do with age? Has maturity got anything to do with experience, with knowledge, with capacity? Has it anything to do with competition and the accumulation of money? If it is not any of these things, then what is maturity? Has it anything to do with time? Don't say no so easily. If you were really free of time, if time had no importance to you whatsoever, what would be the state of your mind? I am not talking about chronological time; that obviously has importance. But if time meant nothing to you in the psychological sense—time to achieve, time to succeed, time to overcome, to conquer, time to become clever, time to grasp, to compare—then wouldn't you be mature? So it is only the innocent mind that is mature, not the mind that has accumulated knowledge for a thousand years. Knowledge is needed and has significance at a certain level, but knowledge does not make for clarity, for innocence. There is innocence only when all conflict has come to an end.

When the mind is no longer moving in any particular direction because all directions have been understood, it is then in that state of originality which is innocence, and from there it can go into the measureless distance where the supreme may be; and only such a mind is mature.

July 23, 1964

Seventh Talk in Saanen

I would like to continue from where we left off the other day. I think it is very important to understand the whole question of action; and I am using that word neither in any abstract sense nor merely as an idea. I mean the actual fact of action, of doing something. Whether you are digging in a garden, going to the office, looking at a tree, following the movement of a river, or just walking along a road without thought, quietly observing things—whatever you are doing, it is part of action. And with most of us, action breeds conflict. Our action, however so-called profound or however superficial, becomes repetitive, tiresome, boring, a mere activity without much significance. So I think it is very important to understand what action is.

To do anything—to walk, to speak, to look, to think, to feel—demands energy; and energy is dissipated when, inherent in the expression of that energy, there is conflict. As we can observe, all our activities, at whatever level, engender some kind of conflict; they create within us a sense of effort, a certain resistance, denial, defense. And is it at all possible to act without conflict, without resistance—and even without effort? That is what I would like to talk about, if I may, this morning.

One sees what is happening in the world. The computers, the electronic brains, and various forms of automation are going to give man more and more leisure, and that leisure is going to be monopolized by organized religion and by organized entertainment. I do not know if there is much difference between the two, but for the moment we will keep them separate. When man has a great deal of leisure, he has more energy—much more energy—and society demands that he utilize that energy rightly, not antisocially. To control the antisocial feeling, he is going to lose himself either in organized religion or in entertainment of every kind. Or he will lose himself in literature, in art, in music—which is another form of entertainment. As a result, man will become more and more superficial. He may read all the books in the world and try to understand the intricacies of theology, of philosophy, of science; he may become familiar with certain facts and truths in literature, but it will still be an external thing, just as the various forms of religion and entertainment are. The organized religions assert that they are seeking the inward things of life, but they demand belief, dogma, ritual, conformity, as we all know.

Now, unless we are very much aware of all these conditions that are inherent in modern civilization, our energies will be consumed by them, and our action will therefore remain very superficial; and because of that superficiality, we shall continue to have conflict within ourselves as well as with other people, with society. In every form of human endeavor—artistic, scientific, mathematical, industrial—and in one's relationship with one's wife or husband, with one's children, with one's neighbor, there will continue to be conflict; and conflict is a waste of energy. To bring about the cessation of conflict, and thereby the conservation of energy, one has to understand for oneself what action is; and without that understanding our life will become more and more outward, and we shall be more and more inwardly empty. This is not a point to be discussed or doubted; it is not a matter of my opinion against your opinion. These are actual facts.

So, first of all, what is action as we know it now? All our action has a subtle or obvious motive, has it not? Either we are pursuing a reward or acting out of fear or trying to gain something. Our action is always an adjustment to a pattern, to an idea, or it is an approximation to some ideal. Conformity, adjustment, approximation, resistance, denial—that is all we know of action, and it implies a series of conflicts.

As I was saying the other day, to commune about something with which we are not deeply related is always rather difficult. I want to commune with you about a state of mind which is the complete antithesis of this conflict which we now call action. There is a total action, an action without conflict, and I want to tell you something about it—not that you should accept it or reject it or be hypnotized by it. You know, one of the most difficult things to do is to sit on a platform talking while others listen—if you do listen at all—and establish the right relationship between the listener and the speaker. You are not here to be mesmerized by a lot of words, nor do I want to influence you in any way whatsoever. I am not doing propaganda for an idea, and it is not my purpose to instruct you. As I have often pointed out, there is neither the teacher nor the taught, there is only a state of learning; and you and I cannot possibly learn if you are waiting to be instructed, to be told what to do. We are not dealing with opinions. I have no opinions. What I am trying to do is just to state certain facts, and you can look at them, examine them for yourself, or not. This means that you and I have to establish the right relationship so that there is a communion which is not merely intellectual but the total perception of a fact at which we are both looking. We are not communing with each other, but rather we are both communing with the fact, and therefore the fact becomes much more important than you and I. It is the fact and our mutual perception of the fact that alone can create the right ambience or atmosphere, and this is bound to affect us profoundly. So it seems to me that to listen to something—to that stream, or to the whisper of those trees, or to one's own thoughts and feelings—becomes extraordinarily important when we are considering the fact itself, and not an idea or an opinion about the fact.

We all know that our action breeds conflict. All action that is based on an idea, a concept, a formula, or that approximates itself to an ideal must inevitably breed conflict. That is obvious. If I act according to a formula, a pattern, a concept, then I am always divided between the fact of what I am, and what I think I should do about that fact; so there is never a complete action. There is always an approximation to an idea or to an ideal, and hence conflict is inherent in all action as we know it—which is a waste of energy and brings about deterioration of the mind. Please observe the state and the activity of your own mind, and you will see that this is true.

Now, I am asking myself: Is there action without idea and therefore without conflict? Or to put it differently: Must action always breed effort, struggle, conflict? For example, I am talking, which is a form of action. Surely, in this action there is conflict only if I am trying to assert myself, trying to be somebody, trying to convince you. So it is tremendously important to find out for oneself whether there is a possibility of living and doing things without the slightest conflict—that is, whether there can be action in which the mind remains intact, without deterioration, without any form of distortion. And there is bound to be distortion if the mind is in any way influenced or if it is caught in conflict, which is a waste of energy. To find out the truth of this matter is of real interest to me, and it must also be to you because what we are trying to do here is to see if it is possible to live without sorrow, without despair, without fear, without any form of activity that brings about deterioration of the mind. If it is possible, then what happens to such a mind? What happens to a mind that is never touched by society, that has no fear, that is not greedy, envious, ambitious, seeking power?

To find out, we have to begin by being aware of our present state of mind, with all its conflicts, miseries, frustrations, perversions, deterioration, despair. We have to be aware of ourselves completely, and thereby gather energy; and the very gathering of that energy is the action which will cleanse the mind of all the rubbish that man has collected through the centuries.

So we are not interested in action for its own sake; we want to find out if there is an action which does not breed contradiction in any form. As we have seen, ideas, concepts, formulas, patterns, methods, dogmas, ideals—it is these that create the contradiction in action. And is it possible to live without idea—that is, without a pattern, without an ideal, without a concept or a belief? Surely, it is very important to find out the truth of this matter for oneself because one can see very well that love is not an idea, a pattern, or a concept. Most of us have a concept of love, but that concept is obviously not love. Either we love, or we do not love.

Is it possible to live in this world and go to the office, cook, wash dishes, drive a car, and do all the other daily things of life which at present have become repetitive and breed conflict—is it possible to do all these things, to live and to act without any ideation, and thereby free action from all contradiction?

I wonder if you have ever walked along a crowded street, or a lonely road, and just looked at things without thought? There is a state of observation without the interference of thought. Though you are aware of everything about you, and you may recognize the person, the mountain, the tree, or the oncoming car, yet the mind is not functioning in the usual pattern of thought. I don't know if this has ever happened to you. Do try it sometime when you are driving or walking. Just look without thought; observe without the reaction which breeds thought. Though you recognize color and form, though you see the stream, the car, the goat, the bus, there is no reaction, but merely negative observation; and that very state of so-called negative observation is action. Such a mind can utilize knowledge in carrying out what it has to do, but it is free of thought in the sense that it is not functioning in terms of reaction. With such a mind—a mind that is attentive without reaction—you can go to the office, and all the rest of it.

Most of us are everlastingly thinking about ourselves from morning till night, and we function within the pattern of that self-centered activity. All such activity, which is a reaction, is bound to lead to various forms of conflict and deterioration. And is it possible not to function within that pattern and yet to live in this world? I don't mean living off by yourself in some mountain cave, and all that kind of thing; but is it possible to live in this world and to function as a total human being from a state of emptiness?—if you will not misunderstand my use of that word. Whether you paint or write poems or go to an office or talk, can you always have inwardly an empty space, and through that empty space, work? For when there is this empty space, action does not breed contradiction.

I think this is a very important thing to discover—and you have to discover it for yourself because it cannot be taught or explained. To discover it, you must first understand how all self-centered action breeds conflict, and then ask yourself whether the mind can ever be content with such action. It may be momentarily satisfied, but when you perceive that, in all such action, conflict is inevitable, you are already trying to find out if there is another kind of action, an action which does not lead to conflict; and then you are bound to come upon the fact that there is.

So the question arises: Why is it that we are always seeking satisfaction? In all our relationships and in whatever we do, there is always the desire to fulfill, the desire to be gratified and to remain with that gratification. What we call discontent arises only when things do not gratify us—and such discontent merely breeds another series of reactions.

Now, it seems to me that a man who is very serious and who sees all this—the way human beings have lived for thousands of years in utter confusion and misery, with never a complete action—must find out for himself whether he is able to function from a mind that is uncontaminated by society; and he can find that out only when he is free from society. I am talking about freedom from the psychological structure of society, which is greed, envy, ambition, and the pursuit of self-importance. When that whole psychological structure has been understood and put aside, one is free from society. One may still go to the office, one may buy a pair of trousers, and all the rest of it; but one is free from the psychological structure which so distorts the mind.

So one comes to a point where one discovers for oneself that complete freedom from the psychological structure of society is complete inaction; and that complete inaction is total action, which does not breed contradiction and therefore deterioration.

I have said what I wanted to say this morning, and perhaps we can now discuss it, or you can ask questions about it.

Question: Can we go to our jobs and work without competition?

KRISHNAMURTI: Can one not, sir? Can you go to the office and keep your job without competing? It is not for me to say that you can or cannot, or that you must, and so on. But you see what competition does, how it breeds antagonism, fear, a ruthless pursuit of your own demands, not only within yourself, but outwardly in the world. You see all that, and you ask yourself if it is possible to live in this world without competition. That means living without comparing; it means doing something which you really love to do, which interests you tremendously. Or, if you are caught in a job which you don't like because you have responsibilities, it means finding out how to do that job efficiently without competing. And that demands a great deal of attention, does it not? You have to be tremendously aware of every thought, of every feeling within yourself; otherwise, you will merely be imposing upon yourself the idea that you must not compete—and then that becomes another problem. But you can be aware of all the implications of competition; you can see the truth of it, how it brings conflict, incessant struggle; you can perceive that competition inevitably leads man—though there may be a great deal of so-called progress and competitive efficiency—to antagonism, to lack of affection. If you see all this, then out of that perception you will act—either competitively or not competitively at all.

Comment: I do not believe that repetitive action is necessarily boring.

KRISHNAMURTI: You know, they are finding out that a man who works in a factory doing the same thing over and over again is not a very productive entity, and I am told that in America they are now experimenting with letting the workers in certain factories learn as they go along. The result is that their work is not so repetitive, and therefore they are producing much more. Even when you take a great deal of pleasure in doing something, if you keep on endlessly repeating that action, it becomes very routine and rather tiresome.

Question: What about the artist?

KRISHNAMURTI: If the artist is merely repeating, surely he has ceased to be an artist. I think we are confusing the two words *repetition* and *creation,* aren't we? What is creation?

Comment: A man who makes good shoes is creative.

KRISHNAMURTI: Making good shoes, baking bread, bearing children, writing poems, and all the rest of it—is that creation? Don't please agree or disagree. Wait just a minute.

Comment: I don't see how one can live in an empty space.

KRISHNAMURTI: Madame, I think we have misunderstood each other. I am sorry. It is possibly due to my choice of words, which is perhaps not as good as it should be, and probably you do not understand exactly what I mean by emptiness. But we are now talking about creation.

You know, I have heard that in a certain university they teach what they call creative writing and creative painting. Can creativity be taught? Will the continuous practice of something bring about the creative spirit? You may learn from a master the technique of playing the violin, but from technique you obviously cannot have genius. Whereas, if one has that creative spirit, it will produce the technique—but not the other way around. Most of us think that by acquiring the technique, we shall find the other. Take a very simple example—though all examples are defective. What is the simple life? The simple life, we say, is to have very few possessions, to eat very little, and to refrain from doing this and doing that. In Asia a man who wears a loincloth, who lives by himself and eats only one meal a day, is considered to be living a very simple life—but inwardly he may be in a volcanic turmoil, burning with his desires, his passions, his ambitions. The simple life of such a man is merely an outward show which everyone can recognize and say, "What a simple man he is!" That is the actual state of most saints: Outwardly they are very simple, but inwardly they are ambitious, disciplining the mind, forcing themselves to conform to a certain pattern, and all the rest of it. So it seems to me that simplicity is first from within, not from without. In the same way, creation cannot come about through expression. One has to be in that state of creation, and not seek it through expression. To be in the state of creation is the discovery of the supreme, and that can happen only when there is no activity of the self in any direction.

To return to what that lady said about emptiness. Most of us, though we are outwardly related to each other, live in isolation—and that isolation is not what I am talking about. Emptiness is something entirely different from isolation. There must be emptiness between you and me in order for us to see each other; there must be space through which I can hear what you are saying, and you can hear what I am saying. Similarly, there must be space in the mind; that is, the mind must not be crowded with so many things that there is no space left at all. Only when there is space within the mind—which means that the mind is not crowded with self-centered activity—only then is it possible to know what it is to live. But to live in isolation—that is not possible.

Question: Will you speak more about energy?

KRISHNAMURTI: To do anything at all, however small, requires energy, does it not? To get up and go out of this tent, to think, to eat, to drive a car—action of every kind demands energy. And for most of us, when we are doing something, there is a form of resistance which dissipates energy—unless what we are doing happens to give us pleasure, in which case there is no conflict, no resistance in the continuity of energy.

As I was saying earlier, one needs energy to be completely attentive, and in that energy there is no resistance as long as there is no distraction. But the moment there is a distraction—that is, the moment you want to concentrate on something, and at the same time you want to look out of the window—there is a resistance, a conflict. Now, the looking out of the window is just as important as any other looking—and when once you see the truth of this, then there is no distraction and no conflict.

To have physical energy, you must obviously eat the right kind of food, have the right amount of rest, and so on. That is something you can experiment with for yourself, and we need not discuss it. Then there is psychological energy, which dissipates itself in various ways. To have that psychological energy, the mind seeks stimulation. Going to church, watching football games, reading literature, listening to music, attending meetings like this one—all these things stimulate you; and if what you want is to be stimulated, it means that you are psychologically dependent. Every form of seeking stimulation implies dependence on something, whether it is a drink, a drug, a speaker, or going to church; and surely dependence on stimulation in any form not only dulls the mind, but also makes for the dissipation of energy. So, to conserve one's energy, every form of dependence on stimulation must disappear; and for the disappearance of that dependence, one has to be aware of it. Whether one depends for stimulation on one's wife or husband, on a book, on one's work in the office, on going to cinemas—whatever may be the particular forms of stimulation one seeks, one has first of all to be aware of them. Merely to accept stimulations and live with them dissipates energy and deteriorates the mind. But if one becomes aware of stimulations and finds out their whole significance in one's life, one can thereby be free of them. Through self-awareness—which is not self-condemnation and all the rest of it, but just being choicelessly aware of oneself—one learns about every form of influence, every form of dependence, every form of stimulation; and that very movement of learning gives one the energy to free oneself from all dependence on stimulation.

July 26, 1964

Eighth Talk in Saanen

Perhaps this morning we could put all our problems aside—our economic problems, our problems of personal relationship, of ill health, and also the many larger problems that surround us, national and international, the problems of war, of starvation, of riots, and so on. Not that we are escaping from them, but if we can put them all aside, for this morning at least, perhaps we shall then be able to approach them differently—with a fresher mind, with keener perception—and thereby tackle them anew, with greater vigor and clarity.

It seems to me that only love can produce the right revolution, and that every other form of revolution—that is, revolution based on economic theories, on social ideologies, and so on—can only bring about further disorder, more confusion and misery. We cannot hope to resolve the basic human problem by reforming and putting together again its many parts. It is only when there is great love that we can have a total outlook and therefore a total action, instead of this partial, fragmentary activity which we now call revolution, and which leads nowhere.

This morning I would like to talk about something that includes the totality of life—something that is not fragmentary but a total approach to the whole existence of man; and to go into it rather deeply, it seems to me that one must cease to be caught in theories, beliefs, dogmas. Most of us plough incessantly the soil of the mind, but we never seem to sow; we analyze, discuss, tear things to pieces, but we do not understand the whole movement of life.

Now, I think there are three things that we have to understand very deeply if we are to comprehend the whole movement of life. They are time, sorrow, and death. To understand time, to comprehend the full significance of sorrow, and to abide with death—all this demands the clarity of love. Love is not a theory, nor is it an ideal. Either you love or you do not love. It cannot be taught. You cannot take lessons in how to love, nor is there a method by the daily practice of which you can come to know what love is. But I think one comes to love naturally, easily, spontaneously, when one really understands the meaning of time, the extraordinary depth of sorrow, and the purity that comes with death. So perhaps we can consider—factually, not theoretically or abstractly—the nature of time, the quality or structure of sorrow, and the extraordinary thing that we call death. These three things are not separate. If we understand time, we shall understand what death is, and we shall understand also what is sorrow. But if we regard time as something apart from sorrow and death and try to deal with it separately, then our approach will be fragmentary, and therefore we shall never comprehend the extraordinary beauty and vitality of love.

So this morning we are going to deal with time, not as an abstraction, but as an actuality—time being duration, the continuity of existence. There is chronological time, hours and days extending into millions of years; and it is chronological time that has produced the mind with which we function. The mind is a result of time as the continuity of existence, and the perfecting or polishing of the mind through that continuity is called progress. Time is also the psychological duration which thought has created as a means of achievement. We use time to progress, to achieve, to become, to bring about a certain result. For most of us, time is a steppingstone to something far greater—to the development of certain faculties, to the perfecting of a particular technique, to the achievement of an end, a goal, whether praiseworthy or not; so we have come to think that time is necessary to realize what is true, what is God, what is beyond all the travail of man.

Most of us regard time as the period of duration between the present moment and some moment in the future when we shall have achieved, and we use that time to cultivate character, to get rid of a certain habit, to develop a muscle or an outlook. For two thousand years the Christian mind has been conditioned to believe in a savior, in hell, in heaven; and in the East a similar conditioning of the mind has been produced over a far longer period. We think that time is necessary for everything that we have to do or understand; therefore, time becomes a burden, it becomes a barrier to actual perception; it prevents us from seeing the truth of something immediately because we think that we must take time over it. We say, "Tomorrow, or in a couple of years, I shall comprehend this thing with extraordinary clarity." The moment we admit time, we are cultivating indolence, that peculiar laziness which prevents us from seeing immediately the thing as it actually is.

We think we need time to break through the conditioning which society—with its organized religions, its codes of morality, its dogmas, its arrogance, and its competitive spirit—has imposed upon the mind. We think in terms of time because thought is of time. Thought is the response of memory—memory being the background which has been accumulated, inherited, acquired by the race, by the community, by the group, by the family, and by the individual. This background is the outcome of the additive process of the mind, and its accumulation has taken time. For most of us the mind is memory, and whenever there is a challenge, a demand, it is memory that responds. It is like the response of the electronic brain, which functions through association. Thought being the response of memory, it is in its very nature the product of time and the creator of time.

Please, what I am saying is not a theory, it is not something that you have to think about. You don't have to think about it, but rather see it, because it is so. I am not going into all the intricate details, but I have indicated the essential facts, and either you see them or you don't see them. If you are following what is being said, not just verbally, linguistically, or analytically, but if you actually see it is so, you will realize how time deceives; and then the question is whether time can stop. If we are able to see the whole process of our own activity—see its depth, its shallowness, its beauty, its ugliness—not tomorrow, but immediately, then that very perception is the action which destroys time.

Without understanding time, we cannot understand sorrow. They are not two different things, as we try to make out. Going to the office, being with one's family, procreating children—these are not separate, isolated incidents. On the contrary, they are all profoundly and intimately related to each other; and we cannot see this extraordinary intimacy of relationship if there is not the sensitivity that love brings.

To understand sorrow we really have to understand the nature of time and the structure of thought. Time must come to a stop; otherwise, we are merely repeating the information we have accumulated, like an electronic brain. Unless there is an end to time—which means an end to thought—there is mere repetition, adjustment, a continual modification. There is never anything new. We are glorified electronic brains—a bit more independent, perhaps, but still machine-like in the way we function.

So, to understand the nature of sorrow and the ending of sorrow, one must understand time; and to understand time is to understand thought. The two are not separate. In understanding time, one comes upon thought; and the understanding of thought is the ending of time, and therefore the ending of sorrow. If that is very clear, then we can look at sorrow, and not worship it as the Christians do. What we don't understand, we either worship or destroy. We put it in a church, in a temple, or in a dark corner of the mind, and hold it in awe; or we kick it, throw it away; or we escape from it. But here we are not doing any of those things. We see that for millennia man has struggled with this problem of sorrow and that he has not been able to resolve it; so he has become hardened to it, he has accepted it, saying it is an inevitable part of life.

Now, merely to accept sorrow is not only stupid, but it makes for a dull mind. It makes the mind insensitive, brutal, superficial, and therefore life becomes very shoddy, a process of mere work and pleasure. One lives a fragmented existence as a businessman, a scientist, an artist, a sentimentalist, a so-called religious person, and so on. But to understand and be free of sorrow, you have to understand time, and thereby understand thought. You cannot deny sorrow or run away, escape from it through entertainment, through churches, through organized beliefs; nor can you accept and worship it; and not to do any of these things demands a great deal of attention, which is energy.

Sorrow is rooted in self-pity, and to understand sorrow, there must first be a ruthless operation on all self-pity. I do not know if you have observed how sorry for yourself you become, for example, when you say, "I am lonely." The moment there is self-pity, you have provided the soil in which sorrow takes root. However much you may justify your self-pity, rationalize it, polish it, cover it up with ideas, it is still there, festering deep within you. So a man who would understand sorrow must begin by being free of this brutal, self-centered, egotistic triviality which is self-pity. You may feel self-pity because you have a disease, or because you have lost someone by death, or because you have not fulfilled yourself and are therefore frustrated, dull; but whatever its cause, self-pity is the root of sorrow. And when once you are free of self-pity, you can look at sorrow without either worshiping it, or escaping from it, or giving it a sublime, spiritual significance, such as saying that you must suffer to find God—which is utter nonsense. It is only the dull, stupid mind that puts up with sorrow. So there must be no acceptance of sorrow whatsoever, and no denial of it. When you are free of self-pity, you have deprived sorrow of all the sentimentality, all the emotionalism that springs from self-pity; and then you are able to look at sorrow with complete attention.

I hope you are actually doing this with me this morning as we go along, and are not just verbally accepting what is being said. Be aware of your own dull acceptance of sorrow, of your rationalizing, your excuses, your self-pity, your sentimentality, your emotional attitude towards sorrow, because all that is a dissipation of energy. To understand sorrow you must give your whole attention to it, and in that attention there is no place for excuses, for sentiment, for rationalization, no place for any self-pity whatsoever.

I hope I am making myself clear when I talk about giving one's whole attention to sorrow. In that attention there is no effort to resolve or to understand sorrow. One is just looking, observing. Any effort to understand, to rationalize, or to escape from sorrow denies that negative state of complete attention in which this thing called sorrow can be understood.

We are not analyzing, we are not analytically investigating sorrow in order to get rid of it, because that is just another trick of the mind. The mind analyzes sorrow, and then imagines it has understood and is free of sorrow—which is nonsense. You may get rid of one particular kind of sorrow, but sorrow will come up again in another form. We are talking about sorrow as a total thing—about sorrow as such—whether it is yours, or mine, or that of any other human being.

As I have said, to understand sorrow there must be the understanding of time and thought. There must be a choiceless awareness of all the escapes, of all the self-pity, of all the verbalizations so that the mind becomes completely quiet in front of something which has to be understood. There is then no division between the observer and the thing observed. It is not that you—the observer, the thinker—are in sorrow and are looking at that sorrow, but there is only the state of sorrow. That state of undivided sorrow is necessary because when you look at sorrow as an observer, you create conflict, which dulls the mind and dissipates energy, and therefore there is no attention.

When the mind understands the nature of time and thought, when it has rooted out self-pity, sentiment, emotionalism, and all the rest of it, then thought—which has created all this complexity—comes to an end, and there is no time; therefore, you are directly and intimately in contact with that thing which you call sorrow. Sorrow is sustained only when there is an escape from sorrow, a desire to run away from it, to resolve it, or to worship it. But when there is nothing of all that because the mind is directly in contact with sorrow, and is therefore completely silent with regard to it, then you will discover for yourself that the mind is not in sorrow at all. The moment one's mind is completely in contact with the fact of sorrow, that fact itself resolves all the sorrow-producing qualities of time and thought. Therefore there is the ending of sorrow.

Now, how are we to understand this thing which we call death, and of which we are so frightened? Man has created many devious ways of dealing with death—by worshiping it, denying it, clinging to innumerable beliefs, and so on. But to understand death, surely you must come to it afresh, because you really do not know anything about death, do you? You may have seen people die, and you have observed in yourself or in others the coming on of old age with its deterioration. You know there is the ending of physical life by old age, by accident, by disease, by murder or suicide, but you do not know death as you know sex, hunger, cruelty, brutality. You do not actually know what it is to die, and until you do, death has no meaning whatsoever. What you are afraid of is an abstraction, something which you do not know. Not knowing the fullness of death, or what its implications are, the mind is frightened of it—frightened of the thought, not of the fact, which it does not know.

Please go into this with me a little bit.

If you died instantly, there would be no time to think about death and be frightened of it. But there is a gap between now and the moment when death will come, and during that interval you have plenty of time to worry, to rationalize. You want to carry over to the next life—if there is a next life—all the anxieties, the desires, the knowledge that you have accumulated, so you invent theories, or you believe in some form of immortality. To you, death is something separate from life. Death is over there, while you are here, occupied with living—driving a car, having sex, feeling hunger, worrying, going to the office, accumulating knowledge, and so on. You don't want to die because you haven't finished writing your book, or you don't yet know how to play the violin very beautifully. So you separate death from life, and you say, "I will understand life now, and presently I will understand death." But the two are not separate—and that is the first thing to understand. Life and death are one, they are intimately related, and you cannot isolate one of them and try to understand it apart from the other. But most of us do that. We separate life into unrelated watertight compartments. If you are an economist, then economics is all that you are concerned with, and you don't know anything about the rest. If you are a doctor whose specialty is the nose and throat, or the heart, you live in that limited field of knowledge for forty years, and that is your heaven when you die.

As I said, to deal with life fragmentarily is to live in constant confusion, contradiction, misery. You have to see the totality of life, and you can see the totality of it only when there is affection, when there is love. Love is the only revolution that will produce order. It is no good acquiring more and more knowledge about mathematics, about medicine, about history, about economics, and then putting all the fragments together—

that will not solve a thing. Without love, revolution only leads to the worship of the state, or the worship of an image, or to innumerable tyrannical corruptions and the destruction of man. Similarly, when the mind, because it is frightened, puts death at a distance and separates it from daily living, that separation only breeds more fear, more anxiety, and the multiplication of theories about death. To understand death you have to understand life. But life is not the continuity of thought—and it is this very continuity which has bred all our misery.

So, can the mind bring death from the distance to the immediate? Do you follow? Actually, death is not somewhere far away—it is here and now. It is here when you are talking, when you are enjoying yourself, when you are listening, when you are going to the office. It is here at every minute of life, just as love is. If once you perceive this fact, then you will find that there is no fear of death at all. One is afraid, not of the unknown, but of losing the known. You are afraid of losing your family, of being left alone without companions; you are afraid of the pain of loneliness, of being without the experiences, the possessions that you have gathered. It is the known that we are afraid to let go of. The known is memory, and to that memory the mind clings. But memory is only a mechanical thing—which the computers are demonstrating very beautifully.

To understand the beauty and the extraordinary nature of death, there must be freedom from the known. In dying to the known, there is the beginning of the understanding of death because then the mind is made fresh, new, and there is no fear; therefore, one can enter into that state which is called death. So, from the beginning to the end, life and death are one. The wise man understands time, thought, and sorrow, and only he can understand death. The mind that is dying each minute, never accumulating, never gathering experience, is innocent, and is therefore in a constant state of love.

I wonder if you care to ask questions about this so that we can go into it in greater detail?

Question: Sir, what is the difference between your thought about love and the Christian thought about love?

KRISHNAMURTI: I am afraid I cannot tell you. I am not thinking about love. You cannot think about love; if you do, it is not love. You know, there is a vast difference between sex, and the thought about sex which stimulates the feeling. The mind that is occupied with the mere enjoyment of sex, that thinks about sex, exciting itself by images, by pictures, by thoughts—the quality of such a mind is destructive. But the other thing, the feeling when there is no thought about it, is entirely different. Similarly, you cannot think about love. You can think about love according to the pattern of your memory, or in terms of what you have been told—that it is good, profane, sacred, and so on. But that thinking is not love. Love is neither Christian nor Hindu, neither Oriental nor Occidental, neither yours nor mine. It is only when you get rid of all these ideas of your nationality, of your race, of your religion, and all the rest of it—it is only then that you will know what it is to love.

You see, I have talked this morning about death so that you might really understand this whole thing—not just while you are here in this tent, but throughout the rest of your life—and thereby be free of sorrow, free of fear, and actually know what it means to die. If now, and in the days to come, your mind is not completely aware, innocent, deeply attentive, then listening to words is utterly futile. But if you are aware, deeply attentive, conscious of your own thoughts and feelings, if you are not interpreting what the speaker is saying but are actually observing yourself as he describes and goes into the problem, then when you leave this tent you will live—live not only with exultation, but with death and with love.

July 28, 1964

Ninth Talk in Saanen

I would like to talk about something this morning which may be rather foreign to most people. It seems to me one of the most important things in life is to clarify the mind, to empty the mind of every experience and thought so that it is made new, fresh, innocent; because it is only the innocent mind, in its freedom, that can discover what is true. This innocence is not a state of permanency. It is not that the mind has achieved a result and remains there. It is a state of a mind that, being utterly free, is capable of renewing itself from moment to moment without effort. And this innocence, this freedom to discover, is of immense significance, because most of us live so very superficially; we live with knowledge and information, and we think that knowledge and information are sufficient. But without meditation, our life is very shallow. By meditation I do not mean contemplation or prayer. To be in a state of meditation, or rather to come by it naturally, easily, without effort, one must begin to understand the superficial, everyday mind, the mind that is so easily satisfied with information. Having accumulated knowledge or acquired some technological capacity that enables us to specialize along a particular line and live in this world rather superficially, most of us are content to live at that level, without understanding whatever psychological problems may arise. So it seems to me very important to observe how superficial the mind now is, and to inquire whether it is possible for the mind to go beyond itself.

The more knowledge and training one has, the greater is one's capacity in daily life—and one must obviously have that knowledge, that training, that capacity, because we cannot put away machinery and science and go back to the ways of ancient times. That would be like those so-called religious people who try to go back to a tradition, or to revive ancient philosophical concepts and formulas, thereby destroying themselves and the world in which they live. Science, mathematics, the technology now available to man—all these things are absolutely necessary. But living in this world of technology, of rapidly expanding knowledge and information, tends to make the mind very superficial; and most of us are content to remain in that superficiality because knowledge and technology give us more money, more comfort, more so-called freedom, all of which are highly respected by a degraded, disintegrating society. So the mind that would go beyond itself must understand the limitations of technology, of knowledge and information, and be free of these limitations.

As one can observe, all our activities, all our emotions, all our neurological reactions are very superficial, on the surface. Living on the surface, as most of us do, we try to seek out the depths, we try to go deeper and deeper below the surface because one soon gets tired of this superficial way of living. The more intelligent, the more intellectual, the more passionate we are, the keener is our awareness of the superficiality of our existence; it becomes rather tiresome, boring, and does not have much significance. So the superficial mind tries to find out the purpose of life, or it seeks a formula that will give life a purpose. It struggles to live according to a concept which it has conceived, or a belief which it has accepted—and its action is therefore still superficial. One must see this fact very clearly.

What we are going to do this morning is to remove layer after layer of superficiality so that one can go to the origin, to the very depth of things. Superficiality perpetuates itself through experience, and that is why it is very important to understand the whole significance of experience.

First of all, one sees how technological specialization of any kind tends to make the mind narrow, petty, limited—qualities which are the very essence of the bourgeois. Then the mind, being superficial, seeks what it calls the significance of life, and thereby projects a pattern which is pleasing, profitable, pleasurable, and conforms to that pattern. This process gives it a certain purpose, a drive, a sense of achievement.

We also have to understand very deeply this thing called experience. Living a very superficial life, we are always seeking wider and deeper experiences. That is why people go to churches, take mescaline, try LSD 25, lysergic acid, and various other drugs—to get a new kick, a new stimulation, a new sensation. The mind also seeks experience through art, through music, through newer, fresher forms of expression.

Now, a mind that would find itself at great depth—find itself, not bring about that state—must understand all these things. To understand is not merely to comprehend intellectually the verbal communication, but rather to see immediately the truth of the matter; and this immediate perception is understanding. No amount of argumentation, of investigating the truth of opinions, can bring about understanding. What is needed is sensitivity, awareness, the quality of hesitancy, of tentativeness, which gives to the mind the capacity to apprehend quickly.

So, what is the nature of experience? We all want new experiences, do we not? We are tired of the old, of the things that have brought us pain or have caused us sorrow. The routine at the office, the church rituals, the rituals of state worship—one is fed up with all that, one is tired of it, exhausted by it, so one wants more experience along different lines and at different levels. But surely it is only the mind that does not seek or accumulate experience—it is only such a mind that can be in a state of complete profundity.

Experience is the outcome of a challenge and a response. The mind's response to a challenge may be adequate or inadequate, depending on its background, its conditioning. That is, we respond to every challenge according to our background, according to our particular conditioning. That response to challenge is experience, and every experience leaves a residue, which we call knowledge.

To put it differently, in going through various experiences the mind acts like a sieve in which each experience leaves a certain sediment. That sediment is memory, and with that memory the next experience is met. So each experience—however wide and deep, however vital—leaves a further deposit of sediment, or memory, and thereby strengthens the mind's conditioning.

Please, this is not an opinion, and it is not a question of your believing what is being said. If you observe yourself, you will see that this is what actually takes place. The speaker is describing the mind's accumulation of experience, and you are watching that process in yourself. So there is nothing to believe, and you are not being hypnotized by words.

So, every experience, whatever it is, leaves a sediment which becomes the past as memory, and in that sediment we live. That sediment is the 'me'; it is the very structure of self-centered activity. Seeing the limited nature of this self-centered activity, we seek more and wider experience, or we demand to know how to break through this limitation in order to find something greater. But all such seeking is still the activity of accumulation, and it merely adds to the remains, to the sediment of experience, whether it be that of a minute, of a day, or of two million years.

Now, you have to see this fact very clearly. You have to be aware of it as you are aware of being hungry. When you are hungry, nobody need tell you about it—it is your own experience. Similarly, you must see very clearly for yourself that every experience—whether it be of affection, of sympathy, of pride, of jealousy, of inspiration, of fear, or what you will—leaves a residue in the mind; and that the constant repetition and overlaying of this residue or sediment is the whole process of our thinking, of our being. Any activity arising from this process, at whatever level, must inevitably be superficial; and a mind that would inquire into the possibility of discovering a state of originality, or a world uncontaminated by the past, must understand this process of experience.

So the question arises: Is it possible to be free of all self-centered activity without effort, without trying to dissolve it and thereby making it into a problem?

I hope I am making the question clear, otherwise what is going to be said presently will be totally unclear.

Now, the word *meditation* generally means to think about, to investigate, or to ponder upon something; or it may mean a state of mind that is contemplative, without the process of thought. It is a word that has very little meaning in this part of the world, but it has extraordinary significance in the East. A great deal has been written on the subject, and there are many schools advocating different methods or systems of meditation.

To me, meditation is none of these things. Meditation is the total emptying of the mind—and one cannot empty the mind forcibly, according to any method, school, or system. Again, one must see the utter fallacy of all systems. The practice of a system of meditation is the pursuit of experience; it is an attempt to achieve a higher experience, or the "ultimate" experience. And when one understands the nature of experience, one brushes all this aside; it is finished forever because one's mind no longer follows anybody; it does not pursue experience, it has no desire for visions. All seeking of visions, all artificial heightening of sensitivity—through drugs, through discipline, through rituals, through worship, through prayer—is self-centered activity.

Our question then is: How is a mind which has been made superficial through tradition, through time, through memory, through experience—how is such a mind to free itself from its superficiality without effort? How is it to be so completely awake that the seeking of experience has no meaning any more? Do you understand? That which is full of light doesn't demand more light—it is light itself. And every influence, every experience which penetrates into that light is burned away from moment to moment so that the mind is always clear, immaculate, innocent. It is only the clear mind, the innocent mind, that can see what is beyond the measure of time. And how is this state of mind to come about?

Have I made the question clear? This is not my question—it is or should be everybody's question, so I am not imposing it on you. If I imposed this question on you, then you would make it into a problem; you would say, "How am I to do it?" This question must be born of your own perception because you have lived, you have watched, you have seen what the world is, and you have observed yourself in operation. You have read, you have gathered information, you have progressed in knowledge. You have seen very clever people with computer-like minds, professors who can reel off an infinite amount of knowledge, and you have met theologians with fixed ideas around which they have built marvelous theories. Having become aware of all this, you must inevitably have asked yourself the question: How is the mind which is a slave of time, a product of the past—how is such a mind to put away the past completely, easily, without effort? How is it to be free of time without any directive or motive, so that it finds itself at the original fountain of life?

Now, when that question is put to you, whether by yourself or by another, what is your response? Don't answer me, please, but just listen. It is an immense question. It is not just a rhetorical question which you can quickly answer or brush off. It is a question of tremendous significance to a mind that has seen through the stupidities of organized religion and has brushed aside all the priests, the gurus, the temples, the churches, the rituals, the incense—thrown them all away. And if you have come to that point, then you must have asked yourself: How is the mind to go beyond itself?

What do you do when you are directly faced with an immense problem, when something tremendous and immediate happens to you? The experience is so vital, so demanding, that it completely absorbs you, does it not? Your mind is taken over by that tremendous happening, so it becomes quiet. That is one form of silence. Your mind responds like a child who has been given a very interesting toy. The toy absorbs him, it causes him to concentrate, so for the moment he ceases to be mischievous, he no longer runs about, and so on. And the same thing happens to grown-ups when they are confronted with a great issue of some kind. Not comprehending the whole significance of it, the mind gives itself over to that experience and becomes numbed, shocked, paralyzed, so that it is fleetingly silent. This is something which most of us have experienced.

Then there is a silence of the mind which comes when the problem is looked at with complete concentration. In that state there is no distraction because for the moment the mind has no other thought, no other interest. It doesn't look anywhere else because it is only concerned with that one thing; there is an intensification of concentration to the exclusion of everything else, and in that effort there is a vitality, a demand, an urgency which also produces a certain quality of silence.

When the mind is absorbed by a toy or loses itself in a problem, it is merely escaping. When images, symbols—words like *God, Savior,* and so on—take over the mind, that also is a deep escape, a flight from the actual, and in that flight there is a certain quality of silence. When the mind sacrifices or forgets itself through complete identification with something, it may be perfectly quiet—but it is then in a neurotic state. The demand to be identified with a purpose, with an idea, with a symbol, with a country, with a race—all that is neurotic, as all would-be religious people are. They have identified themselves with the Savior, with the Master, with this or that, which gives them a tremendous release and brings them a certain beatific outlook on life—which is a totally neurotic attitude.

Then there is the mind that has learned to concentrate, that has taught itself never to look away from the idea, the image, the symbol which it has projected in front of itself. And what takes place in that state of concentration? All concentration is effort, and all effort is resistance. It is like building a defensive wall around yourself with a little hole through which you look at just one idea or thought, so that you can never be shaken, never made uncertain. You are never open, but are always living within your shell of concentration, behind the walls of your inspired pursuit of something, and from this you get a tremendous sense of vitality, a drive which enables you to do extraordinary things—to help people in the slums, to live in the desert, to do all manner of good works; but it is still the self-centered activity of a mind that concentrates on one thing to the exclusion of everything else. And that also gives to the mind a certain quality of peace, of silence.

Now, there is a silence which has nothing whatsoever to do with any of these neurotic states, and that is where our difficulty lies; because unfortunately—and I am saying this very politely—most of us are neurotic. So, to understand what that silence is, one must first be completely free of all neuroticism. In the silence of which I am speaking, there is no self-pity, no pursuit of a result, no projection of an image; there are no visions, and no struggle to concentrate. That silence comes unasked when you have understood the mind's absorption in an idea and the various forms of concentration which it practices, and when you have also understood the whole process of thinking. Out of observing, watching the self-centered activity of the mind, there comes an extraordinarily pliable sense of discipline—and that discipline you must have. It is not a defensive, reactionary discipline; it has nothing to do with sitting cross-legged in a corner and all the other childish stuff, and in it there is no imitation, no conformity, no effort to achieve a result. To observe all the movements of thought and desire, the hunger for new experiences, the process of identifying oneself with something—merely to observe and to understand all that, brings about naturally an ease of discipline in freedom. With this discipline of understanding there comes a peculiar quality of immediate awareness, of direct perception, a state of complete attention. In this attention there is virtue—and that is the only virtue. Social morality, the character that is developed through resistance in conformity with the respectability and ethics of society—this is not virtue at all. Virtue is the understanding of this whole social structure which man has built around himself, and it is the understanding also of the mind's so-called self-sacrifice through identification and control. Attention is born of that understanding, and only in attention is there virtue.

You must have a virtuous mind, but a mind that is merely conforming to the social and religious patterns of a particular society, whether communist or capitalist, is not virtuous. There must be virtue because without virtue there is no freedom; but, like humility, virtue cannot be cultivated. You cannot cultivate virtue, any more than you can cultivate love. But when there is complete attention, there is also virtue and love. Out of complete attention comes total silence, not only at the level of the conscious mind, but also at the level of the unconscious. Both the conscious and the unconscious are really quite trivial, and the perception of their triviality frees the mind from the past as well as from the present. In giving its whole attention to the present, there comes a silence in which the mind is no longer experiencing. All experiencing has come to an end because there is nothing more to experience. Being totally awake, the mind is a light unto itself. In this silence there is peace. It is not the peace of the politicians nor the peace between two wars. It is a peace not born of reaction. And when the mind is thus completely still, it can proceed. The movement of stillness is entirely different from the movement of self-centered activity. That movement of stillness is creation. When the mind is capable of moving with that stillness, it knows death and love; and it can then live in this world and yet be free of the world.

Do you want to ask any questions?

Comment: I yearn for silence, but I find that my attempts to attain it are more and more pitiful as time goes by.

KRISHNAMURTI: First of all, you cannot yearn for this silence; you don't know anything about it. Even if you did know about it, it would not be so because what you know is not *what is*. So one has to be very careful never to say, "I know."

Sir, look. What you know, you recognize. I recognize you because I met you yesterday. Having heard what you then said, and having seen your manner of being, I say that I know you. What I know is already of the past, and from that past I can recognize you. But this silence cannot be recognized; in it there is no process of recognition whatsoever. That is the first thing to understand. To recognize something you must already have experienced it, already known it, or you must have read about it, or somebody must have described it to you; but what is recognized, known, described, is not this silence. And we yearn for this silence because our life is so shallow, so empty, so dull, so stupid that we want to escape from the whole ugly business of it. But we cannot escape from it; we have to understand it. And to understand something, you must not kick it, you must not run away from it. You must have tremendous love, real affection for that which you would understand. If you would understand a child, you cannot compel or force him or compare him with his elder brother. You must look at him, watch him with great care, with tenderness, with affection, with everything that you have. Similarly, we must understand this petty thing we call our life, with all its jealousy, conflict, misery, travail, sorrow. Out of that understanding comes a certain quality of peace which you cannot grope after.

You know, there is a lovely story about a disciple going to the Master. The Master is sitting in a beautiful, quiet, well-watered garden, and the disciple comes and sits near him—not quite in front of him, because to sit directly in front of the Master is not very respectful. So, sitting a little to one side, he crosses his legs and closes his eyes. Then the Master asks, "My friend, what are you doing?" Opening his eyes, the disciple says, "Master, I am trying to reach the consciousness of the Buddha"—and closes his eyes again. Presently the Master picks up two stones and begins to rub them together, making a lot of noise; so the disciple comes down from his great height and says, "Master, what are you doing?" The Master replies, "I am rubbing together these two stones so as to make one of them into a mirror." And the disciple says, "But Master, surely you will never do it, even if you rub them together for a million years." Then the Master smiles and replies, "Similarly, my friend, you can sit like that for a million years, and you will never come to what you are trying to reach." And that is what we are all doing. We are all taking postures; we are all wanting something, groping after something—which demands effort, struggle, discipline. But I am afraid none of these things will open the door. What will open the door is to understand without effort; just to look, to observe with affection, with love. But you cannot have love if you are not humble, and humility is possible only when you do not want a thing, either from the gods or from any human being.

July 30, 1964

Tenth Talk in Saanen

This morning I would like to talk over—not merely to explain verbally, but also to understand deeply—the significance of religion. But before we can penetrate deeply into this question, we shall have to be very clear as to what is the religious mind, and what is the state of a mind that really inquires into the whole question of religion.

It seems to me very important to understand the difference between isolation and aloneness. Most of our daily activity is centered round ourselves; it is based on our particular point of view, on our particular experiences and idiosyncrasies. We think in terms of our family, of our job, of what we wish to achieve, and also in terms of our fears, hopes, and despairs. All this is obviously self-centered, and it brings about a state of self-isolation, as we can see in our daily life. We have our own secret desires, our hidden pursuits and ambitions, and we are never deeply related to anyone, either to our wives, our husbands, or our children. This self-isolation is likewise the result of our running away from our daily boredom, from the frustrations and trivialities of our daily life. It is caused also by our escaping in various ways from the extraordinary sense of loneliness that comes over us when we suddenly feel unrelated to anything, when everything is in the distance and there is no communion, no relationship with anyone. I think most of us—if we are at all aware of the process of our own being—have felt this loneliness very deeply.

Because of this loneliness, out of this sense of isolation, we try to identify ourselves with something greater than the mind—it may be the state, or an ideal, or a concept of what God is. This identification with something great or immortal, something outside the field of our own thought, is generally called religion, and it leads to belief, dogma, ritual, the separative pursuits of competing groups, each believing in different aspects of the same thing; so what we call religion brings about still further isolation.

Then one sees how the earth is divided into competing nations, each with its sovereign government and economic barriers. Though we are all human beings, we have built walls between ourselves and our neighbors through nationalism, through race, caste, and class—which again breeds isolation, loneliness.

Now a mind that is caught in loneliness, in this state of isolation, can never possibly understand what religion is. It can believe, it can have certain theories, concepts, formulas, it can try to identify itself with that which it calls God; but religion, it seems to me, has nothing whatsoever to do with any belief, with any priest, with any church or so-called sacred book. The state of the religious mind can be understood only when we begin to understand what beauty is; and the understanding of beauty must be approached through total aloneness. Only when the mind is completely alone can it know what is beauty, and not in any other state.

Aloneness is obviously not isolation, and it is not uniqueness. To be unique is merely to be exceptional in some way, whereas to be completely alone demands extraordinary sensitivity, intelligence, understanding. To be completely alone implies that the mind is free of every kind of influence and is therefore uncontaminated by society; and it must be alone to understand what is religion—which is to find out for oneself whether there is something immortal, beyond time.

As it is now, the mind is the result of many thousands of years of influence: biological, sociological, environmental, climatic, alimentary, and so on. Again, this is fairly obvious. You are influenced by the food you eat, by the newspapers you read, by your wife or husband, by your neighbor, by the politician, by the radio, the television, and a thousand other things. You are constantly being influenced by what is poured into the conscious as well as into the unconscious mind from many different directions. And is it not possible to be so aware of these many influences that one is not caught in any of them and remains totally uncontaminated by them? Otherwise the mind merely becomes an instrument of its environment. It may create an image of what it thinks is God, or the eternal truth, and believe in that, but it is still shaped by environmental demands, tensions, superstitions, pressures;

and its belief is not the state of a religious mind at all.

As a Christian you were brought up in a church built by man over a period of two thousand years, with its priests, dogmas, rituals. In childhood you were baptized, and as you grew up, you were told what to believe—you went through that whole process of conditioning, brainwashing. The pressure of this propagandist religion is obviously very strong, particularly because it is well-organized and able to exert psychological influence through education, through the worship of images, through fear, and to condition the mind in a thousand other ways. Throughout the East people are also heavily conditioned by their beliefs, their dogmas, their superstitions, and by a tradition which goes back ten thousand years or more.

Now, unless the mind has freedom, it cannot find out what is true—and to have freedom is to be free from influence. You have to be free from the influence of your nationality, and from the influence of your church, with its beliefs and dogmas; and you also have to be free of greed, envy, fear, sorrow, ambition, competition, anxiety. If the mind is not free from all these things, the various pressures from outside and within itself will create a contradictory, neurotic state, and such a mind cannot possibly discover what is true, or if there is something beyond time.

So one sees how necessary it is for the mind to be free from all influence. And is such a thing possible? If it is not possible, then there can be no discovery of what is the eternal, the unnameable, the supreme. To find out for oneself whether it is possible or not, one has to be aware of these many influences, not only here in this tent, but also in one's daily life. One has to observe how they are contaminating, shaping, conditioning the mind. One obviously cannot be aware all the time of the many different influences that are pouring in on the mind, but one can see the importance—and I think this is the crux of the matter—of being free of all influence; and when once one understands the necessity of that, then the unconscious is aware of influence even though the conscious mind may often not be.

Am I making myself clear?

What I am trying to point out is this. There are extraordinarily subtle influences that are shaping your mind, and a mind that is shaped by influences, which are always within the field of time, cannot possibly discover the eternal, or if there is such a thing as the eternal. So the question then is: If the conscious mind cannot possibly be aware of all the many influences, what is it to do? If you put this question to yourself very seriously and earnestly so that it demands your complete attention, you will find that the unconscious part of you, which is not totally occupied when the upper layers of the mind are functioning, takes charge and watches all the influences that are coming in.

I think this is very important to understand because if you merely resist or defend yourself against being influenced, that resistance, which is a reaction, creates a further conditioning of the mind. The understanding of the total process of influence must be effortless, it must have the quality of immediate perception. It is like this: If you really see for yourself the tremendous importance of not being influenced, then a certain part of your mind takes charge of the matter whenever you are consciously occupied with other things, and that part of the mind is very alert, active, watchful. So what is important is to see immediately the enormous significance of not being influenced by any circumstances or by any person whatsoever. That is the real point—not how to resist influence or what to do in case you are influenced. Once you have grasped this central fact, then you will find there is a part of the mind that is always alert and watching, always ready to cleanse itself of every influence, however subtle. Out of this freedom from all influences comes aloneness, which is entirely different from isolation. And there must be aloneness because beauty is outside the field of time, and only the mind that is completely alone can know what beauty is.

For most of us, beauty is a matter of proportion, shape, size, contour, color. We see a building, a tree, a mountain, a river, and we say it is beautiful; but there is still the outsider, the experiencer who is looking at these things, and therefore what we call beauty is still within the field of time. But I feel that beauty is beyond time and that to know beauty there must be the ending of the experiencer. The experiencer is merely an accumulation of experience from which to judge, to evaluate, to think. When the mind looks at a picture, or listens to music, or sees the swift flowing of a river, it generally does so from that background of accumulated experience; it is looking from the past, from the field of time—and to me that is not to know beauty at all. To know beauty, which is to find out what is the eternal, is possible only when the mind is completely alone—and that has nothing whatsoever to do with what the priests say, with what the organized religions say. The mind must be totally uninfluenced, uncontaminated by society, by the psychological structure of greed, envy, anxiety, fear. It must be completely free of all that. Out of this freedom comes aloneness, and it is only in the state of aloneness that the mind can know that which is beyond the field of time.

Beauty and that which is eternal cannot be separated. You may paint, you may write, you may observe nature, but if there is the activity of the self in any form—any self-centered movement of thought—then what you perceive ceases to be beauty because it is still within the field of time; and if you don't understand beauty, you cannot possibly find out what is the eternal because the two go together. To find out what is the eternal, the immortal, your mind must be free of time—time being tradition, the accumulated knowledge and experience of the past. It is not a question of what you believe or disbelieve—that is immature, utterly juvenile, and it has absolutely nothing to do with the matter. But the mind that is in earnest, that really wants to find out, will relinquish totally the self-centered activity of isolation, and will thereby come upon a state in which it is completely alone; and it is only in that state of complete aloneness that there can be the comprehension of beauty, of that which is eternal.

You know, words are dangerous things because they are symbols, and symbols are not the real. They convey a significance, a concept, but the word is not the thing. So when I am talking about the eternal, you have to find out if you are merely being influenced by my words, or caught up in a belief—which would be too infantile.

Now, to find out if there is such a thing as the eternal, one has to understand what is time. Time is a most extraordinary thing—and I am not talking about chronological time, time by the watch, which is both obvious and necessary. I am talking about time as psychological continuity. And is it possible to live without that continuity? What gives continuity, surely, is thought. If one thinks about something constantly, it has a continuity. If one looks at a picture of one's wife every day, one gives it a continuity. And is it possible to live in this world without giving continuity to action, so that one comes to every action afresh? That is, can I die to each action throughout the day so that the mind never accumulates and is therefore never contaminated by the past, but is always new, fresh, innocent? I say that such a thing is possible, that one can live in this way—but that does not mean it is real for you. You have to find out for yourself.

So one begins to see that the mind must be completely alone, but not isolated. In this state of complete aloneness there comes a sense of extraordinary beauty, of something not created by the mind. It has nothing to do with putting a few notes together or using a few paints to create a picture; but because it is alone, the mind is in beauty, and therefore it is completely sensitive; and being completely sensitive, it is intelligent. Its intelligence is not the intelligence of cunning or knowledge, nor is it the capacity to do something. The mind is intelligent in the sense that it is not being dominated, influenced, and is unafraid. But to be in that state, the mind must be able to renew itself every day, which is to die every day to the past, to everything it has known.

Now, as I said, the word, the symbol, is not the real. The word *tree* is not the tree, and so one has to be very alert not to be caught in words. When the mind is free of the word, the symbol, it becomes astonishingly sensitive, and then it is in a state of finding out.

After all, man has been seeking this thing for so long—from very ancient times until now. He wants to find something which is not man-made. Though organized religion has no meaning for any intelligent man, nevertheless the organized religions have always said that there is something beyond; and man has always sought that something because he is everlastingly in sorrow, in misery, in confusion, in despair. Being always in a state of transiency, he wants to find something permanent, something that will last, endure, that will have a continuity, and therefore his seeking has always been within the field of time. But as one can observe, there is nothing permanent. Our relationships, our jobs—everything is impermanent. Because of our tremendous fear of this impermanency, we are always seeking something permanent, which we call the immortal, the eternal, or what you will. But this search for the permanent, the immortal, the eternal, is merely a reaction, and therefore it is not valid. It is only when the mind is free of this desire to be certain that it can begin to find out if there is such a thing as the eternal, something beyond space, beyond time, beyond the thinker and the thing which he is thinking about or seeking. To observe and understand all this requires total attention, and the pliable quality of discipline which comes out of that attention. In such attention there is no distraction, there is no strain, there is no movement in any particular direction because every such movement, every motive, is the result of influence, either of the past or of the present. In that state of effortless attention there comes an extraordinary sense of freedom, and only then—being totally empty, quiet, still—is the mind capable of discovering that which is eternal.

Perhaps you wish to ask questions about what has been said this morning.

Question: How is one to be free from the desire to be certain?

KRISHNAMURTI: The word *how* implies a method, does it not? If you are a builder and I ask you how to build a house, you can tell me what to do because there is a method, a system, a way to set about it. But the following of a method or a system has already conditioned the mind, so just see the difficulty in the use of that word how.

Then we also have to understand desire. What is desire? I went into this the other day, and I hope those of you who were here on that day really caught the significance of what was said, and will not be bored by what is being said now. Because, you know, one can really listen to all these talks a thousand times and each time see something new.

What is desire? As I said the other day, there is seeing or perception, then contact or touching, then sensation, and finally the arising of that which we call desire. Surely this is what takes place. Please follow it closely. There is the seeing, let us say, of a beautiful car. From that very act of seeing, even without touching the car, there is sensation, which creates the desire to drive it, to own it. We are not concerned with how to resist or be free of desire, because the man who has resisted and thinks he is free of desire is really paralyzed, dead. What is important is to understand the whole process of desire—which is to know both its importance and its total unimportance. One has to find out not how to end desire but what it is that gives continuity to desire.

Now, what gives continuity to desire? It is thought, is it not? First there is the seeing of the car, then the sensation, which is followed by the desire; and if thought does not interfere and give continuity to the desire by saying, "I must have that car; how shall I get it?" then the desire comes to an end. Do you follow? I am not insisting that there should be freedom from desire—on the contrary. But you must understand the whole structure of desire, and then you will find there is no longer a continuity of desire, but something else altogether.

So what is important is not desire but the fact that we give it continuity. For instance, we give sexuality a continuity through thought, through images, through pictures, through sensation, through remembrance; we keep the memory going by thinking about it, and all this gives continuity to sexuality, to the importance of the senses. Not that the senses are not important; they are. But we give the pleasure of the senses a continuity which becomes overwhelmingly important in our life. So what matters is not freedom from desire but to understand the structure of desire and how thought gives it continuity—and that is all. Then the mind is free, and you do not have to seek freedom from desire. The moment you seek freedom from desire, you are caught in conflict. Each time you see a car, a woman, a house, or whatever it may be that attracts you, thought steps in and gives desire a continuity, and then it all becomes an endless problem.

What is important is to live a life without effort, without a single problem; and you can live without a problem if you understand the nature of effort and see very clearly the whole structure of desire. Most of us have a thousand problems, and to be free of problems we must be able to end each problem immediately, as it arises. I think we have discussed that enough, and I will not go into it now. But it is absolutely necessary for the mind to have no problems at all, and so live a life without effort. Surely, such a mind is the only religious mind because it has understood sorrow and the ending of sorrow; it is without fear, and is therefore a light unto itself.

August 2, 1964

New Delhi, India, 1964

First Talk in New Delhi

One of our great difficulties is that of communication. Words have an important place in our lives; otherwise, we cannot commune or communicate with each other. We have to use words, but each word has a different meaning for each one of us; the more so when the word is a little abstract—it then demands a greater penetration, a greater insight. But, unfortunately for most of us, we are easily satisfied with superficial words because our whole structure of thinking is based on words. And without understanding the significance of each word, especially when we are dealing with psychological, subtle forms of human behavior, human thought and conduct, it becomes extremely difficult to be really in communication with each other.

So, really to commune with each other—that is, to share, to partake in something together—we must understand the verbal construction, the word. The word plays an extraordinarily important part in our lives. And we are so unconscious of words like the word ***Hindu,*** the word ***Muslim,*** like the words ***God, husband, government, socialism, communism***—these words are all laden with meaning. To go into all these questions of human conflict, human problems, we have to understand the words. We have to go beyond the construction of words, and that seems to be one of our major difficulties. Because in what we are going to talk about during these discourses, talks, or whatever they are called, we will not only use words—because we must use words—but also try, if we can, together to commune over those things which are not contained in the words. The word is static, the word has a definite meaning according to the dictionary; but we interpret the word according to our emotional, psychological structure, according to our temperament, according to our immediate pressures, according to our conditioning. But to commune with each other we have not only to understand the word but also to share that which is contained in, and yet is not, the word. And that seems to be one of our greatest difficulties because unfortunately we do not listen to all the talks.

It is important that you and I share, commune with each other. We really do not know what it means to commune. We have never communed with anybody. We have talked about it; we have conversations, ideas, opinions, the verbal structure of concepts; but we have never communed about anything together. I am sure you have never communed with nature. You have never communed with your wife, with your children, with your friends. To commune is to share, not verbally only, but to penetrate very deeply, to be together active—not you be passive and the speaker active, but together penetrate beyond the words and thereby commune. To commune with each other, you require a certain stability, a certain clarity—not of opinion, but mere clarity to look at things as they are, to look at yourself as you actually are, to look at the world situation not according to your particular group, nationality, section, but to look at all problems of man whether he is in the West or in the East. And to look at the problem is to commune with the problem. You cannot possibly commune with the problem if you have opinions, if you are convinced that this is so and this is not so, if you are steeped in nationalism, if you are caught in politics—then you cannot commune at all at any level with the problem.

We have many problems, immense problems which cannot be solved by anybody except by yourself; and that requires not only the factual understanding of the problem but also to be in communion with that problem. I do not know if you have ever tried to be in communion with anything. You know, if you are a great painter and you want to paint a tree, you must be in communion with the tree. There must be no space between you and the tree—not that you identify yourself with the tree, but there must be no barrier between you and that which you observe, which you paint, with which you are in communion. That is, you as an entity must be totally absent to commune with the tree. To be in communion with nature, with the mountain, with a scene, with a human being—this demands extraordinary attention and a tremendous quality of sensitivity; otherwise, you cannot commune.

As we are going to deal with so many problems during these discourses, you have to take an active part; you have not merely to listen to the speaker, but you have actively to partake in everything that is being said, not agreeing or disagreeing. You cannot partake in something, share something, if you say, "I like you" or "I do not like you." You have to examine critically, be aware of the whole implication of the problem. You have to question, you have to doubt, you have to criticize, and you have to penetrate. That means you must be active, share with the speaker, be in communion with the speaker over the problem. Most of us do not know what it means to be in communion with something because it requires an open heart, a clear mind, a sense of hesitancy, a quality of sensitivity—we have none of these things. We are so full of opinions, so full of judgment, so overwhelmed with what we already know; and with all these we precipitate into the present; therefore, we never understand, we are never in contact intimately, completely, fully, with the problem.

So, if you will be good enough to listen with that quality of attention where you are partaking, you are not merely listening to the speaker, but you are actively, dynamically entering into the problems that are overwhelming the world, especially in this country. As we are going to deal with the problems, you must come to them with a sensitivity, with a hesitancy, with the quality of questioning, asking, demanding, searching. And you cannot do this if you come to it with concepts, with opinions, with the knowledge which already you have accumulated about it. You need a fresh mind.

I am going to talk about these things, not because I am used to talking—I really do not very much like this kind of talks; it is not a habit with me that has caught me up and I go trotting along from country to country—but I see the tremendous problems that are now in the world: the agonies, the despairs, the starvation, the conflicts, the endless sorrow of man, the terrible poison of nationalism, the racial differences and the religious intolerance, and the innumerable gods that break the heart of man. They are there in front of us. We just go along casually with a boredom, with a sense of unawakened despair, and we are caught in it. If we could easily, happily, with a certain quality of intensity, commune together, then perhaps we would be able to understand the problem and resolve and go beyond that. As we were saying, we have many problems not only in this country but throughout the world. And when one comes to this country after a certain time, one sees the extraordinary decline. I do not think one is aware of it: the decline morally, mentally, emotionally, artistically, creatively, the decline of that thing called religion, the utter superstition, the stupidity of the so-called religious mind, the everlasting repetition of what the Gita or somebody else has said, and the desire to escape from the present into the past.

So you see all these. I do not think it is very important to go into the details over these. Perhaps we will, but what is important is: Is it possible for the human mind which has developed for two million years, which is caught in certain habits, in a certain rhythm, can such a mind break away from all these and create for itself a new mind, a new way of action? That is what is needed. You know, in science, in the artistic world, in the world of politics and also in the world of religion, we can go along as we are, improving here and there—little patches of freedom here, little patches of prosperity there, a better government, less corruption or more corruption—the decline of thought, the decline of deep feeling, the utter carelessness. And in the scientific world one observes that the scientists have a few keys which open the doors; and they are always moving in the horizontal direction with these keys, through these doors; and very few are asking: Is there a vertical explosion, not a horizontal process? One sees in the world today a great deal of prosperity, especially in the West, of which we here in this country hardly know anything at all—the throbbing, intense prosperity, money, houses, good food, museums, theatres, cinemas, and excitement. And here we know nothing of all that; here we are not throbbing with a new life, even in the world of economics. So one observes that one can go on indefinitely, becoming a little more prosperous, a little less corrupt, having a better government, a little more intelligent ministers, a better bureaucracy, reading better books, and so on. Indefinitely we can go along on the horizontal line always improving, changing on a minor key; but we have lived that way for two million years. I do not know if you have read or heard or have been told that the scientists have found, the anthropologists have found, that man has lived for two million years and has not solved his problem. He is still in sorrow, he is still in fear, he is still in the agony of despair, in hopeless confusion after two million years; and he can go on that way indefinitely.

I think one has to see this, question this, feel this problem: You, as a human being who has lived for two million years, have not solved your sorrow; you are not free of your despairs, you are not free of this extraordinary thing called death; you have nothing in your life that is creative. We are bound to time, we are bound to a nationality, to a family, to the innumerable corruptions that are going on around us; and we live in that, grow in it, suffer and die, hoping for some future happiness somewhere in some world or to come back here, or having some vague hope based on despair; and we live, quoting some religious book as if it were the final thing. That is how our lives are. So, we have to be aware, we have to be in communion with it; and perhaps we can explode, because that is what is needed—a new mind, a new way of thinking, a new way of acting, a new relationship. For life is movement in relationship, and that demands astonishing awareness, never a moment which is stable, which is firm, to which you are anchored. Life is an endless movement. Unless one understands that movement, one is caught in sorrow.

So, our main question is: How can the mind, your mind—not an abstract mind—how can your mind, living in a world of confusion, misery, in a world of oppression, in a world of poverty, in a world of tremendous authority which destroys the mind; how can this mind which is the result of the influence of two million years of environment, of its conditioning—how can that mind explode and discover something new, not on the horizontal line, but on the vertical? That is really the issue—not whether there is God, whether you believe in this or that: that comes much later. To find reality you must cease to function horizontally—that means, really, that you must be free of your environment. We shall talk about it later. So, the main issue in front of us is this question: We can go on living as we are for another two million years and more, go to the moon, go ten miles deep into the sea, or live under the sea for a month or two in caves (which they are experimenting with) and endlessly live with sorrow—is that the way of life, or is there a new way of living? To live actually, not according to somebody else, not according to the speaker, not according to some formula, not according to an idea or an ideal, not according to a pattern—we have done all these things, and they have led us to where we are.

So, you have to ask yourself whether it is possible to cut yourself off completely from this, from the past, and start anew, not knowing. Because knowledge, however important at a certain level—you must have knowledge at that level, technological knowledge; certain memories are essential—becomes a hindrance for the explosiveness of the new age. So our problem is: Can the mind—do please listen to this, not verbally; look at your own mind, put yourself this question—can your mind which has acquired so much information, so much knowledge, can it put that aside? Knowing that memory, knowledge, is important at a certain level, can it free itself from that knowledge so that it can look, explore into something new? You know, the painters, the musicians, the scientists are trying to find something new. The so-called modern painting, nonobjective painting, is a search for the new; but the new is not possible with the old. They cannot let the old go, they are always battling and discovering something new—a new way of expression, new music, new painting, a new way of finding out.

So, you have to ask yourself the question, the final question: Can the mind, can your mind, liberate itself from the past, not in time, not tomorrow, not ten years later? Either it can be done immediately, or not at all. You know, sirs, we need a surgical operation. We need a tremendous mutation—not a revolution, but a complete mutation—of our mind, our being, which is still animalistic because we are the result of the animal. A great part of our brain is still the animal—the animal is acquisitive, jealous, fearful, anxious, insecure, competing. They are experimenting with animals, and they have discovered all these things. We are very similar to the animals in our behavior, though we might pretend that we are seeking this and that, the super-human—we are not. There is a great deal of us that is still the animal, and unless we operate completely, be free of the animal, we shall still go on for two million years, suffering, in despair, in agony, inventing philosophies that have no value at all in daily existence, seeking God because in our own hearts and minds we are in fear.

So, that seems to be the major issue. Can the mind—our mind, your mind—which has been conditioned for two million years (do listen to this) conditioned, shaped, held ruthlessly by your society, by your priests, by your politicians, by your economists, by your social activities, held by your family—can that mind operate upon itself, cut itself away from the past and discover for itself what this extraordinary mutation is, which is necessary to solve our problems? What to do we shall discuss; we shall commune how to bring about this mutation; we will go into it, step by step; but you must share with me. You cannot sit there, listen, agree or disagree, say that this is right or that is wrong, have fears. Then you and I shan't have any relationship; then you and I are not in communion. You are merely listening to another's talk, which has no meaning at all.

So, first we must see the enormous problem that man has divided the earth into nationalities, into different governments, and thereby is economically suffering. There is the division of nationalities. You know, in Europe, they spit on nationalism now; it means nothing to the intellectual, to the man who is thinking about it; but here we are boiling with that. This country is supposed to be so ancient, so full of wisdom; what they mean by wisdom is being full of words. The world has been cut into nationalities, into economic spheres, into spheres of power. And you have the divisions of religion—Hindu, Muslim, Buddhist, Christian, Catholic, Zen—and there are dozens and dozens of gurus all over the place. So, it is your problem. You cannot leave it alone, you have to solve it. You have to put your mind, your heart, your whole being into it; otherwise, we will go on for another two million years suffering, aching, butchering each other.

So, that is the first thing to realize—that it is you that has to solve the problem and nobody else; you are responsible and nobody else, not your government, not all the politicians—they are a miserable lot anyhow—not the priests, not the gurus, not the sacred books, not the teachers, not your gods and temples. You who are the result of two million years, and you who have suffered, who are suffering, who are in despair, who are everlastingly seeking, asking, begging, demanding to be told what to do—you have to awaken to yourself, you have to become an individual, an individual that sees clearly the problem and breaks away. You know this does not demand courage. When you see something very clearly, then you act; you cannot help acting. It is only when you do not see things clearly that you talk about courage and action. When you see very clearly a poisonous snake, you act. It does not need courage; it demands clarity of perception, clarity of vision. And you cannot have clarity of perception if you are merely caught up in words, in phrases, in beliefs, in dogmas, in all the nonsense that you call modern existence with the terrific amount of religious superstitions, dogmas. So, one has to realize for oneself the total importance of one's own conduct, one's own clarity of perception; one has to be tremendously responsible for oneself. It has to be clear between you and me that I am not, the speaker is not, telling you what to do, that the speaker is not bringing another pattern or another formula according to which you will behave—then we are back again to the old, stupid relationship of a teacher and a follower, which is deadly. But if you and I really, honestly, seriously are in communion over the problem, then we can go together, then we can discuss, and we will point out the extraordinary qualities that lie behind all this—because if one can be free of fear, then the whole problem is solved. And the speaker will explain—not how to follow, but—how to set about for yourself to be completely free of fear. It can be done.

Then the question is: Do you know what it means to be without fear? Have you ever tried in your mind to know what it is to be without any sense of fear? Then your mind becomes extraordinarily clear. And the mind being very clear—it affects the nervous organism; there are no psychosomatic diseases; then the whole body, mind, and everything functions very clearly; then you are not merely mechanically efficient; then you can give your attention to everything that you are doing; with the mind you are attentive. Perhaps, next Sunday, we could go into that, we could talk about this question of fear—what it means to be really free of it and how to set about it.

Now we have to understand, you and I, that we are partaking, we are sharing, that here, there is no authority because authority in any form is destructive. You accept authority because you are afraid. If there were no fear, you would not go to a temple, you would not look at a priest, there would be no guru and all that nonsense; then you would be a free man to look, to search out, to inquire, to ask, to demand, to move. So, this evening, it seems to me, the first thing to realize is that the world is in such a contradictory chaos, in confusion, that nobody can resolve it—no politician, no guru, no teacher, no book—except your own activity. You are responsible for everything, and in you the explosion must take place. This complete mutation must bring about a transformation, and this mutation is not a formula. You know what we mean by mutation? There are two things involved in life—change and mutation. Change implies a continuity of what has been, modified or extended or altered. Change implies a movement from the known to the known, modified. That is what we mean by change. I change my house, I change my way of thinking, because I want to change from what I am to something that I already know—which is a modified continuity of what has been. That is all that most of us are concerned with—change. But we are talking of something entirely different, which has nothing to do with change. Change is the process of time. I am this, today; and if I work on myself, I shall be that, tomorrow. In the interval between today and tomorrow, by the exercise of will, by circumstances, by influences, I shall become that. That is, during the interval of time there is a change. That change is already known, and therefore, it is not mutation. Mutation is something that cannot be known because if you know it already, you have just moved. Please see the importance of this. Mutation is a totally different dimension, and therefore you must have a different eye, a different heart, a different mind—a totally different mind, not a changed mind. We shall go into that, too.

So, what we are talking about is a mind that can use knowledge, but is not a slave to knowledge, a mind that is empty and therefore creative. Because even the scientists, some of them with whom we have talked, are asking this: whether the mind can ever be empty. Because they see that out of emptiness only a new thing takes place, not out of a mind that is burdened, conditioned, and all the rest of it. The new is not conditioned by the old. The new is not recognizable by the old as the new. I shall not go into all this now, at the first talk, because it will probably be too abstract and too difficult. But one can see, one can perhaps verbally grasp, intellectually grasp, what it means to have a mind that is not burdened with knowledge, that is not burdened with all the experience that man has had. Because if the mind is not empty, then it is mechanical; you repeat. It is only out of this extraordinary, awakened, sensitive emptiness that the new can be. The new is, if you can use that word, God; but really it is not God because that word *God* is so misused that it has no meaning, because it is a formula, it is a concept of despair. But it is that mind which is empty, in which creation can take place; it is only there that there is love. We do not know what love means—

we know what sensation means, we know what sex means—because love can never be where there is jealousy; love is not the result, love has no jealousy.

This is not the moment to talk about all this because it is the first talk. You and I have to establish a verbal relationship at least, and then we can proceed. We have got six more talks. During those talks we hope we shall establish a relationship, not that of a listener and a speaker, but of two minds meeting, two minds that have thought out, inquired, searched, asked, demanded, doubted, and awakened. Then only you and I can meet in something that is astonishingly new because out of that or in that, there are no problems; and in that there is the immensity of beauty. Then only we shall understand what that is, and perhaps then, we can function from the unknown in the known.

October 21, 1964

Second Talk in New Delhi

We said that we would talk this evening about fear. But before we go into that, I think we have to understand several things. I am using the word *understand* not verbally or intellectually. It is one of the most difficult things to understand something. Most of us, when we use that word understand, generally mean that we understand the meaning of the word, or we understand intellectually, verbally, or we do not understand because we oppose what we hear with our own opinions, with our own knowledge, with our own judgment. So, understanding becomes a very difficult problem because one is never in contact directly with any issue, with any problem. We approach the problem either verbally, intellectually, or according to a formula; therefore, we are never directly in contact with the problem; therefore, we never understand the issue at all.

So, when we use the word understand, we must be very clear what we mean by that word. It is not a verbal or intellectual understanding. We mean by *understanding* a total comprehension, a total sensitivity to the issue—not a fragmentary approach, not an intellectual, a verbal, or an emotional approach, but a total, comprehensive, complete approach, a complete contact with the problem. That is what we mean when we use the word understand. We have many problems, many issues; and to understand them, we must be directly in contact with them; and we cannot be in contact with them if we approach them intellectually, verbally, or with a prejudice, or with a preconceived idea or a formula—then, there is no contact with the problem, and therefore there is no understanding. So, it has to be clear that we are not playing with words, we are not indulging in ideation, in theories, but are actually trying to understand that which actually is, that with which we can come directly into contact.

As I said, we are going to talk this evening about fear. But before we go into that, we have to understand action and the complex problem of effort. Otherwise, we shall not be able to comprehend or understand or be in total contact with what we call fear, which distorts all our thinking. Fear prevents comprehension, fear brings about various forms of contradiction. So, before we go into fear—whether it is possible at all to be totally free from fear—we have to understand what we mean by action and effort.

As we were saying the other day, life is a movement in relationship, which is action. But, for us, action is the outcome of an idea; we translate what we hear into an idea and then carry out that idea in action. That is all we know as action—an urge either of pleasure or displeasure, which is a reaction, which is translated as an idea, that idea being an organized thought. Idea is an organized thought which is carried out in action. That is all we know of action: that is, we have a formula, a pattern, a concept; and then we try to put that concept, that pattern as closely as possible in action—that is what we call action. We see starvation, soaring prices, exploding population, disintegration; and we want to change all this, we want to put a stop to it; and we conceive a formula, an idea, how to do it, and gather a few people who will agree upon that idea, and then collectively act according to the plan, according to the idea—that is what we consider action.

I think we must be very clear about it because what we are going into presently will be so contradictory to what we hold as the norm, as the pattern of action. So first we must understand what we call action. That is, I see that color and I do not like that color—the idea. And then I act upon that idea. I never look at that color without an idea. When I look, not through the idea of like and dislike, I am immediately in contact with that color. This is important to understand. Idea is the outcome of memory, experience, judgment; and therefore it is either personal or collective, racial, family, as memory. And that idea is carried out in action. Now, is there an action without idea? Otherwise, you are not in contact with action at all; you are acting, approximating that activity to an idea, and therefore it is never an action, it is never a complete, direct, intimate contact with action. It is always through the screen of ideas, and therefore there is a contradiction between action and idea. And we are always trying to bridge the division, this contradiction between idea—which is reasoned, organized thought as an idea—and action which is so separate from the idea; we are trying to bring these two together as closely as possible. Trying to bring together these two—that is, the idea or the formula or the concept and action—is effort. That is all our life. All our life revolves around this.

If you have observed yourself, if you have watched yourself, if you have watched the activities of the politicians, of the gurus, of the saints, of any human being, you will notice that this is going on all the time—the idea, noble or ignoble, well planned, or well reasoned, or unbalanced: how to carry that out in daily life. And to carry out the idea as completely, as totally as possible in action involves effort. So, all our life is one continuous form of activity. Please, it is really important to understand this circle of the human mind, which is all the time perpetuating contradictions. And having perpetuated contradiction, brought it about, the mind tries to overcome that contradiction; and in trying to overcome that contradiction, a great deal of energy, as effort, is involved. And in that way man has lived a million years—the idea, carrying out the idea in action, and therefore living constantly in contradiction. And in being in contradiction, effort is involved.

Please do not translate what we are saying into an idea with which you agree or disagree, but just listen and observe. Because if you, by listening, create another pattern of idea and try to carry out that idea in action, you are back again in the same circle, with different sets of patterns, of ideas and ideologies. We have to understand this process. I am using the word *understand* to mean to be intimately in contact with the process of our thinking, not as an idea, not as a somebody observing the fact from outside, but actually being in contact with the thought process which creates the idea—and again that creates the action which contradicts the idea; so the problem arises. Perhaps many of you have not thought about this, and so perhaps it is not a problem, not an issue. But if you have gone into it, it will become an issue—not imposed by the speaker, but it is a problem for yourself. So, if you have gone into it, or if you are listening actually without an opinion—because we are not dealing with opinions, but we are dealing with actual facts, psychological facts—you will see that the idea predominates and action then follows, and therefore there is contradiction. That is a fact with which you neither agree nor disagree; it is so.

So, one asks oneself: Is it possible to live without effort, at every level of our being, not at fragmentary levels? Is it possible to live our daily life of routine—going to the office, the boredom, the insults, the dirt, the squalor, the beauty of a sunset—to live with all this, our modern life, so completely that there is no effort involved at all? Because when there is an effort of any kind, it is a distortion. You make effort because of an idea, of a memory, of a previous experience, which says, "You must" or "You must not." And is it possible to live, without effort, our daily life, because that is the only life we have, and that is the only thing that matters—not your ideas about God and nirvana, heaven and the future; they have no value at all. What has value, what has significance, what has vitality and energy is your daily life—the ugliness, the squalor, the bitterness, the disappointments, the anxiety, the poverty, the stagnation, the things that are going on in the world, the disintegration in this country with which we have to deal every day. Unless we have a totally different operational approach to this daily existence—not a future utopia, not the lovely communist world or the lovely religious world—unless we understand this present life with all its complexities, we cannot possibly under any circumstances change what is taking place in the world, in the family, and about you.

We need a complete revolution, a complete mutation—not of ideas, not of a formula, however intelligent, however clever, however erudite. We need a complete change of mind, a complete revolution, a mutation of the mind. And it is only such a mind that can stop the disintegration that is going on, that can bring about a new sense of living, a sense of creativeness. Therefore one has to find out whether it is possible to live without effort. Because all effort implies resistance, all effort implies contradiction, all effort involves idea as separate from action; and hence our life, daily living, is a contradiction. Unless that contradiction totally disappears—not in little things; I am not talking about little things but of the contradiction deeply seated in our consciousness, whether conscious or unconscious—we shall disintegrate, we shall be in a state of corruption, and we shall not bring about a different state of mind which can alone solve the immense problems that exist in the world.

So, is it possible to live without effort? Don't say yes or no, don't agree or disagree or say, "Well, all that I know is a life of effort; I do not know anything else; and what you say about a life without effort is silly. We see actually that through opposites, through contradictions, through thesis and antithesis, a synthesis is brought about—which is a constant battle of effort—that is all we know." If you go a little deeper behind this pattern of effort, you see that effort comes about only when there is resistance. I mean by the words *to resist*, "I like, I do not like"—which is merely an opinion according to a memory, according to an idea, according to an experience; and therefore you are not facing facts. When I see that color, I immediately say, "I like it" or "I do not like it"; therefore, I have created a contradiction. Can I look at that color without any judgment? When I merely look at it without any judgment, in that look I am immediately in contact with that color, and therefore there is no contradiction. Please, this is really very subtle but important to understand—as it is to listen to something.

You are listening to me now. I am saying something which you do not know anything about. Your instinctive response is: We cannot do it, or it is nonsense, or he is talking about some stupid, ideological stunt. Therefore, you push it aside—which is resistance. And from that resistance there is a contradiction, and contradiction implies effort, a waste of energy. Whereas, there is no contradiction if you listen to what is being said, not agreeing or disagreeing, not opposing your opinion against the fact, because what I am talking about is a fact, and the issue is whether the pattern of action which we know of can be broken down, not whether you agree or disagree with it. So, you have to listen without creating the pattern of an idea, without agreeing or disagreeing with that idea. Agreeing or disagreeing becomes merely an opinion, and such opinion has no value at all. What has value is that you listen to the fact without agreeing or disagreeing, that you look at it as you would look at the sunset, at a color, at the sky, at the beauty of a person or the loveliness of a tree—just look. Then you are directly in contact, and that contact with something is complete action. A hungry man is not bothered about the idea: how hunger is brought about, how hunger comes. He is concerned about food—food not as an idea but food as a fact—and therefore there is no opinion. You may like a certain food or may not like it, but there is no opinion.

So, you have to listen. And that is very difficult because you are not educated to listen. You never listen. You listen with a mind that is full of opinions, ideas, and contradiction to something which is being said and with which you agree or disagree; and therefore, in that state of mind, you are not listening. But to listen is one of the most difficult things, actually as difficult as seeing. I do not know if you have ever considered what it is to see. Probably most of you are married. Have you ever seen, looked at your wives, or your children, or your neighbors, or your politicians, or your leaders, or your gurus? Have you looked, seen with your eyes—not seeing with the ideas behind the eye? You look at your wife with the ideas which you have collected about her, with the insults, with the hurts, with the pleasures, sex, dozens of things, and you look at her with them in your minds. Therefore, you do not see the things that are being said here, nor do you listen to the things that are being said by the politicians or by the gurus or by anybody. Because you have ideas, because you belong to the party—you are a communist, a socialist, or God knows what else—and because you listen with these ideas to what the other fellow is saying, you are not listening at all. And you never listen to a bird—I do not know whether you have listened to a bird.

To listen to something demands that your mind be quiet—not a mystical quietness, but just quietness. I am telling you something, and to listen to me you have to be quiet, not have all kinds of ideas buzzing in your mind. When you look at a flower, you look at it, not naming it, not classifying it, not saying that it belongs to a certain species—when you do these, you cease to look at it. Therefore I am saying that it is one of the most difficult things to listen—to listen to the communist, to the socialist, to the congressman, to the capitalist, to anybody, to your wife, to your children, to your neighbor, to the bus conductor, to the bird—just to listen. It is only when you listen without the idea, without thought, that you are directly in contact; and being in contact, you will understand whether what he is saying is true or false; you do not have to discuss. So, in the same way, if you can listen this evening—perhaps you will listen not only this evening but every evening, in your life, in your office, in the bus—then you will understand not only yourself, which is a complex entity, but also the whole process of existence.

So, for this evening, please listen without resistance—which does not mean that you are going to follow what is being said—which will be terrible because we are not an authority. Authority is the most destructive thing in life—a leader, a guru, a man who says, "I know and you do not know." That is what has happened in this country. You have ceased to be human beings because you have been led, driven, you have followed the authority of Shankara, the authority of the book, Gita, Upanishads—they have destroyed the mind because you have not thought it out for yourself. You are capable of quoting a dozen books, but you do not know for yourself. You are secondhand human beings, and the problems demand a firsthand mind that is directly in contact with the problem, not a secondhand, dull-witted mind. So, if you can listen to what is being said, without forming an idea, a formula of what you hear, then you will see what is implied in action-without-effort.

Why does the mind create the idea? Instinctively, we have the idea—why? Now, to understand that, we have to go a little bit into the question of memory, experience. What is memory? They, in Europe and America, have been experimenting, investigating into the whole process of memory, how memory is created. You can see it for yourself without being told by the super-expert on neurology and all the rest of it, you can watch it yourself very clearly. If you think about something continuously, that continuity gives the pattern of memory. I like you, I think about you; thinking about you creates the continuity of memory about you, surely. Or I do not like you, I do not think about you; I push it away from me, and that very act of pushing away gives a continuity of dislike. That is psychologically very simple. I see a certain color; in that seeing, the neurological process, the electricity and the nerves, are set going. That is blue, this is red; and I keep on looking at red and blue—which becomes the memory, the idea that it is blue and that this is red. On that all our experiences are based. That is, experience is the action between challenge and response. Am I being too abstract? I hope not. But I cannot help it, and if you do not like it, there it is. What we are trying to say is very simple really.

One sees very clearly that a new mind—a mind which is not fragmented, which is not Indian, which is not European, which is not American, which is not Russian; a mind really without contradiction, without fragmentation; a mind that is not caught in illusion, that is not under any pressure, strain—acts, not indirectly but directly. Such a mind is necessary because it is only such a mind that can understand love. It is only such a mind that can be in a state of creation. And it is only such a mind that can alter completely the present world and its misery, confusion. Such a mind is necessary, and how to bring it about is the problem. Is it at all possible to bring about such a mind? To bring it about, you must understand these things: What is effort, what is fear, what is ambition, What is authority?—understand, not ideologically, not theoretically, but actually; put your teeth into it so that your mind as an individual mind becomes ardent, passionate, clear, so that it is in a state of constant action and therefore it is never in a state of deterioration.

Now, the question is: Our brain is the result of two million years, from the animal to wherever we are now, because we are still the animal; is it possible to free the mind from the animal, without effort? You have to free the mind from the animal—which is greed, envy, fear, ambition, all utter, stupid trivialities which we indulge in and which are all at the animal-instinct level. Is it possible to be free from all that, and to live completely, totally as a human being, not fragmentarily but so completely that all your energy is there? It is only such a mind that can go beyond itself and find out whether there is a reality, whether there is God, whether there is something timeless. And to find that out, you have to begin with the simple things like, "what is action?" and "what is effort?"

Is it possible to be totally, completely free of fear—not only consciously, but also unconsciously, biologically? One has to go into it—not be taught, not be told. You, as a human being, have got to go into it, for yourself, so completely that you become an individual. It is only the individual that is alone, not a slave to environment. It is only the individual who has this mind; it is only the individual that can have it—that can bring about a different world—not the politicians, not the communists, not the theorists. When the individual has understood the whole psychological structure of his being, in that very understanding there is freedom; and it is that freedom that brings about the flowering of the individual.

Why is it that human beings so quickly accept ideas or create ideas? Why do we do it? Have you noticed why ideas have become important in your lives? Ideas as a nationalist, as the family, as God—why? Now, I am going to show it to you, to point it out, not that you must agree or disagree, but just listen. Ideas come into our being because they are not related to action, to immediate action. Ideas are escapes. I will show you something: There is starvation, poverty, misery in this world. You know what is happening in this country—the lack of food, the poverty, the disgrace, the soaring prices, and all the rest of it. Now, science can stop all these, science can give food, clothes, shelter to everybody. But why does it not happen? It is because we are predominated by ideas. That is, you are a Hindu, you are a Muslim, you belong to India, and I belong to Pakistan or to America or Russia, and our nationalism—which is again an idea—predominates; and so we sustain the division through ideas and therefore prevent people from living happily with food, shelter, and clothes. So, ideas are a means of escape from actuality.

I do not know if you have gone into it. I am pointing it out; now don't agree—when you agree with it, you go back again and fall into ideas. If you do not agree or disagree but look, you will see how your nationalism, your racial prejudices, your religious dogmas, all the stupidities are preventing cooperation with human beings. You can cooperate around an idea, and therefore again the same problems arise: you cooperate with certain ideas and I cooperate with other ideas, and therefore there is a contradiction; you are a communist, I am a capitalist, and therefore we battle; and in the meantime the poor chap is suffering.

So, for most of us, the idea is much stronger than action because action demands immediacy. Action is always in the living present; *act* is an active verb. The idea need not be active. It is there; therefore, I do not want to act immediately. But action demands all the time change, breaking down, flowing, living, running—that demands energy, watching, clarity. Whereas, with ideas you can play around everlastingly. Therefore the more idealistic you are, the less active you are, and therefore the 'more' is the contradiction. Therefore, ideas, as most of us know, are a means of escape from total action—we are afraid of total action. If you are really listening, you really cease to be a nationalist, you forget your religion, your prejudices, that you are a Hindu, this and that. Then you are a human being; then you come directly into contact with another human being, and in that direct contact there is action. And that action may create more revolution, more trouble. Therefore we say, "No. Let us deal with ideas, theories, concepts, and we can play with them everlastingly." This is one of the major difficulties.

And also we live fragmentarily. We live at the intellectual level at one time, at an emotional level at another time, at a purely physical level at another time. And most of us worship intellect because knowledge is tremendously important. The more you have read, the more you can quote, the more you can spout out a lot of words about the Gita, this and that, you are respected as an extraordinary human being. It does not matter what kind of a life you lead, what goes on inside you; but as long as you can quote, indulge in intellectual ideas, concepts, you are regarded as a great man—which is again a way of life which is fragmentary. Whereas, a man who lives totally, nonfragmentarily, is not intellectual, emotional, physical, but is all the time a total being. So, that is one of the reasons why we indulge in ideas and why ideas become so dominating.

Is it possible to act without an idea? I hope I am explaining myself clearly. If not, perhaps you will ask questions another day, and we can go more fully in detail with regard to it. One sees that the idea predominates and then action follows, whereas it should be the other way around. There should be only action, not idea; then you are actively living in the present. This demands watchfulness, nonfragmentary action and therefore noncontradiction. Where there is contradiction, there must be effort—which is obvious. So, our whole life goes round and round these three things—idea, action, and contradiction: contradiction being conscious, deliberate, or unconscious, unthought, unknown.

So, when we have to understand fear—which we are going into, perhaps not this evening but another evening—we can then go into it, not as an idea which we have to get rid of, but as a fact which we have to understand and therefore not resist.

What is action without idea? You ask yourself this question: What is action without concept, and is it at all possible? First, don't accept it. Find out, if it is possible, what it means. Because our life is action. You are sleeping, walking, dreaming, going to the office, taking up the pen, signing this or that. The whole of life is action, it is a movement in relationship. And that movement in relationship becomes a contradiction when it is a movement born of idea and therefore unrelated to action. When you discover how ideas are born—which I have tried to explain briefly—and when you understand this process of ideation, then you will see for yourself—nobody can teach you, you have to do it for yourself—you will not create any idea when you look, when you listen; then you are in contact immediately with everything; that immediacy of contact is real action in which there is no contradiction, and therefore does not involve effort of any kind. It is effort that perverts, makes the mind old; contradiction makes the mind old. Most of us have a mind that is already very old and dying because though we may be very young, we live in a state of contradiction, conscious or unconscious.

So, to understand this whole problem of living is the first primary duty of every human being; and after understanding that, one can proceed further because there are things which the mind can never understand if it has not settled these simple problems. To understand that you need tremendous energy; and that energy can only come when there is no contradiction, when one's whole being—physically, emotionally, intellectually—is completely one. Then, with that total energy, the mind can go very deeply and very far. But a mind that is in fragments, that is in contradiction, that is in pain—do what it will; it can go to the temples, to the gurus—such a mind will never go beyond itself; and it must go beyond itself to solve the immense problems that confront every human being.

October 25, 1964

Third Talk in New Delhi

As we said the other day, we are going to talk about fear. To go into that question fully and completely, one must have a great deal of energy—energy to penetrate into all the illusions that one has created round oneself and all the ideas and the innumerable problems that one has built round oneself. Unless one understands these things rightly and deeply for oneself, one will never be able to be free of fear consciously or unconsciously. We are going to take a journey together into this question—I mean together. You and I together are going to penetrate into this whole question, and therefore you and I are going to share together. You are not just sitting there listening to the speaker, agreeing or disagreeing; but we are together at the same level, at the same speed, with the same intensity—together. You and I will have to be in communion with one another—and this needs a great deal of communion, not only verbally, but also with our whole being, intellectually, sensitively, with all the capacity inside and the drive that is necessary to go into this question.

But before we go into it, we must understand also what it is to learn and what it is to acquire knowledge. The two things are completely separate. Learning is one thing and acquiring knowledge is another. Learning is a continuous process, not a process of addition, not a process which you gather and then from there act. Most of us gather knowledge as memory, as idea, store it up as experience, and from there act. That is, we act from knowledge, technological knowledge, knowledge as experience, knowledge as tradition, knowledge that one has derived through one's particular idiosyncratic tendencies; with that background, with that accumulation as knowledge, as experience, as tradition, we act. In that process there is no learning. Learning is never accumulative: it is a constant movement. I do not know if you have ever gone into this question at all: What is learning and what is the acquisition of knowledge? This is very important to understand—not at some future date, but now—because we are going into a very complex problem presently. Therefore, one has to understand what it is to learn. Learning is never accumulative. You cannot store up learning and then, from that storehouse, act. You learn as you are going along. Therefore, there is never a moment of retrogression or deterioration or decline.

The two things—that is, acquiring knowledge and learning—must be very clear in one's mind because what we are going to do together, this evening, is to learn—not to acquire knowledge. We are going to learn together about something which we think we know, but we do not know. That is, we are going to learn together about the quality of energy which is not derived from conflict. All life is energy. And the only energy that we know has a motive; it is the outcome of friction or conflict or a drive towards a particular end; it is the energy derived from something—like eating food and deriving energy, or hating somebody and deriving energy from that hate, or thinking that you love somebody and deriving energy from that. But that energy which is derived from a motive has always in it the seed of conflict, as pleasure and pain.

Please, you are not listening in order to accept an idea, or a formula. We are taking a journey together in inquiring into what this energy is which alone can dissipate all our problems, our conflicts, and our diseases of the mind. We are going to learn together—which means we are going to find out for ourselves what this energy is which is without motive and therefore which is not the outcome of any conflict or of any environment. That energy is by itself and therefore tremendously vital and creative, and has the potency of dissipating every form of illusion, sorrow, and confusion. And to learn about it, one has to understand. I mean by that word *understand,* not verbally or intellectually. One has to understand, to feel one's way into the question of learning, without idea. If you do not know about something which you are given, you have to study it, you have to learn about it, you have to handle it, to put your mind into it and then discover as you go along. We think we know and therefore we have ceased to learn; whereas, learning not being an additive process, one has to approach this learning quite differently. I do not know you, and you do not know me. You have ideas about me, and I have ideas probably about you; but this way I am not learning about you, nor are you learning about me; for me to learn about you and for you to learn about me, we must have a fresh mind, an inquisitive mind, a critical mind, a mind that does not accept or reject.

We are learning, and therefore there is never a judgment, there is no evaluation. When you are learning, your mind is always attentive and never accumulating—therefore, there is no accumulation from which you judge, you evaluate, you condemn and compare. I hope I am making myself clear on this point. Because a mind that is learning is always a fresh mind; it is always an inquiring mind, never a comparative mind, never accepting authority and evaluating action from that authority. Such a mind is young, and such a mind is innocent, fresh, because it is always learning. Now, this evening, the speaker and you are going to learn. Therefore do not judge, evaluate, accept, or deny, or create a pattern of ideas from which to act or to learn.

As we were saying the other day, all our life is conflict. Everything that we do either becomes a routine, a mechanical action, or a repeated pleasure, a resistance, a suppression or so-called sublimation. All our action is based on that, and therefore it is always engendering conflict, breeding conflict. And we have accepted conflict—this friction in life, friction in relationship, friction in the movement of existence—and we say, "That is inevitable, and let us make the best of it." Now, if you do not accept it, if you do not deny conflict in all relationship, at any level, then you can learn about conflict; when you do not say that one must have or must not have conflict, then only can you learn. You cannot learn about conflict if you are judging conflict from that which you have already experienced, known—knowledge. Therefore a mind that is learning is never in a state of experiencing. The moment you experience, you are already in the state of evaluating. Therefore a mind that is learning has no experience because it is moving, acting, driving, going through. So a mind that is actively learning every minute, learning not only about itself but about everything in life, is like a child that looks, asks, demands, and is never satisfied. That learning requires extraordinary energy. And a mind has no energy if it is burdened with knowledge and the demand for further experience.

Now, learning implies discipline—not your discipline which is suppression, control, conformity, the brutality involved in it. The accepting of an ideal as a pattern and trying to conform to it, forcing your mind, your being, your body, everything to conform—that is what you generally call discipline. Like a soldier who is drilled night and day, drilled so hard that he is nothing but a mechanical entity with a straight spine and no head at all. Don't laugh, please. Most of us are that way; only we do not know that we are that way. Society, environment, education—our everyday existence is forcing us to conform to a pattern, to a religious, social, or economic pattern. That discipline to conform is the most destructive form of discipline. The word *discipline,* the root of that word means to learn—not to conform, not to suppress, not to brutalize yourself, but to learn. And learning demands an astonishing discipline—not the discipline of acceptance, not the discipline of authority. Therefore, a mind that is learning has not only to be aware of the environmental influences as much as possible—not to conform, not to resist—but to be aware of its own tendencies, of its own qualities, of its own experiences and not fall into the trap of any of these; and that demands attention.

You know, a boy at school, in a class, wants to look out of the window. A bird is flying by, there is a lovely flower on the tree, or someone goes by. His attention is taken away from the book, and the teacher tells him to look at the book, to concentrate on the book. That is how most of our life is. We want to look, but society, economy, religious doctrines force us to conform; and therefore we lose all spontaneity, all freshness. So, the discipline of learning is something entirely different from the discipline of acquiring knowledge. You need to have a certain discipline when you are acquiring technological knowledge or any other knowledge. You have to pay attention, give your mind to something particular, to specialize in a subject; and that entails a certain discipline of conformity, of suppression, and all the things that are happening in the world through discipline. Now, the discipline which we are talking about has nothing whatsoever to do with the discipline of conformity to a pattern. Please understand all this because we are going into something very, very fundamental; and without understanding this, you will not be able to comprehend that thing which we shall talk of presently.

So we are learning, and that learning is never conformity to a pattern—how can it be? Whether the pattern has been laid down by the Buddha, by Christ, by Shankara, or by your own pet guru, learning has nothing whatever to do with it. Because in that conformity all learning ceases, and therefore there is never originality. And we are discovering through learning, with originality. I do not know whether you see the beauty of what we are talking about. Watching, looking, seeing, listening are all parts of learning. If you do not know how to listen, you cannot learn. If you do not know how to see a flower, you cannot learn about the beauty of that flower. And to listen, to see, to learn implies in itself a discipline which is not conformity. If that is very clear, we are going to go into something now which demands this act of learning; we are going to learn about ourselves.

You are going to learn about yourself. You cannot learn about yourself if you assert that you are God. You cannot learn about yourself if you say you are the higher atma, or if you say you are the result of environment only. You are following what I am talking about? If you say you are the result of environment only—as many do, the communists and so on—then you have stopped learning; if you say that in you there is the atma, the higher self, you are merely repeating something which you do not know at all—at least you are repeating something which you have been told, and it is a very comfortable theory—and so you have stopped learning; and if you say, "I am this, I am something," then also you have stopped learning. To find out about yourself, you must learn about yourself; and therefore you need the highest freedom, intelligence, and critical awareness. Without that, you cannot possibly find yourself or understand yourself. And without understanding yourself, you have no basis for the structure of your being. You might have lots of thoughts, conflicts, pain, pleasure, and all the rest of it; but there is no foundation.

You must know about yourself—not according to Shankara, the Buddha, the Christ, or Freud, or Jung, or anybody, including the speaker. You have to know yourself and therefore to learn about yourself. To learn about yourself, all previous knowledge about yourself must come to an end—which is very difficult because when you say, "I am ugly," that very word *ugly* has the connotation of tradition, and therefore you are judging, and therefore you are not learning. I hope you see this thing: it is very simple. Once you see it, then you can fly with learning; then there is no end, no limit; and that learning is beyond time. A mind that is continually moving from the unknown to the unknown, learning, learning, learning—such a mind is the most extraordinarily sensitive mind and therefore a free mind.

So, we are going to learn about ourselves. And to learn, as we said, there must be no evaluation—naturally. When you evaluate, you judge from that which you have already acquired as knowledge; and when you see yourself, you either condemn or approve or reject, and therefore you are not learning about yourself. Now, if you are learning about yourself, you are learning about the body, the nerves, the responses of the nerves, the memories, the various qualities, the tendencies, the hopes, the fears, the despairs, the agonies, the anger, the lust, the sexual demands, the hope to find something eternal, and all that—you are all those, which are ideas. Are they not? You have ideas about yourself—that you are a good man, that you are the big shot in the town, that you are a Sikh, that you are a Hindu, that you are this and that. You have ideas; and those ideas are the result of your environmental influence, of your knowledge. Therefore when ideas predominate about yourself, you have ceased to learn about yourself. Please, this is very important, very simple. When once you grasp this, you are alive; then tradition, Shankaras, can all be thrown aside; and you become a human being, free to find out, free to inquire, free to learn. So, to learn about yourself is absolutely essential; otherwise, you might create an illusion and live in that illusion.

To learn about himself is the first intelligent action of the human being; it is not that he learns about himself in order to save himself. You are the result of two million years of man with all his experiences, his calamities, his despairs, his sorrows, and his confusion; you are all that. And if you would completely bring about a revolution in yourself, you have to know yourself—not know yourself, but learn about yourself—to understand yourself. You have to learn about yourself. Any fool can say, "I know about myself." But to learn about yourself is extremely difficult because you must look at yourself choicelessly, without any bias, without any criticism, without any condemnation—you must just look. I do not know if you have ever looked at a flower, just looked at it—without idea, without thought. If you have so looked at a tree, at a flower, or at any human being so that in looking the idea does not predominate, then there is a communication between you and the flower—not that you become the flower, or you identify yourself with the flower or with the tree or with the family. But when you look at a flower without the word—if you have ever looked that way, which demands attention—then you will see that the space between you and the flower disappears. You are not that flower; there is only that flower and not you who are looking at it.

Please understand this simple thing because we are going into it still, and if you do not understand all these things, you will not go into it very vitally, dynamically, creatively. So, we have never looked at a flower, actually. We say it is a rose, and by calling it a rose, we have already gone away from looking. To look at that flower, there must be no verbalization; you just look. Look at a cloud of an evening, without a word. There is a vast space between you and that cloud, limitless space. That cloud is full of life and beauty and shape and glory; and you look at it with a narrow mind enclosed by everyday problems, misery and confusion and strife. You never really look. And our life becomes a shadow, a shallow, shoddy thing. So, to learn, we must look.

To learn about myself, I must look—please listen to this—I must look at myself. I can only look at myself when there is no authority of any kind, when I do not say I am the higher self or the lower self, when I do not have any knowledge about myself; I must come to it each day afresh, anew. Now, when I look at myself, there is the looker—the observer, the experiencer—and the thought—the experience, the thing at which I am looking. That is what, with most of us, takes place. Does it not? When I say I look at myself, the observer is different from the thing that is observed. This is simple. I am not going into supermetaphysical and complicated philosophy; that is all too silly—for me, anyhow. There is just the obvious fact: the observer, the I who says, "I am looking," and the thing that is looked at. So, there is the division between the observer and the thing observed. That is, when I say I am angry, the "I" is different from that which I call anger. That is what takes place with most of us. Right? With most people, this is a simple fact: that the thinker is different from thought. And this division is the origin of conflict because the thinker is always trying to change his thought, modify it, control it, shape it, force it, suppress it, sublimate it, or do something about it all the time. If I am to learn about this division, I must question the thinker himself, the observer himself. Right? I must question whether this division is actual, or invented by the mind in order to escape from the actual. I hope this is not too complicated, but if it is, I am sorry.

The speaker sees that to live in conflict at any time, at any level, is destructive. The speaker understands that very clearly—not from experience, but from the actual fact of daily living—how it destroys relationships; how it destroys, corrupts the mind; how it makes the mind mechanical, insensitive, dull, stupid. So, the speaker says that as long as one is in conflict, there can be no sensitivity, and therefore there can be no act of learning. So, for him, conflict is the central factor of distraction, friction. So, he says to himself, "Now, is it possible to live without conflict in life—environment, family, earning a living, the insults, the indignity upon man, and all the rest of it?" He does not say it is possible or it is not possible—which again would be too stupid. He has to learn about it. So, he begins to inquire, to learn about the thinker. And to learn about the thinker, he must observe the thinker, in the same way as he observes a flower without naming it, without giving it a species—he must just observe. Now when he just observes, there is no thinker, there is only observation, and therefore there is no division as the thinker and the thought.

Please don't agree or disagree. I know all the clever things that we say: "The thinker comes first, and thought afterwards; which comes first, the egg or the chicken?" You know all this old business. But if we are going to learn, there is no statement upon which you take a stand. You have to learn. And if you are learning, you will see that there is only thinking and not the thinker. The thinker is created by thought. If you have no thought, there is no thinker, and therefore you destroy radically the root of conflict. There is only thinking, which then begins to create the entity called the thinker, giving it permanency; and that permanency is an idea—it is not an actuality, it is just an idea. Unfortunately, we live by ideas and not by facts, not by action but by ideas carried out in action—which we talked about the other day.

So, there is only thinking. Do you know what happens when you realize that there is only thinking? Please, we are sharing this together; you are not going to sleep. We are taking the journey together. You realize that there is only thinking—which is an obvious fact—and not the entity who thinks, separate from thought. Look! When I say I am angry, for most of us, the "I" is different from anger. But, is not anger part of the "I" which says, "I am angry"? If there were only anger as a reaction, to which you have given the name *anger,* then the whole problem changes.

You understand what I am talking about? There is no entity who says, "I must not be angry" or "I must continue to be angry." There is only that feeling, or that reaction, which we have named as anger. When one realizes that there is no entity who condemns anger, then the whole anatomy of anger changes. Is it too difficult, sirs? I am sorry, because if we do not understand this thing, then, when we talk about fear, you will not be free of fear, and then you and I will part company. That is why I am insisting, I am going into this as deeply and in as great detail as possible. There has to be the realization, the understanding that there is only thought as a reaction of memory, as a reaction of experience—because that is what thought is. I ask you something and you reply quickly, or take time over it. The quickness of the reply indicates that you know the answer very well, you are very familiar, intimate with it. But if I ask you something much deeper, of which you do not know or which you have forgotten, you have to think about it. The thinking is the looking during the time interval.

So, thinking is a mechanical process; it is not something sublime, marvelous. The electronic brains are also doing the thinking. That is, an electronic brain responds to the various information that has been given to it, which is knowledge; and then when you put a question to that electronic brain, it replies. It is exactly the same with us. We act through association, through experience, through previous knowledge; and when that is challenged, it responds, and the response is thinking. If one realizes that all thinking is a response of memory and therefore mechanical—therefore dead, not vital—then our whole structure of conflict changes. Then you begin to learn about thinking. Then you will find out how important it is to understand the whole structure of memory, to learn about it; how our memory is the seat of all response. The scientists have been investigating into the whole problem of memory, how important it is at certain levels. I am saying this: Memory is important at certain levels, and at another level it is completely destructive because memory is of time, of the past; and if you are responding all the time from the past, your thinking is obviously from the past, and therefore you never have the freedom to look at something totally anew.

So a mind that is learning and not acquiring knowledge is concerned with thinking only, not with the thinker, because the thinker is created by thought. Look, it is very simple: I like something, I think about it all the time; the thinking about it gives me pleasure, and therefore I give to that something which I like a continuity, which becomes my memory. And I do not like something and I push it away—which again gives it a continuity. So please look at it, learn about it—that all our thinking is mechanical; and that thought being mechanical, the mere pursuit of thought can never free man; however much you may refine, control, eliminate thought, you can never be free. What you have to do is to learn about thinking and therefore all the time be original. Learning is nonaccumulative.

There is no time to talk about fear—which we shall do next Sunday, or whatever day we meet here. But one has to be very clear about certain things—that the act of learning is entirely different from the act of acquiring knowledge; learning releases energy, whereas accumulating knowledge and acting from that knowledge restricts energy; and this restriction, this bondage of energy is conflict; the real source of conflict is this division between thought and the thinker; and when there is only thought and therefore no condemnation of anything, no resistance of anything, there is merely the act of learning constantly; then that brings about a mind which is young, fresh, innocent; and therefore such a mind is not affected by age.

So a mind that can look, see, that can listen and learn, is a very disciplined mind—the discipline that is born from learning, not from conformity. That very word *discipline* means to learn—which we unfortunately have translated as conforming or suppression and all the rest of it. And to learn there must be attention, not concentration—which we will go into another day. All this requires energy, therefore right food and all the rest of it.

A religious mind is a young mind, which is a mind that is learning and therefore beyond time. Only such a mind is the religious mind. Not the mind that goes to temples—that is not a religious mind. Not the mind that reads books and quotes everlastingly, moralizing—that is not a religious mind. The mind that says prayers, that repeats, repeats, repeats, is frightened at heart and blind with knowledge; therefore, it is not a religious mind. The religious mind is a mind that is learning, and therefore a mind that is never in conflict at any time, and therefore a young mind, an innocent mind. Such a mind is alone. The mind has to be completely alone because only then can it go beyond itself.

October 28, 1964

Fourth Talk in New Delhi

We were talking the other day about learning. Learning obviously implies a state of humility. But humility is not meekness; it is not a low estimation of one's own importance; it is not that "I do not know and you know, so teach me," but rather a mind that is alert and demands to know, to learn; it is not a state of acquiescence, acceptance. Humility is not a virtue. Humility cannot be cultivated—it is there, or it is not there. It is only the vain, proud people who cultivate humility—they put on a mask of humility; but they are not really, in the real sense of that word, humble.

So a mind that is learning must have this quality of not accepting, not denying, not estimating its own importance at any level, at any time; or it must have the quality of denying and really inquiring, asking, questioning, being critical—not only critical of what is being said, but also critical of oneself—critically aware, choicelessly aware of what is being said, and of oneself. Such a mind is necessary to learn. And we need to learn totally anew about our relationships because the world is undergoing an extraordinary transformation, changing rapidly, and old traditions really have no meaning at all any more. Class divisions are disappearing—except perhaps in this country where tradition is very strong, where a certain pattern established by a few people, such as saints and mahatmas and all the rest of it, is followed, but it has no meaning at all.

We must question critically, intelligently the whole problem of relationship, not only relationship with the family, but the relationship of man, between man and man as society; and that demands a mind which is critical, nonaccepting, learning. But, unfortunately, most of us are so eager to be told what to do, so happily follow someone—a political leader or a religious leader or in fact any leader—if he can tell us what to do because we do not want to inquire, learn, ask, demand; we are just satisfied to be led. And a mind that is being led, that is following authority, is incapable of learning and therefore cannot possibly understand the state of humility, which is not humbleness—that word is a dreadful word.

Humility is an energetic state of mind when it is totally aware of itself, of all its intricacies, its limitations, its conditioning, its prejudices, its shortcomings. It is only such a mind that can learn and can understand this extraordinary, complex relationship between man and man, which is called society. Society is progressive, blindly driven by dictators, by revolutions, by economic circumstances, by war, by a few leaders who are really very capable and have drive; and that society is undergoing constant change, evolving. Therefore a mind that is not capable of learning about this movement of social evolution cannot possibly comprehend this vast movement; and therefore it becomes a mind that is dull, stupid, accepting, adjusting. So a mind that is learning is always ahead of society, however much that society is evolving. That is why we have to understand this quality of humility.

What is the state of your mind as you are listening? Are you listening to words, ideas? Are you waiting to be told what to do? Or, do you have a pattern of action which, for you, is very important because it touches your immediate life—and when that pattern is questioned, you resist, you withdraw? You have to find out for yourself what is the state of your own mind, because we are going into the question of fear, and that requires an extraordinarily sharp, clear mind that is capable of learning, questioning, asking, demanding.

As we said just now, society is progressing, evolving. There are those who hinder, who go back; they go back to tradition, to all kinds of ideas which are traditional, old-fashioned—with a mind that is not contemporary, that is not ahead of society. They force society into a particular pattern because they live in ideas, in concepts, in abstractions—as the communists, as the socialists, as the people in this country. They have patterns, concepts which they try to force on people; therefore, such minds are not contemporary minds. I mean by a contemporary mind, a mind that is aware of the whole world situation, not only economically, but politically, scientifically, morally, psychologically, of the world that is torn between the East and the West, of the tremendous powers of destruction. These are facts, and one has to come to them with a fresh mind to understand, to learn—not come to them with a mind that is traditional, pattern driven.

So, before we go into this question of fear, you have to find things out for yourself as a human being—not as an individual, because individuality comes much later. Individuality comes only when you are completely human, not animalistic—with its ambition, greed, envy, hate, and all the rest of it. When the mind is free of all that, then only is it an individual mind. And in that state of mind which is individual, at that moment, something tremendous takes place, and you can go beyond that. You may pretend that you have got a soul, that you are independent, that you are the higher self and all the rest of it: they are just words that have no meaning because you are merely the result of your environment. You are being taught certain patterns of thought; you live in a particular social tribe or race or group or family, and that conditions your mind, and then you repeat that. So a mind that is awake; that is demanding, questioning; that is aware of all the things that are implied in modern existence—such a mind must have the intense quality of humility. It is not a state of underestimation of oneself, or of accepting, acquiescing, adjusting—such a mind is no mind at all. You have to think very clearly, to question very clearly, sharply—not only the speaker, but everybody, all your political, religious, economic leaders so that your mind is made sharp through learning. But that learning is denied when you follow authority.

I do not know if you have not noticed this worship of authority, in yourself and around you—particularly in countries that are old, in countries that have ancient traditions, in countries that are overpopulated. You know, the word *authority* originates, stems from the one who originates something—originates. We are not original because we do not know, or we have not realized, what it is to think clearly, independently of what Shankara, Buddha, or anyone else has said. To think clearly for oneself demands that one has no authority. But, unfortunately, in this country especially—and perhaps in other countries also—we are talking about it. We are not comparing this country with another country: that is an old trick of the politicians; when you say that this country is corrupt, the politicians say that it is better, that it is not so corrupt as the other country, and they think they have done some marvelous thing. What we are talking about is something entirely different. We are not comparing. We are seeing facts. And to see facts there must be no comparison—how can you compare? And to see facts—not intellectually—demands a great deal of affection, a great deal of sympathy, an intense sense of love, empathy. But that affection, love, is denied when you are worshiping authority.

Do consider what the speaker is saying; don't agree with it. Watch what is taking place in your own life because following authority is one of the origins of fear. We have the Gita or some other book, and that book is our authority; that authority has no meaning whatsoever in relation to contemporary existence. Because the mind is afraid to wander away from what, it thinks, is the real—the real as asserted by a certain group of people or by certain persons—it accepts. You accept authority not only spiritually, if I may use that word, but also politically, religiously, in every way. Authority is not in just one particular direction, the authority of the wife over the husband and of the husband over the wife—to dominate. We all want power, and power goes with ambition, and ambition is a form of self-expression. We all want to express ourselves; which is, we want to be somebody in this world—as a writer, as a painter, as a politician, or as a religious leader, and so on and so on. So a mind that is enslaved by authority—whether it is by the wife or by the husband or by society or by the people—a mind that worships authority cannot possibly have either affection, love, or the capacity to learn. You can follow another, and by following another you do not solve your sorrow. You might run away from your sorrow, from your despair, because he might offer a hope, and that hope might be illusory, unreal, nonfactual. Because we are so frightened of existence, we want some hope, and we invest the authority with that hope.

So a mind that would understand fear must understand authority, self-fulfillment, and the demand for power. Function gives power. That is, you are capable of doing something—capable of running a government, capable of putting machines together, capable of running a house properly, cleanly, simply—and that gives you a functional capacity. But, unfortunately, with that capacity goes status which is position, which is money. So a mind that would learn has this intense—I was going to use the words *intensively aggressive humility*. Aggressive humility is, of course, contradictory; but you understand what I mean—such a mind has the intensity of nonacquiescence because humility goes with freedom. And if there is no freedom, you cannot possibly learn. So, to understand fear, you must understand this whole psychological process of authority—which does not mean that you disobey; you have to pay taxes. To understand why you obey is important, not that you must disobey. You obey because inwardly, psychologically, inside your skin you are frightened: you might lose your job if you are not extra polite and kowtow to some big man, the manager or the dictator, the boss or your guru; or you might lose your spiritual values and so on.

Sirs, you are not listening to a lecture. This is not a harangue, a moralizing talk. We are communicating with each other. We are trying to understand this complex problem of living together, and it is a very complex problem. It needs a fresh mind every day to understand your family, your wife or husband, or your children; it needs a fresh mind to learn your job efficiently. So we are trying to understand the problems. They are your problems, and therefore you are not merely listening to words, rejecting, or accepting, or saying it is this, or having opinions. We are together looking, together understanding, together trying to explore this complex problem. So you are as active as the speaker, if not much more active.

So one has to differentiate, when one understands authority, as to why one obeys the law, why one obeys psychologically. One has also to understand function and status because through function one wants status. What we are more concerned with is not function but status. Because status gives us certain privileges, status becomes much more important than function. But if you are only regarding function—not status at all—then the cook is as important as the prime minister. They are merely doing functions, and therefore you approach the two with quite a different mind—you do not kick the cook, nor do you lick the shoes of the prime minister. You treat them as functionaries—and therefore not as machines—as human beings liable to make mistakes. But the moment you think of status, then disrespect comes in; and the moment disrespect comes in, then you are lost; then you show respect to one and disrespect to another. A mind that understands this whole complex, psychological problem of authority must go into all this because that is one of the roots of fear.

We all demand self-fulfillment, we all want to be somebody. Probably you want to be sitting here instead of me; it is there in the mind. Because we all want to be somebody, to be known, to be famous, to have our names appear in the papers, we want to express ourselves—by writing a book, by painting a picture, or through the family, through the wife, through the children, through the work. Through everything, we want to express ourselves. We never question if there is such a thing as self-expression, but we want to express. The moment you begin to question this whole problem of expression, especially of oneself, then you will see that a mind that is seeking self-expression is always in conflict, is always inviting despair and therefore always frightened and therefore resisting, aggressive. So, you have to know, you have to learn, you have to be aware of this urge to self-express. What do you want to express? What do you mean by self-expression? It essentially comes down to this: to be known by the world—which means what?—to be recognized as a big man, as somebody important, somebody who is very clever, who has attained enlightenment, and all that stuff. And we are craving everlastingly to express ourselves in little things, in big things; and therefore there is competition. Out of this competition there is ruthlessness. And we think that this ruthless capacity, efficiency, is progress. Do watch yourselves, please! You are not listening. Please watch your own life. Then you see how the more capacity, the more intelligence, the more drive you have, the more deeply, the more longingly you want to fulfill, you want to be somebody. When you want to be somebody, this desire is to self-fulfill, either in God or in an idea—for God is an idea—or in a state or in the family. What is implied in this self-expression? You want to be, and the "you" is merely an idea, an abstraction, a memory; and that is one of the great sources of fear. So there is ambition, authority, self-expression, and there is the fear of the tomorrow.

Now, what is fear? Fear cannot exist by itself. It is not an abstraction. An abstraction comes into being only when one runs away from fear into an idea, into a concept, into certain activities. Suppose one is afraid, and one's mind is incapable of facing it and seeks an escape from it; then any thought, any activity arising from that escape, from that flight from the fact of fear, breeds an abstraction, a life of contradiction; and a life of contradiction brings more fear, more conflict—all the complexities of existence. So you have to understand fear because fear breeds illusions, fear makes the mind dull. I do not know if you have not noticed, when you are frightened for various reasons, how your mind absolutely withdraws, isolates itself and looks immediately to somebody to help it out; how it builds a wall round itself through various activities, through lies, through every form of activity except facing that fact.

So, we are going to face the fact, this evening—not the speaker's fear, but your fear. How is one to understand that fear? The understanding of that fear is freedom from that fear, and we are going into that. We are going to take a journey, we are going together to commune with that thing which we call fear, because one has to see the importance of understanding fear. It is a necessity to understand it. A mind that lives in fear is a dead mind, is a dull mind; it is a mind that cannot look, see, hear clearly, directly. So, it is very important to understand one's relationships with others, with society, with everything, and to be free of fear, totally—not partially, not fragmentarily, not on various occasions, but completely. I say it is possible, and we will go into that. So, fear is not an abstraction, it is not a thing from which you can run away; it is there. Whether you run away for a day, for a year, for some time, it catches you up wherever you are, and goes with you. You may turn your eyes away from it, but it is there.

Fear exists only in relationship to something else. I am afraid of public opinion, I am afraid of my wife, I am afraid of my boss, I am afraid of losing my job, I am afraid of death, I am afraid of pain; I am not healthy, I would like to be healthy, and I am frightened of going back, of falling ill again; I am frightened because I am lonely; I am frightened because nobody loves me, nobody has a warm feeling for me; I am frightened because I have to be nobody. There are various forms of fear, conscious and unconscious. If you are at all aware—aware, not in the narrow sense, but extensively—you can see the obvious fears: of losing a job and therefore playing up to the man above you, bearing all the boredom of it, his insults, his inhumanities; being frightened of not fulfilling; being frightened of not being somebody, being frightened of going wrong. So we have innumerable fears, and consciously we can know them quite easily. If you spend half an hour consciously, deliberately, to find out your fears, outwardly at least, you can easily stop them. But it is much more difficult to find out the unconscious fears, deep down within you, which have a greater importance and which during your sleep become dreams and all the rest of it. I am not going into all that now.

So one has to understand fear. Now, fear may take different forms: I am afraid of public opinion, I am afraid of falling ill, I am afraid of losing my wife, I am afraid of being nobody, I am afraid of being lonely—do you know what that word means? Have you ever been lonely, have you ever felt what it is to be lonely? Probably not, because you are surrounded by your family, you are always thinking about your job, reading a book, listening to a radio, listening to the infinite gossip of the newspapers. So probably you never know that strange feeling of being completely isolated. You may have occasional intimations of it, but probably you have never come into contact with it directly, as you have with pain, with hunger, with sex. But if you do not understand that loneliness which is the cause of fear, then you will not understand fear and be free of it.

Fear may express itself in many forms—as it does—but there is only one fear. Fear is fear, not how it shows, not what are the mediums through which you are aware of the existence of fear. I may be afraid of public opinion, of death, of losing my job, of a thousand other things; but the fear is the same. Now, whether that fear is conscious or unconscious, one has to find out, one has to go into it. Unfortunately, we have divided life—as has been done by the latest psychologists and so on—as the conscious and the unconscious. Please listen to this: you may not be interested, and probably you have not even thought about it. You might have read about it, if you are interested in psychology, or heard somebody talk about the conscious and the unconscious and so on. But it does not play a great part in your life, as hunger does, as losing a job does, as belonging to a certain class does. So we are going into it briefly for the moment. We are not going into any detail or to explore it at great depth; one can, but we are going into it briefly.

One has divided the mind as the conscious and the unconscious. The conscious mind is the educated mind, the modern technological mind that goes to the office every day, which is bored, which is fed up with all the routine of it, the lack of love of doing something for itself. So the conscious mind becomes the mechanical mind—watch it, sirs—it can think mechanically, it can go to the office and function. It does all the things mechanically—sex, affection, being mechanically conscious of everything, being kind when it pays, kicking when it does not pay; the whole thing, the strange phenomena of modern civilization. Then there is the unconscious which is very deep, which requires great penetration, understanding. Either one can understand the whole thing—both the conscious as well as the unconscious—immediately, with one look, or you take time through analysis, through analyzing all the intimations and hints of the unconscious which arise through dreams and so on. Please follow this.

As I said, you can understand this whole structure of consciousness which is 'you', as a man or a woman, as a human being, the whole consciousness of two million years—not reincarnation—of man, who has evolved from the lowest to the present state. All that development, all that psychological structure of society can be understood immediately, and also the whole psychological structure of society with its greed, envy, ambition, despair, can be completely eliminated. Or you can analyze the whole process of consciousness, analyze it step by step. We feel—not feel, but it is so—that analysis will not free the mind. Then, what will free the mind from ambition, greed, envy, anger, jealousy, and the demand for power?—which are all animalistic. I do not know if you have watched animals. Go to a poultry yard where there are lots of chickens and observe the chickens. You will notice how one pecks the other and how they have established a social order. We also have all the animalistic instincts, consciously as well an unconsciously. And we can understand this whole psychological structure and be totally free of this animalistic, instinctual relationship of man with man, immediately—and this is the only way to do it, not through analysis.

But to understand this thing, to understand this consciousness, one has to be really free, totally, of fear. Fear is the essence of the animal. Now, to understand fear one must come directly into contact with it—that is, nonverbally. Please do take your fear. You are afraid of something: maybe of your wife, husband, children. Take it, look at it, bring it out—not suppress it, not accept it, not deny it, but take hold of it, look at it. To look at it demands a mind fully aware, not a vague, dull mind. Because when you look at fear, either you come directly into contact with it or you go off to an asylum as people do, or you know what to do with it. And we are going into it directly, nonabstractly, nonverbally so that you come directly into contact. We said there are many causes of fear, but fear is always fear. The objects of fear and their relationship with you may vary, but fear is always the same, though it expresses itself in different ways.

Now, most of us do not come into contact with fear. The moment fear shows itself in any form, we run away from it. There is the fear of death. I am not going to talk about death today, but we will do it another day if there is time. When you are afraid of death, your whole defensive psychological machinery is set going immediately; you invent beliefs, you run away from it, you have visions, you have dreams; but you avoid that thing. So the first thing to realize is that any form of escape not only perpetuates and strengthens fear but creates conflict, and therefore the mind is incapable of coming directly into contact with fear. Suppose the speaker is afraid; he has an idea, he has some hope; and that hope, that idea, that escape, becomes much more important than the fear itself because he is running away from the fact, and the running away—not the fear—creates conflict. When a man is directly in contact with something, nonverbally, nonabstractly, without escape, there is no conflict; he is there. It is only the man who has ideas, hopes, opinions, all kinds of defenses—for him there is conflict; and that conflict prevents him from coming directly into contact with fear.

Most people have fear and they have invented a network of escapes—going to the temple, the incessant activity of a restless, stupid mind—they have invented so many fears, so many escapes, and therefore their conflicts increase. So one has to be aware of it—not "How am I to escape?" or "How am I to stop from escaping?" Because the moment you understand that every form of escape from fear only creates more conflict and therefore there is no direct contact with fear, and that it is only with a direct contact with fear that you are free—when you understand that, not intellectually, not verbally, not as something you hear from somebody, but actually, for yourself when you see that—then you do not escape at all. Then the temple, the book, the leader, the round-the-corner guru—all those disappear. Then you are not ambitious.

The escape from fear can be actual—that is through radio, temple, activities. Or it can be through abstractions—that is, the word helps us to escape from fear. Please listen to this, and you will see. Fear is not an abstraction, it is not a word; but, for most of us, the word has taken the place of the fact. You see that? The word *fear,* which is an abstraction, has taken the place of the fact, which is the actual fear, and therefore you are dealing with the abstract word and not with the fact. I hope I am making myself clear. So, you have to understand fear—I mean by "understand" not verbally, not intellectually, but face it—and be completely free of it, totally, right through your being. And you can only do it when there is no escape of any kind—escape through activity, through some form of running away, or escape through the word which, for most people, takes the place of the actual fact. When you understand this, then you are directly in contact with fear. In that contact there is no time interval, there is no saying, "I will get over it" or "I will develop courage"—which is equally stupid—when you are frightened. It is like those people who are violent and everlastingly talking about nonviolence. It is too stupid because it has no validity at all. What has validity is violence, and you can deal with it; but to talk, to go round the world preaching about nonviolence is just a hypnotic, unrealistic mind. So we are dealing with facts, and we cannot deal with *what is* if there is any form of escape, conscious or unconscious.

There is physical fear. You know, when you see a snake, a wild animal, instinctively there is fear; that is a normal, healthy, natural fear. It is not fear, it is a desire to protect oneself—that is normal. But the psychological protection of oneself—that is, the desire to be always certain—breeds fear. A mind that is seeking always to be certain is a dead mind, because there is no certainty in life, there is no permanency. And because you try to establish permanency in your relationship with your wife, with your family, and all the rest of it, you have jealousy and the dreadful thing called family. When you come directly into contact with fear, there is a response of the nerves and all the rest of it. Then, when the mind is no longer escaping through words or through activity of any kind, there is no division between the observer and the thing observed as fear. It is only the mind that is escaping that separates itself from fear. But when there is a direct contact with fear, there is no observer, there is no entity that says, "I am afraid." So, the moment you are directly in contact with life, with anything, there is no division—it is this division that breeds competition, ambition, fear.

So what is important is not "how to be free of fear?" If you seek a way, a method, a system to be rid of fear, you will be everlastingly caught in fear. But if you understand fear—which can only take place when you come directly in contact with it, as you are in contact with hunger, as you are directly in contact when you are threatened with losing your job—then you do something; only then will you find that all fear ceases—we mean all fear, not fear of this kind or of that kind. Because out of the freedom and the understanding and the learning about fear comes intelligence, and intelligence is the essence of freedom. And there is no intelligence if there is any form of conflict, and conflict must exist as long as there is fear.

November 1, 1964

Fifth Talk in New Delhi

As we were saying the other day, it is really very important for a human being to come directly into contact with problems. We have many problems at all the levels of our consciousness, of our being—not only economic, social, but much deeper problems. We live with these problems, and we never seem to transcend and go beyond them. We put up with many problems and drag along as best we can, and then there is the inevitable death at the end. But a mind that lives accepting, putting up with, problems is surely a dull mind, and it is incapable of an efficient, contemporary outlook. One has to solve all the problems; one cannot live with them. Living with a problem is like living with a disease; it either destroys you or you do something about it and you get cured; and if it cannot be cured, you accept it and you do the best you can. Most of us live with problems; we have got used to them. And as the earth is divided into races, groups, nationalities, sexes, religious beliefs, so our minds are divided; and each division has its own problems. It seems to me that a mind that is incapable of solving any of the problems that it is confronted with is a mind that slowly deteriorates, a mind that goes to pieces, a mind that becomes insensitive; and that thereby its problems increase.

So, we have to solve these problems, not as an individual, but as a human being. I think there is a difference between an individual and a human being. We are collective human beings, with our peculiar tendencies, nationalities, religious beliefs, dogmas; we are still the mass. We are not individuals at all; individuality comes much later. When you break through all the conditions—all the national, religious conditions—then you become an individual. But as most people are collective in the mass, one's relationship with society becomes more and more complex, more and more demanding—demanding greater efficiency, a greater, wider outlook. Either one resolves these problems as a whole or one is destroyed. And that happens with all civilizations: when a civilization, when a group of people cannot resolve its problems, then that civilization, that group, is destroyed. These are historical facts. We, as human beings, have many problems. I mean by that phrase "human beings" the entity that is the result of many million years. That entity, that human being, has many problems; and unfortunately he has divided his problems and accepted fragmentary answers.

Please, as I have been saying in all these talks, you are not listening to a lot of words. We are trying to commune with each other, we are trying to understand the problems that each one of us has. And merely listening to a lot of words either intellectually or emotionally, or with a barrier, rejecting or accepting thoughtlessly, stops all communication. We have to commune together, we have to understand the problems that each one of us has. These problems are many, most complex, demanding a solution, demanding that you should come into contact with them and be free of them; and therefore you and I must listen to each other. You are listening to the speaker. But probably you are not listening to your own problems, because when you have a problem, your only desire is to resolve it. And you cannot resolve a single problem by itself; all problems are interrelated. Whether they are scientific problems, religious problems, psychological problems, economic or social problems, whatever the problems may be—they are all interrelated. You cannot solve any problem fragmentarily. You cannot divide your life as a scientist, as an artist, as a writer, as an economist, as a communist, as a socialist, as a capitalist, and try to solve the problems of human beings from that particular, narrow, limited point of view—that way they will never be solved. And I think this is the first thing one has to realize: However clever one is, however much one may accept the latest theory, the latest philosophy, the latest jargon, or however much one may be influenced by society, one has to solve the problems that one has, as a whole—not as a bureaucrat, not as a housewife, not as a communist or a socialist. You have to take man as a whole and resolve those problems as a whole, not separately. I think this is the most important thing to realize: that is, as we have divided the earth into the capitalist and the communist, into the Western and the Eastern bloc, as India and another country, so we have divided our problems, each division trying to solve its own problems unrelated to the whole.

So, if we are going this evening to resolve our problems—it is possible to resolve our problems totally—we will go into them. But to resolve them, you must leave your particular corner which you have so diligently cultivated, and look at the problem as a whole. And you cannot look at the problem as a whole if you do not understand the whole question of time. You know time. There is only one time by the watch, there is no other time. There is actually no tomorrow, except that thought has created tomorrow. Actually there is no tomorrow. Please be patient, I am going into it. It requires a great deal of inquiry—not merely saying, "What nonsense you are talking about! There is a tomorrow. I have to go to the office. I have to have money to buy this and do that. I have to go to a certain place tomorrow." Of course there is a tomorrow, again, chronologically, as twenty-four hours by the watch; but is there any other time? We have made time—not chronological time but psychological time—as a means of resolving our problems: "I will resolve my problem tomorrow; I will do this," and "I will do that." So thought has invented time which is unreal, and that is one of our difficulties.

Please, this requires a great deal of inquiry, not accepting or denying, because all our education, all our ways of thinking—the creation of an utopia which is to sacrifice the present for the future, the development of character, and the idea, "I will be, I will succeed, I will gain, I will become"—are all within the field of time which thought has created. And what thought has created is not real. There is only one time, that is time by the watch.

Why does the mind create this time, this time of the future, tomorrow, the next moment? Why do you say that you *will* do something tomorrow? Why do you say that you *will* give up smoking? The will—that is, "I *will* do something"—which is in time, in the future, is thought out by the mind. When you say, "I will do " or "I will try," when you say, " In the meantime"—all those indicate that you are dealing with an artificial time, but not with chronological time. So the mind invents time first as a postponement—please listen to this—as a means of postponing action. All our education is geared to the future because we are so dissatisfied with the present that we do not understand the present. The present is too complex. The present demands that you give your total attention to everything that you do, to all the thoughts, to all the feelings; it demands the care of everything that you do, the care of your word, the care of your gesture, how you talk, how you look—that demands tremendous energy, that demands great attention. But if you say, "I will be nonviolent some other day," you have nonviolence as an ideal which you practice—as is being done in this country, unfortunately—everlastingly talking about nonviolence when, in your heart, you are violent. You invent this as an idea, as a postponement, as an ideal; and in the meantime you are doing what you want to do: you are violent, you are vicious, you are angry, jealous, envious; but eventually you will get over it.

So, the mind has invented time as gradualness—"gradually I will do that"—psychologically. Suppose I have to learn something. I cannot learn it immediately. I need time. I need several days, perhaps several months—that is by the watch. But that is quite a different time from the time when I say to myself, "I will do this, I will become this, I will develop a character, I will resist, I will suppress." When I say, "I will do this," the future is in the word *will*—the active present is not. The active present is in the verb *is*. Please listen to this. Probably most of you have not thought about this at all. For some probably, it will be something strange and fantastic and unreal; something that cannot be done; therefore, it becomes an ideal, a theory. But if one realizes that there is no psychological tomorrow, no tomorrow, then thought will never say, "I will"—"I will be kind, I will be generous, I will be honest,'' or ''I will be less corrupt.'' When the mind sees clearly this whole question of time as gradation, as gradualness, as a means of gradual progress, then time becomes totally unreal; then you are faced only with the actual chronological time, and there is no other time. Then your whole action is different. The mind has to realize that there is no tomorrow, but an invented tomorrow.

You have many problems that you think you will solve by investigating, by postponing, by asking somebody what to do about it, or by the slow process of analysis—which are all the process of time. If you realize there is no time excepting the chronological time, then you are faced with solving the problem immediately, not postponing it. Sirs, when you have a problem of hunger or a problem of lust—those are very demanding problems—you do not say, ''I will eat tomorrow, I will satisfy my sexual appetite another day,'' because they are very urgent, they demand immediate action. But we, human beings, have invented this time as a means of postponing, as a means of not coming directly into contact with the problem, as a means of evasion.

Look at yourselves, please. Again, let me repeat. To learn you must have a mind that is curious, a mind that demands, questions critically, does not accept or deny. It is an inquiring mind, a mind that has no authority—neither the authority of the government, nor of Moscow, nor of any country in the world, nor of your own guru. It is learning, inquiring, searching, asking—and that is the only way you learn. And you learn only when you deny everything and begin—for most of us, that is very difficult; we would rather live in the muddy, thoughtless, repetitive world, creating many problems and dying with these problems.

So, one has to understand deeply the question of time. That is, one has to live so completely in the present that the mind does not think about the future, because there is no future except what the mind invents. Now to live so completely in the present is one of the most difficult things; it is not accepting the present and just living from day to day in a sloppy, ineffectual, emotional state—a state which does not regard the future or which is not concerned with what is going to happen. Most people, out of their despair, out of their misery, try to push all that away and just live from day to day—that is not living in the present. To live in the present implies that the mind is not thinking of tomorrow at all because it has understood the whole process of time. You cannot live in the present—which demands tremendous energy, great attention—if your mind is conditioned as a Hindu, as a Sikh, or as a Muslim—you know all the stupid divisions that man has made. So one has to be free of all that, to live very ardently, completely in the present. Then time has quite a different significance; time is death.

We are going to talk about death in relation to time, and we are going to talk about death in relation to love. But if you do not understand this whole process of time, you will not come into contact with and therefore understand the whole problem of death. And if you do not understand this extraordinary thing called death, you will not understand what love is. So time, death, and love are interrelated. Naturally one has not the time to go in detail over this question of time. If you had no time as tomorrow, then you would be confronted with your particular problem, you would be intimately in contact with that problem. There is no question of postponing that problem. You have no time for analysis. It must be solved immediately. And it is possible to solve any problem immediately if the mind is not involved in time.

Look! There is a gentleman over there who is wriggling his leg, and he is unaware. If you say, ''Look, watch what you are doing,'' he will stop it for the moment because his attention is drawn to that, and at that moment he is there completely. But a few minutes later, he will forget and begin again the nervous reaction—which means that he has not understood the habit, habit as time.

So, time is the product of thought; time is the result of our desire to do things gradually, psychologically, inwardly to do, to bring about a change, a transformation, gradually, because we are frightened. We are frightened to do something immediately because we do not know what the future is going to be. If we did certain things, we would not know what would happen; therefore, we want to take everything into consideration—the future, the yesterday, the tomorrow—and in the meantime the problems multiply. Whereas, if you had no tomorrow at all, tomorrow being the memory which responds as thought, and if you had understood the whole structure of memory, then you will see that time is a hindrance to immediate action.

Sirs, I see you are all rather puzzled, but that does not matter. Anyhow just listen to this because this requires a great deal of attention, not enlightenment. You know what attention means? To attend, to give your whole being, your whole thought, your whole nerves and everything, at a given moment; in that state there is complete attention, and then every problem, even the smallest problem, ceases. You have to give your attention completely, let us say, to smoking or to your particular habit, sexual or otherwise; and you can only give your complete attention to it if there is no hindrance as "I will do it tomorrow" or "What will be the outcome of it? It must satisfy me" and all the rest of the memories, the responses of memory.

To understand death, you must come into contact with death. Please listen. For most of us, death is something to be avoided; for most of us, death is something far away—at least it may come tomorrow or in ten years' time—it is something in the distance. We do not want it near; therefore, we are frightened to come into contact with that strange thing called death. And because we are frightened, we invent theories: resurrection, reincarnation, hope, and all the rest of it. Because we are actually frightened, thought has made death as something far away, to be avoided; and to escape from it is to have beliefs, dogmas, ideas. To understand death, we must understand life—the two are not separate. Do please listen to this. If you go into it, this thing called death is one of the most extraordinary things in life; and if you do not understand it, you do not understand living. The two are interrelated, they are not two separate events, because if we do not understand living, we do not understand death.

What is your living, actually? Not theoretically, not ideologically, not something which you try to cover up, but actually, daily, every minute of your life, what is it? Have you considered it at all? Caught up in a career, going to the office every day, being insulted, the inhuman indignities, the miseries, the despair, the jealousies, the uncertainties, never being free of anything, but always carrying burdens, always afraid, always competing, being terribly ambitious about nothing at all, being very clever and cunning, being hypocritical, saying something which you do not mean at all, playing along because you cannot get power or position—this is what we call life. A life of confusion, conflict, and misery, a life of deep sorrow, anxiety, despair; and out of that despair, philosophies, hopes—that is our life. And we want to carry that life beyond death. This is what we know, and the other we do not know. We do not know really what is death, but we are frightened of it; therefore, we say, "The misery, the conflict, the travail that I live in—that is good enough." That is you with your stupidities, with your problems, with the person whom you think you love. And unfortunately, you do not know what that word *love* means at all. All that you mean is the person, the family with whom you have lived, with whom you have done things, your companionship, your sexual appetite—all that is identified, and that is all you know, and that is what you call life.

So, we do not understand life. Life is something to be lived, something to be enjoyed—enjoyed, not in terms of pleasure and pain. Life is something that demands complete attention to be lived from moment to moment, not in misery, not in conflict, not in sorrow and despair—to be lived. And you can only live completely in the present when you have no future, when you have no time. You do not understand living because none of you have solved your problems of aching misery, your loneliness, your agonies, your despair. You have not solved your problems; they are there. You may hide them and you may run away from them. You may become a communist working in the service of mankind—which is all nonsense. But in your heart you have not solved a thing, and if you have not solved living, you will not have solved death. You may run away from it, you may have innumerable beliefs, comforts; or you may rationalize death away saying that it is inevitable, that death is part of existence, just as conflict is part of existence. Because we have divided life into living and dying, we understand neither this nor that.

To understand anything, to understand yourself, or to understand the speaker, you must come intimately into contact; you must have no barriers, no fears, no speculative, theological ideas. You must come directly into contact. Do you know what it means to come directly into contact with something? Perhaps you know coming directly into contact sexually and nothing else. You are never in contact with life, with this tremendous movement, with this tremendous change, revolution, mutation that is going on. You are not even in contact with your own agony because you have ideas about it—that it should not be, that it should be, and so on. So, not understanding life which is part of dying, you do not understand death.

What is death? You know what it is to die? The physical organism, because of the many diseases, strains, and stresses and the psychosomatic diseases that exist—the body, the organism, wears out. They may invent a pill, a drug that will give another fifty years more, to lead a sordid, anxious, miserable life. At the end of it, the organism wears itself down through disease, through accidents, through old age. We realize that, and so we say, "I am frightened of it," or "I will live the next life"; our main concern is whether reincarnation is true or false, but not to come directly into contact with the thing called death and understand it.

Now, if you will, please follow the speaker, not in any authoritative sense of that word; do not merely accept or deny what he is saying, but give your full attention. You can only give your full attention if you are really demanding to know what it is to die. If you do not know how to die, you do not know how to live. To die implies the ending of everything as you know it. What you know is memory, is it not? Your pleasures, your pains, your anxiety, your aches, your loneliness, the flatteries, the insults—everything is memory stored up. That is the center from which you function, that is the center from which you act—memory.

Now, you have to die to that memory, to die to your vanity—not argue about your vanity, not find explanations why you should not compete, or why you should compete, or why you should not be ambitious. If you are not ambitious in this world, you are destroyed—this is an argument to support your particular drive of ambition. But you cannot argue with death. It is there; you cannot tell it, "Come another day." So, you have to come to death directly, with tremendous energy, not with just negligent, careless, thoughtless acceptance. But to come to it with tremendous vigor, you need a clear, healthy mind, a sane, rational mind, a mind that is a good mind, not a mind that is beaten, broken. And you can come to death intimately only when you die to the memory of your pleasure, immediately, not to something which you do not like—that, most people can die to—but to something that you love, that you like. Then you will find that the mind is no longer occupied with memory or with cultivating memory, because then memory ceases as time; you may use memory, but it ceases as a means to achieve in the field of time.

So, one has to die to everything, every day, to all relationship. You think it out and see what is implied in it. If you do not die to your relationship, whether it is your wife or your children or your boss, then you merely continue a habit; and a habit dulls the mind, makes the mind insensitive, uncreative. And therefore you are always frightened of death because death is something unknowable. You cannot capture it by the mind, by thought. You cannot capture love by thought, nor can you cultivate love by thought. You can understand love and know what it means to love only when you die to jealousy, to envy, to the narrow field of the family, when thought does not dictate the actions of life. When you love, then you can do anything you want to do because life has no conflict.

A mind that is ambitious, greedy, envious, seeking authority—such a mind has no love, though it may talk a great deal, like all the politicians, like all the gurus—they everlastingly talk about love; but their hearts are empty because they are full of conflict, full of burning desire; they have never a moment when everything in them is dead and when the mind is completely empty. Only when the mind is completely empty is it possible to know or to understand that extraordinary thing called love. When you say, "I love my husband, my child," you do not love; because if your husband turns away or the wife turns away from you, you are jealous, you are angry, you are bitter—and that is what you call love. Love has no attachment. Therefore love is not for the family.

So, to understand this extraordinary flame called love, there must be the understanding of time. And to know what love is, there must be death—death to everything that you have accumulated—otherwise, you will not have a fresh mind. You must have a fresh mind, a young mind, an innocent mind, because the world is moving very fast, and you cannot understand it if you do not come to it with a fresh, young, innocent mind. If you come as a Sikh, as a Hindu, or as a Catholic, or with all the stupid stuff that one carries about with one, how can you understand this extraordinary thing called life which is so vast? To understand the immensity of it, you must die, every day, to everything that you know. Then out of that comes intimacy with death. Then there is no fear. When there is no fear of any kind, then there is love. Then love is not divided as mundane and spiritual; there is only love. And if you have not loved, do what you will, you will not solve the problems of the world, nor your own problems.

Love implies care—care of your children that they have the right education, the right food, right clothing; the care of your servants, if you have servants. But in this country nobody cares; they are full of ideas, speculations, ideals; they will discuss endlessly what love should be, quote innumerable books, but they do not know what it means to love. Love means care, and you cannot care if you are competing, if you are comparing, if you are educating through competition. Therefore, there can only be love when there is this extraordinary sense of care for what you are doing—what you are doing in the office, because the office is not different from your life. It is a miserable office, but it is your life; you cannot shut it away. You spend forty years of your life in that office, but you have to care for it—what you do, how you think, how you are, how you order.

If you do not know what love is, then you will die a miserable human being, not knowing that immensity which we call life. And in the knowing of that fullness of life, there is the fullness of the unknown. And it is only the mind that has seen the significance of time, death, and love—because they are all interrelated—only such a mind can explode into the unknown.

November 5, 1964

Sixth Talk in New Delhi

We would like this evening to talk about something that is as important to understand as time, death, and love which we were talking about the other day. It is necessary to understand it, because in the understanding of what meditation is, we shall also be able to understand the very complex problem of living. Meditation is not something away from living. To understand the content, the significance, the beauty, and the great depth of living—with its sorrows, with its anxieties and fears—one must understand equally the very complex problem or question of what is meditation.

To go into it rather deeply, if one can, in this hour, one must first of all be very clear that we are not laying down any system, any method, any practice, but the very act of exploring, of understanding meditation is meditation. Therefore, one must first be very clear for oneself as to what is not meditation and what is meditation. The two things are distinctly apart: what is and what is not. First we would like to go into what is not meditation, and by the very denial of what is not meditation, we will begin to discover what is meditation.

Now, when we use the phrase *to deny,* we mean by that phrase not an intellectual denial of words but rather the denial of what, one thinks, is the right way of meditation, the denial of all the systems, methods, the petty, little things that the mind invents in the hope of capturing that which is something mysterious. And to deny, you require not only reason, analysis, sanity, but above all intelligence—and all this requires energy. You cannot deny anything merely verbally; then it has no meaning in life. It does not touch the depth of one's being if you casually, sporadically, deny now and then. But if you see the significance of something totally and then, in the understanding of that totality, deny that, then it is out of your system so that you can turn your energy, your face, in a totally different direction. That is what we are going to do this evening.

We are together going to meditate; we are together going to explore what this extraordinary living is—which has very little significance, and therefore man seeks a goal, a purpose for living. We are together trying to find out for ourselves what is the true significance, what is the depth and the beauty and the glory of living. And to do that, one must go into it with a clear mind.

So, first of all we must be very critical, not accept a thing, even one's own experience. Because we are so gullible, we want to believe, we want to accept, we want to be led; and because our own life is so uncertain, so confused, so petty, we hope that some guru, some method—however ancient it be—will help us somehow to get beyond this conflict, this sorrow, and this misery. And so we accept very easily, especially the religious person, the sannyasi, the guru, who gives some kind of method to meditate upon—and that very religious person must be doubted.

You cannot, if you are intelligent, awake, sane, accept any religious person including myself. Because we are so afraid of everything in life—our job, death, the uncertainties, not to do the right thing, not to reach whatever we call God and that mysterious thing that man has sought through the centuries to discover—because our lives are very small, very petty, shallow, and because our minds are also shallow, petty, infantile, we rather accept somebody who says, "I know, you do not; follow me." We do not use our reason, our common sense; and so we remain petty, we remain shallow.

But if you begin to question, doubt, demand, be ruthless with yourself and with the person who gives you a method, if you question that very method, then you are in a position of real inquiry. Unless you inquire very deeply within yourself, you cannot possibly find what is true. Nobody can lead you to it—nobody and therefore no system. Truth is not something that is static, that waits for you through a regular system, through a method which you practice day after day, until you polish your mind, your heart, to arrive at a certain state which you call truth. Truth does not wait for you.

So, one has to see that any method—by whomsoever it is established; by Shankara, Buddha, it does not matter who it is—makes the mind only more petty. Because it practices, day after day, a certain system, the mind becomes mechanical. When it practices something over and over again, it is like those people who do puja every day, endlessly repeating words, words, words, without much meaning; and their puja, their meditation, has nothing whatsoever to do with living. They cheat, they are ambitious, they are greedy, they are full of hate, envy; but they go to their corner in their house and meditate and carry on their daily life of deception. So, such a mind which is already petty, which is already shallow, which is already cheating itself and its neighbor—such a mind, however much it may practice a method hoping to realize its petty gods, will never discover what is true; and therefore they remain everlastingly, day after day, in misery, in sorrow, in a state of utter confusion. So, one has to see very clearly for oneself the utter futility of the mechanical habit, of following a method.

Please, we are investigating this thing together. You are not accepting my word. You are not substituting the speaker for another guru—that would be disastrous. But we are together in communion, to discover what is true, to discover for ourselves the quality of the mind that is in a state of meditation—the quality of the mind, not how to meditate.

As we said, a method, however well established and seasoned in tradition, cannot possibly lead man to anything but to a mechanical result. You can see, you can practice something daily; but it will not free the mind from the ache and the loneliness and the agony of life. We have to understand that, not some spurious god invented by man. All gods are the inventions of man because truth is not to be described; the unknown cannot be put into words; the nameless cannot be named—the mind must come to it unknowingly, innocently, fresh, uncontaminated.

So a method, the repetition of words endlessly repeated, cannot lead one to truth. Nor can prayers, which are merely supplication. You pray because you want happiness, you want pleasure, you want something. Peace on earth you want, and so you pray. You cannot have peace on earth if you pray. What brings peace on earth is that you be peaceful. God is not going to give you peace; you have to be peaceful—that means no competition, no hate, no violence, no divisions of nationalities, not a Muslim and a Hindu and a Sikh and Parsi and a Chinese, a Russian and an

American. You have to be peaceful; then you will have peace on earth.

When in your heart, in your mind, you are peaceful, then you do not pray, then you do not want the help of anybody. So, the prayers of churches and of the leaders and of the saints, which are merely exploiting the people, have no meaning at all, have no validity. Prayers may bring about a certain result, a mechanical result. There are people who pray, not for God or for peace, but for things they want. They want refrigerators, they want houses, prosperity, they want money, they want to pass examinations. And what is the difference between these people and those people who pray for heaven, for peace? There is no difference.

So, one must understand the whole significance of prayer. The man who prays for a refrigerator gets it because he has put all his mind, all his energy on something he wants, something outside of himself. But peace is not outside of yourself. You have to create it, you have to bring it about; you have to cease to be a national. Please, we are communicating with each other; you are not just listening to me. If you want peace, you have to cease to be a Sikh, a Muslim, a Parsi; you have to work for peace. And prayer is an escape.

So methods—the repetition of words, prayers—do not lead man to truth because they are all self-centered processes serving self-interest. And a petty mind praying, asking, soliciting, repeating words cannot possibly find that which is beyond words. You and I this evening are talking about this; we are putting all that aside, not verbally, not intellectually, but actually, because this is the truth—not because the speaker says so, but because it is a fact. And when you see something clearly as a fact, you push it aside; it has no meaning anymore.

The various postures that one takes in so-called meditation, breathing rightly, sitting correctly, and all the rest of those superficial phenomena somewhat help to quieten the body. Naturally, if you breathe regularly, quietly, the physical organism becomes quiet; but the mind is still shallow. You cannot make the mind extensive, wide, deep, healthy, sane, vital, clear, through breathing. You can do it for ten thousand years, and you will still have a petty mind. So, one has to push that also aside.

Then there are all the new drugs that are being tried in America and in Europe: mescaline, LSD 25, and so on. People take them in order to have an extraordinary experience of the real; they think that by taking a pill they can go to nirvana. What these drugs actually do, not that we have tried them is—they make the whole system very sensitive, highly acute for the moment; then the mind is very alert, very sensitive, sharp, clear; it sees things much more vitally; a flower then becomes much more beautiful. But it depends on the person who takes them. If he is already slightly artistic, slightly philosophical, slightly superstitiously religious, he will have his own experience; and that of course gives him an extraordinary sense that he has realized something mysterious. You know, if you take an alcoholic drink, it helps you to break down your inhibitions, and you feel for the moment extraordinarily free to talk easily, cleverly. But the drinker, the person who takes drugs of any kind is no nearer. Perhaps the sinner, the man who does not take drugs, does not follow gurus, does not sit in a posture thinking, meditating, mesmerizing himself—the man whom you call a sinner is probably much nearer because he does not pretend; he knows what he is.

So, none of these systems, prayers, the repetition of words, images, breathing, drugs—none of these will help because your mind is still shallow. So that is the first thing to realize: that a petty mind, a shallow mind, a confused mind—do what it will, trying to escape from itself—will never find the unnameable. So realizing that, one comes back to oneself.

Now, that is what we are going to do, you and I, this evening—not theoretically but actually. You and I are going to face each other, look at ourselves, ruthlessly; and out of this looking at the fact of ourselves—which requires a certain awareness, into which we are going presently—into discovering for ourselves actually what we are, the fact, the *what is,* not what we 'should be', which is just imagination. Then from there we can proceed. And we must do this together.

You are not just listening to me, but we are learning together. To learn, you cannot be confused with systems, methods, prayers, beliefs, and all the rest of it. You must put all those aside, and that is going to be very difficult for most people because they want to believe. The believing mind is the most shoddy mind, is the most stupid mind. You will believe, and what you believe you will experience, naturally.

So, we must understand this whole process of experiencing, into which we are going now. For most of us, daily living is unexciting; there is very little meaning. Going to the office daily, the routine of it, the boredom of it, the little sex that one has, the innumerable problems of anxiety, of fear, of misery, of occasional joy—all that becomes our routine, our life. We want to escape from that; because that is so small, we want different sensations, different experiences, different visions. So we look for something else. So we want greater experiences. Please follow the psychology of this, the reason for this, the sanity of what is being said. So we want wider, deeper, fuller experiences; and we experience according to our background, to our conditioning.

When we talk about experience, we mean the reaction to a challenge, the response to a challenge of society, of a social economy, and all the rest of it—the response to a challenge. And that response to a challenge is experience, and that response is the result of your conditioning as a Hindu, as a Buddhist, as a communist, as a technician, as this or that. That is your background, your temperament, your state of mind; and from that you react, you respond to whatever the challenge is; and that is experience. So, according to your background, according to your conditioning, according to your temperament, according to your emotions, you project; and the projection becomes your experience. And so we are caught in endless experiences, the experiences which are the result of one's own projections, depending upon the challenges which one receives. We will not go into it in very great detail, but you can grasp it quickly if you are at all listening, if you are at all learning.

So, a mind that seeks experiences—follow this, please—is merely escaping from the fact of what it is. So, one has to be tremendously awake not to demand any experience at all. You see what we are doing? We are stripping the mind of everything that is false, we are stripping the mind of beliefs in gods, in priests, in puja, in repetition of prayers, and even of the demand for super-experiences—experiences beyond the senses. We are saying this not illogically, but logically, sanely. There is reason behind what is being said; it is not a fancy, a whim. So, if you are following what is being said nonauthoritatively, then you will see that your own mind is now swept of all the burdens which society, which religions have put upon it; then you are confronted with yourself.

Now, to understand oneself is absolutely necessary. Meditation is the emptying of the mind, and in the emptiness there is explosion into the unknown. A mind that is full, a mind that is burdened with problems, a mind in conflict, a mind that has not explored into the depths of itself, cannot empty itself. And meditation is the emptying of the mind, not eventually, but immediately, out of time.

Now we are going to inquire into the state of the mind that learns about itself. Because if you do not learn about yourself, you have no basis for any inquiry or for any further exploration; if you do not learn about yourself, you are merely deceiving yourself, hypnotizing yourself into all kinds of beliefs, dogmas, prayers, meditative visions. So you must learn about yourself—that is absolutely the foundation. You can learn about yourself on the instant, completely; and that is the only way to learn about yourself, not through a process of analysis or of introspective inquiry—all that takes time. And as we said the other day, there is no tomorrow, there is no next instant; there is only the present, only the now which is tremendously active; and to understand that, you have to put away from your mind this whole question of gradual understanding.

Now, to learn about oneself, there must be a certain awareness. We are not giving any mystical significance to awareness. It is just common, daily awareness: to be aware of the colors, the trees, the dirt, the squalor; to be aware of your wife and your children; to be aware is to watch, to look, to observe what they are, what clothes they have put on, how they talk. Just to be aware—do you know what I mean by that word? When you enter the tent, to be aware of the colors. Please just listen to this. It is a very simple thing: to be aware of the colors, to be aware of the various people sitting, how they are sitting, whether they are yawning, sleepy, tired, forcing themselves to listen, hoping thereby they will get something, the nervous twitches they are going through.

To be aware, not condemning, not judging, just to observe choicelessly, to look without any condemnation, interpretation, comparison—there is great beauty in that, there is great clarity in observation. If you observe yourself in that way, choicelessly, then in that awareness there is attention, there is no entity as the observer and the observed. There is no watcher, looking at the thing which he is watching.

Now, one has to differentiate between concentration and attention. Concentration is a process of effort, exclusion, suppression, forcing all your thought, all your energy in one particular channel for a given moment, excluding every other thought, every other so-called distraction. This concentration most of you practice in your office and when you try so-called meditation. You are brought up from your college days to concentrate, to give or focus your attention on a particular thing: the work you are doing, the page that you are reading. But all the time, other thoughts arise, other impressions come in which you are trying to resist. So concentration is a process of exclusion and attention is not.

To be attentive implies that there is no distraction. When you are attentive, you take in the whole, not the part; you see all the people, the color, the light, the shape of their heads. You are aware and therefore attentive. In that attention, there is neither the observer nor the observed, because there your whole being, your mind, your body, your nerves, your ears, your eyes—everything is attentive; therefore, there is no division. In that state of attention there is an observation of oneself. Therefore, there is no condemnation of oneself. Therefore you are learning. You cannot learn if you condemn. You cannot learn if you compare. You cannot learn if you say, "I will be that tomorrow."

So, a mind that is attentive is in a state of noncontradiction and therefore in a state of no effort at all. And that is absolutely necessary; otherwise, if that is not possible, the mind cannot be emptied—you will see why it is necessary. Most minds are noisy. They are everlastingly chattering. They are everlastingly soliloquizing, or repeating—what it will do, what it has done, what it must do, and so on. It is never quiet. And you think that to produce this quietness in the mind, you must practice some method—which again becomes mechanical.

But if you are aware of every thought as it arises, not judging, not condemning, not accepting—but just being attentive—then you will see that the mind becomes extraordinarily quiet; you have not disciplined it to be quiet—which is a deadly thing. Because if you discipline the mind, the mind becomes shallow, empty, dead. The mind must be free, alive, full, vital.

If you are attentive, out of that attention there comes its own unsolicited, nonrepressive discipline. It is only the mind that is so disciplined through attention, not through compulsion and conformity—it is only such a mind that is clear. Then the mind which is attentive has learned, through attention about itself, its conscious and unconscious motives, fancies, illusions, fears, ambitions, greed, jealousy, competition, and all the rest of the things which we are; when the mind through awareness has learned about itself, then the mind becomes quiet, not disciplined, not drugged, not mesmerizing itself. Such a quiet mind is a still mind. It must be still because otherwise it is not empty.

The mind in all of us is the result of two million years of time. It is conditioned, it is shaped; it is under the compulsion of many impressions, under great strain, conscious as well as unconscious; it is driven by circumstances. So, such a mind, if it is not completely still—still, not demanding, not seeking—it is not empty.

You know, anything new can only take place in emptiness. A new child is conceived in the emptiness of the womb. So, the mind has to be empty, not made empty by restraining thought, controlling thought, suppressing thought—that is not emptiness; that is merely another form of escape from reality. And the reality is yourself, actually what you are, not the super-atma which is an invention of your grandmothers and fathers and Shankaras and Buddhas. All that must go for the mind to be completely empty and still.

Then, in that emptiness, there is a movement which is creation. In that emptiness, there is the energy which the mind needs to go to the ultimate. And this whole process from the beginning of denial to the very end—which is not an escape from life but the very understanding of that life—is meditation. And then you will find that you are meditating all day long, not just one minute of the day; you are meditating wherever you are, in your office, in the bus. Then you are directly in contact with life. You are meditating while you are talking because you are aware, you are attentive to what you are saying, how you are saying it, how you talk to your servant—if you have a servant. You are aware, you are attentive; therefore, the mind which is limited, narrow, petty, shackled by time, breaks through. And it is only such a mind that can find the everlasting.

And that is the beauty of meditation. In that, there is no compulsion of any kind, no effort. And a man who can meditate, a man who has understood what meditation is—he alone can help, and none other.

November 8, 1964

Seventh Talk in New Delhi

We would like this evening to talk about what is a religious life and what is a religious mind—not that they are two separate things. To find out what is a religious life, one has to wander, explore rather extensively. And it seems to me that as our life is so fragmentary, so broken up into departments, into various forms of escapes and activities, unless one finds a central, all-covering activity, we shall not be able to live a coordinated life with passion, with intensity, and with clarity.

To find out what is a really, truly religious life, one has to be totally discontented. And that is one of our great difficulties—to be totally, completely discontented—because we are so easily satisfied with a particular theory or a particular answer that satisfies a problem that can easily be resolved, because we think by following a particular, political or economic pattern we have somewhat satisfied this discontent that most of us have. To sustain this discontent and not to find an easy answer is difficult because most of us want an easy answer, a pill, a tranquilizer to put us to sleep, to guarantee us a certain way of life. We have to be very attentive and watchful, not to accept any form or theory or pattern or concept that will momentarily, or even for many years, satisfy us.

So, the first demand, it seems to me, is to be discontented; and it is one of the most painful things in life to be discontented and not to be easily satisfied. You know, it is very easy to pile up words, listen to many talks, read innumerable books, and we think we have thereby understood something. Probably most of you who have attended these meetings will think you have got something, a little bit here and patches there. I am afraid you will not have completely understood what has been said or what is going to be said if you take a particular field which appeals to you in these talks and are satisfied with the particular answer. We are concerned with the total answer, not with a particular answer. We are concerned with the total comprehension of life, not with a particular comprehension of a particular part of life. So we have to take the whole of it or none of it because what has been said and what is going to be said are related and not fragmentary.

So, to find out what is a religious mind is very important because religion is the only factor that can cover the whole of existence and not fragmentary existence; the whole of our life can be contained in the inquiry and the understanding of what is a religious life. Because religion is not the thing that we know as religion, which is all spurious and sheer unadulterated nonsense. The real inquiry into what is a religious life is necessary because without understanding what is a religious life and living it actually, not theoretically, we shall not be able to solve the many increasing and conflicting problems.

For me the religious life is the key which opens the door to all our problems, and therefore we have to understand it. It is imperative—at least I feel it is imperative—that for human beings who have lived for so long, who have not solved their problems, who are still living in fragments with despair, with anxiety, with no love, broken up, unrelated—for them to bring about a harmonious cohesion in all their activities, in all their thoughts, it is imperative that they understand what is a religious life. And to understand what is a religious life, one must be discontented.

Most of us are discontented because we have not got a good job, we are not so intelligent as somebody else, we do not look so beautiful as that woman next door, we have not got a big car, a better house, a better job, or we have not fulfilled ourselves. And the moment we have a better house, a better car, a better refrigerator, we are satisfied, at least temporarily until a still better refrigerator is invented. So we are discontented with little things and we are so terribly satisfied with little things. One has to be extremely aware of the superficial gratification with petty things, petty answers, quoting innumerable so-called religious teachers. We think we have understood when we quote the Gita, the Koran, or the Bible, or some other book; we think we have captured some spirit of the religious life—which again is utter nonsense. So we must be extremely alert not to be caught in superficial actions, and to remain in and to contain a total discontent with everything—with politics, with religion, with socialists and communists, with any political party. We must be totally discontented; then only can we begin to inquire.

I hope that, this evening at least, you and I are in that state of mind that is not easily gratified, that is capable of intense passion; because it is only when a mind is discontented totally—there is passion, there is intensity. And you need this intensity, the energy of passion to find out what is a religious life. Otherwise, we remain petty, narrow, limited, functioning with a mind that is secondhand and therefore inefficient, never knowing something original. So, this total discontent gives this passion, because real passion has no motive. It is not urged by something objectively or subjectively. It is only when you are completely dissatisfied with everything—with your relationships, with your wife, with yourselves, with society, with every form of escape that you have been offered or that you have invented for yourself—that you have this extraordinary energy; and you need this energy.

To find out what is a religious life is not to find out the pattern of a religious life—what to do, what to wear, what to think and how to control, to be a bachelor, and all that stupid stuff—but to have this energy without a motive, without a direction; and that comes only when there is this deep, unresolved, unsatisfiable discontent. When that is clear—I hope we are communicating or communing with each other nonverbally—if we are in a state of communion with each other, then we can begin to inquire into what is not a religious life; because, you know, the highest form of thinking is negative thinking. When you begin to discard so that your mind is not cluttered up with the so-called positive assertions of so many teachers, of your priests, of politicians, or your gurus, or with what you have read, only then does the mind discern, see clearly the truth in the false—which is negative thinking. Then out of that negative process of looking, observing, attention, you will find out what is true.

Therefore, to find out what is true in the false is the origin of discontent—not only in what the speaker is saying, but in everything, in what every politician says, in what your gurus, your books, your party leaders say—to see what is false and also to see the truth in the false, and to see the truth as true. This can only come about when the mind is in that state of negation and therefore has the capacity to discern, to look, to observe, to see. And that is what we are going to do this evening together—so that our mind is made free to observe, so that it is not cluttered up with innumerable ideas, formulas, concepts. After all, a savage, a very primitive man is so frightened about every little thing: he is frightened of the winds, the stars, the sky, the beauty of a tree at night, thunder. And we too, the so-called sophisticated, educated people, are frightened, and our minds are cluttered up with so many things.

So, to think negatively is the beginning of intelligence. And you need this intelligence to inquire into what is true and what is false in the things which man has learned from childhood as religion, as dogma, as belief, whether it is the belief of the communist with his priests, with his gods—Marx, Lenin, Trotsky and the whole lot of them—or of others with their gods. You need this intelligence to question, to inquire, to find out what is true for yourself, not to be told what is true by another—then you remain a secondhand entity suffering, anxious, constantly in conflict.

So we are going together to commune over the things that are called religion. I am not attacking religion. So you don't have to defend it. I am not attacking you, or asking you to be convinced of something else; but together we are going to examine the mind that gives life a religious significance.

First of all, any belief in any pattern of life, whether it is the communist pattern, the socialist pattern, or the religious pattern, impedes the mind from clear perception. You have innumerable beliefs, obviously, because you are a Hindu, a Sikh, a Muslim, or God knows what else, and you live or try to live along a certain pattern of that belief. If you are a communist, you have certain ideas, certain concepts, and they become the pattern of your existence, and therefore your mind is never free to inquire, to look, to observe, to be passionate. We have beliefs because we are frightened. You believe in God, or you believe in Marx, or you believe in somebody else because you are frightened of existence, of life. Please observe yourself, don't listen to my words only. Please observe the innumerable beliefs that you have and discover for yourself the origin of those beliefs. And you will find that at the root of your beliefs there is fear, despair, the desire to escape from the daily monotony, the daily loneliness, the insufferable insufficiency of existence—it is because of these that we have beliefs, dogmas, rituals, pujas, banners, nationalities.

So a mind that is religious has no belief. It is only concerned with facts and not with beliefs or opinions about the facts. You know, life becomes very simple when you deal with facts, with what is in yourself and outside. When you have no opinions, projections, prejudices, conclusions about the fact, then you can deal with the facts sanely, rationally and with capacity. But if you approach a fact with a lot of opinions, conclusions, what people have said and so on, you approach that fact with confusion, and therefore you never understand that fact. So a mind that is inquiring into the religious life finds that it has no belief, but only facts. The moment you discover that for yourself, you have the energy of freedom, and you can deal unemotionally, without any sentiment, with the fact. But the moment you have sentiment, emotion about the fact, then you are completely lost.

So, that is the first thing to realize—that a mind that is religious has no belief of any kind, at any time; then it is facing facts from moment to moment, and those facts change. Therefore, the mind has to be tremendously alert to move with the fact. When there is no position which you take about the fact, you are always in a state of inquiry and therefore in a state of tremendous discontent. And you will see, in inquiring about the fact, that all religions are based on belief. You believe in God, you believe in salvation, you believe in Jesus, you believe in this and that; and round that belief you can organize.

I do not know if you have ever thought about what is true cooperation. You know, one cannot live in this world if there is no cooperation—one can live in conflict, not as a total human being who willingly cooperates. And when one is capable of real cooperation, he is also capable of not cooperating. For most of us cooperation is based on the compulsion of authority—compelled by reward or punishment—or on what one is going to gain out of it; or circumstances force one to do this, and so one cooperates. Please observe yourself and you will see that what we are talking about is a fact, not an opinion given to you by the speaker. We cooperate round an idea—as the communist idea, or the religious idea, or the idea of nationalism—and we call that cooperation. But true cooperation has no authority; it is not based on reward or punishment; it is based on the realization of the fact, and not on theory.

So all religions are man-made, organized by the priests because they want to give some kind of hope to man, because man's life is utter misery. His life is transient, he lives in agony; and so man invents the priest and the god, and it is organized, as it is in the West. Whether it is the organization of the church called Christian or it is the organization of the church called communism, both the organizations are exactly the same. Because, the one is well organized, well established with the tremendous authority of tradition, property and status, and so on, and offers an escape from life through rituals through dogma, through belief; and the other hopes for utopia, the perfect state.

So, when you see this, see the fact—not that there is God or that there is no God, but the fact—that you want to escape from life, when you realize this, then you do not belong to any religion; you are no longer a Hindu, a Buddhist, a Christian, a Muslim, a communist, or whatever it is, you are no longer caught in the net of beliefs. So you begin to see what is true in the false, the false being what man has created through centuries upon centuries as the religious pattern or the social pattern or the pattern of the family. And when you see that fact, then you are free from all the religious concepts of life—which does not mean that you become a materialist, which you are. What you are really concerned with in life is money, possession, sex, and the enjoyment of a few things; and over that you cover up, you put a lot of words as the spiritual life and all the rest of it.

So, seeing the fact is the beginning of a religious life—not the fact as you want it, not the fact as you hope that it will be: for example, seeing the fact of death, and not having a theory about it. Then you can understand what that extraordinary thing must be. Then you can give your whole energy to it. In the same way, to find out, not repeat endlessly—as one repeats books like the Gita, the Upanishads, the Bible, and all the rest of it—to find out for yourself if there is or if there is not something beyond the measure of man, beyond the things that thought has created—to find out, one must be free of all the religious entanglements, of all the authority of religion, of all the books which teachers have put upon you, so that your mind (your own mind, not somebody else's mind) is capable of finding out if there is something sublime.

To find out, your mind must be free; otherwise, you cannot. If your mind is afraid, if your mind is greedy, ambitious, trivial, frightened, broken up into its own nationality, into its own compartments, how can such a mind be free to inquire? So the religious conditioning must be totally broken down so that out of the breaking down of that conditioning you see the truth in the false and thereby liberate the mind from its own encrustations, from its own fears. So a religious mind has no belief at all, which does not mean that it is atheistic—which is again another form: you believe and somebody else does not believe; they are both the same, and an inquiring mind is not caught in these two.

Then you will find a religious mind does not conform. Most of us are so eager to conform. You observe yourself how, inwardly, we conform to the pattern of social life, the pattern of present-day existence, of greed, of envy. The psychological structure of a society—to that, we conform very easily and so we are caught in conformity. I am not talking of putting on a sari, or a coat, or the superficial things, but I am talking of the deep inner demand to conform. Because in conformity we find satisfaction; in conformity there is a certain sense of security; in conformity there is no fear of losing a job, losing your wife or husband; in conformity you follow the pattern, day after day, so that your mind becomes mechanical, and you do not have to think at all, to question, to ask, to demand. So most of us are so eager to conform.

And this conformity expresses itself in the so-called religious life. The conformity laid down by a religious pattern is that to attain God, you must be a sannyasi or a monk, you must lead a certain kind of life, you must be a bachelor, you must live by yourself—you know the whole pattern established through centuries of what is called a religious life. The so-called religious life of the sannyasi, the monk, and all the rest of it, is an escape from life; it is the denial of life. The sannyasi, the monk, has created that pattern of what he considers—or what others have told him about, which they consider—to be the pattern which will ultimately, through pain, suffering, sacrifice, discipline, control, and all the rest of it, lead him to God.

You must have a fresh mind and not a tortured mind. You must have a clear mind, not a mind that is shoddy, so disciplined, so controlled, so broken up that it becomes a useless thing. So, the religious man, or the religious life, or the religious mind does not escape from life—life being hunger, sex, greed, ambition, joy, and all the travails of life. You cannot escape from it through any form of mysticism. The mystic escapes through some fancy, through some experience; or he mesmerizes himself into a certain state. And the religious man is not a mystical man, he does not go into trances or project something in the future, which hypnotizes him in the present. And when you have realized all this, you will find that you are completely alone.

One has to be alone, not isolated, not put into a corner by life. Because to be alone means that you are free from fear, from greed, from the corrupting influences of envy; then you are alone, you are no longer tortured by your loneliness. And it is necessary for the mind to be alone—which is a tremendous thing. It is not an easy thing because a mind is so easily influenced by what it reads, by what it thinks, by the environment. And one has to be aware of the influences of the environment and walk through them diligently, without being caught in any one of those influences. Then you are alone.

I do not know if you have ever realized or asked yourself what is beauty. Probably you have not had the time or the occasion. Here, in this country, the simple life is considered to be wearing a loincloth, having one meal a day, and not looking at the mountains, the rivers, the flowers, the birds and the heavens that are full of life. You deny beauty. Look at your own life, sirs! Do consider it, don't push aside what is being said; do consider your own life and watch it. Have you ever looked at a tree, enjoyed it, seen the shape of it, the dark color, the leaf in the sun, sparkling, dancing? Have you ever watched the river go by, and communed with the river, have you ever watched the face of another, looked at a woman or a man, seen the beauty in the face? For most of us, beauty is associated with sex, with pleasure; and so the religious mind says, "Don't look at beauty, cut it away from your life. A woman is a disgrace"—you know all the nonsense they talk about. And so we deny beauty.

And we think that a simple life means a loincloth and one meal a day—that is called the simple life. Inside you may be boiling; inside you are burning with desire, with lust, with the desire to dominate, to have power, to be regarded as popular, to be saluted as a great man; but outwardly you have the symbol of simplicity—you have to see the falseness of this, see the truth in the false. Simplicity is within, or without. So, a religious mind knows what true simplicity is. True simplicity is not the disciplined austerity, because to be really inwardly simple you must be austere. Simplicity implies a mind that can be alone, that does not depend for its happiness, for its comfort, for its security on something outside. And it is only the inwardly simple mind that is capable of being alone; and it is only the simple, religious mind that is capable of seeing beauty. Without beauty you have no religious life.

You know, beauty means sensitivity—sensitivity to dirt, to squalor, to disorder, and also, sensitivity to the beauty of a tree, of a person, of a gesture, of a word, of a feeling. If you have no beauty—which is to be sensitive—how can you be sensitive to reality? Reality is beauty, not the images carved out by the mind or by the hand. So a religious mind is sensitive and therefore capable of seeing that which is true in the squalor and seeing that which is beautiful. The religious mind can only see beauty when there is passion. You know, you can look at a tree, you can look at the beautiful face of a man or a woman or a child; but you cannot see the beauty of it if there is no passion behind it. I do not mean by "passion" lust or sexual desire but just to see the rich man go by in a car, to see the bird on the wing, to see a leaf fall down by the road. To see, you must have passion; otherwise, you are merely looking. So, a religious man, a religious life, a religious mind sees the fact and therefore is in a state of sensitivity.

Then it is only the religious mind that knows what the emptiness of the mind is. You know, the empty mind is the mind that is empty, not in the sense of void, but a mind that is astonishingly aware, attentive, a mind that is highly sensitive and therefore a mind that has no center and thereby creates space. It is only the mind that has no center, that has the space of immensity, that is the religious mind; and it is only the religious mind that is a creative mind.

We do not know what it is to be creative. We can invent—we can invent a new machine, a new way of talking, a new concept of life—but there cannot be creation without understanding love. Love, death and creation go hand in hand. Love is not memory; it is not an idea, it is not a concept. Love is neither profane nor divine. Love is not sympathy, sentiment, emotion. Sympathy and emotion are involved in jealousy, hatred. But when hatred, jealousy, envy, greed, ambition and the desire for power cease because one sees the truth in the false, then out of that perception love comes into being. And love cannot exist if there is no death of yesterday and of the minute past—then it is merely a continuity of what has been.

So, a religious mind is a creative mind, not writing a poem, prose, or putting paint on a canvas—that is not a creative mind at all. A creative mind is the mind in which a total mutation has taken place. And then only in this extraordinary state which is not mystical, which is not an escape from life, is it possible for the eternal to be. And such a mind alone can solve the problems of man.

November 11, 1964

Banaras, India, 1964

First Talk at Rajghat

Don't you think it would be wise if I talked for a little while—say for about half an hour or twenty minutes—and then we could discuss what we have talked about?

I mean by "discussion" not merely answering a question that is put but rather to explore together a problem. Not that I explore it for you, but you and I together investigate, uncover the problem or the particular issue that we are going to talk about or discuss, this morning. And to discuss really intelligently and with significance, one has to put away altogether the idea that someone knows and you don't know, that the speaker knows and he will tell you what to do. On the contrary, there is no authority here at all. And I think that is one of the principal things to realize—that every form of authority prevents inquiry. And to discuss intelligently and deeply, every form of assertion, dogmatism, or the maintenance of a particular theory must be put aside as they deny exploration.

That is what we are going to do during all these talks here: we are going together to explore. Therefore there is no person who says, "I know," nor the other who says, "I don't know, teach me." There is no teaching, there is only learning. One cannot learn if one is merely asserting that someone else knows, someone else has realized. But if you and I together learn, then this whole question of authority disappears altogether: there is not the one who maintains a certain position and the other a mere follower—which denies the very inquiry into what is truth. So bearing that in mind, if you will, we shall discuss in the sense we mean, after twenty minutes or so of talking.

I think most of us realize that there must be a radical revolution which will bring about a different dimension of thought, or thinking at a different level altogether, because we can't go on as we are, as we have been, repeating a pattern and functioning within a pattern. A behavior or conduct within a concept—whether this be so-called religious or political, whether of the center, or of the extreme left, or of the extreme right—when one functions within a pattern, it is a continuity of what has been; and I think most of us are aware that this repetitive revolution is no revolution at all.

And one observes in the world—perhaps more so in this country—the deterioration that is going on at all the levels of our existence. And observing this phenomenon unemotionally and in no way sentimentally, one naturally inquires if there is not a different way, a different approach to this whole issue of human existence and relationship, a revolution that will project the whole process of thinking in a different dimension altogether. First of all, I think most of us here and outside in the world are quite clear that there must be some kind of deep radical change in human behavior, in human relationship, and therefore in human thinking.

And how, in what way is this revolution to take place and at what level? You see what is happening in this country: industrially, probably it is advancing a great deal; scientifically, a little behind, perhaps a great deal behind the rest of the West; but morally, intellectually and religiously, it is stagnant—I am not saying something foreign, something extraordinarily outrageous; but this is an obvious, daily fact. And also one observes that the mind, the brain itself, is mechanical and therefore repetitive: teach it a certain behavior pattern, teach it certain ways of conduct, attitudes, desires, ambitions, and so on, and it will function in that groove, in that pattern. You see all this—we are not going into details because it is not significant to go into details, because you can find the details if you observe, if you read a few papers, if you look about you—the squalor, the dirt, the inefficiency, the complete lack of concern about anybody, the utter lack of affection, love, the perpetual repetition of phrases, ideas, theories that there is God or that there is no God, the socialist pattern, the religious pattern, the communist pattern, and so on.

Now, seeing all this, one realizes that there must be a radical change in the quality of the brain itself. The brain, as the anthropologists say, is about two million years old. And we can go on functioning for another two million years repeating the same pattern of sorrow, pain, wife, family, children, husband, quarrels, nationalities, the left, the right, the assertion that there is God, the assertion that there is no God, that we must be virtuous, that we must be this. We can go on indefinitely repeating, repeating, repeating the same pattern—modified slightly, altered, but repeating.

So one can see that the nature of the brain itself must undergo a tremendous revolution—not as an individual who is concerned about his particular little brain, but as a human being. I do not know if one can differentiate between the individual and a human being—at least I want to differentiate. When we are talking about change, we are always talking about the individual change. That is, you change and I change—in our little brain bringing about a different activity, establishing a different pattern—as an individual in a particular position, in a particular relationship; as an individual who has been struggling, struggling, struggling to become a little better, having a little more character, having a little more brain, being a little more kind, having a better job, and so on; as an individual functioning in the limited field of his own consciousness. That is what is generally called an individual; and in that little conditioned existence, if he is at all alert, aware, he does something to bring about a transformation by an action of the will, by control, by suppression; he is doing something all the time within the limited field of his own existence. And that is what we call the individual, who is opposed to the collective—the collective being the many, society, the nation, the race, and so on and so on.

Now, is there such an individual at all, or is there only an artificial division between the collective and himself? If one observes within oneself without any passion, without any emotional impact or reaction, one sees what one is: one is the collective. You are the collective; you are the result of your environment, of your society, of your religious dogmas, of your religious pressures, the climate, the food, the sun—not you as an individual, but as the collective, the group. There is only a total human being outside this pattern of the collective and the individual. You observe it; it is not a matter of your agreeing or disagreeing with me—that has no meaning at all. Because, we are not here discussing theories or opinions with which you agree or disagree. We are looking at facts, and about facts you can't dispute—either you say you don't see the fact or you don't want to see the fact because your own mind is so comfortably settled in a particular groove and keeps on repeating that it does not wish to see anything further. By examining the fact, you may come upon something quite different which is neither the individual nor the collective, but beyond, something far beyond either of these two. And it is only the discovery of that, we feel, that brings about the tremendous mutation in the brain itself.

We are using the brain now in this limited sense—as an individual trying to do something about the collective, or the collective controlling the individual, society shaping the brain in a particular pattern, with religious beliefs, economic beliefs, social beliefs, and so on. And these activities of consciousness within this particular field, however extensive they may be, are still limited, and therefore that consciousness is not truly individual at all. The real individuality, which is the real human being, lies beyond this, and one has to discover it. To discover it, one has to understand the whole mechanism of the brain; and in the very understanding of that brain, there is a mutation—not in time but out of time. This is what I feel to be the most important thing to discuss and to understand. I mean by understand not merely verbally but actually understand, actually realize it, not theoretically, not argumentatively or intellectually or verbally, but actually live with that.

So the question then is really: Is it possible for you and me to bring about this mutation in the use of the brain itself, a revolution which is not a gradual process in time, but a revolution, a mutation that takes place immediately, because it understands immediately? After all, when we talk about understanding we mean—don't we?—that we understand something immediately, not that we will understand it the day after tomorrow. We generally mean by that word *understand*, understand it immediately. Therefore it implies the nonexistence of tomorrow. You understand, not philosophically, not ideationally, but actually; you understand something immediately or not at all. The ideational approach implies that there is time, a period, a distance which has to be traveled to attain understanding, to become good, to become nonviolent. The idea is there; there is the distance; and to cover that distance you must have time, and therefore the gradual process—that is one of the factors of a mind that has been so conditioned by time that it thinks that it will achieve something through time.

Of course one needs time to build a road, to learn a language, to go from here to another place. That is a time which is absolutely necessary. But the ideological time that there is a perfection, a God, or whatever you will, an idea, and that idea is to be achieved only through time—that is one of the old-established patterns of our thought, which is established in the brain itself. And to see the falseness of that is the understanding of the immediate importance of complete mutation now.

I do not know if you have ever thought about it: if there is no tomorrow actually, psychologically, inwardly, then your whole attention is in the present; your whole attitude toward life is so completely integrated, so completely whole, not fragmentary. And that is one of the greatest mutations that can take place. When you see the implication of this whole approach that there is tomorrow and that through tomorrow we will become or we will find out, and when you see the truth that there is no tomorrow psychologically, then the whole mental, emotional, psychological brain structure undergoes a tremendous change. We feel that is the only revolution that is possible nowadays, or perhaps always.

Don't translate what we are talking about in terms of your own Sanskrit words, or what somebody has said, don't say, "By Jove, what he is saying is the same as what somebody has said in the Puranas, Vedas, Upanishads, or whatever it is." When you translate what you hear in terms of what you have already read, you have stopped understanding. Naturally, you are not listening—what you are listening to is what you already know, and you are comparing it with what you hear to see if they both tally; that is all. And if the thing that is being said agrees with what some religious person has said, you get terribly excited, and say, "We are all right, safe!" We are not talking about safety—on the contrary. What we are talking about is the necessity of a tremendous revolution, a revolution which is obviously religious.

I mean by religious revolution a complete, total, nonfragmentary revolution; it is the whole entity. It is not the economic entity, the social entity, the psychological entity—those are fragmentary entities. And any revolution in the fragment will always lead to the repetition of what has been, only modified—which is being proved over and over again. The French Revolution, the Communist Revolution—they are going back to the same old pattern, coming round about; after killing millions and millions of people, they come to the same old pattern, a little higher or a little lower.

So, if you have observed not only yourself but a social revolution, an economic revolution—not ideational or theoretically, but actually observed it in yourself and about you—you will undoubtedly come to the understanding that a complete mutation must take place in the mind, in the brain, if man is to live peacefully, not only with this threat of the atom bomb, but also with all these stupid divisions of nationalities, religious divisions. And one must inevitably see the extraordinary importance of this, not as an individual, but as man as a whole. Man means you, not an individual. In that man there must be a complete revolution. Now how is it to be brought about?

One sees the necessity of such a revolution; one sees the urgency, the maturity and the energy that is demanded for such a revolution. And how is that maturity and that energy to be brought about? You are mature—not in terms of time, old age, all the rest of it—ripe, rich, full, when you have looked, observed, lived without any bitterness, without any fear, without any desire to fulfill—all that is immature. Belonging to a certain class of people, certain religions, certain nationalities—all that is infantile; that has no meaning at all. Because it is only when you slough off all that nonsense that your mind is mature. Then you must have energy—the energy to bring about this tremendous mutation.

So to boil down what we have talked about this morning, it comes to this—that there must be an immediate maturity and that intense energy which goes with that maturity, which alone can bring about this immediate mutation. Now how is it to be done? I have put the problem, perhaps not too clearly, not in too many details—because we can go into it everlastingly, describe the details, but that will get us no further. How is this maturity and energy to be brought about? Or, is it not to be brought about at all? I do not know if you are following all that we are talking about, or am I talking too fast or too generally?

So, if you will, let us this morning limit ourselves to the thing that we have said. We see that a fundamental revolution in the very structure of the brain is necessary—structure not in the biological sense, but the structure in our thinking, the pattern of our thoughts, pursuits, demands. To bring about a fundamental revolution, it needs a great deal of energy; and that energy can only come about when there is maturity—not the maturity of many fragments being put together which, we think, becomes mature. So how is this to be brought about? Perhaps we can discuss this point.

Am I imposing this problem on to you? Would you kindly tell me, am I pushing this problem on to you? No? Just a minute, sir, you say no. If it is a problem to you, not imposed by another, what is your answer to it? Please, do listen to what we are saying. If it is your problem, not my problem which I have transferred to you, what will you do with it? You know, if you have a problem of hunger or a problem of sex, you do something about it—you don't say, "Let us sit down and talk about it." If you are really hungry and food is demanded, you do something. So what will you do with this? Or, rather, what are you doing with it? Or, would you say that it is a problem with you but you don't know what to do—that is more like it, isn't it?

Right, sir? Don't agree with me, please. You see this problem and you say to yourself, "I know all this; I read the newspapers, the magazines, the talks, and all the rest of it; I listen to all that, I read it, I know it, but I don't know what to do." Is that right, sir? Now, who is going to tell you what to do about it? Do you have faith in any leader, including this person who is sitting on the platform? No, don't laugh, sir! Surely, you have given your trust to the politicians, to the teachers, to the religious people; you have put your trust in the books—sacred this and sacred that—and they have no meaning any more, have they? Wars are going on; there is hate, there is misery, there is confusion, there is starvation; and the politicians have their own heaven. And unfortunately, you have nobody you can really trust—actually, not theoretically. So, what will you do? What are you going to do?

Comment: I shall deal with it in the light of my experiences.

KRISHNAMURTI: Is it a matter of experience—what we are talking about? I am pointing it out to you, madame. Is it a matter of experience? You see this outside you, and you see this within. What is there to experience? It is there, right in front of your nose—the squalor, the misery, the whole human mess and misery. You know it is there. Why should you have to experience in order to go through it and thereby understand it and do something about it? It is there.

Sir, look at the issue! What is involved in it? There is a problem, and you want somebody to solve it. Really that is the crux of the whole matter. And is there somebody to solve it for you? You are hungry, and someone is well fed and talks about the nice meal he had. Would that satisfy you? And you are in that position, aren't you? So isn't it important to realize that there is nobody that can help you? It is rather despairing. Can it not be realized that you have yourself to fight through to find out, and that you cannot possibly rely on anybody? You have relied on your gurus, teachers, books, politicians, leaders, your saints, your mahatmas; and where are you now at the end of it all, after two million years? Just the same, old, petty minds. So what will you do, sirs? It is your problem, and you have to do something about it. Please go on with it and you will see what's going to be the outcome of this discussion.

When you understand, realize, that there is no one outside that can help you—no gods, no gurus, no politicians, nobody can help you—aren't you already in a state of maturity? That means you are already free of the fear of making a mistake, free from the fear of not doing the right thing. Aren't you?

So that's the first difficulty we have to face, haven't we?—that no system, a religious system or a communist system, nobody, a religious dictator or political dictator, is going to help us. When one realizes that actually, not theoretically, already there is a revolution in the brain, is there not?

Comment: A teacher can help us to awaken our intuition.

KRISHNAMURTI: You have had umpteen teachers, haven't you? Actually what is the function of a teacher?

Comment: To give us more light.

KRISHNAMURTI: The questioner says, "To give us more light." Now wait a minute, sir. There are different kinds of teachers, are there not? Take the teacher in a class. If the teacher in an educational system is worth his salt, he is not teaching; he is encouraging the student to learn. Obviously! If he says, "I know the distance between here and the moon, and I know the molecules and the atom, and all the rest of it," the boy will repeat after him, but the boy is not learning. A good teacher helps the student to learn, doesn't he? Ask the teachers here and you'll find out. Then there are the teachers who merely assert that there is God, or say, "Do this"; they are not teachers, they are really exploiters, they are really repeaters, and therefore they are in the social pattern. Then there are the teachers whom man establishes as the teacher, like Karl Marx—according to his particular economic, social, religious tendencies, hoping to learn, to find out, from that teacher. This is all obvious.

Now what is the function, apart from all this, of a teacher? What can the teacher do? The teacher says, "Do look in this direction, there may be something in there. Look!" The teacher can't force you, he can't browbeat you; he can only say, "Look, my friend! If you look in that direction, perhaps you will understand things differently." But you must have the energy to look, you must not be afraid to look—so it depends on you. I can go on repeating, as I have been doing for the last forty years; and you come and repeat the same old question to me: "A guru is necessary, he gives us light, he gives us intuition." And where are you at the end of it? So all that one can do is to learn, isn't it, sir?

Comment: If the learning appeals, sir.

KRISHNAMURTI: The gentleman says, "If the learning is pleasurable, gratifying, I learn." But I'm afraid you have to learn about it, whether it's gratifying or painful—that is life. If it is all pleasure, then you do nothing; you don't learn about anything, you just enjoy yourself.

Sir, look! One suffers—we are not going to discuss suffering right now. You suffer, and you can escape from suffering by going to the temples, by turning on the radio, by taking a drink; a dozen things you can do in order to escape from suffering. But suffering keeps on going after you, like a shadow; and whether you like it or not, you have to learn about it, haven't you? Whether it is gratifying or not, you say, "By Jove, I have to learn about this suffering. What does it mean?" You may not like it, but you have to learn about it. Your pleasure and displeasure doesn't enter into this question at all.

So one of the qualities of maturity is that it does not depend on pleasure and pain, but on facts, on *what is* actually. One of the factors of *what is* is that you have trusted so many people, so many politicians, so many books, and they have lost all meaning. Everyone, unless one is blind, unless one wants to keep on repeating the same old pattern—any contemporary, average mind says, "What nonsense all this is, guru and all that!" and throws it all overboard. So is it not one of the signs of maturity that the mind is not dependent on anybody for its understanding?

Comment: I do not see the difference between the individual who is conditioned and man who is not an individual but a human being.

KRISHNAMURTI: The gentleman says that he does not see the difference between the individual who has been conditioned and a man who is thinking not in terms of individuality, but as a human being.

You see the difference, sir, don't you? I can think about myself as an individual. Seeking my own salvation, digging in the backyard, looking after my own character, cultivating virtue, doing all the individual things that we do—pursuing ambition, greed, envy; cultivating my particular quality, gift, and so on. All this is still within the very limited field of what we call an individual. But that individual is also the result of the mass. Every individual all over the world is doing the same thing, and every individual all over the world is the result of his society, his group, his family, his religion, and so on. And to bring about a change in that is no change at all. The change in that is merely a modified change in the pattern, but it is not a radical change, a radical revolution. The radical revolution lies beyond the individual and the mass.

Question: How is this immediate mutation to take place? If we don't know this, we are utterly in despair.

KRISHNAMURTI: Are you in despair, sir? Unfortunately, these are all a lot of words to you, sir—if I may most respectfully point out. A man in despair—do you know what he does?

Now the question is: How is this mutation to take place? First of all, sir, look at the difficulty. If the speaker were to offer you a method, would that bring about a mutation? Sir, if the speaker were to give you a pattern which will bring about a mutation, would that mutation be the right thing?

Comment: No.

KRISHNAMURTI: Why do you say no? But yet, that's what you are all doing in daily life, aren't you? The mind says, "I must change, and how am I to change?" and so it immediately seeks a pattern through which it can bring about this change, a system. Right? One has to understand the futility of the pattern and reject it completely. Because the moment you see something as false, it drops away. So you have to understand the falsity of a pattern, and that will help you to bring about a mutation.

Now, see what is implied in this. When you say that a pattern, a method, a system will bring about a mutation, two things are implied: one, that you know what mutation implies; and the other, that a method will help you to arrive at the mutation. Do you know what mutation means? Obviously not. Verbally you repeat, but do you know what it means, what is involved in it?

Question: Is there anything like a cosmic mind?

KRISHNAMURTI: Now, who is asking it and who is going to reply to it? Suppose I explained, sir, would you understand it? You must also have a cosmic mind to understand what a cosmic mind is. I am not being clever.

Sir, take this simple thing. Most of you, fortunately or unfortunately, believe in God. I don't know why, but you do. Society and various other things have conditioned you to believe or not to believe, and you say, "I would like to reach God." And so people have methods to reach God: you must be a bachelor, you must be this, you must be that, you must control, you must suppress, you must meditate—and a dozen things are laid down, to find God. But who knows God? Does the man who lays down the system know what God is?

Comment: We believe that.

KRISHNAMURTI: You believe in it because the gentleman says that he knows God! You are all rather naive, aren't you, sirs?

To find out God requires an extraordinary mind, doesn't it? First of all you do not say that you believe or that you do not believe. God can't be static. It is only when a thing is static that there can be a method that will lead to it, isn't that so? If it is something that is living, moving, changing, undergoing mutation all the time, you can't have a system that will lead you to it.

Comment: I do not know what God is; but I want to know God.

KRISHNAMURTI: The gentleman says he doesn't know what God is, but he is after it.

Why? Because I'm miserable; my life is frustration; I don't know this existence except through sorrow: this constant flux, uncertainty, the misery, the confusion—I want to escape from all that. I don't want to understand it, to resolve it and put it away; but I want to escape from that to God, who is permanent.

That's all you want. Why do you want God? How can you find God unless you understand life, sir? Life may be God. You can only know it, sir, by being free from all confusion, obviously. If I want to understand you, I must not be in conflict within myself; I must be able to listen to you tranquilly. That's all. Therefore, first bring about order in your life, not according to somebody, but just "order."

Comment: To bring about order, we try one pattern after another until we succeed.

KRISHNAMURTI: That is, you go after one pattern after another until you realize. Right, sir?

Comment: We do not know what to do, sir.

KRISHNAMURTI: The gentleman says that he does not know a thing about anything. That's the only healthy state of mind, isn't it?—to say, "I don't know, but I'm going to learn." And can you learn through a pattern? When you're going to follow patterns, one after another, you will find a hundred patterns according to a hundred men. Do you follow them?

Comment: One after another, until we find the right pattern.

KRISHNAMURTI: Well, sir, good luck to you! Finally for you, sir, there will be at the end of it, death or insanity. So what will you do? There's no use talking, sir; you haven't even thought about it, you just repeat.

Now, let us go back to our question: How do we bring about instant maturity? And with that maturity goes energy; how will you bring it about? Or, is there no method at all, but only seeing the truth: that to depend on anybody, on any system, on any philosophy, on a guru is immature—seeing the truth of it, instantly.

To see the truth of something instantly, one has not to say, "I like or I don't like," as though one knows a great deal and can distinguish, but one has to put away everything and look. Sir, one has to look—for example, to look at that river, look at it. Probably you have never looked at that river. You have seen it, but you have never looked at it because you have associated with that river not only the name but the vast history contained in that river: that river is the Ganga, and that means so much to a Hindu. Therefore all that tradition prevents you from looking very simply at that beautiful river. You have to look at it without all its history which prevents you from looking. In the same way, you have to look at all your misery, at all the confusion, without any pattern, without any idea, without any concept. Surely, that is part of maturity.

I say, it's going to be very difficult to discuss—that is, to inquire. You know, to inquire is quite an art. It's not like saying, "I believe and I want to do this, or I am going to do this." To inquire—that is the scientific method of looking, observing, sensing, taking facts. When you say, "I want to reach God, I'll do this," then, you are immature, you are not a scientific mind. A scientific mind never accepts; it looks, observes, considers. And it is only such a mind that can find.

So, please, as we are going to spend some time together, please understand very clearly what we mean by discussion and inquiry: which is, I want to find out whether the pattern which I accept is right or wrong, not that I want God and therefore accept the pattern—that has no meaning. I can only inquire if there is freedom; otherwise, I can't inquire.

Sir, to find out if there is God, you must be free of the idea of God. To find out, you have to inquire, search out, question, ask. Surely, that is a part of maturity. To ask right questions, to inquire rightly demands energy.

Question: Is it possible to look at something without naming?

KRISHNAMURTI: Why are you asking if it is possible? Try it. Look at a flower. Look at it.

To look at a flower means that there is no verbal interference between your look and the flower. You understand it verbally, first; then also don't name the flower as this species or that species; then don't say, "I like it," or "I don't like it." Don't give it a name, don't give it a color; but just look. And that's an extraordinarily difficult thing to do; most people don't do this.

Comment: One may look in that way only at very rare moments, but not permanently.

KRISHNAMURTI: Sir, why do you want permanency? If you have permanency, you are not looking either. You look from moment to moment. Look at the flower; go, look at it! This is a tremendous art, sir, not just a matter of two words. Then you have to be completely in contact with that flower. And you cannot be in contact with that flower if there is "you" who is the word, you who says, "I like, I don't like." And when you are in contact with the flower, it is not a permanent contact—then there is not a contact at all; then you are merely reducing that contact in terms of time.

Comment: I feel happy, sir, then.

KRISHNAMURTI: Sir, when you observe a flower, when the mind is intimately in contact with that flower, there is no happiness or unhappiness. That moment is of the highest importance. Leave it at that. Don't say that moment must last all the time. If it continues it is merely a memory.

Look, sir! Yesterday evening, the light over the river was very beautiful; it was first silver, then it was gold, then it became deeper gold. At the moment when one was looking at it, there was no naming; one merely observed, and there was not the observer or the thing observed. Don't agree, sir, you know nothing about this. It is one of the most difficult things to do. It was a moment out of time. When the mind which has known that moment says, "I wish it could continue," the desire for that moment to continue becomes memory; and that memory is going to interfere the next time it looks at that river.

So the problem is to look out of time and not demand any further experience at all, just to look. If it remained forever, it would not be the moment when there is no thought. If it is a continuum, then it becomes a thought.

November 20, 1964

Second Talk at Rajghat

If we may, we will continue with what we were talking about the other day when we met here.

We were talking about maturity and the necessity of that energy that goes with maturity, to bring about mutation in the mind. And to go into it fully we must understand, it seems to me, what is action; and in understanding action, we must also find out, for ourselves, what is communication and what is communion.

We see that action in our daily life is so contradictory, so conflicting, so hypocritical. We say one thing and we do another. We believe in certain formulas and do things contrary to those formulas. We are artists, businessmen, politicians, writers, poets, painters, teachers. And at all the levels of our life and of our existence there is this contradictory activity—the ideal and the factual. The ideal has nothing whatsoever to do with the factual—for example, violence has nothing whatever to do with nonviolence. But yet we live in this fragmentary, contradictory activity. At one level we are religious—at least so-called religious—and at another level we are destroying each other, not only in the business world through competition, through ambition, through greed, but also as a group, as a race, as a family.

This is what is happening in our daily life. Every action is so contradictory, so broken up; the activity at one level contradicts it at another level. Such activities must invariably, as we notice in daily life, breed much havoc, breed much misery and confusion and conflict. And to escape from all this contradictory activity, we try to establish a super activity, thorough meditation, through religious scriptures, and all that—which is another escape at another level—quite in contradiction with our daily existence. And realizing this extraordinarily fragmentary, unrelated activity, doesn't one demand naturally—not ideationally, not as an idea or as a theory—doesn't one inquire into an action which is not fragmentary, which is not hypocritical, which is not departmentalized, which is not put in watertight compartments, but which is an action that, in the discovery of it, will function as a whole, in every activity of life?

I mean one must ask this question for oneself: Is there an action, a total action that, wherever it expresses itself, must be total, not contradictory?

Now, if I may, we would like to go into that. First of all, to understand what we are talking about, we must establish the difference between communication and the nature of being in communion. The two, I think, are different—that is, communication is one thing and being in communion with another is quite a different thing. Communication demands either words, gesture, or some form of outward expression which conveys the meaning of the speaker to the listener, or of the listener to the speaker—this is what we mean by communication. When one speaks, one uses certain words as symbols—which means there is a referent. So communication cannot be misunderstood if it is clearly, definitely expressed in words which you and I both understand. Then there can be no equivocation, there can be no misunderstanding; it is clear, definite. You and I both understand English—if we do understand English—and we use the words as a means of conveying certain specific meanings through certain words, certain symbols, certain gestures. And then we both are in a state of understanding of what is being communicated. That, surely, is very clear.

But the other thing is much more difficult: it is to be in communion. As I said, it's much more difficult because most of us are not in *communion* at all with anything. I mean by that word not only the meaning the dictionary gives, but also much more. To be in communion with something implies, does it not, that there is no hindrance between you and the thing you see, the thing you regard, you observe. To be in communion with nature, that is with the birds, with the trees, with the river, with the earth, with the green fields, the squalor on the road—one is not in communion with nature if there is any sense of resistance, any sense of condemnation or disregard, or turning away from it. There is communion when there is no interference of thought between the thing and the observer.

Do please pay a little attention to this because what we are going into presently demands this communion between the speaker and you who are the listener. Otherwise we shall not meet at all; we shall be able to communicate verbally, but we shall not be in a state of communion with each other. And it is necessary, it seems to me, to understand the real significance of action which is not contradictory. So we mean by communion a state of mind which is not to be induced, which allows no barrier to come between you and that which is being heard—which may be contradictory to what you believe—a state of mind which doesn't compare, quote, evaluate, but actually listens, tries to find out.

You know, there is communion between people, between you and nature, when there is a great affection, when I like you and you like me, or when you like one another—in the sense that there is a great deal of sympathy, affection, no sense of condemning, comparing, judging, evaluating. Then in that state the two people are in a state of communion—that is, they are in communion at the same moment, at the same level, with the same intensity—which is, after all, what is called love. So it's only a mind that can put aside every form of opinion, judgment, evaluation, comparison, and so on—it is only such a mind that can be in communion with nature, or with another, or be in communion with itself—which is much more difficult.

And it is necessary to understand this, because, unless you are directly in communion with yourself and therefore with a source of action which is not contradictory, your life will inevitably be a contradiction; do what you will, whatever pattern you may follow, whatever beliefs, whatever concepts you may have, your life will be a contradiction— as in this country where you preach everlastingly ahimsa, nonviolence, and do quite the opposite. You just talk about a nation of peace, of nonviolence, and prepare for war, much more than the other nations—there they don't talk about nonviolence. Here, every politician, every person has this schizophrenia, double entity, double personality, double thinking.

One has ideals, most marvelous ideals which have no relationship whatsoever with daily existence. So one leads such a terribly contradictory, hypocritical life. And this contradictory life makes for greater contradiction, greater misery, greater division between the fact and the theory. And then the problem arises: How to bridge the fact with the theory? And then from that, the everlasting search, the conflict of trying to discipline the mind to conform to the pattern or to the concept, and thereby causing more contradiction, more, wider, deeper division between the fact and the theory. Please, this is what is actually happening in your lives. It is not a theory, I am not condemning it. We are just saying: Observe it, it is a fact.

So, if one is at all serious, one asks oneself, what is a total action? And life is only for the serious. It is only for the man who is very earnest that life has depth, meaning, significance, vitality, energy. But most of us are not serious; we are serious in fragments, little bits of seriousness here and a little bit of seriousness there: it's not a total earnestness. So, you have to find out for yourself what is a total action, not to be told by me, by the speaker—that becomes the pattern, the ideal; and you are back again in contradiction. If you exercise your reason unemotionally, if you exercise whatever capacity you have for understanding, then you will find out for yourself what is this total action, which is not divided as the individual action and the collective action, or the individual paying back to society what society gives him—all these divisions come to a complete end; and the ending of this division in action is the beginning of maturity.

So, this morning we are going to find out for ourselves through exploration, not through conforming, not through being told what it is, not through creating a verbal pattern—all patterns are verbal, except the engineering pattern laid down on a blue paper. Without creating any pattern, ideological or contradictory, we are going to find out, if it is possible, whether there is a total action which, whatever we are doing, will not create a contradictory action and therefore will not create more misery, more sorrow, more confusion.

If that is clear, I think that what I have said this morning is good enough without going into too many details. Therefore first we have to consider what is communication. One has to understand that very clearly because after understanding that we shall go into and find out what is the mind that is in a state of communion. But without understanding what is communication, you will not be able to understand what is communion.

When we have something to communicate to each other, we use words. When I say I like you or I don't like you, I have to use words or a gesture; and that gesture, that word, that symbol gives the meaning, and you interpret that according to your likes and dislikes, or according to your conditioning, or according to your fear. So, communication with words has its own limitation; unless we, both of us, use the same word, with the same meaning with the same clarity on both sides, we do not understand, through communication, what it is that's being said. That's again very clear, isn't it? When we say two and two make four, it is very clear. It is only not clear when your mental state is perverted, refuses to see, when there is imbalance in the mind, when the mind has some fixation, has some definite opinion, ideas, conclusion which says, "No, two and two make six or five." Then such a mind refuses to see the fact and denies the fact because it is already caught in its own conditioning, in its own opinion, in its own experience, belief, and refuses to see the fact that two and two make four.

So see the difficulty of communicating with somebody who is traditional—as most people are—bound by his own ideas, opinions, judgments, by his fears, by his own inept, inefficient thought, by the use of a word to which he gives a specific meaning which the speaker does not. Please see the immense difficulty in communicating verbally. We use certain words like *discipline* and we immediately have certain patterns. You immediately translate that word into your particular terminology, into your particular experience, or as discipline according to some religious leader; and so refuse to understand the meaning that the speaker is giving to that specific word. So, as long as you take a position—an intellectual position, or a verbal position—and refuse to budge from that position, any form of communication is impossible. That's again very obvious.

So it is possible to communicate—I am using the word *communicate,* not *commune*—when the speaker is using an English word, only when you also understand it at the level of that word or give the meaning to that word which the speaker has given, and not translate it into your particular terminology of Sanskrit which has its own associations; then there is a possibility of communicating with each other. Look, sir! Take any word—like the word *discipline,* like the word *effort.* I use the word discipline in its actual sense; it is an English word; and the root of that word means "to learn." But, for you it has quite a different meaning. The moment you hear the word, you translate it, meaning conformity, suppression, control, discipline according to somebody, Shankara or someone else. So you and I have ceased immediately to communicate with each other. Isn't that so? Even to communicate with each other verbally, you must be in a state of trying to find out what that word means according to the speaker, not according to your particular definition.

So it is very difficult to communicate even at the verbal level, and it is much more difficult to be in a state of communion with each other over something which demands an astonishing energy, an astonishing sense of no division but seeing the same thing together at the same time, at the same level, with the same intensity.

Now, we are going to use the word *action.* Action means to do, or having done, or going to do, to act—not according to a pattern, not according to an ideal, not according to what the Gita, or the Buddha, or Shankara have said. I am talking of action, not according to somebody, not according to one's own concept of action. Because concept is not action, idea is not action. By "action" I mean "doing." So, we are not concerned with the idea of what is right action and what is wrong action, or the concept, the formula; but we are only concerned with finding out a total action which does not breed, which has not in it the seed of confusion, the seed of contradiction. Then you and I will be in a state of communion to find out what is action which will be total, complete.

So, first, one has to see actually that our life in action produces the activity which creates contradiction; because life is a movement, and that movement is action. You cannot live without action, whether it is intellectual action, emotional action, physical action, or action in relationship with your wife, with your children, with your husband, with society. Life is a movement, and that movement creates contradiction in action when that movement of life is separated into fragments as the scientific activity, the human activity, the religious activity, the bureaucratic activity, the political activity, the social reform activity, and so on. And when you function in those departments, though there is a movement, that movement creates, or breeds, or brings about contradiction; and from that contradiction the mind seeks to escape through an ideal, such as nonviolence which you consider to be a noble ideal, and so on.

So first we must realize that it is a fact that our life is broken up into fragmentary activities which breed contradiction and therefore more strife, more misery. Not how to escape from it, not what to do about it, but first we must see that fact. Do we see that fact? And then how do you see that fact? Do you see that fact repulsively, saying, "How terrible it is"? The moment you say how terrible it is, you have already stopped understanding it. You know, the fact doesn't demand your opinion, your judgment. The sun rises every day whether you like it or don't like it, whether you have a headache, whether you have slept badly, whether you have hunger or this or that—there it is, a fact. In the same way you have to realize this fact, the *what is,* not 'what should be'.

So, the moment you realize the fact and do not translate the fact into terms of opinion, or what to do about it, then, because your mind is completely concerned with the fact and is not translating that fact according to your conditioning, you are in communion with that fact. Am I making myself clear?

Most of us are never in communion with anything. You are not in communion with your wife, your husband, with your children; you are in communion with the image of your wife, with the memories of your wife, with the sexual pleasures of that wife or husband. You are in communion with the memory but not with the fact that you have a wife or a husband. In the same way if one really wants to go deeply into this extraordinary question of action—not social action or individual action or collective action, not what I should do about society—one has to understand and discover for oneself—or rather, discover and thereby understand—what this total action implies, what it means. One has to be in communion with it. And one can only be in communion with it when one has understood the verbal communication and the difficulties involved in that communication.

And when you have understood verbal communication, then you can go to the next step—not step, the sequence, but the natural movement—which is to be in communion with yourself. Because, after all, that is the source of all action, isn't it? Your desires, your hatreds, your ambition, your greed—that is the source of all your action, and you are not in communion with that at all. You will inevitably follow the movement of life when there is an understanding of the significance of communication; having understood it, you move on to the next question which is: Is it possible to be in communion with anything at all? Or you have your memories of the past—the past may be a thousand years, or the past of yesterday—will those memories interfere all the time, so that you are never in communion with anything? After all, if you are not in communion with anything, you are a dead human being.

You have to be in communion with the river, with the birds, with the trees, with the extraordinary light of the evening, the light of the morning on the water; you have to be in communion with your neighbor, with your wife, with your children, with your husband. I mean by "communion" noninterference of the past, so that you look at everything afresh, anew—and that's the only way to be in communion with something, so that you die to everything of yesterday. And is it possible? One has to find this out, not "How am I to do it?"—that is such an idiotic question. People always ask, "How am I to do this?"—it shows their mentality; they have not understood, but they only want to achieve a result.

So I am asking you if you are ever in contact with anything, and if you are ever in contact with yourself—not with your higher self and lower self and all the innumerable divisions that man has created to escape from the fact. And you have to find out—not to be told, not how to come to this total action. There is no "how," there is no method, there is no system; you cannot be told. You have to work for it. No? I am sorry. I don't mean that word *work:* people love to work; that is one of our fantasies that we must work to achieve something. You can't work when you are in a state of communion—there is no working, it is there, the perfume is there, you don't have to work.

So ask yourself, if I may request you, to find out for yourself whether you are in communion with anything, whether you are in communion with a tree. Have you ever been in communion with a tree? Do you know what it means to look at a tree, to have no thought, no memory interfering with you observation, with your feeling, with your sensibility, with your nervous state of attention, so that there is only the tree, not you who are looking at that tree? Probably you have never done this because for you a tree has no meaning. The beauty of a tree has no significance at all, for to you beauty means sexuality. So you have shut out the tree, nature, the river, the people. And you are not in contact with anything, even with yourself. You are in contact with your own ideas, with your own words, like a human being in contact with ashes. You know what happens when you are in contact with ashes? You are dead, you are burned out.

So the first thing one has to realize is to find out what is the total action which will not create contradiction at any level of one's existence, what it is to be in communion, communion with yourself, not with the higher self, not with the atma, God, and all that, but to be actually in contact with yourself, with your greed, envy, ambition, brutality, deception, and then from there move. Then you will find out for yourself—find out; not be told, which has no meaning—that there is a total action only when there is complete silence of the mind from which there is action.

You know, in the case of most of us, the mind is noisy, everlastingly chattering to itself, soliloquizing or chattering about something or trying to talk to itself to convince itself of something; it is always moving, noisy. And from that noise, we act. Any action born of noise produces more noise, more confusion. But if you have observed and learned what it means to communicate, the difficulty of communication, the nonverbalization of the mind—that is, that communicates and receives communication—then, as life is a movement, you will, in your action, move on naturally, freely, easily, without any effort, to that state of communion. And in that state of communion, if you inquire more deeply, you will find that you are not only in communion with nature, with the world, with everything about you, but also in communion with yourself.

To be in communion with yourself means complete silence so that the mind can be silently in communion with itself about everything. And from there, there is a total action. It is only out of emptiness that there is the action which is total and creative.

Sirs, perhaps we can discuss, or ask questions, explore together what we have said this morning.

Question: Are we not in communion with the contradiction, sir?

KRISHNAMURTI: Are you not in contradiction? Are you not in communion with contradiction—which is the root cause of our existence? All thought, all evolution brings contradiction.

Are you theorizing, or, if I may ask, are you speaking from fact? If you are speaking from fact, have you found out what is the cause of contradiction? What is the cause of contradiction? Do look at it very simply. Don't speculate about it, find out what is the cause of contradiction. May I explore it for you?

What is one of the causes of contradiction? I will develop it as I go along. But go with me, step by step. What is one of the causes of contradiction? One of the major causes of contradiction is having an ideal.

Question: What is the primal cause?

KRISHNAMURTI: Wait, sir, I am coming to that. You want the primal cause, you have not even begun with the first cause. I am saying to myself, "Why does this contradiction arise?"—not the ultimate cause; I want to know the cause at the beginning. I see one of the causes of contradiction is having an ideal. We are examining; we are not saying we must not or we must. We see why we preach nonviolence—at least, you do—and also are violent. Why this contradiction? This contradiction is obvious.

I see one of the primary causes of contradiction is having an ideal. I know you will disagree. You will probably agree with me verbally, but actually you will still have ideals when you leave here. You are bound by, suffocated with, ideals. So I say that the first cause of contradiction is having an ideal. Why do you have ideals? You say that if you did not have ideals, you would not know how to deal with the fact, and that the ideal will help you to alter the fact. That is, if you did not have the ideal of nonviolence, you would not know what to do with violence, and you would be violent. You think that the ideal will help you as a leverage to throw out violence. Does the ideal of nonviolence prevent you from being violent—violence being ambition, domination? Sir, I am explaining it to you, I am showing it to you. This means that, whoever the speaker is, you are not concerned with the understanding of contradiction and being free of it, but you are concerned with ideas.

So, why do we have ideals? First we hope that, by having an ideal, we shall be able to get rid of, or alter, or modify, or change the fact. I am violent and I use the ideal of nonviolence to help me to get rid of my violence. Now look at what has happened! The fact is I am violent, and the ideal is not a fact at all, it is a verbal fact, an idea; and with that idea I hope I can get rid of my violence. The ideal is created because I want to escape from the fact, and so I have created a contradiction; whereas, if I look at the fact—the fact that I am violent—I can deal with that fact, can't I? Either I like violence, or I don't like it. And as most people love violence they keep it. And if it is a fact and you like it, it is all right; you keep it, be violent, and talk about peace and all the rest of it; but know that, by doing this, you are deceiving others and yourself. But if you don't like it, why have the ideal? If you don't like it, you can deal with it now.

Sirs, do you understand how the contradiction arises? Why am I violent? First of all, my education, my society, the climate, the food, the social structure, the phenomena of society, the economic structure and all the rest of it—they all breed in me the sense of violence. And also psychologically I like violence. Being violent I invent the idea of nonviolence in order to escape from it, hoping thereby to postpone, hoping that I will gradually become nonviolent one of these nice days. But if I have no ideal—having an ideal is immature—the mind faces facts and therefore there is maturity. A mature mind has no ideal at all. It faces facts and deals with them, and therefore there is no contradiction in facts. I am violent; either I like it or I don't like it. If I don't like it, I put it away—it is as easy as that. But you cannot put it away if you are pretending to be idealistically nonviolent all the time.

You have to face the fact and you can then deal with the fact. And that is all our life. I am afraid of insecurity, I am afraid of death, I am afraid of public opinion—a dozen things I am frightened of. Why am I frightened of my wife? Why are you frightened of your boss, or your husband, or your neighbor? Because they will hurt you, they will take away something from you. I am frightened of my wife or husband; they belong to me. Legally, morally, brutally, I hold them; and I am frightened. If my wife looks at another, I am jealous; and to prevent that jealousy arising, I put around her various moral laws. So there is the beginning: I am frightened that she may run away from me, that she may not give me the sexual pleasure I want.

Question: Is this not inherent in us, sir?

KRISHNAMURTI: Nothing is inherent, except in the animal—in the animal, some things are inherent. But as we are still animals, as the major part of us is still animalistic, we are frightened. We are dealing with facts. But to say that is a fact, to be satisfied with it is still animalistic. Sir, the animal fights, so does a human being fight; but the human being, still being an animal, is supposed to have evolved two million years from the animal.

Question: You have blazed the path of mutation. Is there another example of a similar mutation?

KRISHNAMURTI: Sirs, we are talking about something else now, so we will leave mutation for the moment.

You know what it is "to learn," sir? What does it mean—to learn? To learn about something, especially about psychological, rather deep and subtle matters, one must be fairly free, and there must be a sense of extraordinary curiosity which is neither acceptance nor denial. It is only then that you can learn, and you learn, not from the speaker only, but you learn from everything. But most of us don't want to learn; because we have accumulated so much knowledge, all that we are concerned with is adding more knowledge to what we already know.

I am trying to point out, to the people listening to me, how difficult, how necessary it is to learn and not to accumulate knowledge. I don't know why we accumulate knowledge at all—it is all in the books. Why not leave it in the books on the shelf? Why carry it in your brain? When you want to know what Shankara said about something, go and have a look at the book in which it is. Why do you carry it in your brain? You carry it, because it gives you a certain spectacular sense of importance, because you can convince somebody that you know much more than somebody else. But such a mind does not learn.

One has to learn. Life is a movement, as I pointed out. You have to learn every minute. And it is only the young, youthful, innocent, clear, good mind that is always learning, learning, learning, never accumulating. So, sir, if you want to learn, you must know what it is to communicate and what it is to be in a state of communion. Learn, discover it for yourself.

And when you know that the word is not the thing, then the word becomes unimportant. The word has its importance, but not this tremendous importance that it now has with most people. Then when the mind is free of the word, then it can look at the tree without the word. You try it sometime, and you will learn the extraordinary beauty of the tree. And when you learn the full meaning and the significance of the word, then there is the same movement which goes on further, deeper, wider. That is, the mind then is in a state of communion. And it is only the mind that is in a state of communion that can understand and discover for itself what it is to act totally at every level of our existence.

November 22, 1964

Third Talk at Rajghat

We were talking the day before yesterday about the question of maturity—which is, really to be in a state of mind which is not in a state of contradiction. And that maturity demands energy. Now this morning, if we may, we would like to talk about the nature of this energy—not as an idea because an idea about energy is entirely different from the fact of energy itself. We have formulas or concepts of how to bring about a quality of energy that is of the highest quality. But the formula is entirely different from the renovating, renewing quality of energy itself.

So we are not talking about the idea but the fact itself. And I think this is where most of us find it difficult. We live so much in ideas, in concepts, in what way or how to bring about the highest form of energy; and then having formed an image, a concept, we work according to that concept to bring about this energy. And therefore the concept and how to bring about this energy and the fact of energy itself are in a state of continuous contradiction. A man who is full of physical energy does not talk about the idea of energy; he is energetic. But the man who has not sufficient energy, who is ill, who is not mentally balanced—he has concepts about how this energy should be brought about. Whereas this morning when we are talking about this energy, we must be very clear that we are not talking about a concept, but the fact itself. We are not talking about the opinion, the assertion, the nature of this energy, or how to bring about this energy. But if we begin to see the fact itself and not the idea, then the contradiction will begin to disappear immediately.

So, we are going to talk about this energy. And the highest form of this energy, the apogee, is the state of mind when it has no idea, no thought, no sense of a direction or motive—that is pure energy. And that quality of energy cannot be sought after. You can't say, "Well, tell me how to get it, the modus operandi, the way." There is no way to it. To find out for ourselves the nature of this energy, we must begin to understand the daily energy which is wasted—the energy when we talk, when we hear a bird, a voice, when we see the river, the vast sky and the villagers, dirty, ill kept, ill, half-starved, and the tree that withdraws of an evening from all the light of day. The very observation of everything is energy. And this energy we derive through food, through the sun's rays. This physical, daily energy which one has, obviously can be augmented, increased, by the right kind of food and so on. That is necessary, obviously. But that same energy which becomes the energy of the psyche—that is, thought—the moment that energy has any contradiction in itself, that energy is a waste of energy.

Please follow this. We will go into it step by step. If we do not follow it logically, sanely, rationally, we won't come to that tremendous force, to the quality of energy that is completely at its highest—because in that alone is movement without time. And we waste our energy, this psychological energy, the energy that brings about thought, the energy that stores up memory, the energy that is the remembrance of things past, the energy that has been and will be—which is all the mechanism of thought. Whenever that energy meets a contradiction and does not understand it and is not free of that contradiction, then that energy is wasted. Contradiction is thinking one thing and doing something else, at the lowest level, not at the highest level but at the level of our daily living. To speak harshly to another and then to regret it later—the regret is a waste of energy which is the outcome of speaking harshly, which is the beginning of the waste of energy; and therefore, this creates the memory that one should not be harsh and that one must be kind; this creates the duality in which the conflict is a waste of energy. Sirs, I hope you are following this.

So, conflict of any kind—physically, psychologically, intellectually—is a waste of energy. Please, it is extraordinarily difficult to understand and to be free of this because most of us are brought up to struggle, to make effort. When we are at school, that is the first thing that we are taught—to make an effort. And that struggle, that effort is carried throughout life—that is, to be good you must struggle, you must fight evil, you must resist, control. So, educationally, sociologically, religiously, human beings are taught to struggle. You are told that to find God you must work, discipline, do practice, twist and torture your soul, your mind, your body, deny, suppress; that you must not look; that you must fight, fight, fight at that so-called spiritual level—which is not the spiritual level at all. Then, socially, each one is out for himself, for his family.

Please watch this yourself; we are going into something very, very, deep. If you will go with the speaker—not follow him, not authoritatively, but walk along with him, take the journey together with him—then you will come upon this extraordinary energy which renews itself without the least effort, which renovates the mind so that the mind remains young, fresh, innocent.

So, religiously, you are taught to make an effort. And sociologically also, you must struggle to attain, to achieve, to become: you must be better than your neighbor, you must have more. Ambition drives you, and that ambition is really a form of self-fulfillment—in the family, in society. That self-fulfillment, identifying itself with the group, with the race, with the nation, makes this constant effort, struggling, struggling, struggling. And there is this effort because of this contradiction; when you are ambitious, when you are fulfilling, there is always the possibility and the inevitability of being frustrated. And that very frustration drives you more, creating greater tension. And if one has the capacity, that tension expresses itself through writing poems or through various forms of distortions from that tension.

Socially, we make effort through our ambition, greed, envy, hate, pleasure; and that effort is the wasting of energy. Please observe it in yourself. And sexually, the very process becomes a tremendous problem for most people. Just see the reason of it, not what to do. We will go into that, and you will understand it as you go into it. Intellectually, you are suffocated; you never think for yourself originally, you repeat; you accumulate knowledge from books, and you can repeat endless phrases from the Gita or the Koran or from the latest writer, or this or that. So, intellectually, you are thwarted, suffocated, controlled, shaped, and there is no release intellectually. Nor emotionally—emotionally in the sense not sentimentally. A sentimental being is an ugly being because he becomes cruel, stupid, insensitive. I am not talking of sentimentality. I am talking of a person who is emotional. That emotion is thwarted when he has no appreciation of beauty.

To see the beauty in the face of a person, the beauty of a river, the beauty of a leaf on the roadside, the beauty of a smile, the beauty of a bird on the wing, you need passion, you need great feeling. But we have no feeling. Feeling implies care—to care for your children, for your neighbor, for your wife, for your servant, if you have a servant—really to care. And we don't care because we have no sense of passion and therefore no intimacy, no communion with beauty. We are suffocated, we are thwarted, because to us beauty is sexuality, and religions throughout the world have said, "To find God, you must not look at a woman." So, emotionally, we are thwarted, we are obstructed; we are destroyed by these sayings, by these half mature mahatmas, gods, and saints.

So the only thing that we have then is sex. Suppressed intellectually, emotionally, there is no outlet, there is no sensitivity. And naturally the only thing that is left is sex. In the office, in daily life, you are insulted. The ugliness of modern existence where you are merely a cog in a vast social machine—do look at yourself, please. So the wife, and the husband and sex—sex becomes extraordinarily important and out of proportion, and therefore sex becomes a problem; in that problem energy is wasted. Because we have no release in our thinking, we create the image, we think about the thing that gives us pleasure in life—which is sex. And physically, we have to go to an office every day, struggle—not having enough food; you know the whole business of existence.

So, all around, we are wasting energy. And that waste of energy in essence is conflict: the conflict between "I should" and "I should not," "I must" and "I must not." Once having created duality, conflict is inevitable. So one has to understand this whole process of duality—not that there is not man and woman, green and red, light and darkness, tall and short; all those are facts. But in the effort that goes into this division between the fact and the idea, there is the waste of energy. I do not know if you have not noticed that people indulge in talk—giving public talks, or talks at home or with themselves—always concerned with ideas: the socialist idea, the communist idea, or the capitalist idea. They are caught in ideas, not in facts. When you are completely concerned with the fact and not with the idea, then there is no conflict.

Please, if you understood this one simple thing in life, then you would understand the nature of conflict and therefore be free of it. Unless one totally eliminates every form of conflict, one is wasting energy completely. And the energy cannot be wasted because the mind needs every cord of energy to keep in with the movement of life—which is action—to flow with life. And to flow with life which is tremendous, which is not an idea, which is not a social reform, which is not the socialist or the communist or the Hindu attitude—to move with this extraordinary thing called life which is a movement, and to keep in with that movement without any friction demands tremendous energy. Therefore one has to understand this—not how to save energy.

If you say, "How am I to save energy?" then you have created a pattern of an idea—how to save it—and then conduct your life according to that pattern; therefore, there begins again a contradiction. Whereas if you perceive for yourself where your energies are being wasted, you will see that the principal force causing the waste is conflict—which is, having a problem and never resolving it, living with a deadly memory of something gone, living in tradition. One has to understand the nature of the dissipation of energy, and the understanding of the dissipation of energy is not according to Shankara, Buddha or some saint, but the actual observation of one's daily conflict in life. So the principal waste of energy is conflict—which doesn't mean that you sit back and be lazy. Conflict will always exist as long as the idea is more important than the fact.

Now we will go into the question of how we waste our energy through fear—I am taking that as an example; you can take any other example: greed, envy, ambition, or what you will. But understanding the structure, the nature and the meaning of fear, we shall be free of the idea and be able to face the fact—which is extraordinarily difficult—not come to the fact with an opinion which may have been remembered as an experience or as an idea or as an opinion, but face that fact; the two things are entirely different.

So we are going to examine fear and see what the fact is and what the opinion is. If you don't like fear, we will take, a little later, violence. We will take, first, fear and then violence. Because most people, practically everybody, have fear; and they are violent, practically everybody, in their thought, in their speech; and if they are not violent in their thought or in their speech, they are violent in their family—if it is not in the family, deep down there is the sense of violence. So I'm going to examine these two facts.

Fear does not exist in itself. Fear exists in relation to something—fear of public opinion, fear of death, fear of one's husband or wife, fear of losing a job. So fear exists in relation to something, it is caused by something. Now you say, "If I can find the cause of the fear, then I shall be free of the fear"; and you then analyze or introspect or examine the cause which brings about fear. Now this analysis, this examination is a waste of energy. Please understand this. Probably you have never thought about all this, so just listen to it, neither accepting nor denying; just look at it.

You say you are afraid and then you try to find a cause; you search, look, examine; and if you can't find a cause, you ask somebody, a psychoanalyst, or your guru; or somewhere you look until you find a cause. Look at what has happened! The fact of it is you are afraid. Then you look to the cause—that is, you have allowed a time interval. The time interval is the analysis, the introspection, the asking, the searching. Then you come upon the cause. Then you say, "How am I to dissolve that cause?" So the fact is one thing, which is fear; and you have wandered right away from it in trying to find out the cause and to eliminate the cause. So you have spent many days or even a minute, and the many days or the minute is a waste of energy. What is important is to understand fear—not the analysis, not the introspective examination, not, after having found the cause, how to get rid of the cause; all this process is a waste of energy.

Don't agree with me, please; watch it. You see, I am working. I am thinking aloud with you and you are not cooperating with me. You want me to lead you, and you are following—that is the misfortune of modern education, the misfortune of religious life and the misfortune of conformity.

So what is the fact in fear? Will the discovery of the cause of fear eliminate fear? Have you ever done it? You could spend a couple of hours or a couple of minutes to find out the cause. You can find it out very simply and very quickly. And after having found it, has the fear gone? Obviously not. You are back where you started. So you say to yourself, "There is something wrong in the process."

So what is the fact of fear? Now how do you find out? Not by running away from it, obviously—taking to drink, going to temples, turning on the radio, chattering endlessly, or reading innumerable books. Every form of escape from fear is a waste of energy. That is taken for granted, so we won't discuss it; that is fairly obvious. So what is the fact of fear? One is afraid of what another says, or one is afraid of the fact of death. Now, what is fear, what is the fact of fear? What is the truth in fear?—not the uncovering of the cause, not running away from it. What is the truth in that fear?

How is the mind to find the truth in fear? First of all, one has to understand that fear is the result of thinking—isn't it? If you did not think, you would not be afraid, would you? That is, if you did not think about death—I am taking that as an example—you would have no fear of death, would you? It is the idea that you are going to die, it is the idea that you have seen others die, it is the idea that you want to put it as far away as you can and not think about it that causes fear—that is, thinking about death causes fear. So you say, is it possible to live in life without thinking? Not go to sleep, not to vegetate, but to see the fact that thinking about death—which is, thought—creates the future. Right? Thought creates the future, thought creates the idea of public opinion and what public opinion is going to say; and that public opinion might deny you, deprive you of your job. So thinking about the future creates fear, breeds fear. And thinking about the past—when you were well, when you were happy, when you have had every comfort, whatever one has had—thinking about that as the past, and thinking about the future is fear. Right?

So, to understand fear, one has to understand the machinery of thought—not how to get rid of fear. As we have pointed out just now, thought breeds fear. And then you will say, "How am I to stop thinking?" You can't stop thinking—that would be too idiotic. But if you understood the whole process of the machinery of thinking, then you would be able to understand what is fear and be rid of fear. Is that clear so far?

So what is thinking? Thinking, as the electronic brain has shown and also as one can observe in oneself, is the response of memory. Thinking is the response or the reaction of the thing that happened yesterday, out of the thing that happened yesterday. An experience, an incident, an insult, flattery, a pain, a remembrance of the things of yesterday—when that reacts, that is the process of thinking. That is, when there is a time interval between the challenge and the response, in that time interval is the process of thinking.

Look, please don't shake your heads, observe it in yourselves; you are not agreeing with me.

That is, all thinking takes place in the interval between the question and the answer—which is, challenge and response. That interval can be lengthened, or that interval can be a split second. In that split second, or in the lengthened interval, is the machinery of memory, looking, searching, asking, demanding, waiting, expecting; and then finding; and then responding. That is, when one is asked a familiar question "What is your name?" the response is immediate because you are very familiar with your name, with your occupation, where you live; there is no time interval. There is a time interval of a split second or a millionth of a second when you hear and immediately respond, but there is still an interval. Then when a question is asked which demands a great deal of inquiry, thinking, so-called thinking, remembering, then the time interval is greater. Right? You are following this? During that time interval your mind, your brain, everything is in operation, looking for the answer.

Then, there is an interval when you say, "I don't know," and you are waiting, looking, searching, asking. It may take a year, it may take a day, but you are waiting, expecting. And then when you find, you say, "This is the answer." Right? You know, sir, I believe that over five thousand books or four thousand books are printed every week. I don't know the exact number. A great many books are printed, and we get information from these books. The distance to the moon, the extraordinary discoveries they are making in science, the doctors, their operations, the medicines, and the extraordinary economic theories—volumes have been written about all these, and one has not the time to learn, to read all these books. If one is alert, awake, if one observes with delight, with sharpness, with clarity, then one does not have to read a book at all; it is there everywhere for one to look and learn. Then one does not depend on authority; then one does not depend on one's own experience either.

So what we are doing this morning is not that the speaker is giving you information, but rather that you and I are exploring together into this question of fear; and in exploring into that, one discovers the whole structure of thinking. So the fact is: thought breeds fear. The understanding of the machinery of thought means facing the fact without a time interval. And facing the fact without a time interval is immediate action. A man who does not allow a time interval to take place but only is concerned with the fact—such a man has no fear. But the time interval is what is really important to understand, and not fear. The time interval is created by thought, which is the word, the symbol, the idea. Most of us are afraid of the word, not of the fact. You are afraid of the idea of death, but not of the fact of death—you don't know the fact. If you were to meet the fact without the time interval then your action would be entirely different; there would be no time interval to be afraid of. I wonder if you are getting all this.

So one sees the time interval as a means of solution of a psychological fact—not the fact of building a bridge; for that, you must have time. Allowing any time interval to creep in is a waste of energy, because in that time interval is conflict. And the time interval is not only the search for the cause of fear, but also the analysis to discover the cause and the determination to be rid of that cause—all that is the time interval in which there is effort, and therefore it is a waste of energy. You see this, sirs?

We said we would also take the question of violence. Most of us are violent—not merely physically: beating somebody, getting angry or ambitious or competitive, which are all violence. Don't fool yourself by saying that violence is merely a physical action. Violence is also this tremendous action: imposing on oneself a discipline, a pattern of discipline; suppression, control, subjugation, domination. It is not just violence, as the thing which we daily experience; it is much more subtle than that. So deep down and superficially, outwardly, we are violent—that is the fact. Because we have grown from the animal, we are frightened; and the stronger the animal the more violent it is.

I do not know if you have not noticed the dogs on this campus. You must have heard them every night, keeping you awake; and how violent they are! You know, there is something extraordinary about noise. The more you fight noise, the more you resist it, the less sleep, the less quiet you have. But if you allow the noise to pass through you as the wind passes through the window, without resisting it, then you will see that the dogs can howl their heads off, and your mind is not disturbed. Please try it.

Most of us are violent, and so we have invented the idea that we must be nonviolent. Look at what has happened! I am violent—in my gesture, in my attitude, in my exclusiveness, in my isolation, in my pride, in my envy, in my ambition. I am violent, conforming to violence, and then I invent the idea of nonviolence. The fact is one thing and the formula, the idea is another thing in which we are caught. Right? This schizophrenia—the double attitude towards life, never facing the fact but always endlessly talking about a fictitious idea which has no reality at all—has created conflict immediately. I am not brotherly; because, to be brotherly, there must be no nationality, no family—family, not in the sense I'll not have a wife and a child, but the idea of the family. The family is, obviously, antisocial immediately; it is always opposed to the rest of the world. We won't go into that.

So being violent and not knowing that we are violent and not being able to resolve that violence, hoping to get rid of that violence through an idea or an ideal, we pursue the ideal. The speaker has no ideal whatever because the speaker only deals with facts and not with ideals. The fact can only be observed when there is no time interval. One has to realize this, as one sees there is violence.

Now one has to find out this: Has the word, *violence*, created violence or the fact itself? Do you understand it? Sirs, the word is not the thing, the word *woman*, the word *child*, the word *door* is not the woman, is not the child, is not the door. For most of us, the word is the door, is the child, is the woman. Look at yourself, consider it yourself and you will see how words play an extraordinarily important part—a communist, a brahmin, a bureaucrat, an engineer, he is an ICS, he earns two thousand—all words. So one has to find out if the word is bringing about the violence, or if there is violence independent of the word. Please examine it for yourself. It requires a great deal of attention to find this out.

Most of us are caught in the word and not in the fact. So the word becomes an abstraction of the fact, and so most of us deal with the abstraction and not with the fact. To deal with the fact is not to allow the time interval between the seeing and the action, and therefore the seeing is the action. And because seeing the fact without the time interval is action, there is no violence. If you have gone into this, you will see how the mind can completely and utterly free itself from every form of violence.

And it is only when the mind is not dissipating in conflict and therefore is not allowing any time interval to intervene between the observer and the fact—only then is there the cessation of the waste of energy; we are thus eliminating every form of conflict—every form of conflict, which is duality. Duality will exist always if the fact is opposed through an opinion, through an idea and through a time interval. When the fact remains without any frills of time, then there is an action which is immediate and instantaneous.

So one begins to see that the waste of energy is caused by conformity to pattern, that the waste of energy is caused by thought—the time interval caught between the past and the future. A mind that is socialistically, politically, communistically trained, can never look at a fact; it always looks at the fact through its opinion, through its conditioning. There is another factor of contradiction which is much more complex, much more demanding of attention: that is the duality between the thinker and the thought—which we have no time to go into now. What we have gone into is sufficient, if you have followed so far. So there will be no waste of energy when the mind is capable of facing a fact without any time interval, whether the fact is the very simple fact of taking away a stone from the road, or mending a road, or taking a thorn out of the way, or whether it is the fact of yourself—what you actually are, not what you think you are, but what actually you are.

The facing of the fact without the time interval is the cessation of the dissipation of energy and therefore the continuous movement of energy. And you will find that in that energy there is no resistance—which I have explained already. That energy does not meet any form of hindrance because it understands, as it goes along, every resistance, every form of conflict, every contradiction—not waiting, asking, demanding—it is moving, living; every moment it is moving. Then, such an energy begins at the lowest level—really there is no lowest, but we will use that expression as a means of conveying our meaning—it begins with daily life. I won't use the word *lowest* because then, of course, you will misuse it. The energy that is in the very action of everyday existence—what you think, what you do, what you feel, what you say and how you say it—when that energy of everyday movement is freed from every form of hindrance, from every form of conflict—which is contradiction—then that very energy moves with such rapidity, with such freedom. And it is only such energy that renovates, makes the mind young, fresh, innocent; and such energy reaches its highest point, and the highest point is the unnameable, the sublime.

Question: Sir, . . .

KRISHNAMURTI: Sir, before you ask the question—I will not interrupt you, you will ask your question—you have not allowed any time interval between your question and what you have heard. You are not even listening, sir. You are so ready to ask your question before I have finished. I have finished, but you have already prepared your question; you are not listening. All right, sir, carry on. What is the question, sir?

Question: What is the time interval that you were explaining and what is that energy? Is it completely in motion, or is that static, sir?

KRISHNAMURTI: How can energy be static? I am afraid I don't understand your question, sir. You began with one thing and you have ended up with another. What are you trying to tell us, sir?

Sir, it is very simple. Why do you complicate a very simple fact? When you say, "I will change," there is a time interval, is there not? When you say, "I will do that tomorrow," there is a time interval, isn't there? I say the time interval is a waste of energy. That is, when something can be done immediately—and all action is in the immediate—why introduce the interval of time? Why do you say, "I will do it"? Take this, for instance, sir: one is angry or jealous. Why don't you deal with that fact immediately, why do you allow a time interval by saying, "I will do it tomorrow; I will get rid of it tomorrow"? Why? Because you are so used to postponing, you are so used to the habit of saying, "I will do it." So, gradually, you have increased the time interval so that you can carry on with the thing you want to do—which may be harmful; but you like it, and therefore you carry on. Why pretend?

Question: Is immediate action total action?

KRISHNAMURTI: That is right, sir. I said, "immediate action." That is one of the most difficult things to understand, so don't just say, "immediate action." You know, there are people who say, "Live in the present." To live in the present is one of the most extraordinary things. To live in the present—which is the immediate action—one has to understand the conditioning which is the past, and not project that past into the future; and one has therefore to eliminate the time interval and live in that extraordinary sense of the immediate. That requires great energy. But that energy is not derived through ideas, sir. Ideas give energy, as you know. Ideas have given energy—the idea as a nation will give you energy to fight another nation. And on that extraordinarily wasteful energy we are living, and we are satisfied with that energy. And when somebody comes along and says, "Don't waste energy," you immediately translate and say, "All right, I must be a bachelor, I must do this"; and thereby again you build contradictions and you get caught in them.

So, to understand this whole question, sir, one must be very simple—not the simplicity of a loincloth, which is the outward exhibition of nonsimplicity, but to be really simple—that is, to go within oneself and commune within oneself all the time, endlessly, without a time interval. You can go to the moon, Mars, Venus—that requires energy. See the astonishing energy of the engineers, the mathematicians, the laborers who put a million things together. I believe it takes a million separate parts to make a rocket, and these million parts must function faultlessly. That requires tremendous energy, and that energy is comparatively easy. But the energy to go within, never having a resting place, never letting that energy stagnate, never letting that energy look back or forward, but keeping it moving endlessly—it is only that energy that has gone so deeply, endlessly within itself, that knows the sublime.

November 24, 1964

Fourth Talk in Rajghat

We would like this morning, if we may, to talk about something that may be a little foreign to you, and perhaps about which you have not thought a great deal. But it must be thought about, it must be inquired into and explored to find for oneself the truth of the matter. Merely to be satisfied with words, or to refer what is being said to what you already know, or to compare it with that which you have already read, will only prevent further understanding and inquiry. So, I would like, before I go into this matter, to prevent—if one can use that word—or stop you from comparing. When you are comparing or referring what you have heard, or what you are going to hear, with what already you have read about, it will actually prevent your immediate understanding. And the immediate understanding is far more important than mere recollection and comparison, than a conclusion.

We are going to inquire into freedom. We are going to inquire into that extraordinary state of mind that has the quality of love. And as we are going to inquire into it, we have to use words. Words prevent one from really coming into immediate contact because the word is not the thing and it never is. What you hear is not *what is.* Unless one has deeply understood the significance of words and is not caught up in words and their influence and their emotional content—unless there is a certain quality of freedom from words, one is caught up in them, and all further inquiry and all further understanding come to an end. So one has to be aware of the extraordinary difficulty of words.

Man throughout the world is being organized—economically, socially, and religiously. He lives in a crowded town or in skyscrapers, living in drawers, in boxes. And men are going to the moon and are living under the sea; they have built huts to live under the sea, on the floor of the sea, for a month, for a week. And being caught in this extraordinary organization of efficiency—and there must be efficiency—man has always sought a further frontier, further space, a feeling of limitless space without horizon, without a border, where there is neither earth nor the sky nor the horizon. Man has always sought space. And without space you and I could not exist.

Please follow this. This is not some kind of vague, abstract subject which we are talking about. We have to understand this thing called space. If there were no space, you would not be able to see, or hear. If you had no space between you and the speaker, you couldn't see the speaker or hear the words that he is using. There must be space between you and that tree, between you and your wife, between you and your neighbor. And there is. And man is getting more and more organized; governments are controlling his thoughts, and religion has denied him his freedom. Religions may assert freedom in another world, but freedom of the mind all religions have denied, actually, because they have imposed on the mind beliefs, dogmas, rituals, fear. And the more there is the explosion of population—as there is in this country and throughout the world—the more people are forced to live together in crowded towns, the more they are organized, controlled, made efficient, and there is less and less space. Space is created, if you observe, by the object as well as without the object.

Please, you have neither to accept nor to reject, but just to observe. The object—you sitting there and me sitting here—creates space round it. This microphone creates space round it; otherwise, it couldn't exist. So, we only know a space because of the object which creates the space. There is the space between the earth and the moon: this space exists because the earth is away from the moon. There is the object, the center; and the observer is the center, is the object looking out.

This is a very difficult subject we are going to discuss—I am going to talk about. And you need all your attention because if you don't follow the thing you won't come to the end of it, you won't flow with it. Man has always sought space outwardly—new frontiers, new countries. And when all the earth has been conquered, explored, as it has now been, he is inquiring into outer space—the space between the earth and the sun, and the moon and the stars. He is always going outward, outward, outward, seeking this space. And inwardly, religions, society, his personal tendencies, fears, the family, circumstances and tensions and pressure of population, and so on, have prevented him from finding the space within. And if you have no space within, you have no freedom. If the object only creates space, then the mind is caught within that space which is bred, brought about by the object. And therefore there is no freedom if one once admits, or allows, or knows that space is created only by the object.

That is, as long as there is a center which creates space round it, and as long as there is no other space except the space which the object creates round itself, there is no freedom for man. You understand? The center is the 'me', which is physical as well as emotional as well as intellectual. The 'me' creates the space round itself because the center exists. And because the center exists and creates the space, and if that is the only space man can ever know, then there is no freedom at all. And if there is no freedom for man, not abstract freedom but freedom in living his daily life: going to the office, doing his daily routine, however pleasurable or painful—if there is no freedom in his daily life, then he is a slave forever: slave to environment, slave to all the pleasures of existence, slave to every form of social influence. And if the object only creates the space, there is no freedom. There can be freedom, obviously, only when there is space without the center, without the object. And that is what we are going to inquire into this morning.

You must have space; otherwise, you have no freedom. Even in a little room, however small it is, you must have space to move about in, to put your things, to do your exercise, to play. To do anything in life, you must have space. And we demand this space outwardly: better houses, more playgrounds, forests, woods, trees, going on boats, and so on. But inwardly we never want space, our minds refuse space, because we are frightened.

We are going to inquire, not abstractly, whether it is possible for a mind to be completely free and therefore to have space without a center—only that space without a center is free. The space is translated by the scientist as a field: electromagnetic field, gravitational field, nuclear field, and so on. We are not talking of a field as the scientist knows it. But we are talking about the space which is beyond the scientific investigation of fields as the scientist knows it; we are inquiring into something much more human, which has relationship with human thought, and not merely into scientific facts. So you must first see the problem very clearly, even intellectually, verbally. That is, man must have space. Modern society with an ever exploding population, the atomic fears, wars, threats, forces man to go out, outwardly.

And we only know space because there is the observer, the center, the object, which creates the space. A piece of furniture creates the space round it—so also a wall, a house—and that is the only space you know: the space that you observe with your eyes when you look out from the earth to the moon, to the stars.

So we are going to inquire into this problem of space without the object. And only in that space is freedom; that space without the object is freedom. In inquiring into space and freedom we are also going to discover for ourselves what is love. Because without love there is no freedom. Love is not sentimentality, love is not emotionality. Love is not being in an emotional state, nor is it devotional.

So we going to find out for ourselves. To find out, we must create space in the mind. We must empty the mind, obviously, so as to give space: not space in a limited field of thought, but space without limit and space within, if we can so divide it—that is, space in the mind and in the heart; otherwise, there is no love, no freedom. And without love and freedom man is doomed. You may live very comfortably on the fifteenth floor of the skyscraper or live most miserably in a filthy little village; but you will be doomed unless there is this extraordinary, limitless space within the mind and the heart, within the whole of your being.

Now, as I said, we are going to inquire. I am going to go into it. Probably you have not thought about this at all. I am going to go into it, and you have to be sufficiently awake, alert, watchful, forceful, energetic, if we are to travel together. But if you just sit there agreeing, disagreeing, nodding your head in approval or in denial, you will be left behind.

Now, this inquiry into space is meditation. Please listen carefully. I am using the word *meditation,* not in your sense—so don't take a posture immediately, don't sit up straight. I said the inquiry into and the understanding of this space demands meditation. But the meditation with which is associated posture, breath, repetition of words, concentration, various forms of having visions, heightened sensitivity, is not meditation. It is all a form of self-hypnosis. You may say, "Well, aren't you making a rather sweeping statement, a vast general statement?" I am not. We haven't the time this morning to go into it all step by step. And I shall go into it very briefly because there is much more to be said about it than the mere repetition of fairly obvious things.

So meditation is the inquiry into, and the discovery of, this space without a center. Therefore it is not an experience at all. You understand? If you experience that space, you have a center from which you are experiencing; therefore, you are a slave to the center which creates the space, and therefore you are not free. So you have to understand this thing that man demands, which is experience. He wants more and more experience because he is fed up with the daily routine experience of going to an office, sex, the everyday boredom of life. As he wants more experience, he turns to drugs, to various forms of stimulants, which will give him new experience, new visions, new states of heightened sensitivity, which will bring about further experience.

So, a mind that is seeking more experience is only perpetuating the center which is creating the space, and therefore it is never free. And experience comes only when there is a challenge and a response. And the inadequacy of that response demands further experience. Please, you have not thought about all this; just listen, go into it, as I am going along. So a mind that is seeking experience is a mind that wishes or wants or has not understood that experience—this only further enslaves the mind. You have had the experience of going to an office for forty or fifty years. You have had the experience of hunger, of sex. You have had the experience of your peculiar devotions to peculiar idols made by the hand or by the mind. And you live in those experiences and pretty soon you get tired of them, bored with them—whether it be Jesus, or Krishna, or any other man-made thing. So you want more experience, further experience away from all this stupid stuff. So you call that a mystical, extraordinary state. A man who is seeking experience and calls it mysticism is deluding himself; he is only projecting his own desires, his own conditionings, his own unfulfilled, agonizing demands, clothed in virtue, in nobility, in visions.

So one has to be free of this demand for experience because, as I have explained, the moment you want experience, you are strengthening the center, the observer, and creating a little space round it and living in that space. In that space you have your relationship, your family, the design of morality and everything; and that little space will never bring freedom, do what you will.

Similarly, the escape through prayers, through repetition of words, is fairly obvious. Because you are dissatisfied with life, there is agony, there is misery, conflict, the agonizing existence of life. And you pray for somebody—for what you call God—to give you relief. You shed tears, you beg, you are suffocated by your own thirst of ignorance. You pray and you never find satisfaction. When you do pray, you are supplicating, you are asking, you are begging, you are putting out your hand for somebody to fill it; and there generally is somebody to fill it—that is the most peculiar part of life, it is always filled by somebody. Because you are seeking to be filled, you are asking, begging, searching for someone to give you something to fill your hands, your heart, your mind; and you are filled. There are people who pray for refrigerators. Don't laugh; they are just like you; only their prayer is much more concrete. You want happiness, you want experience, you want something which you call much better than worldly goods—it is exactly the same thing as asking for a refrigerator, a better house. So a mind that begs can never be free.

Please, we are inquiring into freedom and space and love, and this inquiry is a process of meditation. Therefore I am putting away the things which are not meditation—such as experience, prayer, repetition of words, mantras, turning over beads endlessly. The repetition of words, turning over beads calms the mind. You know, if you repeat something over and over again like a machine, naturally your mind becomes quiet—that is, your mind becomes dull, stupid, heavy. But that is not meditation. Sitting in the right position, with a straight back, breathing regularly—that gives a certain quietness to the body, but that is not meditation; if you sit straight, blood can flow easier to the head, and that is all there is to it, nothing else. A petty mind, a shallow mind, a narrow mind, a mind that is jealous, furious, angry, bitter, agonizing, suffocating—a mind that has no sense of beauty, such a mind can sit straight with a straight back, breathe regularly, do all the tricks, and think it is doing meditation—it is not meditating, it is dying in its own putrefaction. None of these things is meditation because meditation is something that comes into being naturally—you do not have to pursue it. A man who deliberately sits to meditate is merely cultivating a habit, wanting a certain experience, a certain state of mind—and he will get it; but that is not meditation, that is only a form of hypnosis.

So, we are inquiring into this extraordinary thing of space without object. And that space must exist; otherwise, there is no freedom and love. And it is only when you see the false as the false, and the truth in the false, that you are beginning to empty the mind—that is, then the mind is emptying itself. Then you will see the truth in the falseness that experience is going to liberate you. When you see the truth of experience, the whole implication of experience, then you are free of it; you are no longer asking, demanding, panting after experience—which does not mean that you are satisfied, content like a cow. And when you see the falseness and therefore the truth in prayers, in postures, in deliberate methods invented by man with a definite goal, in doing certain definite practices which you call by so many names—all that only makes the mind dull, stupid, heavy; and therefore the mind is never free. So when you see the falseness and the truth in that falseness, then you are free of it, you do not have to struggle, you do not have to say, "How am I to get rid of this stupid thing?"—because you see it is stupid, it is gone.

So, the mind realizes that without space, without infinite space, there is no freedom, and that there is infinite space only when there is no object which creates the space. You see the beauty of it? Space is infinite the moment there is no object; and therefore, freedom is infinite. And when there is this sense of space without borders, without limit, infinite, out of that infiniteness comes love—not the love of God, not the love of man, but love which shares, which watches, which nourishes, which protects, which guides, which helps, which shows.

Meditation is not being absorbed by a toy invented by man. You know, a child is absorbed by a toy, and he is quiet because the toy is so interesting; he is taken over by the toy, and he won't be mischievous; he will behave for the time being because the toy is new and delightful to play with and because his whole attention is concentrated there. And so are men; the grown-up people have their toys, the toys of images, the toys of ideas, of Masters, pictures, visions; by those visions, by those Masters, by those toys they are absorbed; and during that period they behave very nobly, very quietly, decently. So absorption by a toy is not meditation.

Nor is concentration meditation. We all learn to concentrate. Apparently that is one of the most important things taught by the various stupid schools that preach, talk, teach meditation. Think of anybody teaching another how to meditate—as though you can be taught! See the fallacy of it. You can learn, you can be taught how to drive a car, how to learn a language, how to acquire a particular technique. But you cannot be taught—through a method, through a system—how to meditate. If you are taught, if you have learned that particular method of meditation, you are caught in it. Therefore again there is no freedom.

So, through the understanding of experience and seeing the truth of that, the mind is free from the demand for experience. By understanding and observing, seeing the falseness of prayer, various forms of postures, breathing—seeing the falseness and the truth of it, you are free. And also you are free of this supplication, of this being absorbed by toys—toys created by another or by yourself. And also you are free of this terrible thing called concentration, because concentration is a process of exclusion. When you want to concentrate on what you think is right, on your particular image, God, or idea, phrase, you focus your mind on that; but the mind wanders off, and you pull it back; again it wanders off, and again you pull it back; you play this game for the rest of your life. And that is what you call meditation, this battle—forcing the mind when it is not interested in something, and trying to control it. And if you saw that, if you understood the truth of this matter or the falseness of this process, then you would never concentrate, whether you are in a school learning a particular subject, or whether you are teaching in a school. Do not concentrate, when you are in your office, or when you are trying to meditate. Do not concentrate; that only excludes, creates a resistance, a focus, giving greater strength to the center and therefore limiting space.

Now, if you understand all this, then out of this understanding comes awareness, which is nothing mysterious. Just to be aware: to be aware of that river when you are near it, not from here, to watch the sail of a boat, to see the current go by, to see that bridge, to hear the train going over it making a noise, to see the tree—just to see it, not to compare it, not to judge it, not to say, "I like" or "I don't like"—just to observe. And from the outside you come inside, come inside the room, and you observe the shape of the room; don't compare it, don't say, "It is ugly" or "It is beautiful, I wish I were living in it," or "I wish I had that carpet, that furniture"; but just look at the colors, the shape, the beauty, the ugliness of the curtains, the light out of the window, and the people, their faces, their expressions, without judging, without comparing, without analyzing—you just observe, choicelessly.

And with that awareness, starting from the outside—the dirt, the squalor, the poverty; the national divisions; the religious separations; the battle between the tribes, between the nations, between the groups, between the families; the family within itself, the husband, the wife against each other, the brutality, the sexual demands, the unfulfilled appetites, agonies—observing that awareness from the outside, come in. It is all one movement. And as you come in you go deeper; from the room you go into yourself—what you think, what you feel; don't judge it, don't say, "This is noble" or "This is ignoble" or "I shouldn't be this" or "I shouldn't be that" or "I am Supreme God, I am atma"—all that is sheer nonsense, created by your own mind to give you a certain satisfaction. Just observe what you are. What you are is the fact—the fact that you are jealous, anxious, envious, brutal, demanding, violent. That is what you are. Look at it, be aware; don't shape it, don't guide it, don't deny it, don't have opinions about it. By looking at it without condemnation, without judgment, without comparison, you observe; out of that observation, out of that awareness comes affection.

Now, go still further. And you can do this in one flash. It can only be done in one flash—not first from the outside and then working further and deeper and deeper and deeper; it does not work that way, it is all done with one sweep, from the outermost to the most inward, to the innermost depth. Out of this, in this, there is attention—attention to the whistle of that train, the noise, the coughing, the way you are jerking your legs about; attention whereby you listen to what is said, you find out what is true and what is false in what is being said, and you do not set up the speaker as an authority. So this attention comes out of this extraordinarily complex existence of contradiction, misery, and utter despair. And when the mind is attentive, it can then give focus, which then is quite a different thing; then it can concentrate but that concentration is not the concentration of exclusion. Then the mind can give attention to whatever it is doing, and that attention becomes much more efficient, much more vital, because you are taking everything in.

So that is the beginning of meditation—that is, the mind which has sought space and searched for it outwardly, having understood outward space, moves with that same energy, with that same intensity as is required to go to the moon, and turns inward within itself and looks. And denying the false—not verbally, but actually, ruthlessly cutting out, like a surgeon, all the stupid things that man has invented in order to make the mind quiet—the mind comes to a quietness, to a very still state. And the mind is no longer seeking, asking, demanding, because it has understood all that. So the mind then becomes naturally, without any enforcement, without any pressure, quiet, completely still. A mind is only still when there is no object in that stillness to experience. Please understand, you cannot experience this stillness; the moment you say, "I must experience stillness," you are no longer still. And I have explained what the implication of experiencing is. So it is not to be experienced. And such a still mind, which knows what space is without the object, is an empty mind. It is empty of every effort, of every struggle, of every demand, of every agony, of despair, because it is free of the psychological structure of society—which is the animal still, which is greedy, envious, acquisitive, competitive, seeking power, domination, and all the rest of it.

It is only such a mind that has understood—not verbally but actually—this extraordinary space and emptiness. Then, if the mind can go still further—there is no further really, it is part of the same thing—then you will understand what it is to love. Really you have no love. You have pleasure, you have sensation, you have sexual attachments, such as the family, the wife, the husband, the attachment to a nation. But attachment is not love. And love is not something divine and profane: it has no division. Love means something to care for: to care for the tree, for your neighbor, for the child—to see that the child has the right education, not just put him in a school and disappear; the right education, not just technological education—and to see that the children have the right teachers, right food, that they understand life, that they understand sex. Teaching children merely geography, mathematics, or a technical thing which will give them a job—that is not love. And without love you cannot be moral—you may be respectable; that is, you may conform to society: that you will not steal, that you will not chase your neighbor's wife, that you will not do this and you will not do that. But that is not morality, that is not virtue, that is merely the conformity of respectability. Respectability is the most terrible, disgusting thing on earth because it covers so many ugly things. Whereas when there is love, there is morality. Do what you will, it is moral if there is love.

And love, like freedom, can only be when you have understood meditation. Therefore, when a mind is empty of all the things and pressures of two million years which man has lived in, out of that comes this extraordinary thing called emptiness and space. It is only then that the mind can be quiet. And it is only then that there is love and that extraordinary thing called creation.

November 26, 1964

Fifth Talk at Rajghat

From recent discoveries of the anthropologists man has apparently been living on this earth for about two million years. And man has left in caves, for about seventeen thousand years, records of the struggle, the battle, the unending sorrow of existence—the battle between good and evil, between brutality and the thing he seeks everlastingly, which is love. And man has not apparently solved his problems: not mathematical problems, not scientific or engineering problems, but human problems of relationship—how to live in this world peaceably, how to be in intimate contact with nature and see the beauty of a bird on a naked branch.

Coming down to modern times, our problems, human problems, are increasing more and more; and these problems we try to resolve according to certain patterns of morality, behavior, and according to the various commitments that one has given one's mind to. According to our commitments, patterns of behavior, religious formulas and sanctions, we try to solve our problems, our agonies, our despair, our inconstancy and the contradictions of our life. We take up a certain attitude as a communist, a socialist, this or that; and from that attitude, from that platform as it were, we try to solve our problems piecemeal, one after the other—this is what we do in our lives.

One may be a great scientist, but that very scientist in his laboratory is entirely different from the scientist at home, who is a national, who is bitter, angry, jealous, envious, competitive with his fellow scientists for a greater name, for greater popularity and for more money. He is not concerned with human problems at all; he is concerned with the discovery of various forms of matter and the truth of all that.

And we too, being ordinary human beings, not experts, not specialists along any particular line, are committed to a certain pattern of behavior, to certain religious concepts, or to national poison; and from that we strive to solve the ever increasing, multiplying problems.

You know there is no end to talking, no end to reading. Words can be piled upon words, and the phrasing, the beauty of the language, the reason or the illogicity of what is being said either persuades you or dissuades you. But what is important is not the piling up of words and listening to talks and discourses and reading but rather resolving the problem—the human problem, your problem—not piecemeal, not as it arises, not according to circumstances, not according to the pressures and strains of modern existence, but from a totally different activity. There are the human problems of greed, envy, the dull spirit of the mind, the aching heart, the appalling insensitivity of man, the brutality, the violence, the deep despair and agony. And during the two million years we have lived, we have tried to solve these problems according to different formulas, different systems, different methods, different gurus, different ways of looking, asking, questioning; and yet we are where we are, caught in this endless process of agony, confusion, and endless despair.

Is there a way of resolving the problems entirely, completely, so that they never arise, and if they do arise, we can meet them instantly and resolve them, dissipate them, put them away? Is there a total way of life that gives no soil to problems, is there a way of living—not the pattern of a way, of a method, of a system, but a total way of living—so that no problem at any time will arise, and if it does arise, it can be resolved instantly? Because a mind that carries the burden of problems becomes a dull, heavy, stupid mind. I do not know if you have watched your own mind and the minds of your wives, husbands, and your neighbors. When the mind has problems of any kind, those very problems—even mathematical problems, however complex, however painful, however intriguing, intellectual—make the mind dull. By the word *problem* I mean a difficult question, a difficult relationship, a difficult issue which remains unresolved, and which is carried from day to day. So we are asking if there is a way of living, if there is a state of mind which, because it understands the totality of existence, has no problem, and which, when a problem does arise, can resolve it immediately. Because the moment a problem is carried over even for a day, even for a minute, it makes the mind heavy, dull, and the mind has no sensitivity to look, to observe.

So, is there a total action, a state of mind that resolves every problem as it arises, and has no problem in itself, at whatever depth, conscious or unconscious? I do not know if you have ever asked that question of yourself. Probably not, because most of us are so sunk, so held in the problems of everyday existence—earning a livelihood and the demands of a society which psychologically builds a structure of ambition, greed, acquisitiveness—that we have no time to inquire. This morning we are going to inquire into this, and it depends upon you how deeply you inquire, how earnestly you demand, with what clarity and intensity you observe.

We have apparently lived for two million years—a terrible idea! And probably, as human beings are, we shall live another two million years, caught in the everlasting pain of existence. Is there a way, is there something that will free man from this, entirely, so that he will not live even a second in agony, will not invent a philosophy which satisfies him in his agony, will not have a formula which he applies to all the problems that arise, thereby increasing those problems? There is! There is a state of mind that can resolve problems immediately, and therefore, the mind, in itself, has no problem, conscious or unconscious.

And we are going to inquire into that this morning. And though the speaker is going to use words and penetrate as far as possible through the communication of words, you have to listen and understand. You are a human being, not an individual, because you are still the world, the mass; you are part of this terrible structure of society. There is individuality only when there is a state of mind when the mind has no problems, when it has completely extricated itself from the social structure of acquisitiveness, greed, ambition.

We say that there is a state of mind that can live without any problem and can resolve instantly any problem that arises. You have to see how important it is not to carry a problem over, even for a day or for a second. Because the more you have a problem unresolved, the more you give it soil in which it can take root, the more the mind, the heart, the nervous sensitivity is destroyed. So it is imperative that the problem should be resolved immediately.

Is it possible, after having lived for two million years with the conflicts, the misery, the remembrance of many yesterdays—is it possible for the mind to free itself from that so that it is complete, whole, not broken up? And to find that out, one has to inquire into time because problems and time are closely related.

Please, you are not listening to me, you are not listening to my words and descriptions. Don't be mesmerized by my words, by the speaker on the platform. This is not propaganda, because propaganda is a lie; there is no truth in repetition.

So, you are inquiring into your own mind, into your own heart, as a human being who has lived for so long, with so much anxiety and despair and fear. The speaker is only indicating. We are walking together. And you have to walk, not sit back and say, "Proceed ahead of me and tell me all about it"—we are not in that relationship. Therefore, when we walk together we have to see the same things together—see the same bird, smell the same breeze that is bringing the freshness of the river, see the same tree, see the same dirt, the people who are dirty, squalid. We have to see everything that is seen, together, at the same time, with the same intensity; otherwise, you and I cannot commune about something which demands tremendous inquiry, not verbal acceptance or denial. So if you and I are going to take the journey together into this question, you have to be much more alert, vital, awake, intense than the speaker himself; only then can you proceed.

So we are going to inquire into time. That is, after having lived for two million years, must we go on living another two million years in sorrow, pain, anxiety, everlasting struggle, death? Is that inevitable? Society is progressing, is evolving that way—evolving through war, through pressure, through this battle of East and West, through the various contentions of nationality, the common market, the blocks of this power and that power. Society is moving, moving, moving—slowly, in a sense asleep, but it is moving. Well, perhaps in two million years, society will come to some kind of state where it can live with another human being without competition, with love, with gentleness, with quiet, with an exquisite sense of beauty. But must one wait two million years to come to that? Must one not be impatient? I am using the word *impatient* in the right sense—being impatient, having no patience with time. That is, can we not resolve everything, not in terms of time but immediately?

Do think about this. Do not say it is not possible or it is possible. What is time? There is chronological time, time by the watch—that is obvious, that is necessary; when you have to build a bridge, you have to have time. But every other form of time—that is, "I will be, I will do, I must not"—is not true; it is just an invention of a mind that says, "I will do it." If there is no tomorrow—and there is no tomorrow—then your whole attitude is different. And actually there is no such time—when you are hungry, sexual, or lustful, you have no time; you want that thing immediately. So the understanding of time is the resolution of problems.

Please see the intimate relationship between the problem and time. For instance, there is sorrow. You know what sorrow is—not the supreme sorrow, but the sorrow of being lonely, the sorrow of not achieving something you want, the sorrow of not seeing clearly, the sorrow of frustration, the sorrow of having lost somebody whom you think you love, the sorrow of seeing something very clearly, intellectually, and not being able to do it. And beyond this sorrow, there is a still greater sorrow—the sorrow of time. Because it is time that breeds sorrow. Do please listen to this. We have accepted time; which is the gradual process of life, the gradual way of evolving, the gradual change from this to that, from anger to a state of nonanger gradually. We have accepted the gradual process of evolution, and we say that is part of existence, that is part of life, that is God's plan or the communist plan or some other plan. We have accepted it, and we live with that not ideationally, but actually.

Now, for me, that is the greatest sorrow—to allow time to dictate the change, the mutation. Have I to wait ten thousand years and more, have I to go through this misery, conflict, for another ten thousand years, and slowly, gradually change little bit by little bit, take my time, move slowly? And to accept that and to live in that state is the greatest sorrow. If I lose my son, my wife, my husband; if I fulfill or if I don't fulfill—those are all very trivial things. I can resolve all sorrow if I understand the greatest sorrow which time breeds.

Please listen to all this. Most of you, being conditioned to the acceptance of time, say, "In some future life I will change, I will be good; not in this life, it is too much; I have ten thousand lives more, why hurry?" So the moment you accept time as a means of change, you do not see the falseness in that fact and therefore the truth of that—that is the greatest sorrow. Not, if I fail or if I don't fail, if I become a rich man or a poor man—that is all so utterly petty in relation to something much vaster. So is sorrow, grief—the loss of something good, the loss of something beautiful, the fear of what might be, the fear of what is called evil, this sorrow we live with. A mind that is in sorrow is a dull mind. Whether it is the sorrow of the Christ for mankind, and he bearing his sorrow—it is still a dull mind.

Is it possible to end that sorrow immediately? That is the real crux of the matter. Because once I resolve sorrow, everything is over—sorrow in the deeper sense of that word. Because a mind in sorrow can never know what it means to love.

For most people sorrow is self-pity—I have lost my son and I am left; and I am pitying myself that I have been left lonely, with nobody to help me fulfill—you know the whole business of self-pity. So is it possible to end that sorrow immediately, and not allow this habit of gradually getting rid of sorrow? That sorrow is not resolved by time, and we know that sorrow cannot be resolved by time. You can live ten thousand years or ten days, or one day, or a split second more: but time will not resolve sorrow. So, one has to learn immediately, not gradually, because there is no learning anything gradually—psychologically. If I learn a language, it will take time, many days, because I have to get used to the rhythm of the words, the sound of a strange word, the grammar, the syntax, how to put the words together, how to use the right word, the right verb, and so on. But here, if I allow time, sorrow will increase. So I have to learn about sorrow immediately, and the very act of learning is the complete cutting away of time. To see something immediately, to see the false immediately—that very seeing of the false is the action of truth which frees you from time.

I am going a little bit into this question of seeing. As we came in just now, there was a parrot—green, bright, with its red beak, on a dead branch against the blue sky. We do not see it at all; we are too occupied, we are too concentrated, we are disturbed, so we never see the beauty of that bird on the dead branch against the blue sky. The act of seeing is immediate—not "I will learn how to see." If you say, "I will learn," you have already introduced time. So, not only to see that bird but also to hear that train, to hear the coughing, this nervous coughing that is going on all the time here—to hear that noise, to listen to it is an immediate act. And it is an immediate act to see very clearly, without the thinker—to see that bird, to see what one is, actually—not the theories about super-atma and all the rest of it, but to see actually what one is.

To see implies a mind that has no opinion, that has no formula. If you have a formula in your mind, you will never see that bird, that parrot on that branch against the sky, you will never see the total beauty of it. You will say, "Yes, that is a parrot of such and such a species, and the dead branch is of such and such a tree, and the blue of the sky is blue because of light, specks of dirt"; but you will never see the totality of that extraordinary thing. And to perceive the totality of that beauty, there is no time. In the same way, to see the totality of sorrow, time must not come in at all.

I will show you, sirs! I have lost my son and I am in sorrow. What is involved in that sorrow? I am going to analyze it, a little bit quickly. First, there is the shock of losing somebody in whom I have invested myself. Please, I am being ruthless—not sentimental. I have invested in my son my hopes, my immortality, my continuity; he is the heir to my property if I have a property; he is going to fulfill much more than I. And suddenly that son is cut off, and I am left without an entity in whom I have invested my own personal hopes, fears, everything. So I am lonely. Then, being lonely, I begin to have self-pity, and say, "Oh, how terrible!" I begin this whole circle of self-pity, and I begin to cry over my son. Really I am crying over my own state of emptiness, loneliness, self-pity, the sense of being frustrated, and so on.

Now, to see the whole of that, to see this whole process how sorrow comes out of the death of a particular person whom I have identified with myself as "my son," to see the totality of that, the loneliness, the sense of being frustrated, my investment, self-pity, to see the whole of that at one glance, not analytically—if you see it immediately, then you have put a stop to time, haven't you, and therefore to sorrow. Because it is time that breeds this sorrow—"Oh, I had hoped my son would be that; I had hoped my son would become much bigger than me; I had invested my immortality, the continuity of the name through him." You have used time to further your own existence, and when that further existence identified with your son is cut off, you are caught in time. I don't know if you are following all this.

So if you see the totality of this whole process, then you are no longer in sorrow—you are in a state of high sensitivity, observing. And that observation is prevented when you say, "My son will be reborn and we shall be reunited," which is again "time." So what is important is to see immediately, and to demand—not just say, "Well, I will learn about it"—that you must see everything immediately, clearly, that you must see your own states, the social condition, that you must see everything about you, not according to your likes and dislikes, not according to the particular pattern of the social structure that you know, but see everything clearly, without any center, without any opinion. Then you will see that the noninterference of time with the fact will never create problems.

Please look at it in another way. You know, actually we have no love—that is a terrible thing to realize. Actually we have no love; we have sentiment; we have emotionality, sensuality, sexuality; we have remembrances of something which we have thought as love. But actually, brutally, we have no love. Because to have love means no violence, no fear, no competition, no ambition. If you had love you would never say, "This is my family"—you may have a family and give them the best you can; but it would not be "your family" which is opposed to the world. If you love, if there is love, there is peace. If you loved, you would educate your child not to be a nationalist, not to have only a technical job and look after his own petty little affairs; you would have no nationality. There would be no divisions of religion, if you loved. But as these things actually exist—not theoretically, but brutally—in this ugly world, it shows that you have no love. Even the love of a mother for her child is not love. If the mother really loved her child, do you think the world would be like this? She would see that he had the right food, the right education, that he was sensitive, that he appreciated beauty, that he was not ambitious, greedy, envious. So the mother, however much she may think she loves her child, does not love the child.

So we have not that love. Now love cannot be cultivated, obviously; it is like cultivating humility—it is only the vain man, the man of arrogance, who can cultivate humility; that is a cloak to hide his vanity. As humility cannot be cultivated, so love cannot be cultivated. But you must have it. If you don't have it, you cannot have virtue, you cannot be orderly, you cannot live with passion—you may live with lust, which we all know. So if you have no love, you have no virtue; and without virtue there is disorder.

Now, how are you going to get love? You understand the problem? You must have love, as you must have water when you are thirsty. How are you going to get it? With time? In a future life, the future life of tomorrow, or when you die, or in the next life? Or the next second, which is still the future? Will that give you this sense of love with care, which means beauty? Love and beauty go together—they are not separate. Unfortunately, for most of us, beauty means sensuality, sexuality. Your scriptures, your saints, your gurus, your sannyasis—all of them have done this to you, so you have no feeling, no beauty, no love. I do not know if you realize what a tragedy it is!

And since you must have love as a human being, what will you do? There is no time. You can't say, "Well, I can't have it. I can live without love because I have lived without love for two million years, and I will live another two million years without love"—that means perpetual sorrow for the next two million years. So what can you do? You understand my question now? Sorrow cannot be put away or be resolved through time, nor can love be invited through time. And time is: ten days ahead, or the next minute, or the next second. What will you do? Will you jump in the lake? Unless you find love, you are already in the lake. And you have to find it, as you have to find food. This is a much more demanding, much more strenuous thing that demands intense vitality.

So what will you do? If you say, please tell me what to do, then you are missing the bus entirely. But you have to see the importance, the immensity, the urgency of that question—not tomorrow, not the next day or the next hour, but see it now while you are sitting. And to see that, you must have energy. So just see immediately—the catalyst that makes the liquid into solid or vaporizes it immediately does not take place if you allow time, even a second. All our existence, all our books, all our hope is tomorrow, tomorrow, tomorrow. This admittance of time is the greatest sorrow.

So the issue is with you, not with the speaker from whom you are expecting to get the answer. There is no answer. That is the beauty of it. You can sit cross-legged, breathe rightly, or stand on your head for the next ten thousand years. Unless you have put this question to yourself—not superficially, not verbally, not intellectually, but with your whole being—you will live with it for two million years—those two million years may be only tomorrow. So problems and time are intimately related—do you see it now?

And as sorrow and love cannot be resolved, or love cannot exist through time, what is the state of your mind that has put this question? I am putting the question: What is that state of your mind? But if you put that question to yourself—not casually, not sporadically, not when you have little time to spare, but actually put it with an intensity, with vitality and energy—are you waiting for an answer? If you wait, back again there is the whole repetition. If you ask somebody what is the answer, you go back into the proposition that somebody knows and you don't know, and he will tell you what to do. And that is the most terrible thing to demand of a man or of yourself—for you to be told about something which nobody can tell you. I can tell you that you must love, I can tell you that love is not a thing to be cultivated. If you cultivate love, it becomes sympathy, kindliness, social work and all that petty, little stuff; it is as good as going to church; but it is not love. And one must have love.

Now, if you have put that question, then, what is the state of your mind that has put this question? Is it expecting an answer, is it waiting, is it looking into its memory to see where it can find an answer? All that admits of time, and therefore, if you are doing that, you have merely put the question verbally—and a drowning man looking for a straw has no meaning. So if you put that question with alacrity, with urgency, with potency, then what takes place in the mind? Because the mind will not allow time to come and interfere. And a mind that is not caught in time does not belong to society—which does not mean it runs off, becomes a hermit, a sannyasi, a monk; that is just an escape from life, escape in its own, self-induced hypnotic visions and mysticism; that has nothing to do with reality. Reality is to see human existence every minute of the day, with fullness, with vitality, with urgency. And it is only such a mind that is the religious mind—no other mind.

So what takes place when you do not allow time, when the mind does not allow time to come in, though the mind itself is the product of time? You are following? Because, your brain is the result of two million years and much more, probably; and the mind is asking that brain not to be controlled by time, not to be shaped by time, not to respond to time. Certain parts of the brain are still animalistic—I won't go into all that; you can read a book and you will know about it, or you can observe yourself which is much simpler and much quicker and more direct, and you can see that a certain part of the brain which is still animalistic. And there is a great part of the brain which is not touched by civilization, by culture, by the animalistic brain; and if you allow time, that part will also be cultivated, will also be covered by the human experience of miseries, and you will be sunk for the rest of your life.

So, a mind that demands an answer to this question has not only to understand that it is the result of time, but also to deny itself so that it can be outside the structure of time, of society. If you have listened—really listened with urgency, with intensity, you will have come into this—not only verbally, but actually—that you are no longer held in the clutches of time. The mind, though it is the result of two million or more years, is out, because it has seen the whole process and understood it immediately. Up to this one can come—that is fairly obvious. When one sees this thing, that is child's play. Though you are all grown-up people, the moment you see it, you say, "What have I been doing with my life!" Then the mind has no deception, has no pressures.

When the mind has no problems, no tensions, no direction, then such a mind has space, an infinite space both in the mind and in the heart; and it is only in that infinite space that there can be creation. Because sorrow, love, death, and creation are the substance of this mind; this mind is free of sorrow, is free of time; and so this mind is in a state of love; and when there is love, there is beauty; and in that sense of beauty, in that sense of vast, infinite space, there is creation. And still further—further not in the sense of time—there is a sense of vast movement.

Now you are all listening to it, hoping to capture it verbally; but you won't—any more than you can capture love by listening to a talk about love. To understand love, you must begin very near—which is yourself. And then when you understand, when you take the first step—and that very first step is also the last step—then you can go very far, much further than the rockets to the moon or to Venus or to Mars. The whole of this is the religious mind.

November 28, 1964

Questions

Banaras, 1963

1.	Does the recognition of a thing prevent one from observing it? You may not name it.	51
2.	What is the significance of words? Have words any significance? If we cannot use words, how do we communicate?	52
3.	You have said that ideas prevent action. Is not that statement itself an idea?	53
4.	Is it not helpful to have a teacher, a guru, to instruct and guide me?	53
5.	Scientific or technological progress is made by the new knowledge that has been learned being added to the old knowledge. How can you say that this is not learning?	54
6.	It requires a good deal of energy to observe oneself. How is one to get that energy?	55
7.	Is it possible to be free from conflict without ending it?	55
8.	When you decide to do something, why is there conflict in that decision?	55
9.	Not to choose is also a choice—is it not?	56
10.	My memory is inherent in me, it is part of me. How can I get rid of it?	59
11.	It is only with my memory that I can recognize something. Can I recognize you if I have no memory of you?	59
12.	Does this not imply that, if I have been robbed once by somebody, I should not allow that memory to operate when I meet him again, and thus I allow myself to be robbed again by that person?	60
13.	Does mutation come about naturally, spontaneously? Or is it caused by an outside agency?	60
14.	Sir, you have not explained why we divide.	60
15.	If the mutation you talk of takes place, how can I do my present job, how can I maintain my present relationship with persons and things?	61
16.	What is the use of your talking? Why do you talk?	61
17.	What is the aim of human life? What is the purpose of human life?	61
18.	Is it possible to be free of fear?	61
19.	Are we not the creatures of destiny?	64
20.	Is everything preordained? What is the truth of it?	64
21.	Is there not a middle course?	64
22.	But lukewarm may be the truth. It is life.	65
23.	What is really the difference between the brain and the mind?	65

24. But in the physical body, the brain is the medium. 65
25. You have said that one must look at the unconscious without interpretation; but the interpretation arises from the unconscious. What is one to do? 65
26. How can you understand a human being without interpreting? 66
27. Is there anything to do after watching? 66
28. We are infants in observation. Should we not have some help from people who know how to observe? 70
29. When you wrote *At the Feet of the Master,* did you not follow the double lines? 71
30. What is the right understanding for the attainment of bliss? 71
31. At certain periods, the mind is very alert, sees everything, sees every detail—the ants, the flowers, the birds, and so on—with clarity, with simplicity, with care; it sees everything. At other moments it is dull, weary. Why? 72
32. Is the conflict within oneself not better than the conflict outside? Is it not more significant, better manageable, more worthwhile, more significant than the conflict in society outside? 72
33. If life is continuous action, how can there be inaction? 73
34. We understand you intellectually, but we do not really understand you. What can we do about it? 73
35. How does one get that alert mind which you talk about? 73
36. What is the function of a teacher in a school or in a college? 73
37. How can we avoid the decline, the disintegration of the mind, due to old age and disease? 74
38. The individual is related to society. And when there is so much conflict within society, how can an individual be completely free from it? 74
39. You see some persons very rich and others very poor. Don't you want to do something about it? 74
40. Is what you have said any different from what the Gita says? 75
41. If I watch violence passionately with care, will that free me from violence? 75
42. What is philosophy, and is it useful for us? 76

Saanen, 1964

1. I can't understand why you say that money is not a problem. 176
2. Are you saying that when an embarrassing or inconvenient situation exists, like the lack of money, the mind can rise above it? 177
3. I am illiterate through a disability in childhood, and this has been a great problem to me throughout my life. How can I solve it? 177
4. When we are incapable of seeing all that is involved in a problem, how can we go to the root of it and resolve it? 178
5. Can there be desire without an object? 180
6. As far as I have experienced, thinking condemns me to isolation, because it prevents me from communing with the things around me, and it also prevents me from going to the roots of myself. Therefore I should like to ask: Why do human beings think? What is the function of human thinking? And why do we so greatly exaggerate the importance of thinking? 191

7. Is the feeling of having an individual will the cause of fear? 197
8. What is maturity? 202
9. Can we go to our jobs and work without competition? 206
10. I do not believe that repetitive action is necessarily boring. 206
11. I don't see how one can live in an empty space. 207
12. Will you speak more about energy? 208
13. Sir, what is the difference between your thought about love and the Christian thought about love? 213
14. I yearn for silence, but I find that my attempts to attain it are more and more pitiful as time goes by. 218
15. How is one to be free from the desire to be certain? 223

Banaras, 1964

1. A teacher can help us to awaken our intuition. 276
2. I do not see the difference between the individual who is conditioned and man who is not an individual but a human being. 277
3. How is this immediate mutation to take place? If we don't know this, we are utterly in despair. 277
4. Is there anything like a cosmic mind? 277
5. I do not know what God is; but I want to know God. 278
6. We do not know what to do, sir. 278
7. Is it possible to look at something without naming? 279
8. One may look in that way only at very rare moments, but not permanently. 279
9. Are we not in communion with the contradiction, sir? 285
10. What is the time interval that you were explaining and what is that energy? Is it completely in motion, or is that static, sir? 295
11. Is immediate action total action? 295

Index

Acceptance: of authority, 246; and dulled feelings, 34; as hindrance to meditation, 33; of problems, 181; of religious authority, 258–59

Accumulation: dying to, 257; of experience, 215–16; of knowledge, 170–71; versus learning, 73, 239, 241, 243

Action, 203–8, 231–37, 280–85; as both collective and individual, 56; and crisis, 152; defining, 68, 231–32, 283; divided, 20–21; and emptiness, 118; and facts, 1; and freedom, 139; and gradual self-knowing, 155; and ideas, 21, 53, 68–70, 135–36, 139, 194–95; and life, 68, 70; and looking, 234; and the movement of life, 290; and the need for clarity, 229–30; and the postponement of time, 253; as the present, 13; psychological, 68; and revolution, 44; and seeing the fact, 294; and time, 149; types of, 135; and violence, 293; and watching, 66; and the will, 189–90

Action and ideas: and contradiction, 231–34; division between, 44–45; and the gap between, 20–21; gulf between, 58. *See also* Action; Conflict; Ideals; Ideas

Adjustment: and cooperation, 164; as destructive, 124. *See also* Conditioning; Conformity

Affection: and awareness, 301; and communion, 281. *See also* Caring; Love

Alert mind: and observation, 73. *See also* Clear mind; Fresh mind

Alertness: and self-observation, 138. *See also* Alert mind; Awareness

Aloneness: and cooperation, 117–18; and discovery of the truth, 172; and freedom from fear, 268; and freedom from influences, 220–22; and the mind, 222–23; and mutation, 167; and the religious mind, 117; and the simple mind, 269; as a state of mind, 118; and understanding religion, 220, 221. *See also* Isolation; Loneliness

Ambition: and conflict, 10; as hindrance to love, 61; versus love, 91; and self-fulfillment, 289; and time, 150–51. *See also* Comparison; Competition

America. *See* Authority; Conditioning; Divisions; Society; World problems

Amnesia: and thought, 158. *See also* Memory

Analysis: of fear, 291; hindrance to the unconscious, 38; and relationships, 249–50; and time, 190

Analyzer and the analyzed: and duality, 190. *See also* Analysis; Thinker and the thought

Animal: freeing the mind from, 235; and human behavior, 228; and human evolution, 199; and inherent fear, 287; and the social order, 249–50; and violence, 293

Answers: nonexistence of psychological, 14; and problems, 182. *See also* Inquiry

Apes: and human behavior, 199. *See also* Animal

Artists: and communion, 182; and knowledge, 138; and the search for the new, 228. *See also* Creative

Arts: and expression versus creation, 166; and leisure, 203; and the search for experiences, 215; and the search for the new, 196–97. *See also* Artists

Atheism: and belief, 267; and the communist world, 130. *See also* Belief; Religion

Atma: and conditioning, 36; and learning, 240; meaning of, 16; as nonexistent, 107; and time, 158

Attention: and the absence of the fragmentary, 202; and the aware mind, 240; and awareness, 111; and caring, 127; and communion, 128; and death, 256; defining, 62, 255; and energy, 88, 156; and knowing the unconscious, 62; and learning, 244; and listening, 20, 48, 186, 193; and meditation, 301–2; and nonrepressive discipline, 263; and passion, 154; and the sense of freedom, 223; and sorrow, 211; and understanding, 82; and understanding conflict, 10; and virtue, 46, 218; and the whole, 262

At the Feet of the Master: and followers, 71

Austerity: defining, 27; and observation, 27–28; and self-knowing, 117; and continuity, 45; and simplicity, 268–69

Authority, 244–47; absence of, 1; acceptance of the religious, 258–59; and beauty, 308; and conformity, 268; and confusion, 12; versus cooperation, 266; and criticism, 33–34; and desire, 97; desire to receive help from, 163; as destructive, 230, 235; and followers, 28; forms of, 171; freedom from, 18–20, 116–17, 130–31, 172–73; as hindrance to clarity, 229; as hindrance to learning, 170–71, 246; and the imposition of formulas, 142; and inquiry into deterioration, 29–30; and inquiry into the true, 265; and knowledge, 86, 87; and learning, 171, 292; and looking at the self, 242; and the loss of inquiry, 75; versus new thinking, 5; versus observation, 18,

19–20; and the old mind, 15, 20; placing trust in, 275–77; and prayer, 156; and religion, 6, 86–87; and the religious life, 267; and the search for security, 129–30; and security, 130; and sex, 166; and understanding fear, 246–47; understanding the anatomy of, 86–87; and the willingness to be led, 244–45; worship of, 162, 166

Automation: and leisure, 162, 203. *See also* Technology

Awareness: and attention, 159–60; and austerity, 45; of comparison, 194; and conflict, 10, 12; of the conscious, 62–63, 65; of consciousness, 7; of death and love, 213–14; and discipline, 4, 218; of the disintegrating mind, 28; of duality, 36; and the empty mind, 269; and freedom from the past, 216–17; of inner conflict, 48; and learning, 178; and learning about the self, 262; and listening, 8, 122–23; meaning of, 69; and meditation, 263; of the mind, 205; and observation, 301; of the present, 28–29; of the problem of living, 41–42; and the quiet mind, 38–39; of the self, 16–18; of the structure of conflict, 13

Beauty: and clarity, 106; and feeling, 289; inability to cultivate, 199–200; insensitivity to, 153; loss of, 137; and love, 308–9; meaning of, 268–69; and religion, 166; and the religious mind, 45; and the state of aloneness, 220–22; state of mind of, 110; and time, 222; understanding, 222. *See also* Caring; Death; Love

Becoming. *See* Ambition

Belief: versus awareness of existence, 77; versus clear perception, 266; and death, 104; and fear, 24; and God, 131; and religion, 43, 220; and the religious mind, 116; as the stupid mind, 261. *See also* Conditioning

Bible. *See* Authority; Books; Knowledge; Religion

Bliss: and understanding conflict, 71–72

Books, 86; and the accumulation of knowledge, 287; and authority, 116, 246; as hindrance to thinking, 75; and intelligence, 143; and leisure, 203; and learning, 292–93; and originality, 149–50; and repetition, 138, 267

Boredom: life as, 115; and the search for the new, 196. *See also* Escape

Brain: and animal origins, 228; function of, 171; and the human as animal, 235; as lazy, 135; and mutation, 273; and the need for radical change, 272, 274–75; as part of the mind, 65, 136; and time, 309

Brotherliness: and the family, 293–94. *See also* Relationships; World Problems

Buddha. *See* Authority; Conditioning; Divisions; Religion; Society; World Problems

Capitalism. *See* Authority; Divisions; Progress; Society; World problems

Caring: without condemnation, 125–26; and cooperation, 123; defining, 79; and feeling, 289–90; listening, 127; and love, 257–58; meaning of, 123, 302; as solution, 18

Caring mind: and observation, 79. *See also* Caring; Mind

Catholic. *See* Authority; Conditioning; Divisions; Religion; Society; World problems

Catholicism: and communion. *See also* Catholic

Cause: of the dull mind, 29; of psychological problems, 179

Cause and effect: absence of, 112. *See also* Challenge and response

Center: and experience, 299; and freedom, 297, 300; as hindrance to inner space, 298, 300; movement toward, 198–200, 202; as the original source, 202; and the religious mind, 269. *See also* Self

Challenge: and conflict, 133; to the self, 159. *See also* Challenge and response

Challenge and response: and conflict, 136; and experience, 37, 158–59, 215, 299; and the interval of thought, 292–93; and problems, 176

Change: and adaptation, 9; and caring, 302; and conflict, 13; defining, 169, 172, 230; and ideas, 236; individual, 272, 277; as limited, 188; meaning of, 187–88; and the mind, 57–58; and mutation, 5; and obsolescence, 2–3; and patterns, 277; and time, 13, 306; *See also* Revolution

Children: mother's love for, 307; and observation, 18, 19

China. *See* Authority; Conditioning; Divisions; Society; World problems

Choiceless awareness: and learning, 244; and observation, 111; and passion, 117; and the spontaneous mind, 59. *See also* Attention; Awareness

Christ. *See* Christianity

Christianity: and conditioning, 156, 221. *See also* Authority; Divisions; Religion; Society; World problems

Chronological time: and the mind, 209; as the only time, 253–54. *See also* Time

Church: and conditioning, 190. *See also* Religion

Civilization: and the resolution of problems, 252. *See also* Society; World problems

Clarity: and the absence of authority, 246; and action, 229; and communion, 226, 229; defining, 108; and freedom from fear, 229–30; and living without formulas, 147; and the mind, 29; through observation, 143; and space, 112; and *what is*, 106–7. *See also* Clear mind

Clear mind: and the absence of conflict, 9, 10, 82; and the absence of fear, 3; achieving, 88; and coming to death, 257; and discipline, 146; and discovery of the true, 9; and drugs, 260; and negation, 108. *See also* Clarity; Free mind; Fresh mind; Mind

Collective: and society, 252. *See also* Collective and the individual

Collective and the individual, 41, 272, 277; and conflict, 48; as one, 56. *See also* Individual; Society

Comfort: and security, 81. *See also* Permanency

Commitment: as escape, 115–16; and identity, 131. *See also* Identification; Naming

Commune: defining, 225–26. *See also* Communication; Communion

Communication, 280–85; versus communion, 280–81; without comparing, 84; conditions for, 42; defining, 180, 182, 281, 282–83; difficulty of, 127–28, 283;

and the meaning of the word, 15–16; 280–85. *See also* Naming; Words
Communion: approach to, 128; and clarity, 27–28; defining, 180–81, 281; versus ideas, 195; intensity of, 100; and listening, 192; meaning of, 185–86, 189; and the meaning of words, 114; and psychological security, 184, 186; and total action, 288; and understanding words, 225. *See also* Communication
Communism: and the failure of utopia, 118; as religion, 267. *See also* Authority; Divisions; Revolution; Society; World problems
Communist Revolution: as fragmentary, 274
Comparison: and the absence of conflict, 11, 13; as basis for behavior, 193–94; as breeder of fear, 193–94; versus caring, 19. *See also* Ambition; Competition
Competition: versus caring, 257; as hindrance to love, 173; and psychological security, 185; and ruthlessness, 247; at work, 206. *See also* Ambition; Comparison; Education; Society
Compulsion: versus meditation, 263. *See also* Contradiction; Effort
Computer: function of, 86; and mechanical learning, 73–74; and mechanistic human activity, 57. *See also* Electronic brain
Concentration: versus attention, 62; and distraction, 201–2; and effort, 262; and exclusion, 111; freedom from, 301; versus meditation, 300–301; and silence, 217; understanding, 159–60
Concepts. *See* Ideals; Ideas
Condemnation: as hindrance to learning, 172; looking at the self without, 241–42; and observation, 17–18. *See also* Comparison; Interpretation
Conditioned mind. *See* Conditioning; Dull mind; Mind
Conditioning: and the acceptance of time, 306; and authority, 86; and challenge and response, 37; and change, 190; and the collective and the individual, 56; and control, 110; and crisis, 156; and discipline, 4; and experience, 215, 261; and facing the fact, 294; as hindrance to living in the present, 254; as hindrance to the new mind, 15; as hindrance to sensitivity, 5; and images, 108; influence of, 190; and living in the present, 295; and meditation, 35; versus the new, 8; and religion, 221; and response, 22–23, 136–37; by society, 79, 126; and thought, 107, 110; and time, 209; understanding, 185; and words, 7–8, 40. *See also* Conformity; Freedom
Conflict, 7–13, 78–82, 129–34; and acquiring knowledge, 87; and action, 203–6, 239; and the action and idea, 21, 69; approach to, 49–50; and the belief in security, 132; causes of, 10; and comparative thinking, 196; and the confused mind, 106; and daily life, 30; and decision making, 55–56; defining, 129; and desire, 96–98, 183; and the desire for security, 131; and destiny, 64; as destructive, 242; and the deteriorating mind, 175; and disintegration, 28; through division, 160; and divisions in the thinker and the thought, 242–44; and duality, 293; elimination of, 294; and energy, 6, 208; and escape, 250–57; between fact and ideas, 290; between formulas and *what is*, 142; freedom from, 55; and habits, 144–45; as hindrance to energy, 78, 295; as hindrance to observation, 42–43; as hindrance to the new mind, 49; as hindrance to the religious spirit, 43; as hindrance to understanding life, 278; and innocence, 202; in the individual and the world, 124; inside and outside, 72–73; inward and outward, 47–48; and learning, 239; and love, 257; meaning of, 50, 81; and meditation, 35; and motive, 238; and passion, 95; physical effects of, 74; versus the religious man, 29; and the search for self-expression, 247–48; source of, 244; and the thinker and the thought, 36, 92–93; as torture, 142; and truth, 57; understanding, 81, 124–25; understanding the structure of, 71; and the waste of energy, 289–90, 293, 295
Conformity: and conflict, 203–4; and discipline, 144–46, 239–40; and ideals, 91; versus the religious life, 267–68; and society, 90, 145; and the wasting of energy, 294. *See also* Authority; Conditioning; Dull mind; Society
Confusion: and conflict, 11–12; and the desire for authority, 163; expulsion of, 143; versus the new, 58; and problems, 174. *See also* Contradiction
Conscience: and the unconscious, 131
Conscious: awareness of, 62–63, 65; and conflict, 10, 11; defining, 140; and fear, 249, 251. *See also* Brain; Conscious and unconscious; Mind; Unconscious
Conscious and unconscious: and fear, 94; as one movement, 20; as trivial, 190, 201. *See also* Conscious mind
Conscious mind: and authority, 19–20; defining, 19–20; as the superficial mind, 38. *See also* Consciousness
Consciousness: divisions in, 62; and experience, 158; and fear, 250; and the 'me' and the whole as one, 77; as not individual, 273; and time, 62; understanding, 249–50
Contact: as necessary to understanding, 256; and permanency, 279–80; with the self, 284–85
Contemporary mind: defining, 245. *See also* Mind; New; New mind
Continuity: and the conscious and the unconscious, 190; and the creation of formulas, 147; and desire, 180, 183, 224; ending of, 153; and misery, 213; and sorrow, 26, 307; and thinking, 243; and thought, 24, 25, 26, 102, 105, 184; and time, 209, 223. *See also* Death; Fear; Security
Contradiction: acceptance of, 90; and action, 205, 283; and action and ideas, 13, 232–33; cause of, 286; and conflict, 10, 11, 79, 81, 125; and energy, 6; between the fact and the idea of energy, 288; between the factual and the ideal, 280–82; and fragmentation, 284; freedom from, 91; as hindrance to observation, 50–51; and knowledge, 87; and problems, 186; and resistance, 234; and the thinker and the thought, 294; and understanding problems, 175, 177, 179–80; and the waste of energy, 288–89, 295. *See also* Divisions
Control: as hindrance to discovery, 110; understanding, 157–58. *See also* Discipline; Resistance

Cooperation: absence of, 123; hindrances to, 236; and ideas, 266; as life, 164; and passion, 95; and the state of aloneness, 117–18; true, 266; and truth, 42; understanding, 34
Corruption: and the absence of fear, 193, 196; levels of, 123; prevalence of, 162–63. *See also* Authority; Religion; Society; World problems
Creation: and the creative, 207; and emptiness, 263; movement of, 112; and the new mind, 235–36; and self-discovery, 196–97; and space, 309; state of, 161, 207; and stillness, 218. *See also* God; Truth; Unknown
Creation, death, and love: as interrelated, 269. *See also* Creation
Creative: and creation, 207; and the religious mind, 46, 269; and uncertainty, 133
Creative mind: versus conflict, 78. *See also* New mind
Crisis: and attention, 156; and the disappearance of the past, 151; and time, 102
Critical awareness: and communion, 226. *See also* Awareness
Critical observation: need for, 33. *See also* Observation
Curiosity: and learning, 287

Daily existence: as brutalizing, 133; escape from, 39–40. *See also* Daily life
Daily life: and contradiction, 280–82, 284; and effort, 233; and energy, 295; and freedom, 297
Danger: and outward fear, 90. *See also* Security
Dead mind: and the search for permanency, 251. *See also* Continuity; Dull mind
Death, 31–33; approaches to, 31–32; as the decline of the mind, 28; fear of, 64, 195, 250, 292; and fear of living, 30–32; and humility, 27; theories about, 255; understanding, 256. *See also* Continuity; Creation; Life; Love; Sorrow; Time
Death and life: relationship between, 255. *See also* Death
Death, love, and creation: as interrelated, 269. *See also* Creation; Death; Love
Death, love, and time: as interrelated, 254, 257–58. *See also* Death; Love; Time
Death, sorrow, and time, 100–106; as interrelated, 147–54, 208–14. *See also* Death; Sorrow; Time
Decay: and time, 102. *See also* Deterioration
Decline. *See* Deterioration
Denial: defining, 258; and discovering meditation, 258. *See also* Negation
Desire, 96–100; and the creation of contradiction, 179–80; and the loss of beauty, 137; and the object of, 183; process of, 146; and self-contradiction, 182–83; understanding, 222–24
Destiny: achieving freedom from, 64; questioning, 64
Deterioration: and comparison, 194, 196; and conflict, 78; and imitation, 29; increasing, 77; and the need for revolution, 271–72; versus observation, 28; physiological and psychological, 66–67, 69–70
Devotion: versus passion, 95
Dialectical approach, 145; meaning of, 51
Discipline: and the clear mind, 263; and conflict, 11; and conformity, 239–40; defining, 4, 91–92, 144, 218; and energy, 6; implications of, 145; and learning, 146, 239–40, 244; and observation, 36–37, 51; and the religious spirit, 46; types of, 4; understanding, 173; and understanding fear, 194. *See also* Conditioning; Resistance
Disciplined mind: as the dead mind, 145. *See also* Discipline; Mind
Discontent: causes of, 264; and the fact, 266; and gratification, 206; and the religious life, 264–65. *See also* Satisfaction; Security
Discovery: of the fact, 8; and the new mind, 83; of truth, 121–22, 124, 127
Discussion: without authority, 271. *See also* Communication; Communion
Disintegration: and conflict, 87. *See also* Deterioration
Distraction: and energy, 208; as escape, 121; as hindrance to understanding, 66; and inattention, 201–2; and observation, 52. *See also* Attention, Concentration; Meditation
Disturbance: and desire, 96. *See also* Conflict
Divisions: between the collective and the individual, 56, 272; in daily life and ideals, 282; between death and living, 31, 33, 212, 256; in the earth, 252; ending of, 282; and fear, 251; as hindrance to peace, 259–60; between the individual and the world, 79; of the inner and outer, 60; and inward and outward movement, 2; and nationalism, 150; national, religious and technological, 78; in nations and people, 220; of nations and religions, 229; between the observer and the observed, 157, 242–44; and sorrow, 211–12; between the thinker and the thought, 92–93; and the wasting of energy, 290; and world problems, 26–27. *See also* Conflict; Contradiction
Dogma: as hindrance to clarity, 229. *See also* Belief
Dreams: and the unconscious
Drugs: and consciousness, 5; and the desire for experience, 37; and the expansion of consciousness, 159; and "instant mysticism," 109–10; as nirvana, 260; and the search for answers, 41; and the search for experiences, 215; and visions, 108–9
Duality: and conflict, 290, 294; and schizophrenic attitudes toward life, 281, 293; and the thinker and the thought, 36. *See also* Contradiction; Divisions
Dull mind: cause of, 29; and conflict, 124, 126, 131, 183; and fear, 248; as hindrance to understanding, 85; and the past, 85; and problems, 185, 251–52, 303–4; and sorrow, 210–11, 306; and stimulation, 208. *See also* Fresh mind; Mind; Petty mind
Dying: daily, 105, 153; to the known, 32–33, 213; to memory, 256–57; to the past, 222–23. *See also* Continuity; Death

Earnestness: and the serious mind, 51
East. *See* Authority; Conditioning; Divisions; Society; World problems
East and West: and search, 198, 201
Education: and competition, 257; and the function of teachers, 276; as repetition, 115. *See also* Knowledge; Learning
Efficiency: and organization, 296

Effort: and change, 188; and conflict, 183, 289; and contradiction, 232–34, 289; and control of thought, 157–58; and desire, 97; life as constant, 97; living without, 224, 232–33; and the wasting of energy, 289. *See also* Meditation
Electronic brain: and knowledge, 243; and memory, 210; and the response of memory, 23; role of, 151. *See also* Dull mind; Mind
Emotions: as hindered, 166; suppression, 289–90
Emptiness: and creation, 263; and freedom, 140; function from a state of, 205; listening in the state of, 122; and the religious mind, 269; and self-knowing, 76; and space in the mind, 207–8; and total action, 285. *See also* Empty mind; Meditation; Mutation
Empty mind: and the absence of fear, 118; as creative, 230; and love, 257; and meditation, 160, 216, 261–63; and mutation, 164; and seeing the true and the false, 300; and space, 298, 302; and total freedom, 134; and understanding the supreme, 94. *See also* Mind
Ending: of authority, 18, 20; and the beginning of innocence, 153; of conflict, 49–50; of experience, 218; of the experiencer, 222; of the fear of death, 31–32; of imitation, 30; of problems, 23–24, 176, 184; of sorrow, 22, 25–26, 105, 147–48, 210, 306–7, 309; of thought, 26, 112, 192, 210, 212. *See also* Continuity
Energy, 288–96; and the absence of effort, 10; and attention, 88; through clarity, 157–58; versus conflict, 133, 203; creative, 46; defining, 201; and denial, 258; and deterioration, 29; and discontent, 265; and the discovery of truth, 124; and the hindrance of time, 308; and identification, 115; and inquiry, 279; and knowledge, 244; and learning, 239, 244; and listening, 143, 165; and the listening mind, 87; living with, 104; and maturity, 274–75, 278; and motive, 238; motiveless, 238; need for, 113; neurotic, 115; and observation, 6, 55; and the perception of the new, 1; and resistance, 208; of self-knowing, 111; and seriousness, 78; and stimulation, 208; and the teacher and the taught, 170; types of, 6, 208; through work, 166–67
England. *See* Authority; Conditioning; Divisions; Society; World problems
Enslavement: and freedom, 297
Entertainment: and leisure, 162. *See also* Organized entertainment
Entity: permanent, 158
Environment: adjustment to, 124; and the collective and the individual, 272; as conditioner, 245; freedom from, 135; and the individual, 162; and the individual as one, 126. *See also* Society
Escape: through belief, 267; from conflict, 10–11, 79, 280; and energy, 55; from fear, 62, 250–51, 291; forms of, 77; futility of, 219; and habits, 144; as hindrance to the religious mind, 113, 117, 118; and ideals, 284, 286; and ideas, 3, 236; from loneliness, 103–4; and meditation, 155; through prayers, 299; and problems, 174–75, 177–78, 182; and religion, 162; and the religious life, 268; from routine, 261; from sorrow, 24, 26–27, 103, 149, 212; and time, 150, 305; types of, 114–15; through utopia
Eternal: and beauty, 222; and the creative mind, 269; and time, 222. *See also* God; Reality; Truth; Unknown
Evolution: man as the sum of, 135–36. *See also* Brain
Existence: and time, 102; understanding the implications of, 81. *See also* Life
Experience: as challenge and response, 136; and dealing with problems, 275; direct, 101; ending of, 37–38, 39, 218; freedom from, 300; inquiry into, 109–10; and knowledge, 84; and learning, 53–54; and meditation, 37–38, 159, 298–99; and memory, 215–16; and momentary silence, 217; and naming, 106; versus observation, 18; process of, 158–59, 215–16; and the process of thought, 158; and recognition, 52; as response to challenge, 261; search for, 298–99; and the second-hand mind, 37; and security, 185; and superficiality, 215, 216; understanding, 39
Experiencer: ending of, 222. *See also* Experience
Experiencing: and the boredom of routine, 261; versus learning, 239. *See also* Experience
Experimenting: and seeking, 198
Exploration: and attention, 122; and freedom, 108. *See also* Discovery

Fact: and the absence of conflict, 87; versus abstractions, 57; versus belief, 266–67; and the collective and the individual, 273; communion with, 284; versus comparison, 246; and conditioning, 282, 286; and cooperation, 266; and energy, 55, 288, 290; and escape from conflict, 10; and escape from life, 267; and escape through ideals, 69; facing, 25–26; and facing problems, 177; and fear, 291; versus formula, 293; and freedom from fear, 195; and the futility of the will, 189; and the hindrance of conclusions, 40–41; and the hindrance of conditioning, 1–2; hindrance of interpretation, 191; and ideals, 286; versus the idea of fear, 194–95; importance of, 204; of insecurity, 132–34; living with, 88; and maturity, 286–87; need to see, 284, 287; observing, 301; and the religious life, 267; and the search for help, 163; and the state of sensitivity, 269; and the symbol, 99; and the time interval, 294; and understanding thought, 293; versus the word, 52–53, 106, 294. *See also What is*
False: need to see, 44; seeing, 306; stripping the mind of, 261. *See also* False and true; True
False and true: and belief, 267; and discontent, 265. *See also* False; True
Fame: and comparison, 193. *See also* Ambition; Competition; Comparison
Family, 293–94; and corruption, 123; and desire for psychological security, 186; and permanency, 251. *See also* Children; Cooperation; Society
Fear, 61, 63–64, 88–94, 192–97, 248–51, 290–93; absence of, 213; and aloneness, 268; in animals and humans, 287; and authority, 230; and belief, 266; and death, 31–32, 212–13, 255; and the desire for security, 30–31; and deterioration, 29; and the

duration of time, 24; and facing facts, 287; forms of, 248–49; freedom from, 169, 229–30; versus freedom from authority, 20; of the future, 248; as hindrance to understanding, 231; of living and dying, 31–32; and love, 257; and the religious mind, 116–17; and solving the problem, 229; of total action, 236; of uncertainty, 171; and understanding authority, 246–47; of the unknown, 152–53; and the waste of energy, 290–91; and words, 7

Feelings: and caring, 289–90; intensity of, 94; and the loss of beauty, 137; and observation, 71; and sensitivity, 143; and sorrow, 34. *See also* Love

Followers, 170–73; and religion, 166. *See also* Authority

Formulas: creation of, 147; as hindrance to the free mind, 8; imposed by others, 142; understanding, 147. *See also* Conditioning; Discipline; Patterns

Fragmentary mind: and problems, 181–82. *See also* Mind; Total action; Whole

Fragmentation: and conflict, 125, 280, 284; of life, 263, 64; of problems, 252–53; in the world. *See also* Fragmentary mind

Freedom, 82–88, 134–40, 296–302; and the absence of problems, 181; achieving, 86–87; from authority, 172; from conflict, 9, 10, 11–12, 290; from the corrupt society, 166; defining, 83, 140; demand for, 173; from desire, 224; and discipline, 4, 5; and the discovery of truth, 82–83, 85; and the dull mind, 85; and energy, 295; as essential for mutation, 169, 173; from fear, 61, 64–65, 89, 92, 116–17, 193, 196, 229–30, 248, 291; from the formula of words, 7–8; and the hindrance of accumulation of knowledge, 170–71; and humility, 246; and the individual, 236; from influences, 221–22; and inquiry, 279; and intelligence, 179; from the known, 152, 213; lack of, 162; meaning of, 88; as necessity, 176; and observation, 18, 20; from the old mind, 14–15, 20; from the past, 228; and problems, 174, 175–76, 304; and progress, 83; from the psychological structure of society, 64, 206; search for, 16–17; through self-knowing, 167; from self-pity, 211; and standing alone, 164; from superficiality, 216; from time, 63, 306, 309; through total understanding, 72; and truth, 145; types of, 134; and the unconscious, 19–20; understanding, 164; from violence, 294

Free man: and the search for help, 163–64. *See also* Freedom

Free mind: and the ability to seek, 57; and conflict, 13; defining, 135; and discipline, 92; and discovery, 8; and the eternal, 223; and the hindrance of words, 7–8; as the individual mind, 245; and inquiry, 267; and learning, 241; and seeing, 132. *See also* Dull mind; Freedom; Mind

French Revolution: as fragmentary, 274. *See also* Revolution French

Fresh mind: and communion, 226; and the dull mind, 85; and dying to the known, 213; and learning, 171, 239; and observation, 58–59; and seeing, 86; and understanding authority, 87; and understanding problems, 247; and world problems, 59. *See also* Free mind

Friction: and the mind, 69, 70

Frontier: search for, 296–97. *See also* Space

Function and status, 247

Future: and fear, 196, 292; and time, 253–54. *See also* Past

Germany. *See* Authority; Conditioning; Divisions; Society; World problems

Gita: as hindrance to thinking, 75. *See also* Authority; Books; Knowledge; Religion

God: belief in, 278, 279; and desire, 96; desire to know, 278, 279; and effort, 289; as fiction, 15; finding, 36, 44; and illusion, 68; and loneliness, 220; as man-made, 126; and the new, 230; as not original, 117; as the perfect security, 129; and reality, 115; search for, 116–17, 141–43; and security, 130; seeking, 57; and suffering, 211; and time, 209. *See also* Authority; Truth

Gods: as man's inventions, 259; as security, 81. *See also* God

Goodness: versus becoming good, 89. *See also* Humility; Virtue

Government: and problems, 162; and thought control, 297. *See also* Authority; Nationalism; Society; World problems

Gradual: acceptance of, 305–6; and the immediate, 262; and time, 253–55

Gratification: and learning, 276. *See also* Satisfaction; Security

Gullibility: and the desire for security, 108

Guru. *See* Authority

Habits: and conflict, 12, 144–45; dying to, 32; and fear of death, 257; and mechanical action, 70; and the mind, 29. *See also* Conditioning; Conformity; Security

Happiness: as a goal of the future, 227. *See also* Feelings; Sorrow; Time

Hatred: and fear, 193–94; and the fear of evil, 195; as unifier, 34. *See also* Conflict; Divisions

Healthy mind: defining, 142–43; and inquiry into total living, 121; interests of, 57. *See also* Fresh mind; Mind; New mind

Hearing: and attention without resistance, 90; and communion, 128; and listening, 84–85, 122. *See also* Communication

Hidden mind: and consciousness, 62. *See also* Mind

Higher self. *See* Atma

Hindu: and conditioning, 156. *See also* Authority; Divisions; Religion; Society; World problems

Hope: and authority, 246; and organized religion, 266–67. *See also* Ideas

"How": as nonexistent, 12. *See also* Patterns

Human being: defining, 251; versus the individual, 251; and individuality, 273, 277; as the world, 304

Human existence: sensitivity to, 45–46; and the unconscious, 63

Human problems: ending of, 23; as world problems, 3

Humans: as computers, 57; and freedom from the animal past, 228; as highly evolved animals, 199

Humility: achieving, 46, 219; defining, 27; and fear, 89; and freedom, 246; as an immediate state, 89; and

learning, 171, 244; and meditation, 155; as necessary to inquiry, 89; state of, 245; and truth, 28. *See also* Virtue
Hypnosis: and meditation, 155–56, 160

'I'. *See* 'Me'; Self
Ideals: and action, 21; and contradiction, 286; fiction of, 47–48; freedom from, 91; and immaturity, 286; as myth, 69; nature of, 87; pursuit of, 294; reasons for having, 286; understanding the process of, 91; vested interest in, 192–93; versus *what is*, 139. *See also* Belief; Ideas; Patterns
Ideas, 231–37; and action, 21, 53, 68–70, 118, 135–36, 139, 194–95, 204–5, 231–33, 242–43, 283; and conflict, 13; and cooperation, 266; and effort, 233; and energy, 295; and the failure of utopian communities, 118; and fear, 292; as hindrance to energy, 288, 290; as nonexistent, 57; and nonviolence, 293; and the search for God, 141–42; and self-knowing, 241; and time, 253; versus *what is*, 107. *See also* Belief; Ideals; Patterns
Ideas and action: division between, 144–45; and the gap between, 13; gulf between, 58. *See also* Action; Ideals
Ideation. *See* Ideals
Identification: as escape, 115; and inward security, 130; and loneliness, 220; and looking, 137–38; and the mind, 217; and security, 131; and self-fulfillment, 289. *See also* Communication; Naming; Words
"I do not know": and the process of thought, 22–23. *See also* Knowledge; Learning
Ignorance: meaning of, 16
Illusion: and conflict, 78, 81; and learning, 241. *See also* Ideals; Ideas
Images: and escape, 217.
Imitation: defining, 30. *See also* Discipline; Resistance
Immediate: and fear of the future, 255; learning about the self, 262; versus postponement, 254; and resolution of sorrow, 306–7, 309. *See also* Meditation; Mutation; New
Immediate action: and crisis, 68; and the time interval, 293; as total action, 295; and world problems, 26. *See also* Immediate
Immediate perception, 210; and understanding influences, 221. *See also* Immediate; Perception
Immediate understanding: and mutation, 273. *See also* Immediate
Inaction: as action, 118; and time, 151–52; as total action, 206; and the world of ideas, 73
Inattention: and distraction, 201–2. *See also* Attention; Concentration
India. *See* Authority; Conditioning; Divisions; Society; World problems
Individual: as alone, 236; birth of, 140; and the collective, 41; and collective conflict, 48; defining, 272, 277; versus human being, 251; and inward conflict, 124–25; meaning of, 197; and responsibility, 229–30; role of, 77; as society, 72–73; as the solver of problems, 229–30; and world chaos, 230
Individual and the collective: as one, 56. *See also* Individual
Individual and the world, 14, 17; as one, 49–50, 79, 80, 126. *See also* Individual
Individuality: achieving, 245; and aloneness, 133; and mutation, 273; and freedom from problems, 304. *See also* Individual
Individual, mutation, and the individual: relationship between, 161–67. *See also* Individual
Industrialization: and freedom, 82–83. *See also* Technology
Infinite: freedom as, 300; space as, 300. *See also* Meditation; Mutation
Influences: awareness of, 268; on the mind, 220–22; understanding, 60. *See also* Environment; Society
Inner and outer space, 297. *See also* Inward and outward
Innocence: and creation, 197; importance of, 214; state of, 202–3. *See also* Humility; Innocent mind; New Mind
Innocent mind: and the absence of psychological time, 202; achieving, 33; and discovery of the true, 214, 216; and the immeasurable, 6; and love, 153; and sorrow, 27; and the timeless, 37, 39
Inquiry: art of, 279; into decline, 67; into deterioration, 29–30; and energy, 112–13; and fact, 266; and freedom, 16–17; and the hindrance of books, 75; and the hindrance of patterns, 266; and humility, 89; and learning, 244, 254; and listening, 20; and negation, 43; into problems, 304; and the religious life, 264–65, 267; and security, 132; and self-knowing, 107; into space, 298; and the state of listening, 86; and total freedom, 121; into truth, 23, 259; and the unconscious, 38
Insensitive: versus attentive, 88. *See also* Sensitivity
Inside and outside: as one conflict, 72–73. *See also* Inward and outward
Integration: nonexistence of, 14
Intellectual: suppression, 289–90; understanding, 73. *See also* Knowledge; Learning
Intelligence: and awareness of the superficial, 214; and beauty, 223; defining, 2; and the discipline of learning, 146; living with, 145; and negative thinking, 265; and sensitivity, 143–44, 145, 146; and understanding problems, 179
Intensity: and communion, 27, 114; loss of, 96–97. *See also* Feelings; Passion
Interest: as necessary to observation, 51; and the problems of daily existence, 56
Interpretation: and the conscious and unconscious, 65; as distraction, 65
Interpreter. *See* Authority
Interval: between action and time, 149–50; between the question and answer, 292–93. *See also* Thought
Invention: versus creativity, 269
Inward and outward: as one, 167
Inward movement: through understanding the outward, 2
Inward security: and conflict, 81; and the invention of gods, 130
Isolation: versus aloneness, 117; versus emptiness, 207–8; and escape from boredom, 219–20; and fear,

153; and religion, 220; as self-imposed, 116; and thought, 191. *See also* Loneliness

Jobs: and competition, 206; security in, 81, 133
Judgment: as hindrance to learning, 239. *See also* Comparison; Competition

Knowing: as the present, 138. *See also* Self-knowing
Knowledge: accumulation of, 79–80; adding to, 287; as authority, 18; defining, 238; and discipline, 240; as fragmented, 212; and freedom, 16, 86; and function of material things, 151; as hindrance and necessity, 107; as hindrance to the new, 228; increase of, 16; and learning, 170–71; and the mind, 230; as necessary to daily life, 214; as the past, 138; and problems, 178; without reaction, 205; and response, 136–37
Known: and drugs, 159; dying to, 32; fear of losing, 213; freedom from, 105; as preferable to the unknown, 152; and the search for the unknown, 196–97. *See also* Continuity
Koran. *See* Authority; Books; Knowledge; Religion
Krishna. *See* Authority; Conditioning; Divisions; Religion; Society; World problems

Law: and authority, 19; obedience to, 247. *See also* Society
Laziness: facing the fact of, 113
Leaders: absence of, 3. *See also* Authority
Learning, 238–44; and the absence of despair, 94; versus accumulation, 6–7; versus acquiring knowledge, 137; without authority, 271; without condemnation, 262–63; versus conformity, 240; and curiosity, 287; defining, 27, 73, 238, 240; and discipline, 91–92, 144, 173; and energy, 170; and evolution of society, 245; and the hindrance of accumulation, 79–80; and humility, 89; versus instruction, 178, 204; and life, 276; and love, 173; as noncumulative, 171–72; and observation, 139; and obstruction, 1, 2, 3–4; and problems, 178; process of, 53–54, 170–71; and the teacher, 51–53, 276. *See also* Attention; Knowledge; Listening
Leisure: effects of more, 203; and technological progress, 162
Liberty: desire for, 135. *See also* Freedom
Life: as action, 68, 70; avoidance of, 12; as a battle, 70; as conflict, 126, 239; as the continuity of existence, 102; and continuity of thought, 213; as continuous activity, 232; and contradiction in action, 283; defining, 33; as drab, 155; as energy, 238; fear of, 255; importance of knowing, 152; and inward and outward desires, 130; and living in the present, 256; looking at, 19; and love, 258; as mechanical, 151; and the movement to the center, 198, 202; and the need for passion, 95; need to understand, 278; as a problem, 23; purpose of, 61, 115; and relationship, 123, 227; uncertainty of, 129. *See also* Death
Life and death: as one, 104–5, 212–13; relationship between, 255. *See also* Death; Life
Listening: approach to, 48; art of, 8–9, 82, 90; and attention, 149; beauty in, 96; and communion, 128, 186, 192; without conflict, 43; and desire, 100; difficulty of, 234; without division, 13; and the empty mind, 165; with a free mind, 134; and hearing the words, 84–85; without ideas, 234; importance of, 20; inwardly, 127; as a miracle, 96–97; negatively, 192; nonverbally, 193; and observation, 138–39; and seeing, 85; state of, 143; and time, 122. *See also* Learning
Livelihood: and living without habit, 145
Living: without conflict, 131; with death, 31–32, 152; describing, 30–31; at different levels, 68; by dying to the past, 105; without effort, 232–33; and fear, 30; and freedom from the known, 33; and the hindrance of knowledge, 80; without ideas, 205; in the present, 94; as a problem, 114–15; and sensitivity, 105; as a total problem, 121; with uncertainty, 133, 134; understanding the significance of, 40. *See also* Life
Loneliness: versus aloneness, 117; and escape, 116; and fear, 249; and the lack of communion, 219–20; and self-pity, 307; understanding, 103–4. *See also* Isolation
Looking: and the hindrance of memory, 280; and the hindrance of naming, 137–38; without judgment, 233–34; without naming, 279–80; without tradition, 279; without verbalization, 241–42. *See also* Observation; Seeing
Love: absence of, 165, 307; achieving, 308–9; versus ambition, 91; and caring, 123–24; and communion, 281, 286; versus conflict, 78; defining, 269; and the empty mind, 230–31; and feelings, 34; and freedom, 179, 298; futility of thinking about, 213; and the hindrance of sorrow, 306; as immediate, 44; and infinite space, 300; as instant action, 21; and life without conflict, 257; meaning of, 153; as the new, 196–97; and observation, 17–18, 76; and order, 212; and sensitivity, 131; versus sentiment, 27; without sorrow, 61; state of, 167; and time, 308–9; and time, sorrow, and death, 209; and total action, 208–9; understanding, 99–100, 219, 302, 307–9; and understanding death, 106
Love, death, and creation: as interrelated, 267. *See also* Creation; Death; Love
Love, death, and time: as interrelated, 254, 257–58. *See also* Death; Love; Time
LSD: and the role of drugs, 260

Marx, Karl: and freedom, 176
Masters: and self-absorption, 160. *See also* Authority
Materialism: and religion, 267. *See also* Progress; Technology
Material progress: and human problems, 5. *See also* Materialism
Mature mind: and aloneness, 160; and energy, 274–75, 278; and understanding conflict, 58. *See also* Empty mind; Free mind; Maturity; Mind
Maturity: and the denial of authority, 275–77, 278; and the ending of divisions, 282; and energy, 288; and facing facts, 286; meaning of, 202. *See also* Mature mind

'Me': choiceless awareness of, 107; and communion, 182; as self-centered activity, 215; and the state of mutation, 137; and time, 149. *See also* Center; Self
Mechanical brain: and adaptation to society, 124. *See also* Conditioning
Mechanical mind: as the conscious, 249; and discipline, 144–45; and repetition, 230. *See also* Dull mind; Mind
Meditation, 33–39, 106–12, 154–61, 258–61, 298–302; versus absorption, 300; and the empty mind, 118; and the ending of thought, 26; and inquiry into space, 298; meaning of, 216; and the new mind, 34–35; and repetition, 299; versus the shallow mind, 214. *See also* Attention; Mutation; Observation
Memory: and authority, 86; as background, 210; and the desire for continuity, 280; dying to, 256–57; and the electronic brain, 151; explaining, 235; as hindrance to seeing, 58–59; as hindrance to understanding, 58, 59; as the 'I', 158; and the idea of fear, 194; and ideas, 232; and knowledge, 16, 18; as the known, 213; and learning, 170; and the mind, 215–16; and naming, 137–38; as necessary and as hindrance, 243; and observation, 107; and problems, 178–79; and the process of thought, 191–92; and recognition, 51–52; response of, 22–23; and security, 185; as the self, 16–17; and sorrow, 104; and thinking, 292; and thought, 243; understanding, 59; and the word, 106. *See also* Past; Time
Memory and perception: relationship between, 58. *See also* Memory; Perception
Mescaline: and the role of drugs, 260. *See also* Experience
Method: and the petty mind, 259; versus truth, 259. *See also* Conditioning; Discipline; Patterns
Mind: and the absence of gratification, 201; and action, 21; alone, 39; and aloneness, 268; and authority, 171, 246; and awareness, 240; and awareness of conflict, 11; brain as part of, 65; and communion, 288; and concentration, 217; as conditioned, 263; in conflict, 81, 175, 204–5; and the conscious and the unconscious, 190–91, 249; and constant change, 58; and crisis, 151–52; defining, 28, 136; deterioration, 28, 194; and discovery of the new, 228; divisions in, 251; Eastern and Western, 198; and the effect of problems, 99; effortless state, 262–63; and the ending of thought, 212; enslaved by words, 89; and fear, 292; and the fear of death, 213; and the formation of ideas, 142; and freedom, 174, 300; and freedom from conflict, 9; and freedom from fear, 94; and freedom from influences, 220–22; and freedom from time, 217; free from authority, 130–31; free from fear of insecurity, 133; free from memory, 59; free from the past, 87; and friction, 69, 70; going beyond itself, 217; and going beyond the word, 53; and the idea, 235; and immediate freedom from the past, 228–29; and inquiry, 254; and knowledge, 215; and listening, 8; and loneliness, 220; without loss of clarity, 29; and meditation, 106, 302; and memory, 215–16; and the need for energy, 290; and the need to be critical, 244–45; and new action, 227; and observation, 5–6; and problems, 182; and psychological freedom, 83; reasons for changes in, 72; reasons for decline of, 67, 70; and the search for authority, 116–17; and the search for experience, 299; and seeing, 306; and seeking experiences, 261; and the shaping of formulas, 146; as slave to the environment, 135; and society, 245; and space, 140–41, 207–8, 309; and time, 63, 150, 152, 200, 209, 309; as total, 72; and the unknown, 153; untouched by society, 205
Modified continuity: as change, 187. *See also* Continuity
Moment to moment: and learning, 172. *See also* Immediate
Money: and psychological problems, 176–77
Monk. *See* Authority
Morality: and the discipline of society, 144; and humans and the apes, 199; and love, 302. *See also* Humility
Mother: and love for the child, 307. *See also* Family
Motive: and action, 204; and change, 187–88; and comparison, 194; and energy, 238; as hindrance to energy, 118; and pain and pleasure, 95; and passion, 265; and sorrow, 26. *See also* Effort; Resistance
Movement of life: need to understand, 227–28. *See also* Life
Muslim: and conditioning, 156. *See also* Authority; Divisions; Religion; Society; World problems
Mutation: and the absence of time, 5; achieving, 60, 140, 191–92, 277–78; and the active present, 13; and the brain, 273; and the cessation of thought, 8; and the collective and the individual, 273; and the conscious and unconscious as unimportant, 190–91; and the creative mind, 269; and creativeness, 233; defining, 59, 230; and the hindrance of systems, 278; and the hindrance of the mind, 15; and the hindrance of time, 305; and immediate action, 135; as motiveless, 9; need for, 228–29; and the need for contact, 256; and the need for freedom, 169; and the need for total revolution, 274; and observation, 58–59; and self-knowing, 172; out of time, 59; as part of daily living, 61; as revolution, 35; and space in the mind, 140; versus time, 188. *See also* Change
Mutation, religion, and the individual: as interrelated, 161–67. *See also* Individual; Religion
Mysticism: as escape, 268; as self-delusion, 299

Naming: as hindrance, 138; as hindrance to observation, 50, 111; and insensitivity, 137; and looking, 279–80. *See also* Communication; Communion; Words
Nationalism: and divisions, 229; as hindrance, 150; and ideas, 236; and problems, 41; and security, 186; and starvation, 75. *See also* Society; World problems
Nature: communion with, 226
Negation: and seeing completely, 201–202; state of, 192
Negative approach: and religion, 44
Negative thinking: and discovery of the true, 265
Neurosis: and fear, 94; and identification, 217–18; and uncertainty, 132
New: without the animal background, 200; and communion, 284; and emptiness, 164, 263; and the hindrance of the past, 52; and learning, 54–55; and living totally, 80; versus memory, 59; and the mind,

83; as not conditioned, 230; search for, 196–97. *See also* New mind; Mutation
New entity. *See* New; New mind
New human being: immediate need for, 30. *See also* New
New man: achieving, 6; and observation, 4–5. *See also* New
New mind: and the absence of conflict, 49; and criticism, 34–35; and the hindrance of fragmentation, 14; need for, 14–17, 47; for new relationships, 227–28; and time, 5; and understanding experience and thought, 37; and understanding love, 335–36. *See also* Empty mind; Mutation; New; Religious mind
Noisy mind: and action, 285; versus the empty mind, 262–63. *See also* Dull mind
Nonfiction: and the pursuit of the fiction, 48
Nonverbal: and listening, 193. *See also* Communion; Words
Nonviolence. *See* Violence

Obedience: and authority, 247; and security, 130. *See also* Conditioning; Conformity
Object: and space, 293, 300. *See also* Center
Observation, 1–7; with care, 79–80; and the clear mind, 3; without condemnation, 12; and conflict, 125–26; and the conscious mind, 63, 65; and consciousness, 38–39; and desire, 183; and discipline, 4; and discovering the true and false, 27; and the ending of conflict, 42; and the ending of sorrow, 307; and the ending of violence, 76; and energy, 288; as exploration, 108; and facing the fact, 26; without formula, 143–44, 146; and freedom, 18, 19–20, 139; and the hindrance of accumulation, 107; of human conflict, 43; without judging, 301; of the inner and outer world, 79; and learning, 1–4, 54–55, 80; meaning of, 50; and meditation, 33, 35, 36–37; of the mind, 29; without naming, 280; and the need for gurus, 70–71; and the problem, 182; process of, 50–52; without resistance, 138–39; of the self, 17–18; and space, 140; without thought, 205; and understanding conflict, 79; and understanding the world, 17; of *what is*, 1–2. *See also* Attention; Awareness
Observer. *See* Observer and the observed; Thinker and the thought
Observer and the observed: and communion, 185–86, 189; and looking at the self, 242; as one, 195; and sorrow, 211; and understanding thought, 36. *See also* Thinker and the thought
Occident. *See* Authority; Conditioning; Divisions; Society; World problems
Old: and authority, 20; and the new, 230
Old mind, 14–15, 20. *See also* Dull mind; Petty mind
Opinions: versus communion, 226; versus facts, 145; as valueless, 234; and words, 50. *See also* Comparison; Competition
Order: need for, 278
Organization: increase in, 296–97
Organized entertainment: and leisure, 203
Organized religion: and leisure, 203; as propaganda, 43. *See also* Religion
Orient. *See* Authority; Conditioning; Divisions; Society; World problems
Original: and freedom from time, 150; need to be, 149–50; and the religious man, 117. *See also* Conditioning; New
Originality: and learning, 240. *See also* Original
Outer space: and exploration, 297. *See also* Space
Outward movement: of life, 1–2
Overpopulation: and worship of authority, 246

Pain: and motive, 95; physical, 90; and time, 103. *See also* Pleasure; Sorrow
Painter: and communion, 226, *See also* Arts
Parsi. *See* Authority; Conditioning; Divisions; Religion; Society; World problems
Passion, 95–100; and action, 70; and discontent, 265; and the discovery of truth, 124; and energy from *what is*, 113; and the hindrance of acceptance, 33–34; need for, 60–61, 154; and the need for reason, 154; and seeing beauty, 269. *See also* Intensity; Sensitivity
Passionate mind: as the empty mind, 118. *See also* Religious mind
Past: and action, 149; and communion, 284; in the conscious and the unconscious, 138; defining, 151; and fear, 94; freedom from, 87, 228; as hindrance to the new, 243; as hindrance to the new mind, 35; as hindrance to the young mind, 85; living in, 88; as a response to thought, 190; and time, 102; as the unconscious, 63. *See also* Memory; Time
Past, present, and future: and time, 101. *See also* Past
Patience: meaning of, 100
Patterns: and change, 277; and contradiction, 281; as hindrance to change, 188; as hindrance to radical revolution, 271; and memory, 170; and satisfying discontent, 264; search for, 278; and society, 245. *See also* Conditioning; Conformity; Discipline
Peace: achieving, 13, 259–60; versus becoming, 133–34; desire for inward, 129; and prayer, 259–60; and the still mind, 218–19
Perception: and conflict, 12–13; and desire, 180; and energy, 290; and time, 210; and total freedom, 134, 135; and the word, 189. *See also* Awareness; Observation
Perception and memory: relationship between, 58. *See also* Memory; Perception
Permanency: and the dead mind, 251; desire for, 279; as an idea, 242; and organized religion, 223; search for, 223. *See also* Continuity; Death; Security
Permanent entity: and thought, 158
Permanent state: desire for, 129, 132
Petty mind: and avoidance of problems, 94–95; and the meaning of bliss, 72; as the mechanical mind, 259; and meditation, 299–300; and problems, 81–82. *See also* Dull mind
Philosophy: defining, 76; as immature, 198; and the meaning of life, 40
Physical energy: sources of, 288. *See also* Energy
Physical security: urge for, 184. *See also* Security

Planned revolution: versus revolution, 44. *See also* Mutation
Pleasure: dying to, 32, 153; and dying to memory, 257; and love, 165; and motive, 95. *See also* Sorrow
Poems: and tension, 289. *See also* Arts
Politicians: and fragmentation, 3; and world confusion, 12. *See also* Authority; Society; World problems
Politics: versus the religious mind, 117. *See also* Politicians
Poor: and the pseudo-religious, 26. *See also* Starvation; World problems
Population: effects of increasing, 297. *See also* World problems
Positive movement: versus seeing immediately, 200, 202
Poverty: desire to alleviate, 74–75; and world problems, 2. *See also* Poor
Power: desire for, 246; evil of, 74. *See also* Ambition; Competition; Society; World problems
Prayer: as escape, 299; and freedom, 300–301; function of, 259–60; and meditation, 108–109, 156. *See also* God; Religion
Prejudice: as hindrance to learning, 1–2
Present: and action, 139, 236; and attention, 273; defining, 28; versus gradual understanding, 262; living in, 94, 178–79, 254; as meaningless, 40; observing in, 4; and total attention, 253. *See also* Future; Past; Time
Problems, 174–80, 180–87, 251–58; approach to, 14–15, 161–66; awareness of, 41–42; critical awareness of, 226; of daily existence, 56; defining, 188, 304; and the destruction of clarity, 174; and the dull mind, 126; immediate resolution of, 133, 304, 308, 309; increase of, 303; and India, 272; and the individual, 229–30; as interrelated, 14, 252; living with, 224; need to solve, 251–52; and reliance on authority, 275–76; and the religious life, 264; resolving, 303–4, 309; rethinking, 40; understanding, 99; unresolved, 290. *See also* World problems
Progress: as comparative, 193; technological, 162
Propaganda: function of, 8; and organized belief, 127. *See also* Influences
Prosperity: of the West, 227. *See also* Poor; Technology; World problems
Psyche: and the mind, 136, 140; need to understand, 140; revolution in, 5
Psychological energy: as the highest form, 288. *See also* Energy
Psychological fact: and the time interval, 293. *See also* Fact
Psychological freedom: from society, 74. *See also* Freedom
Psychological security: and competition, 184; desire to understand, 184; need for, 30; and starvation, 75. *See also* Security
Psychological structure: need to understand, 72–73
Psychological structure of society: and conditioning, 156; and the conscious mind, 38; denial of, 163, 166; freedom from, 64, 74, 302. *See also* Society
Psychological superstructure: and religions, 44
Psychological time: and continuity, 24. *See also* Time
Psychosomatic diseases: versus the clear mind, 230; and conflict, 74; and relationships, 174
Public opinion: fear of, 292

Questioning: and the process of thought, 22–23. *See also* Inquiry
Quiet brain: and sensitivity, 111–12. *See also* Quiet mind
Quiet mind: achieving, 38–39; and awareness of the conscious, 63, 65; and consciousness, 38–39; and drugs, 108–9; and listening, 234; and love, 302; and observation, 19–20; and seeing immediately, 202; and sorrow, 211; and the state of freedom, 174; and the unconscious, 38–39; as vital, 263. *See also* Meditation; Mind; Mutation

Radical revolution: versus continuity, 271; need for, 7. *See also* Mutation; Revolution
Rama: and conditioning, 156. *See also* Authority; Divisions; Religion; Society; World problems
Reaction: and desire, 97; and experience, 110; and freedom, 135. *See also* Challenge; Challenge and response; Response
Reality: and beauty, 269; defining, 309; and freedom, 83; and freedom from the environment, 228; and the hindrance of escape, 115; and relief from sorrow, 82; and the search for God, 115; versus the tortured mind, 142. *See also* Love; Truth
Reason: defining, 154
Recognition: meaning of, 51–52; and memory, 59–60; and the new, 196–97; and silence, 219. *See also* Identification; Naming; Words
Reincarnation: and the nature of death, 153, 255, 256. *See also* Continuity
Relationships: as action, 68; changing, 244; and communion, 204; and cooperation, 95; and disintegration, 67; dying to, 257; and fear, 248; of problems, 181; time, death, and sorrow as interrelated, 208–14
Religion, 263–69; absence of, 124; and belief, 220; and conditioning, 221; defining, 6, 124; and desire, 96, 97; and divisions, 229; and effort, 289; and escape, 115; failure of, 3, 127; and freedom of the mind, 297; function of, 81–82; and the imposition of formulas, 141–42; loss of the significance of, 40; negative approach to, 44; only, 6; and symbolism, 52–53; and transformation, 126; and the whole existence, 264. *See also* Empty mind; Mutation; New mind; Religious mind; Truth
Religion, the individual, and mutation: as interrelated, 161–67. *See also* Religion; Individual; Mutation
Religious life, 263–69; response to, 78. *See also* Religion
Religious man: versus conflict, 29; and fragmentation, 3; and freedom from fear, 195; and the new mind, 16; as nonmystic, 268; and the secondhand, 117. *See also* Religion
Religious mind, 112–19, 263–69; defining, 9, 309; and freedom from authority, 20; as the revolutionary mind, 45–46; understanding, 42–46; and world problems, 82. *See also* Religion
Religious organizations: as escape, 115. *See also* Religion

Religious people: and understanding the inner and the outer, 2. *See also* Religion
Religious revolution: defining, 274; and intelligence, 45. *See also* Religion
Religious spirit: loss of, 78–79; as the only, 42–43. *See also* Religion
Religious thinking: and world problems, 3. *See also* Religion
Repetition: and boredom, 206; and deterioration, 29; and meditation, 156, 299
Resistance: and concentration, 217; and conditioning of the mind, 221; and conflict, 11–12; and desire, 224; and effort, 233–34; and energy, 208; as hindrance to communion, 281; as hindrance to energy, 294; as hindrance to learning, 92, 234–35
Resolution: as escape from problems, 178; of problems, 181, 252
Respect: and authority, 247; versus humility, 89
Respectability: versus morality, 302
Response: and action, 21; and conditioning, 136–37; and memory, 22–23, 243; to problems, 99; and thought, 292. *See also* Cause and effect; Challenge; Challenge and response
Responsibility: for individual conduct, 229–30
Resurrection: and death, 255. *See also* Continuity
Revolt: versus revolution, 34–35; types of, 135. *See also* Change
Revolution: achieving, 126–27; and action, 44; and betrayal, 163–64; and the brain, 272, 274–75; and the breakdown of conditioning, 9; and the denial of the psychological structure of society, 34–35; and the individual, 140; and the limits of the known, 188; need for inward, 126; and the problem of living, 5; and religious, 43; and time, 126. *See also* Change; Mutation
Revolutionary change: need for, 188. *See also* Revolution
Rich life: defining, 30
Right meditation. *See* Meditation
Routine: escape from, 261; and time, 102, 104
Russia. *See* Authority; Conditioning; Divisions; Society; World problems
Ruthlessness: and competition, 247. *See also* Ambition; Comparison

Saints: and austerity, 45; and confusion, 12; and desire, 98; and simplicity, 207. *See also* Authority; Religion
Samadhi, 118. *See also* Meditation
Sannyasi: and the formula of belief, 141; as a symbol, 138. *See also* Authority
Satisfaction: and conformity, 267–68; versus discontent, 264; search for, 206. *See also* Discontent; Self-fulfillment
Science: and change, 187; as necessary, 214; and the search for solutions, 40. *See also* Scientists; Technology
Scientific mind: and inquiry, 279. *See also* Mind
Scientists: and defining space, 297; and energy, 55; and knowledge, 138; and the need to discover, 48; and problems, 303; and the search for the new, 228. *See also* Science
Secondhand human beings: and authority, 235
Security, 129–34; and communion, 186; and conformity, 267–68; desire for, 184; and dullness, 28; and fear, 196; forms of, 186; inward and outward, 81, 129; as nonexistent, 130; and the old mind, 15; and problems, 184–85; and the psychological acceptance of authority, 33; pursuit of, 129. *See also* Conformity; Conditioning
Seeing: as immediate, 306; and memory, 58–59. *See also* Looking; Observation
Seeing and listening: as one, 85. *See also* Listening; Seeing
Seeking: meaning of, 197–98. *See also* Exploration
Self: as authority, 172; and communion, 285; contact with, 284–85; defining, 16; learning about, 240–42, 262; as teacher, 178; as the world, 201. *See also* Knowing; Knowledge; 'Me'
Self-awareness: and observation, 6; and stimulation, 208; and *what is*, 91. *See also* Awareness; Self
Self-centered activity: and concentration, 218; and conflict, 205–6; and isolation, 220, 222; and the search for experience, 215–16.
Self-communion: and listening, 183–86. *See also* Communion
Self-contradiction: and understanding desire, 183. *See also* Contradiction
Self-discovery: of the true, 143–44. *See also* Awareness; Self-knowing
Self-expression: questioning, 47–48. *See also* Arts; Creativity
Self-fulfillment: demand for, 247–48; and effort, 289. *See also* Ambition; Competition; Comparison
Self-hypnosis: and meditation, 35, 110, 298, 300
Self-knowing: and awareness, 167; difficulty of, 136; effect of, 172; and freedom, 116; and the healthy mind, 57; importance of, 201; and learning, 240–41; and listening, 127; and meditation, 107–8, 155–56; as the most difficult task, 138; and the religious life, 78; and the total human being, 139; and wisdom, 76. *See also* Observation; Self-knowledge; Self-observation
Self knowledge: defining, 136; and the ending of sorrow, 26; need for, 78. *See also* Self-knowing
Self-observation: and change, 58, 59; and choiceless awareness, 262; and fear, 89; and listening, 136; need for, 132. *See also* Self-knowing
Self-pity: and sorrow, 25–26, 104, 211, 306–7
Self-understanding: and love, 18. *See also* Self-knowing
Sensation: and the beginning of desire, 180. *See also* Experience
Senses: and continuity, 224; and learning, 240
Sensitive mind: and the hindrance of fear, 131; and meditation, 35. *See also* Empty mind; Quiet mind; Sensitivity
Sensitivity: and beauty, 45, 269; and caring, 123; defining, 143; and desire, 180; and discipline, 146; versus escape, 99; and the hindrance of suppression, 290; and listening, 127; loss of, 10–11; and love, 76; as necessary to living, 105; need for, 143; and observation, 71; and passion, 95; and understanding desire, 100. *See also* Sensitive mind

Sentiment: versus love, 307
Serious: defining, 41. *See also* Serious mind
Serious mind: and conflict, 82; and world problems, 80. *See also* Seriousness
Seriousness: and the alive mind, 124; and listening, 84–85; meaning of, 78; and the search for truth, 121–22; versus the superficial, 172–73; and understanding the world, 81
Sex: and desire, 96; as escape, 114–15; problems of, 165–66; and thought, 213; and the wasting of energy, 289–90
Sexuality: and continuity, 224. *See also* Sex
Shallow life: and the desire for death, 31–32
Shankara. *See* Authority; Conditioning; Divisions; Religion; Society; World problems
Sikh. *See* Authority; Conditioning; Divisions; Religion; Society; World problems
Silence: achieving, 218–19; and achieving understanding, 66; and attention, 159–60; and communion, 180–86, 285; and meditation, 160; types of, 217–18; unasked, 218. *See also* Empty mind; Quiet mind
Simple life: and saints, 207; meaning of, 268. *See also* Simplicity
Simplicity: and the clear mind, 147; meaning of, 29; and the religious mind, 117, 268–69; and the time interval, 295
Slave. *See* Enslavement
Sleep: and dreams, 111. *See also* Mind; Unconscious
Smoking: and conflict, 144; and the conflict of contradiction, 125. *See also* Habits
Socialism. *See* Authority; Divisions; Revolution; Society; World problems
Social morality: versus virtue, 218. *See also* Morality; Society
Social order: and animals, 249–50. *See also* Society
Society: and comparison, 193; and conditioning, 56, 79; and conditioning in belief, 278; and conflict, 72–73; and conformity, 90, 145; and conformity to patterns, 239–40; and corruption in, 162; and effort, 289; evolving of, 245; freedom from, 74, 206; as a history of suffering, 302–5; and the imposition of formulas, 142; and the individual and the collective, 41; individual as the result of, 277; and the lessening of freedom, 82–83; and organized religion, 117; and relationships, 162–63, 252; and the relationship to man, 245; and the second-hand mind, 37; and time, 210. *See also* Authority; World problems
Soldier: and the mechanical mind, 144–45. *See also* Conditioning
Sorrow: collective and the individual, 6; greatest, 305–6, 308; as hindrance to love, 61; as loss, 306–7; resolution of, 305–7, 309; and time, 305–9; types of, 25, 26, 148; understanding, 21–22; as the unsolved human problem, 227. *See also* Death; Thought
Sorrow, death, and time, 100–106; as interrelated, 147–54, 208–14. *See also* Sorrow
Sorrow, thought, and time: as interrelated, 20–27. *See also* Sorrow
Soul: and the field of thought, 105
Space, 296–302; and action, 205; defining, 140; existence of, 165; and the mind, 207–8; in the mind and heart, 309; and mutation, 164; as necessary to existence, 296–98; and the observer and the observed, 167; and the quiet brain, 112; and the religious mind, 269; search for, 296–97. *See also* Emptiness; Freedom
Specialists: and the failure of religion and science, 40. *See also* Authority
Specialization: and the lazy brain, 135
Spiritual essence: as a product of thought, 105
Spontaneity: and change, 57–58; and perception, 122
Starvation: desire to eradicate, 74–75; and the hindrance of ideas, 236; and world problems, 41. *See also* Poor; Technology
State: worship of, 213. *See also* Nationalism; Society; World problems
Status and function, 247
Still mind: and the absence of experience, 112; and learning, 88. *See also* Quiet mind; Silence
Stillness: and awareness, 159–61; and discovery of the true, 39; state of, 302. *See also* Still mind
Stimulation: and psychological dependence, 208. *See also* Experience
Subconscious. *See* Unconscious
Success: and comparison, 193. *See also* Ambition; Competition
Suffering: ending of, 61; and learning, 276. *See also* Pain; Sorrow
Superficial action: and conflict, 203. *See also* Action
Superficial mind: and consciousness, 62; going beyond, 214, 216; and the purpose of life, 214–15. *See also* Mind
Suppression: and desire, 97–98. *See also* Discipline; Resistance
Supreme self. *See* Atma
Symbol: and fact, 52, 99, 195; and the word, 222–23. *See also* Communication; Communion; Naming
Systems: and belief in God, 278; and the empty mind, 216; putting aside, 261. *See also* Conformity; Patterns

Teachers: function of, 73, 276; and learning, 53–54; and observation, 70–71. *See also* Education
Teaching: versus learning, 271. *See also* Teachers
Technological knowledge: as accumulation, 80; and human understanding, 54. *See also* Science; Technology
Technological specialization: and the bourgeois mind, 215. *See also* Technological knowledge
Technology: advances in, 124; and change, 2; and comparison as progress, 193; and leaders, 3–4; limitations of, 214; and the need for authorities, 171
Theology: as immature, 198. *See also* Religion
Thinker: and conflict, 92–93; created by thought, 242–43. *See also* 'Me'; Self; Thinker and the thought
Thinker and the thought: and conflict, 36, 242–44; division between, 157–58; and fear, 92–93. *See also* Observer and the observed; Thinker; Thinking
Thinking: and fear, 292–93; as a mechanical process, 243; process of, 22–23, 35; as the response of

memory, 292; structure of, 292–93; and time, 150. *See also* Thinker; Thought
Thought: and the atma, 158; attempt to control, 36; as breeder of sorrow, 103; and conditioning, 107, 110; and continuity, 102, 105, 184, 190, 222; control of, 110, 157–58; and desire, 180, 183, 224; ending of, 26; and facing the fact, 26; and fact, 195; and fear, 292–93; as hindrance to mutation, 189, 191; and negative observation, 205; as the origin of fear, 63–64; and the past, 151; process of, 191–92; as reaction, 164; as a reaction to memory, 243; as the response to memory, 22–23; and the solution of problems, 161; and sorrow, 22, 149, 211; and time, 93, 210, 253–55; understanding the machinery of, 112; as unoriginal, 150
Thought, time, and sorrow: as interrelated, 20–27. *See also* Sorrow; Thinker; Thought; Time
Time: and authority, 19; and change, 13, 230; chronological and psychological, 24, 93, 101; and contact, 279–80; and death, 254; and degeneration, 200; and the ending of conflict, 49; falseness of, 273; and fear, 63–64; freedom from, 306, 309; and freedom from fear, 291; as hindrance to action, 255; as hindrance to mutation, 35, 188–89; as hindrance to the eternal, 221–22; and the innocent mind, 202; as an invention of the mind, 305; and love, 308–9; and the mind, 309; and mutation, 59; and the new mind, 5; and problems, 304–5, 308; and the process of thinking, 292–93; and the process of thought, 22–23; as a psychological continuity, 222; and psychological fear, 93; and the resolution of problems, 23, 253; and revolution, 126; and seeing, 306; and seeking experience, 110; and self-understanding, 155; and sorrow, 305–9; and the structure of the conscious and unconscious, 62; types of, 149; and the unconscious, 63; and understanding conflict and security, 134; and virtue, 89. *See also* Future; Memory; Past; Present
Time, death, and love: as interrelated, 254, 257–58. *See also* Death; Love; Time
Time, death, and sorrow: as interrelated, 100–106, 147–54, 208–14. *See also* Death; Sorrow; Time
Time interval: and fear, 293; and observation of the past, 294; between seeing and action, 294; and the wasting of energy, 293–95. *See also* Time
Timeless: and the religious spirit, 46; and the state of understanding, 84. *See also* God; Meditation; Mutation; Reality; Unknown
Time, thought, and sorrow: as interrelated, 20–27. *See also* Sorrow; Thought; Time
Today. *See* Present; Time
Tomorrow: absence of psychological, 273; as nonexistent, 305; and time, 151. *See also* Future; Past; Time
Torture: and the search for God, 141–43
Total action, 280; and observation, 2; and problems, 304; and understanding, 81. *See also* Action
Total answer: versus the particular answer, 264. *See also* Problems
Total human being: and the resolution of the psyche, 5. *See also* Human beings
Totality of life: versus fragmentation, 212; need to understand, 12; and resolving of problems, 303–4; and understanding death, sorrow, and time, 209. *See also* Life
Total revolution: versus beliefs, 77. *See also* Revolution
Tradition: and communication, 283. *See also* Belief; Conditioning; Conformity
Traditional religion: abandoning of, 161. *See also* Religion; Tradition
Transformation: through comprehension, 122–23; and the mind, 191; and revolution, 126. *See also* Change; Mutation
Translation: as hindrance to understanding, 274. *See also* Communication
True: discovery of, 42; and energy, 6; and freedom from influences, 221. *See also* False; False and true; God; Reality; Truth
True and false: and belief, 267; and discontent, 265; and the empty mind, 300; and freedom, 169. *See also* True
Truth: and the absence of authority, 12, 81; and the absence of conflict, 57; defining, 21; discovery of, 81–82, 83, 84; and discovery of moment to moment, 28; and effortless listening, 165; and the fact, 25; and freedom, 145; and the healthy mind, 142–43; as immediate, 21; and immediate perception, 2, 200, 215; and inquiry, 23; versus knowledge, 86; as a living thing, 18; versus the petty mind, 259; and prayer, 260; search for, 7, 9; seeing instantly, 279; self-discovery of, 121–22, 124, 127, 143–44, 171–72; and self-knowledge, 78; and time, 200; as timeless, 118–19; and understanding, 82; and understanding the inner and outer, 2. *See also* Eternal; Reality; True; Unknown

Uncertainty: and the accumulation of knowledge, 170–71; as the human state, 132–34. *See also* Permanency; Security
Unconscious: and authority, 19–20, 131; and conflict, 10, 11; defining, 111, 140; and escape, 114; and fear, 249; and freedom from the past, 190; and influences on the mind, 221; need to know, 62; and silence, 218; understanding, 63, 65. *See also* Brain; Conscious
Unconscious mind: and conditioning, 38. *See also* Mind; Unconscious
Understand: defining, 1–2, 9–10, 71–72, 80–81, 101, 231, 239
Understanding: achieving, 66; action, 68, 70, 203–8, 231–37, 280–85; and the act of listening, 8; authority, 244–47; and the cessation of escape, 115; communication, 280–85; communion, 280–85; conflict, 7–13, 78–82, 124–26, 129–34; death, 31–33; death, sorrow, and time, 100–106, 147–54, 208–14; defining, 152; desire, 96–100; discipline, 144–46; effect of the word, 53; emotionally and intellectually, 73; energy, 288–96; fear, 88–94, 192–97, 248–51, 290–93; formulas, 141–47; freedom, 82–88, 134–40, 296–302; as hindrance to disintegration, 67; ideas, 231–37; as immediate, 13, 273; and immediate perception, 2, 215; individual,

religion, and mutation, 161–67; language, 238–44; living, 256; meaning of, 189; meditation, 33–39, 106–12, 154–61, 258–63, 298–302; mutation, religion, and the individual, 161–67; and the new mind, 17; observation, 1–7; passion, 95–100; problems, 174–80, 180–87; relationship of sorrow, thought, and time, 20–27; religion, 263–69; religion, mutation, and the individual, 161–67; religious life, 263–69; religious mind, 42–46, 112–19, 263–69; security, 129–34; self, 201; sorrow, death, and time, 100–106, 147–54, 208–14; violence, 293–94; world passions, 161–63

Unknown: and creation, 196–97; and death, 31–33; and death, love, and time, 258; fear of, 152; and learning, 241; and the silent mind, 112. *See also* God; Reality; Truth

Upanishads. *See* Authority; Books; Knowledge; Religion

Utopia: failure of, 117–18

Values: and observation, 19

Verbalization: and communication, 284; looking without, 241–42. *See also* Communion; Naming; Words

Violence, 293–94; attempt to escape from, 47–48; and facts, 69, 251; freedom from, 75–76; and the ideal of nonviolence, 90–91; and ideals, 139; prevalence of, 291, 293. *See also* Conflict; Contradiction; Problems

Violence and nonviolence: and contradiction, 11, 13, 281, 286. *See also* Violence

Virtue: and attention, 7; and humility, 89; inability to cultivate, 155; and love, 100, 308; and meditation, 106–9; and self-knowing, 108–9; as timeless, 27, 46; understanding, 218; and wisdom, 116

War: and sorrow, 26; as the ultimate escape, 125. *See also* Violence; World problems

Watching: as the greatest action, 66. *See also* Looking; Observation; Seeing

Welfare state: and the loss of freedom, 82. *See also* Society

West. *See* Authority; Conditioning; Divisions; Society; World problems

What is: and energy, 113; escape from, 156; facing, 116, 142; and fact versus ideas, 91; versus fiction of ideals, 47; importance of observing, 139; and living without destructive discipline, 146; and maturity, 276–77; and observation, 1–2, 87; perceiving, 123; and self-observation, 136; understanding the significance of, 40; and violence, 251; and words, 296

What is and 'what should be': and conflict, 11, 129, 139; and meditation, 35. *See also What is*

'What should be': as the ideal, 91. *See also What is* and 'what should be'

Whole: and the cessation of the positive movement, 202; 'me' as part of, 77–78; and problems, 14; and problem solving, 252–53. *See also* Fragmentation; Total action

Will: and change, 126; defining, 188; and desire, 98; structure of, 189–90; and the thinker, 36; and the ending of sorrow, 104

Wisdom: and the ending of sorrow, 152; and self-knowing, 76, 116. *See also* Humility; Virtue

Words: apart from action, 39–40; beyond, 14, 67, 114; and communication, 225, 286, 282–83; and communion, 285; and the creation of fear, 93; difficulty of, 296; as distraction, 50; as distraction to observation, 65; dynamics of, 7–8; enslavement to, 134; and fear, 250, 293; importance of, 287–88; interpretation of, 225; and listening, 90; and loneliness, 117; and meditation, 106; as not the thing, 52, 97; significance of, 7–8; slaves to, 88–89; and symbol, 222–23; translating, 283; unimportance of, 189; and violence, 294. *See also* Naming

World: and change, 9; defining, 131–32; as the individual, 14, 17; and the individual as one, 49–50, 108; need to understand, 17, 126–27; and outward conflict, 124–25; retreat from, 79. *See also* World problems

World chaos: and the individual, 230. *See also* World problems

World problems, 226–27; and authority, 275–76; and corruption, 123; and fragmentation, 2–3; and the fresh mind, 59; increase of, 47; and the interrelationship of people, 41; and psychological revolution, 15; and the religious life, 79; and revolution, 126–27; and the serious mind, 80; and the state of man, 133; understanding, 98

Worship: of authority, 246; without love, 213; of sorrow, 103, 210

Yesterday. *See* Memory; Past; Time

Yogis: and desire, 98. *See also* Authority

Young mind: achieving, 244; and energy, 295; and learning, 287; and meditation, 167. *See also* Dull mind; Empty mind; Free mind; Mind; Quiet mind; Religious mind

Youth: and passion, 97

Zen. *See* Authority; Conditioning; Divisions; Religion; Society; World problems

www.ingramcontent.com/pod-product-compliance
Lightning Source LLC
Chambersburg PA
CBHW080429140626
46572CB00003B/6

* 9 7 8 1 9 3 4 9 8 9 4 7 0 *